COMPREHENSIVE STRUCTURED COBOL

OR
Touch Typing

L. WAYNE HORN
GARY M. GLEASON

Pensacola Junior College

BOYD & FRASER PUBLISHING COMPANY
BOSTON

Credits:

Editor: Tom Walker
Development editor: Sharon Cogdill
Ancillaries editor: Donna Villanucci
Composition: IPS Publishing, Inc.
Project manager: Laura Welch
Production manager: Rebecca D. Evans
Cover photo: Winchester disks. © Jon Goell, 1980.

Library of Congress Cataloging in Publication Data

Horn, Lister Wayne.
    Comprehensive structured COBOL.

    Combined ed. of Beginning structured COBOL and
Advanced structured COBOL by the authors.
    Includes index.
    1. COBOL (Computer program language)
2. Structured programming. I. Gleason, Gary M.
II. Horn, Lister Wayne. Beginning structured COBOL.
III. Horn, Lister Wayne. Advanced structured COBOL.
IV. Title.
QA76.73.C25H673 1986   001.64'24   84-29336
ISBN 0-87835-154-X

CONTENTS

Contents

DIRECTORY OF PROCEDURES

DIRECTORY OF PROGRAMS

PREFACE

The purpose of *Comprehensive Structured COBOL* is to teach structured programming concepts and practices in the context of ANSI 74 COBOL. It is based on the many years of teaching experience of the authors and others who have taught COBOL and used and class tested previously published parts of this text: *Fundamentals of Structured COBOL* and *Advanced Structured COBOL: Batch and Interactive*. The reading and conceptual levels of this text are closely matched with the abilities of average college students. The numerous programming examples and exercises are based on realistic business applications. The text and instructor's manual have been carefully designed and include many pedagogical features to facilitate the teaching/learning task.

Many changes in accepted standards and practices—for example, the release of the ANSI 85 COBOL Standard—have occurred in recent years and are reflected in this edition. *Comprehensive Structured COBOL* satisfies the requirements of a two- or three-semester course in COBOL programming, such as that described by the DPMA in its Model Computer Information Systems Curriculum CIS '86, Course CIS86-3 and CIS86-4 (Introduction to and Intermediate Business Application Programming) or its Associate-Level Model Curriculum, Courses COMP. 4 and 5 (Programming Language I and II).

The first half of the text is oriented towards the fundamentals of COBOL and the basic techniques of top-down program design and structured programming. The second half of the text (beginning in Chapter 10) stresses a broader systems approach. The focus is on the relationship of individual programs to a data processing system, providing students with an understanding of a program as an element of a complete system rather than as an isolated entity.

This systems approach is evident in the second half of the text in other, less obvious ways as well. For example, the student is asked to consider the impact of an applications programs/system on the computing system. Various trade-offs are considered when the impact of a program or system on the resources of the computer is a critical issue. Topics such as the establishment of audit trails, back ups, transaction logs, and error recovery procedures are covered. *Cmprehensive Structured COBOL* bridges the gap between the attention to the details of the language which usually occupies much of the student's first exposure to COBOL to the broader considerations of the tasks that mush be accomplished with the language and the environment in which the resulting programs will be written and executed.

- The text includes many completely coded and tested programs, which provide superior models for students' own programs. All programs in the text are reproduced from actual program listings in an effort to assure that they execute. Important sections of these programs are highlighted in blue to help students readily identify these program segments.

- There is early and continuing emphasis on structured problem solving. Each programming example uses the same format, which closely parallels the way a student must solve a programming problem:

    Problem statement
    Problem analysis
    Problem solution

    Top-down program design is emphasized throughout the problem analysis. The problem solution contains the actual program and a narrative describing important features of the COBOL code.

- There is an early and continuing emphasis on the theory and practice of structured programming. Students are introduced to good, top-down structured design techniques with every program example. The structure diagrams used throughout the book conform to modern standards widely used today.

- A limited but logically complete subset of the language is introduced early in the text, so students are able to begin writing meaningful programs very early in the course. Immediately seeing the results of their efforts motivates students to keep learning as topics are expanded in later chapters, building on previous knowledge and covering successively higher levels of detail.

- Because the design of printed reports is important in business and industry, each program in the text is illustrated with a completed printer spacing chart. A supply of blank printer spacing charts is perforated and bound into the end of this text for students to use for their programming assignments. Students using these charts will be able to produce professional-looking output for their programs.

- Each chapter contains a variety of realistic business-type programming assignments, enabling instructors to meet the needs of students with varying interests and levels of ability. Some of the end-of-chapter programming assignments contain sample data to ease the instructor's task of checking student programs. Other assignments do not supply data to encourage students to practice the art of creating adequate sample test data.

- For those instructors who prefer to have students write programs which use the same data or are a part of the same data processing system during the entire course, *Comprehensive Structured COBOL* includes three such systems. The programming assignments and data sets in Appendix E (Personnel System) or Appendix F (Sales Accounting System) can easily serve as the basis for all programming assignments needed in Chapters 1-9. The third system in Appendix G (Subscription System) is for use with Chapters 10-17. These appendices may be used in place of or in addition to the end-of-chapter programming assignments.

- Both batch and interactive systems are presented. The importance of interactive systems is often ignored or relegated to relative insignificance in COBOL-oriented texts, yet COBOL is equally well suited for the development of programs in both kinds of systems.

- A brief chapter on data base management systems in included, reflecting the increasing importance of such systems in developing applications software.

- A complete description of picture codes and editing appears in chapter four and is illustrated with numerous figures and examples.

- The presentation of table concepts includes extensive explanations of one-, two-, and three-level tables, and the representation of table data reflects the results of recent research on the best pedagogical device for this purpose.

- Every chapter (except the first and last) contains a "Debug Clinic," which covers in detail debugging techniques, caution notes, style notes, and warnings to students about potential problems as well as possible solutions. These sections help students become more efficient and professional in their approach to the art of computer programming.

- Each chapter contains a full complement of "Self-Test Exercises." These short-answer questions test vocabulary, basic skills, and programming techniques. They enhance the learning process by providing students with immediate feedback, as all Self-Test answers appear in a separate section at the end of the book.

Appendices

- The text covers ANSI 74 standard COBOL. The student is provided with a complete general syntax of the language in Appendix C. The instructor only needs to provide details of modifications required to run programs on the system students will be using.

- Appendix B presents the most significant changes offered by the new ANSI 85 Standard COBOL.

- Report Writer is described in Appendix A, included for those instructors who wish to cover this feature.

- Of help to users of IBM OS systems, Appendix D includes detailed explanations of execution time error messages produced by these systems.

- The text contains a complete glossary of terms and their definitions.

ANCILLARIES

Instructor's Manual

The Instructor's Manual to Accompany Comprehensive Structured COBOL and *Fundamentals of Structured COBOL* (available to adopters from our publisher, boyd & fraser) is a complete pedagogical package. Divided into two parts, it includes the following:

- Chapter-by-chapter teaching objectives

- Estimated lecture times corresponding to each chapter of the text

- Vocabulary words from each chapter

- Complete section-by-section lecture outlines, including special notes to the instructor

- Chapter-by-chapter testing objectives and numerous test questions, including true/false, short-answer, fill-in and multiple choice, as well as additional programming assignments.

Transparency Masters

Also available to adopters is an extensive set of over 400 transparency masters. These masters include enlargements of figures, programs and tables from the following Horn and Gleason texts published by boyd & fraser publishing company:

> *Fundamentals of Structured COBOL*
> *Advanced Structured COBOL: Batch and Interactive*
> *Comprehensive Structured COBOL*

L. W. H.
G. M. G.

ACKNOWLEDGMENTS

Fundamentals of Structured COBOL has been designed as a complete teaching/ learning system. Systems of any sort must be "fine tuned" from time to time. Many people have helped make this book the best it can be. We are indebted to all of those individuals who have contributed to the success of this text. Deserving very special thanks and praise are those who reviewed various drafts of the manuscript and whose comments and suggestions were invaluable. Among them are: Professor Janice Guarnieri of Trenton State College, Professor Hossein Saiedian of Flint Hills Vo-Tech, Professor Robert England of the University of Southern Mississippi, Professor Donald P. George and Thomas A. Emch of Youngstown College of Business, Professor Lou R. Goodman of the University of Wisconsin, Professor Barbara Kreaseck of Atlantic Union College, Professor Thomas McKee of Belmont College, Professor William Jarosz of Boston University, Professor Cynthia Hanchez of Oklahoma Baptist University, Professor Jerry G. Booher of Scottsdale Community College, Professor George C. Fowler of Texas A & M University, Marjorie Leeson, Educator/Consultant, Professor Michael Michaelson of Palomar College, Professor Ramona J. Richardson of San Diego City College, Professor John F. Schrage of Southern Illinois University-Edwardsville, and Professor Eileen Wrigley of Community College of Allegheny County.

We reserve our special thanks for Mary Lynch of University of Florida-Gainsville and Paul Ross of Millersville University. Not only did their detailed comments and suggestions significantly improve the text over several drafts, but we remain indebted to them for their invaluable help in preparing what is surely the best Instructor's Manual to accompany any COBOL text.

In addition, we express our thanks to Mr. Terry McClarren of IBM Corporation for helping to ensure the accuracy of certain IBM-specific material included in the text.

Finally, we extend our appreciation to the editorial and production staffs at boyd & fraser: to Tom Walker, editor-in-chief, for conceiving this book and encouraging us to write it; to Sharon Cogdill, development editor, whose talents added appreciably to the book's readability; to Donna Villanucci, ancillaries editor, for her work in the development of a strong ancillary package; and to Laura Welch and Rebecca Evans at IPS Publishing for diligently guiding this book through the various stages of production.

NOTES

1) Generic COBOL is used in this text in the hope that it will apply to as many different systems as possible. You may need to make minor modifications to the programs to make them run on your system.
2) The examples of code in the text use generic identifier names. In your own coding, use descriptive data names, for example, PART-NUM-IN instead of DATA-IN.
3) The COBOL element descriptors are italicized when they are used in the text.
4) A caret (^) is used to designate the implied position of a decimal point in a field.
5) The answers to all the Self-Test Exercises, as well as a Glossary, are in the back of the book.
6) You will find Appendix C, General Formats of COBOL Elements, and Appendix D, IBM OS Execution-Time Error Messages, helpful for quick reference.
7) A Directory of Programs and a Directory of Procedures are found right after the Table of Contents.
8) The following conventions are used to describe the general form of COBOL elements:
   a) All capitalized words are COBOL reserved words.
   b) All underlined capitalized words are required. Capitalized words that are not underlined may be included at the discretion of the programmer. Their general purpose is to improve readability.
   c) Words written in small letters indicate elements that are to be supplied by the programmer.
   d) Ellipses (...) are used when more than one element of the preceding type may be included.
   e) Brackets ([ ]) indicate elements which are optional.
   f) Braces ({ }) indicate that one of the enclosed elements, which are placed on separate lines, must be chosen.

COMPUTERS AND STRUCTURED PROGRAMMING 1

1.1 WHAT IS A COMPUTER?

From astronomy to zoology, from business to medicine, from art to engineering, computers have become very important tools in almost all areas of human endeavor. Since the first primitive automatic computing machines were devised in the 1940's, computers have undergone steady improvement. Each substantial improvement yielded more computing power and greater reliability at less cost, resulting in a greater number of applications for which the computer could be cost effective. Presently, computers are available in sizes ranging from the microcomputer, contained in an electronic chip smaller than a fingernail, to super computers which fill a large room. Computer prices range from one hundred dollars for a microcomputer, to several million dollars for a super computer. In between, computers are available in a wide range of sizes, shapes, and prices (with an equally wide variety of capabilities). Today it is possible to choose a computer for almost any application at a reasonable cost.

What do such diverse devices have in common that enables us to classify them all as computers? All computers execute sequences of instructions called *programs*. Programs are written to solve specific problems; they are placed in the computer's memory, which recalls the programs when they are needed. Thus, the same computer can solve different problems simply by changing the program it executes.

All computers share a basic logical organization composed of five logical components called *units* (Fig. 1.1):

    1) Input Unit
    2) Output Unit
    3) Memory Unit
    4) Control Unit
    5) Arithmetic/Logical Unit

The *input* unit transfers data from some external medium, such as a keyboard or magnetic tape, into the computing system. The *output* unit

1

Figure 1.1   Organization of a computer

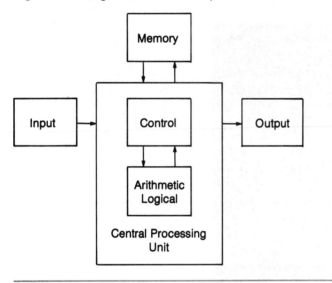

transfers data from the system onto some external medium, such as paper or magnetic tape. Data is stored in the *memory* unit. The memory unit also stores the sequence of instructions (the program) required to manipulate the data to produce the desired results.

Memory is composed of storage locations, each of which has an *address*. The content of any location is made available to other units of the computing system by specifying to the memory unit the address of the desired data. Data is stored in a location by specifying to the memory unit the content and the address of the location into which the data is to be placed. The commands that order data to be placed, moved or used in various ways are given to the computer in *programs* discussed at length in later chapters.

The control unit executes each program one instruction at a time. When the program requires data, the control unit activates the input unit. When a program instruction requires that data be written out, the control unit activates the output unit. When a program requires that computations be performed, the control unit activates the *arithmetic/logical* unit, which performs all the arithmetic and logical operations. The control and arithmetic/logical units are often referred to collectively as the *central processing unit*, or *CPU*.

The hardware for these components varies greatly among computing systems; the central processing unit ranges from an electronic chip in a microprocessor (Fig. 1.2), to a small box in a microcomputer system (Fig. 1.3), to a larger unit in other computers (Fig. 1.4).

Input and output devices are available for a great variety of input and output media. A commonly used input/output device is the computer terminal, which contains a typewriterlike keyboard by which data is entered into the computing system. Some terminals have a video screen (also called a *cathode ray tube* or *CRT*) on which information is displayed to the operator (Fig. 1.5). Other terminals have the capability of printing data on paper in much the same fashion as a typewriter. As terminals allow the user to enter data and receive information, they serve as both input and output devices.

Figure 1.2 CPU for a microcomputer

Figure 1.3 An IBM-PC computing system

Figure 1.4   An IBM medium-scale computing system (IBM 4341)

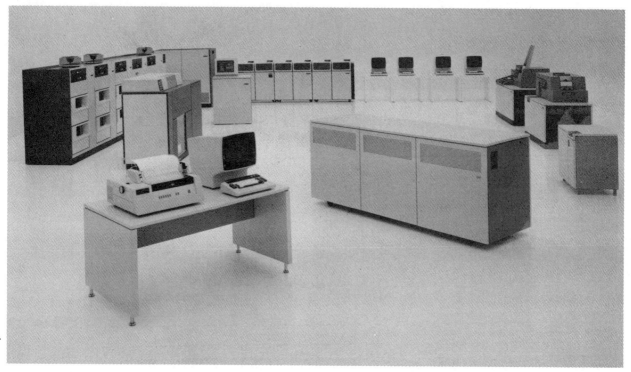

Courtesy IBM

Figure 1.5   A CRT terminal

Courtesy Digital Equipment Corporation

Figure 1.6   A diskette

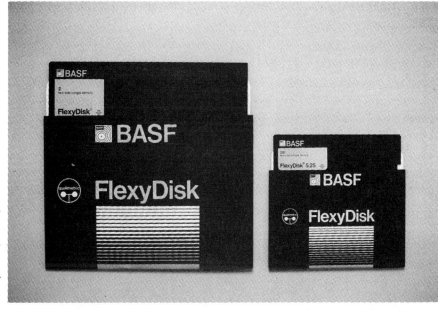

Courtesy BASF System Corporation

Another common input device is the diskette data station. Data is recorded on a *diskette* (also called a *floppy disk*) as shown in Figure 1.6. A diskette data station similar to a terminal is used for this purpose. When the user has completed recording data on the diskette, the data station is used to transmit the data to the computer for processing. Because diskettes are inexpensive, easily portable, and highly reliable, they often are used in academic computing systems.

Most computer systems have one or more high-speed line printers used for applications that require a high volume of output. Printers such as the one shown in Figure 1.7 can produce printed output at rates varying from 300 to 1600 lines per minute.

Most computing systems have mass storage devices capable of storing many millions of characters in a form that can be readily accessed by the CPU. The two most common types of mass storage devices are magnetic tape drives (Fig. 1.8) and magnetic disk drives (Fig. 1.9). Both devices have the capability of writing data onto a magnetic medium (tape or disk) and reading data from the medium at a later time; hence, they function as both output and input units. Magnetic tapes most often are used for long-term storage of large volumes of data. Magnetic disks usually are used for program libraries and short-term low volume data storage. Disks are indispensable in providing direct access to data required in an interactive computing environment. At one time the punched card was used for communicating with computing systems, and it still may be found in some installations.

1.2   COMPUTER PROGRAMMING LANGUAGES

The term *hardware* refers to the physical devices which make up a computing system. The devices pictured in Figures 1.8 and 1.9 are examples of computer hardware. The programs and their supporting documents required to

Figure 1.7   A high-speed printer

Courtesy IBM

Figure 1.8   Magnetic tape drives

Courtesy IBM

Figure 1.9 Magnetic disk drives

Courtesy IBM

make the hardware function are referred to as *software*. Computer hardware is completely useless without software.

There are two basic types of software: *system* and *application*. System software consists of programs that control the operation of the computer, perform routine tasks needed by computer users, and provide facilities for the development of programs. Application software consists of programs that are designed to help the user solve problems and perform data processing tasks related to specific needs of the individual or organization.

Computer programs must be expressed in a *language* the computer hardware can read and use. Each central processing unit "understands" programs in machine language. Machine language is numerical (binary); the operation to be performed and the data to be operated on are expressed numerically. Machine languages tend to be very different from one computer to another, depending on the design of the CPU, and programs written in machine language for one particular computer usually cannot be executed by a computer built by a different manufacturer. It is very hard to write programs in machine language because every detail must be turned into a coded expression built of numbers.

As there are a great many disadvantages to machine language, other languages (generally called *high-level languages*) have been devised for constructing programs. Programs written in high-level languages use words and other symbols to represent both the operations to be performed and the addresses of data items to be operated on. COBOL, an acronym for

*CO*mmon
*B*usiness
*O*riented
*L*anguage

is one example of a high-level language. Other commonly available programming languages include:

BASIC (*B*eginners' *A*ll-purpose *S*ymbolic *I*nstruction *C*ode)
FORTRAN (*FOR*mula *TRAN*slation)
RPG (*R*eport *P*rogram *G*enerator)
PASCAL (named for French mathematician Blaise Pascal)
WATBOL (*WAT*erloo CO*BOL*)
C (developed by AT&T for use on UNIX-based systems)
ADA (developed by Defense Department)

A program written in a high-level language must be translated into machine language before it can be executed. Programs called *compilers* perform this task. A COBOL program, called a *source program*, is submitted to the COBOL compiler, which automatically translates the program into an equivalent machine language program, called the *object program*. The object program then can be executed by the computing system. In addition to translating the program into machine language, the compiler also produces a listing of the source program and checks its content for correctness.

There are many advantages to writing programs in high-level languages. The languages are symbolic rather than numeric in nature, thereby enabling the programmer to formulate a problem solution in somewhat familiar terms. The more a language resembles ordinary speech, the faster the programmer can work. The details of the exact form of machine language are handled by the compiler; the programmer can be concerned only with the logic of his program. Furthermore, programs written in a high-level language tend to be transportable (i.e., they can be used on machines of many different designs and manufacturers), whereas machine language programs are specific to individual types of machines.

1.3 COMMUNICATING WITH THE COMPUTER

The computer user must communicate his or her program and data to be processed to the computing system. As noted earlier, no two computing installations are completely the same in all particulars, so it is impossible to provide the reader with complete details of all that he or she will need to know in order to enter a program and data for processing at an installation. All installations have manuals or handouts that explain procedures to be followed at that installation; the reader must secure these instructions before attempting the first program. The following is a brief survey of common types of systems encountered in academic computing centers.

On Line/Off Line

The term *on line* means that a device is in direct communication with a computing system; *off line* means that a device is acting on its own without direct communication with a computing system. Most computer terminals are on line; all data and instructions entered by the user are communicated directly to the system. Diskette data stations may be on line or off line. In most installations utilizing these devices, the station is off line during the time when the user is recording programs and data on the diskette. The station is then turned on line (or the user takes his or her diskette to a station that is on line) to transmit the program and data to the computer. A key punch is another example of an off line device; a program prepared in punched card form must be read by an on line punched card reader in order to be processed by the computer system.

The term *batch computing* implies that data is collected for some period of time before being submitted for processing; *interactive computing* implies that the computer and user engage in a dialogue in which the user enters commands and/or data for immediate processing by the system. Punched card and diskette systems are batch systems. The user must completely prepare the program and data files to be processed utilizing off line devices. (A *file* is a collection of records. Each record contains a collection of data items pertaining to one entity, e.g., person, inventory item, bank transaction, or program statement.) Only when the program and data are completed can the system accept the program for compilation and execution.

Systems utilizing terminals usually offer interactive computing. A program called an *editor* enables the user to build a file containing the program to be executed. Once the user is satisfied with the program, he or she can give commands to execute the compiler and, if there are no errors, execute the program itself. The program can process data from a data file (which has been created utilizing the editor) or from the user who enters data at the terminal in response to messages from the program. If errors are encountered by the compiler or during execution, the user can use the editor to modify the program file and/or data file and repeat the compilation-execution process.

In an interactive computer system the entire program development process typically is carried out by the computer and user while the user is sitting at a terminal. In a batch system the user typically prepares his program and data at one station, submits the task to the computer at a second, and then waits for the output to be produced at a third. Some systems combine interactive and batch processing. Such systems generally use an interactive terminal for the user to enter a program and data; however, once the program and data are entered, the tasks of compiling and executing the program are treated as in batch computing (i.e., the user must wait until the system can perform the tasks and produce the desired output).

Single User/Multiuser Systems

Some computing systems, particularly smaller systems, are single user systems because they can communicate with only one user at a time. Other systems are classified as multiuser systems because they can engage in simultaneous communications with several users. Multiuser systems behave as though each person is the sole user of the system; however, in most systems the computer is engaged in *timesharing* (i.e., allocating a small slice of time to each of many users, usually on a rotating basis).

Most multiuser systems require that each user be assigned an account number and a password before he or she can utilize the system. The purpose of the account number is to enable the computing system to keep track of who uses what resources and in what quantity. The password protects one user's files from others, so it must be kept secret. Both the account number and the password must be entered using a *sign on* (or *log on*) procedure, when a user initiates communication with the computer. There are also *sign off* (or *log off*) procedures required when the user terminates communication. Details of these procedures are quite specific to individual computing systems.

1.4   PROGRAM FLOWCHARTS

A program is a sequence of instructions describing actions to be taken by the computer. A *program flowchart* is a visual representation of these steps. Each type of instruction is represented in a flowchart by a different type of symbol, called a *block*. Inside each block, the programmer writes a description of the instruction to be executed. Figure 1.10 illustrates types of instructions and their corresponding blocks.

Figure 1.10   A summary of program flowchart symbols

Block   *Purpose*

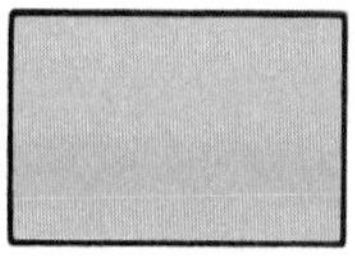

Processing
    Describes all data
    movement and
    computations.

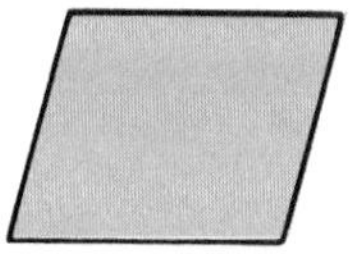

Input/Output
    Describes all input
    and output operations.

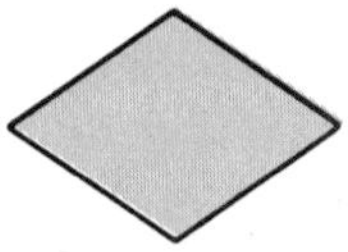

Decision
    Describes all decisions
    involving comparison of
    data items.

Flow Lines
    Describes which
    instruction is to be
    executed next.

Connector
    Indicates point at which
    two flow lines converge.

Termination
    Describes the beginning
    and ending points.

Predefined Process
    Describes execution of a
    procedure defined
    elsewhere.

Examples

Move the content of
location N to location M.

Multiply 4 by the content
of HOURS and place the
result in PAY.

Input a record from the
file SALES–IN.

Write the PRINT–OUT
record.

If the value of HOURS is
greater than 40 take YES
path otherwise take NO
path.

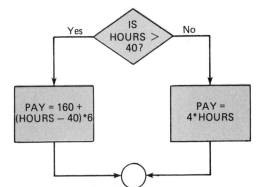

If the value of HOURS is
> 40 pay time and one-
half for overtime; other-
wise pay is computed
at $4 per hour.

The start of the program.

Processing should stop.

Return to statement which
caused this procedure to
be executed.

Execute HEADING–
ROUTINE.

An oval-shaped symbol is used to describe the beginning and ending points in a flowchart. The instruction START typically denotes the beginning, while the instruction STOP or END denotes the ending point.

Flowlines such as → describe the direction of flow, that is, which instruction is to be executed next. All blocks in a flowchart are connected to others by flowlines.

A parallelogram-shaped symbol is used to describe input and output operations. The instruction READ is used to denote an input operation; the instruction WRITE is used for output. The name of the file may also be used in the block to define the file to which the instruction pertains. For example, a complete flowchart for a program to read a record from the file INPUT-FILE would be:

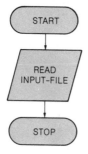

The rectangle is used to describe processing such as movement of an input record, as in the flowchart which follows:

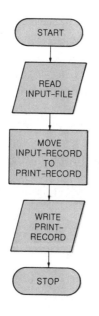

A program flowchart to compute pay at $4 per hour for an employee is shown below:

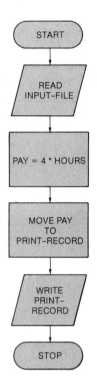

The diamond-shaped symbol is used to denote decisions. Decisions involve relations such as greater than (>), less than (<), and equal to (=) between data items. If the relation is true, the "yes" path from the decision block is followed to determine the next instruction. If the relation is false, the "no" path from the decision block is followed. For example, suppose we wish to pay time and one-half for overtime hours worked by an employee. If the value of HOURS is less than 40, we shall pay him at $4 per hour. If the value of HOURS is more than 40, we shall pay him $4 times 40 equals $160 plus $6 for all hours in excess of 40. This program could be described by the following flowchart:

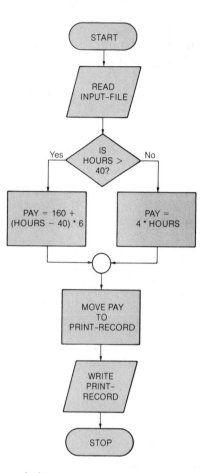

In some flowcharts it is useful to draw separate flowcharts for some complicated procedures and indicate that the procedures are to be executed by using the predefined process block:

For example, let's construct a separate procedure called COMPUTE-PAY to take care of the details of determining the appropriate value of PAY based on HOURS.

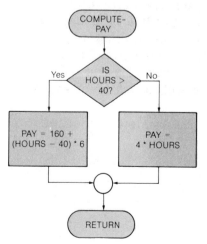

Note that the termination block is used with the procedure name to note the entry to the procedure and the statement **RETURN** to note the end of the procedure.

Using this procedure, the program to compute an employee's pay can now be written as:

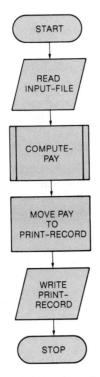

Program flowcharts are a useful means of describing a program in a rough form prior to writing the program in a programming language. They are also used as a form of documentation to enable a person unfamiliar with a program to understand how it works.

1.5   PSEUDOCODE

Pseudocode (from *false* code) is an alternative program preparation technique that has become a very important tool for COBOL programmers. Pseudocode is an informal language that omits many of the details required in a real programming language, but which expresses the procedure to be implemented in a useful preliminary form. The syntax of pseudocode is nonstandard; each programmer uses a version with which he or she is comfortable.

For example, the following pseudocode expresses a procedure for computing an employee's pay at $4 per hour:

> *Pay employee*
> Read input file
> Pay = 4 * hours
> Move pay to print record
> Write print record
> Stop

A different programmer might express the procedure in a different form; the important point when using pseudocode is that the overall logical flow be correct, not the exact syntax or even the level of detail included.

Decisions are expressed in pseudocode using an If/Else structure that has the general form:

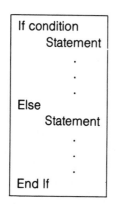

```
If condition
        Statement
            .
            .
            .
Else
            Statement
            .
            .
            .
End If
```

For example, suppose pay is computed at $4 an hour for hours less than or equal to 40 but $6 an hour for hours over 40. This procedure can be expressed in pseudocode as

```
If hours > 40
        Pay = 160 + (hours − 40) * 6
Else
        Pay = 4 * hours
End If
```

The procedure Pay employee would now appear as:

Pay employee
```
        Read input file
        If hours > 40
                Pay = 160 + (hours - 40) * 6
        Else
                Pay = 4 * hours
        End If
        Move pay to print record
        Write print record
        Stop
```

Note the use of indentation to visually delineate two statements—one of which will be carried out if the condition hours > 40 is true and the other which will be carried out if hours > 40 is false. Note also the use of the words "End If" to specify the end of the statements controlled by the If statement.

Execution of another procedure is signified in pseudocode using the Do statement with general form:

```
Do procedure name
```

This statement signifies that the named procedure should be carried out and at its end, control should return to the statement following the Do statement. For example, the payroll procedure described above could be specified as two procedures:

Pay employee
> Read input file
> Do Compute pay
> Move pay to print record
> Write print record
> Stop

Compute pay
> If hours > 40
>> Pay = 160 + (hours − 40) * 6
>
> Else
>> Pay = 4 * hours
>
> End If

Within the general outlines given above, you are at liberty to express program specifications in pseudocode using any syntax you desire. Often pseudocode specifications undergo many transformations between the first rudimentary document and the final design for a program. Remember to include only essential elements of a procedure in pseudocode; leave as many details of the final program as possible to the program itself. The purpose of pseudocode, like flowcharting, is to enable the programmer to express the overall problem and its proposed solution in a form more expressive and convenient to use than actual programs.

1.6   PROGRAM DEVELOPMENT

The task of developing a program involves much more than simply writing COBOL code, although this is a necessary step. In practice, more time usually is spent analyzing the problem at hand before writing the program, and in testing the actual program usually requires more time than coding it. The task of developing a program may be viewed as a seven-step process:

1) **Define the problem.** Answer the following questions: What is the purpose of the program? What data is to be processed? What output is desired? What is input? How will the program accomplish the desired goals?
2) **Design test data.** Only if the program is executed with an adequate amount of test data and the output produced is compared to the output desired, can the programmer be reasonably sure that a program is correct. At this step, test data that will thoroughly test all aspects of the program should be designed.
3) **Design the program.** Decide on names for all files, records and fields that will be needed in the program. Draw a flowchart or write the pseudocode for the procedure required.
4) **Code the program.** Write the COBOL equivalent of the program designed in step 3 above.
5) **Compile the program.** Submit the program for compilation and correct any syntax errors.
6) **Test the program.** Run the program with the test data from step 2 above. If the output produced is not correct, revise the program and return to step 5.

7) **Document the program.** A properly written COBOL program has a great deal of built-in documentation; however, other forms of documentation such as structure diagrams, record layouts, and user manuals also may be needed.

1.7   WHY STRUCTURED PROGRAMMING?

When computers first were put into use, the users tried to make them as efficient as possible to justify costs and prove the value of the systems. From the beginning, however, people who bought computers had to deal with not only the cost of using the hardware to solve a problem (hardware cost), but also the cost of preparing programs for the machine to execute (program development costs). At first, hardware costs were much greater than program development costs (Fig. 1.11). The emphasis on machine efficiency often forced programmers to use complicated logic and programming tricks that resulted in very efficient programs, but the programs were difficult to debug and also difficult for any other programmer to modify. Documentation (detailed explanations supplied with a program) provided a partial solution to the problem, but the documentation was often incomplete and sometimes incorrect.

In recent years hardware costs have become much lower than program development costs, and there has been a corresponding shift in programming philosophy. Programmer productivity has become a higher priority than the machine efficiency of the programs written. Programmers are now encouraged to develop straightforward solutions to problems and to concentrate on building programs in such a way that debugging, additional coding, and future enhancements will require minimal effort.

Structured programming is a way of writing programs which, if followed carefully, will result in programs that are easy to

1) Read
2) Understand
3) Debug
4) Modify

Figure 1.11   Relative costs of computing equipment and programming personnel

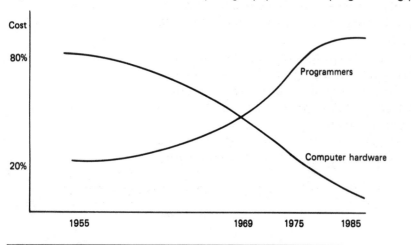

A structured program can be understood clearly not only by its author but also by anyone else who needs to understand or change it. Structured programming decreases programming costs, particularly when applied to large programming projects. This cost decrease is apparent not only in the initial programming stages but also later on when the programs must be modified to suit new requirements. Also there tend to be fewer detected and undetected logical errors in structured programs, so testing, debugging, and maintenance times are reduced. Structured programming, in short, has gained wide acceptance as a standard programming technique.

1.8 WHAT IS STRUCTURED PROGRAMMING?

Structured programming is a general approach to the programming task that has gained a considerable following during the past decade. The concept of structured programming can be traced to the work of Bohm and Jacopini in the 1960s. The early emphasis in the movement was on program modularity. Edsger Dijkstra was also a pioneer in the field. His letter, "Go To Statement Considered Harmful," was published in a 1968 issue of *Communications of the ACM*. In this letter, Professor Dijkstra observed that program complexity is largely a function of the use of GO TO statements. He recommended that the GO TO statement be eliminated from programming languages in the interest of forcing programmers to develop simpler program designs. There is, however, much more to structured programming than modularity and the elimination of GO TO statements. Concepts of program control structures, programmer productivity aids, program design techniques, and techniques for enhancing maintainability have been incorporated under the general framework of "structured programming."

One of the first large-scale implementations of this philosophy was made by IBM in developing a data processing system for the *New York Times*. The project was widely reported as a success because of the unusually low error rate in the programs that made up the system. Gradually, structured programming concepts and practices have emerged from theory and experimental use to become standards for the industry.

Although some of the problems associated with designing and developing software have yet to be solved, structured programming offers significant advantages over previous practices. Programming systems designed and written by these methods tend not only to be error-free but also easy to maintain by subsequent programmers, who must make minor modifications to accommodate changes in the systems.

A fundamental proposition of structured programming is that program design is the single most important aspect of the program development process. A well-designed program will be easy to code, debug and maintain; a poor program design cannot result in a "good" program, no matter how much effort goes into subsequent program development steps.

In programming, "structure" refers to the way in which statements are related to one another. Only three program structures are needed for program development:

1) Sequence
2) If/Then/Else (Decision)
3) Iteration (Loop)

In fact, in structured programming, only these three structures are permitted.

In a Sequence structure, each statement is executed in succession. A sequence structure is shown as:

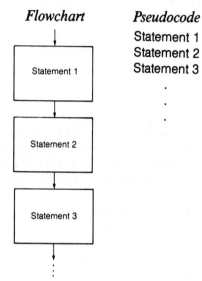

Flowchart   *Pseudocode*

Statement 1
Statement 2
Statement 3

After statement 1 is executed, statement 2 is executed, followed by the execution of statement 3, and so on.

The If/Then/Else structure describes a test condition and two possible resulting paths. Only one path is selected, and executed depending on the evaluation of the given test condition. The decision structure is shown as:

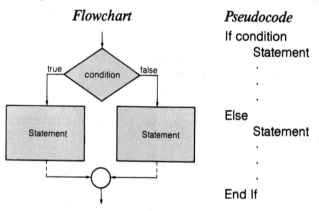

Flowchart   *Pseudocode*

If condition
    Statement

Else
    Statement

End If

The Iteration structure causes the repetition of one or more statements until a given condition is met. The iteration structure is shown as:

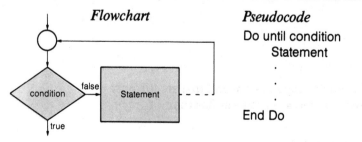

Flowchart   *Pseudocode*

Do until condition
    Statement

End Do

Structured programming has come to mean much more than simply programs that use only the three basic structures. In a COBOL environment, concepts of top down program design and standards for program coding are usually considered to be part of the overall concept referred to as "structured programming."

1.9 SELF-TEST EXERCISES

1. Matching

1. program	a.	computer and user engage in a dialogue
2. input unit	b.	communicates directly with a computing system
3. output unit	c.	program which enables user to build and modify files
4. memory unit	d.	procedure used to identify a user to a computing system
5. control unit	e.	device used to communicate with computing system in an interactive mode
6. arithmetic/logical unit		
7. CPU	f.	carries out arithmetic and logical instructions
8. microcomputer	g.	program written in machine language
9. CRT	h.	Central Processing Unit
10. terminal	i.	general term for computing machinery
11. diskette	j.	collection of records
12. line printer	k.	program written in a high-level language
13. hardware	l.	computer based on an electronic chip
14. software	m.	carries out instructions which transfer data from outside into memory
15. high-level language	n.	video terminal
16. source program	o.	data is accumulated over a period of time before processing
17. object program	p.	high speed printed output device
18. compiler	q.	stores currently active programs and data
19. on line	r.	computer engages in communication with more than one user
20. batch computing	s.	carries out instructions which transfer data from memory to the outside world
21. interactive computing		
22. file	t.	symbolic language such as COBOL
23. editor	u.	set of instructions for a computer
24. time sharing	v.	executes each program instruction
25. sign on	w.	general term for computer programs
26. mass storage	x.	small disk often used in academic computing systems
	y.	program which translates a source program into an object program
	z.	magnetic tape and disk

2. Matching

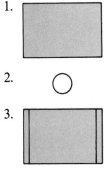

a. termination
b. decision
c. input/output
d. connector
e. processing
f. predefined process

3. List three structures that are sufficient for any program and that are the only structures used in a structured program. Draw a program flowchart for each one.

4. List the seven steps of program development.

References

Bohn, C., and G. Jacopini. "Flow Diagrams, Turing Machines and Languages with Only Two Formation Rules." *Communications of the ACM*. Vol. 9, no 5 (May 1966), pp. 366-71.

Dijkstra, Edsger. "Go To Statement Considered Harmful," *Communications of the ACM*. Vol. 11, no. 2 (Feb. 1968), pp. 147-48.

Stevens, W. P., G. J. Meyers, and L. L. Constantine. "Structured Design." *IBM Systems Journal*. Vol. 13, no. 2 (1974).

Yourdon, E., and L. L. Constantine. *Structured Design*. Englewood Cliffs, N.J.: Prentice-Hall, 1979.

INTRODUCTION TO COBOL 2

2.1 ORIGIN AND DEVELOPMENT OF COBOL

The origin of COBOL lies in the development in the late 1950s of programming systems that were better suited to commercial applications than the algebraic languages then in use. Much of the early work was carried out by Dr. Grace Hopper, at that time a commander in the Navy. Beginning in 1959 a series of meetings among concerned individuals of the Department of Defense, academic institutions, and computer manufactures resulted in the organization of CODASYL (*CO*nference on *DA*ta *SY*stems *L*anguages). The avowed purpose of this group was the development and standardization of a commercial programming language.

CODASYL has developed several versions of the COBOL language. The earliest version was known as COBOL-60. This was superseded by COBOL-68 and then by COBOL-74, in 1968 and 1974 respectively. The American National Standards Institute formally adopts standards for the language; hence, these versions of the language are often referred to as ANSI-68 and ANSI-74 respectively. A new standard, ANSI-85, has recently been adopted but is unavailable at the time of this writing. At this time, COBOL-74 remains the most widely used version of the language.

The original intent in the development of COBOL was to design a language that was:

1) naturally suited to commercial data processing,
2) self-documenting (anyone should be able to read and understand a COBOL program), and
3) extensible (the language should be designed so as to permit later versions to add features without fundamental change in the structure or syntax of the language).

Objective 1 was attained by organizing every COBOL program around the data files which are to be processed. The files, records within files, and fields within records are described very explicitly. Objective 2 was met by allowing very long data-names which can completely describe a data item, by allowing operations (such as ADD, SUBTRACT, and so on) to be specified verbally rather than in symbolic form, and by insisting on a paragraph/sentence structure for each program segment. Objective 3 also was met by the original designers because COBOL has been redesigned and extended to include a multitude of features never envisaged by the original group, yet the fundamental organization and structure of COBOL programs remain the same now as in the beginning.

2.2 ORGANIZATION OF A COBOL PROGRAM

All COBOL programs are organized into major subordinate parts called DIVISIONs. The four DIVISIONs required in a COBOL program are:
1) IDENTIFICATION DIVISION
2) ENVIRONMENT DIVISION
3) DATA DIVISION
4) PROCEDURE DIVISION

Each division begins with a division header consisting of the division name, the word DIVISION, and a period.

Some divisions are divided into SECTIONs. A section is preceded by a section header which consists of the section name, the word SECTION, and a period. For example, the ENVIRONMENT DIVISION is divided into two sections:
1) CONFIGURATION SECTION
2) INPUT–OUTPUT SECTION

The DATA DIVISION is divided into two sections:
1) FILE SECTION
2) WORKING–STORAGE SECTION

Another basic unit of subdivision is the *paragraph*. A paragraph is preceded by a paragraph header which consists of a paragraph name followed by a period. In the IDENTIFICATION and ENVIRONMENT DIVISIONs the paragraph headers are specified by the COBOL syntax; in the PROCEDURE DIVISION the programmer names the paragraphs.

The next lower unit of subdivision is the *sentence*. A sentence consists of a series of COBOL clauses followed by a period. A clause may be as simple as one entry specifying a name for the program or programmer in the IDENTIFICATION DIVISION or as complex as a series of commands describing how data is to be processed in the PROCEDURE DIVISION.

COBOL programs are made up of two basic types of entries: COBOL-reserved words which are specified to have a specific meaning in the language and programmer-defined entries that are made up by the programmer. A list of COBOL reserved words is printed inside the front and back covers of this text. Reserved words are included for DIVISION, SECTION and paragraph headings, commands, and various other entries. Reserved words may not be used for programmer-defined entries. The programmer defines names for files, records, data items, the program name, and various other entries.

Program Example

Let us write a COBOL program to create a copy of a file. A program such as this is used to create a backup of a file so that the original file can be re-created if needed. (Errors in data or system problems can make it necessary to recall a file in its previous state.)

The program will process two files, which we shall call INPUT-FILE and OUTPUT-FILE. These names are arbitrary; a programmer can use any suitable names for files. The records associated with each file will also require names; we shall call the records INPUT-REC and OUTPUT-REC; these names are also programmer-defined. The program will read a record from INPUT-FILE and write it on OUTPUT-FILE, repeating the process until all records from INPUT-FILE have been processed.

The IDENTIFICATION DIVISION for this program is shown in Figure 2.1. The purpose of the IDENTIFICATION DIVISION is to identify the program, its author, and other related information.

Figure 2.1   IDENTIFICATION DIVISION for backup program

```
100        IDENTIFICATION DIVISION.
200
300        PROGRAM-ID. FILE-BACKUP.
400        AUTHOR. HORN.
500
```

Line 100 contains the division header. Line 200 is a blank line inserted to enhance readability of the program. Most compilers allow the programmer to insert blank lines in programs for this purpose; such lines have no effect on the function of the program. Line 300 contains a name (FILE-BACKUP) that is assigned to the program; this name is determined by the programmer and will change from program to program. The program name is preceded by a paragraph header PROGRAM-ID. This entry will be present in every COBOL program. Line 400 contains an entry that is used to specify the name of the programmer. The programmer's name is preceded by the paragraph header AUTHOR.

The ENVIRONMENT DIVISION for the backup program is shown in Figure 2.2. The purpose of the ENVIRONMENT DIVISION is to identify the computing "environment" in which the program will function.

Figure 2.2   ENVIRONMENT DIVISION for backup program

```
600        ENVIRONMENT DIVISION.
700
800        CONFIGURATION SECTION.
900
1000       SOURCE-COMPUTER.
1100       OBJECT-COMPUTER.
1200
1300       INPUT-OUTPUT SECTION.
1400
1500       FILE-CONTROL.
1600
1700           SELECT  INPUT-FILE ASSIGN TO DISK.
1800           SELECT OUTPUT-FILE ASSIGN TO DISK.
1900
```

Line 600 contains the division header. Line 800 contains the section header for the CONFIGURATION SECTION. The CONFIGURATION SECTION contains two paragraphs: SOURCE-COMPUTER (line 1000) and OBJECT-COMPUTER (line 1100). The SOURCE-COMPUTER entry specifies the computer that will be used to compile the program; the OBJECT-COMPUTER entry specifies the computer that will be used to execute the program. In most instances the entries in these paragraphs will be the same. The exact entry required in these paragraphs varies from computing system to computing system and often the entry can be omitted altogether. You will need to determine what entry is required in your system for these paragraphs. In the programs of this text these paragraphs have been included, but the computer name entries have been omitted.

Line 1300 contains the section header for the INPUT-OUTPUT SECTION. This section is used to describe the data files that the program is going to process. It contains one paragraph—FILE-CONTROL. Line 1500 contains the paragraph header FILE-CONTROL. One sentence beginning with the reserved word SELECT is required for each file the program is going to process. Line 1700 contains the SELECT entry for INPUT-FILE; line 1800 contains the SELECT entry for OUTPUT-FILE. The words ASSIGN TO are COBOL reserved words. The word DISK signifies the device in the system that will contain the file. This entry will change depending on the requirements of individual computing systems.

The DATA DIVISION for the backup program is shown in Figure 2.3. The purpose of the DATA DIVISION is to describe the data records and other data items the program will require.

Figure 2.3   DATA DIVISION for backup program

```
2000      DATA DIVISION.
2100
2200      FILE SECTION.
2300
2400      FD  INPUT-FILE
2500          LABEL RECORDS ARE STANDARD
2600          DATA RECORD IS INPUT-REC.
2700
2800      01  INPUT-REC   PIC X(80).
2900
3000      FD  OUTPUT-FILE
3100          LABEL RECORDS ARE STANDARD
3200          DATA RECORD IS OUTPUT-REC.
3300
3400      01  OUTPUT-REC PIC X(80).
3500
3600      WORKING-STORAGE SECTION.
3700
3800      01  FLAGS.
3900          02  END-OF-FILE    PIC X(3) VALUE "NO".
4000
```

Line 2000 contains the division header. The DATA DIVISION is divided into two sections—the FILE SECTION (line 2200) and the WORKING-STORAGE SECTION (line 3600). The FILE SECTION is used to describe the files the program will process and their associated data records. Each file must be described by an FD entry (an abbreviation for *File Description*) which consists of the characters FD followed by the name of the file and various clauses that describe the file. The FD entry constitutes a sentence that begins with FD and ends with a period. The FD entry for INPUT-FILE begins with line 2400 and ends on line 2600; most COBOL sentences may be coded on one or more lines as desired. Often each clause of a sentence is placed on a separate line to improve readability. Line 2500 contains the LABEL RECORDS clause for the INPUT-FILE. LABEL RECORDS ARE STANDARD will be the most common entry here, although for files assigned to certain devices (e.g., printers) the entry LABLE RECORDS ARE OMITTED may be required. Line 2600 contains the DATA RECORD clause, which is used to specify the name of the data record (DATA-REC) associated with INPUT-FILE.

Line 2800 contains a description of DATA-REC. This entry consists of a level number (01) followed by the data name (DATA-REC) and the reserved word PIC (which is an abbreviation for PICTURE), and the picture codes X(80). The code X signifies that the record contains alphanumeric data (any combination of alphabetic and numeric characters); the numbers 80 signify the length of the record. The length 80 is quite common for a record but each file in a system will have a record length determined by the nature of the data contained in the file and/or the requirements of the operating system.

Lines 3000 through 3200 contain the FD entry for OUTPUT-FILE. Note the similarity of this entry to the FD entry for INPUT-FILE. Line 3400 contains the record description for OUTPUT-REC, which closely resembles the description for INPUT-REC. Remember that the purpose of this program is to create a duplicate of INPUT-FILE, so this resemblance would be expected.

Line 3600 contains the section header WORKING-STORAGE SECTION. The purpose of the WORKING-STORAGE SECTION is to define data items that are required in the program but which are not a part of the records the program will process. In this case the program will need a data item to signify that all of the data from INPUT-FILE has been read. We shall call the item END-OF-FILE and define it to contain three alphanumeric characters (PIC X(3)) and specify that its initial value will be "NO" because initially the end of the file has not been reached. This task is carried out in lines 3800 and 3900. Line 3800 contains an 01 entry setting up a data-name FLAGS. This is an overall data-name for entries which follow at the higher levels. In this case only one subordinate entry is required (02 END-OF-FILE . . .) but in general other entries of the same type could also be included here. Line 3900 contains the entry defining the data-item END-OF-FILE. Note that the 02 entry is indented below the 01 entry of which it is a part. The VALUE clause is used to establish the initial value of the data-item (VALUE "NO"). During the execution of the program the value of the item will be changed to "YES" when the end of INPUT-FILE is encountered.

The purpose of the PROCEDURE DIVISION is to describe the processing steps required to accomplish the objective of the program. In developing a program it is usually beneficial to have a preliminary description of the tasks that the PROCEDURE DIVISION must accomplish before attempting to code this portion of the program. Either a program flowchart or pseudocode can be used for this preliminary plan. The plan for this program is shown in Figure 2.4. You will probably prepare only one or the other of these types of plans; both are shown here for reference. The actual PROCEDURE DIVISION for this program is shown in Figure 2.5.

Figure 2.4   Plan for file program

Pseudocode

Major processing

    Open files
    Read input file
    Do Build file until end of file = "YES"
    Close files
    Stop

Build File

    Move input record to output record
    Write output record
    Read input file

Program flowchart

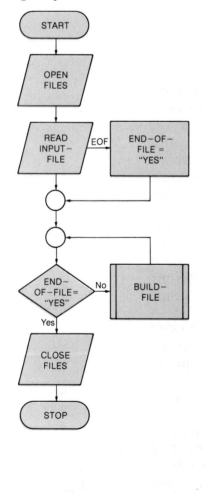
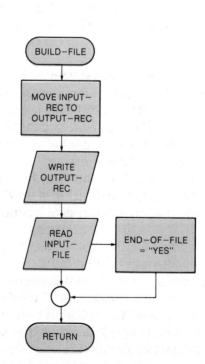

Figure 2.5 PROCEDURE DIVISION for backup program

```
4100      PROCEDURE DIVISION.
4200
4300      1000-MAJOR-PROCESSING.
4400
4500          OPEN INPUT  INPUT-FILE
4600              OUTPUT OUTPUT-FILE.
4700          READ INPUT-FILE
4800              AT END MOVE "YES" TO END-OF-FILE.
4900          PERFORM 2000-BUILD-FILE
5000              UNTIL END-OF-FILE = "YES".
5100          CLOSE INPUT-FILE
5200              OUTPUT-FILE.
5300          STOP RUN.
5400
5500      2000-BUILD-FILE.
5600
5700          MOVE INPUT-REC TO OUTPUT-REC.
5800          WRITE OUTPUT-REC.
5900          READ INPUT-FILE
6000              AT END MOVE "YES" TO END-OF-FILE.
```

Line 4100 contains the division header. The PROCEDURE DIVISION is divided into two paragraphs—1000-MAJOR-PROCESSING (lines 4300 through 5300) and 2000-BUILD-FILE (lines 5500 through 6000). In the PROCEDURE DIVISION, paragraph names are defined by the programmer. It is customary to use names that begin with a sequence of numeric digits (1000 and 2000 in this case) to signify the actual sequence of the paragraphs in the program. In a short program this may not appear to be necessary but in a long program this practice aids the reader in locating a paragraph. The rest of the paragraph name chosen should be as descriptive as possible of the task that will be accomplished in that paragraph.

Lines 4500 and 4600 contain the OPEN statement for the files to be processed by the program. The OPEN statement requires that the OPEN mode for a file be specified (INPUT or OUTPUT). Thus INPUT-FILE is opened in INPUT mode and OUTPUT-FILE is opened in OUTPUT mode. Note that the OPEN statement is one sentence but contained on two lines for readability. A file must be opened before it can be processed by a COBOL program.

Lines 4700 and 4800 contain a READ statement for INPUT-FILE. The READ statement addresses the file by name and includes the AT END clause, which specifies the action to be taken when no more data is contained in the file. In this case we specify MOVE "YES" TO END-OF-FILE when this event occurs. This means that the data item END-OF-FILE will be replaced by "YES" (remember that we initially defined this item to contain "NO").

Lines 4900 and 5000 contain the PERFORM statement that causes the program to enter a loop and continue its work until all the data from INPUT-FILE has been processed. The paragraph 2000-BUILD-FILE will be executed repeatedly until the condition END-OF-FILE = "YES" becomes true. Initially this condition is false (if there is any data in INPUT-FILE).

Lines 5100 and 5200 contain the CLOSE statement for the files processed by the program. This statement consists of the reserved word CLOSE followed by a list of the files to be closed. These are placed on separate lines to improve readability.

Line 5300 contains the STOP RUN statement, which terminates the execution of the program.

Line 5500 contains the paragraph header for 2000-BUILD-FILE. This paragraph handles the details of processing the data record from INPUT-FILE that has just been read by the program and reading the next record from INPUT-FILE. The processing steps involve moving data from INPUT-REC to OUTPUT-REC (line 5700) and writing that record to the file (line 5800). Note that the WRITE statement addresses the record associated with a file, not the file itself. Lines 5900 and 6000 contain the READ statement to cause the next record from INPUT-FILE to be read. The same AT END clause as was used earlier is repeated; when there is no more data in the file, the value of END-OF-FILE is replaced by the characters "YES" so that the condition END-OF-FILE = "YES" on the PERFORM statement will become true and processing of records from INPUT-FILE will terminate.

Program 2.1 displays the completed program. In order to help you understand the difference between entries required by COBOL and entries you the programmer will construct, the required entries are screened. These entries will be virtually the same in every COBOL program that you write.

Program 2.1   Backup program

```
100      IDENTIFICATION DIVISION.
200
300      PROGRAM-ID. FILE-BACKUP.
400      AUTHOR. HORN.
500
600      ENVIRONMENT DIVISION.
700
800      CONFIGURATION SECTION.
900
1000     SOURCE-COMPUTER.
1100     OBJECT-COMPUTER.
1200
1300     INPUT-OUTPUT SECTION.
1400
1500     FILE-CONTROL.
1600
1700         SELECT  INPUT-FILE ASSIGN TO DISK.
1800         SELECT OUTPUT-FILE ASSIGN TO DISK.
1900
2000     DATA DIVISION.
2100
2200     FILE SECTION.
2300
2400     FD  INPUT-FILE
2500         LABEL RECORDS ARE STANDARD
2600         DATA RECORD IS INPUT-REC.
2700
```

Program 2.1 (continued)

```
2800    01  INPUT-REC   PIC X(80).
2900
3000    FD  OUTPUT-FILE
3100        LABEL RECORDS ARE STANDARD
3200        DATA RECORD IS OUTPUT-REC.
3300
3400    01  OUTPUT-REC  PIC X(80).
3500
3600    WORKING-STORAGE SECTION.
3700
3800    01  FLAGS.
3900        02  END-OF-FILE    PIC X(3) VALUE "NO".
4000
4100    PROCEDURE DIVISION.
4200
4300    1000-MAJOR-PROCESSING.
4400
4500        OPEN INPUT  INPUT-FILE
4600             OUTPUT OUTPUT-FILE.
4700        READ INPUT-FILE
4800            AT END MOVE "YES" TO END-OF-FILE.
4900        PERFORM 2000-BUILD-FILE
5000            UNTIL END-OF-FILE = "YES".
5100        CLOSE INPUT-FILE
5200              OUTPUT-FILE.
5300        STOP RUN.
5400
5500    2000-BUILD-FILE.
5600
5700        MOVE INPUT-REC TO OUTPUT-REC.
5800        WRITE OUTPUT-REC.
5900        READ INPUT-FILE
6000            AT END MOVE "YES" TO END-OF-FILE.
```

2.3 A REPORT PROGRAM

A file which is part of an accounting system contains records for each customer's account. Each record that is 80 characters in length has the following fields:

Positions	Description
1-9	Account number
10-19	Customer last name
20-29	Customer first name
30	Customer middle initial

Other record positions contain data that are not used in this problem.

A report listing the content of this file is desired. Figure 2.6 contains a printer spacing chart showing the desired positions of the various fields on the output report.

Figure 2.6   Printer spacing chart for Program 2.2

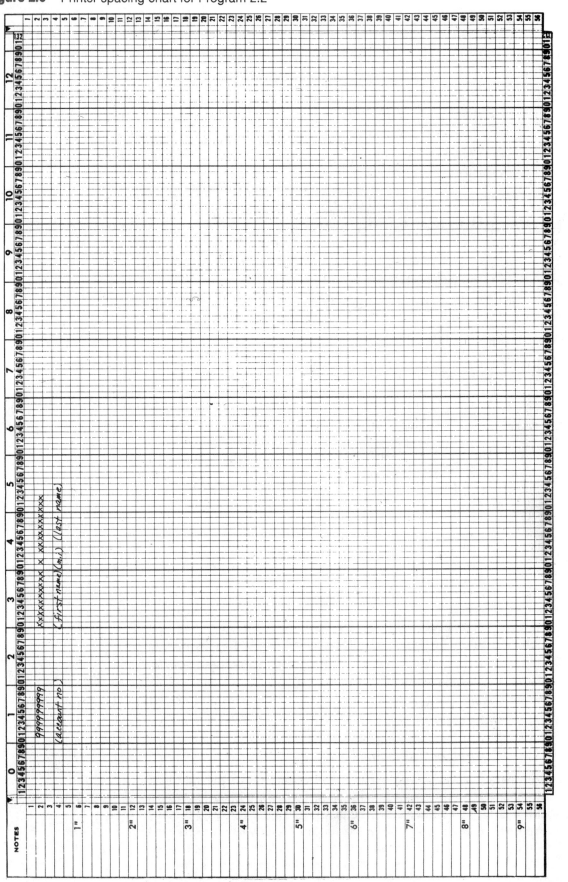

Problem Analysis

The required program must process a data file, which we call ACCOUNT-MASTER, to produce a printed report that we call REPORT-FILE. ACCOUNT-MASTER will be contained on disk while REPORT-FILE will be assigned to a printer. The program will require a flag that can be used to control the processing loop in much the same way as was needed in Program 2.1. This flag will be defined in the WORKING-STORAGE SECTION of the DATA DIVISION. In this case, the form of the output record is different from the form of the input record, so it will be necessary to move individual fields from the input record into related fields on the output record. Many positions on the output record are not used, therefore it is necessary to move spaces into the record before moving individual data items into the record; otherwise undesired characters may be printed in these unused areas. The procedure for solving this problem is summarized in Figure 2.7.

Figure 2.7   Plan for Program 2.2

Main logic

    Open files
    Read account master file
    Do Sub logic until end of file
    Close files
    Stop

Sub logic

    Move spaces to output record
    Move fields from input record to output record
    Write output record
    Read account master file

Problem Solution

Program 2.2 produces the desired report. Lines 2800 through 3300 contain the description of INPUT-RECORD. Note that each data name in INPUT-RECORD uses the suffix IR. This convention makes it possible to determine quickly where a given data item is defined. For example, note that the name of each field in OUTPUT-RECORD is given the suffix OR. INPUT-RECORD contains one numeric field (the account number) and three alphanumeric fields (the parts of the name). A numeric field is defined using the picture code 9. In this case ACCOUNT-NUMBER-IR is defined as PIC 9(9). This means that the field consists of nine (the number in parentheses) numeric digits (signified by the picture code 9). An alternative way to represent this picture is:

```
02 ACCOUNT-NUMBER-IR        PIC 999999999.
```

Lines 3900 through 4800 contain the description of OUTPUT-RECORD. This description is coded directly from the printer spacing chart shown in Figure 2.6. A numeric field is described using the picture code 9; alphanumeric fields are described using the picture code X. The unused positions within the record are described using the reserved work FILLER in place of a programmer-defined data name. Such entries are commonly given alphanumeric picture codes. In describing a record, positions that will not be explicitly referenced

Program 2.2   Customer list program

```
100      IDENTIFICATION DIVISION.
200
300      PROGRAM-ID. CUSTOMER-LIST.
400      AUTHOR. GARY.
500
600      ENVIRONMENT DIVISION.
700
800      CONFIGURATION SECTION.
900
1000     SOURCE-COMPUTER.
1100     OBJECT-COMPUTER.
1200
1300     INPUT-OUTPUT SECTION.
1400
1500     FILE-CONTROL.
1600
1700         SELECT ACCOUNT-MASTER ASSIGN TO DISK.
1800         SELECT REPORT-FILE ASSIGN TO PRINTER.
1900
2000     DATA DIVISION.
2100
2200     FILE SECTION.
2300
2400     FD  ACCOUNT-MASTER
2500         LABEL RECORDS ARE STANDARD
2600         DATA RECORD IS INPUT-RECORD.
2700
2800     01  INPUT-RECORD.
2900         02 ACCOUNT-NUMBER-IR        PIC 9(9).
3000         02 LAST-NAME-IR             PIC X(10).
3100         02 FIRST-NAME-IR            PIC X(10).
3200         02 MIDDLE-INITIAL-IR        PIC X.
3300         02 FILLER                   PIC X(50).
3400
3500     FD  REPORT-FILE
3600         LABEL RECORDS ARE OMITTED
3700         DATA RECORD IS OUTPUT-RECORD.
3800
3900     01  OUTPUT-RECORD.
4000         02 FILLER                   PIC X(11).
4100         02 ACCOUNT-NUMBER-OR        PIC 9(9).
4200         02 FILLER                   PIC X(10).
4300         02 FIRST-NAME-OR            PIC X(10).
4400         02 FILLER                   PIC X.
4500         02 MIDDLE-INITIAL-OR        PIC X.
4600         02 FILLER                   PIC X.
4700         02 LAST-NAME-OR             PIC X(10).
4800         02 FILLER                   PIC X(79).
4900
5000     WORKING-STORAGE SECTION.
5100
5200     01  FLAGS.
5300         02  EOF-FLAG        PIC X(3) VALUE "NO".
```

Program 2.2 (continued)

```
5400
5500      PROCEDURE DIVISION.
5600
5700      1000-MAIN-LOGIC.
5800
5900          OPEN INPUT ACCOUNT-MASTER
6000              OUTPUT REPORT-FILE.
6100          READ ACCOUNT-MASTER
6200              AT END MOVE "YES" TO EOF-FLAG.
6300          PERFORM 2000-SUB-LOGIC
6400              UNTIL EOF-FLAG = "YES".
6500          CLOSE ACCOUNT-MASTER
6600              REPORT-FILE.
6700          STOP RUN.
6800
6900      2000-SUB-LOGIC.
7000
7100          MOVE SPACES TO OUTPUT-RECORD.
7200          MOVE ACCOUNT-NUMBER-IR      TO ACCOUNT-NUMBER-OR.
7300          MOVE FIRST-NAME-IR          TO FIRST-NAME-OR.
7400          MOVE MIDDLE-INITIAL-IR      TO MIDDLE-INITIAL-OR.
7500          MOVE LAST-NAME-IR           TO LAST-NAME-OR.
7600          WRITE OUTPUT-RECORD AFTER ADVANCING 1 LINES.
7700          READ ACCOUNT-MASTER
7800              AT END MOVE "YES" TO EOF-FLAG.
```

Figure 2.8 Sample output from customer list program (Program 2.2)

```
000001111      JOHN     M   SMITH
000003333      MARY     C   BROWN
000005555      JAMES    A   WHITE
000007777      LINDA    L   GREEN
000008888      DONNA    F   WHITE
```

by name within a program are assigned the data name FILLER. For example, in this program the description of INPUT-RECORD contains the entry:

```
    02 FILLER      PIC X(50).
```

to represent the 50 unused positions in the record. It is important that a record description describe all of the positions of the actual input or output record. In this case, the record in the file to be processed contains 80 characters; therefore the program must account for all 80 characters. The output record for the printer contains 132 characters (which is a common record length for printers); therefore the record description for this file accounts for all 132 positions. The record length for printers varies depending on the actual hardware in use at a particular installation. You must check the documentation for your system to determine the record length of the printer available to you.

The PROCEDURE DIVISION of this program resembles the PROCEDURE DIVISION of Program 2.1 in many respects. The primary difference in this program is the processing steps required to produce the desired output. Before any other data is moved to OUTPUT-RECORD it is necessary to ensure that the entire record contains blanks. This task is accomplished by the MOVE statement at line 7100:

```
MOVE SPACES TO OUTPUT-RECORD.
```

The word SPACES is called a *figurative constant*. (Other types of constants are numeric constants such as 1 and alphanumeric constants such as "NO".) This MOVE statement will move to this area of memory the number of spaces required to fill the OUTPUT-RECORD. Any content that previously occupied these locations will be destroyed. If this statement is omitted, undesirable characters may be printed in the positions described in the output record as FILLER, representing the contents of memory in these locations at the time the program was executed. Moving spaces into the entire record prior to filling up individual parts of it is similar to wiping a chalkboard clean prior to writing on it; the purpose is to ensure that the previous contents do not detract from the new.

The statements at lines 7200 through 7500 cause the individual fields from INPUT-RECORD to be moved to corresponding fields in OUTPUT-RECORD. Note that except for the suffixes, data items that hold the same information are assigned the same names. Thus, the field that will hold the first name is called FIRST-NAME-IR in INPUT-RECORD and FIRST-NAME-OR in OUTPUT-RECORD. Note also that the order of the fields can be changed in moving data to the output record. In this case, INPUT-RECORD contains data in this order: last name, first name, middle initial. The output record has data in this order: first name, middle initial, last name. The program can process all of an input record or any parts of it in any order as required to produce the needed output.

2.4 PREPARING A COBOL PROGRAM FOR COMPILATION

A COBOL program may be prepared and entered into the computer in a variety of ways. Regardless of the method used, a COBOL program initially may be written on coding sheets such as that shown in Figure 2.9. A supply of COBOL coding sheets in included with this text. Each line of the coding sheet represents one input record. Each line is divided into fields used in entering COBOL statements. Positions 1 through 6 are used for a sequence number. The first record could be numbered 001010, the second record would then be 001020, and so on.

When terminals are used to enter a program, it is more useful to assign sequence numbers consecutively using increments of 10 or 100, as shown in Programs 2.1 and 2.2 Sequencing by 10s or 100s allows statements to be added later.

Positions 73 through 80 are used for an identification sequence. The programmer may enter the program name here or choose to leave these positions blank. Position 7 is used in the continuation of a non-numeric literal from one line to another (see Chap. 5, Section 5.7 for details). If the character "*" is entered in position 7, the entire line is treated by the compiler as a comment (i.e., the line is listed on the program listing but is not translated into machine language). Comments are useful to provide documentation regarding the function and purpose of the program. If it is not used for either of these purposes, position 7 is left blank. Most compilers allow the

Figure 2.9   Sample COBOL coding sheet

COBOL CODING FORM

PROGRAM	*Customer List*			REQUESTED BY		PAGE	OF	
PROGRAMMER	*Gary*			DATE		IDENT	73	80

PAGE NO.	LINE NO.	A	B														Z

Ø Ø 1	01Ø Ø	IDENTIFICATION DIVISION.
Ø Ø 1	02Ø Ø	
Ø Ø 1	03Ø Ø	PROGRAM-ID. CUSTOMER-LIST.
Ø Ø 1	04Ø Ø	AUTHOR. GARY.
Ø Ø 1	05Ø Ø	
Ø Ø 1	06Ø Ø	ENVIRONMENT DIVISION.
Ø Ø 1	07Ø Ø	
Ø Ø 1	08Ø Ø	CONFIGURATION SECTION.
Ø Ø 1	09Ø Ø	
Ø Ø 1	10Ø Ø	SOURCE-COMPUTER.
Ø Ø 1	11Ø Ø	OBJECT-COMPUTER.
Ø Ø 1	12Ø Ø	
Ø Ø 1	13Ø Ø	INPUT-OUTPUT SECTION.
Ø Ø 1	14Ø Ø	
Ø Ø 1	15Ø Ø	FILE-CONTROL.
Ø Ø 1	16Ø Ø	
Ø Ø 1	17Ø Ø	SELECT ACCOUNT-MASTER ASSIGN TO DISK.
Ø Ø 1	18Ø Ø	SELECT REPORT-FILE ASSIGN TO PRINTER.
	19	
	20	

insertion of blank records in the program to provide for visual separation of various groups of statements in the final program listing.

Positions 8 through 72 are used for the content of the COBOL statement. There are two margins (A and B) delineated on the coding form. Some COBOL statements must begin in margin A (position 8), while others may not begin before margin B (position 12).

Those entries which begin in margin A are:

DIVISION headers
SECTION headers
paragraph names
FD entries
01 entries

All other entries begin at or to the right of margin B.

Note the placement of COBOL statements in Programs 2.1 and 2.2. The rules for placement of statements permit a statement which may begin in margin B to be placed anywhere on the line after margin B. In particular, record description entries (02 through 49) may begin anywhere on the line. However, it is common practice to show the breakdown of data records by indenting subordinate items as shown in Programs 2.1 and 2.2.

Many words in a COBOL program are reserved words. They have a meaning automatically assumed by the COBOL compiler, and must be used only in a given context. A complete list of these words is included on the inside of the covers of this text. Many other words including names of:

    programs
    files
    records
    data items
    paragraphs

are chosen by the programmer. A programmer-defined word must not be the same as a COBOL reserved word. For example, a programmer could not choose to call a paragraph "MOVE" because MOVE is a reserved word. Programmer-defined names should be chosen to be as descriptive of the element being named as possible.

2.5 IDENTIFICATION DIVISION ENTRIES

The general form of the IDENTIFICATION DIVISION is shown in Figure 2.10. This format is used throughout the text to represent the general form for COBOL program elements. All capitalized entries are COBOL reserved words. Entries which are underlined, if used, must be present as shown. All punctuation marks such as "-" and "." must be present as shown. Any entry which is capitalized but not underlined may be included at the programmer's discretion. Any entries described in lower case characters are supplied by the programmer. Any entry enclosed in brackets ([ ]) is an optional entry. For example, a complete IDENTIFICATION DIVISION might be:

```
IDENTIFICATION DIVISION.
PROGRAM-ID. SAMPLE.
```

All other paragraphs in the division are optional.

Figure 2.10 General form of the IDENTIFICATION DIVISION

```
IDENTIFICATION DIVISION.

PROGRAM-ID. program-name.

[AUTHOR. [comment-entry] . . . ]

[INSTALLATION. [comment-entry] . . . ]

[DATE-WRITTEN. [comment-entry] . . . ]

[DATE-COMPILED. [comment-entry] . . . ]

[SECURITY. [comment-entry] . . . ]
```

Various operating systems place restrictions on the program-name specified in the PROGRAM-ID paragraph. Check with locally available documentation for further details.

Ellipses (. . .) used on the general format specifications indicate that more than one element of the preceding type may be present. Note, for example, that all of the paragraphs except for PROGRAM-ID may contain as many sentences as desired.

The general purpose of the IDENTIFICATION DIVISION is to identify the program, programmer, when and where the program was written, and the purpose for writing the program.

1) The PROGRAM-ID paragraph specifies to the operating system a name for the program.
2) The AUTHOR paragraph specifies the name(s) of the programmers.
3) The INSTALLATION paragraph specifies where the program was written.
4) The DATE-WRITTEN paragraph specifies the date on which the program was written.
5) The DATE-COMPILED paragraph specifies when the program was compiled. Most compilers will insert an appropriate date into this paragraph replacing whatever entry was made by the programmer.
6) The SECURITY paragraph is used in sensitive application areas to specify the security level required for personnel to have access to the program.

Figure 2.11 illustrates a completely coded IDENTIFICATION DIVISION for Program 2.2. Note the inclusion of an additional "paragraph" in this example. The REMARKS paragraph is actually a comment because of the asterisk placed in column 7. ANSI-68 COBOL provided for a REMARKS paragraph at this point; the specification was omitted in ANSI-74 COBOL.

The REMARKS comments may be used for any purpose the programmer desires. They are typically used to describe in general terms the purpose served by the program. This paragraph also may be used to document changes made by subsequent programmers.

2.6 ENVIRONMENT DIVISION ENTRIES

The ENVIRONMENT DIVISION describes the computing system and the files which will be required by the program. The ENVIRONMENT DIVISION may be composed of two sections, CONFIGURATION SECTION and INPUT-OUTPUT SECTION, as shown in Figure 2.12. Note that the INPUT-OUTPUT SECTION is optional.[1] The CONFIGURATION SECTION is used to specify the SOURCE-COMPUTER, which is the computer that will be used to compile the source program; the OBJECT-COMPUTER, is the computer that will be used to execute the object program; and SPECIAL-NAMES, which will be recognized within the program. Entries in these paragraphs vary somewhat from one compiler to another.

All data to be processed and all output produced by a COBOL program must be organized into sets of data records called *files*. The FILE-CONTROL paragraph of the INPUT-OUTPUT SECTION is used to describe the files which the

---

1. Many compilers also allow you to omit the CONFIGURATION SECTION as well.

Completely coded IDENTIFICATION DIVISION for Program 2.2

COBOL CODING FORM

PROGRAM	Customer List		REQUESTED BY	PAGE OF
PROGRAMMER	Gary		DATE	IDENT. 73 80

```
01  IDENTIFICATION DIVISION.
02  PROGRAM-ID. CUSTOMER-LIST.
03  AUTHOR. GARY.
04  INSTALLATION. ABC DEPT. STORES INC.
05  DATE-WRITTEN. JULY 27, 1985.
06  DATE-COMPILED. AUGUST 1, 1985.
07  SECURITY. NONE.
08 *REMARKS. PROGRAM PRODUCES A LISTING
09 *          OF ACCOUNT MASTER FILE.
```

Figure 2.12 General form of the ENVIRONMENT DIVISION

```
ENVIRONMENT DIVISION.

CONFIGURATION SECTION.

SOURCE-COMPUTER. computer-name.

OBJECT-COMPUTER. computer-name.

[SPECIAL-NAMES. special-names-entry.]

INPUT-OUTPUT SECTION.

[FILE-CONTROL.
    SELECT select-entry . . .]

[I-O-CONTROL.
    i-o-control-entry . . .]
```

program will process. There will be one SELECT entry for each file. For example, refer to the two SELECT sentences defining the two files in program of Figure 2.1. The I-O-CONTROL paragraph of the INPUT-OUTPUT SECTION is used to describe special procedures to be used by the program in processing files.

The only entry that will be found in the ENVIRONMENT DIVISION of most COBOL programs will be the FILE-CONTROL paragraph of the INPUT-OUTPUT SECTION. Each file to be processed must be described in a SELECT sentence. The general form of the most useful parts of the SELECT sentence is:

```
SELECT file-name ASSIGN TO system-name.
```

where the *file-name* is the name of the file that will be used within the COBOL program and the *system-name* is a description of the file that is communicated to the operating system. The general form of system-names varies from one computer installation to another; the manual for your installation will contain details.

2.7 DATA DIVISION ENTRIES

Data items that will be required in a program must be described in the DATA DIVISION. Generally programs require three distinct types of data items:

1) Input—these items will be a part of an input record description;
2) Output—these items will be a part of an output record description; and
3) Working—these items are required temporarily by the program but are not on an input record or an output record.

When a record from a file is read, data from the file is placed in the input record area. Before a record can be written onto an output file, that data must be placed in the output record. All other items needed by the program will be classified as working terms.

File Section

The general form of the DATA DIVISION is shown in Figure 2.13. The FILE SECTION contains a description of each file to be processed and a description of each

Figure 2.13

```
DATA DIVISION.

 [ FILE SECTION.

  [FD file-description-entry .. ] ...
  [record-description-entry ... ] ...

  [ WORKING-STORAGE SECTION.

   [record-description ....]
```

record to be found in file. In Program 2.1 there is an input file description followed by a description of the input record and an output file description followed by an output record description, The WORKING-STORAGE section contains a description of working data items. In Program 2.2 there is a control variable (EOF-FLAG) defined in WORKING-STORAGE. (Subsequent programs will require more extensive entries in WORKING-STORAGE.)

Figure 2.14 shows the general form of the most useful entries of the FD (*File Description*) entry. The use of { } indicates that one and only one of the entries contained within may be chosen.

Figure 2.14   General form of the FD entry. Note: The recording mode clause is extension not included in ANSI standards specification.

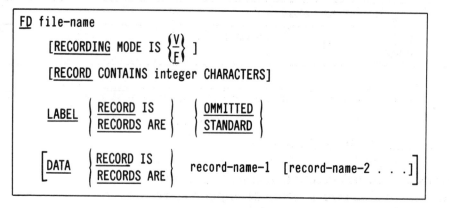

The RECORDING MODE clause is an IBM extension of ANSI COBOL standards; it is required only by IBM compilers and may not be allowed by other compilers. The most common entry is RECORDING MODE IS F, which designates *fixed length* records. Each record in a file having fixed length records contains the same number of characters as all other records. (The entry V would designate variable length records.) The RECORD CONTAINS clause is used to describe the length of the record(s) associated with this file; the clause is optional. If the RECORD CONTAINS clause is omitted, the compiler will assume a record length equal to the number of characters in the specified record name. The LABEL RECORDS clause usually is required; it describes to the COBOL compiler the way in which the program should process the first record in the file. If the LABEL RECORD IS STANDARD is specified, the first record in the file is assumed to be a label record containing a file identification, expiration date, file description, access keys and other such information. Label records are used to control access to a file to ensure that files are not destroyed by mistake and that unauthorized programs do not have access to the file. If LABEL RECORDS ARE OMITTED is specified, the first record on a file is assumed to be a data record. The DATA RECORD clause specifies the name of one or more records that will be found in the file. A detailed description of each type of record must follow the FD entry.

Figure 2.15   General form of the RECORD DESCRIPTION entry

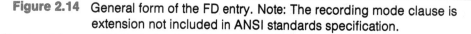

A *record-description-entry* has the form shown in Figure 2.15 where *level-number* is a two-digit number in the range 01 to 49; *data-name* is the name that identifies with the item; and *picture* is a description of the number and type of characters that will make up the item. The level-number 01 is classed as the highest level; level-numbers 02, 03, . . . 49 are used on data-items that are subdivisions of items with higher level-numbers. In Program 2.2 the input record is given the overall name INPUT-RECORD and is subdivided into items (also called fields) which include ACCOUNT-NUMBER-IR, LAST-NAME-IR and so forth. The reserved word FILLER is used as the data-name for a field that does not need to be referenced by any subsequent part of the program. The input record may be visualized as a sequence of characters as follows:

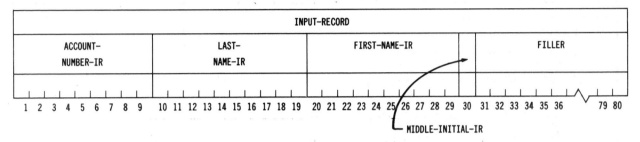

Any reference to the data-name INPUT-RECORD refers to the entire 80 characters; a reference to ACCOUNT-NUMBER-IR or LAST-NAME-IR refers to a specific subset of these characters. A record description entry which contains a PICTURE clause is an *elementary data item*; a record description entry which does not contain a PICTURE clause is a *group item*. Group data items may be subdivided; elementary data items may not. INPUT-RECORD is a group data item; ACCOUNT-NUMBER-IR and LAST-NAME-IR are elementary data items.

A data-name in COBOL must be composed only of the characters 0 through 9, A through Z, and - (hyphen). At least one character in the name must be alphabetic. Embedded hyphens are permitted; however, a hyphen may not be the first character nor the last character in a name. A name is terminated by a space or other mark of punctuation; embedded spaces are not permitted. The maximum length for a data-name is 30 characters. All other programmer-defined names such as file-names, record-names, condition-names, paragraph-names, and so on are subject to the restrictions specified for data-names.

A requirement of structured programming is that data-names be as descriptive as possible to aid the reader in understanding a program. Fields that will contain the same data at some point in the program are customarily assigned essentially the same name. A suffix (or prefix) is used to provide unique data names and to indicate which record contains the field. For example, in Program 2.2 the data item ACCOUNT-NUMBER is present both on INPUT-RECORD and OUTPUT-RECORD. The data-name ACCOUNT-NUMBER-IR is used for the field on INPUT-RECORD (IR is an abbreviation for INPUT-RECORD) while ACCOUNT-NUMBER-OR is used for the field on OUTPUT-RECORD.

A picture clause is made up of a sequence of characters called *picture codes* which are used to describe:

1) the length of the field, and
2) the type of data contained in the field.

The picture code 9 is used to describe a numeric character; the picture code X is used to describe an alphanumeric character. (An alphanumeric character is any representable character (digit, letter or other); whereas a numeric character is any character 0 through 9.) The total number of 9s or Xs used in the picture defines the length of the field. Thus, in the program in Figure 2.2, the field ACCOUNT-NUMBER-IR with a picture 9(9) is described as a nine-digit numeric item; the field LAST-NAME-IR with a picture X(10) is a ten-digit alphanumeric field. All of the FILLER entries are given alphanumeric pictures of varying lengths. A repetition factor enclosed in parentheses may be used in a picture. When the repetition factor is used, the preceding character is repeated the specified number of times. For example, the entry PIC 9(4) is equivalent to PIC 9999.

Working-Storage Section

Entries in the WORKING-STORAGE SECTION are data items which are used in the program but are not specifically included in an input record or an output record. The VALUE clause may not be used to establish an initial value to a data item in the FILE-SECTION; its use for this purpose is restricted to elementary data items in the WORKING-STORAGE SECTION. For example, the initial value of EOF-FLAG in Program 2.2 is specified to be "NO". The value of an item may be specified as any one of the following:

1) numeric constant (e.g., VALUE IS 0);
2) alphanumeric constant (e.g., VALUE IS "NO"); or
3) figurative constant (e.g., VALUE IS SPACES).

Numeric constants are written as a sequence of digits (e.g., 0, 123); alphanumeric constants are written as a sequence of characters enclosed in quotes (e.g. "NO", "YES"); figurative constants are COBOL reserved words that represent a specific value such as ZERO and SPACES. (See. Chap. 4, Section 4.11, Fig. 4.13 for a complete list of figurative constants). In some systems alphanumeric constants are enclosed in single quotes (') rather than the double quotes (") used in this text. The reader must check locally available documentation to find out which character is accepted by his or her compiler.

2.8 PROGRAM EXAMPLE

Problem Statement

Records in a file contain the following fields:

Positions	Description
1-6	Old balance (2 decimal places implied)
9-15	Check amount (2 decimal places implied)

A program is needed to produce a report showing the new balance for each account. The new balance is computed by adding the old balance and check amount. Headings are required in the report as shown in Figure 2.16.

Problem Analysis

This program is required to process a file on disk which we shall call AMOUNT-FILE to produce a file on the printer which we shall call REPORT-FILE. There are three primary differences between this program and Program 2.2:

Figure 2.16 Printer spacing chart for Program 2.3

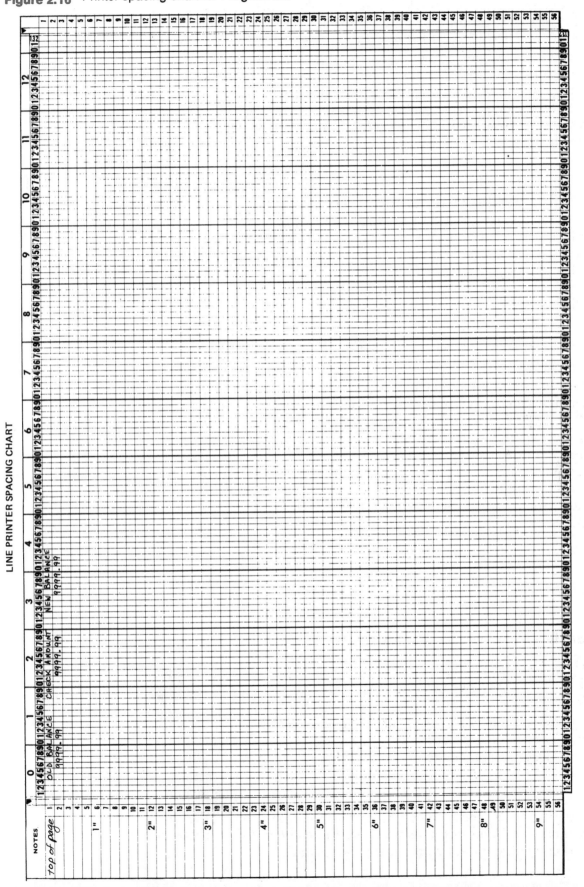

1) Headings must be printed
2) Arithmetic operations must be performed
3) Numeric data contains an implied decimal point and must be edited for output

The appropriate time to produce headings is after files have been opened and before processing the first data record. As part of the processing of each record, the value of the old balance must be added to the check amount and the result must be placed on the output record. Appropriate editing of the output must be performed to ensure that an actual decimal point is printed even though the input data only contained an implied decimal point. That is, an input item such as:

0 1 2 3 4 5

in which the implied position of the decimal point in between the 3 and the 4 thereby representing a value 123.45 must be printed as

0 1 2 3 . 4 5

A plan for this program is shown in **Figure 2.17**.

Figure 2.17   Plan for Program 2.3

Main logic

    Open files
    Write heading
    Read amount file
    Do Sub logic until end of file
    Close files
    Stop

Sub logic

    Move input fields to output record
    Compute new balance
    Write detail line
    Read amount file

Problem Solution

The required program is shown in Program 2.3. Note the use of the V picture code in the descriptions of the numeric fields OLD-BALANCE-IR and CHECK-AMOUNT-IR (lines 2900 and 3100). Each of these fields is six digits in length with two implied decimal positions. The picture code V is used to represent the position of the implied decimal point. Thus a picture code such as:

    PIC 9999V99

describes a field containing six characters. The V does not represent a character in the field. When computation is performed on numeric items, COBOL automatically aligns decimal positions to take into account implied decimal positions within a field.

This program requires that two different types of output lines be printed—a heading line and detail lines. This requirement is handled by defining a "dummy" output record for the printer files called OUTPUT-RECORD consisting of 132 undifferentiated characters and defining areas in WORKING-STORAGE for the actual records to be used. This strategy is very useful because it allows us to define the actual records using the VALUE clause to establish the content of the record. (Recall that the VALUE clause cannot be used for this purpose in the FILE SECTION of the DATA DIVISION.) In this program two records are defined in WORKING-STORAGE:

HEAD-LINE (lines 4500-5100) and
DETAIL-LINE (lines 5300-5900)

Note that in both records the VALUE clause is used to establish the initial value of all areas except those that will be filled from input fields (OLD-BALANCE-DL and CHECK-AMOUNT-DL) and the field that will be computed (NEW-BALANCE-DL). In order to actually print the content of a WORKING-STORAGE area, it is necessary to move it to OUTPUT-RECORD before writing OUTPUT-RECORD. This is done in Program 2.3 at lines 6700-6800 for HEAD-LINE and at lines 8200-8300 for DETAIL-LINE. Note the use of the clause AFTER ADVANCING PAGE in the WRITE statement at line 6800. This causes this output to be produced at the top of a new page, which is desirable for the headings being printed at this point in the program.

In order to print an actual decimal point, the edit picture code "." is used in the description of output fields. For example, the field OLD-BALANCE-DL is described as:

PIC 9999.99.

The 9s represent numeric positions as before. The decimal point represents an actual printed decimal point taking up one position in the field. Thus, this field requires seven positions within the output record. When numeric data is moved into a field described using the edit picture code "." the decimal point is inserted in place of the implied decimal point. Note however, that the new field is not numeric. Arithmetic computations cannot be performed on a field described using edit picture codes. An edited item can be used to receive the result of a computation if that result is not needed in further computations as is the case in Program 2.3.

The requirement that the two fields from the input record be added is accomplished by the ADD statement at line 8100:

ADD OLD-BALANCE-IR CHECK-AMOUNT-IR GIVING NEW-BALANCE-DL.

This statement will cause the computer to add the content of two fields and place the result in the location specified in the GIVING clause, in this case into NEW-BALANCE-DL.

2.9 SUMMARY OF PROCEDURE DIVISION ENTRIES

The PROCEDURE DIVISION describes the processing of the data files. It is the "action part" of any COBOL program. The PROCEDURE DIVISION of Program 2.3 has two paragraphs, 1000-MAIN-LOGIC and 2000-SUB-LOGIC. Each sentence in the PROCEDURE DIVISION is made up of one or more statements. A statement

---

Program 2.3   Balance report program

```
100      IDENTIFICATION DIVISION.
200
300      PROGRAM-ID. BALANCE.
400      AUTHOR.
500
600      ENVIRONMENT DIVISION.
700
800      CONFIGURATION SECTION.
900
1000     SOURCE-COMPUTER.
1100     OBJECT-COMPUTER.
1200
1300     INPUT-OUTPUT SECTION.
1400
1500     FILE-CONTROL.
1600
1700         SELECT AMOUNT-FILE ASSIGN TO DISK.
1800         SELECT REPORT-FILE ASSIGN TO PRINTER.
1900
2000     DATA DIVISION.
2100
2200     FILE SECTION.
2300
2400     FD  AMOUNT-FILE
2500         LABEL RECORDS ARE STANDARD
2600         DATA RECORD IS INPUT-RECORD.
2700
2800     01  INPUT-RECORD.
2900         02 OLD-BALANCE-IR    PIC 9999V99.
3000         02 FILLER            PIC XX.
3100         02 CHECK-AMOUNT-IR   PIC 9999V99.
3200         02 FILLER            PIC X(66).
3300
3400     FD  REPORT-FILE
3500         LABEL RECORDS ARE OMITTED
3600         DATA RECORD IS OUTPUT-RECORD.
3700
3800     01  OUTPUT-RECORD        PIC X(132).
3900
4000     WORKING-STORAGE SECTION.
4100
4200     01  FLAGS.
4300         02 EOF-FLAG          PIC X(3)  VALUE "NO".
4400
4500     01  HEAD-LINE.
4600         02 FILLER            PIC X(3)   VALUE SPACES.
4700         02 FILLER            PIC X(11)  VALUE "OLD BALANCE".
4800         02 FILLER            PIC X(3)   VALUE SPACES.
4900         02 FILLER            PIC X(12)  VALUE "CHECK AMOUNT".
5000         02 FILLER            PIC X(3)   VALUE SPACES.
5100         02 FILLER            PIC X(11)  VALUE "NEW BALANCE".
5200
```

Program 2.3 (continued)

```
5300      01  DETAIL-LINE.
5400          02  FILLER          PIC X(5)     VALUE SPACES.
5500          02  OLD-BALANCE-DL  PIC 9999.99.
5600          02  FILLER          PIC X(9)     VALUE SPACES.
5700          02  CHECK-AMOUNT-DL PIC 9(4).99.
5800          02  FILLER          PIC X(7)     VALUE SPACES.
5900          02  NEW-BALANCE-DL  PIC 9(4).99.
6000
6100      PROCEDURE DIVISION.
6200
6300      1000-MAIN-LOGIC.
6400
6500          OPEN INPUT AMOUNT-FILE
6600               OUTPUT REPORT-FILE.
6700          MOVE HEAD-LINE TO OUTPUT-RECORD.
6800          WRITE OUTPUT-RECORD AFTER ADVANCING PAGE.
6900          READ AMOUNT-FILE
7000               AT END MOVE "YES" TO EOF-FLAG.
7100          PERFORM 2000-SUB-LOGIC
7200               UNTIL EOF-FLAG = "YES".
7300          CLOSE AMOUNT-FILE
7400                REPORT-FILE.
7500          STOP RUN.
7600
7700      2000-SUB-LOGIC.
7800
7900          MOVE OLD-BALANCE-IR TO OLD-BALANCE-DL.
8000          MOVE CHECK-AMOUNT-IR TO CHECK-AMOUNT-DL.
8100          ADD OLD-BALANCE-IR CHECK-AMOUNT-IR GIVING NEW-BALANCE-DL.
8200          MOVE DETAIL-LINE TO OUTPUT-RECORD.
8300          WRITE OUTPUT-RECORD AFTER ADVANCING 1 LINES.
8400          READ AMOUNT-FILE
8500               AT END MOVE "YES" TO EOF-FLAG.
```

Figure 2.18   Sample output from Program 2.3

```
OLD BALANCE    CHECK AMOUNT    NEW BALANCE
   1500.00        0200.00        1700.00
   0800.00        0125.00        0925.00
   0750.00        0286.00        1036.00
   0777.00        0444.00        1221.00
```

begins with a COBOL reserved word describing the operation to be performed. Statements used in Program 2.3 include:

```
OPEN      PERFORM
MOVE      CLOSE
WRITE     STOP RUN
READ      ADD
```

The OPEN statement causes the designated files to be opened (i.e., readied for processing). A file must always be opened before any READ or WRITE operations may be performed on it.

The MOVE statement causes data to be moved from one data item (the sending item) to another (the receiving item). A MOVE replaces the contents of the receiving item but does nothing to the sending item.

The WRITE statement causes the specified output record to be written onto the appropriate file. The AFTER clause designates the vertical spacing of paper for a printer file. A general form of the WRITE statement with the AFTER clause is shown in Figure 2.19.

Figure 2.19   General form of the WRITE/AFTER statement

```
                    ┌                       ┌         ┌┌ LINE  ┐┐ ┐
WRITE record-name   │ AFTER ADVANCING    │ integer  ││ LINES ┘│ │
                    └                    │ PAGE                   ┘
```

When the AFTER clause is used, PAGE is used to skip to the top of a new page, 0 is used to skip no lines before printing, 1 is used to skip one line before printing, 2 is used to skip two lines before printing, and 3 is used to skip three lines before printing.

The READ statement causes a record to be read from the specified file. When the record is read, a check is made to determine if it is the system end-of-file record. The purpose of the system end-of-file record is to mark the end of the data records so that a program will not inadvertently process data belonging to another file. When the end-of-file record is read, the statement(s) in the AT END clause of the READ statement wil be executed. In Program 2.1 the READ statement:

```
READ INPUT-FILE AT END MOVE "YES" TO END-OF-FILE.
```

will cause the contents of the data item END-OF-FILE to be set to "YES" when the end-of-file record for the file INPUT-FILE is read.

The PERFORM statement causes the sentences of the designated paragraph to be executed if the condition given in the UNTIL clause is *not* met. For example, the statement:

```
PERFORM 2000-SUB-LOGIC UNTIL EOF-FLAG = "YES".
```

will case a test of EOF-FLAG to be made. If EOF-FLAG = YES, the next statement will be executed. If EOF-FLAG ≠ "YES", the paragraph 2000-SUB-LOGIC will be executed. After execution of the paragraph, the condition is tested again and the procedure is repeated. In Programs 2.1, 2.2, and 2.3 this logic is used to process each record of the input file and to stop processing when the end-of-file record has been read. The CLOSE statement is used to terminate processing of designated files. Any file that is opened should always be closed before the program stops execution. The STOP RUN statement is used to terminate execution of the program. The ADD statement is used to perform the arithmetic operation of addition on designated data items and place the results in a location specified in the GIVING clause. For example:

```
ADD OLD-BALANCE-IR CHECK-AMOUNT-IR GIVING NEW-BALANCE-DL.
```

will cause the sum of OLD-BALANCE-IR and CHECK-AMOUNT-IR to be placed in NEW-BALANCE-DL.

Figure 2.20   Summary of a simple COBOL program

```
IDENTIFICATION DIVISION.
```
The program, author, and other identifying information is given.
```
ENVIRONMENT DIVISION.
```
The computing system(s) to be used and the files to be processed are specified.
```
DATA DIVISION.
FILE SECTION.
```
The input and output files and the records for these files are described.
```
WORKING-STORAGE SECTION.
```
Other data items required by the program are described.
```
PROCEDURE DIVISION.
```
The files are opened. Each record of the input file is processed and the appropriate line of output is written. When all the records have been processed, the files are closed and the execution of the program is terminated.

2.10   DEBUG CLINIC

It is almost inevitable that there will be errors in COBOL programs when they are first submitted for compilation. Errors may be classed as either *syntax errors* or *logical errors*. A syntax error is an error in constructing a COBOL statement. The compiler will alert the programmer that syntax errors have been made by printing appropriate messages as part of the program listing. A logical error is an error in the logic of the program; the program does not perform the desired function. These errors become apparent as the programmer examines the output produced from the processing of sample data. *Debugging* is the process of removing syntax and logical errors from programs.

Syntax Errors

Program 2.4 is an example of a program with syntax errors. The error messages produced by the compiler follow the statement that contains the error. Usually the messages immediately follow the line of code that contains the error, but occasionally other lines of code may intervene. One error may produce one error message or several error messages. Common sources of syntax errors are omission of periods, omission or misspelling of reserved words and misspelling of data names.

Example

The error message following line 4800 in Program 2.4 was caused by the omission of the reserved word PIC in line 4800:

```
02  FILLER          X(3)    VALUE SPACES.
```

This error caused the compiler to generate the error messages following line 4900 as well.

Program 2.4   Program with syntax errors

```
000100 IDENTIFICATION DIVISION.
000200


000300 PROGRAM-ID. BALANCE.
000400 AUTHOR. PAULA.
000500
000600 ENVIRONMENT DIVISION.
000700
000800 CONFIGURATION SECTION.
000900
001000 SOURCE-COMPUTER.
001100 OBJECT-COMPUTER.
001200
001300 INPUT-OUTPUT SECTION.
001400
001500 FILE-CONTROL.
001600
001700     SELECT AMOUNT-FILE ASSIGN TO DISK.
001800     SELECT REPORT-FILE ASSIGN TO PRINTER.
001900
002000 DATA DIVISION.
002100
002200 FILE SECTION.
002300
002400 FD  AMOUNT-FILE
002500     LABEL RECORDS ARE STANDARD
002600     DATA RECORD IS INPUT-RECORD.
002700
002800 01  INPUT-RECORD.
002900     02 OLD-BALANCE-IR   PIC 9999V99.
003000     02 FILLER          PIC XX.
003100     02 CHECK-AMOUNT-IR  PIC 9999V99.
003200     02 FILLER          PIC X(66).
003300
003400 FD  REPORT-FILE
003500     LABEL RECORDS ARE OMITTED
003600     DATA RECORD IS OUTPUT-RECORD.
003700
003800 01  OUTPUT-RECORD      PIC X(132).
003900
004000 WORKING-STORAGE SECTION.
004100
004200 01  FLAGS.
004300     02  EOF-FLAG       PIC X(3)  VALUE "NO".
004400
004500 01  HEAD-LINE.
004600     02 FILLER          PIC X(3)    VALUE SPACES.
004700     02 FILLER          PIC X(11)   VALUE "OLD BALANCE".
004800     02 FILLER              X(3)    VALUE SPACES.
```

ERROR   000 : UNRECOGNIZED CONSTRUCT*** X

```
004900     02 FILLER          PIC X(12)   VALUE "CHECK AMOUNT".
```

ERROR   088 : ELEMENTARY ITEM MUST HAVE SIZE*** 02
ERROR   168 : ITEM CANNOT BE ZERO SIZE*** 02

Program 2.4

```
005000      02 FILLER            PIC X(3)    VALUE SPACES.
005100      02 FILLER            PIC X(11)   VALUE "NEW BALANCE".
005200
005300 01 DETAIL-LINE.
005400      02 FILLER            PIC X(5)    VALUE SPACES.
005500      02 OLD-BALANCE-DL    PIC 9999.99.
005600      02 FILLER            PIC X(9)    VALUE SPACES.
005700      02 CHECK-AMOUNT-DL   PIC 9(4).99.
005800      02 FILLER            PIC X(7)    VALUE SPACES
005900      02 NEW-BALANCE-DL    PIC 9(4).99.
```
ERROR   000 : UNRECOGNIZED CONSTRUCT*** 02
ERROR   027 : DUPLICATE OR INCOMPATIBLE CLAUSE *** PIC
```
006000
006100 PROCEDURE DIVISION.

006200
006300 1000-MAIN-LOGIC.
006400

006500      OPEN INPUT AMOUNT-FILE
006600          OUTPUT REPORT-FILE.
006700      MOVE HEAD-LINE TO OUTPUT-RECORD.
006800      WRITE OUTPUT-RECORD AFTER ADVANCING PAGE.
006900      READ AMOUNT-FILE
007000          AT END MOVE "YES" TO EOF-FLAG.
007100      PERFORM 2000-SUB-LOGIC
```
ERROR   159 : PROCEDURE-NAME DOES NOT OCCUR*** 2000-SUB-LOGIC
```
007200          UNTIL EOF-FLAG = "YES".
007300      CLOSE AMOUNT-FILE
007400          REPORT-FILE.
007500      STOP RUN.
007600
007700 2000-SUB-LOICG.
007800
007900      MOVE OLD-BALANCE-IR TO OLD-BALANCE-DL.
008000      MOVE CHECK-AMOUNT-IR TO CHECK-AMOUNT-DL.
008100      ADD OLD-BALANCE-IR CHECK-AMOUNT-IR GIVING NEW-BALANCE-DL.
```
ERROR   046 : QUALIFIER OR NAME HAS NOT APPEARED BEFORE*** NEW-BALANCE-DL
ERROR   254 : NUMERIC RECEIVING FIELD OPERAND EXPECTED*** NEW-BALANCE-DL
```
008200      MOVE DETAIL-LINE TO OUTPUT-RECORD.
008300      WRITE OUTPUT-RECORD AFTER ADVANCING 1 LINES.
008400      READ AMOUNT-FILE
008500          AT END MOVE "YES" TO EOF-FLAG.
```

```
DID NOT COMPILE
NUMBER OF ERRORS DETECTED = 0008
LAST ERROR AT 008100
TOTAL CARD COUNT: 85
COMPILER COMPILED WITH FOLLOWING OPTIONS: FEDLEVEL.
COMPILE TIMES:     ELAPSED     CPU      I-O     RPM
                   0015.886 0000.980 0003.180 05201
```

Line 5800 is in error because the period is omitted at the end of the line:

```
02  FILLER           PIC X(7)    VALUE SPACES
```

This error caused the error messages listed after line 5900. Because the period is missing on line 5800, the compiler tried to interpret line 5900 as a part of the statement which began on line 5800.

Example

The error message following line 7100 is produced because the paragraph referred to in the preceding line 2000-SUB-LOGIC does not exist. The probable cause of this error is the misspelling of the paragraph name in line 7700.

Example

The error messages following line 8100 are caused by the omission of the period in line 5800. Because of this error, the data name NEW-BALANCE-DL was never defined in the program.

Unfortunately there are no standards for error messages; each compiler uses a different set. Usually a programmer's guide is available containing detailed information about the error messages for the COBOL compiler used at a given computer center.

Logical Errors

Even if a program is compiled without syntax errors, logical errors in the program may remain. The programmer must devise a set or sets of test data and execute the program with the test data in order to ensure that the program correctly performs the function(s) specified for it. It is a good idea to design the test data very early in the program development process; when the expected output with a set of test data is known in advance, the output actually produced by the program can be analyzed easily.

2.11 STANDARDIZATION OF COBOL

This text describes the version of the language generally called COBOL-74, which is currently the most widely available implementation. Even though the language is standardized, each implementation of COBOL is somewhat different. Differences that exist among implementations are of three varieties:

1) There are different requirements in areas specified in the COBOL standard as implementor-defined. (Example: the entry in the ASSIGN clause of the SELECT entry in the ENVIRONMENT DIVISION.)

2) There are additional clauses required by certain compilers but not others. (Example: IBM compilers require the RECORDING MODE clause in an FD entry in the DATA DIVISION.)

3) There are different levels of implementation of standard COBOL. The ANSI standard describes the language as a Nucleus that contains the minimum set of functions required of a COBOL compiler and a set of functional processing modules:

>   Table Handling
>   Sequential I-O
>   Relative I-O
>   Indexed I-O
>   Sort-Merge
>   Report Writer
>   Segmentation
>   Library
>   Debug
>   Inter-Program Communication
>   Communication

Within each module there are two or more levels of implementation. The standard defines a minimal implementation of COBOL as low levels of the Nucleus, Table Handling and Sequential I-O. A full implementation includes a high-level Nucleus and all of the functional processing modules. A subset implementation includes any level of the Nucleus and any combination of functional processing modules from a minimal implementation up to a full implementation. Most implementations of COBOL are of this latter variety.

Because of the wide variety of implementations of standard COBOL, users must have access to the implementor's reference manual for the COBOL compiler with which they will be dealing. This text will describe full ANSI-74 COBOL. Not all of the features described here will work on all systems. Minor modifications to the programs in this text will probably be required to make them run on a particular computing system. Your best guide is the reference manual.

2.12 SELF-TEST EXERCISES

1. Matching

   1. CODASYL
   2. ANSI
   3. DIVISION
   4. ENVIRONMENT
   5. DATA
   6. IDENTIFICATION
   7. PROCEDURE
   8. sequence number
   9. continuation
   10. Margin A
   11. MOVE
   12. PROGRAM-ID
   13. CONFIGURATION SECTION
   14. INPUT-OUTPUT SECTION
   15. SOURCE-COMPUTER
   16. OBJECT-COMPUTER
   17. SELECT
   18. FILE SECTION
   19. WORKING-STORAGE SECTION
   20. FD
   21. level-number
   22. FILLER
   23. OPEN
   24. PERFORM
   25. CLOSE
   26. AFTER

   a. Assigns name to a COBOL program
   b. entry used in FILE SECTION of the DATA DIVISION
   c. used on WRITE statements addressed to printer
   d. computer used to compile the program
   e. largest unit of subdivision of a COBOL program
   f. column 7
   g. column 8
   h. assigns a file to a system component
   i. columns 1-6
   j. Conference on Data Systems Languages
   k. terminates processing of a file by a COBOL program
   l. section of DATA DIVISION in which records associated with files are defined
   m. division of a COBOL program which defines data to be processed
   n. American National Standards Institute
   o. statement which readies a file for processing
   p. computer used to execute the program
   q. identifier used to indicate levels of subdivision of data
   r. division of a COBOL program which identifies the program and the programmer
   s. division of a COBOL program which specifies the computing environment in which the program will function
   t. instruction used to copy data from one memory location to another
   u. reserved word used to define unused positions of a record
   v. command used to execute a COBOL paragraph
   w. portion of the DATA DIVISION used to define data not directly a part of an input or output record
   x. portion of ENVIRONMENT DIVISION used to define the computing system
   y. division used to describe the processing of data
   z. portion of ENVIRONMENT DIVISION used to define files to be processed

2. Write a complete IDENTIFICATION DIVISION for Program 2.3.

3. Draw a program flowchart for Program 2.3.

4. List entries which must begin in Margin A.

5. Classify each of the following data-names as valid or invalid:
   a. INPUT-REC
   b. 100-32
   c. 300 -PARA
   d. PARA-
   e. INPUT-DATA-TO-BE-PROCESSED-BY-THIS-PROGRAM
   f. INPUT REC

6. The following list of items were taken from Program 2.3. Match each item with the applicable terms from the list of descriptive terms below.

   1. HEAD-LINE
   2. PROCEDURE DIVISION
   3. MOVE
   4. AMOUNT-FILE
   5. INPUT-OUTPUT SECTION
   6. CHECK-AMOUNT-DL
   7. 1000-MAIN-LOGIC
   8. ASSIGN
   9. EOF-FLAG
   10. "OLD BALANCE"
   11. 1
   12. SPACES
   13. X(5)
   14. 9999.99
   15. FILLER
   16. ADD
   17. AUTHOR

   a. division header
   b. section header
   c. paragraph header
   d. group data name
   e. elementary data name
   f. alphanumeric constant
   g. figurative constant
   h. numeric constant
   i. reserved word
   j. picture
   k. file name

7. Write DATA DIVISION entries to define a record containing the following fields:

Positions	Content
1-20	customer name
21-35	street address
36-45	city
46-47	state
48-52	zip code
53-80	unused

8. Classify each file-name, record-name and data-name defined in Program 2.3 using the following table:

Where Defined in DATA DIVISION

Type of Item	FILE SECTION		WORKING-STORAGE SECTION		
	Used for Input	Used for Output	Used for Input	Used for Control	Used for Output
File					
Record					
Field					

2.13 PROGRAMMING EXERCISES

1. Write a program to create a file on disk containing the data shown below:

Customer Name	Address				Current Balance
JONES, JAMES	123 A ST.	ANYWHERE	FL	32504	23.00
SMITH, MARY	100 MAIN PL.	SOMEWHERE	AL	34501	78.00
DOE, JANE	502 OAK RD.	ANYWHERE	FL	32504	2.90
JIMENEZ, JAMES	1000 JONES CT.	OVERTHERE	GA	49206	632.00
CHAI, LE	695 MAPLE	OVERHERE	LA	59600	.95

Record Layout

Positions	Content
1-20	Customer name
21-35	Street address
36-45	City
46-47	State
48-52	Zip code
53-57	Current balance (2 decimal places implied)

2. Write a program to list the data file created in Exercise 1 above. Include appropriate headings.

3. Write a program to produce address labels from the input data defined in Exercise 2 above. Output should be of the form:

Name
Street Address
City   State   Zip

4. Write a program to process a file containing records as follows:

Positions

3-4	Grade-1
6-7	Grade-2
10-11	Grade-3

Compute the sum of the grades and list them with appropriate headings.

5. Jones Furniture Co. maintains four warehouse facilities. Inventory records show the quantity of a given item on hand in each facility. The format for each record is:

Positions

1-5	Inventory number
6-15	Item description
16-17	Quantity on hand warehouse 1
18-19	Quantity on hand warehouse 2
20-21	Quantity on hand warehouse 3
22-23	Quantity on hand warehouse 4

Produce a report showing the total quantity of each item on hand.

STRUCTURED PROGRAMMING IN COBOL 3

3.1 STRUCTURED PROGRAMMING GOALS AND STRATEGIES

One of the most onerous problems in utilizing computer-based data processing systems is the cost of developing and maintaining software for the system. Most development and maintenance costs are labor-related because programming is highly labor-intensive. Other costs result from errors in the system's programs that may cause lost productivity or lost opportunity. A primary goal of structured programming is to decrease overall costs of developing and maintaining a system. Structured programming methodology has been demonstrated to be a successful tool to

1) reduce initial development costs and time by increasing programmer productivity
2) produce programs that are virtually error-free
3) simplify the tasks of program maintenance and reduce the associated costs.

A variety of strategies, some of them new and some adapted from engineering and other disciplines, are used to achieve these goals. A primary strategy of structured programming is to create programs that are simple and easy to comprehend. A program with a simple overall design is of much greater value than one with a complex design, because the person who must maintain the program will spend less time learning the mechanics of the program in order to determine where changes must be made. Also, the original programmer is less likely to make logical errors if the design is simple, and errors that do occur should be easier to correct. The virtual elimination of the GO TO statement, as recommended by Dijkstra, and the implementation of only a selected set of program structures contribute greatly to program simplicity.

A structured program must be readable. Readability makes the job of debugging and maintenance easier by reducing the time spent learning what the program is doing and how the task is being accomplished.

Readability is achieved by using descriptive data and procedure names and by using rules for alignment and indention of program elements. A side benefit of readability is that the program becomes largely self-documenting, which reduces the need for most other forms of documentation.

A structured program must be designed and coded in a modular fashion. A *program module* is a segment of code having a well-defined purpose and a single entry and single exit point. A complex task is decomposed into a set of modules; a structured program is a set of modules linked together by a control structure, which determines the order in which the modules are executed. If a program is divided into well-thought-out modules, the debugging process is easier because errors are readily traced to a particular module. Maintainability is also enhanced because the maintenance programmer can readily locate the particular section of the program which must be changed by matching the required change to the program module "responsible" for that function.

The general thrust in data processing over the past few years has been towards developing a professionalism among programmers, analysts and other data processing personnel. Calling programmers "software engineers" emphasizes the parallel between developing computer programs and developing mechanical or electronic systems. Many practices that have long been associated with engineering, including

- well-defined methodology
- emphasis on product design
- standards for product testing
- modular decomposition of complex systems

have increasingly been adopted by data processing professionals. The day of brilliant but eccentric programmers who develop programs in total isolation, using their own unique methods, is largely in the past. Current programming techniques emphasize simplicity, readability, modularity and program maintainability. The resulting program may not have the hallmark of creativity that characterized programs of the past, but the programs work well, are easy to read and maintain, and help hold down the cost of developing and maintaining computing systems.

3.2   TOP-DOWN PROGRAM DESIGN

Structured programming is really a programming discipline. It encompasses techniques used to develop program logic and standards for the actual coding of the program. The technique used for program development generally is referred to as *top-down program design*. In top-down program design, a program is specified as a set of procedures to be executed in some chosen sequence; a procedure may be relatively simple (opening a file) or complex (accumulating the sum of a sequence of data items). A complex procedure will in turn be broken down into a sequence of simpler procedures until at last the COBOL code for the program can be written.

3.3   PROGRAM EXAMPLE

Problem Statement

A data file contains records with a field in positions 10-14 representing a whole number quantity (no decimal places). A program is needed that will list these quantities and calculate their total. A printer spacing chart for the desired report is shown in Figure 3.1.

Problem Analysis

The entire program could be summarized as one rather complex procedure:

> Compute the sum of a set of data items

This statement amounts to little more than a restatement of the problem to be solved. In order to design a suitable program, it is necessary to respecify the program as a sequence of simpler procedures:

> Open files
> Read the first data record
> Do until no more data
>   Accumulate the sum of each data item
> End Do
> Write the sum
> Close files
> Stop

At this point it is apparent that the procedure "Accumulate the sum of each data item" is still quite complex and must be respecified as follows:

> Add the data item to the sum
> Read the next data record

Thus the complete program now has the form:

> Open files
> Read the first data record
> Do until no more data
>   Add the data item to the sum
>   Read the next data record
> End Do
> Write the sum
> Close files
> Stop

Upon examination of this procedure we realize that an important requirement of the program specification has been omitted—the program should produce a list of the items read. During the processing of each record, the value of the data item should be written on the printer. Because the COBOL program requires that the actions controlled by the Do-until-structure be coded as separate procedures, we should revise the design one more time as follows:

> *Main logic*
>   Open files
>   Read the first data record
>   Do Loop control until end of file
>   Write the sum
>   Close files
>   Stop
>
> *Loop control*
>   Add data item to sum
>   Write data item
>   Read the next record

Figure 3.1 Printer spacing chart for Program 3.1

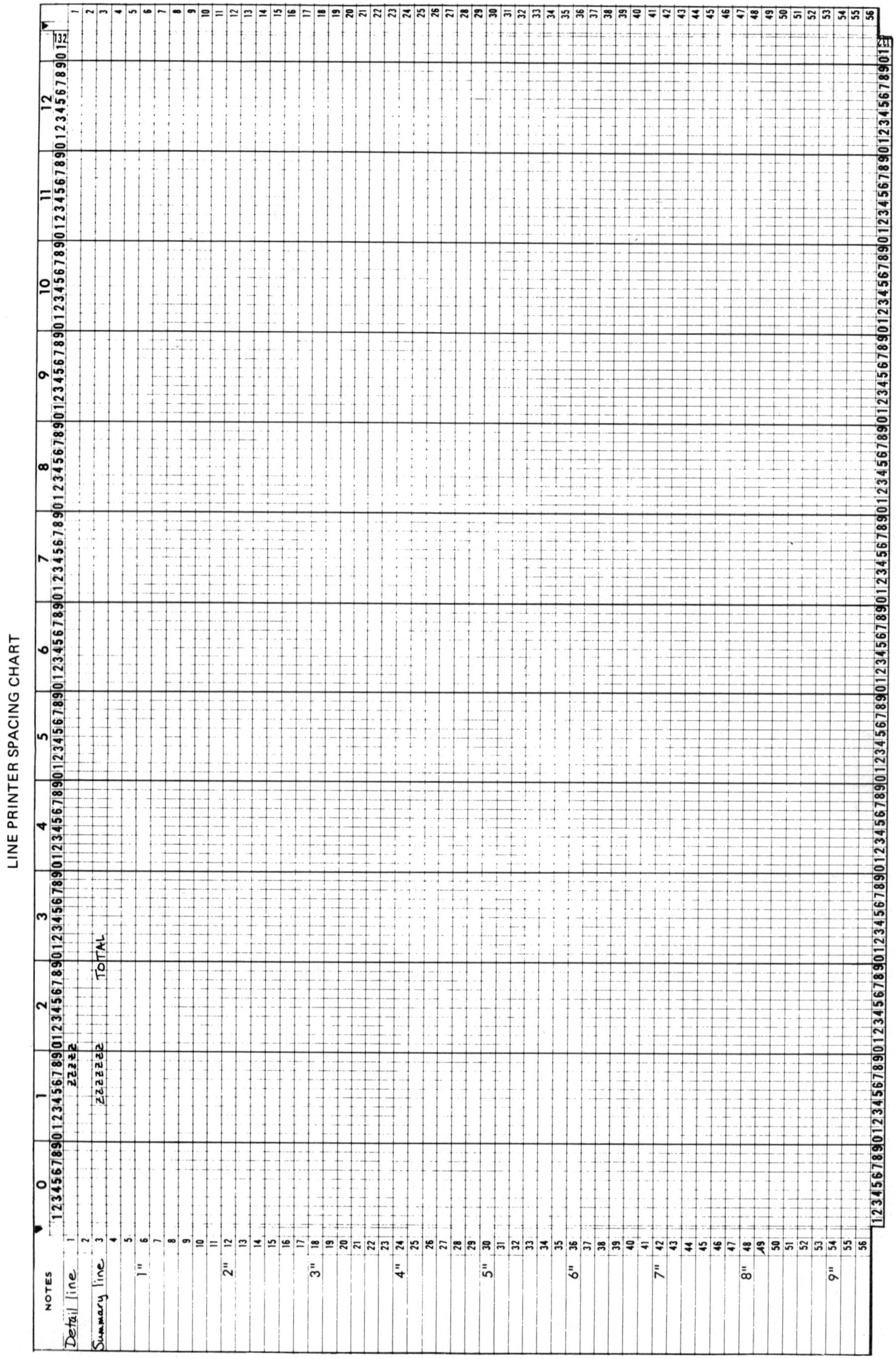

LINE PRINTER SPACING CHART

This plan is now sufficiently complete for the programmer to begin writing the actual program. The process by which this plan was derived is an example of top-down program design. At each successive stage in the process, one or more complex tasks are broken down into a series of simpler tasks. At some stage the plan is expressed in simple enough terms that the program can be written.

This problem requires the use of a programming technique called *accumulation* in order to compute the required total. In accumulation, a data item is used to store a running total, that is, each new value is added to the accumulator and the results replace the old value. The accumulator must have the initial value of zero before any values are added to it. An easy way to accomplish this task is to use the VALUE IS ZERO clause when the accumulator is defined in WORKING-STORAGE. (ZERO is another figurative constant; the clause VALUE IS 0 would be equivalent.)

Problem Solution

A solution to this problem is shown in Program 3.1. This program processes an input file called AMOUNT-FILE and produces a printed report on REPORT-FILE. As in Program 2.3, the two different output records are defined in WORKING-STORAGE: DETAIL-LINE (lines 4700-4900) and SUMMARY-LINE (lines 5100-5500). Prior to printing either of these records, the record is moved to PRINT-LINE, which is the record defined in the FILE SECTION for REPORT-FILE. (See, for example, line 6800-6900 and 7800-7900.)

The accumulator in this program is called GRAND-TOTAL and is defined in WORKING-STORAGE as follows (lines 4400-4500):

```
01  TOTALS.
    02  GRAND-TOTAL        PIC 9(7) VALUE ZERO.
```

The item GRAND-TOTAL is a numeric field with initial value zero. It is defined as being subordinate to the group item TOTALS so that if a subsequent programmer wishes to add other accumulators to the program, all of them will be grouped together for easy reference.

The actual task of accumulating the total is carried out by the ADD statement at line 7600:

```
ADD IR-NUMBER TO GRAND-TOTAL.
```

This statement causes the value of IR-NUMBER to be added to GRAND- TOTAL and the result to replace GRAND-TOTAL. The statement is equivalent to the ADD statement:

```
ADD IR-NUMBER GRAND-TOTAL GIVING GRAND-TOTAL.
```

It is imperative that GRAND-TOTAL be a numeric item in order for this computation to be carried out. That is why a separate entry in the DATA DIVISION is required for GRAND-TOTAL and SL-GRAND-TOTAL—the field used to store that value on the SUMMARY-LINE. SL-GRAND-TOTAL is defined as an edited field and, hence, is non-numeric. The content of SL-GRAND-TOTAL could not have arithmetic operations performed on it. Prior to moving SUMMARY-LINE to PRINT -LINE for printing, the content of GRAND-TOTAL is moved to SL-GRAND-TOTAL (line 6700).

Program 3.1 Accumulation Program

```
100      IDENTIFICATION DIVISION.
200
300      PROGRAM-ID. SAMPLE-ACCUMULATION.
400      AUTHOR. GARY GLEASON.
500
600      ENVIRONMENT DIVISION.
700
800      CONFIGURATION SECTION.
900
1000     SOURCE-COMPUTER.
1100     OBJECT-COMPUTER.
1200
1300     INPUT-OUTPUT SECTION.
1400
1500     FILE-CONTROL.
1600
1700         SELECT AMOUNT-FILE ASSIGN TO DISK.
1800         SELECT REPORT-FILE ASSIGN TO PRINTER.
1900
2000     DATA DIVISION.
2100
2200     FILE SECTION.
2300
2400     FD  AMOUNT-FILE
2500         LABEL RECORDS ARE STANDARD
2600         DATA RECORD IS INPUT-RECORD.
2700
2800     01  INPUT-RECORD.
2900         02 FILLER              PIC X(9).
3000         02 IR-NUMBER           PIC 9(5).
3100         02 FILLER              PIC X(66).
3200
3300     FD  REPORT-FILE
3400         LABEL RECORDS ARE OMITTED
3500         DATA RECORD IS PRINT-LINE.
3600
3700     01  PRINT-LINE             PIC X(132).
3800
3900     WORKING-STORAGE SECTION.
4000
4100     01  FLAGS.
4200         02  EOF-FLAG           PIC X(3) VALUE "NO".
4300
4400     01  TOTALS.
4500         02  GRAND-TOTAL        PIC 9(7) VALUE ZERO.
4600
4700     01  DETAIL-LINE.
4800         02 FILLER              PIC X(15) VALUE SPACES.
4900         02 DL-NUMBER           PIC ZZZZZ.
5000
5100     01  SUMMARY-LINE.
5200         02 FILLER              PIC X(13) VALUE SPACES.
5300         02 SL-GRAND-TOTAL      PIC ZZZZZZZ.
```

```
5400        02 FILLER           PIC X(7) VALUE SPACES.
5500        02 FILLER           PIC X(5) VALUE "TOTAL".
5600
5700    PROCEDURE DIVISION.
5800
5900    1000-MAJOR-LOGIC.
6000
6100        OPEN INPUT AMOUNT-FILE
6200             OUTPUT REPORT-FILE.
6300        READ AMOUNT-FILE
6400             AT END MOVE "YES" TO EOF-FLAG.
6500        PERFORM 2000-LOOP-CONTROL
6600             UNTIL EOF-FLAG = "YES".
6700        MOVE GRAND-TOTAL TO SL-GRAND-TOTAL.
6800        MOVE SUMMARY-LINE TO PRINT-LINE.
6900        WRITE PRINT-LINE AFTER ADVANCING 2 LINES.
7000        CLOSE AMOUNT-FILE
7100             REPORT-FILE.
7200        STOP RUN.
7300
7400    2000-LOOP-CONTROL.
7500
7600        ADD IR-NUMBER TO GRAND-TOTAL.
7700        MOVE IR-NUMBER TO DL-NUMBER.
7800        MOVE DETAIL-LINE TO PRINT-LINE.
7900        WRITE PRINT-LINE AFTER ADVANCING 1 LINES.
8000        READ AMOUNT-FILE
8100             AT END MOVE "YES" TO EOF-FLAG.
```

Program 3.1 (continued)

Figure 3.2   Sample output from Program 3.1

```
100
150
200
250

700        TOTAL
```

In this program the edit picture code Z is used to provide editing of numeric output fields. The picture code Z causes suppression of leading non-significant zeroes. Thus instead of output such as:

0 0 0 1 2 3

which would result using a picture such as 9(6), we are able to produce output like:

1 2 3

by using a picture Z(6). The leading zeroes are replaced by spaces in the edited field.

3.4 STRUCTURED PROGRAMMING STYLE

A major goal of structured programming is readability and ease of understanding. Unstructured programs sometimes get too complicated to be readable; one reason for this is the use of the unconditional branching statement GO TO. The GO TO statement causes a branch to a specified location within a program *with no provision for returning*. By contrast, the PERFORM statement causes a branch to a specified location, but when the paragraph is completed, control returns to the PERFORM statement. In a structured program, virtually all branching will be controlled by the PERFORM and IF statements. The GO TO statement, if used at all, is used in a very restricted and controlled manner, described later in this book. In fact, it is possible to write any program using only the three types of structures outlined above, and none of these structures requires the GO TO statement in COBOL implementation. For this reason structured programming is sometimes referred to as "go-to-less" programming; the avoidance of the use of the GO TO statement is an important principle of structured programming.

The goals of readability and ease of understanding lead to certain restrictions and practices in the coding of a structured COBOL program. For example, it is important to use meaningful names for data items, paragraphs and other names defined by the programmer. In COBOL, data-names and paragraph names may range in length from one to thirty characters, thus giving the programmer a wide latitude in the assignment of names. In a particular program, for example, a programmer might choose to call two data-names X and Y, or he might choose PAY-RATE and HOURS-WORKED. It is obvious that the latter choice is more descriptive and would aid in understanding the type of data stored in each data-name. In a similar spirit, the names of paragraphs should describe the functions performed in each paragraph. For example, in Program 3.2 the paragraph names 1000-MAJOR-LOGIC, 2000-INITIALIZATION, 3000-LOOP-CONTROL, 4000-READ, 5000-ACCUMULATE-SUM, 6000-WRITE-DETAIL-LINE, and 7000-END-OF-JOB were chosen to aid the reader in understanding the program. The paragraph numbers 1000, 2000, and so on help the reader to locate the paragraph quickly.

Comprehension and readability are enhanced considerably by the use of short single function paragraphs in a program. For example, Program 3.1 is rewritten in Program 3.2 to contain a number of short single-function paragraphs. Note that Program 3.1 contains only two paragraphs, while Program 3.2 contains seven paragraphs. Which program do you find easier to read and understand? In this simple example you may prefer Program 3.1. However, as programs become longer and more complex, the practice of coding reasonably short single-function paragraphs can result in a more understandable and readable program. A rule of thumb is that no paragraph should be longer than one page of print or one screen of CRT display, whichever is appropriate. There is nothing to prevent paragraphs from being shorter to increase readability and understandability.

The discussion above suggests that there are good ways and not-so-good ways to write a correct COBOL program. Style is important in programming, as it is in writing reports, letters, or novels. A good program is distinguished by more than correctness; the style in which it is written determines whether people can read and understand the program with ease. A well-written program is far more valuable than another program which, though it performs the same task, is written in a way which makes it unreadable and difficult to understand.

We cannot set down an exhaustive list of rules regarding style for writing a structured COBOL program, as there are no universally agreed-upon standards for style. You will find a number of programs in this text which, though imperfect, are written in "good" structured programming style. If you discover ways in which you can improve on our style, feel free to practice your improvements in your own programs. Any organization such as a large business which uses structured COBOL programming extensively will have a style book outlining rules and practices expected in coding programs at that installation.

In summary, the following rules form the bases for structured programming:

1) Use top-down program design techniques.
2) Use only the sequence, decision, and loop structures.
3) Use unconditional branching (the GO TO) with restraint if at all.
4) Follow standards of program readability and understandability.

By following the examples of structured COBOL programs in this text and applying the major rules above, you can become adept at writing structured COBOL programs. Although structured programming may place an added burden on you initially because you have to learn rules for structure as well as rules for COBOL language, the benefits of the structured approach far outweigh the disadvantages.

3.5 THE PERFORM STATEMENT

The PERFORM statement causes a program to execute a paragraph and, when the paragraph is completed, to return either to the PERFORM statement itself or to the statement following the PERFORM statement. A general form for the PERFORM statement is:

PERFORM paragraph-name [UNTIL condition]

Note the use of brackets ([ ]) in this general form. Brackets mean that the enclosed portion of the statement is optional.

If the UNTIL clause is omitted, the PERFORM statement causes the specified paragraph to be executed and, upon completion of that paragraph, control returns to the statement following the PERFORM statement. For example, in the partial program illustrated in Figure 3.3, the statement

```
PERFORM 2000-WRITE-SUMMARY-LINE.
```

in the paragraph 1000-MAIN-LOGIC causes the paragraph 2000-WRITE-SUMMARY-LINE to be executed. The three sentences in the paragraph will be executed in sequential order; then, the statement immediately following the PERFORM statement will be executed. In flowchart form this structure would be shown as:

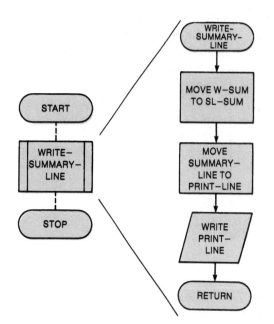

The result would be the same if the statements in the executed paragraph were inserted in place of the PERFORM statement. For example, consider the statement PERFORM 5000-ACCUMULATE-SUM at line 7500 of Program 3.2. The statement (line 8600)

    ADD IR-NUMBER TO GRAND-TOTAL.

(which is the only statement in 5000-ACCUMULATION-SUM that could be inserted in place of the statement PERFORM 5000-ACCUMULATE-SUM) to give the same results. In general, if you wish to cause the execution of a paragraph one time, you will use the PERFORM statement without the UNTIL option.

Figure 3.3 Example of the use of the PERFORM statement

```
1000-MAIN-LOGIC
    .
    .
    .
    PERFORM 2000-WRITE-SUMMARY-LINE.
    .
    .
    .
    STOP RUN.
2000-WRITE-SUMMARY-LINE.
    MOVE W-SUM TO SL-SUM.
    MOVE SUMMARY-LINE TO PRINT-LINE.
    WRITE PRINT-LINE AFTER ADVANCING 2 LINES.
```

If, however, you desire to cause the execution of a paragraph to be repeated a number of times until some condition is satisfied, you include the UNTIL clause in the PERFORM statement. In this case the condition is tested before execution of the paragraph. If the condition is not met (the condition is false), the statement following the PERFORM statement is executed next. When the named paragraph has been executed, the condition is tested again; if the condition now is met, the statement following the PERFORM is executed. Otherwise execution of the paragraph is repeated.

Figure 3.4 PERFORM/UNTIL program example

```
WORKING-STORAGE SECTION.
01  EOF-FLAG PIC XXX VALUE "NO".
    .
    .
    .
PROCEDURE DIVISION.
1000-MAJOR-LOGIC
    .
    .
    .
    PERFORM 2000-LOOP-CONTROL UNTIL EOF-FLAG = "YES".
    .
    .
    .
    STOP RUN.
2000-LOOP-CONTROL.
    .
    .
    READ INPUT-FILE AT END MOVE "YES" TO EOF-FLAG.
```

Figure 3.4 illustrates the use of this version of the PERFORM statement. The condition being tested involves the value of a data-name called EOF-FLAG. A data-name such as this is sometimes called a "program switch" because it has two values—"NO" and "YES"—in much the same way as a light switch has two positions—off and on. The value "NO" corresponds to the switch being set in the "off" position; the value "YES" represents the "on" position. Program switches are used as communications links among paragraphs of a program.

The program switch in Figure 3.4 is used to detect when the last record from the input file has been read. So long as the last record has not been read, the switch remains in the "off" position. When the last record is read, the switch is turned to the "on" position. The occurrence of the reading of the last record is in the paragraph 2000-LOOP-CONTROL; the fact that the last record has been read is communicated to the paragraph 1000-MAJOR-LOGIC via the setting of the program switch EOF-FLAG. The statement

```
    PERFORM 2000-LOOP-CONTROL UNTIL EOF-FLAG = "YES".
```

will cause control to be passed to the paragraph 2000-LOOP-CONTROL as long as the switch is "off" (i.e., it has value other than YES). The switch is in the "off" position in the WORKING-STORAGE SECTION where the data item is defined:

```
    01 EOF-FLAG PIC XXX VALUE "NO".
```

The switch is turned to the "on" position in the paragraph 2000-LOOP-CONTROL in the AT END clause of the READ statement. Figure 3.5 illustrates in flowchart form the logic of this use of the PERFORM statement. In general, any paragraph executed by a PERFORM/UNTIL statement must modify the condition being tested, or the program will enter an *infinite loop*. An infinite loop is formed when a sequence of statements is executed repeatedly with no possibility for the program to exit the sequence. Most computing systems contain provision for terminating programs after a reasonable period of time to protect the system from programs which are caught in an infinite loop.

Figure 3.5 Flowchart of the PERFORM/UNTIL in Figure 3.4

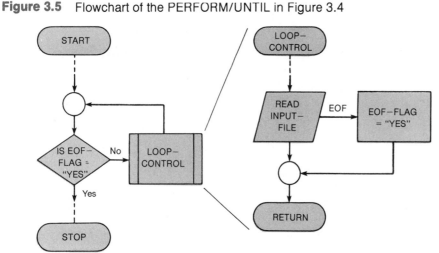

3.6 A MODULAR EXAMPLE

Recall that Program 3.1 lists and calculates the sum of a sequence of values which are contained in a data file where each record in the file contains one value. Program 3.1 illustrated the process of accumulation, which is used to compute the sum of a sequence of data items. The process essentially is one of maintaining a "running" total (i.e., adding one data item at a time into the total). In the beginning, a data item (GRAND-TOTAL) to be used to contain the total is assigned an initial value of zero; a data item used in this way is called an *accumulator*. When each data record is read, the data item from that record is added to the accumulator in the statement (line 7600):

```
ADD IR-NUMBER TO GRAND-TOTAL.
```

When all records have been read, the accumulator holds the accumulated sum of the values. A similar process can be used to count the occurrence of specific items, except that the value 1 is added to the accumulator. An accumulator used in this fashion is often referred to as a *counter*.

Program 3.2 contains Program 3.1 redone in an expanded modular form. Note that the PROCEDURE DIVISION of Program 3.1 contains two paragraphs, while Program 3.2 contains seven paragraphs. The 3000-LOOP-CONTROL paragraph of Program 3.2 calls upon other paragraphs to do various functions, whereas in Program 3.1 instructions for these functions are written into the LOOP-CONTROL paragraph. For example, in place of the statement

ADD IR–NUMBER TO GRAND–TOTAL (line 7600 of Prog. 3.1) we find PERFORM 5000–
ACCUMULATE–SUM (line 7500 of Prog. 3.2). The content of the paragraph 5000–
ACCUMULATE–SUM is the statement ADD IR–NUMBER TO GRAND–TOTAL (line 8600 of
Prog. 3.2).

Program 3.2   Modular program example

```
100      IDENTIFICATION DIVISION.
200
300      PROGRAM-ID. ACCUMULATION-MODULAR-FORM.
400      AUTHOR. GARY GLEASON.
500
600      ENVIRONMENT DIVISION.
700
800      CONFIGURATION SECTION.
900
1000     SOURCE-COMPUTER.
1100     OBJECT-COMPUTER.
1200
1300     INPUT-OUTPUT SECTION.
1400
1500     FILE-CONTROL.
1600
1700         SELECT AMOUNT-FILE ASSIGN TO DISK.
1800         SELECT REPORT-FILE ASSIGN TO PRINTER.
1900
2000     DATA DIVISION.
2100
2200     FILE SECTION.
2300
2400     FD   AMOUNT-FILE
2500         LABEL RECORDS ARE STANDARD
2600         DATA RECORD IS INPUT-RECORD.
2700
2800     01   INPUT-RECORD.
2900         02 FILLER          PIC X(9).
3000         02 IR-NUMBER       PIC 9(5).
3100         02 FILLER          PIC X(66).
3200
3300     FD   REPORT-FILE
3400         LABEL RECORDS ARE OMITTED
3500         DATA RECORD IS PRINT-LINE.
3600
3700     01   PRINT-LINE        PIC X(132).
3800
3900     WORKING-STORAGE SECTION.
4000
4100     01   FLAGS.
4200         02  EOF-FLAG       PIC X(3) VALUE "NO".
4300
4400     01 TOTALS.
4500         02  GRAND-TOTAL    PIC 9(7) VALUE ZERO.
4600
```

Program 3.2 *(continued)*

```
4700    01  DETAIL-LINE.
4800        02 FILLER              PIC X(15) VALUE SPACES.
4900        02 DL-NUMBER           PIC ZZZZZ.
5000
5100    01  SUMMARY-LINE.
5200        02 FILLER              PIC X(13) VALUE SPACES.
5300        02 SL-GRAND-TOTAL      PIC ZZZZZZZ.
5400        02 FILLER              PIC X(7) VALUE SPACES.
5500        02 FILLER              PIC X(5) VALUE "TOTAL".
5600
5700    PROCEDURE DIVISION.
5800
5900    1000-MAJOR-LOGIC.
6000
6100        PERFORM 2000-INITIALIZATION.
6200        PERFORM 3000-LOOP-CONTROL
6300            UNTIL EOF-FLAG = "YES".
6400        PERFORM 7000-END-OF-JOB.
6500        STOP RUN.
6600
6700    2000-INITIALIZATION.
6800
6900        OPEN INPUT AMOUNT-FILE
7000             OUTPUT REPORT-FILE.
7100        PERFORM 4000-READ.
7200
7300    3000-LOOP-CONTROL.
7400
7500        PERFORM 5000-ACCUMULATE-SUM.
7600        PERFORM 6000-WRITE-DETAIL-LINE.
7700        PERFORM 4000-READ.
7800
7900    4000-READ.
8000
8100        READ AMOUNT-FILE
8200            AT END MOVE "YES" TO EOF-FLAG.
8300
8400    5000-ACCUMULATE-SUM.
8500
8600        ADD IR-NUMBER TO GRAND-TOTAL.
8700
8800    6000-WRITE-DETAIL-LINE.
8900
9000        MOVE IR-NUMBER TO DL-NUMBER.
9100        MOVE DETAIL-LINE TO PRINT-LINE.
9200        WRITE PRINT-LINE AFTER ADVANCING 1 LINES.
9300
9400    7000-END-OF-JOB.
9500
9600        MOVE GRAND-TOTAL TO SL-GRAND-TOTAL.
9700        MOVE SUMMARY-LINE TO PRINT-LINE.
9800        WRITE PRINT-LINE AFTER ADVANCING 2 LINES.
9900        CLOSE AMOUNT-FILE
10000            REPORT-FILE.
```

The modular style used in Program 3.2 is the style preferred among most programmers. Each paragraph is concise and carries out a single well defined function; the name assigned to the paragraph is descriptive of the paragraph's function. The art of writing "good" structured programs begins with breaking down the task at hand into a manageable set of functions, each of which can be implemented in COBOL program by a paragraph of reasonable size and complexity. The remainder of this text contains many examples of structured programs which the reader may use as models.

3.7   STRUCTURE DIAGRAMS

Structure diagrams represent the relationships among paragraphs in a program. Each paragraph is represented as a block in the diagram; the paragraph name is written in the block. If one paragraph is executed via the `PERFORM` statement from another, a line connecting the two blocks is drawn. For example, in Figure 3.6 `PARA-B` is executed (`PERFORM`ed) from `PARA-A` so a line in the structure diagram connects the block labeled `PARA-B`. The structure diagram for Program 3.1 is shown in Figure 3.7.

Figure 3.6   Example of structure diagram

COBOL Code   *Structure Diagram*

```
PROCEDURE DIVISION
PARA-A.
    .
    .
    .
    PERFORM PARA-B UNTIL EOF-CODE = "YES".
    .
    .
    .

PARA-B.
    .
    .
    .
```

```
      ┌──────────┐
      │  PARA-A  │
      └─────┬────┘
            │
      ┌─────┴────┐
      │  PARA-B  │
      └──────────┘
```

Figure 3.7   Structure diagram for Program 3.1

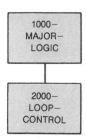

For a program such as this with a very simple structure, the diagram provides little new insight into the program. However, consider the structure diagram for Program 3.2 shown in Figure 3.8. In this case, because of the numerous paragraphs the diagram shows at a glance which paragraphs are used primarily to control the functioning of the program and which paragraphs carry out the operations (such as input, output, computation) required by the program.

Paragraphs which function primarily to provide control appear in the structure diagram with several lines leading from them to other paragraphs. In this case 1000-MAJOR-LOGIC and 3000-LOOP-CONTROL are examples of control paragraphs. Paragraphs which function primarily as operations appear in the structure diagram with few or no lines leading from them. In this case 2000-INITIALIZATION, 4000-READ, 5000-ACCUMULATE-SUM, 6000-WRITE-DETAIL-LINE and 7000-END-OF-JOB are operational paragraphs.

Figure 3.8 Structure diagram for Program 3.2

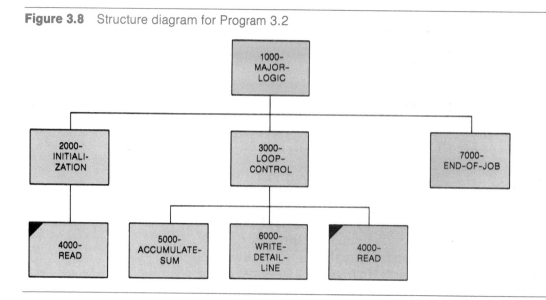

A structure diagram clearly shows the hierarchy into which paragraphs of a program are divided. A paragraph which is executed from a paragraph directly via a PERFORM, or indirectly by way of a paragraph which is PERFORMed, is *subordinate* to that paragraph. Thus, in Figure 3.8, it is clear that all other paragraphs are subordinate to 1000-MAJOR-LOGIC while 5000-ACCUMULATE-SUM, 6000-WRITE-DETAIL-LINE, and 4000-READ are subordinate to 3000-LOOP-CONTROL.

The triangular shading in the blocks labeled 4000-READ signifies that this paragraph is PERFORMed from more than one place in the program.

3.8   DEBUG CLINIC

The PERFORM Statement

A fundamental restriction on the use of the PERFORM statement is that no paragraph may PERFORM itself. The following code would be invalid:

COBOL code   *Structure Diagram*

```
PARA-A.
    .
    .
    .
    PERFORM PARA-A.
```

In general COBOL compilers will not detect violations of this rule; however, when the program is executed an infinite loop will result.

A more general restriction on the PERFORM statement is that no paragraph may PERFORM another paragraph that results in a PERFORM of the original paragraph. For example, consider the following code:

COBOL code   *Structure Diagram*

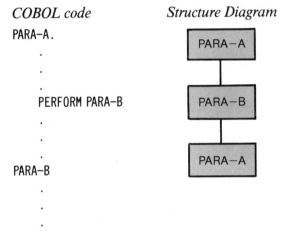

```
PARA-A.
    .
    .
    .
    PERFORM PARA-B
    .
    .
    .
PARA-B
    .
    .
    .
    PERFORM PARA-A
```

PARA-A PERFORMs PARA-B which in turn PERFORMs PARA-A. As before, this code results in the creation of an infinite loop during execution. The error is perhaps more obvious from the structure diagram than from the COBOL code itself. This does not mean that a given paragraph may not occur several times in the structure diagram. For example, in Figure 3.8 4000-READ occurs twice; the first time it is subordinate to 2000-INITIALIZATION; the second time it is subordinate to 3000-LOOP-CONTROL. However, note that in Figure 3.8, no paragraph is subordinate to itself.

Program Structure

As we discussed earlier, constructing "good" structured programs is as much an art as a science; however, certain guidelines should be observed. We have already discussed some of them: use of three fundamental structures; use of descriptive data-names and paragraph-names; segmentation of the program into control and operational paragraphs; and so on. The segmentation of a program has been the subject of a great deal of research, with the result that there is now general agreement on two principles, both of which have close analogs in organization theory.

In an organization, a manager should not be responsible for too many subordinates. The manager's "span of control" reaches an optimal limit; it is counter-productive to ask a manager to control more than that limit. In a similar way a control paragraph in a COBOL program has maximum "span of control." There is a limit to the number of subordinate paragraphs which a given paragraph should control directly. A structure diagram such as

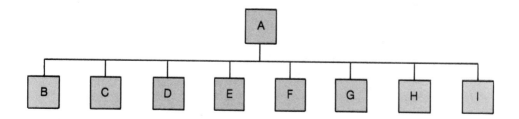

probably represents a paragraph with too many subordinates; its span of control is too large. It would be better to substitute an organization such as

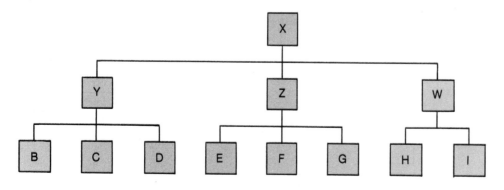

in which each control paragraph has a more restricted span of control.

There is no general agreement as to the number of paragraphs which represents an appropriate span of control in a COBOL program. It seems clear that ten subordinates are probably too many, but where the line is drawn is a matter of personal opinion.

In a management hierarchy there are levels ranging from the chief executive officer at the top through various levels of middle management to the lowest level employee. As the number of levels of bureaucracy grows, problems of communication and control may develop. In a similar way, problems of communication and control may develop within a COBOL program which has too many levels of subordination. Thus, a structure such as

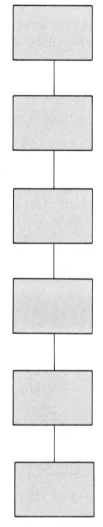

which has six levels should probably be redesigned to have fewer levels. A structure such as

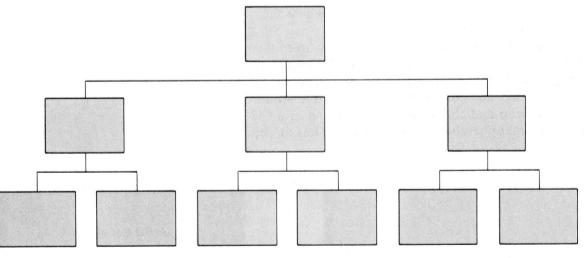

which has only three levels is preferable to the six-level structure above.

The COBOL programmer should analyze the structure diagrams of programs he or she writes to determine if each control paragraph has an appropriate span of control, and if there are an appropriate number of levels of subordination within the program. It is usually possible to redesign any program that fails either of these tests.

Loop Control

In a structured program, loops are created by the iteration structure implemented in COBOL by the PERFORM/UNTIL statement. Recall that PERFORM/UNTIL causes execution of the specified paragraph until a condition is met. There are three possible errors which may occur: the paragraph is never executed at all; the paragraph is executed exactly one time; and the paragraph is executed continuously without a proper end, creating an infinite loop. Consider the PERFORM/UNTIL statement from Program 3.2 (lines 6200-6300)

```
PERFORM 3000-LOOP-CONTROL
    UNTIL EOF-FLAG = "YES".
```

In flowchart form this would appear as

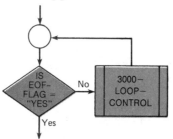

In one instance, suppose analysis of output from the program showed that the paragraph 3000-LOOP-CONTROL was never executed at all. What would be the probable cause? The only reason is that EOF-FLAG is equal to "YES". This could happen in one of two ways: either the initial value of EOF-FLAG was specified to be "YES" in WORKING-STORAGE; or the program has caused the value of EOF-FLAG to become "YES" prior to execution of the PERFORM/UNTIL statement. A probable cause of this latter condition is that there were no records in the file so that when 4000-READ is PERFORMed in 2000-INITIALIZATION (Prog. 3.2 line 7100), the AT END clause on the READ statement causes the value "YES" to be moved to EOF-FLAG. In the first case the programmer should rewrite the definition of EOF-FLAG in WORKING-STORAGE; in the second case he or she must ensure that there are records in the file to be processed.

On the other hand, suppose analysis of the output showed that the paragraph 3000-LOOP-CONTROL was executed exactly one time. If there was only one record in the file being processed, this is obviously the way the program should behave. If, however, there was more than one record in the file, there is an error in the program. One likely source of error is the omission of the UNTIL clause on the PERFORM statement. The statement PERFORM 3000-LOOP-CONTROL would cause 3000-LOOP-CONTROL to be executed exactly one time. If the UNTIL clause is in its proper place, another cause for this error would be a statement within 3000-LOOP-CONTROL which sets the value of EOF-FLAG to "YES" by mistake.

Or, suppose analysis of the output from the program led us to believe that the program had entered an infinite loop. For example, the program has been terminated because of excessive elapsed time or a message has been produced indicating that an attempt has been made to read past end-of-file (i.e., an attempt to read more records than the file contained). If the value of EOF-FLAG never becomes "YES", the PERFORM/UNTIL statement will cause 3000-LOOP-CONTROL to be executed forever.

There are two possible causes for this condition; either the READ operation has been omitted with 3000-LOOP-CONTROL; or the AT END clause on the READ statement does not set EOF-FLAG equal to "YES". Omission of the READ operation within the loop will cause the program to appear to process the first record again and again. This the most probable cause if the program terminates because of excessive time used. Failure of the program to set EOF-FLAG to "YES" when end-of-file is reached will generally result in an attempt to read past end-of-file.

3.9 SELF-TEST EXERCISES

1. What purpose do the numbers used with paragraph names have? Are the numbers required by COBOL syntax or are they a part of structured programming style?

2. What is a "switch"? Why are switches used?

3. What is an "accumulator"? Why are accumulators used?

4. Rewrite the PROCEDURE DIVISION of Program 2.2 in the modular form described in this chapter. Draw the associated structure diagram. Classify each paragraph as providing a control or operation function.

5. The PROCEDURE DIVISION of Program 2.1 has been rewritten in Figure 3.9. Find logical errors in the code.

Figure 3.9 Program with logical errors

```
Line
  1     PROCEDURE DIVISION.
  2     1000-MAIN-LOGIC.
  3         PERFORM 2000-INITIALIZATION.
  4         PERFORM 3000-BUILD-FILE.
  5         PERFORM 5000-TERMINATE.
  6         STOP RUN.
  7     2000-INITIALIZATION.
  8         OPEN INPUT INPUT-FILE
  9             OUTPUT OUTPUT-FILE.
 10         PERFORM 4000-READ-INPUT-FILE.
 11     3000-BUILD-FILE.
 12         MOVE INPUT-REC TO OUTPUT-REC.
 13         WRITE OUTPUT-REC.
 14     4000-READ-INPUT-FILE.
 15         READ INPUT-FILE
 16             AT END MOVE "YES" TO END-OF-FILE.
 17     5000-TERMINATE.
 18         CLOSE INPUT-FILE
 19             OUTPUT-FILE.
```

3.10 PROGRAMMING EXERCISES

1. Rewrite the program assigned to you from Chapter 2 in the modular form described in this chapter.

2. A file contains daily sales records for a small retail business. The format for each record is

   Positions

1-4	Department number
5-10	Date
11-15	Amount of sale

   Write a program to list these records with appropriate headings. Compute the total of the sale amounts and print a line at the conclusion of the report containing this total.

3. A real estate office maintains a file containing a record for each property it handles. The records have the following format:

   Positions

1-10	Multiple Listing Service Number (MLS Number)
11-18	Sale price

   Write a program to compute and print the total price for the properties, and the total number of properties. Use the following test data:

MLS Number	Sale Price
0123456789	$45,000.00
1111111111	$95,950.00
2222222222	$135,760.00

INPUT, OUTPUT AND DATA MOVEMENT 4

4.1 PROGRAM EXAMPLE

Problem Statement

The ABC Department Store maintains an inventory file showing the stock number, description, quantity on hand and unit cost for each item it stocks. The sales clerks need a listing of the file so that they can ascertain quickly the availability of items. The purchasing agent needs a listing of the file to aid in making decisions on which items should be reordered. The president of the store has expressed curiosity about the total number of different items carried by the store; he feels the information could be used in an advertising campaign he is planning. Figure 4.1 shows a printer spacing chart for the desired report.

Problem Analysis

Note that the report is made up of the following elements:

> Report headings
> Column headings
> Detail lines
> Summary line

This organization is quite typical of most reports written for business purposes. Report headings and column headings must be written before any detail lines are produced. The report requires one detail line for each record in the file being processed. The summary line is printed after all records in the file have been processed.

This program requires a form of accumulation called *counting*. For each record read, a data item is incremented by one. When the program finishes processing the file, the value in this item (called a *counter*) is equal to the number of records processed. A plan for this program is shown in Figure 4.2.

Figure 4.1 Printer spacing chart for Inventory Report

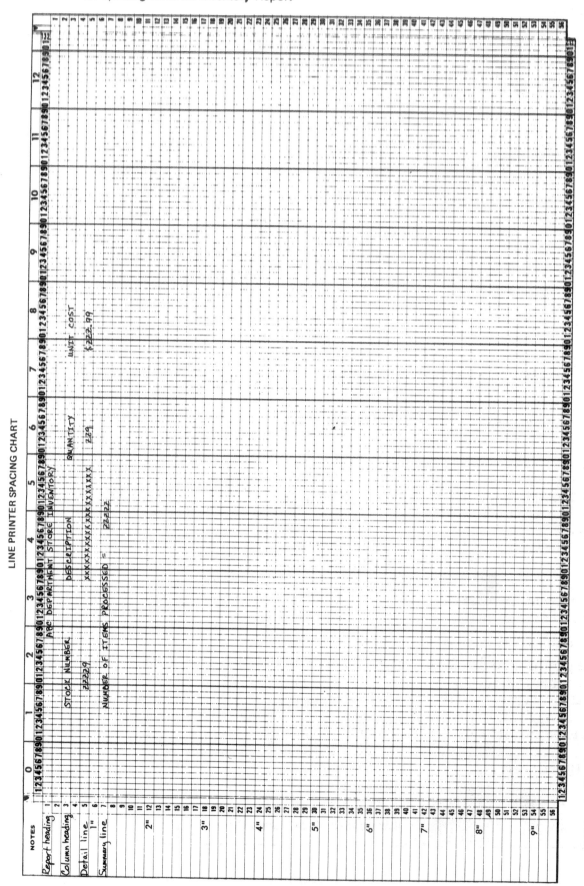

Figure 4.2 Plan for Inventory Report program

Main logic

    Open files
    Write headings
    Read product file
    Do Loop control until end of file
    Write summary line
    Close files
    Stop

Loop control

    Add 1 to number items processed
    Move input fields to detail line
    Write detail line
    Read product file

Problem Solution

A program for this problem is shown in Program 4.1. Figure 4.3 shows the structure diagram for this program. Note that the output routines (6000-WRITE-DETAIL-LINE and 5000-RECORD-DETAIL-LINE) involve several statements. Structuring these routines as separate paragraphs aids in keeping the paragraphs containing the primary logic of the program (1000-MAIN-LOGIC and 3000-LOOP-CONTROL) simple, short and easy to understand.

4.2 THE SELECT AND FD ENTRIES

Every file to be processed by a program also must be defined in a SELECT statement in the FILE-CONTROL paragraph of the INPUT-OUTPUT SECTION of the ENVIRONMENT DIVISION. The purpose of the SELECT statement is to associate the file with a particular type of physical device. The general form of the SELECT statement is:

> <u>SELECT</u> file-name <u>ASSIGN</u> TO system name.

For example, in Program 4.1, the file PRODUCT-FILE is associated with a disk file in the statement (line 1700)

    SELECT PRODUCT-FILE ASSIGN TO DISK.

The particular system-names associated with particular devices vary from one compiler to another. You must check with your instructor or with the local system manual to find out what system-names to use.

    One FD entry is required in the FILE SECTION of the DATA DIVISION for each file to be processed. A general form for the FD entry is:

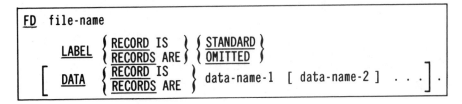

Program 4.1   Inventory Report program

```
100      IDENTIFICATION DIVISION.
200
300      PROGRAM-ID. MONTHLY-INVENTORY.
400      AUTHOR.     GARY GLEASON.
500
600      ENVIRONMENT DIVISION.
700
800      CONFIGURATION SECTION.
900
1000     SOURCE-COMPUTER.
1100     OBJECT-COMPUTER.
1200
1300     INPUT-OUTPUT SECTION.
1400
1500     FILE-CONTROL.
1600
1700         SELECT PRODUCT-FILE ASSIGN TO DISK.
1800         SELECT REPORT-FILE ASSIGN TO PRINTER.
1900
2000     DATA DIVISION.
2100
2200     FILE SECTION.
2300
2400     FD  PRODUCT-FILE
2500         LABEL RECORDS ARE STANDARD
2600         DATA RECORD IS INPUT-RECORD.
2700
2800     01  INPUT-RECORD.
2900         02  IR-STOCK-NUMBER      PIC 9(5).
3000         02  IR-DESCRIPTION       PIC X(20).
3100         02  IR-QUANTITY          PIC 9(3).
3200         02  IR-UNIT-COST         PIC 999V99.
3300         02  FILLER               PIC X(47).
3400
3500     FD  REPORT-FILE
3600         LABEL RECORDS ARE OMITTED
3700         DATA RECORD IS PRINT-LINE.
3800
3900     01  PRINT-LINE               PIC X(132).
4000
4100     WORKING-STORAGE SECTION.
4200
4300     01  FLAGS.
4400         02  EOF-FLAG             PIC X(3) VALUE "NO".
4500
4600     01  TOTALS.
4700         02  RECORDS-IN           PIC 9(5) VALUE ZERO.
4800
4900     01  MAJOR-HEADING.
5000         02  FILLER               PIC X(27) VALUE SPACES.
5100         02  FILLER               PIC X(30) VALUE
5200         "ABC DEPARTMENT STORE INVENTORY".
```

Program 4.1 (continued)

```
5300
5400        01  MINOR-HEADING.
5500            02  FILLER    PIC  X(15)    VALUE SPACES.
5600            02  FILLER    PIC  X(12)    VALUE "STOCK NUMBER".
5700            02  FILLER    PIC  X(10)    VALUE SPACES.
5800            02  FILLER    PIC  X(11)    VALUE "DESCRIPTION".
5900            02  FILLER    PIC  X(10)    VALUE SPACES.
6000            02  FILLER    PIC  X(8)     VALUE "QUANTITY".
6100            02  FILLER    PIC  X(10)    VALUE SPACES.
6200            02  FILLER    PIC  X(9)     VALUE "UNIT COST".
6300
6400        01  DETAIL-LINE.
6500            02  FILLER                PIC X(8) VALUE SPACES.
6600            02  DL-STOCK-NUMBER       PIC ZZZZ9.
6700            02  FILLER                PIC X(14) VALUE SPACES.
6800            02  DL-DESCRIPTION        PIC X(20).
6900            02  FILLER                PIC X(4) VALUE SPACES.
7000            02  DL-QUANTITY           PIC ZZ9.
7100            02  FILLER                PIC X(13) VALUE SPACES.
7200            02  DL-UNIT-COST          PIC $ZZZ.99.
7300
7400        01  TOTAL-LINE.
7500            02  FILLER                PIC X(15) VALUE SPACES.
7600            02  FILLER PIC X(27)      VALUE "NUMBER OF ITEMS PROCESSED =".
7700            02  FILLER                PIC X(4) VALUE SPACES.
7800            02  TL-RECORDS-IN         PIC Z(5).
7900
8000        PROCEDURE DIVISION.
8100
8200        1000-MAIN-LOGIC.
8300
8400            PERFORM 2000-INITIALIZATION.
8500            PERFORM 3000-LOOP-CONTROL
8600                UNTIL EOF-FLAG = "YES".
8700            PERFORM 7000-TERMINATION.
8800            STOP RUN.
8900
9000        2000-INITIALIZATION.
9100
9200            OPEN INPUT PRODUCT-FILE
9300                 OUTPUT REPORT-FILE.
9400            MOVE MAJOR-HEADING TO PRINT-LINE.
9500            WRITE PRINT-LINE AFTER PAGE.
9600            MOVE MINOR-HEADING TO PRINT-LINE.
9700            WRITE PRINT-LINE AFTER 2 LINES.
9800            PERFORM 4000-READ.
9900
10000       3000-LOOP-CONTROL.
10100
10200           ADD 1 TO RECORDS-IN.
10300           PERFORM 5000-RECORD-DETAIL-LINE.
10400           PERFORM 6000-WRITE-DETAIL-LINE.
10500           PERFORM 4000-READ.
10600
```

Program 4.1 (continued)

```
10700    4000-READ.
10800
10900         READ PRODUCT-FILE
11000             AT END MOVE "YES" TO EOF-FLAG.
11100
11200    5000-RECORD-DETAIL-LINE.
11300
11400       MOVE IR-STOCK-NUMBER    TO  DL-STOCK-NUMBER.
11500       MOVE IR-DESCRIPTION      TO  DL-DESCRIPTION.
11600       MOVE IR-QUANTITY         TO  DL-QUANTITY.
11700       MOVE IR-UNIT-COST        TO  DL-UNIT-COST.
11800
11900    6000-WRITE-DETAIL-LINE.
12000
12100       MOVE DETAIL-LINE TO PRINT-LINE.
12200       WRITE PRINT-LINE AFTER 2.
12300
12400    7000-TERMINATION.
12500
12600       MOVE RECORDS-IN TO TL-RECORDS-IN.
12700       WRITE PRINT-LINE FROM TOTAL-LINE AFTER ADVANCING 2 LINES.
12800       CLOSE PRODUCT-FILE
12900              REPORT-FILE.
```

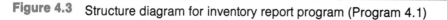

Figure 4.3   Structure diagram for inventory report program (Program 4.1)

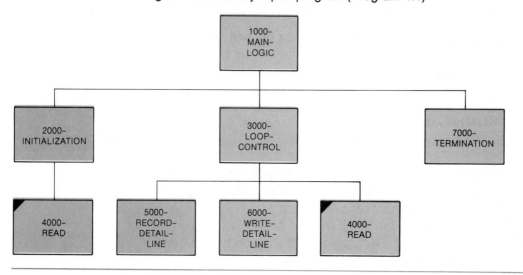

For example, Program 4.1 processes two files, so two FD entries are required: one for the file PRODUCT-FILE (lines 2400-2600) and one for the file REPORT-FILE (lines 3500-3700). A record description must be provided following the FD entry. The record description may be quite simple, such as the description of the record PRINT-LINE (line 3900) as a sequence of 132 characters, or complex such as the description of the record INPUT-RECORD (lines 2800-3300) which is subdivided into a number of fields.

In general a record will contain several fields. If the description of these fields is not written in the FILE SECTION, then it is written as a part of WORKING-STORAGE. This approach is used with the file REPORT-FILE in Program 4.1. There are four different types of output records for this file. The description of these records MAJOR-HEADING (lines 4900-5200), MINOR-HEADING (lines 5400-6200), DETAIL-LINE (lines 6400-7200) and TOTAL-LINE (lines 7400-7800) is placed in the WORKING-STORAGE SECTION. The program moves the appropriate record to the output record before writing a record on the file PRINT (for example, lines 9400, 9600, and 12100.) Note that these descriptions make use of the VALUE clause to specify the content of a number of fields. The VALUE clause may *not* be used in a record-description-entry in the FILE SECTION; its use is restricted to definitions of data items in the WORKING-STORAGE SECTION. If you wish to define a record which will contain constant data, you will employ the technique used with the file REPORT-FILE in Program 4.1:

1) Define the data-record as an elementary data item of appropriate length in the FD entry.
2) Define records and their content in the WORKING-STORAGE SECTION.
3) Move data to the data-record defined in the FD entry before processing.

This procedure is usually followed for output files, as they are likely to contain records having constant data.

4.3 THE OPEN AND CLOSE STATEMENTS

Before any file in a program can be processed, it must be opened. The OPEN statement causes the computing system to perform various initialization procedures required before the file can be processed. The general form of the OPEN statement is:

```
OPEN    { INPUT  file-name-1    [file-name-2] . . . }  . . .
        { OUTPUT file-name-3    [file-name-4] . . . }
```

The programmer must specify whether a file is being opened as an INPUT or an OUTPUT file. It is permissible to READ records from a file opened as an INPUT file, and it is permissible to WRITE records onto a file opened as an OUTPUT file. It is not permissible to WRITE a record onto a file opened as INPUT or to READ a record from a file opened as OUTPUT; an attempt to perform either of these operations will result in an execution time diagnostic message and the program will be cancelled.

Examples

To open the INCOME-RECORDS as an INPUT file, use the statement

```
OPEN INPUT INCOME-FILE.
```

To open the file PRINTED-REPORT as an OUTPUT file, use the statement

```
OPEN OUTPUT PRINTED-REPORT.
```

More than one file at a time may be opened by an OPEN statement. For example, the statement

```
OPEN OUTPUT PRINTED-REPORT NEW-MASTER-FILE.
```

will cause the files PRINTED-REPORT and NEW-MASTER-FILE to be opened as OUTPUT files.

The CLOSE statement causes a file to become unavailable for further processing. Any file which is opened in a program should also be closed before the program terminates. The general form of the CLOSE statement is:

```
CLOSE file-name . . .
```

One or more files may be closed in a CLOSE statement. Consider, for example the following CLOSE statements:

```
CLOSE INPUT-FILE OUTPUT-FILE. (2 files are closed)
CLOSE PRINTED-REPORT. (1 file is closed)
```

Any file that has not been opened is assumed to be closed. A file may be opened and closed any number of times in a program. However, a file must be closed before it can be opened. In a typical file processing program such as the one shown in Program 4.1, files are opened (2000-INITIALIZATION) and processed (3000-LOOP-CONTROL). After all inputs and outputs have been performed, the files are closed (7000-TERMINATION).

4.4   THE READ STATEMENT

A READ statement causes the computer to read one record from a specified file. The contents of the record are placed in the record area specified in the FD entry for the file. A general form for the READ statement is:

```
READ file-name [INTO data-name] AT END statement. . .
```

The file addressed in a READ statement must be currently opened as an INPUT file. When the end-of-file record is read, the statement(s) at the AT END clause of the statement are executed. For example, the statement

```
READ INPUT-FILE
    AT END CLOSE INPUT-FILE
        STOP RUN.
```

will cause the statements CLOSE INPUT-FILE and STOP RUN to be executed when the end-of-file is reached on INPUT-FILE. In a structured program a switch is often set when the end-of-file record is read. (A switch is a data item which has only two possible values, e.g., 1 and 0, "yes" and "no", "on" and "off.") A typical READ statement in a structured program would be:

```
READ INPUT-FILE
    AT END MOVE "YES" TO EOF-FLAG.
```

The contents of the switch (EOF-FLAG in this case) can be tested in subsequent instructions to determine whether the record should be processed (if not end-of-file) or whether processing should be terminated (if end-of-file has been reached). See, for example, the paragraph 1000-MAIN-LOGIC in Program 4.1.

When the INTO clause is included on a READ statement, data is placed in the record area specified in the FD entry for the file and also into the specified data-name. This feature often is used to allow the placement of a detailed description of an input record in the WORKING-STORAGE section. For example, in Program 4.1 the FD entry for the file PRODUCT-FILE could be rewritten as:

```
FD  PRODUCT-FILE
    LABEL RECORDS ARE STANDARD
    DATA RECORD IS IN-RECORD.
01  IN-RECORD PIC X(80).
```

The following entries (which define the fields contained on the record) could be added to the WORKING-STORAGE section:

```
01  IN-RECORD-DESCRIPTION.
    02  IR-STOCK-NUMBER   PIC 9(5).
    02  IR-DESCRIPTION    PIC X(20).
    02  IR-QUANTITY       PIC 9(3).
    02  IR-UNIT-COST      PIC 999V99.
    02  FILLER            PIC X(47).
```

With these changes, the READ statement at lines 10900-11000 in Program 4-1 would be changed to:

```
READ PRODUCT-FILE INTO IN-RECORD-DESCRIPTION
    AT END MOVE "YES" TO EOF-FLAG.
```

Data would be placed into the input-record IN-RECORD *and* into IN-RECORD-DESCRIPTION.

Your instructor may wish for you to follow this practice in the programs you write.

4.5   THE MOVE STATEMENT

The MOVE statement causes the transfer of data from one location in memory to another. The general form of the MOVE statement is:

```
MOVE data-name-1 TO data-name-2 . . .
```

The data at the location from which the information is moved (the sending item) is not changed; the data at the target location (the receiving item) is replaced by new data. For example, suppose FLDA and FLDB are as shown in Figure 4.4. After execution of the statement

```
MOVE FLDA TO FLDB
```

sending   receiving
item   item

the contents of FLDA is unchanged; the contents of FLDB is the same as FLDA. More than one item may be designated as a receiving item. In this case the contents of the sending item are moved to each of the receiving items. For example, the statement

```
MOVE FLDA TO FLDB FLDC FLDD.
```

will cause FLDB, FLDC and FLDD to receive identical data from FLDA.

Figure 4.4   Results of the execution of MOVE FLDA TO FLDB

Contents before MOVE

FLDA   FLDB

J,O,E,_,_,   X,Y,Z,W,_

Contents after MOVE

FLDA   FLDB

J,O,E,_,_,_,   J,O,E,_,_,_

4.6   THE WRITE STATEMENT

The WRITE statement causes one record to be written onto an output file. A general form of the WRITE statement is shown in Figure 4.5.

Figure 4.5   General form of the WRITE statement

```
WRITE record-name    [FROM identifier-1]

    ⎡                      ⎧⎧⎧identifier-2⎫ ⎡LINE ⎤⎫⎫
    ⎢ ⎧BEFORE⎫              ⎪⎪⎨           ⎬ ⎢     ⎥⎪⎪
    ⎢ ⎨      ⎬   ADVANCING ⎨⎪⎩integer    ⎭ ⎣LINES⎦⎪⎬
    ⎢ ⎩AFTER ⎭              ⎪⎧mnemonic-name⎫      ⎪
    ⎣                      ⎩⎨PAGE         ⎬       ⎭
                            ⎩             ⎭
```

Remember that the WRITE statement always addresses a record, while a READ statement addresses a file. The *record-name* used in the WRITE statement must be the same as the record declared in the FD entry for the file. The contents of the record are transferred to the appropriate file. The file addressed in a WRITE statement must be currently open as an output file.

If the printer is the device assigned to the file, the BEFORE/AFTER clause is used to specify the vertical spacing of the printed output line. The AFTER option causes vertical spacing to be performed prior to writing a new line. The BEFORE option causes the line to be written first, and then the vertical spacing is performed. In either case the PAGE entry will cause the advancement of paper to the top of a new page; the use of an integer (such as 0, 1, 2, 3) causes the printer to skip the specified number of lines.

Data to be written onto a file must be present in the output record area before the WRITE statement is executed. In Program 4.1 there are four types of output lines defined in the WORKING-STORAGE SECTION: MAJOR HEADING (line 4900), MINOR-HEADING (line 5400), DETAIL-LINE (line 6400), and TOTAL-LINE (line 7400). Prior to the WRITE operation for the first three types of lines, the contents of each appropriate output line are moved to the output record area. For example, in lines 9400 and 9500 one finds:

```
MOVE MAJOR-HEADING TO PRINT-LINE.
WRITE PRINT-LINE AFTER PAGE.
```

Use of the FROM clause can simplify output operations of this type. When the FROM clause is included, the contents of the designated data-name are automatically moved to the output record area before the WRITE operation is performed. For example, the two statements above could be combined as follows:

```
WRITE PRINT-LINE FROM MAJOR-HEADING AFTER PAGE.
```

The contents of MAJOR-HEADING are moved to PRINT-LINE before the output record is written. The FROM clause is used in Program 4.1 in writing the TOTAL-LINE (line 12700):

```
WRITE PRINT-LINE FROM TOTAL-LINE AFTER ADVANCING 2 LINES.
```

4.7   DATA TYPES

Any field may be classified either 1) numeric, 2) alphanumeric, 3) numeric edited or 4) alphanumeric edited, depending on the type of picture codes used in the PICTURE clause associated with the field.

A numeric field may contain only numeric data. A numeric field is defined using the picture codes 9, V, and S. The 9 specifies a numeric digit, (i.e., a single number). The V specifies the position of the decimal point. The S specifies that the item is to be signed (i.e., may become negative).

Examples

```
03 SAL-CODE PIC 9.
```

SAL-CODE is a one-digit numeric field. For instance salary paid for a particular project is coded as a single-digit "6".

```
03 SALARY PIC 999V99.
```

SALARY is a five-digit field such as 423.78 (dollars). The decimal point is assumed to be placed between the third and fourth digits. Note that such salaries cannot be negative.

```
01 AMOUNT PIC S9(4)V9(3).
```

AMOUNT is a seven-digit field. The decimal point is placed between the fourth and fifth digits. The item may become negative since the S is present. (If an S is not present in the picture codes of a numeric item, then the item is assumed always to be positive.) If used, an S must precede other codes used in describing the item. In Program 4.1, IR-STOCK-NUMBER (line 2900), IR-QUANTITY (line 3100), IR-UNIT-COST (line 3200), and RECORDS-IN (line 4700) are numeric items.

An alphanumeric field may contain any string of numeric, alphabetic, or special characters. Alphanumeric fields may be defined in two ways:

1) All group items are considered as alphanumeric regardless of the definition of the elementary items in the group. Recall that a group item is an item which is subdivided into one or more elementary data items. The specification of group items does not contain a PICTURE clause. For example, in Program 4.1 MAJOR-HEADING, MINOR-HEADING, DETAIL-LINE, TOTAL-LINE, INPUT-RECORD, FLAGS, and TOTALS are group items and, hence, are classed as alphanumeric.

2) Fields defined using the picture code X are alphanumeric. The X represents an alphanumeric character. For example, in Program 4.1 IR-DESCRIPTION (line 3000), PRINT-LINE (line 3900), EOF-FLAG (line 4400),

and all of the FILLER entries are alphanumeric because of the picture code X.

Fields defined using the picture codes Z, ., $, and so on are numeric edited items. The purpose of these codes is to prepare a numeric item for readability on a report. For example, in Program 4.1, the items DL-STOCK-NUMBER (line 6600), DL-QUANTITY (line 7000), DL-UNIT-COST (line 7200) and TL-RECORDS-IN (line 7800) are given numeric edited pictures and hence are non-numeric items. The Z provides for the substitution of a blank in place of a nonsignificant leading zero. The decimal point is inserted in place of the assumed position of the decimal point. The $ is printed to label items which represent dollar amounts.

Alphanumeric edited fields are used to edit alphanumeric fields for output. Picture codes used to specify an alphanumeric edited field include X, B (for blank insertion), 0 (for zero insertion), and / (for slash insertion).

Arithmetic operations can be performed only on numeric type data items. Arithmetic operations, therefore, cannot be performed on data which are alphanumeric, numeric edited or alphanumeric edited.

4.8 DATA MOVEMENT

Programming involves moving a lot of data around. Sometimes you have to move alphanumeric data from one data item to another; more often you have to move numeric data to a numeric edited field. All would be easy enough if the receiving fields always have as many characters (or elements, or numbers, or letters) as did the data, but that does not always happen. For instance, a check writing machine in a major Blue Cross plan does not have very many spaces assigned for the name of the person receiving the check. So instead of his full name, which the computer has in its subscriber file—properly spelled and listed with his name, address and policy number—Alphonse Hornswogger will get a check made out to HORNS, A. Clearly, the data item in the check writing program has fewer spaces than the name file in the program feeding it.[1] The rules for fitting data into spaces too large or too small depend on the kind of data you are using, as detailed below.

When alphanumeric data are moved from one field to another, characters are moved from left to right. If the sending field and receiving field have exactly the same length, the receiving field becomes an exact duplicate of the sending field.

Example

```
MOVE FLDA TO FLDB.

 A B C D          A B C D

FLDA PIC X(4)     FLDB PIC X(4)
```

---

1. Hornswogger endorses his check by writing HORNS, A. first; then underneath it, he writes his full and correct name. Can truncating (cutting off) a name lead to confusion? No, because the Blue Cross computer is really reading the subscriber account number, for which there are always enough data spaces. It does not pay much attention to Mr. Hornswogger's name.

If the receiving field is no longer than the sending field, blanks are added to the right most positions of the receiving field.

Example

```
MOVE FLDA TO FLDB.
                              These blanks are inserted because FLDB is longer than FLDA
 1 A 3 B          1 A 3 B  ⌣⌣

FLDA PIC X (4)    FLDB PIC X(6)
```

If the receiving field is shorter than the sending field, the *rightmost* characters are truncated.

Example

```
MOVE FLDA TO FLDB.

 1 A 3 B          1 A

FLDA PIC X(4)    FLDB PIC XX
```

The JUSTIFIED RIGHT clause can be used in the definition of an alphanumeric item in the DATA DIVISION to cause data moved to the field to be right justified with truncation and padding on the left.

Example

```
MOVE FLDA TO FLDB.

 1 A 3 B              1 A 3 B

FLDA PIC X(4)    FLDB PIC X(6) JUSTIFIED RIGHT

MOVE FLDA TO FLDB.

 1 A 3 B            3 B

FLDA PIC X(4)    FLDB PIC X(2) JUSTIFIED RIGHT
```

The rules for alphanumeric data movement are summarized by the examples in Figure 4.6.

Numeric data

When numeric data is moved to a numeric type data item, the digits to the left of the decimal point are moved from right to left. If the receiving field is too short, truncation of excess *leftmost* digits will be performed. If the receiving field is too long, zeros will be inserted in the unused leftmost digits.

Figure 4.6 Examples of alphanumeric data movement: MOVE FLDA TO FLDB

FLDA		FLDB		Comment
Definition	*Content*	*Definition*	*Content After* MOVE	
PIC XXX	A B C	PIC XXXX	A B C	Data is left-justified with blanks inserted on the right.
PIC XXX	A B C	PIC XX	A B	Rightmost characters are truncated.
PIC XXX	A B C	PIC X(4) JUSTIFIED RIGHT	A B C	Data is right-justified with blanks inserted on the left.
PIC XXX	A B C	PIC XX JUSTIFIED RIGHT	B C	Leftmost characters are truncated.
PIC XXX	A B C	PIC XXX JUSTIFIED RIGHT	A B C	When fields have the same width, the JUSTIFIED RIGHT clause has no effect.

Example

```
MOVE FLDA TO FLDB.
```

0 1 2 3 4   0 1 2 3 4

FLDA PIC 99999   FLDB PIC 9(5)

0 1 2 3 4   0 0 0 0 1 2 3 4   Extra zeroes inserted because FLDB is
                                                                   longer than FLDA
FLDA PIC 99999   FLDB PIC 9(8)

0 1 2 3 4   2 3 4   Truncation occurred since FLDB is
                                                      shorter than FLDA
FLDA PIC 99999   FLDB PIC 999

Digits to the right of the decimal point are moved from left to right. If the receiving field is too short, truncation of excess *rightmost* digits will be performed. If the receiving field is too long, zeroes will be inserted in the unused rightmost digits. In the following examples, the caret symbol represents the assumed position of the decimal point.

Example

```
MOVE FLDA TO FLDB.
```

1 2 3 0   1 2 3 0
^   ^
FLDA PIC V9999   FLDB PIC V9(4)

1 2 3 0   1 2 3 0 0 0   Extra zeroes inserted since FLDB is
^   ^   longer than FLDA
FLDA PIC V9999   FLDB PIC V9(6)

1 2 3 0   1 2   Truncation of rightmost digits occurred
^   ^   since FLDB is shorter than FLDA
FLDA PIC V9999   FLDB PIC V99

Decimal points in two numeric fields are aligned before transferring digits in the MOVE operation. Transfers of digits to the left and to the right of the decimal point are carried out independently.

Example

```
MOVE FLDA TO FLDB.
```

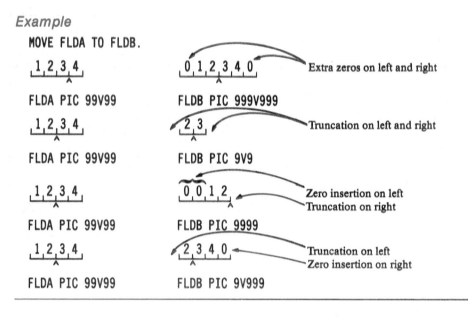

Internally, the sign of a data item is expressed as a code in the rightmost digit of the item. For purposes of illustration in this book we shall show the sign by a raised − or + above the rightmost digit.

Example

```
  1 2 3 4 5̄
  └─┴─┴─┴─┘
      ^
FLDA PIC S999V99          The value of FLDA is negative.

  0 0 1 2 3̇
  └─┴─┴─┴─┘
      ^
FLDB PIC S999V99          The value of FLDB is positive.
```

If a signed data item is moved to an unsigned data item the sign is lost. The value of the resulting field is unsigned and hence positive.

Example

```
MOVE FLDA TO FLDB.

  1 2 3 4 5̄          1 2 3 4 5
  └─┴─┴─┴─┘          └─┴─┴─┴─┘
      ^
FLDA PIC S999V99   FLDB PIC 999V99
```

If an unsigned data item is moved to a signed item the resulting value is assumed to be positive.

Example

```
MOVE FLDA TO FLDB.
```

1 2 3 4 5		1 2 3 4 5̇

```
FLDA PIC 999V99    FLDB PIC S999V99
```

P Picture Code

The P picture code can be used to scale numeric data read from a data record. The P takes the place of a decimal digit with assumed value zero.

Example

Suppose a record has a three-digit field representing the population of a city in thousands. An appropriate description of such a field would be

```
03  POPULATION    PIC    999PPP.
```

For example, if the content of the field were

| 1 2 3 |

the value of the item POPULATION would be 123,000 for purposes of computation and data movement.

Example

Suppose a record has a two-digit field representing a measurement in units of hundred-thousandths. An appropriate description would be

```
03  MEASUREMENT   PIC    VPPP99.
```

Thus, if the content of the field was

| 1 2 |

the value would be .00012.

When data is moved to or from a scaled field the digits represented by P are used to align the decimal points prior to the movement of the data.

Example

```
MOVE FLDA TO FLDB
```

| 3 4 | | 0 3 4 0 0 0 |

```
FLDA PIC 99PPP     FLDB PIC 999999.
```

For computational purposes, the value of FLDA and FLDB will be the same—34,000.

The movement of numeric data is summarized in Figure 4.7.

Figure 4.7 Examples of numeric data movement MOVE FLDA TO FLDB

Note: the symbol ^ is used to show the implied position of the decimal point.

FLDA		FLDB		*Comment*
PICTURE	*Content*	**PICTURE**	*Content After MOVE*	
9999	0123^	999999	000123^	Extra zeros inserted on left.
9999	0123^	99	23^	Truncation of leftmost digits.
99V99	01^23	999V999	001^230	Extra zero on left and right.
99V99	01^23	9V9	1^2	Truncation on left and right.
S99V99	01^23	99V99	01^23	Sign lost due to unsigned receiving field.
99V99	01^23	S99V99	01^23	Unsigned data becomes positive.
99PP	12^	9999V99	1200^00	The value of FLDA is 1200.
PIC 9(6)	123456^	PIC 999PPP	123^	Scaling truncates rightmost digits.
PIC V9(6)	^000123	PIC VPPP99	^12	Scaling truncates leftmost digits.

4.9 EDITING

The only time numeric data is moved into a non-numeric field is for purposes of editing the data for report output. The receiving field is described using numeric edited picture codes. Numeric edited picture codes such as Z, $, and . react with the numeric digits moved into the field, resulting in an appropriately edited character string.

Decimal Point Insertion (.)

The use of the decimal point (.) in a numeric edited picture causes the decimal point to be inserted in the indicated position in the item. The implied position of the decimal point in the numeric sending item is aligned with the indicated position in the numeric edited receiving item. Zeroes will be inserted into the resulting field on the left or right if the receiving item is longer than the sending item. Digits also may be truncated on the left or right if the receiving item is too short to receive all of the digits of the sending field.

Example

```
MOVE FLDA TO FLDB.
```

1 1 2 3 4	0 1 2 . 3 4
FLDA PIC 999V99	FLDB PIC 999.99
0 1 2 3 4	0 0 1 2 . 3
FLDA PIC 999V99	FLDB PIC 9999.9
0 1 2 3 4	2 . 3 4 0
FLDA PIC 999V99	FLDB PIC 9.999

If a V is used in an edited picture the decimal point is *not* included in the receiving field although it is used to align the implied decimal positions between the sending and receiving fields.

Example

```
MOVE FLDA TO FLDB.
```

0 1 2 3 4	2 3 4 0
FLDA PIC 999V99	FLDB PIC 9V999

If FLDB is printed only the characters 2340 would appear on the page.

Zero Suppression (Z)

The character Z in a numeric edited picture will cause substitution of blanks in place of leading zeroes in the sending item. When a nonzero digit is encountered, that digit and all subsequent digits (zero or nonzero) are moved to the receiving field.

Example

```
MOVE FLDA TO FLDB.
```

0 1 0 3 4	1 0 . 3 4	Blank is inserted in place of leading zero
FLDA PIC 999V99	FLDB PIC ZZZ.99	
0 0 0 0 0	. 0 0	Decimal point will be inserted if the digit to the immediate right is not suppressed
FLDA PIC 999V99	FLDB PIC ZZZ.99	
0 0 0 0 0		Decimal point is not inserted since digits to right are suppressed
FLDA PIC 999V99	FLDB PIC ZZZ.ZZ	
1 0 0 0 0	1 0 0 . 0 0	
FLDA PIC 999V99	FLDB PIC ZZZ.ZZ	

The use of the decimal point and Z picture codes is summarized in Figure 4.8.

Dollar Sign Insertion ($)

The character $ used as the first character in a numeric edited picture will cause the $ to be the first character in the receiving item.

Example

```
MOVE FLDA TO FLDB.
```

0 1 0 3 4 $ 1 0 . 3 4

FLDA PIC 999V99   FLDB PIC $ZZZ.99

If more than one $ is used in the numeric edited picture, the character will cause zero suppression in each position in which it occurs, and the $ will be inserted immediately in front of the first nonsuppressed character.

Example

```
MOVE FLDA TO FLDB.
```

0 1 0 3 4 $ 1 0 . 3 4

FLDA PIC 999V99   FLDB PIC $$$$.99

0 0 0 0 0 $. 0 0

FLDA PIC 999V99   FLDB PIC $$$$.99

Check Protection (*)

The character * used in a numeric edited picture will cause the asterisk to be inserted in place of each leading zero or other suppressed character. The * is used chiefly in prefacing the dollar amount on checks.

Examples of decimal point insertion and zero suppression: MOVE FLDA TO FLDB

FLDA		FLDB		Comment
Definition	*Content*	*Definition*	*Content After* MOVE	
PIC 999V99	0 1 2 3 4	PIC 999.99	0 1 2 . 3 4	Decimal point insertion.
PIC 999V99	0 1 2 3 4	PIC 99.999	1 2 . 3 4 0	Digits truncated on left and padded on right.
PIC 999V99	0 1 0 3 4	PIC ZZZ.99	1 0 . 3 4	Blank inserted in place of leading zero.
PIC 999V99	0 0 0 0 0	PIC ZZZ.ZZ		If value is zero, the field contains blanks.
PIC 999V99	0 0 0 0 2	PIC ZZZ.ZZ	. 0 2	If value is not zero, the decimal point is not suppressed.

Example

```
MOVE FLDA TO FLDB.
  0 0 0 1 2 3 4           * * * 1 2 . 3 4
         ^
FLDA PIC 99999V99      FLDB PIC *****.99
  1 2 3 4 5 6 7          $ 1 2 3 4 5 . 6 7
         ^
FLDA PIC 99999V99      FLDB PIC $*****.99
  0 0 0 0 0              $ * * * . * *
       ^
FLDA PIC 999V99        FLDB PIC $***.**
```

The character "," used in a numeric edited picture will cause the comma to
be inserted in the appropriate position in the receiving field if the character
immediately preceding is not a suppressed zero.

```
MOVE FLDA TO FLDB.
  0 0 1 2 3 4 5          0 , 0 1 2 , 3 4 5
         ^
FLDA PIC 9(7)          FLDB PIC 9,999,999
  0 0 1 2 3 4 5                1 2 , 3 4 5
         ^
FLDA PIC 9(7)          FLDB PIC Z,ZZZ,ZZZ
  0 0 0 0 1 2 3                    1 2 3
         ^
FLDA PIC 9999999       FLDB PIC Z,Z(3),Z(3)
  0 0 0 1 2 3 4                  1 , 2 3 4
         ^
FLDA PIC 9999999       FLDB PIC Z,ZZZ,ZZZ
  0 0 1 2 3 4 5 6 7        $ 1 2 , 3 4 5 . 6 7
           ^
FLDA PIC 9(7)V99       FLDB PIC $$,$$$,$$$.99
  0 0 1 2 3 4 5 6 7      $ * * * 1 2 , 3 4 5 . 6 7
           ^
FLDA PIC 9999999V99    FLDB PIC $*,***,***.99
```

Use of the *, $ and comma for editing is summarized in Figure 4.9.

Figure 4.9 Examples of the of $, * and , for numeric editing: MOVE FLDA TO FLDB

FLDA		FLDB		Comment
Definition	*Content*	*Definition*	*Content After* MOVE	
PIC 999V99	0 1 0 3 4	PIC $$$$.99	$ 1 0 . 3 4	Single dollar sign acts as an insertion character.
PIC 999V99	0 0 1 3 4	PIC $$$$.99	$ 1 . 3 4	Multiple dollar signs will float.
PIC 9(5)V99	0 0 0 1 2 3 4	PIC *****.99	* * * 1 2 . 3 4	Asterisk replaces leading zeroes.
PIC 9(5)V99	0 0 0 0 0 0 0	PIC *(5).**	* * * * * . * *	Asterisk replaces all suppressed characters except decimal point.
PIC 9(7)	0 0 1 2 3 4 5	PIC 9,999,999	0 , 0 1 2 , 3 4 5	Comma inserted in each position.
PIC 9(7)	0 0 1 2 3 4 5	PIC Z,ZZZ,ZZZ	1 2 , 3 4 5	Comma is suppressed if digit to right is suppressed.
PIC 9(7)V99	0 0 1 2 3 4 5 6 7	PIC $$,$$$,$$$.99	$ 1 2 , 3 4 5 . 6 7	Comma may be used with $.
PIC 9(7)V99	0 0 1 2 3 4 5 6 7	PIC $*,***,***.99	$ * * * 1 2 , 3 4 5 . 6 7	Comma may be used with *.
PIC 9(3)V99	1 2 3 4 5	PIC $$$.$$	$ 2 3 . 4 5	Note suppression of leading digit.
PIC 9(3)V99	0 0 0 0 0	PIC ZZZ.99	. 0 0	
PIC 9(3)V99	0 0 0 0 0	PIC ZZZ.99 BLANK WHEN ZERO		Value moved to FLDB has value zero, hence field is replaced by spaces.

Sign Insertion (+ and −)

The character "−" used as the first or last character in a numeric edited picture will cause the minus sign to be inserted in the appropriate position of the receiving field if the sending item is negative. If the sending field is positive or unsigned, a blank is inserted.

Example

```
MOVE FLDA TO FLDB.
```

```
  1 2 3 4 5̄          - 1 2 3 . 4 5
        ^
FLDA PIC S999V99    FLDB PIC -999.99
```

```
  0 1 2 3 4̄            1 2 . 3 4 -
        ^
FLDA PIC S999V99    FLDB PIC ZZZ.99-
```

```
  1 2 3 4 5̇          1 2 3 . 4 5
        ^
FLDA PIC S999V99    FLDB PIC ZZZ.ZZ-
```

The character "+" may be used in exactly the same way as the character "−" except that the plus sign will be inserted whenever the sending item is positive or unsigned, and the minus sign will be inserted if the sending item is negative.

Example

```
MOVE FLDA TO FLDB.
```

```
  1 2 3 4 5̇          + 1 2 3 . 4 5
        ^
FLDA PIC S999V99    FLDB PIC +ZZZ.ZZ
```

```
  0 1 2 3 4̄          -   1 2 . 3 4
        ^
FLDA PIC S999V99    FLDB PIC +ZZZ.ZZ
```

```
  0 0 0 1 2                  . 1 2 +
        ^
FLDA PIC 999V99     FLDB PIC ZZZ.99+
```

The use of more than one − (or +) as the first characters in an edit picture will cause zero suppression. It will also give you the appropriate sign preceding the first nonsuppressed character.

Example

```
MOVE FLDA TO FLDB.
```

```
  0 0 0 1 2 3 4̄           - 1 2 . 3 4
            ^
FLDA PIC S99999V99      FLDB PIC -(6). 9 9
```

```
  0 0 0 0 0 1 2̄                  - . 1 2
            ^
FLDA PIC S99999V99      FLDB PIC +++++.99
```

The characters CR and DB used as the last two characters in an edit picture will cause CR or DB to be inserted in the receiving field if the sending field is negative. Otherwise, blanks will be inserted.

Example

```
MOVE FLDA TO FLDB.
```

```
0 1 2 3 4̄            1 2 . 3 4 C R
```

FLDA PIC S999V99   FLDB PIC ZZZ.99CR

```
0 1 2 3 4̇            1 2 . 3 4
```

FLDA PIC S999V99   FLDB PIC ZZZ.99CR

```
0 0 0 1 2̄              $ . 1 2 D B
```

FLDA PIC S999V99   FLDB PIC $$$$.99DB

Further examples of editing numeric data are shown in Figure 4.10.

Figure 4.10   Examples of editing signed data: MOVE FLDA TO FLDB

FLDA		FLDB		*Comment*
Definition	*Content*	*Definition*	*Content After* MOVE	
PIC S999	0 1 2̄	PIC −ZZZ	− 1 2	Sending field is negative. Minus sign is inserted.
PIC S999	0 1 2	PIC ZZZ−	1 2	Sending field is positive, minus sign is suppressed.
PIC S999	0 1 2̄	PIC ZZZ+	1 2 −	Sending field is negative, plus sign is replaced by minus.
PIC S999	0 1 2̇	PIC +ZZZ	+ 1 2	Sending field is positive, plus sign is inserted.
PIC S9(6)	0 0 0 1 2 3̄	PIC −(7)	− 1 2 3	Minus may float.
PIC S9(6)	0 0 0 1 2 3̄	PIC ++++,+++	+ 1 2 3	Plus may float.
PIC S999V99	0 1 2 3 4̄	PIC ZZZ.99CR	1 2 . 3 4 C R	Sending field is negative; CR is inserted.
PIC S999V99	0 1 2 3 4	PIC $$$$.99BCR	$ 1 2 . 3 4	Sending field is positive; CR is suppressed. B acts as insertion character.
PIC S999V99	0 1 2 3 4̄	PIC $ZZZ.99BDB	$ 1 2 . 3 4 D B	Sending field is negative; DB is inserted.
PIC S999V99	0 1 2 3 4̇	PIC $$$$.99DB	$ 1 2 . 3 4	Sending field is positive; DB is suppressed.

Blank Insertion (B)

The character B used in an edit-type picture will cause a blank to be inserted in the receiving field.

Example

```
MOVE FLDA TO FLDB.
```

1 2 3 4 5 6 7 8 9	1 2 3 4 5 6 7 8 9
FLDA PIC 9(9)	FLDB PIC 999B99B9999
0 1 2 3 4̄	1 2 . 3 4 C R
FLDA PIC S999V99	FLDB PIC ZZZ.99BCR

Alphanumeric data as well as numeric data can be edited using the code B.

Example

```
MOVE FLDA TO FLDB.
```

A B C D	A B C D
FLDA PIC X(4)	FLDB PIC XXBBXX

FLDB in this case is classed as an alphanumeric edited field.

Slash Insertion (/)

The character slash (/) used in an edit-type picture will cause the character to be inserted in the receiving field. The primary use for this code is for editing date fields.

Example

```
MOVE DATE-IN TO DATE-OUT
```

0 3 0 5 8 2	0 3 / 0 5 / 8 2
DATE-IN PIC 9(6)	DATE-OUT PIC 99/99/99

The slash can be used to edit alphanumeric as well as numeric data.

Example

```
MOVE FLDA TO FLDB.
```

A B C D	A / B / C D
FLDA PIC XXXX	FLDB PIC X/X/XX

Zero Insertion (0)

The character 0 in an edit picture will cause 0 to be inserted in the receiving field. Zero insertion can be performed on numeric and alphanumeric fields.

Example

```
MOVE FLDA TO FLDB.
```

1 2 3 4		1 2 0 0 3 4

FLDA PIC 9(4)   FLDB PIC 990099

```
MOVE FLDA TO FLDB.
```

A B C D		A 0 B C D

FLDA PIC X(4)   FLDB PIC X0XXX

Further examples of the use of the picture codes B, / and 0 are shown in Figure 4.11.

Figure 4.11 Examples of B, 0 and /: MOVE FLDA TO FLDB

FLDA		FLDB		*Comment*
Definition	*Content*	*Definition*	*Content*	
PIC X(4)	A B 1 2	PIC XXBXX	A B 1 2	Insertion of blank in alphanumeric field.
PIC X(4)	A B 1 2	PIC XXXX0	A B 1 2 0	Insertion of zero in alphanumeric field.
PIC X(4)	A B 1 2	PIC XX//XX	A B / / 1 2	Insertion of slash in alphanumeric field.
PIC 999999	0 1 2 0 8 6	PIC 99/99/99	0 1 / 2 0 / 8 6	Slash insertion in alphanumeric field.
PIC 9(9)	1 2 3 4 5 6 7 8 9	PIC 999B99B9(4)	1 2 3 4 5 6 7 8 9	Blank insertion in alphanumeric field.
PIC 999	1 2 3	PIC 999000	1 2 3 0 0 0	Zero insertion in numeric field.

A summary of all possible cases of data movement is shown in Figure 4.12. The result of a data movement operation in those cases described as "not permitted" depends on the system in use. In most cases the compiler will treat such MOVE instructions as syntax errors. In any case, these types of moves are most likely logical errors because the result will be of no value to the program. While the movement of a numeric field to a field described as alphanumeric is permitted and handled in the same way as an alphanumeric to alphanumeric move, this type of movement is performed rarely in practice. Numeric data is usually moved to another numeric field or to a numeric edited field in preparation for output.

Figure 4.12   Summary of data movement by type

		Receiving Field Type			
		Alphanumeric	*Numeric*	*Numeric edited*	*Alphanumeric edited*
Sending Field Type	*Alphanumeric*	Characters moved left to right with truncation and padding on right except when JUSTIFIED RIGHT is used with receiving field	Not permitted	Not permitted	Appropriate characters are inserted in receiving field
	Numeric	Same as alphanumeric to alphanumeric	Decimal points in fields are aligned. Digits right of decimal point are moved left to right. Digits left of decimal point are moved right to left. Truncation/padding of leading/trailing digits in receiving field.	Same as numeric to numeric except editing of numeric digits is performed	Not permitted
	Numeric edited	Same as alphanumeric to alphanumeric	Not permitted	Not permitted	Not permitted
	Alphanumeric edited	Same as alphanumeric to alphanumeric	Not permitted	Not permitted	Not permitted

4.10   FIGURATIVE CONSTANTS

The COBOL language provides a number of *figurative constants* which are assigned reserved word names (Fig. 4.13). Any of these figurative constants may be used in any place the corresponding nonfigurative constant would be appropriate. Examples of using the figurative constants ZERO and SPACES are abundant in Program 4.1.

Example

The following are equivalent:

```
03   DATA-A PIC X(5)   VALUE ALL "*".
03   DATA-A PIC X(5)   VALUE"*****".
```

In both cases the content of DATA-A will be:

```
* * * * *
└─┴─┴─┴─┘
    DATA-A
```

Figure 4.13 Figurative constants

Reserved Word	*Value*
ZERO ZEROS ZEROES	0
HIGH-VALUE HIGH-VALUES	the largest value which can be represented in the computer (binary 1's)
SPACE SPACES	one or more blanks
LOW-VALUE LOW-VALUES	the smallest value which can be represented in the computer (binary 0's)
ALL "character"	a string of appropriate length consisting entirely of the specified character
QUOTE QUOTES	quotation mark(s)

Example

Suppose you desire to describe the character string "XYZ" for inclusion on an output line. The following code could be used:

```
02  DATA-B.
    03  FILLER  PIC X    VALUE QUOTE.
    03  FILLER  PIC XXX  VALUE "XYZ".
    03  FILLER  PIC X    VALUE QUOTE.
```

The content of DATA-B will be:

```
" X Y Z "
```
DATA-B

Use of the figurative constant QUOTE is a convenient way to specify this character (the ") in the string since quotes are used in coding non-numeric constants in COBOL.

The following statements are equivalent:

```
MOVE 0    TO FLD.
```
and
```
MOVE ZERO TO FLD.
```

The figurative constants HIGH-VALUE(S) and LOW-VALUE(S) are used in certain instances for passing values between a program and the operating system.

4.11 SIGNED NUMBERS

As noted earlier, the picture code S must be the first code in the picture of any data-name which may be negative. For example, the following DATA division declarations specify FLD-A and FLD-B as signed variables:

```
01   REC-DESC.
     03  FLD-A    PIC S9999.
     03  FLD-B    PIC S9V99.
     03  FILLER   PIC X(73).
```

Suppose REC-DESC specified in the preceding example is the description of a data record. FLD-A and FLD-B may be positive or negative. If a value is entered in a field in the ordinary fashion, it is stored as an unsigned value (i.e. positive). But what about a negative quantity? There are two ways to enter negative data: entering the sign as a part of the rightmost digit in the field, and entering the sign as a separate character.

Sign in Rightmost Digit

As discussed in Section 4.8, the sign of a value is associated with the rightmost digit in the field. This practice originated at a time when punched cards were used as input. When using punched cards, the sign was punched in conjunction with the rightmost digit in the field. An 11 zone together with the digit in the rightmost position is used for a negative value. A 12 zone and the appropriate digit is used for a positive value.

If a data card containing the characters

record position 1 2 3 4 5 6 7 8 9   80
                 0 0 3 M 4 0 A

were read using the record description above the content of FLD-A and FLD-B will be:

0 0 3 4̄   4 0 1̇

FLD-A   FLD-B

The absence of any zone punch will also signify a positive value. When output is produced for a signed field, the character equivalent of the punch combination will be used. For example, if the content of FLD-A and FLD-B were printed without editing, the output would appear as:

0 0 3 M   4 0 A

FLD-A   FLD-B

The appearance of alphabetic characters in the rightmost position of the fields is caused by the inclusion of zones in the output. (11-4 is the code for M and 12-1 is the code for A.) The movement of a signed field to an edited field is necessary to suppress this inclusion of a sign zone along with the digit in the rightmost position.

Example

```
MOVE FLDA TO FLDB FLDC.
```

$$\underbrace{0\,3\,\overset{+}{4}}_{\wedge} \qquad \underbrace{0\,3\,4}_{\wedge} \qquad \underline{\quad 3\,4\quad}$$

FLDA PIC S999   FLDB PIC 999   FLDC PIC ZZZ

Those who use terminals and diskettes to enter data must perform the logical equivalent of supplying a 12 or 11 zone in the rightmost position of a signed numeric field. This is done by using the character equivalent of the punch combination (Fig. 4.14.)

Figure 4.14   Representation of signed data

Punched card code	Character	Meaning for Signed Data
12-1	A	$\overset{+}{1}$
12-2	B	$\overset{+}{2}$
12-3	C	$\overset{+}{3}$
12-4	D	$\overset{+}{4}$
12-5	E	$\overset{+}{5}$
12-6	F	$\overset{+}{6}$
12-7	G	$\overset{+}{7}$
12-8	H	$\overset{+}{8}$
12-9	I	$\overset{+}{9}$
11-1	J	$\overline{1}$
11-2	K	$\overline{2}$
11-3	L	$\overline{3}$
11-4	M	$\overline{4}$
11-5	N	$\overline{5}$
11-6	O	$\overline{6}$
11-7	P	$\overline{7}$
11-8	Q	$\overline{8}$
11-9	R	$\overline{9}$

Thus, in order to enter FLDB and FLDC with values −34 and +4.01 respectively, the terminal or diskette user would enter:

$$\underline{0\;0\;3\;M} \qquad \underline{4\;0\;A}$$

FLD−A   FLD−B

Note that characters representing $\overset{+}{0}$ and $\overline{0}$ are omitted from the list above. Details as to how these characters are to be entered vary from one system to another. The reader must check the user's manual or other local documentation to determine the appropriate procedure.

The SIGN IS Clause

The sign of a data item may be entered as a leading or trailing character in the field if the item is defined using the SIGN IS clause (Fig. 4.15.)

Figure 4.15 General form of the SIGN IS clause

```
[SIGN IS] { LEADING  } [SEPARATE CHARACTER]
          { TRAILING }
```

When this clause is used in the definition of the item, the S picture code, which must be present, is counted as a position in the field.

A field A is 4 characters in length and the user desires to enter the sign of the field as a leading character. The field would be defined by

```
A  PIC S999  SIGN IS LEADING SEPARATE.
```

If the characters $-,1,0,2,$ are entered on the input record, the value of A will be -102. If the characters $\quad -,3$ are entered, the value of A will be -3.

Example

A field B is 6 characters in length; the user will enter the sign in the rightmost character of the field. The field would be defined by

```
B  PIC S99999  SIGN IS TRAILING.
```

If the characters $1,0,2,-$ are entered on the input record, the value of B will be -102.

4.12 DEBUG CLINIC

File, Record, Field References

A very common mistake made by beginning programmers is to reference a file, record or field by two different names in the same program. It is important to remember that all references to the same file, record or field must use the same data-name.

For example, consider the lines in Program 4.1 that are screened. Note that the name PRODUCT-FILE is used in the SELECT entry, FD entry, OPEN statement, READ statement and CLOSE statement, and also that the name INPUT-RECORD is used both in the DATA RECORD clause and the following 01 entry. Failure to use the same file, record or field name in each reference will be treated by the compiler as a syntax error.

Mixing WRITE/BEFORE and WRITE/AFTER

Care must be exercised in utilizing both options of the WRITE statement in the same program. Recall that the BEFORE option causes lines to be printed prior to advancing the paper (WRITE . . . BEFORE ADVANCING) while the AFTER option cause paper to be advanced prior to writing the line (WRITE . . . AFTER ADVANCING).

In a given program, if WRITE/BEFORE is used for all WRITE statements the printer normally will be on a new line for each output. The same observation is true if WRITE/AFTER is used for all WRITE statements. If a program uses a WRITE/AFTER followed by a WRITE/BEFORE, the WRITE/AFTER leaves the paper on the line printed. The following WRITE/BEFORE causes another line to be printed and then the paper is advanced. The second line of print will be printed on top of the first one!

In order to avoid problems of this kind, most COBOL programmers employ only WRITE/AFTER in a given program.

Editing

When performing editing of numeric data, make sure the receiving field contains a sufficient number of positions for all digits in the sending field. In general, when a numeric field is moved to an edited field, the decimal points are aligned. Leading and trailing digits are truncated or padded with zeroes, depending on number of positions in the edited field.

Example

Suppose the instruction

        MOVE FLDA TO FLDB.

is executed.

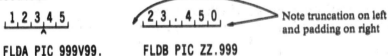

        1 2 3 4 5   2 3 . 4 5 0   Note truncation on left
                                                    and padding on right

        FLDA PIC 999V99.   FLDB PIC ZZ.999

In this case, FLDB contains too few digits on the left to accommodate all digits of FLDA, resulting in truncation of the leading digit. FLDB contains more digits on the right of the decimal point than FLDA; hence, FLDB is padded on the right with a zero.

        1 2 3 4 5 $ 1 2 3 . 4 5   Note leading space

        FLDA PIC 999V99   FLDB PIC $$$$$.99

FLDB contains space for four digits to the left of the decimal point. Since FLDA has only three digits left of the decimal point, FLDA is padded on the left with a zero. Because of the editing function the leading zero is then suppressed.

        1 2 3 4 5 $ 2 3 . 4 5   Note truncation

        FLDA PIC 999V99   FLDB PIC $$$.99

FLDB contains space for only two digits left of the decimal point because the dollar sign uses one space and is never suppressed. This results in the truncation of the leading digit of FLDA.

The programmer must be careful to construct edit pictures which are sufficiently long to accommodate all digits of the field to be edited.

Signed Fields

Recall that a field which will be signed (i.e., may become negative) must be described in the DATA DIVISION by a picture which contains the picture code S as its first character. Thus if the data 032J is read into a field described as S9999, the resulting value is −321. Suppose signed data is entered into a field which is not described using the S picture code: for example, the data 032J is read into a field described as 9999. In this case the value stored will be 321—a positive value! In order for a field to store a negative value it *must* be described using the S picture code.

Remember also that when a signed field is specified without the SIGN IS clause, S is *not* counted as a part of the number of characters in the field. If the SIGN IS clause is used, the S *is* counted as a character in the field.

Examples

    Q PIC S999.

The size of the field is three.

    R PIC S999 SIGN IS LEADING.

The size of the field is four.

4.13 SELF-TEST EXERCISES

1. Consider the following information about a file:

        File-name: SALES-RECORD
        Device type: disk
        Record-name: SALESMAN

   a. Write an FD entry for the file.
   b. Write an OPEN statement for the file.
   c. Write a READ statement for the file.
   d. Write a CLOSE statement for the file.

2. Consider the following information about a file:

        File-name: PAYROLL
        Device type: printer
        Record-name: NET-PAY

   a. Write an FD entry for the file.
   b. Write an OPEN statement for the file.
   c. Write a READ statement for the file.
   d. Write a CLOSE statement for the file.

3. Show the result of the statement MOVE ITM1 TO ITM2 for ITM1 and ITM2 as shown below:

a. 1 2 3 4 5
         ^

   ITM1 PIC 999V99

   ITM2 PIC 9(5)

   ITM2 PIC 9(3)   ITM2 PIC 9PP

   ITM2 PIC 9(8)

   ITM2 PIC 999V9999

   ITM2 PIC 9999V999

b. 0 1 2 3 4 5 0
           ^

   ITM1 PIC 9(4)V999

   ITM2 PIC ZZZZZ

   ITM2 PIC $$$$$$.99

   ITM2 PIC ****.9

c. 4 3 2 1

   ITM1 PIC X(4)

   ITM2 PIC X(6)   ITM2 PIC X(6) JUSTIFIED RIGHT

   ITM2 PIC XX   ITM2 PIC XX JUSTIFIED RIGHT

d. 0 0 1 2 3 4̄
          ^

   ITM1 PIC S9(4)V99

   ITM2 PIC -(5).99

   ITM2 PIC +(5).++

   ITM2 PIC Z(5).99CR

   ITM2 PIC $Z,ZZZ.99BDB

e. 0 0 0 1 2 3̄
          ^

   ITM1 PIC S9(4)V99

   ITM2 PIC 9(4)

   ITM2 PIC +Z(4).ZZ

   ITM2 PIC ZZZZ.99-

   ITM2 PIC ZZZZ.ZZDB

f. 1 2 3 4 5 6 7 8
             ^

   ITM1 PIC 9(6)V99

   ITM2 PIC $(5).99

   ITM2 PIC Z(6).9999

   ITM2 PIC ZZ,ZZZ.9

g. 0 1 2 3 4

   ITM1 PIC 9(5)

   ITM2 PIC X(6)   ITM2 PIC 9909909

   ITM2 PIC X(4)   ITM2 PIC 99B999

h. 0 3 1 1 8 2

   ITM1 PIC 9(6)

   ITM2 PIC ZZ/99/99

4. Draw a program flowchart for the paragraph of Program 4.1 which will terminate the processing of the loop. What will cause this termination?

5. List types of output lines found in most reports.

6. In each cell of the following table classify each type of move as permitted or not permitted.

		Receiving Field			
		Alphanumeric	*Numeric*	*Numeric edited*	*Alphanumeric edited*
Sending Field	*Alphanumeric*				
	Numeric				
	Numeric edited				
	Alphanumeric edited				

4.14 PROGRAMMING EXERCISES

1. Write a program to produce an appropriately edited report listing each item from data records in the following format:

Positions

1-20	Name
21-34	Street address
35-41	City
42-46	ZIP code
47	Marital status code
50-60	Yearly salary (two decimal places implied)

Write a line at the conclusion of your report specifying the total number of records processed.

Use the following data to test your program:

Name	*Street address*	*City*	*ZIP*	*Marital Status Code*	*Yearly Salary*
JOHN DOE	123 A ST.	MOBILE	34712	S	$16,000.00
MARY SMITH	1400 MAPLE	NEW ORLEANS	51760	M	$27,500.00
JAMES BROWN	72 MAIN AVE.	JACKSONVILLE	32571	W	$17,895.85
SUSY QUEUE	1900 OAK ST.	TROY	47501	M	$15,970.00

2. Write a program to process a file containing records in the following format and produce a report listing sales in each department. The last line of the report should contain the totals for each column of the report.

Positions

1-6	Date
10-19	Sales in shoe department
20-29	Sales in ladies' clothing
30-39	Sales in men's clothing
40-49	Sales in children's clothing
50-59	Sales in jewelry department

3. A real estate company maintains the following records for each listed property.

   Positions

1-8	Multiple listing number
9-10	Zone
11-25	Address
26	Number of bedrooms
27-28	Number of baths (9V9)
29	Total number of rooms
30	Number of cars in carport
31	Number of cars in garage
32-40	Elementary school name
41-49	Junior high school name
50-58	High school name
59-63	Taxes (9999)
64-68	Price (999999)
69-74	Amount of existing mortgage (999999)
75-77	Amount of payment on existing mortgage (999)
78-80	Interest rate on existing mortgage (V999)

   Write a program to list this file using a format similar to the following:

   ```
   MULTIPLE LISTING NUMBER xxxxxxxx     ZONE xx
   ADDRESS            xxxxxxxxxxxxxxx   PRICE $xxxxxx
   ROOMS x     BEDROOMS x     BATHS x.x
   CARPORT x     GARAGE x
       .
       .
       .
   etc.
   ```

4. The managers of Burgers, Inc. which operates a franchise system of hamburger restaurants, are concerned with the profitability of a number of the company's outlets. They have requested a report showing basic data about each store. The format for the input records is:

   Positions

1-10	Franchise number
11-25	Location
26-40	Manager's name
41-48	Previous year's profits (S999999V99)
	(Field could be negative if the store lost money.)

   The manager of the computer at ABC Furniture, Inc. prepares a record in the following format for each supply requisition he makes:

   Positions

1-6	Date
7-25	Description
26-31	Amount (9999V99)

   At the end of each month, he collects all the requisitions and runs a program to list each requisition and the total for the month. Write a program for the manager to use for this task.

ARITHMETIC STATEMENTS 5

Arithmetic statements are used to perform computations in a COBOL program. Two types of arithmetic statements can be used. One type uses the verbs ADD, SUBTRACT, MULTIPLY, and DIVIDE to specify the arithmetic operation to be performed; the other type uses the verb COMPUTE and allows the programmer to specify arithmetic operations using the symbols + (for add), − (for subtract), * (for multiply), / (for divide), and ** (for exponentiation). The programmer may choose whichever type of statement he or she finds most advantageous.

5.1 THE ADD STATEMENT

The ADD statement is used to perform addition of numeric data items. Figure 5.1 shows a general form for the ADD statement.

Figure 5.1 A general form of the ADD statement

$$\underline{ADD} \left\{ \begin{array}{l} \text{data-name-1} \\ \text{constant-1} \end{array} \right\} \cdot \cdot \cdot \left\{ \begin{array}{l} \underline{TO} \\ \underline{GIVING} \end{array} \right\} \text{data-name-n}$$

Any number of data items may be added; the result is placed in *data-name-n*. If the TO option is used, the receiving item participates as an addend. If the GIVING option is used, the calculated sum is moved to the receiving item and does not participate in the addition.

Example

Add credit to present balance to get new balance.

```
ADD CREDIT  BAL GIVING NEW-BAL
```

| 0 3 2 0 0 | 0 0 4 0 0 0̄ | 0 0 0 8 0 0̄ |

```
CREDIT PIC 999V99   BAL PIC S9999V99   NEW-BAL PIC S9999V99
```

Calculation: $32.00 + (-40.00) = -8.00$

Example

Add the constant 3.2 to the values contained in X and Y to get Z. In this case, suppose X = 23.0 and Y = 123.

```
ADD 3.2  X  Y  GIVING Z
```

| 2 3 0 | 1 2 3 | 0 1 4 9 2 |

```
X PIC 99V9   Y PIC 999   Z PIC 9(4)V9
```

Calculation: $3.2 + 23.0 + 123 = 149.2$

Example

Add 1 to the present value of the data item KOUNT.

```
ADD 1 TO KOUNT
```

Before Execution

| 0 0 3 |

```
KOUNT PIC 999
```

After Execution

| 0 0 4 |

```
KOUNT PIC 999
```

Example

Add the constant 3.2 and the contents of X and Y, to Z, whose values in this case are 23.0, 123 and 149.2.

```
ADD 3.2  X  Y TO Z
```

Before Execution

| 2 3 0 | 1 2 3 | 0 1 4 9 2 |

```
X PIC 99V9   Y PIC 999   Z PIC 9(4)V9
```

After Execution

| 2 3 0 | 1 2 3 | 0 2 9 8 4 |

```
X PIC 99V9   Y PIC 999   Z PIC 9(4)V9
```

Calculation: $3.2 + 23.0 + 123 + 149.2 = 298.4$

Note that this example could be rewritten as

```
ADD 3.2  X  Y  Z GIVING Z.
```

The results would be exactly the same.

When the computer executes the ADD (and SUBTRACT) instruction, data items are adjusted to align decimal positions; the operation is performed, taking into account the sign of the field (if any); and the result is placed in the receiving fields. In all arithmetic instructions (as in the MOVE instruction), data is moved to the receiving field from the decimal point to the right and also from the decimal point to the left. *Truncation* occurs on the leftmost digits of the integer portion and of the rightmost digits of the fractional portion if the receiving field is too short. Padding with zeroes occurs on the left and right if the receiving field is too long.

Example

Add the regular hours (40) to overtime hours (6.5) to get total hours. The regular and overtime hours may contain fractions, but total hours does not.

```
ADD REG-HR  OV-HR GIVING TOT-HR
```

   4,0,0   0,6,5   0,4,6

REG-HR PIC 99V9   OV-HR PIC 99V9   TOT-HR PIC 999

Calculation: 40.0 + 6.5 = 46.5 ← Truncated when result is moved to TOT-HR.

Example

Add regular sales (30.40) to special sales (245.00) to get total sales.

```
ADD REG-SALES  SPECIAL-SALES GIVING TOTAL-SALES
```

  0,3,0,4,0   2,4,5,0,0

REG-SALES PIC 999V99   SPECIAL-SALES PIC 999V99

  0,0,0,2,7,5,4,0   The first three

TOTAL-SALES PIC 9(6)V99   zeroes pad out the field of whole dollars.

5.2 THE SUBTRACT STATEMENT

The SUBTRACT statement is used to perform subtraction of numeric data items, as shown in general form in Figure 5.2

Figure 5.2   General form of the SUBTRACT statement

```
SUBTRACT  {data-name-1}  . . .  FROM  {data-name-n [GIVING data-name-m]}
          {constant-1  }               {constant-n   GIVING  data-name-m }
```

The result is placed in the last *data-name* specified. The GIVING clause is optional when the subtrahend (the value subtracted from) is specified as a data-name, but required when it is specified as a constant.

Example

Subtract FICA tax (26.00) from pay (400.00) to get net pay.

```
SUBTRACT FICA FROM PAY GIVING NET-PAY
```

```
FICA PIC 999V99    PAY PIC 9999V99   NET-PAY PIC 9999V99
```

Calculation: $400.00 - 26.00 = 374.00$

Example

Subtract FICA tax (26.00) from pay (400.00).

```
SUBTRACT FICA FROM PAY
```

Before Execution

```
FICA PIC 999V99              PAY PIC 9999V99
```

After Execution

```
FICA PIC 999V9               PAY PIC 9999V99
```

Any number of items may be subtracted. The sign (if any) is considered in the operation.

Example

Subtract 3.2 and X (-1.2) from Y (.32) to get Z.

```
SUBTRACT 3.2  X FROM Y GIVING Z
```

```
X PIC S99V99     Y PIC S99V99     Z PIC S99V99
```

Calculation: $.32 - 3.2 - (-1.2) = -1.68$

When you subtract from a constant, the GIVING clause *must* be specified, since it is not permissible to store a different value into a constant.

Subtract contents of Field A (20) from 25. The following statement is *invalid*:

The following statement is *valid*:

```
SUBTRACT FLDA FROM 25 GIVING FLDB
```

```
FLDA PIC 99V99        FLDB PIC 99V99
```

5.3 THE MULTIPLY STATEMENT

The MULTIPLY statement is used to perform multiplication of two numeric items (Fig. 5.3).

Figure 5.3 General form of the MULTIPLY statement

```
MULTIPLY  { data-name-1 }  BY  { data-name-2   [GIVING data-name-3] }
          { constant-1  }      { constant-2     GIVING data-name-3  }
```

The result is placed in the last *data-name* specified.

Example

Multiply pay (400.00) by the constant .075 to get FICA tax. (Note that you are multiplying by a constant, so the GIVING clause is required.)

```
MULTIPLY PAY BY 0.075 GIVING FICA
```

|0|4|0|0|0|0| |0|3|0|0|0|

PAY PIC 9999V99   FICA PIC 9999V99

Computation: $400 \times .075 = 30.00$

Example

Multiply price (20.00) times percent (25%) to get sale price. (Note that most sales are based on a percent-off figure, not a direct percent as in this example.)

```
MULTIPLY PRICE BY PCT GIVING SALE-PRICE
```

|0|2|0|0|0| |2|5|0| |0|0|5|0|0|

PRICE PIC 999V99   PCT PIC V999   SALE-PRICE PIC 999V99

Computation: $20.00 \times .250 = 5.00$

Example

Multiply the contents of FLDA (12.3) by the contents of FLDB (2.3) and store the results in FLDB.

```
MULTIPLY FLDA BY FLDB
```

Before Execution

1	2	3

FLDA PIC 99V9

0	2	3

FLDB PIC 99V9

After Execution

1	2	3

FLDA PIC 99V9

2	8	2

FLDB PIC 99V9

Computation: $12.3 \times 2.3 = 28.29$ ← This last digit will be truncated when the result is moved to FLDB.

5.4   THE DIVIDE STATEMENT

Recall the terminology used in arithmetic division:

$$
\text{Divisor} \longrightarrow \quad 7\overline{)15} \quad
\begin{array}{l}
\longleftarrow \text{ Quotient} \\
\longleftarrow \text{ Dividend}
\end{array}
$$
$$
\underline{14}
$$
$$
1 \quad \longleftarrow \text{ Remainder}
$$

The DIVIDE statement has two formats as shown in Figure 5.4.

Figure 5.4   General form of the DIVIDE statement

Format 1

```
DIVIDE {data-name-1} INTO data-name-2
       {constant-1 }
```

Format 2

```
DIVIDE {data-name-1}{INTO}{data-name-2} GIVING data-name-3 [REMAINDER data-name-4]
       {constant-1 }{BY  }{constant-2 }
```

When the INTO option is specified, the divisor is specified first and the dividend is specified next. If the GIVING clause is omitted, then the quotient replaces the dividend.

Example

Divide the kount (20) into a total (100) to get the average.

```
DIVIDE KOUNT INTO TOTAL GIVING AVERAGE
        ↑         ↑              ↑
     Divisor   Dividend       Quotient

   ⌊2⌄0⌋     ⌊0⌄1⌄0⌄0⌋     ⌊0⌄5⌋
      ^           ^            ^
KOUNT PIC 99  TOTAL PIC 9999  AVERAGE PIC 99
```

Example

Divide the contents of FLDA (12.3) into FLDB (4.6).

```
DIVIDE FLDA INTO FLDB⬎
        ↑        ↑         ↘
     Divisor  Dividend   Quotient
```

Before Execution

```
  ⌊1⌄2⌄3⌋          ⌊0⌄4⌄6⌋
      ^                ^
 FLDA PIC 99V9      FLDB PIC 99V9
```

Computation: $4.6 \div 12.3 = .3$

After Execution

```
  ⌊1⌄2⌄3⌋          ⌊0⌄0⌄3⌋
      ^                ^
 FLDA PIC 99V9      FLDB PIC 99V9
```

When the BY option is specified, the dividend is specified first and the divisor is specified next. The GIVING clause *must* be used in this case.

Example

Divide the total (100) by the kount (20) to get the average.

```
DIVIDE TOTAL BY KOUNT GIVING AVERAGE
        ↑        ↑           ↑
     Divisor  Dividend    Quotient

  ⌊0⌄1⌄0⌄0⌋    ⌊2⌄0⌋      ⌊0⌄5⌋
      ^           ^           ^
TOTAL PIC 9999  KOUNT PIC 99  AVERAGE PIC 99
```

If the REMAINDER option is included, the remainder after the division will be placed in the specified data name. The remainder is computed by subtracting the product of the quotient and divisor from the dividend.

Example

Given a number of ounces, compute the number of pounds and ounces. For example, 20 ounces is equal to 1 pound, 4 ounces. The number of ounces left over is equal to the remainder after dividing by 16 and subtracting the number of ounces in 1 pound.

```
DIVIDE OUNCES BY 16 GIVING POUNDS REMAINDER OUNCES
```
           ↑   ↑   ↑   ↑
        Dividend Divisor   Quotient   Remainder

Before Execution

| 0 | 2 | 0 | | ? | ? |

OUNCES PIC 999   POUNDS PIC 99

Computation of quotient: 20 ÷ 16 = 1
                          ↑   ↑   ↑
                      Dividend Divisor Quotient

Computation of remainder: 20 − (16 × 1) = 4
                           ↑   ↑   ↑   ↖
                       Dividend Divisor Quotient Remainder

After Execution

| 0 | 0 | 4 | | 0 | 1 |

OUNCES PIC 999   POUNDS PIC 99

Example

Divide the dividend (62.8) by the contents of FLDA to get FLDB, and place any remainder in FLDC.

```
DIVIDE 62.8 BY FLDA GIVING FLDB REMAINDER FLDC
```
         ↑   ↑   ↑   ↑
      Dividend Divisor   Quotient   Remainder

Before Execution

| 0 | 1 | 3 | | ? | ? | ? | | ? | ? |

FLDA PIC 9V99   FLDB PIC 999   FLDC PIC V99

Computation of quotient: 62.8 ÷ .13 = 483
                          ↑   ↑   ↑
                      Dividend Divisor Quotient

Computation of remainder: 62.8 − (.13 × 483) = .01
                           ↑   ↑   ↑   ↑
                       Dividend Divisor Quotient Remainder

After Execution

| 0 | 1 | 3 | | 4 | 8 | 3 | | 0 | 1 |

FLDA PIC 9V99   FLDB PIC 999   FLDC PIC V99

5.5   THE COMPUTE STATEMENT

The COMPUTE statement is used to perform any desired sequence of arithmetic operations. The symbols used for operations are:

+   Add
−   Subtract
*   Multiply
/   Divide
**   Exponentiation

The general form of the COMPUTE statement is

> <u>COMPUTE</u> data-name = expression

The value of the expression is placed in the location specified by the *data-name*. An *expression* is either a constant, a variable, or any valid combination of constants and/or variables linked by arithmetic operations and parentheses. Arithmetic operation symbols, and the "=" sign must be preceded and followed by at least one blank.

Move the value 42 to FLDA.

```
COMPUTE FLDA = 42
```

Place the value of FLDA into FLDB.

```
COMPUTE FLDB = FLDA
```

Multiply content of FLDA by 3 and place the result in FLDC.

```
COMPUTE FLDC = 3 * FLDA
```

Divide the TOTAL by KOUNT and place the result in AV.

```
COMPUTE AV = TOTAL / KOUNT
```

Add A and B; subtract C from the result.

```
COMPUTE VALUE = A + B - C
```

Multiply A times itself three times to get the cube of A or A^3.

```
COMPUTE X = A ** 3
```

Parentheses may be used to control the order in which operations are carried out. Expressions within parentheses are evaluated first. For some compilers a left parenthesis "(" must be preceded by a blank and a right parenthesis ")" must be followed by a blank or a period.

Example

Add 3 to the contents of FLDB. Then multiply the sum by 6.

Note absence of blanks in these positions.

COMPUTE FLDA = (3 + FLDB) * 6

Note the presence of blanks in these positions.

3 is added to FLDB and the result is multiplied by 6.

As many sets of parentheses as are necessary may be used.

Example

Compute the result of adding Z to Q; then subtract that sum from Y; then multiply what is left by 6.

    COMPUTE X = (Y - (Z + Q)) * 6

The expression in the innermost set of parentheses is evaluated first.

An expression is evaluated by performing operations in order of precedence (Figure 5.5). Operations with equal precedence (such as multiplication and division or addition and subtraction) are performed in a left-to-right order.

Figure 5.5   Precedence of arithmetic operations

Expressions in parentheses		Highest precedence
**	Exponentiation	↓
*/	Multiplication and division	
+−	Addition and subtraction	Lowest precedence

Example

Compute B × C first. Then add A.

    COMPUTE X = A + B * C

Multiplication has higher precedence than addition; therefore, B and C are multiplied first and only then is the result added to A.

Example

Compute the exponential 2^3 first. Then divide the result into the product of 4 × 2.

    COMPUTE FLDA = 4 * 2 / 2 ** 3

Exponentiation has highest precedence; hence, the first operation to be performed is 2^3. Then, as multiplication precedes division and they are both of the same order of precedence, the next operation is 4×2. Finally the division is performed, giving 1 as a value of the expression.

Example

Compute 3×2 and add it to 4. Then compute $3 \times 3 \times 3$ and multiply that result by 2. Subtract the last answer from the first (3×2 plus 4). (Your answer will be -8.)

```
COMPUTE A = 4 + 3 * 2 - 3 ** 3 * 2
```

This is equivalent to

```
COMPUTE A = (4 + (3 * 2)) - ((3 ** 3) * 2)
```

5.6 THE ROUNDED OPTION

The ROUNDED option may be used with any of the arithmetic statements. When it is specified, rounding of the computed result will be performed by the computer before it places the value in the receiving field. Rounding is performed by adding 5 to the digit immediately following the rightmost decimal digit to be stored, and then truncating excess decimal digits as usual.[1] For example, suppose the calculated result for an arithmetic operation is 12.347, and this value will be stored in a location with picture 99V99. Rounding will be performed as follows:

```
  12.347      If this last digit is 0, 1, 2, 3, or 4, rounding has no effect on the
+     5      value stored. If this digit is 5, 6, 7, 8 or 9, rounding causes a
  ------      carry of one into the next position and does affect the
  12.352      value stored.

  1,2,3,5,          2 is lost due to truncation
      ^
PIC 99V99
```

If the receiving field had picture 99V9, the rounding would result in

```
  12.345      This digit is less than 5; rounding has no effect on the
+     5      value stored.
  ------
  12.395  ———————— 95 is lost due to truncation

  1,2,3,
     ^
PIC 99V9
```

---

1. Negative quantities are rounded by first taking the absolute value of the field, performing the rounding operation, and then making the resulting field negative. For example,

```
12.347    absolute value        12.347
                              +      5
12.35    result is negative    ------
                                12.352
  1,2,3,5,
PIC S99V99
```

The placement of the ROUNDED option in each of the arithmetic statements is shown below in general formats (Fig. 5.6):

Figure 5.6   General form of arithmetic statements

```
ADD   {data-name-1} . . . {TO     } data-name-n   [ROUNDED]
      {constant-1 }       {GIVING }

SUBTRACT {data-name-1}  . . . FROM {data-name-n [GIVING data-name-m]}  [ROUNDED]
         {constant-1 }            {constant-n   GIVING data-name-m    }

MULTIPLY {data-name-1} BY {data-name-2 [GIVING data-name-3]}  [ROUNDED]
         {constant-1 }    {constant-2   GIVING data-name-3   }

DIVIDE {data-name-1} INTO data-name-2   [ROUNDED]
       {constant-1 }

DIVIDE {data-name-1}{INTO}{data-name-2} GIVING data-name-1 [ROUNDED] [REMAINDER data-name-4]
       {constant-2 }{BY  }{constant-3 }

COMPUTE   data-name [ROUNDED] = expression
```

Example

Add 6.2, 4.52, and 7.892 to get an answer rounded to the nearest whole number.

```
ADD 6.2  4.52  7.892 GIVING X ROUNDED
```

Computation: 6.2
                                4.52
                              +7.892
                             ───────
                              18.612
                              + 5
                             ───────
                              19.112

After Execution

  1 9
 └─┴─┘
      ^

X PIC 99

Example

Multiply the contents of FLDA (12.3) times the contents of FLDB (3.4) and round the answer to tenths.

```
MULTIPLY FLDA BY FLDB ROUNDED
```

Before Execution

  1 2 3   0 3 4
 └─┴─┴─┘   └─┴─┴─┘
       ^   ^

FLDA PIC 99V9   FLDB PIC 99V9

Computation:
$$\begin{array}{r} 12.3 \\ \times\ \ 3.4 \\ \hline 492 \\ 369\ \ \ \\ \hline 41.82 \\ +\ \ \ \ 5 \\ \hline 41.8\cancel{7} \end{array}$$

After Execution

|_4_|_1_|_8_|
    ^

FLDB PIC 99V9

Example

Add 4.2 to 8.97 and round the answer to tenths.

    COMPUTE XYZ ROUNDED = 4.2 + 8.97

Computation:
$$\begin{array}{r} 4.2\ \ \\ +\ 8.97 \\ \hline 13.17 \\ +\ \ \ \ 5 \\ \hline 13.2\cancel{2} \end{array}$$

|_1_|_3_|_2_|
    ^

XYZ PIC 99V9

5.7 PROGRAM EXAMPLE

Problem Statement

The XYZ Company requires a payroll register to be constructed showing gross pay and net pay for its employees. Input consists of records containing the following fields:

Employee number
Employee name
Regular hours worked
Overtime hours worked
Pay rate
Federal withholding rate
Other deductions

The program must calculate and print:

Gross pay
Amount of federal income tax to withhold
Amount of FICA taxes to withhold
Net pay

The program must also accumulate and print appropriate totals. The printer spacing chart for the required report is shown in Figure 5.7.

Figure 5.7 Printer spacing chart for payroll register

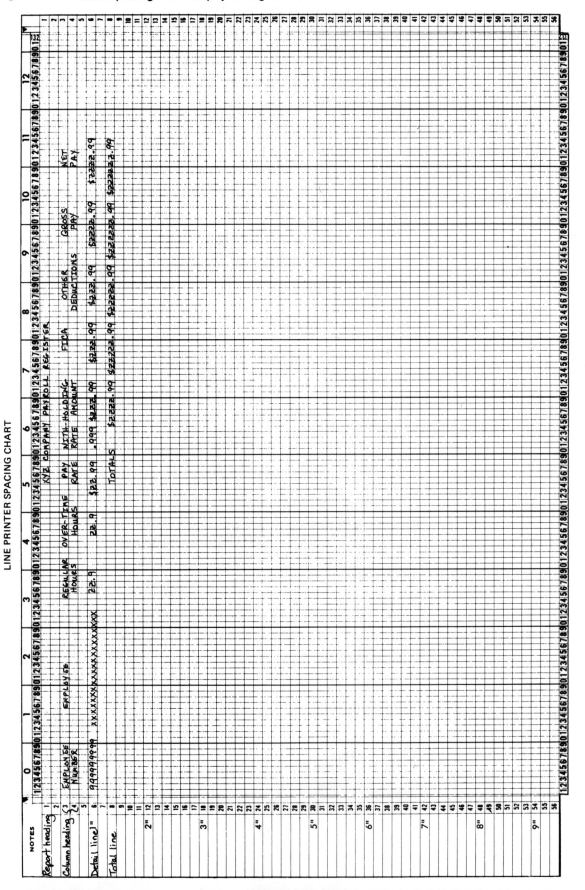

Problem Analysis

This problem requires that a data file, which we may call PAY-FILE, be processed to produce a printed report that we call PAY-REGISTER. The processing of each record entails the computation of four amounts—withholding, FICA, gross pay, and net pay. It will be necessary to define numeric fields for these amounts (in addition to the edited fields on the output record) because they are involved in further computations. Totals must be accumulated for five different fields; therefore, five accumulators will be needed.

The overall structure of this problem resembles those examples presented previously. The primary difference in this program is the number of computations required. A plan for this program is shown in Figure 5.8.

Figure 5.8   Plan for payroll register program

Main Logic

    Open files
    Write headings
    Read pay file
    Do Process read until end of file
    Write total line
    Close files
    Stop

Process read

    Compute amounts for detail output
    Accumulate totals
    Write detail line
    Read pay file

Problem Solution

Program 5.1 makes extensive use of the arithmetic statements described in this chapter, particularly in the paragraph 5000-COMPUTATIONS (lines 18400 through 19600). The program also illustrates several new COBOL features and structured programming practices.

Program 5.1 Payroll register

```
100     IDENTIFICATION DIVISION.
200
300     PROGRAM-ID. PAYROLL-REGISTER.
400     AUTHOR. HORN.
500
600     ENVIRONMENT DIVISION.
700
800     CONFIGURATION SECTION.
900
1000    SOURCE-COMPUTER.
1100    OBJECT-COMPUTER.
1200
1300    INPUT-OUTPUT SECTION.
1400
1500    FILE-CONTROL.
1600
1700        SELECT PAY-FILE ASSIGN TO DISK.
1800        SELECT PAY-REGISTER ASSIGN TO PRINTER.
1900
2000    DATA DIVISION.
2100
2200    FILE SECTION.
2300
2400    FD  PAY-FILE
2500        LABEL RECORDS ARE STANDARD
2600        DATA RECORD IS INPUT-RECORD.
2700
2800    01  INPUT-RECORD.
2900        03  EMPLOYEE-NUMBER-IR      PIC 9(9).
3000        03  EMPLOYEE-NAME-IR        PIC X(20).
3100        03  REG-HRS-IR              PIC 99V9.
3200        03  OT-HRS-IR               PIC 99V9.
3300        03  PAY-RATE-IR             PIC 99V99.
3400        03  WITH-RATE-IR            PIC V999.
3500        03  OTHER-DEDUCTIONS-IR     PIC 999V99.
3600        03  FILLER                  PIC X(33).
3700
3800    FD  PAY-REGISTER
3900        LABEL RECORDS ARE OMITTED
4000        DATA RECORD IS PRINT-LINE.
4100
4200    01  PRINT-LINE              PIC X(132).
4300
4400    WORKING-STORAGE SECTION.
4500
4600    01  FLAGS.
4700        02  EOF-FLAG                PIC X(3) VALUE "NO".
4800
4900    01  CONSTANTS.
5000        02  FICA-FACTOR             PIC 9V9999 VALUE 0.0750.
5100
5200    01  COMPUTED-AMOUNTS.
5300        03  WITH-AMT                PIC 999V99  VALUE ZERO.
```

Program 5.1 (continued)

```
5400          03 NET-PAY                 PIC 9999V99 VALUE ZERO.
5500          03 GROSS-PAY               PIC 9999V99 VALUE ZERO.
5600          03 FICA                    PIC 999V99  VALUE ZERO.
5700
5800       01 ACCUMULATED-TOTALS.
5900          03 TOTAL-NET               PIC 9(6)V99 VALUE ZERO.
6000          03 TOTAL-WITH              PIC 9(4)V99 VALUE ZERO.
6100          03 TOTAL-OTHER             PIC 9(5)V99 VALUE ZERO.
6200          03 TOTAL-FICA              PIC 9(5)V99 VALUE ZERO.
6300          03 TOTAL-GROSS             PIC 9(6)V99 VALUE ZERO.
6400
6500       01 HEADING-LINE.
6600          03 FILLER                  PIC X(54) VALUE SPACES.
6700          03 FILLER                  PIC X(28) VALUE
6800                                     "XYZ COMPANY PAYROLL REGISTER".
6900       01 SUB-HEAD-1.
7000          03 FILLER                  PIC X     VALUE SPACES.
7100          03 FILLER                  PIC X(8)  VALUE "EMPLOYEE".
7200          03 FILLER                  PIC X(6)  VALUE SPACES.
7300          03 FILLER                  PIC X(8)  VALUE "EMPLOYEE".
7400          03 FILLER                  PIC X(11) VALUE SPACES.
7500          03 FILLER                  PIC X(7)  VALUE "REGULAR".
7600          03 FILLER                  PIC X(2)  VALUE SPACES.
7700          03 FILLER                  PIC X(9)  VALUE "OVER-TIME".
7800          03 FILLER                  PIC X(3)  VALUE SPACES.
7900          03 FILLER                  PIC X(3)  VALUE "PAY".
8000          03 FILLER                  PIC X(2)  VALUE SPACES.
8100          03 FILLER                  PIC X(12) VALUE "WITH-HOLDING".
8200          03 FILLER                  PIC X(5)  VALUE SPACES.
8300          03 FILLER                  PIC X(4)  VALUE "FICA".
8400          03 FILLER                  PIC X(5)  VALUE SPACES.
8500          03 FILLER                  PIC X(5)  VALUE "OTHER".
8600          03 FILLER                  PIC X(6)  VALUE SPACES.
8700          03 FILLER                  PIC X(5)  VALUE "GROSS".
8800          03 FILLER                  PIC X(7)  VALUE SPACES.
8900          03 FILLER                  PIC X(3)  VALUE "NET".
9000
9100       01 SUB-HEAD-2.
9200          03 FILLER                  PIC X(2)  VALUE SPACES.
9300          03 FILLER                  PIC X(6)  VALUE "NUMBER".
9400          03 FILLER                  PIC X(9)  VALUE SPACES.
9500          03 FILLER                  PIC X(4)  VALUE "NAME".
9600          03 FILLER                  PIC X(14) VALUE SPACES.
9700          03 FILLER                  PIC X(5)  VALUE "HOURS".
9800          03 FILLER                  PIC X(5)  VALUE SPACES.
9900          03 FILLER                  PIC X(5)  VALUE "HOURS".
10000         03 FILLER                  PIC X(4)  VALUE SPACES.
10100         03 FILLER                  PIC X(4)  VALUE "RATE".
10200         03 FILLER                  PIC X(2)  VALUE SPACES.
10300         03 FILLER                  PIC X(4)  VALUE "RATE".
10400         03 FILLER                  PIC X(2)  VALUE SPACES.
10500         03 FILLER                  PIC X(6)  VALUE "AMOUNT".
10600         03 FILLER                  PIC X(12) VALUE SPACES.
10700         03 FILLER                  PIC X(10) VALUE "DEDUCTIONS".
10800         03 FILLER                  PIC X(4)  VALUE SPACES.
10900         03 FILLER                  PIC X(3)  VALUE "PAY".
```

Program 5.1 *(continued)*

```
11000        03  FILLER                PIC X(8)  VALUE SPACES.
11100        03  FILLER                PIC X(3)  VALUE "PAY".
11200
11300    01  DETAIL-LINE.
11400        03  FILLER                PIC X     VALUE SPACES.
11500        03  EMPLOYEE-NUMBER-OUT   PIC 9(9).
11600        03  FILLER                PIC X(2) VALUE SPACES.
11700        03  EMPLOYEE-NAME-OUT     PIC X(20).
11800        03  FILLER                PIC X(3) VALUE SPACES.
11900        03  REG-HRS-OUT           PIC ZZ.9.
12000        03  FILLER                PIC X(6) VALUE SPACES.
12100        03  OT-HRS-OUT            PIC ZZ.9.
12200        03  FILLER                PIC X(3) VALUE SPACES.
12300        03  PAY-RATE-OUT          PIC $ZZ.99.
12400        03  FILLER                PIC X(2) VALUE SPACES.
12500        03  WITH-RATE-OUT         PIC .999.
12600        03  FILLER                PIC X     VALUE SPACES.
12700        03  WITH-AMT-OUT          PIC $ZZZ.99.
12800        03  FILLER                PIC X(3) VALUE SPACES.
12900        03  FICA-OUT              PIC $ZZZ.99.
13000        03  FILLER                PIC X(3) VALUE SPACES.
13100        03  OTHER-DEDUCTIONS-OUT  PIC $ZZZ.99.
13200        03  FILLER                PIC X(3) VALUE SPACES.
13300        03  GROSS-PAY-OUT         PIC $Z(4).99.
13400        03  FILLER                PIC X(3) VALUE SPACES.
13500        03  NET-PAY-OUT           PIC $Z(4).99.
13600
13700    01  TOTAL-LINE.
13800        03  FILLER                PIC X(54) VALUE SPACES.
13900        03  FILLER                PIC X(6)  VALUE "TOTALS".
14000        03  FILLER                PIC X(4)  VALUE SPACES.
14100        03  TOTAL-WITH-OUT        PIC $Z(4).99.
14200        03  FILLER                PIC X     VALUE SPACES.
14300        03  TOTAL-FICA-OUT        PIC $Z(5).99.
14400        03  FILLER                PIC X     VALUE SPACES.
14500        03  TOTAL-OTHER-OUT       PIC $Z(5).99.
14600        03  FILLER                PIC X     VALUE SPACES.
14700        03  TOTAL-GROSS-OUT       PIC $Z(6).99.
14800        03  FILLER                PIC X     VALUE SPACES.
14900        03  TOTAL-NET-OUT         PIC $Z(6).99.
15000
15100    PROCEDURE DIVISION.
15200
15300    1000-MAIN-LOGIC.
15400
15500        PERFORM 2000-INITIALIZATION.
15600        PERFORM 3000-PROCESS-READ
15700            UNTIL EOF-FLAG = "YES".
15800        PERFORM 7000-TERMINATION.
15900        STOP RUN.
16000
16100
16200    2000-INITIALIZATION.
16300
16400        OPEN INPUT PAY-FILE
16500             OUTPUT PAY-REGISTER.
16600        WRITE PRINT-LINE FROM HEADING-LINE AFTER PAGE.
```

```
16700          WRITE PRINT-LINE FROM SUB-HEAD-1 AFTER 2.
16800          WRITE PRINT-LINE FROM SUB-HEAD-2 AFTER 1.
16900          MOVE SPACES TO PRINT-LINE.
17000          WRITE PRINT-LINE AFTER 1.
17100          PERFORM 4000-READ.
17200
17300      3000-PROCESS-READ.
17400
17500          PERFORM 5000-COMPUTATIONS.
17600          PERFORM 6000-DETAIL-OUTPUT.
17700          PERFORM 4000-READ.
17800
17900      4000-READ.
18000
18100          READ PAY-FILE
18200              AT END MOVE "YES" TO EOF-FLAG.
18300
18400      5000-COMPUTATIONS.
18500
18600          COMPUTE GROSS-PAY ROUNDED = REG-HRS-IR * PAY-RATE-IR +
18700              OT-HRS-IR * PAY-RATE-IR * 1.5.
18800          MULTIPLY WITH-RATE-IR BY GROSS-PAY GIVING WITH-AMT ROUNDED.
18900          MULTIPLY FICA-FACTOR BY GROSS-PAY GIVING FICA ROUNDED.
19000          SUBTRACT WITH-AMT, FICA, OTHER-DEDUCTIONS-IR
19100              FROM GROSS-PAY GIVING NET-PAY.
19200          ADD WITH-AMT              TO TOTAL-WITH.
19300          ADD FICA                  TO TOTAL-FICA.
19400          ADD OTHER-DEDUCTIONS-IR   TO TOTAL-OTHER.
19500          ADD GROSS-PAY             TO TOTAL-GROSS.
19600          ADD NET-PAY               TO TOTAL-NET.
19700
19800      6000-DETAIL-OUTPUT.
19900
20000          MOVE EMPLOYEE-NUMBER-IR     TO EMPLOYEE-NUMBER-OUT.
20100          MOVE EMPLOYEE-NAME-IR       TO EMPLOYEE-NAME-OUT.
20200          MOVE REG-HRS-IR             TO REG-HRS-OUT.
20300          MOVE OT-HRS-IR              TO OT-HRS-OUT.
20400          MOVE PAY-RATE-IR            TO PAY-RATE-OUT.
20500          MOVE WITH-RATE-IR           TO WITH-RATE-OUT.
20600          MOVE OTHER-DEDUCTIONS-IR    TO OTHER-DEDUCTIONS-OUT.
20700          MOVE WITH-AMT               TO WITH-AMT-OUT.
20800          MOVE FICA                   TO FICA-OUT.
20900          MOVE GROSS-PAY              TO GROSS-PAY-OUT.
21000          MOVE NET-PAY                TO NET-PAY-OUT.
21100          WRITE PRINT-LINE FROM DETAIL-LINE AFTER 1.
21200
21300      7000-TERMINATION.
21400
21500          MOVE TOTAL-WITH  TO TOTAL-WITH-OUT.
21600          MOVE TOTAL-FICA  TO TOTAL-FICA-OUT.
21700          MOVE TOTAL-OTHER TO TOTAL-OTHER-OUT.
21800          MOVE TOTAL-GROSS TO TOTAL-GROSS-OUT.
21900          MOVE TOTAL-NET   TO TOTAL-NET-OUT.
22000          WRITE PRINT-LINE FROM TOTAL-LINE AFTER 2.
22100          CLOSE PAY-FILE
22200              PAY-REGISTER.
```

Continuation of Non-numeric Literals

Lines 6700-6800 illustrate a common situation that arises when defining long non-numeric literals in the DATA DIVISION. The string of characters is too long to fit on 1 line in the usual fashion. Two solutions to the problem are possible. One solution is to bring the entire character string to a second line, an approach used in Program 5.1. An alternative is to continue the literal from the first line to the second, as shown in Figure 5.9.

Figure 5.9   Continuation of non-numeric literals

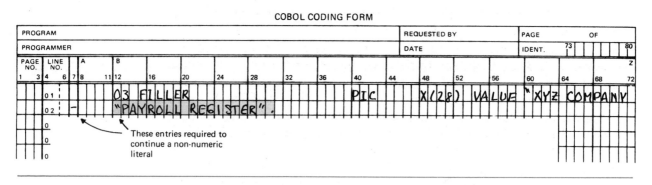

As shown in Figure 5.9, the literal XYZ COMPANY PAYROLL REGISTER is broken into two parts: the first part on line 1 extends from positions 61 through 72; the second part is on line 2 positions 13 through 28. The two parts are connected by placing a dash ("–") in position 7 and quotes in the B area (position 12) of the continuation line. In general, the placement of a "–" in position 7 of a line will cause the content of that line to be treated as a continuation of the preceding line. When using this mechanism to continue non-numeric literals,[2] the remaining characters of the literal must be preceded by a quote in the B area. Note that there are no quotes following the literal on the first line; all of the characters from the opening quote through position 72 are treated as part of the literal.

Grouping of Related Fields in WORKING–STORAGE

A number of data-names in addition to the usual output records are defined in WORKING–STORAGE (lines 5200 through 6300). All of the data-names could be defined as 01 items; however, current structured programming practice requires that related items that describe the relation be grouped under 01 items. Thus, under COMPUTED–AMOUNTS the items WITH–AMT, NET–PAY, GROSS–PAY and FICA are defined, and under TOTALS all the data-names used as accumulators are defined. This practice makes the program easier to read.

VALUE Clause for all Data-names

In Program 5.1 the data-names listed under TOTALS are all accumulators. The VALUE clause is used to ensure that the initial value of each data-name is zero

---

2. Although other COBOL elements including data-names, numeric-constants, and reserved words can be continued by use of a "–" in position 7, the continuation facility is recommended only for non-numeric literals.

so that the accumulation process will function properly. The data-names listed under COMPUTED-AMOUNTS are also initialized to zero. This is not a requirement of the logic of the program since the value in each of them is replaced by appropriate statements in 5000-COMPUTATIONS (see lines 18600-19100).

All elementary numeric items defined in WORKING-STORAGE should be given an initial value. The reason for this practice lies not in an absolute requirement for logical correctness but in making the program easier to debug and update.

Suppose, for example, that a programmer omits the initialization of some data-name such as FICA-AMT. Suppose further that the statement computing FICA-AMT is omitted in the PROCEDURE DIVISION. In this case the first reference to FICA-AMT usually will cause the program to terminate because of invalid data. The source of such an error usually is difficult to locate. However, if FICA-AMT had been initialized, the reference to the data-name would have been processed with a value zero and the program would have continued in a normal fashion. When the programmer noted that the value of FICA-AMT was zero on the same output, he or she could surmise that the computation in the PROCEDURE DIVISION was either incorrect or omitted. Thus, the debugging process is simplified considerably.

This practice also results in programs that are easier to update. If a subsequent revision of the program results in the deletion of the statement that computes a value for the data-name, the remaining statements can be left unaltered because the data-name will have no effect on the computations.

Constants in WORKING-STORAGE

Consider the data item FICA-FACTOR defined in line 5000 of Program 5.1. This value is used in the computation of the FICA withholding amount at line 18900. The practice of defining constants such as this in WORKING-STORAGE makes programs easier to change when the value of the constant changes. If this practice is followed, a programmer performing maintenance has to make only a single change in a well-defined easily located WORKING-STORAGE entry. Otherwise, the maintenance programmer must search through the PROCEDURE DIVISION and change every instance where the constant is used. This is a particular burden if the constant is used more than once. There is always the chance that one value will be changed, but another will not be, resulting in a potentially difficult debugging problem.

5.8 THE ON SIZE ERROR OPTION

The ON SIZE ERROR option causes the program to test for errors and to take appropriate action when two types of errors are found during execution of an arithmetic statement:

1) Division by a divisor having value zero.
2) A receiving field which is too small to accept all the significant digits to the left of the decimal point of the calculated result.

The programmer is responsible for specifying data items that are sufficiently large to hold any valid results. The programmer also needs to ensure that the computer is not asked to attempt the impossible operation of dividing by zero. However, such errors do occur because of errors in data and/or programmer oversight. The ON SIZE ERROR option allows the program to take appropriate action when such errors are detected during execution of a program. If the ON SIZE ERROR option is included in the arithmetic statement, the statement in that clause will be executed if either of the errors is detected. The general form of the clause is

> ON SIZE ERROR statement. . .

Any number of statements may be included in an ON SIZE ERROR clause. The clause is placed after the main body of each of the arithmetic statements.

Example

Add X (78.3) and Y (87.2) to get Z; also, if a size error appears write an appropriate message.

```
ADD X, Y GIVING Z
    ON SIZE ERROR
        WRITE OUTLINE FROM ERROR-MSG-LINE AFTER 1.
```

Before Execution

7 8 3		8 7 2		1 2 3
^		^		^
X PIC 99V9		Y PIC 99V9		Z PIC 99V9

Computation:

$$
\begin{array}{r}
78.3 \\
+87.2 \\
\hline
165.5
\end{array}
$$

Size error detected

Since a size error has occurred, the WRITE statement will be executed; that is, the program will now print a message explaining that the answer field is too small.

After Execution

1 2 3
^
Z PIC 99V9

The content of ERROR-MSG-LINE will be written on the printer. An appropriate message would be ARITHMETIC OVERFLOW HAS OCCURRED.

Example

Divide the contents of FLDA (2.3) by the contents of FLDB (0) to get FLDC. Also, if a size error occurs, move both FLDA and FLDB to a report line that explains the error.

```
DIVIDE FLDA BY FLDB GIVING FLDC
    ON SIZE ERROR
        MOVE FLDA TO FLDA-OUT
        MOVE FLDB TO FLDB-OUT
        WRITE OUT-LINE FROM ERR-LINE AFTER 1.
```

Another option for this statement would be

```
DIVIDE FLDA BY FLDB GIVING FLDC
    ON SIZE ERROR
        PERFORM ERROR-MESSAGE-OUTPUT.
```

The paragraph ERROR-MESSAGE-OUTPUT would contain the required statements to produce the error message.

Before Execution

| 0 | 2 | 3 | | 0 | 0 |
|---|---|---| |---|---|

FLDA PIC 99V9   FLDB PIC 99

Since the value of the divisor is zero, the statements in the ON SIZE ERROR clause will be executed; the division will not be performed.

In each of the above examples, the sentence following the arithmetic statement will be executed next after the ON SIZE ERROR statements have been executed. In flowchart form, the ON SIZE ERROR option is shown as:

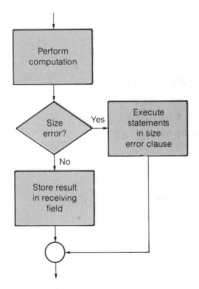

If a division by zero is attempted by a statement and the ON SIZE ERROR clause is not a part of the statement, the program is halted by the operating system, which prints an appropriate error message. If a receiving field is too small to accept the significant digits to the left of the decimal point and the ON SIZE ERROR clause is not a part of the statement, the results are moved to the receiving field and the leftmost digits will be truncated.

Example

Add the content of a data item X, to another, Y, to get the result Z.

```
ADD X, Y GIVING Z.
```

Before Execution

```
  7 8 3            8 7 2           ? ? ?
     ^                 ^                ^

X PIC 99V9     Y PIC 99V9    Z PIC 99V9
```

Computation: 78.3
                87.2
              ——————
               165.2

After Execution

```
  7 8 3            8 7 2        leftmost digits of   6 5 5
     ^                 ^        receiving field          ^
                               have been
X PIC 99V9     Y PIC 99V9      truncated            Z PIC 99V9
```

One area in programming in which size errors are particularly prevalent is in the accumulation of totals. The programmer has little control over the number of records the program will process or the size of the values that fields will contain. Inflation, which causes values to increase, is a partial cause of this problem; a program which performed adequately in the past may be faced with an overflow in accumulation of totals because of newly inflated values.

One way in which the programmer can warn the user of a report in which overflow has occurred is by placement of flags beside fields in which there has been overflow. For example, suppose the TOTAL-LINE from Program 5.1 (lines 13700 through 14900) is replaced with the following:

```
01  TOTAL-LINE.
    03  FILLER               PIC X(54)    VALUE SPACES.
    03  FILLER               PIC X(6)     VALUE "TOTALS".
    03  FILLER               PIC X(4)     VALUE SPACES.
    03  TOTAL-WITH-OUT        PIC $(6).99
    03  ERROR-IN-WITH-FLAG    PIC X        VALUE SPACES.
    03  TOTAL-FICA-OUT        PIC $(6).99
    03  ERROR-IN-FICA-FLAG    PIC X        VALUE SPACES.
    03  TOTAL-OTHER-OUT       PIC $(6).99
    03  ERROR-IN-OTHER-FLAG   PIC X        VALUE SPACES.
    03  TOTAL-GROSS-OUT       PIC $(7).99
    03  ERROR-IN-GROSS-FLAG   PIC X        VALUE SPACES.
    03  TOTAL-NET-OUT         PIC $(8).99
    03  ERROR-IN-NET-FLAG     PIC X        VALUE SPACES.
```

Each accumulated total has been provided with a field into which an appropriate character such as "*" can be placed if overflow occurs. The statements which compute these totals in the PROCEDURE DIVISION (lines 19200 through 19600) can be replaced by:

```
ADD WITH-AMT TO TOTAL-WITH
    ON SIZE ERROR MOVE "*" TO ERROR-IN-WITH-FLAG.
ADD FICA TO TOTAL-FICA
    ON SIZE ERROR MOVE "*" TO ERROR-IN-FICA-FLAG.
ADD OTHER-DEDUCTIONS-IR TO TOTAL-OTHER
    ON SIZE ERROR MOVE "*" TO ERROR-IN-OTHER-FLAG.
ADD GROSS-PAY TO TOTAL-GROSS
    ON SIZE ERROR MOVE "*" TO ERROR-IN-GROSS-FLAG.
ADD NET-PAY TO TOTAL-NET
    ON SIZE ERROR MOVE "*" TO ERROR-IN-NET-FLAG.
```

If a size error occurs in any of the accumulation statements, the character "*" will be moved to the appropriate output field. Output from this program might appear as

```
TOTALS    $1129.30 $304.00    $3222.19  $5241.14*$1035.91*
```

in which overflow has occurred in accumulation of the last two items—TOTAL-GROSS and TOTAL-NET.

5.9 DEBUG CLINIC

Computation With Non-numeric Items

Note that in Program 5.1, several data items appear to be defined twice. For example, consider GROSS-PAY (line 5500). GROSS-PAY is defined as a numeric item (PIC 9999V99), while GROSS-PAY-OUT is defined as numeric edited (PIC $Z(4).99). This dual definition is necessary because after GROSS-PAY is computed (line 18600), it is required for further computations (lines 18800 through 19500). In general a computation statement may place results in a numeric edited field. For example,

```
COMPUTE GROSS-PAY-OUT ROUNDED =
    REG-HRS-IR * PAY-RATE-IR +
    OT-HRS-IR * PAY-RATE-IR * 1.5.
```

would be a valid statement. The result would be computed and the value would be edited when placed in GROSS-PAY-OUT. But GROSS-PAY-OUT is a non-numeric item because of the editing process. Because it is non-numeric, it cannot be a part of a numeric operation. Thus, a statement such as

```
ADD GROSS-PAY-OUT TO TOTAL-GROSS.
```

would be invalid.

Items used as accumulators are used both as the receiving field and as a part of the computation, so accumulators must be defined as numeric fields as well as edited output fields. In preparation for output, the numeric field that has acted as an accumulator is moved to an appropriately edited output field. Any other item that will be used in further computations after a value is placed in it must be defined both as a numeric field and as a separate edited field. Remember:

> Computations cannot be performed on numeric edited data items.

Testing Programs

As programs become longer and more complex, the job of providing adequate test data becomes more demanding. In fact, it may be necessary to test programs with more than one set of data records to make sure that the program will function properly in all sets of circumstances. A common practice is to test each program at least three times: once with no data (that is, with an input file that contains no data records); again with "good" data (data that results in no error conditions); and finally with "bad" data (data that tests the program's ability to handle error conditions). The development of a set of data records that provides a thorough test of a program's logic should be started early in the program development cycle. This task is one that beginning programmers often do not perform adequately because it can be tedious and time-consuming; however, the success or failure of a programming project often hinges as much on thorough testing of the finished product as it does on imaginative program design or meticulous coding. Placing a program into production before it has been adequately tested surely will be embarrassing for the programmer and perhaps expensive for the organization. The old engineering maxim "there is never time to do it right but always time to do it over" often applies to programming.

5.10   SELF-TEST EXERCISES

1. Write COBOL statements for each of the following:
   a. Add A and B
   b. Subtract EXPENSE from INCOME and store result in BALANCE
   c. Store the product of A and D in A
   d. Divide SALES by 12 and store the quotient in MONTHLY-AVERAGE
   e. Compute the volume of a sphere ($V = 4/3 \, \pi \, r^3$)
   f. $I = P \times R \times T$
   g. $a = 25\%$ of b
   h. $A = P(1 + r)^n$

2. Show the contents of each data item after execution of each of the following statements:
   a. ADD A B GIVING C ROUNDED

      |0,2,3| |0,4,5,6| | |

      A PIC 99V9   B PIC 99V99   C PIC 99

   b. SUBTRACT A FROM C GIVING B

      |0,3,2| |1,7,0| | |

      A PIC 99V9   C PIC S99V9   B PIC 99

   c. MULTIPLY C BY B

      |0,3,2,1| |0,4,2|

      C PIC S 99V99   B PIC S999

d. DIVIDE C BY B GIVING A ROUNDED REMAINDER D

　0,6,0̄　　　　　1,2,0̇　　　　└─┴─┴─┘　　　└─┴─┘

C PIC S99V9　　B PIC S999　　A PIC S99V9　　D PIC S99

e. COMPUTE A = B ** 3

　0,3̄　　　　　└─┴─┴─┘

B PIC S99　　A PIC S999

f. COMPUTE A ROUNDED = C + B * A ON SIZE ERROR MOVE 0 TO A

　0,5　　　　1,2,3　　　　1,6

C PIC 99　　B PIC 99V9　　A PIC V99

g. COMPUTE A = A + (B – C) / B
　　ON SIZE ERROR
　　　MOVE 0 TO A

　3,2,0　　　　0,0　　　　0,1,2

A PIC 99V9　　B PIC 99　　C PIC 999

h. MULTIPLY A BY B GIVING C ROUNDED

　3,2,0̄　　　　0,1,0,2　　　　└─┴─┘

A PIC S99V9　　B PIC 99V99　　C PIC 99

i. DIVIDE A INTO B

　3,2,0　　　　6,4,0̇

A PIC S99V9　　B PIC S99V9

3. Draw a structure diagram for Program 5.1. Identify each paragraph as a control or operation paragraph.

4. With respect to the operation of Program 5.1, what purpose is served by each of the following:
   a. line 5200
   b. The VALUE clause on line 5300
   c. line 5000
   d. The ROUNDED option on line 18600

5. Given a date in the form *mmdd* compute the equivalent approximate Julian date. Julian date refers to the day of the year: Jan. 1 has Julian date 1, Dec. 31 has Julian date 365, and so on.

5.11 PROGRAMMING EXERCISES

1. Write a program to compute the amount of money one will earn if he or she invests P dollars at an interest rate R for N years with interest compounded daily. The formula required is:

$$A = P \times (1 + R/360)^{360 \times N}$$

2. Write a program to produce an end-of-year sales summary for a retail store. Input consists of records containing the following fields:

   Department name and number
   Amount of sales in first quarter
   Amount of sales in second quarter
   Amount of sales in third quarter
   Amount of sales in fourth quarter

Output should consist of all input data and the total sales for each department as well as the total yearly sales for the store.

3. Write a program that could be used by a department store to determine the value of items in stock. Input consists of records containing:

> Quantity
> Item (including stock number and name)
> Unit cost

Output should consist of all data read in and the value of each item (quantity * unit cost) as well as the total value of all items in stock.

4. An inventory file contains records in the following format:

> *Positions*
>
> 1-6   Item number
> 7-20   Description
> 21-26   Cost
> 27-32   Selling price

A sale is planned with progressive discounts from selling price of 10%, 15%, and 20%. Write a program to list all of the input data and the three discounted selling prices.

5. A daily sales file contains records with the following fields:

> Department number (1, 2, 3, or 4)
> Date
> Item description
> Selling price for each item
> Cost of each item

Write a program to list all input data and compute total amount of sale and profit for each sale. Accumulate and print totals of sales and profits.

6. A check digit is an extra digit of an account number that is computed as a function of the other digits. Its purpose is to enable the verification of valid account numbers. If any digits are mispunched or transposed, the check digit computed by the program will not match the check digit of the account number, thus enabling the identification of an invalid account number. There are a number of schemes for computation of check digits. One of the most effective methods uses the following sequence of steps:
   a. Suppose the account number contains 5 digits and a sixth check digit:

   $$d_1 d_2 d_3 d_4 d_5 d_{ck}$$

   b. Compute $S = d_1 + 2 \times d_2 + 3 \times d_3 + 5 \times d_4 + 7 \times d_5$ (the multipliers are purposely chosen to be prime numbers; this system has been shown to yield very good error detection capabilities).
   c. The check digit d_{ck} is the one's digit of S.

Write a program to input a sequence of account numbers and compute the check digit.

Example

Suppose the account number is 23576.

$$S = 2 + 2 \times 3 + 3 \times 5 + 5 \times 7 + 7 \times 6 = 100$$

The ones digit of 100 is 0, hence $d_{ck} = 0$. The complete account number is 235760. Suppose that in the transcription process two digits of the account number are transposed (a very common error); for example, 237560 is entered instead of 235760. The check digit computation for 235760 is $S = 2 + 2 \times 3 + 3 \times 7 + 5 \times 5 + 7 \times 6 = 96$; hence, the check digit for this account number would be 6, not 0: The erroneous account number has been detected.

7. Write a program to generate seven–digit account numbers beginning with 1000001 using the method of check digit computation described in Exercise 6 above. Often the check digit is inserted as middle digit in the account number, e.g., 10001000. check digit. Modify your program to list the account numbers in this fashion.

8. Write a program to list the number of bills of each denomination required to make up the pay envelopes for a payroll. Input consists of the net amount to be paid in dollars. Output should consist of the number of twenties, tens, fives, and ones required for that amount. Compute and list the total number of bills of each denomination which will be required. For example, $273 would be made up of

13 twenties	= $260
1 ten	= $ 10
0 fives	= $ 0
3 ones	= $ 3
	$273

9. Write a program to calculate the amount of monthly payment required to pay a mortgage based on the following input data:

Principal (P)   The required formula is

Interest rate (R)

Time in years (T)

$$\frac{P \times \dfrac{R}{12}}{1 - \left[\dfrac{1}{1 + \dfrac{R}{12}}\right]^{(T \times 12)}}$$

Use the following test data:

P	R	T	Expected Value of Monthly Payment
$10,000	.08	20	$83.64
$65,000	.16	30	$874.09
$105,000	.175	25	$1551.41

Note: Your computed values may vary slightly from those shown because of internal differences among computers.

THE IF STATEMENT AND CONDITIONS 6

6.1 PROGRAM EXAMPLE

A company maintains a personnel file, each record of which contains the following items:

Employee identification number
Employee name
Sex code (M = male, F = female)
Employee date of birth (*mmddyy*)
Date employee was hired (*mmddyy*)

The personnel manager needs a list of employees hired after 1980 and also wishes to know how many of them there are. A printer spacing chart for the required report is shown in Figure 6.1.

Problem Analysis

The required report contains report and column headings, a detail line, and a summary line. The report and column heading must be written as part of initialization prior to entering the loop, which will process each record in the file. The summary line must be written after all records in the file have been processed. In order to place the required information on the summary line, it is necessary to count the records that meet the specified condition; this will require a counter initialized to zero (NUMBER-EMPLOYEES). Each time an employee who was hired after 1980 is encountered, the value of NUMBER-EMPLOYEES will be increased by one.

So far, the program required for this problem resembles other programs that process a data file and produce a report. The major difference in this program is that not all records in the file are to be counted. Only records for employees who were hired after 1980 are of interest. This task requires the selection program structure. In pseudocode, selection is expressed using the following form:

Figure 6.1   Printer spacing chart for Program 6.1

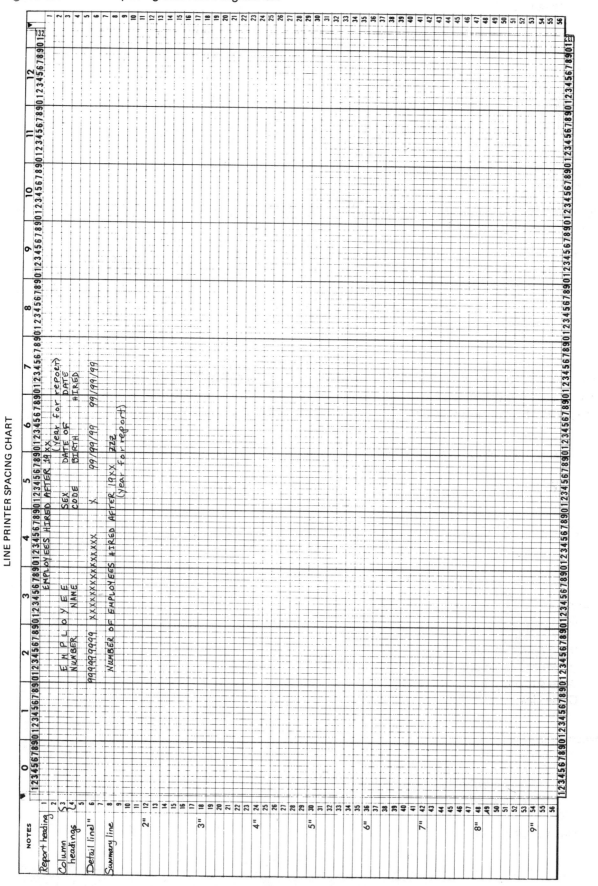

```
If condition
    Statement-1
    Statement-2          }  These statements executed if condition is true
         .
         .
         .
Else
    Statement-n
    Statement-n+1        }  These statements executed if condition is false
         .
         .
         .
End If
```

When there are no actions to be taken if the condition is false, the Else clause can be omitted as shown below:

```
If condition
    Statement-1
    Statement-2          }  These statements executed if condition is true
         .
         .
         .
End If
```

This form suits the present problem as we wish to process records that meet the required condition and will ignore the remainder. Thus, part of the design for this program will be:

```
If year hired > 80
    Add 1 to number of employees
    Move employee data to detail line
    Write detail line
End If
```

A complete plan for this program is shown in Figure 6.2.

Figure 6.2 Plan for employee report

Main routine
```
    Open files
    Write headings
    Read employee file
    Do Process read until end of file
    Write summary line
    Close files
    Stop run
```

Process read
```
    If date hired > 80
        Add 1 to number employees
        Move employee data to detail line
        Write detail line
    End If
    Read employee file
```

Problem Solution

The program for this problem is shown in Program 6.1. The structure diagram for this program is shown in Figure 6.3. The IF statement in lines 12500 through 12700 implements the selection structure required in the plan. The syntax for the COBOL IF statement resembles the syntax of the pseudocode. The reserved word IF is followed by a condition, which is followed by the actions to be carried out if the condition is true at the time the statement is executed. In this case, the IF statement appears as:

```
IF DATE-HIRED-PDR IS GREATER THAN YEAR-FOR-REPORT
    ADD 1 TO NUMBER-EMPLOYEES
    PERFORM 5000-EMPLOYEE-REPORT.
```

The condition

```
DATE-HIRED-PDR IS GREATER THAN YEAR-FOR-REPORT
```

will be true when DATE-HIRED-PDR has a value of 81, 82, etc. because the value of YEAR-FOR-REPORT is set to 80 via the VALUE clause in WORKING-STORAGE (see line 4700). Note that the IF statement is terminated by a period. This period corresponds to the "End If" line in the pseudocode. The period determines the scope of the IF statement. All of the statements following the condition and preceding the period will be carried out when the condition is true. (In this case there are two statements in this clause, but in general there could be many.) A more complete description of the IF statement is presented in the next section.

Program 6.1   Employee report program

```
100       IDENTIFICATION DIVISION.
200       PROGRAM-ID. EMPLOYEE-REPORT.
300       AUTHOR. PAULA.
400
500       ENVIRONMENT DIVISION.
600
700       CONFIGURATION SECTION.
800
900       SOURCE-COMPUTER.
1000      OBJECT-COMPUTER.
1100
1200      INPUT-OUTPUT SECTION.
1300
1400      FILE-CONTROL.
1500
1600          SELECT PERSONNEL-DATA-FILE ASSIGN TO DISK.
1700          SELECT EMPLOYEE-REPORT ASSIGN TO PRINTER.
1800
1900      DATA DIVISION.
2000
2100      FILE SECTION.
2200
2300      FD  PERSONNEL-DATA-FILE
2400          LABEL RECORDS ARE STANDARD
2500          DATA RECORD IS PERSONNEL-DATA-RECORD.
2600
```

```
2700      01  PERSONNEL-DATA-RECORD.
2800          03 ID-NUM-PDR        PIC 9(9).
2900          03 NAME-PDR          PIC X(15).
3000          03 SEX-PDR           PIC X.
3100          03 BIRTH-DATE-PDR    PIC 9(6).
3200          03 DATE-HIRED-PDR.
3300             05 MONTH-HIRED-PDR    PIC 99.
3400             05 DAY-HIRED-PDR      PIC 99.
3500             05 YEAR-HIRED-PDR     PIC 99.
3600          03 FILLER            PIC X(43).
3700
3800      FD  EMPLOYEE-REPORT
3900          LABEL RECORDS ARE OMITTED
4000          DATA RECORD IS OUTPUT-RECORD.
4100
4200      01  OUTPUT-RECORD        PIC X(132).
4300
4400      WORKING-STORAGE SECTION.
4500
4600      01  YEAR.
4700          02 YEAR-FOR-REPORT PIC 99 VALUE 80.
4800
4900      01  FLAGS.
5000          02  EOF-FLAG         PIC X(3) VALUE "NO".
5100
5200      01  COUNTERS.
5300          02 NUMBER-EMPLOYEES PIC 999 VALUE 0.
5400
5500      01  HEAD-LINE.
5600          03 FILLER            PIC X(35) VALUE SPACES.
5700          03 FILLER            PIC X(24) VALUE
5800             "EMPLOYEES HIRED AFTER 19".
5900          03 YEAR-FOR-REPORT-HL PIC 99.
6000
6100      01  SUB-HEAD-1.
6200          03 FILLER            PIC X(21) VALUE SPACES.
6300          03 FILLER            PIC X(15) VALUE "E M P L O Y E E".
6400          03 FILLER            PIC X(13) VALUE SPACES.
6500          03 FILLER            PIC X(3) VALUE "SEX".
6600          03 FILLER            PIC X(5) VALUE SPACES.
6700          03 FILLER            PIC X(7) VALUE "DATE OF".
6800          03 FILLER            PIC X(5) VALUE SPACES.
6900          03 FILLER            PIC X(4) VALUE "DATE".
7000
7100      01  SUB-HEAD-2.
7200          03 FILLER            PIC X(21) VALUE SPACES.
7300          03 FILLER            PIC X(6) VALUE "NUMBER".
7400          03 FILLER            PIC X(5) VALUE SPACES.
7500          03 FILLER            PIC X(4) VALUE "NAME".
7600          03 FILLER            PIC X(13) VALUE SPACES.
7700          03 FILLER            PIC X(4) VALUE "CODE".
7800          03 FILLER            PIC X(4) VALUE SPACES.
7900          03 FILLER            PIC X(5) VALUE "BIRTH".
8000          03 FILLER            PIC X(6) VALUE SPACES.
8100          03 FILLER            PIC X(5) VALUE "HIRED".
```

Program 6.1 (continued)

```
8200
8300     01  EMPLOYEES-OUT.
8400         03  FILLER           PIC X(19) VALUE SPACES.
8500         03  ID-NUM-OUT       PIC 9(9).
8600         03  FILLER           PIC X(2) VALUE SPACES.
8700         03  NAME-OUT         PIC X(15).
8800         03  FILLER           PIC X(4) VALUE SPACES.
8900         03  BIRTH-DATE-OUT   PIC 99/99/99.
9000         03  FILLER           PIC X(3) VALUE SPACES.
9100         03  DATE-HIRED-OUT   PIC 99/99/99.
9200
9300     01  SUMMARY-LINE.
9400         02  FILLER                   PIC X(22) VALUE SPACES.
9500         02  FILLER                   PIC X(34) VALUE
9600             "NUMBER OF EMPLOYEES HIRED AFTER 19".
9700         02  YEAR-FOR-REPORT-SL       PIC 99.
9800         02  FILLER                   PIC X VALUE SPACES.
9900         02  NUMBER-EMPLOYEES-SL      PIC ZZZ.
10000
10100    PROCEDURE DIVISION.
10200
10300    1000-MAIN-ROUTINE.
10400
10500        PERFORM 2000-INITIALIZATION.
10600        PERFORM 3000-PROCESS-READ
10700            UNTIL EOF-FLAG = "YES".
10800        PERFORM 8000-SUMMARY.
10900        PERFORM 9000-TERMINATION.
11000        STOP RUN.
11100
11200    2000-INITIALIZATION.
11300
11400        OPEN INPUT PERSONNEL-DATA-FILE
11500            OUTPUT EMPLOYEE-REPORT.
11600        MOVE YEAR-FOR-REPORT TO YEAR-FOR-REPORT-HL.
11700        MOVE HEAD-LINE TO OUTPUT-RECORD.
11800        WRITE OUTPUT-RECORD AFTER PAGE.
11900        WRITE OUTPUT-RECORD FROM SUB-HEAD-1 AFTER 2.
12000        WRITE OUTPUT-RECORD FROM SUB-HEAD-2 AFTER 1.
12100        PERFORM 4000-READ.
12200
12300    3000-PROCESS-READ.
12400
12500        IF DATE-HIRED-PDR IS GREATER THAN YEAR-FOR-REPORT
12600            ADD 1 TO NUMBER-EMPLOYEES
12700            PERFORM 5000-EMPLOYEE-REPORT.
12800        PERFORM 4000-READ.
12900
13000    4000-READ.
13100
13200        READ PERSONNEL-DATA-FILE
13300            AT END MOVE "YES" TO EOF-FLAG.
13400
13500    5000-EMPLOYEE-REPORT.
13600
```

```
13700        MOVE ID-NUM-PDR         TO ID-NUM-OUT.
13800        MOVE NAME-PDR           TO NAME-OUT.
13900        MOVE BIRTH-DATE-PDR     TO BIRTH-DATE-OUT.
14000        MOVE DATE-HIRED-PDR     TO DATE-HIRED-OUT.
14100        MOVE EMPLOYEES-OUT TO OUTPUT-RECORD.
14200        WRITE OUTPUT-RECORD AFTER 2.
14300
14400    8000-SUMMARY.
14500        MOVE NUMBER-EMPLOYEES TO NUMBER-EMPLOYEES-SL.
14600        MOVE YEAR-FOR-REPORT  TO YEAR-FOR-REPORT-SL.
14700        WRITE OUTPUT-RECORD FROM SUMMARY-LINE.
14800
14900    9000-TERMINATION.
15000
15100        CLOSE PERSONNEL-DATA-FILE
15200              EMPLOYEE-REPORT.
```

Program 6.1 (continued)

Figure 6.3   Structure diagram of Program 6.1

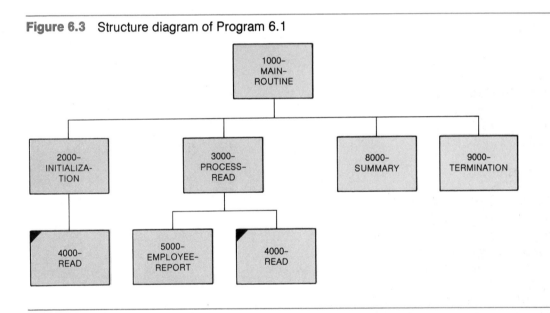

6.2   THE IF STATEMENT

The general form of the IF statement is shown in Figure 6.4.

Figure 6.4   General form of the IF statement

```
IF condition
   { statement-1 . . . }
   { NEXT SENTENCE   }
[ELSE
   { statement-2 . . . }
   { NEXT SENTENCE   }]
```

If the condition is true, only the statement(s) before the ELSE clause will be executed. If the condition is false, the statements following ELSE will be executed; the statements preceding ELSE will *not* be executed. When the statement(s) either before the ELSE clause or in the ELSE clause are completed, control is given to the sentence following the IF statement. A flowchart of the IF statement is shown in Figure 6.5.

Figure 6.5   Flowchart of the IF statement

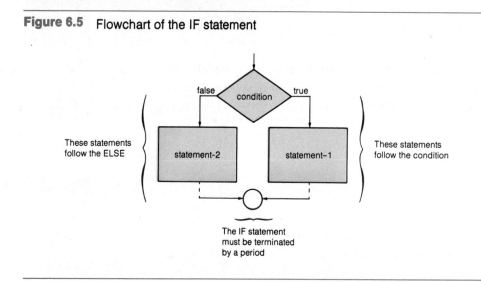

Example

If the value of HOURS is greater than 40, execute OVERTIME-PAY; otherwise, execute REGULAR-PAY.

```
IF HOURS > 40
     PERFORM OVERTIME-PAY
ELSE
     PERFORM REGULAR-PAY.
```

Example

If A = B, then execute COMPUTE-PROC and OUTPUT-1 sequentially, and then execute the next sentence. If A ≠ B, perform OUTPUT-2 four times and then execute the next sentence.

```
IF A = B
     PERFORM COMPUTE-PROC
     PERFORM OUTPUT-1
ELSE
     COMPUTE KOUNT = 1
     PERFORM OUTPUT-2 UNTIL KOUNT > 4.
```

If no action needs to be taken when a true (or false) condition is encountered, the statement NEXT SENTENCE is used to pass control to the sentence following the IF statement.

Example

If the value of the variable KODE is equal to 0, the next sentence is executed; otherwise, one is added to KOUNT and OUTPUT-ROUTINE is executed and then the next sentence is executed.

```
IF KODE EQUAL 0
    NEXT SENTENCE
ELSE
    ADD 1 TO KOUNT
    PERFORM OUTPUT-ROUTINE.
```

The above example is equivalent to adding 1 to KOUNT and executing OUTPUT-ROUTINE when the value of KODE is *not* equal to zero. The following statement is thus equivalent to the preceding sentence:

```
IF KODE NOT EQUAL 0
    ADD 1 TO KOUNT
    PERFORM OUTPUT-ROUTINE
ELSE
    NEXT SENTENCE.
```

The ELSE clause of the IF statement is optional. If the ELSE clause is omitted and the condition is false, the sentence following the IF statement is executed. (The statements following the condition are executed only when the condition is true.)

Example

If AGE is greater than 25, move AGE and NAME to an output record and write the output record.

```
IF AGE IS GREATER THAN 25
    MOVE AGE TO AGE-OUT
    MOVE NAME TO NAME-OUT
    WRITE OUT-REC AFTER 1.
```

Example

If the value of KODE is not equal to 0, add 1 to KOUNT and execute OUTPUT-ROUTINE.

```
IF KODE NOT EQUAL 0
    ADD 1 TO KOUNT
    PERFORM OUTPUT-ROUTINE.
```

This code is equivalent to

```
IF KODE NOT EQUAL 0
    ADD 1 TO KOUNT
    PERFORM OUTPUT-ROUTINE
ELSE
    NEXT SENTENCE.
```

The rules of COBOL syntax do not require that each statement in an IF state-ment be placed on a separate line, nor that the word ELSE be aligned with IF as shown in the above examples. However, this placement does aid in readability, and it is a recommended structured programming practice.

6.3 RELATIONAL CONDITIONS

The preceding examples contained many examples of the use of relational conditions. Relational conditions are used to compare two entities (see Figure 6.6).

Figure 6.6 General form of relational conditions.

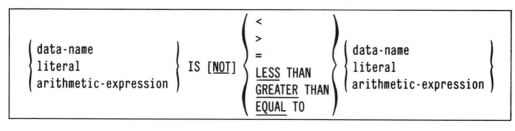

Note that the relation being tested may be expressed either symbolically using the symbols <, >, or =, or verbally as LESS THAN, GREATER THAN, or EQUAL TO. (The use of the words THAN and TO in the verbal expressions is optional.) The meanings of the symbols are shown below:

Symbol	Verbal Expression
<	Less than
>	Greater than
=	Equal to

When writing a condition a programmer may choose a symbol or the corres-ponding verbal expression at his or her option; the meaning of the resulting condition will be the same.

Example

The following conditions are equivalent:

```
HOURS > 40
HOURS GREATER THAN 40
HOURS GREATER 40
```

The word IS may be included in a condition at the option of the program-mer; the purpose of the word is to aid in readability.

Example

The following conditions are equivalent to each other and to those in the previous example:

```
HOURS IS > 40
HOURS IS GREATER THAN 40
HOURS IS GREATER 40
```

To negate any of the relations, write NOT before the type of relation. For example, the condition

    HOURS IS NOT GREATER THAN 40

is true when the value of HOURS is 0, 1, 2, 3, . . ., 38, or 40 and false if HOURS has value of 41 or larger.

Examples

4 IS EQUAL TO KODE ↑ ↑ literal data-name	This condition will be true when the value of KODE is 4 and false otherwise.
NAME-FIELD NOT EQUAL SPACES ↑ ↑ data-name literal	This condition will be false when all the characters in NAME-FIELD are blanks and true otherwise.
X + Y < Z ↑ ↖ expression data-name	The value of the expression X + Y will be computed and this value will be compared to the value in Z.

Occasionally it is necessary to write conditions of the form A ≤ B (A less than or equal to B) or A ≥ B (A greater than or equal to B). This can be done easily by using the NOT option. The COBOL equivalent of A ≤ B is

    A NOT GREATER THAN B

or

    A NOT > B

Example

If the value of SALES is 600 or greater, compute COMMISSION as 10% of SALES.

    IF SALES NOT LESS THAN 600
        MULTIPLY 0.10 BY SALES GIVING COMMISSION.

The values 600, 601, 602, . . . satisfy the condition SALES NOT LESS THAN 600.

6.4 NESTED IF STATEMENTS

In many instances, actions will depend on conditions being satisfied. For example, suppose we want to count the number of males and females in a set of data that contains a SEX-CODE having value M for males and F for females. If the value of SEX-CODE is neither M nor F, the data record contains an error, and we perform an error routine to take appropriate action. This error routine is performed when the sequence of conditions SEX-CODE = "M" and SEX-CODE = "F" are both false. The flowchart for this task would be:

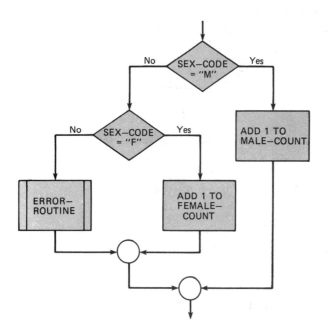

The following COBOL code could be used to perform this task.

```
IF SEX-CODE = "M"
    ADD 1 TO MALE-COUNT
ELSE
    IF SEX-CODE = "F"
        ADD 1 TO FEMALE-COUNT
    ELSE
        PERFORM ERROR-ROUTINE.
```

Note that the terminal collector blocks in the above flowchart correspond to the period that terminates the IF statement in the COBOL code. In this example, the ELSE clause of the IF statement which tests the condition SEX-CODE = "M" contains another IF statement which tests the condition SEX-CODE = "F". If both of these conditions are false, then ERROR-ROUTINE will be executed. This is an example of an IF statement that contains another IF statement. Statements of this sort are called *nested* IF statements. This example also shows a useful way to test conditions that exclude one another; a person is either male or female, but not both. When an IF statement is nested, an ELSE clause must be included for each IF. For example, suppose we wish to obtain a list of the names of males and females who are over 20 years of age together with the notation OVER 20 and MALE or FEMALE. The flowchart for this task would be:

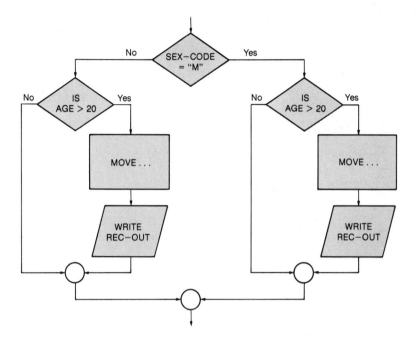

This flowchart would be translated into COBOL as:

```
IF SEX-CODE = "M"
    IF AGE > 20
        MOVE "OVER 20" TO AGE-OUT
        MOVE NAME TO NAME-OUT
        MOVE "MALE" TO SEX-OUT
        WRITE REC-OUT AFTER 1
    ELSE
        NEXT SENTENCE
ELSE
    IF AGE > 20
        MOVE "OVER 20" TO AGE-OUT
        MOVE NAME TO NAME-OUT
        MOVE "FEMALE" TO SEX-OUT
            WRITE REC-OUT AFTER 1
    ELSE
        NEXT SENTENCE.
```

Note the importance of the ELSE clause after WRITE REC-OUT AFTER 1. If this clause were omitted, the next ELSE clause would have been associated with the test on AGE rather than the test on SEX-CODE. The preceding coding could be simplified (and improved) as follows:

```
IF AGE > 20
    MOVE "OVER 20" TO AGE-OUT
    MOVE NAME TO NAME-OUT
    IF SEX-CODE = "M"
        MOVE "MALE" TO SEX-OUT
        WRITE REC-OUT AFTER 1
    ELSE
        MOVE "FEMALE" TO SEX-OUT
        WRITE REC-OUT AFTER 1.
```

The flowchart for this code would be:

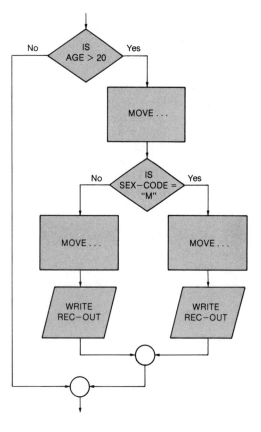

In the preceding example, the statement WRITE REC-OUT AFTER 1 occurs in both clauses of the SEX-CODE test. We might wonder if this could not be simplified by placing the common statement after the IF statement, so that no matter which branch of the test is taken, the common statement will still be executed. This is not the case at all, because after either clause of an IF statement is concluded, the following *sentence* is executed next. In the above example, the output is to be performed only if AGE is greater than 20. If the output statement followed the entire IF statement, it would be produced for all values of AGE. If the logic of a problem makes this type of structure necessary, the entire sequence of statements should be placed into a separate paragraph. The preceding code could be written as:

```
IF AGE > 20
    PERFORM OVER-20-ROUTINE.
    .
    .
    .
OVER-20-ROUTINE.
    MOVE "OVER 20" TO AGE-OUT.
    MOVE NAME TO NAME-OUT.
    IF SEX-CODE = "M"
        MOVE "MALE" TO SEX-OUT
    ELSE
        MOVE "FEMALE" TO SEX-OUT.
    WRITE REC-OUT AFTER 1.
```

6.5   SIGN AND CLASS CONDITIONS

Thus far, all conditions used in our examples have been relational. Such tests as

```
IF KOUNT IS GREATER THAN 13. . .
IF AMOUNT < 0. . .
IF SEX-CODE = "M". . .
```

use conditions of this type. Remember that alphanumeric as well as numeric tests may be made with the relational condition. Two additional types of conditions may be used: the sign condition and the class condition.

Sign Condition

The sign condition is a convenient way to test the sign (positive, negative, or zero) of a data-name or expression. The general form of this condition is demonstrated in Figure 6.7

Figure 6.7   General form of the sign condition

$$
\left\{ \begin{array}{l} \text{data-name} \\ \text{expression} \end{array} \right\} \text{ IS [\underline{NOT}]} \left\{ \begin{array}{l} \text{POSITIVE} \\ \underline{\text{ZERO}} \\ \text{NEGATIVE} \end{array} \right\}
$$

Example

```
IF KODE IS ZERO. . .

PERFORM PARA-X UNTIL A + B IS POSITIVE. . .

IF AMOUNT-DUE NEGATIVE. . .

IF BALANCE IS NOT NEGATIVE. . .
```

Note that NOT NEGATIVE is equivalent to testing for greater than or equal to zero, and NOT POSITIVE is equivalent to testing for less than or equal to zero. If a field tested for sign has not been defined using the S picture code, it will never be negative.

Class Condition

The class condition is used to test whether a data-name contains alphabetic data or numeric data. Figure 6.8 shows the general form of this condition.

Figure 6.8   General form of the class condition

$$
\text{data-name} \quad \text{IS [\underline{NOT}]} \left\{ \begin{array}{l} \underline{\text{NUMERIC}} \\ \text{ALPHABETIC} \end{array} \right\}
$$

The numeric test can be performed on fields with numeric or alphanumeric pictures. If the data-name contains any characters other than 0, 1, 2, . . . 9, then the numeric test will be false.

Example

```
IF IN-FLD IS NUMERIC. . .
ELSE. . .
```

      1 2 3 4   1 2 3

     IN-FLD PIC X(4)   IN-FLD PIC X(4)

Numeric test is true. | Numeric test is false because the field contains a blank—a non-numeric character.

When testing signed fields with the numeric test, the condition will be true if the field contains a valid sign and numeric digits.

Example

```
IF FLDA IS NUMERIC. . .
ELSE. . .
```

   0 1 2 3̇   0 1 2 3 −

FLDA PIC S9(4)   FLDA PIC S9(4) SIGN IS
                                 TRAILING SEPARATE CHARACTER

In both cases the numeric test is true.

The alphabetic test may be performed on fields with alphanumeric or alphabetic pictures. If the field contains solely characters A,B,C, . . ., Z or blank, then an alphabetic test will be true; otherwise it will be false.

Example

```
IF NAME IS ALPHABETIC. . .
ELSE. . .
```

 J O H N J O N E S

NAME PIC X(15)

Alphabetic test is true.

 J . J O N E S   J . J O N E S 3 R D

NAME PIC X(15)   NAME PIC X(15)

Alphabetic test is false because of the period. | Alphabetic test is false because of the "3".

Fields that should contain only numeric characters but do not, and fields that should contain only alphabetic characters or spaces but do not, may occur because of error in data preparation or entry. It is important that data processing systems be provided with error-free data. The class condition is a useful tool to enable the COBOL program to take alternate action when it encounters data containing errors.

6.6 COMPLEX CONDITIONS

All of the conditions described to this point—relational, sign, and class—are called *simple conditions*. The logical operations NOT, AND, and OR may be used to construct *complex conditions* based on simple conditions.

NOT

The NOT operation acts on a single condition with the general form:

> **NOT** condition

The resulting compound condition is true when the condition is false and false when the condition is true.

Example

Write a condition that will be true when the value of HRS is not greater than 40:

```
NOT HRS > 40

  3 2
 |_|_|
    ^
HRS PIC 99     Since HRS > 40 is false, NOT HRS > 40 is true.
```

Example

Write a condition which will be true when NET-PAY is non-negative (i.e., greater than or equal to zero):

```
NOT NET-PAY IS NEGATIVE
  0 0 3 6 0 0
 |_|_|_|_|_|_|
          ^
NET-PAY PIC S9999V99     The condition NET-PAY IS NEGATIVE is true;
                         therefore, NOT NET-PAY IS NEGATIVE is false.
```

AND

The AND operation connects two conditions with the general form:

> condition-1   **AND**   condition-2

The resulting complex condition is true only in the case when both condition-1 and condition-2 are true. It is false in all three other cases (that is, it is false if either condition-1 or condition-2 or both are false).

Example

Write a condition which will be true when both A < 10 and B = 4.

```
A < 10 AND B = 4
  0 6         0 3
 L__|__      L__|__
     ʌ            ʌ
A PIC 99     B PIC 99
```

The condition A < 10 is true but B = 4 is false, therefore the complex condition is false.

Example

Write a condition that will check the validity of both HRS and RATE, which are numeric fields.

```
HRS IS NUMERIC AND RATE IS NUMERIC
```

Both HRS and RATE must be numeric for the compound condition to be true.

OR

The OR operation, which connects two conditions, has the general form:

```
condition-1    OR    condition-2
```

The resulting complex condition is true when either condition-1 or condition-2 (or both) are true (three cases), and false only in the one case when both condition-1 and condition-2 are false.

Example

Write a condition that will be true when either A < 10 or B = 4 or both:

```
A < 10 OR B = 4
  0 6         0 3
 L__|__      L__|__
     ʌ            ʌ
A PIC 99     B PIC 99
```

Example

Write a complex condition that will be true if either HRS or RATE is not numeric.

```
HRS IS NOT NUMERIC OR RATE IS NOT NUMERIC
```

For both the AND and OR operations there are four possible combinations: both conditions being true; either one being false; or both conditions being false. These together with the value of resulting complex conditions are summarized in Figure 6.9. The operation NOT acts only on one condition hence there are only two possibilities—the condition is true or false. The value of the resulting compound condition is summarized in Figure 6.10.

Figure 6.9   Summary of logical operations AND and OR

condition-1	condition-2	condition-1 AND condition-2	condition-1 OR condition-2
true	true	true	true
true	false	false	true
false	true	false	true
false	false	false	false

Figure 6.10   Summary of the logical operation NOT

condition	NOT condition
true	false
false	true

Complex conditions may be used either in IF statements or in the PERFORM statement. For example, suppose we wish to repeat execution of a routine continually until either of two conditions is met. The following code illustrates the use of a complex condition in the PERFORM statement to accomplish this objective:

```
PERFORM ROUTINE
    UNTIL CONDITION-1-FLAG = "YES" OR CONDITION-2-FLAG = "YES".
```

Similarly, if repetition of a routine is desired until both of two conditions are true, the following code could be used:

```
PERFORM ROUTINE
    UNTIL CONDITION-1-FLAG = "YES" AND CONDITION-2-FLAG = "YES".
```

Suppose, for example, we wish to modify Program 6.1 to produce a listing of male employees who were hired after 1980. Lines 12500-12700 in Program 6.1 could be rewritten as

```
IF SEX-PDR = "M" AND YEAR-HIRED-PDR > YEAR-FOR-REPORT
    ADD 1 TO NUMBER EMPLOYEES
    PERFORM 5000-EMPLOYEE-REPORT.
```

If more than one logical operation is present in a complex condition, the order in which the operations are evaluated will determine the value of the condition. The same problem arose in the evaluation of arithmetic expressions containing more than one arithmetic operation. Recall that arithmetic operations are assigned precedence. In evaluating an arithmetic expression, arithmetic operations with higher precedence are performed before operations with lower precedence. In a similar fashion, logical operations are assigned precedence to control the order of evaluation in complex conditions. Figure 6.11 gives the rules of precedence for logical operations.

Figure 6.11   Precedence for evaluation of complex conditions

```
        simple condition              high precedence
complex condition in parentheses             ↑
              NOT                            |
              AND                            ↓
              OR                      low precedence
```

For example, suppose a data-item A has a value of 6 and B has a value of 3. Consider the complex condition:

```
NOT A < 10 and B = 4
```

As NOT has higher precedence than AND, the condition NOT A < 10 is evaluated before the condition involving AND. The entire condition will be evaluated as follows:

```
NOT A < 10 AND B = 4
    ‿‿‿‿‿‿    ‿‿‿‿‿
     true      false
    ‿‿‿‿‿‿‿‿‿
     false
   _____
         false
```

In evaluating a complex condition, the simple conditions, which may be relational, class, or sign conditions are evaluated first. In this example, the simple conditions are A < 10 and B = 4, which are evaluated as true and false respectively. Then the logical operation with highest precedence is evaluated. In this case NOT has highest precedence, so the NOT condition is evaluated next. Finally, the next highest operation is evaluated, in this case an AND condition that results in the final value of the entire condition.

Example

Consider the following condition with the values of fields as shown:

```
A < 10 OR B = 4 AND A IS NOT POSITIVE
|0,6|           |0,3|
  ∧               ∧
A PIC 99     B PIC 99
```

The above condition is evaluated as follows:

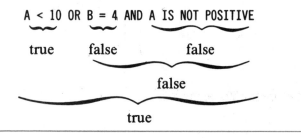

The AND condition is evaluated before the OR condition because AND has higher precedence than OR.

If two or more operators with equal precedence are present (two or more ORs, for example), the conditions are evaluated in order from left to right.

Example

Consider the following condition with the values of fields as shown:

```
AGE < 29 AND YRS-EXPERIENCE > 5 AND DEPT-CODE = 3
```

```
  2 8              0 7                      4
 |__|A            |__|A                    |_|A

AGE PIC 99    YRS-EXPERIENCE PIC 99    DEPT-CODE PIC 9
```

The above expression is evaluated as follows:

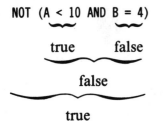

```
AGE < 29 AND YRS-EXPERIENCE > 5 AND DEPT-CODE = 3

    true             true                false

              true

                    false
```

If you want to write a logical expression that requires an order of evaluation different from the normal order, use parentheses. Conditions within parentheses are evaluated before conditions outside parentheses.

Example

Consider the following condition with contents of fields as shown:

```
NOT (A < 10 AND B = 4)
```

```
  0 6              0 3
 |__|A            |__|A

A PIC 99       B PIC 99
```

The above expression is evaluated as follows:

```
NOT (A < 10 AND B = 4)

       true     false

             false

     true
```

In this case, note that the AND condition is evaluated before the NOT because of the parentheses.

Example

Consider the following condition with the contents of fields as shown:

```
AGE < 29 AND (YRS-EXPERIENCE > 5 OR DEPT-CODE = 3)
```

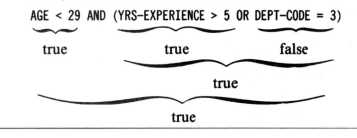

```
AGE PIC 99     YRS-EXPERIENCE PIC 99     DEPT-CODE PIC 9
```

The above expression is evaluated as follows:

```
AGE < 29 AND (YRS-EXPERIENCE > 5 OR DEPT-CODE = 3)
```

| | | |
| true | true | false |

true

true

Example

The XYZ Department Store has decided to give a Christmas bonus to its employees. The amount of the bonus is subject to the following considerations:

- Employees with less than one year of experience will be given a flat $100 bonus.
- Employees with one to three years of experience will receive $100 plus 10 percent of their monthly paycheck for each year of experience.
- Employees with three to twenty years experience will receive 20 percent of their monthly paycheck plus 5 percent of the monthly pay for each year of experience.
- Employees with more than twenty years experience will receive the same bonus as twenty-year employees.

Let us assume that data records are to be processed containing the following fields:

```
YEARS          number of years experience
MONTHLY-PAY    amount of monthly pay
```

The routine required to compute the amount of the Christmas bonus is shown in Figure 6.12. Notice that by use of complex conditions, it is possible to perform the computations without the use of nested IF statements, which would otherwise be required.

Figure 6.12   Christmas bonus computation.

```
IF YEARS = 0
    COMPUTE BONUS = 100.
IF YEARS > 0 AND YEARS NOT > 3
    COMPUTE BONUS = 100 + YEARS * 0.1 * MONTHLY-PAY.
IF YEARS > 3 AND YEARS NOT > 20
    COMPUTE BONUS = 0.2 * MONTHLY-PAY +
                        YEARS * 0.05 * MONTHLY-PAY.
IF YEARS > 20
    COMPUTE BONUS = 1.2 * MONTHLY-PAY.
```

6.7   NAMED CONDITIONS

Named conditions are useful in documenting the meaning of a programmer written test. Suppose, for example, that data being processed contains a code having value M if sex is male and F is sex is female. The PROCEDURE division statement

```
IF KODE = "M"
    PERFORM MALE-ROUTINE
ELSE
    IF KODE = "F"
        PERFORM FEMALE-ROUTINE
    ELSE
        PERFORM ERROR ROUTINE.
```

could be used to differentiate in the processing of males and females. The meaning of the tests KODE = "M" and KODE = "F" is not apparent from the statement of the condition itself. It is possible to assign a name to the conditions KODE = "M" and KODE = "F". The 88 level used in the DATA DIVISION defines these names as follows:

```
03  KODE PIC X.
    88  SEX-IS-MALE VALUE "M".
    88  SEX-IS-FEMALE VALUE "F".
```

The condition SEX-IS-MALE is true if KODE has a value of 1 and false otherwise. The condition SEX-IS-FEMALE is true when the KODE has a value of 2 and false otherwise. The PROCEDURE DIVISION code above could now be rewritten as:

```
IF SEX-IS-MALE
    PERFORM MALE-ROUTINE
ELSE
    IF SEX-IS-FEMALE
        PERFORM FEMALE-ROUTINE
    ELSE
        PERFORM ERROR-ROUTINE.
```

The general form of the 88-level entry is shown in Figure 6.13. Any number of 88-level entries may follow an elementary data item definition in the DATA DIVISION.

Figure 6.13 General form of the 88-level entry

```
88  condition-name  { VALUE IS  }  literal-1  [ { THROUGH }  literal-2 ]
                     { VALUES ARE}             { THRU    }

    [ literal-3  [ { THROUGH }  literal-4 ] ] . . . . .
                  { THRU    }
```

Example

A common usage of named conditions is in end-of-file testing. For example, in Program 6.1, suppose the definition of EOF-FLAG at lines 4800-5000 is replaced by

```
01  FLAGS.
    02  EOF-FLAG    PIC X(3) VALUE "NO".
        88 END-OF-FILE    VALUE "YES".
```

Then the code at lines 10600-10700, which is currently

```
PERFORM 3000-PROCESS-READ
    UNTIL EOF-FLAG = "YES".
```

can be replaced by

```
PERFORM 3000-PROCESS-READ
    UNTIL END-OF-FILE.
```

The latter code is more readable and is completely equivalent to the first code, as END-OF-FILE is a name for the condition

```
EOF-FLAG = "YES".
```

Note that more than one value can be included in a VALUE clause.

Example

Suppose a company has numbered its stores 1, 2, 3, 7, 10, and 20. The program that checks the validity of the store-number on an input record could use the following code:

```
03  STORE-NUMBER PIC 99.
    88  VALID-STORE-NUMBER
            VALUES ARE 1  2  3  7  10  20.
```

The condition VALID-STORE-NUMBER will be true when the value of STORE-NUMBER is 1, 2, 3, 7, 10, or 20. The definition of the named condition VALID-STORE-NUMBER enables the program statement

```
IF  STORE-NUMBER = 1  OR
    STORE-NUMBER = 2  OR
    STORE-NUMBER = 3  OR
    STORE-NUMBER = 7  OR
    STORE-NUMBER = 10 OR
    STORE-NUMBER = 20
    PERFORM PROCESS-DATA
ELSE
    PERFORM INVALID-STORE-NUMBER.
```

to be replaced by the much more readable and compact code

```
IF  VALID-STORE-NUMBER
      PERFORM PROCESS-DATA
ELSE
      PERFORM INVALID-STORE-NUMBER.
```

This mechanism also makes the task of program maintenance easier, as new store numbers can be added or existing numbers deleted by making a simple change in the DATA DIVISION only; it is not necessary to make modifications to the PROCEDURE DIVISION.

The THROUGH clause is useful for including a sequence of values. For example, the above 88-level entry could also be written as:

```
88  VALID-STORE-NUMBER
          VALUES ARE 1 THROUGH 3  7  10  20.
```

The clause 1 THROUGH 3 is equivalent to 1, 2, 3.

Example

The following code could be used to define a condition INVALID-STORE-NUMBER which would include all possible values of STORE-NUMBER except 1, 2, 3, 7, 10, and 20:

```
03  STORE-NUMBER PIC 99.
      88  INVALID-STORE-NUMBER
            VALUES ARE 0  4 THRU 6  8  9
                          11 THRU 19  21 THRU 99.
```

6.8 ABBREVIATED RELATIONAL CONDITIONS

Relational conditions are made up of three parts:

1) subject
2) relation
3) object

For example, in the relational condition

$$A + B < 32$$

the subject is A + B, the relation is < and the object is 32. When relational conditions are linked by AND or OR to form complex conditions, it is possible to abbreviate the condition when the subject, or the subject and the relation, are the same. Abbreviation is accomplished by omitting the common subject or subject and relation in subsequent relations. Figure 6.14 gives the general form of an abbreviated complex condition.

Figure 6.14 General form of the abbreviated complex condition

$$\text{relation-condition} \left\{ \left\{ \frac{AND}{OR} \right\} [\underline{NOT}] [\text{relation}] \text{ object} \right\} \ldots$$

Example

Non-abbreviated Form	Abbreviated Form	Comment
A < B AND A < 3	A < B AND 3	Both the subject and relational operator omitted in abbreviated form
A > 16 OR A NOT < C	A > 16 OR NOT < C	Subject is omitted in abbreviated form
A < B AND A < C OR A > D	A < B AND C OR > D	Subject and relation are omitted for the first abbreviation; only the subject is omitted in the second abbreviation.

It is *not* possible to omit objects in forming abbreviations. For example, the correct abbreviation for A < B OR A = B is A < B OR = B, not the common mistake A < OR = B.

6.9 DATA VALIDATION

Errors can enter a data processing system in many ways. Wrong values for data fields can be entered at the source of the data. For example, a clerk sells an item for $10, but writes $9 on the sales ticket. Another source of errors occurs at the point that someone prepares a machine-readable document that will ultimately be processed by the computing system. The data-entry person could make any number of errors in keying the data; digits within a field could be transposed, an alphabetic character could be entered in what should be a numeric field, or a numeric character could be entered in what should be an alphabetic field, to list a few examples. A well-written program will attempt to test the data it processes to detect as many errors as possible in the data items.

Data fields that contain characters of an inappropriate type (i.e., a numeric field that contains an alphabetic character or an alphabetic field that contains a numeric character) are said to contain *invalid data*. The class test is a convenient means for checking the validity of input data fields. Each data item on an input record can be checked using the appropriate class test. If the item does not contain the correct type of data, an error message concerning the record can be written, and processing of the data can be bypassed. For example, consider the following input record description:

```
01  INPUT-RECORD.
    03 EMP-NUM-IR      PIC 9(9).
    03 EMP-NAME-IR     PIC X(20).
    03 HRS-WORKED-IR   PIC 99V99.
    03 PAY-RATE-IR     PIC 99V99.
    03 FILLER          PIC X(43).
```

The code required to check the validity of data in this record might be as shown in Figure 6.15. The structure diagram for this program is illustrated in Figure 6.16.

Figure 6.15 Simple validation program

```
1000-MAIN-LOGIC.
     PERFORM 2000-INITIALIZATION.
     PERFORM 3000-PROCESS-READ
         UNTIL EOF-FLAG = "YES".
     PERFORM 8000-TERMINATION.
     STOP RUN.
2000-INITIALIZATION.
     .
     .
     .
3000-PROCESS-READ.
     PERFORM 4000-ERROR-CHECK-ROUTINE.
     IF ERROR-FLAG = "NO"
         PERFORM 5000-NORMAL-PROCESS
     ELSE
         PERFORM 6000-ERROR-PROCESS.
     PERFORM 7000-READ-INPUT-FILE.
4000-ERROR-CHECK-ROUTINE.
     MOVE "NO" TO ERROR-FLAG.
     IF EMP-NUM-IR NOT NUMERIC
         MOVE "YES" TO ERROR-FLAG.
     IF EMP-NAME-IR NOT ALPHABETIC
         MOVE "YES" TO ERROR-FLAG.
     IF HRS-WORKED-IR NOT NUMERIC
         MOVE "YES" TO ERROR-FLAG.
     IF PAY-RATE-IR NOT NUMERIC
         MOVE "YES" TO ERROR-FLAG.
5000-NORMAL-PROCESS.
     .
     .
     .
6000-ERROR-PROCESS.
     .
     .
     .
7000-READ-INPUT-FILE.
     .
     .
     .
8000-TERMINATION.
     .
     .
     .
```

Figure 6.16   Structure diagram for simple validation program

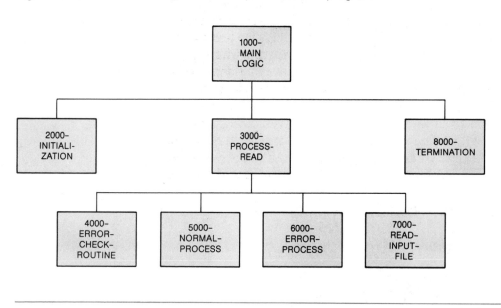

In this program note the use of the switch ERROR-FLAG. The switch is set to value "NO" or "YES" in 4000-ERROR-CHECK-ROUTINE. It is then used by 3000-PROCESS-READ to determine the appropriate action to take for the record.

Data validation also may take the form of checking that data in fields is within valid ranges. For example, suppose the maximum and minimum pay-rates are defined in WORKING-STORAGE as:

```
01  PAY-RATES.
    03 MAXIMUM-RATE  PIC 99V99 VALUE 30.00.
    03 MINIMUM-RATE  PIC 99V99 VALUE 3.50.
```

To detect a field outside this range the following statements could be added to the 4000-ERROR-CHECK-ROUTINE paragraph:

```
IF PAY-RATE-IR > MAXIMUM-RATE OR PAY-RATE-IR < MINIMUM-RATE
    MOVE "YES" TO ERROR-FLAG.
```

Another means by which this range check can be accomplished is to add a named condition INVALID-PAY-RATE to the description of INPUT-RECORD as shown below:

```
01  INPUT-RECORD.
    03 EMP-NUM-IR    PIC 9(9).
    03 EMP-NAME-IR   PIC X(20).
    03 HAS-WORKED-IR PIC 99V99.
    03 PAY-RATE-IR   PIC 99V99.
       88 INVALID-PAY-RATE VALUES ARE
           0 THRU 3.49  30.01 THRU 99.99.
    03 FILLER        PIC X(43).
```

It would now be possible to add the following statement to 4000-ERROR-CHECK-ROUTINE:

```
IF INVALID-PAY-RATE
    MOVE "YES" TO ERROR-FLAG.
```

The use of a simple two-value switch will result in a record being flagged as an error, although no indication will be given as to which field is in error or the type of error that may be present. It is indeed possible to write a complete description of the errors encountered in a data record; it is also possible to generate a code that would indicate which fields are in error and what type of error was encountered. For example, in this case, there are four items to be tested, so let's assume that ERROR-CODE is a four-digit number. The first digit would indicate an error in the first field; the second digit would indicate an error in the second field, and so on. Assume that 1 in a given position would indicate that the wrong type of data is present. A 2 would mean that the value of the data item is out of range. (If there were more types of errors, we could easily extend the list of codes.) The 4000-ERROR-CHECK-ROUTINE could now be coded as:

```
4000-ERROR-CHECK-ROUTINE.
    MOVE 0 TO ERROR-CODE.
    IF EMP-NUM-IR NOT NUMERIC
        ADD 1000 TO ERROR-CODE.
    IF EMP-NAME-IR NOT ALPHABETIC
        ADD 100 TO ERROR-CODE.
    IF HRS-WORKED-IR NOT NUMERIC
        ADD 10 TO ERROR-CODE.
    IF PAY-RATE-IR NOT NUMERIC
        ADD 1 TO ERROR-CODE
    ELSE
        IF PAY-RATE-IR > MAXIMUM-RATE
            ADD 2 TO ERROR-CODE
        ELSE
            IF PAY-RATE-IR < MINIMUM-RATE
                ADD 2 TO ERROR-CODE.
```

Naturally, the out-of-range test does not apply to alphabetic information. Therefore, if PAY-RATE-IR is NOT NUMERIC, the testing for an out-of-range value should not be performed. Thus, if EMP-NUM-IR is not numeric and the PAY-RATE is out of range, the ERROR-CODE generated would be 1002. The value of ERROR-CODE could be written out along with the data in the 6000-ERROR-PROCESS. A programmer-prepared guide for the user (commonly called an operations manual) could explain the meaning of the code used in the flag. In the following example more detailed descriptions of errors are produced.

6.10 PROGRAM EXAMPLE

Problem Statement

At the XYZ Gas Company data gathered by meter readers is loaded into a title called GAS-USAGE. Each record in this file contains:

> Account number
> Customer name
> Previous meter reading
> Present meter reading

This data will ultimately be used to compute monthly bills. However, before this can be done the data must be validated to prevent the production of

erroneous bills. In particular, data records with any of the following conditions are suspect and should not be processed:

  Any numeric field containing non-numeric data
  Customer-name field contains nonalphabetic data
  The amount of gas used is unreasonably high (>10,000,000)

A program is needed to process the data in the file GAS-USAGE and prepare a
report showing all suspect records. Any record which is not suspect should
be written to a file VALID-GAS-USAGE which will be used to produce the actual
bills. Specific descriptions of each error encountered in a record are to be
written in a report format shown in Figure 6.17.

Problem Analysis

Programs encountered thus far in this text always have processed two files—
an input file and an output file. This is not, however, a general rule. In this
problem, the program processes three files—one input file and two output
files. In general, a program may process any number of input and/or
output files.

   The computation of the amount of gas used in this problem is not as
straightforward as we might initially expect. At first glance there is a tempta-
tion to compute the amount of usage by subtracting the previous reading
from the present reading. This procedure is fine most of the time; however,
meters count only up to some maximum (999999 in our example) before they
roll over and begin again at zero. If this happens, the present reading will
actually appear to be less than the previous reading. For example, suppose
the previous reading was 999980 and the present reading is 000020. The
amount of usage is actually 40. To handle this case, the formula for computing usage is:

  Usage = (present reading + 1000000) − previous reading

For the above data the computation would yield:

  Usage = (20 + 1000000) − 999980
          = 1000020 − 999980
          = 40

The procedure for computing usage can be expressed as

  If previous reading < present reading
     Usage = present reading − previous reading
  Else
     Usage = (present reading + 1000000) − previous reading
  End If

   When non-numeric characters are present in a numeric field, the computer will use the numeric equivalent of the character in any computations
with that field. The numeric equivalent is based on the internal representation of the character. When the field is edited for output by usual methods
the content of the field will appear to be numeric. This problem can be
solved by treating each numeric field as both numeric and alphanumeric,
since in an alphanumeric field, each character is preserved. By defining
each numeric field as a group item with a numeric elementary data item subordinate to it, it is possible to work with an alphanumeric field (the group
item) or a numeric field (the elementary item) as needed. (Recall that all

Figure 6.17   Printer spacing chart for Program 6.2

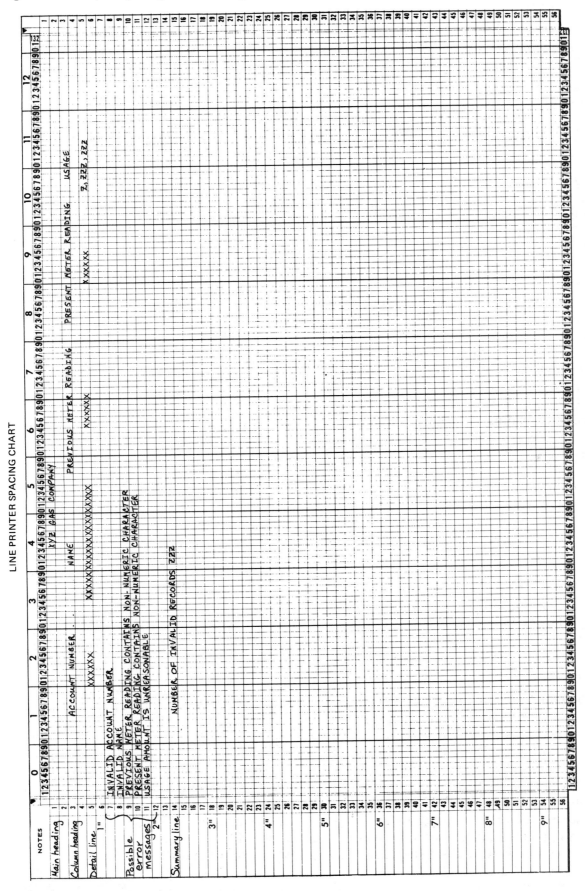

group items are classed as non-numeric.) This approach will be needed in the present program.

(Recall that all group items are classed as non-numeric.) This approach will be needed in the present program.

When one of the reading fields contains an invalid character, the computation of usage is of no value since the basic data is flawed. Hence, the program should compute the value of usage only if the two readings contain valid data.

At this point, it would be helpful to summarize the procedure required to solve this problem based on the preceding considerations as shown in Figure 6.18.

Figure 6.18   Preliminary plan for data validation program

Main routine

    Open files
    Write headings
    Read gas usage file
    Do Process read until end of file
    Write summary line
    Close files
    Stop

Process read

    Do Validate account number
    Do Validate name
    Do Validate previous reading
    Do Validate present reading
    If previous reading and present reading valid
            Do Compute usage
    Else
            Move 0 to usage
    End If
    Do Validate usage
    If record is invalid
            Add 1 to number of invalid records
            Do Invalid record output
    Else
            Do Valid record output
    End If
    Read gas usage file

Compute usage

    If previous reading < present reading
            Usage = present reading − previous reading
    Else
            Usage = (present reading + 1000000) −
                        previous reading
    End If

Invalid record output

    Write detail line
    Write appropriate error messages

Valid record output

    Move gas usage record to valid gas usage record
    Write valid gas usage record

Notice that we have not yet addressed the problem of controlling the production of the report—a detail line is to be included in the output only if one or more errors is found in a record. The error messages must occur *after* the related detail line. For a given record, a number of error messages may be written.

A simple way of carrying out this task is to use five flags, one for each possible error:

```
INVALID-ACCT-NUMBER-FLAG
INVALID-NAME-FLAG
INVALID-PREVIOUS-FLAG
INVALID-PRESENT-FLAG
INVALID-USAGE-FLAG
```

For each record, all of the flags are be set to "NO". Then the various validity tests are performed on the data. Each test procedure can change the appropriate flag to "YES" if an error is found. After all tests are completed, the program writes the detail line if any of the flags are set to "YES"; if all of them remain set to "NO", there are no errors in the record. If the record contains invalid data, the program then tests each of the flags in succession to write the appropriate set of error messages. With this technique in mind, it is now possible to refine the preliminary plan (Figure 6.18) to form a more complete plan as shown in Figure 6.19.

Figure 6.19   Plan for data validation program

Main routine

>Open files
>Write headings
>Read gas usage file
>Do Process read until end of file
>Write summary line
>Close files
>Stop

Process read

>Move "NO" to all invalid flags
>Do Validate account number
>Do Validate name
>Do Validate previous reading
>Do Validate present reading
>If previous reading and present reading valid
>>Do Compute usage
>Else
>>Move 0 to usage
>End If
>Do Validate usage
>If record is invalid
>>Add 1 to number of invalid records
>>Do Invalid record output
>Else
>>Do Valid record output
>End If
>Read gas usage file

Compute usage

    If previous reading < present reading
            Usage = present reading − previous reading
    Else
            Usage = (present reading + 1000000) −
                        previous reading
    End If

Invalid record output

    Write detail line
    If invalid account number
            Write invalid account number message
    End If
    If invalid name
            Write invalid name message
    End If
    If invalid previous
            Write non-numeric previous message
    End If
    If invalid present
            Write non-numeric present message
    End If
    If invalid usage
            Write invalid usage message
    End If

Valid record output

    Move gas usage record to valid gas usage record
    Write valid gas usage record

Validate account number

    If account number is not numeric
            Move "YES" to invalid account number flag
    End If

Validate name

    If name is not alphabetic
            Move "YES" to invalid name flag
    End If

Validate previous

    If previous reading not numeric
            Move "YES" to invalid previous flag
    End If

Validate present

    If present reading not numeric
            Move "YES" to invalid present flag
    End If

Validate usage

    If usage > 1000000
            Move "YES" to invalid usage flag
    End If

Problem solution

The program for this problem is shown as Program 6.2, with the structure diagram in Figure 6.20. Note the technique used to secure alphanumeric and numeric data names for the same data item. For example, at lines 2900-3000 the field for account number is defined as:

```
02  ACCOUNT-NUMBER-AN.
    03  ACCOUNT-NUMBER-GUR PIC 9(6).
```

Because ACCOUNT-NUMBER-AN is a group data item, it is classed as alphanumeric. When this field is moved to the output line at line 21000, the alphanumeric item is moved to an alphanumeric field. This is necessary so that any alphabetic characters in the field will not be printed using the numeric equivalent (which is what would have happened if the numeric item ACCOUNT-NUMBER-GUR had been used for output purposes). Notice, however that it is the numeric ACCOUNT-NUMBER-GUR which is tested to see if it contains all numeric characters at line 17600. The numeric test must be performed only on fields classed as numeric. (By the same token, the alphabetic test can only be used on fields classed as alphanumeric.)

The pseudocode statement

If record is invalid . . .

is implemented in the program at lines 16600-16700:

```
IF INVALID-ACCOUNT-NUMBER OR INVALID-NAME OR INVALID-PREVIOUS
    OR INVALID-PRESENT OR INVALID-USAGE
```

This is a complex condition that will be true if any one of the named conditions which make it up is true. Each of these named conditions will be true if the associated error flag is equal to "YES" (see lines 5200-6400).

The pseudocode statement:

Move "NO" to all error flags

is implemented at lines 15200 through 15600:

```
MOVE "NO" TO INVALID-ACCOUNT-NUMBER-FLAG
             INVALID-NAME-FLAG
             INVALID-PREVIOUS-FLAG
             INVALID-PRESENT-FLAG
             INVALID-USAGE-FLAG.
```

Recall that when multiple receiving fields are specified in a MOVE statement, the sending field value is moved to each of the receiving fields.

Figure 6.20   Structure diagram for program 6.2

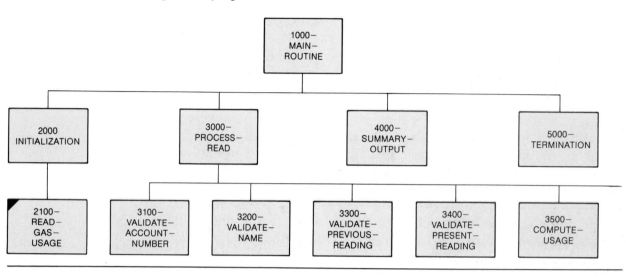

Program 6.2   Data validation

```
100      IDENTIFICATION DIVISION.
200      PROGRAM-ID. DATA-VALIDATION.
300      AUTHOR. PAULA.
400
500      ENVIRONMENT DIVISION.
600
700      CONFIGURATION SECTION.
800
900      SOURCE-COMPUTER.
1000     OBJECT-COMPUTER.
1100
1200     INPUT-OUTPUT SECTION.
1300
1400     FILE-CONTROL.
1500
1600         SELECT GAS-USAGE-FILE ASSIGN TO DISK.
1700         SELECT INVALID-DATA-REPORT ASSIGN TO PRINTER.
1800         SELECT VALID-GAS-USAGE-FILE ASSIGN TO DISK.
1900
2000     DATA DIVISION.
2100
2200     FILE SECTION.
2300
2400     FD  GAS-USAGE-FILE
2500         LABEL RECORDS ARE STANDARD
2600         DATA RECORD IS GAS-USAGE-RECORD.
2700
2800     01  GAS-USAGE-RECORD.
2900         02 ACCOUNT-NUMBER-AN.
3000             03 ACCOUNT-NUMBER-GUR   PIC 9(6).
3100         02 NAME-GUR                 PIC X(20).
3200         02 PREVIOUS-READING-AN.
3300             03 PREVIOUS-READING-GUR PIC 9(6).
```

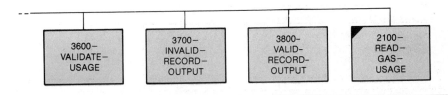

Program 6.2 (continued)

```
3400          02 PRESENT-READING-AN.
3500             03 PRESENT-READING-GUR  PIC 9(6).
3600          02 FILLER                  PIC X(42).
3700
3800    FD  INVALID-DATA-REPORT
3900        LABEL RECORDS ARE OMITTED
4000        DATA RECORD IS PRINT-LINE.
4100
4200    01  PRINT-LINE        PIC X(132).
4300
4400    FD  VALID-GAS-USAGE-FILE
4500        LABEL RECORDS ARE STANDARD
4600        DATA RECORD IS VALID-GAS-USAGE-RECORD.
4700
4800    01  VALID-GAS-USAGE-RECORD    PIC X(84).
4900
5000    WORKING-STORAGE SECTION.
5100
5200    01  FLAGS.
5300        02 EOF-FLAG                      PIC X(3) VALUE "NO".
5400           88 END-OF-FILE             VALUE "YES".
5500        02 INVALID-ACCOUNT-NUMBER-FLAG PIC X(3) VALUE "NO".
5600           88 INVALID-ACCOUNT-NUMBER VALUE "YES".
5700        02 INVALID-NAME-FLAG             PIC X(3) VALUE "NO".
5800           88 INVALID-NAME           VALUE "YES".
5900        02 INVALID-PREVIOUS-FLAG         PIC X(3) VALUE "NO".
6000           88 INVALID-PREVIOUS       VALUE "YES".
6100        02 INVALID-PRESENT-FLAG          PIC X(3) VALUE "NO".
6200           88 INVALID-PRESENT        VALUE "YES".
6300        02 INVALID-USAGE-FLAG            PIC X(3) VALUE "NO".
6400           88 INVALID-USAGE          VALUE "YES".
6500
6600    01  COMPUTED-AMOUNTS.
6700        02  AMOUNT-USED            PIC 9(7) VALUE ZERO.
6800        02  NUMBER-INVALID-RECORDS PIC 999 VALUE ZERO.
```

Program 6.2 *(continued)*

```
6900
7000      01  HEADING-LINE-1.
7100          02 FILLER            PIC X(43) VALUE SPACES.
7200          02 FILLER            PIC X(15) VALUE
7300             "XYZ GAS COMPANY".
7400
7500      01  HEADING-LINE-2.
7600          02 FILLER            PIC X(14) VALUE "ACCOUNT NUMBER".
7700          02 FILLER            PIC X(12) VALUE SPACES.
7800          02 FILLER            PIC X(4)  VALUE "NAME".
7900          02 FILLER            PIC X(12) VALUE SPACES.
8000          02 FILLER            PIC X(22) VALUE "PREVIOUS METER READING".
8100          02 FILLER            PIC X(4) VALUE SPACES.
8200          02 FILLER            PIC X(21) VALUE "PRESENT METER READING".
8300          02 FILLER            PIC X(4) VALUE SPACES.
8400          02 FILLER            PIC X(10) VALUE "USAGE".
8500
8600      01  DETAIL-LINE.
8700          03 FILLER               PIC X(4) VALUE SPACES.
8800          03 ACCOUNT-NUMBER-DL    PIC X(6).
8900          03 FILLER               PIC X(8) VALUE SPACES.
9000          03 NAME-DL              PIC X(20).
9100          03 FILLER               PIC X(12) VALUE SPACES.
9200          03 PREVIOUS-READING-DL  PIC X(6).
9300          03 FILLER               PIC X(19) VALUE SPACES.
9400          03 PRESENT-READING-DL   PIC X(6).
9500          03 FILLER               PIC X(12) VALUE SPACES.
9600          03 USAGE-DL             PIC Z,ZZZ,ZZZ.
9700
9800      01  POSSIBLE-ERROR-MESSAGES.
9900          02 MESSAGE-LINE-1.
10000            03 FILLER            PIC X(22) VALUE
10100            "INVALID ACCOUNT NUMBER".
10200
10300          02  MESSAGE-LINE-2.
10400            03 FILLER            PIC X(12) VALUE
10500            "INVALID NAME".
10600
10700          02  MESSAGE-LINE-3.
10800            03 FILLER            PIC X(54) VALUE
10900            "PREVIOUS METER READING CONTAINS NON-NUMERIC CHARACTER".
11000
11100          02  MESSAGE-LINE-4.
11200            03 FILLER            PIC X(53) VALUE
11300            "PRESENT METER READING CONTAINS NON-NUMERIC CHARACTER".
11400
11500          02  MESSAGE-LINE-5.
11600            03 FILLER            PIC X(28) VALUE
11700            "USAGE AMOUNT IS UNREASONABLE".
11800
11900      01  SUMMARY-LINE.
12000          02 FILLER                     PIC X(14) VALUE SPACES.
12100          02 FILLER                     PIC X(26) VALUE
12200             "NUMBER OF INVALID RECORDS ".
12300          02 NUMBER-INVALID-RECORDS-SL  PIC ZZZ.
```

Program 6.2 (continued)

```
12400
12500    PROCEDURE DIVISION.
12600
12700    1000-MAIN-ROUTINE.
12800
12900        PERFORM 2000-INITIALIZATION.
13000        PERFORM 3000-PROCESS-READ
13100            UNTIL END-OF-FILE.
13200        PERFORM 4000-SUMMARY-OUTPUT.
13300        PERFORM 9000-TERMINATION.
13400        STOP RUN.
13500
13600    2000-INITIALIZATION.
13700
13800        OPEN INPUT GAS-USAGE-FILE
13900            OUTPUT INVALID-DATA-REPORT
14000                    VALID-GAS-USAGE-FILE.
14100        WRITE PRINT-LINE FROM HEADING-LINE-1 AFTER PAGE.
14200        WRITE PRINT-LINE FROM HEADING-LINE-2 AFTER 2.
14300        PERFORM 2100-READ-GAS-USAGE.
14400
14500    2100-READ-GAS-USAGE.
14600
14700        READ GAS-USAGE-FILE
14800            AT END MOVE "YES" TO EOF-FLAG.
14900
15000    3000-PROCESS-READ.
15100
15200        MOVE "NO" TO INVALID-ACCOUNT-NUMBER-FLAG
15300                     INVALID-NAME-FLAG
15400                     INVALID-PREVIOUS-FLAG
15500                     INVALID-PRESENT-FLAG
15600                     INVALID-USAGE-FLAG.
15700        PERFORM 3100-VALIDATE-ACCOUNT-NUMBER.
15800        PERFORM 3200-VALIDATE-NAME.
15900        PERFORM 3300-VALIDATE-PREVIOUS-READING.
16000        PERFORM 3400-VALIDATE-PRESENT-READING.
16100        IF NOT INVALID-PREVIOUS AND NOT INVALID-PRESENT
16200            PERFORM 3500-COMPUTE-USAGE
16300        ELSE
16400            MOVE ZERO TO AMOUNT-USED.
16500        PERFORM 3600-VALIDATE-USAGE.
16600        IF INVALID-ACCOUNT-NUMBER OR INVALID-NAME OR INVALID-PREVIOUS
16700            OR INVALID-PRESENT OR INVALID-USAGE
16800                ADD 1 TO NUMBER-INVALID-RECORDS
16900                PERFORM 3700-INVALID-RECORD-OUTPUT
17000        ELSE
17100                PERFORM 3800-VALID-RECORD-OUTPUT.
17200        PERFORM 2100-READ-GAS-USAGE.
17300
17400    3100-VALIDATE-ACCOUNT-NUMBER.
17500
17600        IF ACCOUNT-NUMBER-GUR IS NOT NUMERIC
17700            MOVE "YES" TO INVALID-ACCOUNT-NUMBER-FLAG.
17800
```

Program 6.2 *(continued)*

```
17900        3200-VALIDATE-NAME.
18000
18100           IF NAME-GUR NOT ALPHABETIC
18200               MOVE "YES" TO INVALID-NAME-FLAG.
18300
18400        3300-VALIDATE-PREVIOUS-READING.
18500
18600           IF PREVIOUS-READING-GUR NOT NUMERIC
18700               MOVE "YES" TO INVALID-PREVIOUS-FLAG.
18800
18900        3400-VALIDATE-PRESENT-READING.
19000
19100           IF PRESENT-READING-GUR NOT NUMERIC
19200               MOVE "YES" TO INVALID-PRESENT-FLAG.
19300
19400        3500-COMPUTE-USAGE.
19500
19600           IF PREVIOUS-READING-GUR < PRESENT-READING-GUR
19700               SUBTRACT PREVIOUS-READING-GUR  FROM PRESENT-READING-GUR
19800                   GIVING AMOUNT-USED
19900           ELSE
20000               COMPUTE AMOUNT-USED = PRESENT-READING-GUR  + 1000000
20100                   - PREVIOUS-READING-GUR.
20200
20300        3600-VALIDATE-USAGE.
20400
20500           IF AMOUNT-USED > 1000000
20600               MOVE "YES" TO INVALID-USAGE-FLAG.
20700
20800        3700-INVALID-RECORD-OUTPUT.
20900
21000           MOVE ACCOUNT-NUMBER-AN      TO ACCOUNT-NUMBER-DL.
21100           MOVE NAME-GUR               TO NAME-DL.
21200           MOVE PREVIOUS-READING-AN    TO PREVIOUS-READING-DL.
21300           MOVE PRESENT-READING-AN     TO PRESENT-READING-DL.
21400           MOVE AMOUNT-USED            TO USAGE-DL.
21500           MOVE DETAIL-LINE            TO PRINT-LINE.
21600           WRITE PRINT-LINE AFTER 2.
21700           IF INVALID-ACCOUNT-NUMBER
21800               WRITE PRINT-LINE FROM MESSAGE-LINE-1 AFTER 1.
21900           IF INVALID-NAME
22000               WRITE PRINT-LINE FROM MESSAGE-LINE-2 AFTER 1.
22100           IF INVALID-PREVIOUS
22200               WRITE PRINT-LINE FROM MESSAGE-LINE-3 AFTER 1.
22300           IF INVALID-PRESENT
22400               WRITE PRINT-LINE FROM MESSAGE-LINE-4 AFTER 1.
22500           IF INVALID-USAGE
22600               WRITE PRINT-LINE FROM MESSAGE-LINE-5 AFTER 1.
22700
22800        3800-VALID-RECORD-OUTPUT.
22900
23000           MOVE GAS-USAGE-RECORD TO VALID-GAS-USAGE-RECORD.
23100           WRITE VALID-GAS-USAGE-RECORD.
23200
```

```
23300    4000-SUMMARY-OUTPUT.
23400
23500        MOVE NUMBER-INVALID-RECORDS TO NUMBER-INVALID-RECORDS-SL.
23600        MOVE SUMMARY-LINE            TO PRINT-LINE.
23700        WRITE PRINT-LINE AFTER 2.
23800
23900    9000-TERMINATION.
24000
24100        CLOSE GAS-USAGE-FILE
24200              INVALID-DATA-REPORT
24300              VALID-GAS-USAGE-FILE.
```

Program 6.2 (continued)

6.11 DEBUG CLINIC

The Case of the Missing Period

One of the most common errors made when using the IF statement is the omission of the period required to terminate the statement. For example, suppose we want to write code to implement the following flowchart:

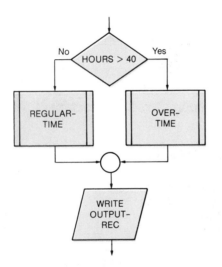

The correct code is:

```
IF HOURS > 40
     PERFORM OVER-TIME
ELSE
     PERFORM REGULAR-TIME.
WRITE OUTPUT-REC AFTER 1.
```

However, suppose the program is coded (erroneously) as:

```
IF HOURS > 40
    PERFORM OVERTIME
ELSE
    PERFORM REGULAR-TIME              (note missing period)
WRITE OUTPUT-REC AFTER 1.
```

The result will be to include the WRITE statement as a part of the ELSE clause of the IF statement, as though the flowchart had been written:

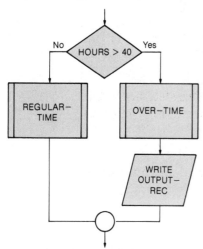

The alignment of the WRITE statement in the same column as the IF and ELSE entries indicates to the reader that the WRITE statement is not a part of the ELSE clause of the IF statement, but the compiler ignores the placement of statements. The period is required to terminate the IF statement.

Conditional and Imperative Statements

A *conditional* statement is a statement which

1) contains one or more statements in a clause, and
2) selects the action(s) to be taken next depending on the evaluation of some condition.

It is clear that the IF statement is a conditional statement. Other statements also are classed as conditional, including:

- any arithmetic statement with the ON SIZE ERROR option
- READ statement with the AT END option

In all of these statements, the action to be taken depends on the evaluation of some condition. In the case of the arithmetic statement with the ON SIZE ERROR option, the statements in the ON SIZE ERROR clause are executed if there is overflow or division by zero; otherwise, execution continues with the next sentence. The statement(s) in the AT END clause of a READ statement are executed at end-of-file; otherwise, the next sentence is executed. Conditional statements are always terminated by a period.

Any statement that is not a conditional statement is an *imperative* statement. Examples of imperative statements include:

- arithmetic statements without the clause ON SIZE ERROR
- WRITE statement
- PERFORM statement
- MOVE statement

Imperative statements are terminated either by a period or a COBOL verb signifying the start of another statement.

A single COBOL PROCEDURE DIVISION sentence may be made up of many imperative statements.

Example

The following two coding sequences are equivalent:

```
MOVE A TO A-OUT          MOVE A TO A-OUT.
MOVE B TO B-OUT          MOVE B TO B-OUT.
COMPUTE OUT = A + B      COMPUTE OUT = A + B.
WRITE OUT-REC AFTER 1.   WRITE OUT-REC AFTER 1.
```

On the left is a single sentence composed of four imperative statements. On the right there are four sentences, each sentence containing a single imperative statement and ends with a period.

Clauses within conditional statements may be made up of any number of imperative statements.

Examples

```
COMPUTE A = B + C
    ON SIZE ERROR
        MOVE "ERROR IN COMP" TO MSG-OUT
        WRITE OUT-REC FROM ERR-REC AFTER 1
        MOVE 0 TO A.
```

In the example above, the ON SIZE ERROR clause is made up of three imperative statements.

```
READ IN-FILE
    AT END
        MOVE 999 TO A
        MOVE "YES" TO EOF-FLAG.
```

In this example the AT END clause is made up of two imperative statements.

Care must be taken that every conditional statement ends with a period. If the period is omitted, succeeding statements will be erroneously included as a part of a clause of the conditional statement.

Example

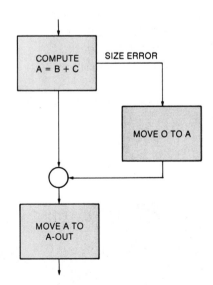

The correct code terminates the conditional COMPUTE statement with a period:

```
COMPUTE A = B + C
    ON SIZE ERROR
        MOVE 0 TO A.
MOVE A TO A-OUT.
```

If the conditional COMPUTE statement is not terminated with a period, as in

```
COMPUTE A = B + C
    ON SIZE ERROR
        MOVE 0 TO A
MOVE A TO A-OUT.
```

the result is to include the statement MOVE A TO A-OUT as a part of the ON SIZE ERROR clause as though the flowchart had been written like this:

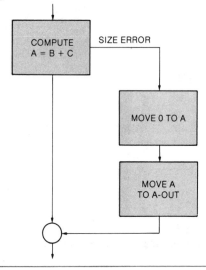

Embedding a conditional statement into a clause of another conditional statement is possible only if the embedded conditional statement is the last one in a clause.

Example

Suppose we wish to implement the following flowchart:

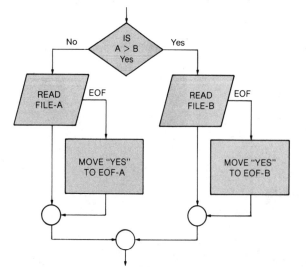

It would be correct to code this flowchart as

```
IF A > B
    READ FILE-B AT END MOVE "YES" TO EOF-B
ELSE
    READ FILE-A AT END MOVE "YES" TO EOF-A.
```

The conditional statement READ FILE-B is terminated by ELSE; the conditional statement READ FILE-A and the IF statement itself are terminated by the period.

Example

Suppose we wish to implement the following flowchart:

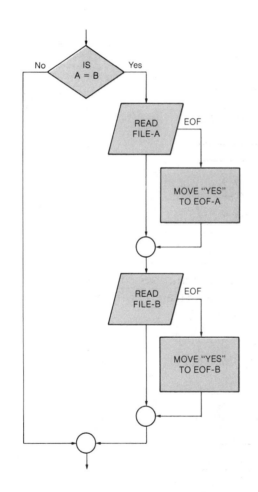

The best way to code this logic is to write separate paragraphs for READ FILE-A and READ FILE-B and PERFORM these paragraphs, as in:

```
IF A = B
    PERFORM READ-FILE-A
    PERFORM READ-FILE-B.
```

This IF statement has a clause made up of two imperative statements. If one attempts to embed two conditional statements into the IF statement, as in

```
IF A = B
    READ FILE-A AT END MOVE "YES" TO EOF-A
    READ FILE-B AT END MOVE "YES" TO EOF-B.
```

the code would be in error because the READ FILE-B statement would be a part of the AT END clause of the statement READ FILE-A. The above code would be executed as though the flowchart had read as shown below on the left:

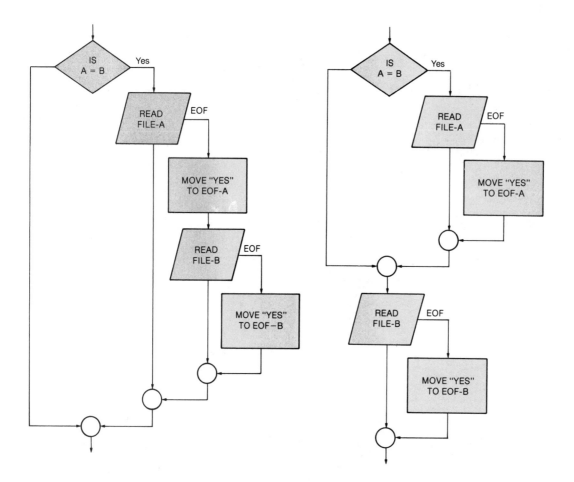

Note that a clause in a conditional statement is made up of statements, *not* sentences. If a programmer tried to salvage the above code by placing a period at the end of the first READ statement, as in

```
IF A = B
    PERFORM READ-FILE-A.
    PERFORM READ-FILE-B.
```

the coding would be in error because the added period would terminate not only the READ statement but also the IF statement. The result would be as though the flowchart read as shown above on the right

The programmer should break a program into paragraphs to avoid inclusion of conditional statements in a clause of another conditional statement.

6.12 SELF-TEST EXERCISES

1. Evaluate each of the following conditions based on the following data names:

   | 1,4,5̄ | | 3,5 | | B,E,T,A, |

   X PIC S99V9   Y PIC 99   Z PIC X(5)

   Example: X IS NEGATIVE OR Y > 30

            True   True

              The condition is True

   a. X < Y OR Y IS NEGATIVE
   b. Z IS ALPHABETIC
   c. X IS NUMERIC AND Z IS NOT ALPHABETIC
   d. NOT Y IS POSITIVE
   e. NOT X IS ZERO OR Y IS NOT NEGATIVE
   f. NOT (X > 25 OR Y < 39)
   g. X > Y OR X IS ZERO AND Y > 1
   h. X < Y AND (Y < 0 OR X > 30)

2. Evaluate each of the following conditions:

   | 2 | | | A,B, |

   03 FLDA PIC 9.   03 FLDB PIC XXX.
     88 ITEM-TYPE-1 VALUE 1.   88 XYZ VALUE "ABC" "AB".
     88 ITEM-TYPE-2 VALUE 2.
     88 ITEM-TYPE-OTHER VALUE 0 3 THRU 9.

   Example: NOT ITEM-TYPE-1

              False

              True

   a. ITEM-TYPE-1
   b. ITEM-TYPE-1 OR ITEM-TYPE-2
   c. XYZ
   d. NOT XYZ
   e. NOT (ITEM-TYPE-1 OR ITEM-TYPE-2)
   f. XYZ AND NOT ITEM-TYPE-1
   g. NOT XYZ AND ITEM-TYPE-1 OR NOT ITEM-TYPE-2
   h. NOT ITEM-TYPE-OTHER

3. When possible, write an abbreviated version of each of the following conditions:
   a. A < B AND A EQUAL C
   b. A < B OR C AND A > D
   c. A < B AND C < B
   d. A IS GREATER THAN B OR A < D
   e. A LESS THAN B AND A < C
   f. A NOT > B AND A < C AND A NOT = C

4. Write an IF statement to compute minimum payment defined by:

$$\text{minimum payment} = \begin{cases} \text{balance, if balance} \le \$20 \\ \$20 + 10\% \text{ of (balance} - \$20), \text{ if } \$20 < \text{balance} \le \$100 \\ \$36 + 20\% \text{ of (balance} - \$100), \text{ if balance} > \$100 \end{cases}$$

5. Write COBOL code to implement each of the following flowcharts.
   a.

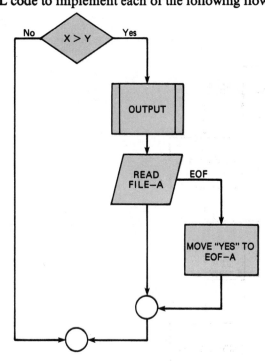

   b.

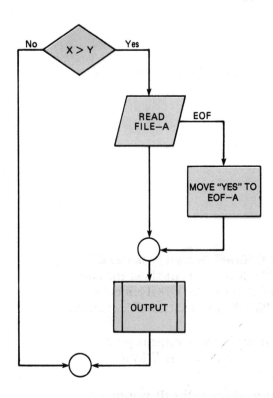

c.

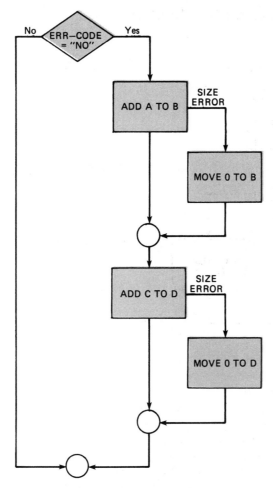

6. Write a data validation routine to check the validity of the following data record:

```
01  DATA-REC.
    03  ACCOUNT-NUM-DR        PIC 9(9).
    03  CUSTOMER-NAME-DR      PIC X(20).
    03  CUSTOMER-ADDRESS-DR.
        05  STREET-ADDRESS-DR PIC X(15).
        05  CITY-DR           PIC X(8).
        05  STATE-DR          PIC XX.
        05  ZIP-DR            PIC 9(9).
    03  BALANCE-FORWARD-DR    PIC 9999V99.
```

The fields ACCOUNT-NUM-DR, ZIP-DR and BALANCE-FORWARD-DR must be numeric. The fields CUSTOMER-NAME-DR, CITY-DR and STATE-DR must be nonblank and contain only alphabetic data. Move "YES" to a field VALIDITY-ERROR if errors are found; otherwise, move "NO" to VALIDITY-ERROR. Why is it not possible to check the validity of STREET-ADDRESS-DR?

7. The PERFORM UNTIL statement is classed as an imperative statement, yet it involves checking a condition and taking alternative actions. Why is the PERFORM UNTIL statement classed as imperative?

8. How would the program of Program 6.1 be modified to list all women employees born between 1920 and 1940?

9. Write the PROCEDURE DIVISION and necessary additional DATA DIVISION entries to modify the program of Program 6.1 to

   - list all female employees
   - count and print the number of male and female employees
   - compute and print the average age for males and females.

6.13 PROGRAMMING EXERCISES

1. The managers of Burgers, Inc., a franchise system of hamburger restaurants, are concerned with the profitability of a number of the company's outlets. They have requested a report showing basic data about each store and have a flag for stores showing profits less than $20,000. The format for the input records is:

Positions

1-10	Franchise number
11-25	Location
26-40	Manager's name
41-48	Previous year's profits (S999999V99)
	(Field could be negative if the store lost money.)

Print a row of asterisks (e.g., "*****") as a flag for each store with low profits.

2. At ABC Furniture Store, Inc. the manager of the computing center has separately budgeted amounts for computer supplies, office supplies, computer equipment, and office equipment. He needs to keep track of his cumulative expenditures in each of these categories. He has created a data file with records in the following format:

Positions

1-6	date of purchase
7-25	description of purchase
26-32	amount (2 decimal places)
33	account code
	1 = computer supplies
	2 = office supplies
	3 = computer equipment
	4 = office equipment

Write a program to list each purchase in an appropriately labeled column. Accumulate and print totals for each account.

Sample Data:

Date	Description	Amount	Account code
1/1/86	office chair	95.00	4
1/2/86	calculator	259.50	4
1/2/86	continuous paper	593.00	1
1/13/86	typewriter ribbons	9.00	2
1/14/86	terminal	3000.00	3
1/15/86	ribbon	359.00	1

3. The FHA insures home mortgages up to $85,000. The down-payment schedule is as follows:

   > 3% of the first $45,000
   > 10% of the next $10,000
   > 20% of the remainder

   Write a program to accept input records containing an applicant's name and the amount of the loan requested. Output should consist of all input fields and the amount of the down-payment required. Reject any application that is for more than $85,000. Also compute the total amounts of loans and down-payments.

4. Using the file described in Program 6.2, write a program to compute the amount of the monthly bill. Output should consist of all input data and the amount of the bill based on the following schedule:

   > $6.00, if amount used is less than 50
   > $6.00 + .10 × (amount used − 50), if 50 ≤ amount used ≤ 200
   > $21.00 + .08 × (amount used − 200), if amount > 200

5. Write a program that could be used to determine a weekly payroll. The input file contains one record per employee with the following fields: employee name, employee number, hourly rate of pay and hours worked. Have your program list the employee name, employee number, hourly rate of pay, number of hours worked and gross pay. Remember to pay time and one-half for all hours over 40 worked in the week.

6. Jones Hardware, Inc. maintains an accounts receivable file with records of the following format:

   Positions

1-6	Account number
7-25	Customer name
26-31	Date of last purchase (*mmddyy*)
32-37	Date of last payment (*mmddyy*)
38-43	Balance of account
44-55	Address
55-65	City
66-67	State
68-73	Zip Code

   Write a program to produce a report that will be used by clerks who will write letters to customers requesting either their continued business for inactive accounts or payment of a past due balance. If the date of last purchase indicates that no purchase has been made in the past three months and the balance is zero, indicate that a letter requesting continued patronage should be written. If the balance of the account is greater than $1 and no payment has been made in the previous two months indicate a letter requesting payment. If the balance is greater than $100 and no payment has been made in the previous four months, indicate a stronger letter threatening that legal action will be taken if payment is not forthcoming. For purposes of this program, assume that the current date is 03/30/86.

7. Write a program to list all three-bedroom houses with more than one bath in the price range $65,000 to $95,000 using the file described in Chapter 4, Section 4.15, Exercise 3.

8. Write a program to list all accounts with a past due balance using the file described in Exercise 6 above. Count the number of accounts which have had no payment made in the previous month, the previous two months, the previous three months and the previous four or more months. Write these amounts after processing the entire file.

9. When a house is listed and sold by real estate brokers, the commission is divided among four people: the listing broker (firm which lists and advertises the house), the listing salesman (the person who secures the listing from the owner), the selling salesman (person who sells the house), and the selling broker (firm for whom the selling salesman works).

    In Happy Valley, which has six real estate brokers and many salesmen, commissions are divided as follows: When the listing salesman and selling salesman work for the same broker, the commission is divided 25 percent to the listing salesman, 30 percent to the selling salesman, and 45 percent to the broker. When the listing salesman and selling salesman work for different brokers, the commission is divided 25 percent to the listing salesman, 35 percent to the listing broker, 20 percent to the selling salesman, and 20 percent to the selling broker.

    Design the input record and write a program to calculate real estate commissions for the city of Happy Valley.

10. Modify the program written for Chapter 5, Exercise 9 to produce an amortization schedule for the loan. There should be one line of output for each month's payment showing:

    Payment number
    Payment to interest
    Payment to principal
    Total monthly payment
    New balance

Accumulate and print the total of the interest payments. (The last month's payment may be slightly more or less than the other payments.) For example, for principal of $105,000, interest rate of 17.5 percent and time of 25 years, the expected output would be similar to:

Number	Principal	Interest	Pmt	Balance
1	20.16	1531.25	1551.41	104980.00
2	20.45	1530.96	1551.41	104959.00
3	20.75	1530.66	1551.41	104939.00
4	21.05	1530.36	1551.41	104918.00
5	21.36	1530.05	1551.41	104896.00
6	21.67	1529.74	1551.41	104875.00
7	21.99	1529.42	1551.41	104853.00
8	22.31	1529.10	1551.41	104830.00
9	22.64	1528.77	1551.41	104806.00
.				
.				
.				
295	1422.56	128.85	1551.41	7413.10
296	1443.3	108.11	1551.41	5969.80
297	1464.35	87.06	1551.41	4505.45
298	1485.71	65.70	1551.41	3019.74
299	1507.37	44.04	1551.41	1512.37
300	1512.37	22.06	1534.43	0.00
TOTAL INTEREST	$360,406.00			

SEQUENTIAL FILES AND SORTING 7

Up to this point we have used data files with little regard to the characteristics of the device used or to the various options available to optimize the operation of programs that access the data. We also have neglected procedures by which data files can be changed to reflect the current status of the subject of the file. This chapter presents a detailed discussion of these very important topics as they relate to the most commonly used types of mass storage: magnetic tape and magnetic disk.

7.1 TAPE CONCEPTS

Data records stored on magnetic tape are separated by an *Inter-Record-Gap* (IRG) as shown in Figure 7.1. The IRG is an unused block of tape that is typically six-tenths of an inch long. When a magnetic tape drive is started, some tape (about three-tenths of an inch) will move past the read/write head before operating speed is reached. When a tape drive is stopped, approximately three-tenths of an inch of tape will move past the read/write head before the tape comes to a stop. The IRG is an allowance for the tape, required in both starting and stopping the drive, in order to minimize errors in reading and writing data.

It is often convenient to create physical data records on the tape that contain more than one logical data record. This arrangement is called *blocking*. Two or more logical data records may make up a physical record on the tape. For example, if the blocking factor is three, the data would appear on the tape as shown in Figure 7.2. The gap between used portions of tape is often called an *Inter-Block-Gap* (IBG), to denote the separation of blocks of data rather than logical records.

The use of blocked records serves to utilize as much tape as possible and also to minimize access time. The programmer must know the size of the blocking factor when he or she is writing a program to process a file. If a file is being created by a program, the programmer should choose as large a blocking factor as possible. The maximum size for a blocking factor is limited by the amount of main memory available. When a physical record is read, all of the data contained on it must be stored in memory.

Figure 7.1   Inter-Record-Gap for records stored on magnetic tape

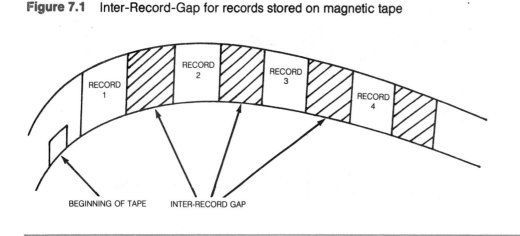

Figure 7.2   Blocked records with a label record on magnetic tape

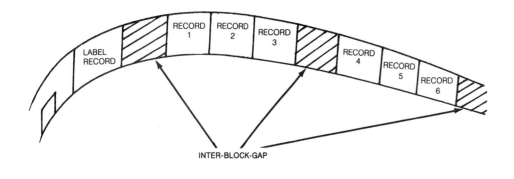

There is a provision for creating a record at the beginning of the tape that will contain identifying data about the file. This record is called a *label record* (Fig. 7.2). The label record is created by the operating system when the file is opened as an output file. When the data file is used as an input file, the operating system will check the content of the label record to verify that the correct tape has been mounted.

The existence of blocked records and/or label records must be noted in the FD entry written for the file. The BLOCK clause has the general form:

$$\underline{\text{BLOCK}} \text{ CONTAINS integer } \left\{ \begin{array}{l} \text{CHARACTERS} \\ \underline{\text{RECORDS}} \end{array} \right\}$$

The BLOCK clause is used to specify the size of the physical data block. The LABEL clause has the general form:

$$
\text{LABEL} \left\{ \begin{array}{l} \underline{\text{RECORD}} \text{ IS} \\ \underline{\text{RECORDS}} \text{ ARE} \end{array} \right\} \left\{ \begin{array}{l} \underline{\text{OMITTED}} \\ \underline{\text{STANDARD}} \end{array} \right\}
$$

This clause is used to specify whether the label record is to be found on the file. For example, the FD entry for the file illustrated in Figure 7.2 would be:

```
FD  DATA-FILE
        BLOCK CONTAINS 3 RECORDS
        LABEL RECORD IS STANDARD
        DATA RECORD IS DATA-RECORD.
```

The programmer does not need to make any modifications to the logic of the program because of the label record and/or blocked records. The operating system performs the required label record creation/checking and deblocks the physical data record into logical records (as described in the DATA DIVISION FDs), which are made available to the program for processing one at a time.

The computer requires that you tell it not only which file to use but also what equipment to use to access the file. The SELECT statement is used to associate the file with a physical device. The general form of a SELECT statement is:

$$
\underline{\text{SELECT}} \text{ file-name } \underline{\text{ASSIGN}} \text{ TO system-name.}
$$

The form taken by the *system-name* differs widely among different versions of COBOL. The reader must check the system COBOL manual supplied by the manufacturer for specific details.

7.2 DISK CONCEPTS

A disk contains one or more recording surfaces. Each surface is organized into *tracks* on which data is recorded. The tracks on a surface may be thought of as a series of concentric circles (Fig. 7.3). There may be anywhere from 40 to 400 or more tracks per surface, depending on the size of the disk. A track may store from 1000 to 8000 or more characters, depending on the size of the disk. Data is organized on each track into records. As with data stored on tape, there is typically an IRG between records. A typical track containing records is shown in Figure 7.4. Data is read from and written onto a disk one record at a time. In order to optimize access time and utilization of space on the disk, records may be blocked in much the same fashion as was done on tape files.

Figure 7.3 A disk recording surface

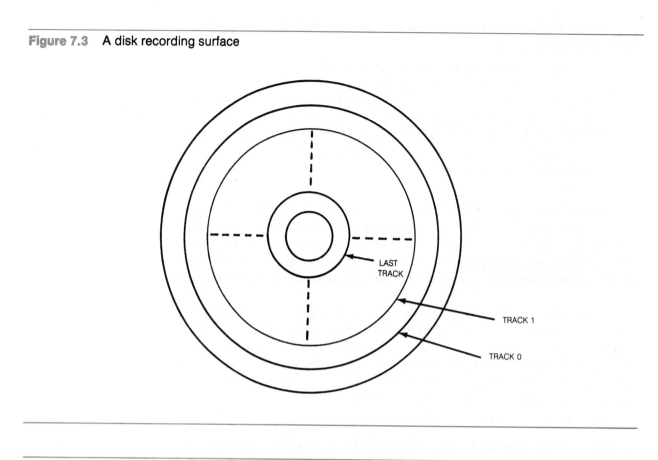

Figure 7.4 A typical track containing data records

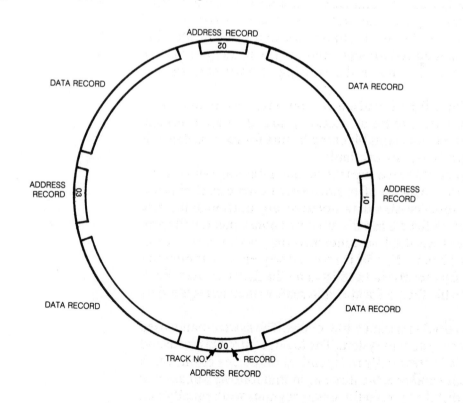

A typical sequence of events required to read a record on disk includes the following steps:

1) A program requests a record from a disk file.
2) The operating system (which keeps track of the physical disk address of files and records) instructs the disk drive to read a particular record from a specified surface and track.
3) The disk drive moves its read/write head to the track and when the disk surface has rotated into position for reading the required record, the data is read.

A similar sequence of events occurs when a record is written onto a disk file. One entire physical record is read/written at a time. The operating system handles the details of accumulating a sufficient number of logical records before writing a physical record, and making logical records available to a program one at a time after reading a block of data from the file.

A disk usually contains many files. The operating system maintains a directory of existing files on a disk. This directory contains such information as the location and name of each file. The directory information is the logical equivalent of the label record found on the tape. While the label record is an optional feature for a tape file, the directory information is a required part of creating and accessing a file on disk. Hence, the clause

LABEL RECORD IS STANDARD

usually *must* be included in the FD for a file found on disk. On come compilers (including the one used to prepare programs for this text), the LABEL RECORD IS STANDARD clause is assumed if the LABEL RECORD clause is omitted from an FD entry. On the other compilers, the LABEL RECORD clause must be included in FD entries for all files. The ANSI-74 standard for COBOL indicates that the LABEL RECORD clause is required for all FD entries. The reader must check specifications for the compiler he or she is using to determine what is required.

Blocking records for a disk file will ensure optimum performance from the computing system when programs accessing that data are executed. Documentation specifying optimum blocking factors for records depending on the record length is usually available.

The nature of magnetic tape requires the sequential storage and accessing of the records. However, because of its movable read/write mechanism, a disk has the capability for accessing data stored on any portion of the disk upon demand. This feature figures in a discussion of nonsequential file processing. For the moment we shall be concerned only with the storage of sequential files on disk. When a disk file is accessed sequentially, the operating system locates the first record in the file when the file is opened. Each successive record in the file then is located and read/written as required by the program.

The SELECT entry is used to assign a file to disk. The system-name used for a disk file varies from system to system. The logic required to create and process a sequential file is essentially independent of the device on which the file is stored. For convenience, the discussion that follows will assume that the files will be on disk, but you could make programs work equally well for tape storage simply by changing the SELECT statement.

7.3   THE OPEN STATEMENT

The OPEN statement causes the operating system to make a file available for processing. A file must be opened before any input or output operation can be performed on it. A sequential file can be opened in one of four modes: INPUT, OUTPUT, I–O, and EXTEND (Fig. 7.5).

Figure 7.5   General form of the OPEN statement

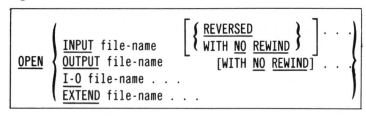

When a file is opened in INPUT mode, the records from the file are made available to the program one at a time, from first to last. The file must exist on the device specified in the SELECT statement for the file. Two options exist for tape files opened as INPUT mode: WITH NO REWIND and REVERSED. These options are ignored if the file is assigned to a disk. Ordinarily, a tape reel is rewound from the takeup reel onto its original reel and positioned at the first record in the file when the file is opened. The NO REWIND clause can be used when a reel of tape contains multiple files and you want to process each file in succession. When the first file is closed, it must not be rewound, so that the reel is left in position for the next file to be opened. The WITH NO REWIND clause would then be used to open the second file. The REVERSED option will cause the file to be positioned at its last record and read in reverse order from last to first. The REVERSED and NO REWIND options are not included in all COBOL compilers.

When a file is opened in OUTPUT mode, the file is assumed to have no data records in it. WRITE statements cause records to be placed in the file sequentially from first to last. If records already were present in the file, they would be destroyed. The WITH NO REWIND clause has the same effect here as it does for the INPUT mode.

When a file is opened in I–O (Input-Output) mode, it is assumed to exist and may be processed by READ and REWRITE statements. The REWRITE statement will cause the content of a record that has been read (and perhaps changed by the processing program) to be rewritten, thereby destroying the content of the original. This mode can be used for disk files only; it is not valid for tape files.

When a file is opened in EXTEND mode, records are written in the file following the last record in the file. When the file is opened, the operating system locates the last record in the file; any record written in the file will follow that record. EXTEND mode may not be implemented on all compilers.

7.4   THE CLOSE STATEMENT

The CLOSE statement terminates processing of a file. The file must be open at the time of execution of a CLOSE statement. After a file has been closed, no

further input or output operations may be executed. A general form of the
CLOSE statement is shown in Figure 7.6.

Figure 7.6   General form of the CLOSE statement

$$\underline{\text{CLOSE}}\text{ file-name}\left[\text{WITH}\left\{\begin{array}{c}\underline{\text{NO REWIND}}\\\underline{\text{LOCK}}\end{array}\right\}\right]\text{. . .}$$

When a file is assigned to tape, the NO REWIND clause will prevent the reel
of tape from being repositioned to the beginning of the file. Repositioning of
the tape reel (rewinding) is performed as part of the CLOSE operation if the NO
REWIND clause is omitted.

The LOCK option will prevent the current program (or any subsequent
program in the job) from reopening the file. The LOCK option should be
invoked if it would be an error for any further processing of the file to take
place. In some operating systems the LOCK phrase has the additional function
of causing the file to become permanent, if the file is being created by this
program. For these operating systems a file will be purged from the disk at
the end of the program unless the LOCK option is used.

7.5   MULTIPLE TYPES OF INPUT RECORDS

In many instances there will be more than one type of data record format in a
file to be processed. For example, suppose you wish to process a file containing records in the following two formats:

Name and Address Record

Positions
1-9	Identifying number
10-25	Name
26-40	Street address
41-50	City
51-52	State
53-57	Zip Code
58	Record identification code (1)

Time Record

Positions
1-9	Identifying number
10-15	Hours worked
16-21	Date
22-57	Blank
58	Record identification code (2)

When a file contains records having different formats, there must be some
way for the program to determine which type of record has been read after a
READ operation takes place. One way to accomplish this is to place a specific
code in a field common to the two records. In the example above, position 58
is used as a record-identification-code field. This field has the value 1 on a
name-and-address record and the value 2 on the time record.

It is possible to define the different types of input records in either the FILE section of the DATA division or in the WORKING-STORAGE section of the DATA division. Description of the records in the FILE section requires that all record descriptions be placed following the FD entry for the file, and that the names of the records be included in the DATA RECORDS clause of the FD entry. For example, the following code could be used for the preceding data file:

```
FD  DATA-FILE
    LABEL RECORDS ARE STANDARD
    DATA RECORDS ARE NAME-ADDRESS-RECORD TIME-RECORD.
01  NAME-ADDRESS-RECORD.
    03 ID-NUM-NAR       PIC 9(9).
    03 NAME-NAR         PIC X(16).
    03 STREET-ADR-NAR   PIC X(15).
    03 CITY-NAR         PIC X(10).
    03 STATE-NAR        PIC X(2).
    03 ZIP-NAR          PIC 9(5).
    03 REC-ID-NAR       PIC 9.
01  TIME-RECORD.
    03 ID-NUM-TR        PIC 9(9).
    03 HOURS-TR         PIC 9(4)V99.
    03 DATE-TR          PIC 9(6).
    03 FILLER           PIC X(37).
    03 REC-ID-TR        PIC 9.
```

Note that there is only one area in memory allocated for the data record for a given file regardless of the number of data records declared for the file. The data record area for this file may be visualized as:

When a file is read, the content of a data record is placed in the memory locations allocated as the data record area for that file. The program may then choose to use any of the descriptions of that record that have been specified. For example, if the record is a name-and-address record, then the fields NAME-NAR, STREET-ADR-NAR, CITY-NAR, and so on would be processed. However, if the record is a time record, the fields HOURS-TR and DATE-TR would be processed.

The program must decide which of the data descriptions is appropriate for this record. In our example, the decision can be made based on the content of REC-ID-NAR or REC-ID-TR, as these names describe the same field on the record. The following code could be used to make this decision:

```
PROCESS-DATA-READ.
    IF REC-ID-NAR = 1
        PERFORM PROCESS-NAME-ADDRESS-RECORD
    ELSE
        PERFORM PROCESS-TIME-RECORD.
    READ DATA-FILE
        AT END MOVE "YES" TO EOF-FLAG.
```

As there is only one memory area allocated to the data record, the content of all of the fields will change each time a new record is read; data from the new record replaces the data from the previous record. Suppose, for example, that the first record is a name-and-address record and the second record is a time record. The content of the fields NAME-NAR, STREET-ADR-NAR, CITY-NAR, and so forth will change when the second record is read, as characters from the second record now occupy the locations in the data record as read. This will cause no inconvenience if the data from the name-and-address record is moved immediately to another location when the program determines that name-and-address record has been read. In the above example, the content of the paragraph PROCESS-NAME-ADDRESS-RECORD could be as follows:

```
PROCESS-NAME-ADDRESS-RECORD.
    MOVE ID-NUM-NAR     TO ID-NUM-HOLD.
    MOVE NAME-NAR       TO NAME-HOLD.
    MOVE STREET-ADR-NAR TO STREET-ADR-HOLD.
    MOVE CITY-NAR       TO CITY-HOLD.
    MOVE STATE-NAR      TO STATE-HOLD.
    MOVE ZIP-NAR        TO ZIP-HOLD.
        .
        .
        .
```

The fields with suffix HOLD would, of course, be defined in the WORKING-STORAGE section.

When there are a great many record types, moving fields to different locations can become a nuisance. As an alternative, multiple records may be described in the WORKING-STORAGE section. Using this technique, a minimal description of the record is made in the FILE section; the only field that needs to be specified is the record identification field. Detailed description of the records is given in the WORKING-STORAGE section.

When a record is read, the contents are moved to the appropriate location, based on the record identification. For the previous example, this technique could be implemented by the following code:

```
DATA DIVISION.
FILE SECTION.
FD  DATA-FILE
    LABEL RECORDS ARE STANDARD
    DATA RECORD IS DATA-RECORD.
01  DATA-RECORD.
    03 FILLER        PIC X(79).
    03 RECORD-ID     PIC 9.
WORKING-STORAGE SECTION.
    .
    .

    .
01  NAME-ADDRESS-RECORD.
    03 ID-NUM-NAR     PIC 9(9).
    03 NAME-NAR       PIC X(16).
    03 STREET-ADR-NAR PIC X(15).
    03 CITY-NAR       PIC X(10).
    03 STATE-NAR      PIC X(2).
    03 ZIP-NAR        PIC 9(9).
01  TIME-RECORD.
    03 ID-NUM-TR      PIC 9(9).
    03 HOURS-TR       PIC 9(4)V99.
    03 DATE-TR        PIC 9(6).
PROCEDURE DIVISION.
1000-MAIN-ROUTINE.
    .
    .

    .
    READ DATA-FILE
        AT END MOVE "YES" TO EOF-FLAG.
    PERFORM 2010-PROCESS-DATA-READ
        UNTIL EOF-FLAG = "YES".
    .
    .

    .
2010-PROCESS-DATA-READ.
    IF RECORD-ID = 1
       MOVE DATA-RECORD TO NAME-ADDRESS-RECORD
       PERFORM PROCESS-NAME-ADDRESS-RECORD
    ELSE
       IF RECORD-ID = 2
          MOVE DATA-RECORD TO TIME-RECORD
          PERFORM PROCESS-TIME-RECORD
       ELSE
          PERFORM DATA-RECORD-ERROR.
    READ DATA-FILE
        AT END MOVE "YES" TO EOF-FLAG.
```

One advantage to the preceding method is that the contents of NAME–ADDRESS–RECORD are changed only when a new record of the same type is read; a disadvantage is the necessity of allocating memory locations in addition to the record area required for the file. If records are lengthy and/or there are many different types of records in the file, this excess memory requirement may be a significant factor, particularly in systems with limited memory available.

7.6 INTRODUCTION TO SORTING

A set of data items in either ascending sequence or descending sequence are said to be in *sorted order*. *Sorting* refers to the process of transforming unsorted data items into sorted order. For example, consider the data items:

16, 25, 90, 42, 70

They are neither in ascending sequence (each item smaller than its successor) nor in descending sequence (each item larger than its successor). If the data items were rearranged as

16, 25, 42, 70, 90

they would be sorted into ascending sequence. If the data items were rearranged as

90, 70, 42, 25, 16

they would be sorted into descending sequence.

In a data processing situation it is often desirable to have data records in some sequence based on one or more fields within the record. The field used for this sequencing is called the *key* field. For example, consider the following set of data records:

Employee Number	Name		Age	Department
123	DOE	JOHN	32	3
492	SMITH	MARY	40	4
479	JAMES	JOHN	19	4
333	QUE	SUSY	40	2
695	BROWN	JAMES	25	2

This data could be sorted into sequence in a number of different ways. Each of the four fields could be used individually as a key field. If the employee number is chosen as the key field and descending sequence is desired, the resulting set of data would be:

	Employee Number	Name		Age	Department
Descending sequence	695	BROWN	JAMES	25	2
	492	SMITH	MARY	40	4
	479	JAMES	JOHN	19	4
	333	QUE	SUSY	40	2
	123	DOE	JOHN	32	3

Using the name as the key field and sorting for ascending sequence would result in:

Employee Number		Name		Age	Department
695		BROWN	JAMES	25	2
123	Ascending	DOE	JOHN	32	3
479	sequence	JAMES	JOHN	19	4
333		QUE	SUSY	40	2
492		SMITH	MARY	40	4

It is possible to sort a file using more than one key field. For example, we might want a listing of the above data to be grouped by department number. Also, within each department, the data should be listed in ascending sequence based on employee name. In this case, the department number is called the *primary key* (or *major key*) and the name field is the *secondary key* (or *minor key*). The resulting data would be:

Employee Number		Name		Age	Department	
695		BROWN	JAMES	25	2	
333	Ascending	QUE	SUSY	40	2	Ascending
123	sequences	DOE	JOHN	32	3	sequence
479	(three)	JAMES	JOHN	19	4	
492		SMITH	MARY	40	4	

Many other combinations using two or more key fields could conceivably be of value depending on the logical requirements of the problem being solved.

7.7 FILE SEQUENCE CHECKING

For many types of applications it is imperative that a file be organized in sequence by a key field. Many versions of COBOL have a SORT verb which allows you to resequence a file. The COBOL sort facility is described later in this chapter. Prior to executing a program which depends on a file being in a particular sequence one could

1) sort the file or
2) remove out of sequence records from the file

Sorting a file, particularly a large file is likely to be very time-consuming. It may be advantageous to perform a much simpler sequence check and remove out-of-sequence records from the file. The out-of-sequence records (if any) could be treated as new data and used to update the file by facilities already available in the system. This latter approach is particularly useful if the probability of finding out-of-sequence records is small. This technique is used in the following program example.

Figure 7.7 Printer spacing chart for Program 7.1

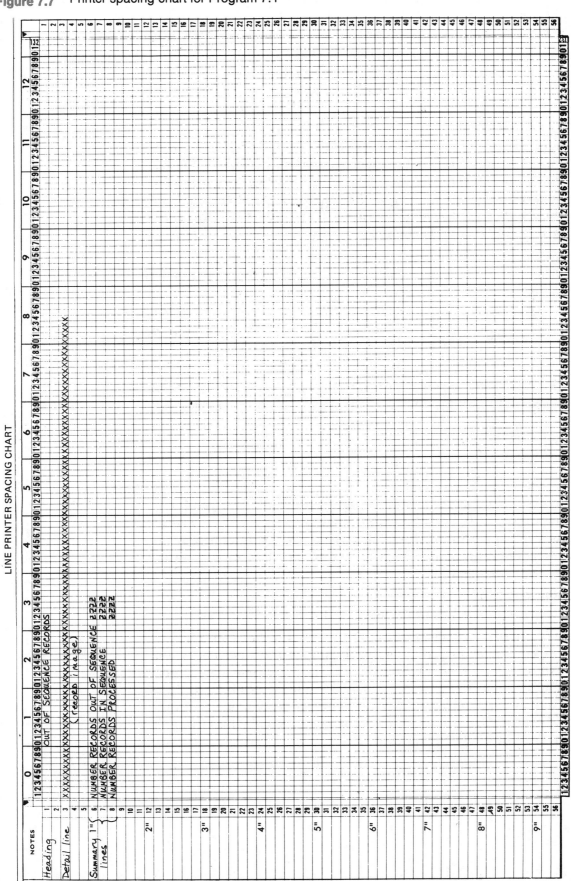

Problem Statement

Data records in the file CUSTOMER-FILE contain the following fields:

Positions	Content
1-9	Account number
10-29	Name
30-44	Street address
45-59	City
60-61	State
62-66	Zip code
67-72	Amount owed (2 decimal places)
73-78	Credit maximum (2 decimal places)
79-84	Date of last payment (*mmddyy*)

The file should be in sequence by account number. Write a program to process this file placing all properly sequenced records in a file ACCOUNTS-RECEIVABLE-FILE. Create a report as shown in Figure 7.7 showing those records that are out of sequence.

Problem Analysis

This program must process one input file (CUSTOMER-FILE) and produce two output files—ACCOUNTS-RECEIVABLE-FILE and a report which we shall call ERROR-FILE. In order to detect an out-of-sequence record, it is necessary to compare the content of account number on the record just read with the account number of the record just processed. This task will require the use of a holding field (ACCOUNT-NUMBER-HOLD) which will be initialized to the value of the account number of the first record. During the processing of succeeding records the program must compare the content of account number from the record just read to the content of ACCOUNT-NUMBER-HOLD. If the account number from the record is greater than ACCOUNT-NUMBER-HOLD, the record can be written to ACCOUNTS-RECEIVABLE-FILE and the account number from that record moved to ACCOUNT-NUMBER-HOLD. If the account number from the record is not greater than ACCOUNT-NUMBER-HOLD, then the record is out of sequence and must be written on ERROR-FILE. The report requires two counters: the number of records out of sequence and the number of records in sequence. These counters must be incremented at appropriate points in the processing of each data record. After all records have been processed, the summary lines can be written. A plan for this program is shown in Figure 7.8.

Figure 7.8 Plan for sequenced file creation program

Main logic

    Open files
    Read customer file
    Write accounts receivable record from input record
    Add 1 to records in sequence
    Move customer number from input record to customer number hold
    Read customer file
    Do Write read until end of file
    Write summary lines
    Close files
    Stop

Write read

> If account number from input record > account number hold
>> Add 1 to records in sequence
>> Write accounts receivable record from input record
>> Move account number from input record to account number hold
> Else
>> Add 1 to records out of sequence
>> Write error record from input record
> End If
> Read customer file

Problem Solution

The program that performs this task is shown in Program 7.1 with structure diagram in Figure 7.9. Note in this program that two records from the input file must be read before entering the processing loop. If the second record had not been read, then the value of ACCOUNT-NUMBER-IR and ACCOUNT-NUMBER-HOLD would be equal at line 13900 since the value of ACCOUNT-NUMBER-IR would not have been replaced by data from a new record. This would cause the first record to be considered out of sequence. Note also the importance of moving the value of ACCOUNT-NUMBER-IR to ACCOUNT-NUMBER-HOLD each time an in sequence record is processed (see line 14100). This causes the value of ACCOUNT-NUMBER-HOLD to store the account number of the preceding record each time through the loop. If this statement had been omitted, the effect would have been to compare each record to the account number from the first record only; not to the account number of the preceding record.

Program 7.1 Sequenced file creation program

```
100     IDENTIFICATION DIVISION.
200
300     PROGRAM-ID. FILE-CREATION.
400     AUTHOR. GARY GLEASON.
500
600     ENVIRONMENT DIVISION.
700
800     CONFIGURATION SECTION.
900
1000    SOURCE-COMPUTER.
1100    OBJECT-COMPUTER.
1200
1300    INPUT-OUTPUT SECTION.
1400
1500    FILE-CONTROL.
1600
1700        SELECT CUSTOMER-FILE ASSIGN TO DISK.
1800        SELECT ACCOUNTS-RECEIVABLE-FILE ASSIGN TO DISK.
1900        SELECT ERROR-FILE ASSIGN TO PRINTER.
2000
```

Program 7.1   (continued)

```
2100      DATA DIVISION.
2200
2300      FILE SECTION.
2400
2500      FD  CUSTOMER-FILE
2600          BLOCK CONTAINS 84 CHARACTERS
2700          LABEL RECORDS ARE STANDARD
2800          DATA RECORD IS INPUT-RECORD.
2900
3000      01  INPUT-RECORD.
3100          02  ACCOUNT-NUMBER-IR       PIC 9(9).
3200          02  NAME-IR                 PIC X(20).
3300          02  ADDRESS-IR.
3400              03  STREET-IR           PIC X(15).
3500              03  CITY-IR             PIC X(15).
3600              03  STATE-IR            PIC X(2).
3700              03  ZIP-CODE-IR         PIC 9(5).
3800          02  AMOUNT-OWED-IR          PIC 9(4)V99.
3900          02  CREDIT-MAXIUM-IR        PIC 9(4)V99.
4000          02  DATE-OF-LAST-PAYMENT-IR.
4100              03  MONTH-IR            PIC 99.
4200              03  DAY-IR              PIC 99.
4300              03  YEAR-IR             PIC 99.
4400
4500      FD  ACCOUNTS-RECEIVABLE-FILE
4600          BLOCK CONTAINS 84 CHARACTERS
4700          LABEL RECORDS ARE STANDARD
4800          DATA RECORD IS ACCOUNTS-RECEIVABLE-RECORD.
4900
5000      01  ACCOUNTS-RECEIVABLE-RECORD.
5100          02  ACCOUNT-NUMBER-ARR      PIC 9(9).
5200          02  NAME-ARR                PIC X(20).
5300          02  ADDRESS-ARR.
5400              03  STREET-ARR          PIC X(15).
5500              03  CITY-ARR            PIC X(15).
5600              03  STATE-ARR           PIC X(2).
5700              03  ZIP-CODE-ARR        PIC 9(5).
5800          02  AMOUNT-OWED-ARR         PIC 9(4)V99.
5900          02  CREDIT-MAXIUM-ARR       PIC 9(4)V99.
6000          02  DATE-OF-LAST-PAYMENT-ARR.
6100              03  MONTH-ARR           PIC 99.
6200              03  DAY-ARR             PIC 99.
6300              03  YEAR-ARR            PIC 99.
6400
6500      FD  ERROR-FILE
6600          LABEL RECORDS ARE OMITTED
6700          DATA RECORD IS PRINT-LINE.
6800
6900      01  PRINT-LINE          PIC X(132).
7000
```

Program 7.1 (continued)

```
7100        WORKING-STORAGE SECTION.
7200
7300        01  FLAGS.
7400            02  EOF-FLAG              PIC X(3) VALUE "NO".
7500
7600        01  HOLD-FIELDS.
7700            02  ACCOUNT-NUMBER-HOLD   PIC 9(9) VALUE ZERO.
7800
7900        01  TOTALS.
8000            02  RECORDS-OUT-OF-SEQUENCE  PIC 9(4) VALUE ZERO.
8100            02  RECORDS-IN-SEQUENCE      PIC 9(4) VALUE ZERO.
8200            02  RECORDS-PROCESSED        PIC 9(4) VALUE ZERO.
8300
8400        01  MAIN-HEADING.
8500            02  FILLER               PIC X(9) VALUE SPACES.
8600            02  FILLER               PIC X(23) VALUE
8700              "OUT OF SEQUENCE RECORDS".
8800
8900        01  SUMMARY-LINE-1.
9000            02  FILLER               PIC X(31) VALUE
9100              "NUMBER RECORDS OUT OF SEQUENCE".
9200            02  FILLER               PIC X VALUE SPACES.
9300            02  OUT-OF-SEQUENCE-SL1  PIC Z(4).
9400
9500        01  SUMMARY-LINE-2.
9600            02  FILLER               PIC X(26) VALUE
9700              "NUMBER RECORDS IN SEQUENCE".
9800            02  FILLER               PIC X(5) VALUE SPACES.
9900            02  IN-SEQUENCE-SL2      PIC Z(4).
10000
10100       01  SUMMARY-LINE-3.
10200           02  FILLER               PIC X(24) VALUE
10300             "NUMBER RECORDS PROCESSED".
10400           02  FILLER               PIC X(7) VALUE SPACES.
10500           02  RECORDS-PROCESSED-SL3  PIC Z(4).
10600
10700       PROCEDURE DIVISION.
10800
10900       1000-MAIN-LOGIC.
11000
11100           PERFORM 2000-INITIALIZATION.
11200           PERFORM 3000-WRITE-READ
11300               UNTIL EOF-FLAG = "YES".
11400           PERFORM 7000-WRITE-SUMMARY.
11500           PERFORM 9000-TERMINATION.
11600           STOP RUN.
11700
11800       2000-INITIALIZATION.
11900
12000           OPEN INPUT CUSTOMER-FILE
12100               OUTPUT ACCOUNTS-RECEIVABLE-FILE
12200                     ERROR-FILE.
12300           WRITE PRINT-LINE FROM MAIN-HEADING AFTER PAGE.
12400           PERFORM 2500-FIRST-RECORD.
12500
```

```
12600    2500-FIRST-RECORD.
12700
12800        READ CUSTOMER-FILE
12900            AT END MOVE "YES" TO EOF-FLAG.
13000        ADD 1 TO RECORDS-IN-SEQUENCE.
13100        MOVE INPUT-RECORD TO ACCOUNTS-RECEIVABLE-RECORD.
13200        WRITE ACCOUNTS-RECEIVABLE-RECORD.
13300        MOVE ACCOUNT-NUMBER-IR TO ACCOUNT-NUMBER-HOLD.
13400        READ CUSTOMER-FILE
13500            AT END MOVE "YES" TO EOF-FLAG.
13600
13700    3000-WRITE-READ.
13800
13900        IF  ACCOUNT-NUMBER-IR > ACCOUNT-NUMBER-HOLD
14000            ADD 1 TO RECORDS-IN-SEQUENCE
14100            MOVE ACCOUNT-NUMBER-IR TO ACCOUNT-NUMBER-HOLD
14200            WRITE ACCOUNTS-RECEIVABLE-RECORD FROM INPUT-RECORD
14300        ELSE
14400            ADD 1 TO RECORDS-OUT-OF-SEQUENCE
14500            WRITE PRINT-LINE FROM INPUT-RECORD AFTER 1.
14600        READ CUSTOMER-FILE
14700            AT END MOVE "YES" TO EOF-FLAG.
14800
14900    7000-WRITE-SUMMARY.
15000
15100        ADD RECORDS-OUT-OF-SEQUENCE RECORDS-IN-SEQUENCE
15200            GIVING RECORDS-PROCESSED.
15300        MOVE RECORDS-OUT-OF-SEQUENCE TO OUT-OF-SEQUENCE-SL1.
15400        MOVE RECORDS-IN-SEQUENCE      TO IN-SEQUENCE-SL2.
15500        MOVE RECORDS-PROCESSED        TO RECORDS-PROCESSED-SL3.
15600        WRITE PRINT-LINE FROM SUMMARY-LINE-1 AFTER 1.
15700        WRITE PRINT-LINE FROM SUMMARY-LINE-2 AFTER 1.
15800        WRITE PRINT-LINE FROM SUMMARY-LINE-3 AFTER 1.
15900
16000    9000-TERMINATION.
16100
16200        CLOSE CUSTOMER-FILE
16300            ACCOUNTS-RECEIVABLE-FILE LOCK
16400            ERROR-FILE.
```

Figure 7.9 Structure diagram for Program 7.1

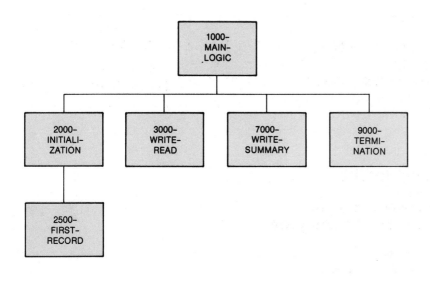

7.8 THE SORT WORK-FILE

The COBOL programmer may make use of the COBOL SORT feature in order to sort a file on one or more key fields into any desired sequence. The SORT statement is used in the PROCEDURE division. It specifies the source of the records to be sorted, the key field(s), the sequencing desired (ascending or descending), the destination for the sorted records, and the name of a *sort work-file* that will be used by the computing system in the performance of the sort. Setting up the sort work-file must be done in the ENVIRONMENT and DATA division in preparation for utilization of the SORT statement in the PROCEDURE division.

A sequential disk file is required as a sort work-file for utilization of the COBOL SORT command. First, the SORT statement causes records to be read from some source file and copied into the sort work-file. Second, the records are sorted and then, third, copied from the sort work-file into some specified destination. Setting up the sort work-file requires a SELECT sentence in the ENVIRONMENT division for the file in exactly the same manner as for any other file. The description of the file in the DATA division requires the use of an SD (Sort Description) rather than an FD entry. The general form for an SD entry is shown in Figure 7.10.

Figure 7.10 General form of the SD entry

```
SD    file-name
         [RECORD CONTAINS [integer-1 TO] integer-2 CHARACTERS]
      [DATA {RECORD IS    } data-name. . .].
            {RECORDS ARE  }
```

The file description used in an SD entry is much the same as in an FD entry. The record described for the sort work-file must contain data-names for any desired key fields.

Example

Problem Statement

Write a program to sort a file (EMPLOYEE-FILE) that contains data described in the preceding example. Sort in ascending sequence by employee name. The sorted data should be placed in another file (SORTED-EMPLOYEE-FILE).

Problem Analysis

The program will require three files: the two files described in the problem statement and a sort work-file.

Problem Solution

Program 7.2 performs the desired function. In this case the sort work-file is called SORT-WORK-FILE, however any suitable name could have been used. Note that the SELECT entry for the sort-work-file varied slightly from the SELECT entry for other files. This requirement is system dependent; the entry required by your system may vary. The following section describes the SORT statement in detail (lines 6100-6400).

Program 7.2   Sort program with USING and GIVING

```
100      IDENTIFICATION DIVISION.
200
300      PROGRAM-ID. EMPLOYEE-SORT1.
400      AUTHOR. HORN.
500
600      ENVIRONMENT DIVISION.
700
800      CONFIGURATION SECTION.
900
1000     SOURCE-COMPUTER.
1100     OBJECT-COMPUTER.
1200
1300     INPUT-OUTPUT SECTION.
1400
1500     FILE-CONTROL.
1600
1700         SELECT EMPLOYEE-FILE ASSIGN TO DISK.
1800         SELECT SORT-WORK-FILE ASSIGN TO SORT DISK.
1900         SELECT SORTED-EMPLOYEE-FILE ASSIGN TO DISK.
2000
```

Program 7.2 (continued)

```
2100    DATA DIVISION.
2200
2300    FILE SECTION.
2400
2500    FD  EMPLOYEE-FILE
2600        LABEL RECORDS ARE STANDARD
2700        DATA RECORD IS EMPLOYEE-RECORD.
2800
2900    01  EMPLOYEE-RECORD.
3000        03  EMP-NUM-ER              PIC 9(9).
3100        03  EMP-NAME-ER             PIC X(20).
3200        03  EMP-AGE-ER              PIC 99.
3300        03  EMP-DEPT-ER             PIC 9.
3400        03  FILLER                 PIC X(52).
3500
3600    SD  SORT-WORK-FILE
3700        DATA RECORD IS SORT-WORK-RECORD.
3800
3900    01  SORT-WORK-RECORD.
4000        03 EMP-NUM-SWR              PIC 9(9).
4100        03 EMP-NAME-SWR             PIC X(20).
4200        03 EMP-AGE-SWR              PIC 99.
4300        03 EMP-DEPT-SWR             PIC 9.
4400        03 FILLER                   PIC X(52).
4500
4600    FD  SORTED-EMPLOYEE-FILE
4700        LABEL RECORDS ARE STANDARD
4800        DATA RECORD IS SORTED-EMPLOYEE-RECORD.
4900
5000    01  SORTED-EMPLOYEE-RECORD.
5100        03 EMP-NUM-SER              PIC 9(9).
5200        03 EMP-NAME-SER             PIC X(20).
5300        03 EMP-AGE-SER              PIC 99.
5400        03 EMP-DEPT-SER             PIC 9.
5500        03 FILLER                   PIC X(52).
5600
5700    PROCEDURE DIVISION.
5800
5900    1000-MAIN.
6000
6100        SORT SORT-WORK-FILE
6200            ON ASCENDING KEY EMP-NAME-SWR
6300            USING  EMPLOYEE-FILE
6400            GIVING SORTED-EMPLOYEE-FILE.
6500    STOP RUN.
```

7.9   THE SORT STATEMENT

The SORT statement is used in the PROCEDURE division to activate the sort procedure. A general form for the SORT statement is shown in Figure 7.11.

Figure 7.11   General form of SORT with USING and GIVING

```
SORT       sort-work-file-name

       ON  { ASCENDING  } KEY data-name-1 . . .
           { DESCENDING }
      [ON  { ASCENDING  } KEY data-name-2 . . .] . . .
           { DESCENDING }
              USING file-name-1  . . .
              GIVING file-name-2
```

The *sort-work-file-name* must be specified in an SD entry in the DATA DIVISION. The ON. . .KEY clause gives the programmer the choice of specifying ASCENDING sequence or DESCENDING sequence for the records. The data-name(s) must be defined within the record associated with the sort work-file. If more than one key field is specified, the first field is the primary key and the following fields are secondary keys. The USING clause specifies the source of the data, the GIVING clause specifies the destination of the sorted data records. In execution, the SORT command performs the following three functions in sequential order:

1) Read the file or files specified in the USING clause and place the records in the sort work-file.
2) Sort the sort work-file on the specified key field(s).
3) Copy the sorted records from the sort work-file into the file specified in the GIVING clause.

For example, the following code could be used to sort the data defined above into alphabetic sequence by name:

```
SORT   SORT-WORK-FILE
          ON ASCENDING KEY EMP-NAME-SWR
          USING EMPLOYEE-FILE
          GIVING SORTED-EMPLOYEE-FILE.
```

To sort the records into ascending alphabetic sequence within departments, the following code could be used:

```
SORT   SORT-WORK-FILE
          ON ASCENDING KEY EMP-DEPT-SWR EMP-NAME-SWR
          USING SORTED-EMPLOYEE-FILE
          GIVING SORTED-EMPLOYEE-FILE.
```

In this example the department number is declared to be the primary key and the employee's name is a secondary key. As many secondary keys as desired may be specified. Furthermore, it is possible to include as many ON. . .KEY clauses as desired. For example, suppose we want to sort the data into descending sequence by age within ascending department number sequence. In this example, the arrangement of the data desired is:

Employee Number	Name		Age			Department	
333	QUE	SUSY	40	Descending	2		
695	BROWN	JAMES	25	sequences	2	Ascending	
123	DOE	JOHN	53	(three)	3	sequence	
492	SMITH	MARY	40		4		
497	JAMES	JOHN	19		4		

The required code is:

```
SORT  SORT-WORK-FILE
      ON ASCENDING KEY EMP-DEPT-SWR
      ON DESCENDING KEY EMP-AGE-SWR
      USING SORTED-EMPLOYEE-FILE
      GIVING SORTED-EMPLOYEE-FILE.
```

The sequence of clauses governs the sequence of keys—primary to secondary.

It is possible to sort more than one file with the same SORT statement. For example, to sort DATA-FILE and NEW-DATA-FILE into ascending sequence by employee number, the following statement could be used:

```
SORT  SORT-WORK-FILE
      ON ASCENDING-KEY EMPLOYEE-NUM-SWR
      USING DATA-FILE NEW-DATA-FILE
      GIVING SORTED-EMPLOYEE-FILE.
```

This statement would have the effect of merging the records from the two input files into one output file. This facility can be used to add records to an existing file while preserving the sequencing of the records.

For example, to add the records contained in NEW-DATA-FILE to those contained in SORTED-EMPLOYEE-FILE, the following statement could be used:

```
SORT  SORT-WORK-FILE
      ON ASCENDING KEY EMPLOYEE-NUM-SWR
      USING SORTED-EMPLOYEE-FILE NEW-DATA-FILE
      GIVING SORTED-EMPLOYEE-FILE.
```

The new version of SORTED-EMPLOYEE-FILE will contain all of the records from the old version plus all of the records from NEW-DATA-FILE and will be in sequence by employee number.

7.10   A COMPLETE EXAMPLE

Problem Statement

The procurement system of a company uses a file containing purchase request records. Each record corresponds to an item that must be purchased by the company. Each record contains the following fields:

Supplier identification number
Item number
Item description
Item cost
Order quantity

Before purchase orders to be sent to the various suppliers can be printed, it is necessary to resequence the file so that all of the requests for a supplier are grouped together. It is also useful to have the records for each supplier in sequence by item number.

Problem Analysis

Two files must be defined in the program: the file containing the data to be sorted (PURCHASE-REQUEST-FILE) and a sort work-file (SORT-FILE). PURCHASE-REQUEST-FILE will be specified in both the USING and GIVING clauses of the SORT statement. Two keys will be needed in the ON. . .KEY clause of the SORT statement. The primary key will be the supplier identification number, the secondary key will be the item number. In this way the new file will have all records for each supplier in a continuous group. Within each group the records will be in sequence by item number.

Problem Solution

The required program is shown in Program 7.3. An alternative way in which the sort-work record could have been described is:

```
01   SORT-RECORD.
     03 SUPPLIER-ID-NUMBER-SR    PIC X(5).
     03 ITEM-NUMBER-SR           PIC X(5).
     03 FILLER                   PIC X(74).
```

Only fields that are to be used as key fields in the SORT verb must be described in the sort-work record. Describing other fields does, however, make it easier to later modify the SORT statement to sort on other fields.

Program 7.3   Sort of purchase request file

```
100      IDENTIFICATION DIVISION.
200
300      PROGRAM-ID. PURCH-REQUEST-SORT2.
400      AUTHOR. GARY.
500
600      ENVIRONMENT DIVISION.
700
800      CONFIGURATION SECTION.
900
1000     SOURCE-COMPUTER.
1100     OBJECT-COMPUTER.
1200
1300     INPUT-OUTPUT SECTION.
1400
1500     FILE-CONTROL.
1600
1700         SELECT PURCHASE-REQUEST-FILE ASSIGN TO DISK.
1800         SELECT SORT-FILE ASSIGN TO SORT DISK.
1900
```

Program 7.3 (continued)

```
2000     DATA DIVISION.
2100
2200     FILE SECTION.
2300
2400     FD  PURCHASE-REQUEST-FILE
2500         LABEL RECORDS ARE STANDARD
2600         DATA RECORD IS PURCHASE-REQUEST-RECORD.
2700
2800     01  PURCHASE-REQUEST-RECORD.
2900         03  SUPPLIER-ID-NUMBER-PRR          PIC X(5).
3000         03  ITEM-NUMBER-PRR                 PIC X(5).
3100         03  ITEM-DESCRIPTION-PRR            PIC X(10).
3200         03  ITEM-COST-PRR                   PIC 999V99.
3300         03  ORDER-QUANTITY-PRR              PIC 9(3).
3400         03  FILLER                          PIC X(56).
3500
3600     SD  SORT-FILE
3700         DATA RECORD IS SORT-RECORD.
3800
3900     01  SORT-RECORD.
4000         03  SUPPLIER-ID-NUMBER-SR           PIC X(5).
4100         03  ITEM-NUMBER-SR                  PIC X(5).
4200         03  ITEM-DESCRIPTION-PRR            PIC X(10).
4300         03  ITEM-COST-SR                    PIC 999V99.
4400         03  ORDER-QUANTITY-SR               PIC 9(3).
4500         03  FILLER                          PIC X(56).
4600
4700     PROCEDURE DIVISION.
4800
4900     1000-MAIN.
5000
5100         SORT SORT-FILE
5200             ON ASCENDING KEY SUPPLIER-ID-NUMBER-SR
5300                              ITEM-NUMBER-SR
5400             USING  PURCHASE-REQUEST-FILE
5500             GIVING PURCHASE-REQUEST-FILE.
5600         STOP RUN.
```

7.11 PROCEDURE DIVISION SECTIONS

The SORT feature also provides a means by which a programmer can construct his/her own routines for storing the records to be sorted on the sort work-file (an INPUT PROCEDURE) and copying the sort records from the sort work-file (an OUTPUT PROCEDURE). The routine to be used in this fashion must be placed in a separate PROCEDURE DIVISION section.

Up to this point the PROCEDURE DIVISION of a program has consisted only of a sequence of paragraphs and no mention has been made of sections in the PROCEDURE DIVISION. It is possible to segment a PROCEDURE DIVISION into named sections, each of which consists of one or more paragraphs. The paragraphs in a section usually are related in some way. For example, they may perform related computations or they may constitute an input or output routine. It is the latter usage which is important when writing an INPUT PROCEDURE or OUTPUT PROCEDURE for a SORT verb. In order to segment paragraphs of a PROCEDURE DIVISION, each group of paragraphs must be preceded by a section header which has the general form:

```
section-name SECTION.
```

For example, suppose a PROCEDURE DIVISION is made up of the paragraphs 1100-MAIN-LOGIC, 2100-INITIALIZATION, 2200-CONTROL, 2300-TERMINATION, 3100-READ-FILE-A, and 3200-READ-FILE-B. The following code divides these paragraphs into three sections: 1000-MAIN, 2000-SECONDARY, and 3000-INPUT-OUTPUT:

```
PROCEDURE DIVISION.
1000-MAIN-SECTION.
1100-MAIN-LOGIC.
     .
     .
     .

2000-SECONDARY-SECTION.
2100-INITIALIZATION.
     .
     .
     .

2200-CONTROL.
     .
     .
     .

2300-TERMINATION.
     .
     .
     .

3000-INPUT-OUTPUT SECTION.
3100-READ-FILE-A.
     .
     .
     .

3200-READ-FILE-B.
     .
     .
     .
```

Dividing a PROCEDURE DIVISION into sections in no way affects the logic of a program or the way in which statements within a program are executed. For example, a statement in one section may PERFORM a paragraph in another section; after execution of the last statement in the paragraph, control passes back to the PERFORM statement.

If a section is referenced in a PERFORM statement, the paragraphs of that section will be executed in succession and the program will return to the PERFORM statement only after the last statement in the last paragraph of the section has been completed. For example, if the statement

```
PERFORM 3000-INPUT-OUTPUT
```

were executed in the above example, all of the statements in 3100-READ-FILE-A and 3200-READ-FILE-B would be executed in sequence. Only after both paragraphs have been completed will the program return to the statement following the PERFORM.

In the theory of structured programming, a *module* is defined as a procedure that carries out a well-defined task and has a single entry point and a single exit. All of our programs thus far have been composed of single paragraph modules. Each paragraph carried out a well-defined function; execution of each paragraph began at its first statement and continued through its last. Dividing a PROCEDURE DIVISION into sections enables us to construct modules consisting of more than one paragraph; the module begins with the first statement of the first paragraph and concludes with the last statement of the last paragraph. It is often advantageous to build multiparagraph modules because each individual paragraph still is usable as a single paragraph module. For example, in the above program it is still possible to use statements such as PERFORM 3100-READ-FILE-A or PERFORM 3200-READ-FILE-B; in either case, control returns to the PERFORM statement when the last paragraph has been completed.

The programmer must exercise caution when writing sections containing several paragraphs. If the entire section is performed, when the first paragraph of the section is complete control passes to the next paragraph, and so on. Only by branching to the last paragraph in the section can the module return control to the performing statement. This usually necessitates the use of the GO TO statement.

7.12   GO TO AND EXIT

The general form of the GO TO statement is shown in Figure 7.12.

Figure 7.12   General form of the GO TO statement

```
GO TO { paragraph-name }
      { section-name   }
```

When the GO TO statement is executed, an immediate branch is made to the specified paragraph/section. Control does not return automatically at the end of the execution of the paragraph/section as it does when branching takes place via the PERFORM statement. The GO TO statement causes an unconditional branch with *no* provision for return; the PERFORM statement causes an unconditional branch *with* provision for return.

Unstructured programs frequently use GO TO statements. Structured programs also use the GO TO statement, in a more restricted and disciplined fashion. A primary usage of the GO TO statement in structured COBOL programming is to transfer control to the last paragraph in a multiparagraph section that has been performed. Typically, the last paragraph contains the single statement EXIT and serves only to return control to the PERFORM statement. A typical situation is shown on the next page.

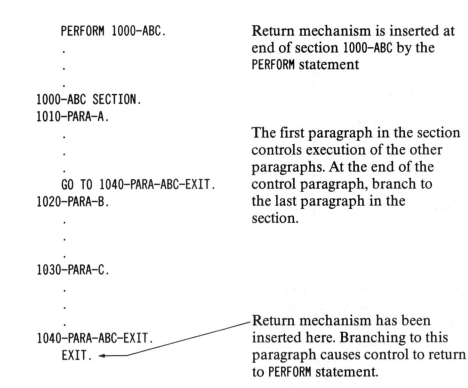

```
        PERFORM 1000-ABC.
              .
              .
              .
        1000-ABC SECTION.
        1010-PARA-A.
              .
              .
              .
           GO TO 1040-PARA-ABC-EXIT.
        1020-PARA-B.
              .
              .
              .
        1030-PARA-C.
              .
              .
              .
        1040-PARA-ABC-EXIT.
           EXIT.
```

Return mechanism is inserted at end of section 1000-ABC by the PERFORM statement

The first paragraph in the section controls execution of the other paragraphs. At the end of the control paragraph, branch to the last paragraph in the section.

Return mechanism has been inserted here. Branching to this paragraph causes control to return to PERFORM statement.

The technique used above requires that the last paragraph in the section exist, yet there is no work for it to accomplish. COBOL syntax requires that each paragraph have at least one sentence. The EXIT sentence is provided for this contingency. The general form of EXIT is:

```
EXIT.
```

When used, the EXIT sentence must be the *only* sentence in the paragraph.

The EXIT sentence is used in paragraphs which are required by COBOL syntax but which otherwise serve no function. When large programs are designed and developed in parts, it is often necessary to include in early versions of the program paragraphs which will be developed later. In order to begin testing the program at early stages of development programmers frequently include unfinished paragraphs with an EXIT statement as their only content. In this way the program can be compiled and tested without syntax errors resulting from references to missing paragraphs. Of course, the program will not perform all of its required functions until all dummy paragraphs have been replaced with code required to perform their designated functions.

7.13 INPUT/OUTPUT PROCEDURES

A complete form of the SORT statement is shown in Figure 7.13.

Figure 7.13 General form of the SORT verb

```
SORT    sort-work-file-name
        ON { ASCENDING  } KEY   data-name-1
             DESCENDING
        [ON { ASCENDING  } KEY   data-name-2]. . .
              DESCENDING
        { USING       file-name-1 . . .            }
        { INPUT PROCEDURE  IS section-name-1       }
        { GIVING      file-name-2                   }
        { OUTPUT PROCEDURE  IS section-name-2      }
```

When the INPUT PROCEDURE option is used, the SORT procedure performs the specified INPUT PROCEDURE section prior to sorting the records in the sort work-file. It is the task of the section to store the desired records on the sort work-file. When the OUTPUT PROCEDURE option is used, the SORT procedure performs the specified OUTPUT PROCEDURE section after sorting the records in the sort work-file. The records in the sort work-file are available to the program for further processing in any desired fashion.

The RELEASE and RETURN statements are used, instead of ordinary WRITE and READ statements. The RELEASE statement has the general form shown in Figure 7.14.

Figure 7.14 General form of the RELEASE statement

```
RELEASE sort-record-name [FROM data-name]
```

The RELEASE statement is used instead of a WRITE statement, and causes a record to be written onto the sort work-file.

The RETURN statement has the general form shown in Figure 7.15.

Figure 7.15 General form of the RETURN statement

```
RETURN sort-file-name RECORD [INTO data-name]
       AT END statement . . .
```

It is used instead of a READ statement. The RETURN statement causes a record to be read from a sort work-file. The statements in the AT END clause are executed when the end of the sort work-file is reached.

For example, Program 7.4 could be used to sort the employee data described in Section 7.7.

Program 7.4   Input procedure example

```
100      IDENTIFICATION DIVISION.
200
300      PROGRAM-ID. EMPLOYEE-SORT3.
400      AUTHOR. HORN.
500
600      ENVIRONMENT DIVISION.
700
800      CONFIGURATION SECTION.
900
1000     SOURCE-COMPUTER.
1100     OBJECT-COMPUTER.
1200
1300     INPUT-OUTPUT SECTION.
1400
1500     FILE-CONTROL.
1600
1700         SELECT EMPLOYEE-FILE ASSIGN TO DISK.
1800         SELECT SORT-WORK-FILE ASSIGN TO SORT DISK.
1900         SELECT SORTED-EMPLOYEE-FILE ASSIGN TO DISK.
2000
2100     DATA DIVISION.
2200
2300     FILE SECTION.
2400
2500     FD  EMPLOYEE-FILE
2600         LABEL RECORDS ARE STANDARD
2700         DATA RECORD IS EMPLOYEE-RECORD.
2800
2900     01  EMPLOYEE-RECORD.
3000         03  EMP-NUM-ER               PIC 9(9).
3100         03  EMP-NAME-ER              PIC X(20).
3200         03  EMP-AGE-ER               PIC 99.
3300         03  EMP-DEPT-ER              PIC 9.
3400         03  FILLER                   PIC X(52).
3500
3600     SD  SORT-WORK-FILE
3700         DATA RECORD IS SORT-WORK-RECORD.
3800
3900     01  SORT-WORK-RECORD.
4000         03  EMP-NUM-SWR              PIC 9(9).
4100         03  EMP-NAME-SWR             PIC X(20).
4200         03  EMP-AGE-SWR              PIC 99.
4300         03  EMP-DEPT-SWR             PIC 9.
4400         03  FILLER                   PIC X(52).
4500
```

```
4600    FD  SORTED-EMPLOYEE-FILE                        Program 7.4 (continued)
4700        LABEL RECORDS ARE STANDARD
4800        DATA RECORD IS SORTED-EMPLOYEE-RECORD.
4900
5000    01  SORTED-EMPLOYEE-RECORD.
5100        03  EMP-NUM-SER                 PIC 9(9).
5200        03  EMP-NAME-SER                PIC X(20).
5300        03  EMP-AGE-SER                 PIC 99.
5400        03  EMP-DEPT-SER                PIC 9.
5500        03  FILLER                      PIC X(52).
5600
5700    WORKING-STORAGE SECTION.
5800
5900    01  EOF                             PIC 9 VALUE 0.
6000
6100    PROCEDURE DIVISION.
6200
6300    0000-MAIN SECTION.
6400
6500    1000-CONTROL.
6600
6700        SORT SORT-WORK-FILE
6800            ON ASCENDING KEY EMP-NAME-SWR
6900            INPUT PROCEDURE IS 2000-READ-AND-STORE-RECORDS
7000            GIVING SORTED-EMPLOYEE-FILE.
7100        STOP RUN.
7200
7300    2000-READ-AND-STORE-RECORDS SECTION.
7400
7500    2010-READ-STORE-CONTROL.
7600
7700        OPEN INPUT EMPLOYEE-FILE.
7800        READ EMPLOYEE-FILE AT END MOVE 1 TO EOF.
7900        PERFORM 2020-RELEASE-AND-READ UNTIL EOF = 1.
8000        CLOSE EMPLOYEE-FILE.
8100        GO TO 2030-READ-STORE-EXIT.
8200
8300    2020-RELEASE-AND-READ.
8400
8500        RELEASE SORT-WORK-RECORD FROM EMPLOYEE-RECORD.
8600        READ EMPLOYEE-FILE AT END MOVE 1 TO EOF.
8700
8800    2030-READ-STORE-EXIT.
8900
9000        EXIT.
```

Note that the INPUT PROCEDURE in this program is completely self-contained (i.e., it does not perform any paragraph outside the section). This conforms to a restriction on INPUT/OUTPUT PROCEDURES: An INPUT or OUTPUT PROCEDURE must not transfer control (via GO TO or PERFORM) to a point outside the procedure.

For the example above, the SORT verb causes the following sequence of tasks to be executed:

1) The section 2000-READ-AND-STORE-RECORDS is PERFORMed. At the end of the procedure, control returns to the SORT verb.
2) The file SORT-WORK-FILE is sorted.
3) The content of SORT-WORK-FILE is copied onto SORTED- EMPLOYEE-FILE.

In this example, there seems to be no advantage to using the INPUT PROCEDURE option, as the USING option would have an identical effect. However, note that the logic contained in 2000-READ-AND-STORE-RECORDS could process the data contained in DATA-RECORD in any desired way. For example, a listing of the data could be produced, or fields within the data record could be validated, or any desired computations could be performed.

Suppose you want to print a listing of the records and to sort the records alphabetically by name within descending age sequence. Program 7.5 could be used.

Program 7.5   Output procedure example

```
100     IDENTIFICATION DIVISION.
200
300     PROGRAM-ID. EMPLOYEE-SORT4.
400     AUTHOR. HORN.
500
600     ENVIRONMENT DIVISION.
700
800     CONFIGURATION SECTION.
900
1000    SOURCE-COMPUTER.
1100    OBJECT-COMPUTER.
1200
1300    INPUT-OUTPUT SECTION.
1400
1500    FILE-CONTROL.
1600
1700        SELECT SORT-WORK-FILE ASSIGN TO SORT DISK.
1800        SELECT SORTED-EMPLOYEE-FILE ASSIGN TO DISK.
1900        SELECT HARDCOPY-FILE ASSIGN TO PRINTER.
2000
2100    DATA DIVISION.
2200
2300    FILE SECTION.
2400
2500    SD  SORT-WORK-FILE
2600        DATA RECORD IS SORT-WORK-RECORD.
2700
2800    01  SORT-WORK-RECORD.
2900        03 EMP-NUM-SWR              PIC 9(9).
3000        03 EMP-NAME-SWR             PIC X(20).
3100        03 EMP-AGE-SWR              PIC 99.
3200        03 EMP-DEPT-SWR             PIC 9.
3300        03 FILLER                   PIC X(52).
3400
```

Program 7.5 (continued)

```
3500   FD  SORTED-EMPLOYEE-FILE
3600       LABEL RECORDS ARE STANDARD
3700       DATA RECORD IS SORTED-EMPLOYEE-RECORD.
3800
3900   01  SORTED-EMPLOYEE-RECORD.
4000       03 EMP-NUM-SER                  PIC 9(9).
4100       03 EMP-NAME-SER                 PIC X(20).
4200       03 EMP-AGE-SER                  PIC 99.
4300       03 EMP-DEPT-SER                 PIC 9.
4400       03 FILLER                       PIC X(52).
4500
4600   FD  HARDCOPY-FILE
4700       LABEL RECORDS ARE OMITTED
4800       DATA RECORD IS PRINT-RECORD.
4900
5000   01  PRINT-RECORD                    PIC X(132).
5100
5200   WORKING-STORAGE SECTION.
5300
5400   01  EOF-SWF                         PIC 9 VALUE 0.
5500
5600   PROCEDURE DIVISION.
5700
5800   0000-MAIN SECTION.
5900
6000   1000-CONTROL.
6100
6200       SORT SORT-WORK-FILE
6300           ON DESCENDING KEY EMP-AGE-SWR
6400           ON ASCENDING  KEY EMP-NAME-SWR
6500           USING SORTED-EMPLOYEE-FILE
6600           OUTPUT PROCEDURE IS 4000-PRINT-FILE-LISTING.
6700       STOP RUN.
6800
6900   4000-PRINT-FILE-LISTING SECTION.
7000
7100   4010-PRINT-LISTING-CONTROL.
7200
7300       OPEN OUTPUT HARDCOPY-FILE.
7400       RETURN SORT-WORK-FILE AT END MOVE 1 TO EOF-SWF.
7500       PERFORM 4020-WRITE-RETURN UNTIL EOF-SWF = 1.
7600       CLOSE HARDCOPY-FILE.
7700       GO TO 4030-PRINT-LIST-EXIT.
7800
7900   4020-WRITE-RETURN.
8000
8100       WRITE PRINT-RECORD FROM SORT-WORK-RECORD AFTER 1.
8200       RETURN SORT-WORK-FILE AT END MOVE 1 TO EOF-SWF.
8300
8400   4030-PRINT-LIST-EXIT.
8500
8600       EXIT.
```

In this program the following sequence of events will occur:

1) The content of SORTED-EMPLOYEE-FILE will be copied onto SORT-WORK-FILE.
2) The SORT-WORK-FILE will be sorted into prescribed sequence.
3) The section 4000-PRINT-FILE-LISTING will be executed. At the termination of this procedure, control passes to the statement following the SORT statement.

Of course, it is possible to specify both an INPUT PROCEDURE and an OUTPUT PROCEDURE in a SORT statement. An example of this code would be:

```
SORT   SORT-WORK-FILE
       ON ASCENDING KEY EMP-NAME-SWR
       INPUT PROCEDURE 2000-READ-AND-STORE-RECORD
       OUTPUT PROCEDURE 4000-PRINT-FILE-LISTING.
```

Note that in an INPUT/OUTPUT PROCEDURE it is necessary to OPEN the files from which data is to be read or onto which data is to be written, but it is *not* necessary to OPEN the sort work-file. The sort work-file *must not* be opened or closed. The operations are a built-in part of the SORT verb.

7.14   SORT UTILITIES

The task of sorting is fundamental to any data processing system. Most computer installations have utility programs available to perform this task. A utility program is a program designed to perform a specified task (or group of related tasks) on data of any description. In order to use a utility program, the user specifies the exact nature of the data files and the specifics of the task and allows the utility program to do the rest. For example, in order to use a typical sort utility to perform the simple sort tasks described in Programs 7.2 and 7.3 user would specify:

- the name of the input file and the characteristics of its records
- the name of the output file and the characteristics of its records
- the name of the output file and the characteristics of its records
- the location and number of the key fields
- the nature of the data in the key fields (numeric or alphanumeric)
- the desired sequencing

Typically, it is much quicker to write the specifications for the sort utility than to code a COBOL program to perform the same task. More important, the sorting algorithm used by the utility may be more efficient in use of time and/or space than the sort procedure used by COBOL. This is possible because the utility is usually more complex than the routine used to carry out a COBOL SORT; the utility can therefore use a more sophisticated sort algorithm, which can accomplish the sort process in less time. Also, because the utility is more complex, it is able to make better use of space on the mass storage device than the relatively simpler routine supplied by the COBOL SORT verb.

Most major manufacturers of computers provide sort utilities. There are many other companies, specializing in software rather than hardware, that sell sort utilities. Some of the better-known packages are listed in Figure 7.16. Manufacturers of these packages usually advertise that their software is more efficient or easy to use than others, particularly the utilities supplied by the computer manufacturers. A large percentage of commercial data processing computer installations own one or more sort packages distributed by outside software companies.

Figure 7.16 Some common sort/merge software packages

Package Name	Supplier	Comments
Alternate Sort	The Alternate Source	TRS-80/4 under TRS-DOS
CA SORT	Computer Associates	IBM mainframes
Autosort-C/CR (Sort Merge Select)	Computer Control Systems, Inc.	CP/M operating system
SORT/1000	Corporate Computer Systems, Inc.	Hewlett-Packard 100
SORT PLUS	Ecosoft, Inc.	Hewlett-Packard 100
FSORT3/VSORT	Evans Griffiths and Hart, Inc.	DEC PDP-11/VAX-11
SORT ROUTINE	Inmark	Perkin Elmer OS
SORT-I-PLUS	Oregon Software, Inc.	DEC VAX
SPEEDSORT/11	Pennington Systems, Inc.	DEC PDP-11
WORKPERFECT SORTER	Satellite Software Inter.	IBM PC
FLEX-I-SORT	Bean Computers, Inc.	CP/M & MP/M
INFO-SORT	Info Pros	IBM PC
SUPERSORT	Micropro International Corp.	CP/M & MS/DOS
SYNCSORT	Syncsort, Inc.	IBM OS/VS
PRIME	Prime	Primos
SORMER	Sormer Sort	Primos

7.15 DEBUG CLINIC

The SORT verb and multiparagraph sections are very powerful features; however, there are a number of restrictions on their use. Failure to observe these restrictions will result in debugging problems. Some of the most common errors result from failure to observe the following rules:

1) *Sort work-files must not be opened or closed.* The SORT verb takes care of opening and closing the sort work-file. The OPEN and CLOSE statements are invalid for sort work-files.

2) *Use RETURN and RELEASE rather than READ and WRITE for a sort work-file.* Use of READ and WRITE verbs for a sort work-file is invalid. Use of RETURN and RELEASE for ordinary files is also invalid.

3) *Define the sort work-file with an SD rather than an FD entry.* A file defined with an FD entry cannot be used as a sort work-file.

4) *An INPUT/OUTPUT PROCEDURE cannot contain a SORT statement.* The SORT verb causes the execution of a specific routine; this routine cannot be asked to execute itself.

5) *A file used in the USING or GIVING clause must not be open.* A file to be used in USING or GIVING must be closed at the time the SORT statement is executed. Of course, these files may be opened and processed in other parts of the program.

6) *A sort work-file must be assigned to disk.* A special designation used in the system name may be used in the ASSIGN entry for a sort work-file. The reader must check local documentation for specific details.

7) *An* INPUT/OUTPUT PROCEDURE *may not reference a paragraph or section outside the procedure.* INPUT/OUTPUT PROCEDUREs must be wholly self-contained sections; there must not be any PERFORM or GO TO statements that address paragraphs or sections external to the section being used to specify the INPUT/OUTPUT PROCEDURE.

8) *In order to exit a multiparagraph section, branch to its last paragraph.* When a section is executed either with a PERFORM statement or SORT statement, the return mechanism is inserted following the last statement of the last paragraph of the section. The GO TO statement is used to branch from the controlling paragraph to the last paragraph to effect a return; omission of the GO TO statement will result in the sequential execution of the paragraphs in the section. Omission of the GO TO statement almost always will be an error, because the paragraphs which will be executed have already been performed under control of the first paragraph of the section.

9) *Use the* GO TO *statement only to branch to the last paragraph of a multiparagraph section.* Unrestricted use of the GO TO statement results in unstructured program modules. This usage of the GO TO is necessary to create a single entry/single exit module from a section that is composed of more than one paragraph.

7.16 SELF-TEST EXERCISES

1. Draw structure diagrams for Programs 7.4 and 7.5. How will you handle multiparagraph sections? (Structure diagrams should reflect relationships among program modules rather than paragraphs.)

2. List the actions taken by the SORT statements in lines 5100 through 5500 of Program 7.3.

3. Fill in the blanks:
   a. A sort work-file is defined in the FILE SECTION by a(n) _____.
   b. A field used to govern the sequence of records in a file is called a(n) _____.
   c. A primary difference between the GO TO and PERFORM statements is _____.
   d. A PROCEDURE DIVISION section is declared by _____.
   e. In structured programming a procedure that carried out a well-defined task has a single entry and a single exit is called a(n) _____.
   f. One permitted use of the GO TO statement is to _____.
   g. The equivalent of READ for a sort work-file is _____.
   h. The equivalent of WRITE for a sort work-file is _____.
   i. The EXIT statement is used as _____.
   j. Two statements that cannot be used in an INPUT/OUTPUT PROCEDURE are _____ and _____.
   k. In order to exit a multiparagraph section, a program must _____.
   l. A sort work-file must be assigned to a(n) _____.

4. Consider the following file descriptions:

```
FILE SECTION.
FD  DATA-FILE
    LABEL RECORDS ARE STANDARD
    DATA RECORD IS DATA-RECORD.
01  DATA-RECORD.
    03 SS-NUM-DR    PIC 9(9).
    03 NAME-DR      PIC X(20).
    03 ST-ADDR-DR   PIC X(20).
    03 CITY-DR      PIC X(10).
    03 STATE-DR     PIC XX.
    03 ZIP-DR       PIC 9(5).
SD  SORT-FILE
    DATA RECORD IS SORT-RECORD.
01  SORT-RECORD.
    03 SS-NUM-SR    PIC 9(9).
    03 NAME-SR      PIC X(20).
    03 ST-ADDR-SR   PIC X(20).
    03 CITY-SR      PIC X(10).
    03 STATE-SR     PIC XX.
    03 ZIP-SR       PIC 9(5).
```

Assume that DATA-FILE is assigned to DISK.
a. Write a SORT statement to sort DATA-FILE into ascending sequence by social security number.
b. Write a SORT statement to sort DATA-FILE into sequence by zip code, and within each zip code order the records alphabetically by name.

5. Add the following file description to those given in Exercise 4:

```
FD  NEW-DATA-FILE
    LABEL RECORDS ARE STANDARD
    DATA RECORD IS NEW-DATA-RECORD.
01  NEW-DATA-RECORD.
    03 NAME-NDR     PIC X(20).
    03 SS-NUM-NDR   PIC X(20).
    03 ZIP-NDR      PIC 9(5).
    03 ST-ADDR-NDR  PIC X(20).
    03 CITY-NDR     PIC X(10).
    03 STATE-NDR    PIC XX.
```

Write a SORT statement to sort NEW-DATA FILE into ascending sequence by state. Place the sorted data in DATA- FILE.

6. Write a SORT statement using the files defined in Exercises 4 and 5 to merge the content of DATA-FILE and NEW-DATA-FILE, placing the resulting file into DATA-FILE in descending sequence by zip code.

7.17 PROGRAMMING EXERCISES

1. Modify Program 7.3 to include an OUTPUT PROCEDURE that lists all of the data in PURCHASE-REQUEST-FILE.

2. Modify Program 7.3 to include an INPUT PROCEDURE that selects from PURCHASE-REQUEST-FILE only items costing under $10.00.

3. The records in an employee file contain (among other items) the employee name, sex, date of birth, and date of hire by a company. Write COBOL programs to produce these required reports:
   a. A list sorted by seniority.
   b. An alphabetic list of all employees over 60 years old.
   c. Separate lists of men and women sorted in alphabetic order.
   d. A list of employees sorted into descending order by seniority (highest seniority first).
   e. Separate lists of men and women sorted into descending order by seniority.

4. The records of an inventory file contain the following items: product code, description, selling price, cost, number on hand. Write COBOL programs to:
   a. List the items sorted by product code.
   b. List the items that have a markup in excess of 20 percent, sorted by product code.
   c. List the "big ticket" items (selling price greater than $200) sorted by description.

REPORTS AND CONTROL BREAKS 8

8.1 REPORT REQUIREMENTS

Businesses require many reports, so it is no surprise that many COBOL programs are written to produce reports that summarize and make available the data in files. There are several features shared by such report writing programs that require special logic. Among these features and requirements are:

Feature	Requirement
1) Headings	Is there a major heading?
	What column headings are required?
2) Page Numbers	Are pages to be numbered?
3) Page Totals	Are page totals required for some items?
4) Subtotals	Are subtotals required for segments of data?
	How many levels of subtotals are required?
5) Grand Totals	What items require grand totals?

In this chapter we shall concentrate on program logic necessary to fulfill these requirements.

8.2 REPORT-WRITING TECHNIQUES

When you write a program to generate a report, you will want to give the reader guidance in interpreting the information contained in the report. Usually you will want to print a heading at the top of every page. Occasionally a major heading—the company name and the report title, for example—is required on the first page but not on succeeding pages. Generally there will be column headings on every page to identify the data contained on the lines of the report.

A very useful technique to control the generation of headings is *line counting*. A typical page of computer output contains 64 lines of print, although this varies greatly among computing systems. (Check the size of the printed page generated on your computer.) The program uses a line counter to keep track of the number of lines of print generated. When a line is written, an appropriate value (1 for single spacing, 2 for double spacing, and so on) is added to the line counter. After each output operation, the value of the line counter is tested against the maximum number of lines allowed on a page. If the page is full, headings are written at the top of a new page, the line counter is re-initialized, and processing proceeds.

Page numbers often are required in reports. The writing of page numbers can be accomplished by the routine used to print the report headings. A page counter is initialized to value zero. Each time the heading routine is entered, the page counter is incremented by 1, and this value is moved to the appropriate field on the page heading line.

Page totals are totals of data items occurring on a page. Data-names used to accumulate page totals should be re-initialized in the page total routine. Page totals should be printed when the program detects that a page is full before page headings for a new page are printed.

Grand totals are printed after all data has been processed. As each record is processed, items are added to appropriate totals. When end-of-file is detected, both page totals (if any) and grand totals should be printed. The last page is usually not a full page of data; hence, page totals would not have been printed at the usual point in the program.

8.3 PROGRAM EXAMPLE

Problem Statement

Management of the ABC Company desires a report showing each employee's name, employee number, department and salary. The report should have appropriate headings on each page and pages should be numbered. Each page should list the total of the salaries of the employees on that page; the final page should list the total number of employees and the total salaries of all employees. The data for the required report is contained in the file ALPHABETIC-FILE, which contains records in alphabetic sequence for all employees of the company. A printer spacing chart for the required report is shown in Figure 8.1.

Problem Analysis

This problem requires the following major report features:

Major heading at top of each page
Page number
Column heading on each page
Page total for salary
Grand total for salary and number of employees

An appropriate technique to control pagination and page numbers is line counting. This technique requires a field LINE-COUNT defined in WORKING-STORAGE and initialized to value zero. Additional data items in WORKING-STORAGE are required for the page total (PAGE-TOTAL), the grand total of salaries (SALARY-TOTAL), and the number of employees (NUMBER-OF-EMPLOYEES). All of these fields are used as accumulators and hence must be initialized to zero. An

Figure 8.1 Printer spacing chart for alphabetic employee report

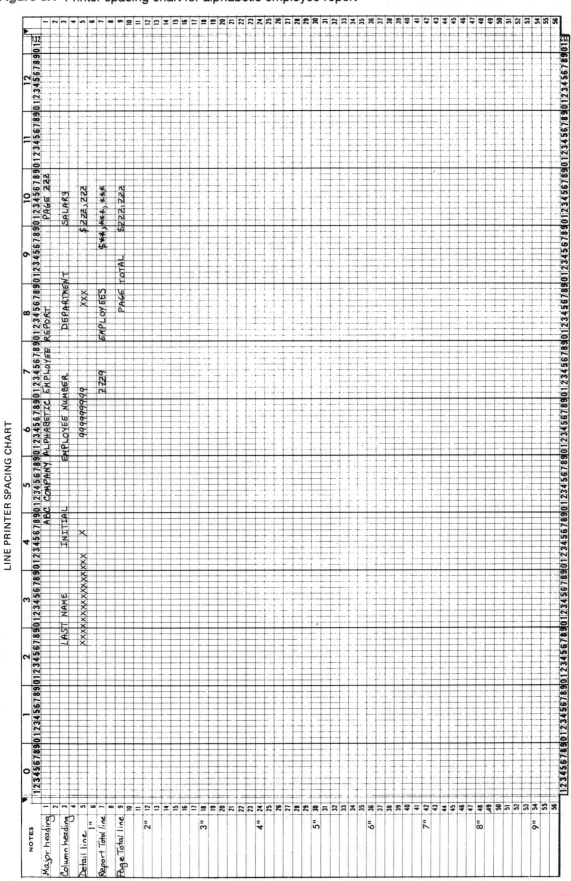

additional field is required for the actual page number (PAGE-COUNT). This item will be initialized to value zero and incremented by one each time a page heading is written. We shall assume that there are 46 lines of print per page, a constant coded into WORKING-STORAGE using the data name LINES-PER-PAGE. (This practice enables the report to be readily adapted to pages of different length without changing any code in the PROCEDURE DIVISION.)

The program must produce page headings before any data has been processed. Thereafter, before any output operation is performed, the content of LINE-COUNT is compared to LINES-PER-PAGE. If the content of LINE-COUNT is greater than LINE-PER-PAGE this means that the page is full of data and new page headings must be printed before the current output can be printed. The page heading procedure must increment PAGE-COUNT, write the page headings, and re-initialize LINE-COUNT to the number of lines used in producing the page headings—in this case 3 lines are used. After output is written, the value of LINE-COUNT must be incremented by the number of lines used. A preliminary plan for the desired program showing the technique required for pagination is shown in Figure 8.2.

Figure 8.2   Preliminary plan for alphabetic report program

Main logic

        Open files
        Do Write headings
        Read alphabetic file
        Do Control until end of file
        Close files
        Stop

Control

        If line count > lines per page
                Do Write headings
        End If
        Write detail line
        Add 1 to line count
        Read alphabetic file

Write headings

        Add 1 to page count
        Write major heading
        Write column heading
        Move 3 to line count

Note that in this preliminary plan there is no provision for page totals or grand totals. Page totals must be written after a page break is detected (i.e., when the program determines that a page is full) and before page headings for a new page are produced. After the page total is written, the accumulator PAGE-TOTAL must be re-initialized to zero for the next page. The processing of each record must include adding the salary to the accumulator's PAGE-TOTAL and SALARY-TOTAL and adding one to the counter NUMBER-OF-EMPLOYEES. The revised plan for this program shown in Figure 8.3 includes the logic required for these features.

Figure 8.3   Final plan for alphabetic report program

Main logic

> Open files
> Do Write headings
> Read alphabetic file
> Do Control until end of file
> Do Page total output
> Write summary line
> Close files
> Stop

Control

> If line count > lines per page
> > Do Page total output
> > Do Write headings
> End If
> Add salary to total salary
> Add 1 to number employees
> Add salary to page total
> Write detail line
> Add 1 to line count
> Read alphabetic file

Write headings

> Add 1 to page count
> Write major heading
> Write column heading
> Move 3 to line count

Page total output

> Write page total line
> Move 0 to page total

Problem Solution

The program for this problem is shown in Program 8.1 with structure diagram in Figure 8.4. Note the way in which the requirements for the report are implemented in the program. The requirement that a heading be produced at the top of each page is handled by performing 8000-WRITE-HEADINGS from 2000-INITIALIZATION (see line 12300) to produce the heading at the top of the first page. Page headings at the top of succeeding pages are produced by checking the value of LINE-COUNT in 3000-CONTROL (see lines 12800-13000). When the value of LINE-COUNT exceeds LINES-PER-PAGE, headings are written again. Page numbers are implemented using the counter PAGE-COUNT, which is initialized to zero at line 4800 and incremented each time headings are written at line 16300. The page totals are implemented using an accumulator PAGE-TOTAL, which is initialized to zero at line 5200, incremented at line 15300, printed each time a new page heading is produced (see line 12900), and re-initialized to zero after it is printed (line 18000). The grand totals are implemented using the accumulator SALARY-TOTAL, which is initialized to zero at line 5100, and the counter NUMBER-OF-EMPLOYEES, which is initialized to zero at line 5000. As each record is processed, the value of IR-SALARY is added to SALARY-TOTAL (line 15200) and NUMBER-OF-EMPLOYEES is incremented (line 15100). The fields are printed after end-of-file has been reached (see line 18500).

Program 8.1   Alphabetic employee report program

```
100      IDENTIFICATION DIVISION.
200
300      PROGRAM-ID. APHABETIC-LIST.
400      AUTHOR. GARY GLEASON.
500
600      ENVIRONMENT DIVISION.
700
800      CONFIGURATION SECTION.
900
1000     SOURCE-COMPUTER.
1100     OBJECT-COMPUTER.
1200
1300     INPUT-OUTPUT SECTION.
1400
1500     FILE-CONTROL.
1600
1700         SELECT ALPHABETIC-FILE ASSIGN TO DISK.
1800         SELECT ALPHABETIC-LIST ASSIGN TO PRINTER.
1900
2000     DATA DIVISION.
2100
2200     FILE SECTION.
2300
2400     FD  ALPHABETIC-FILE
2500         LABEL RECORDS ARE STANDARD
2600         DATA RECORD IS INPUT-RECORD.
2700
2800     01  INPUT-RECORD.
2900         02  IR-NAME              PIC X(16).
3000         02  IR-INITIAL           PIC X.
3100         02  IR-EMPLOYEE-NUMBER    PIC 9(9).
3200         02  IR-DEPARTMENT        PIC X(3).
3300         02  IR-SALARY            PIC 9(6).
3400         02  FILLER               PIC X(45).
3500
3600     FD  ALPHABETIC-LIST
3700         LABEL RECORDS ARE OMITTED
3800         DATA RECORD IS PRINT-LINE.
3900
4000     01  PRINT-LINE               PIC X(132).
4100
4200     WORKING-STORAGE SECTION.
4300
4400     01  CONSTANTS.
4500         03 LINES-PER-PAGE        PIC 99 VALUE 46.
4600
```

Program 8.1 (continued)

```
4700    01  ACCUMULATED-TOTALS.
4800        03  PAGE-COUNT              PIC 999 VALUE ZERO.
4900        03  LINE-COUNT             PIC 999 VALUE ZERO.
5000        03  NUMBER-OF-EMPLOYEES    PIC 999 VALUE ZERO.
5100        03  SALARY-TOTAL          PIC 9(8) VALUE ZERO.
5200        03  PAGE-TOTAL            PIC 9(6) VALUE ZERO.
5300
5400    01  FLAGS.
5500        02  EOF-FLAG               PIC X(3) VALUE "NO".
5600            88  END-OF-FILE    VALUE "YES".
5700
5800    01  MAJOR-HEADING.
5900        02  FILLER                 PIC X(47) VALUE SPACES.
6000        02  FILLER                 PIC X(11) VALUE "ABC COMPANY".
6100        02  FILLER                 PIC X    VALUE SPACES.
6200        02  FILLER                 PIC X(10) VALUE "ALPHABETIC".
6300        02  FILLER                 PIC X    VALUE SPACES.
6400        02  FILLER                 PIC X(8) VALUE "EMPLOYEE".
6500        02  FILLER                 PIC X    VALUE SPACES.
6600        02  FILLER                 PIC X(6) VALUE "REPORT".
6700        02  FILLER                 PIC X(15) VALUE SPACES.
6800        02  FILLER                 PIC X(5) VALUE "PAGE ".
6900        02  MH-PAGE-NUMBER         PIC ZZZ.
7000
7100    01  SUBHEADING.
7200        02  FILLER                 PIC X(26) VALUE SPACES.
7300        02  FILLER                 PIC X(9) VALUE "LAST NAME".
7400        02  FILLER                 PIC X(8) VALUE SPACES.
7500        02  FILLER                 PIC X(7) VALUE "INITIAL".
7600        02  FILLER                 PIC X(8) VALUE SPACES.
7700        02  FILLER                 PIC X(15) VALUE "EMPLOYEE NUMBER".
7800        02  FILLER                 PIC X(8) VALUE SPACES.
7900        02  FILLER                 PIC X(10) VALUE "DEPARTMENT".
8000        02  FILLER                 PIC X(8) VALUE SPACES.
8100        02  FILLER                 PIC X(6) VALUE "SALARY".
8200
8300    01  DETAIL-LINE.
8400        02  FILLER                 PIC X(26) VALUE SPACES.
8500        02  DL-NAME                PIC X(16).
8600        02  FILLER                 PIC X(3)  VALUE SPACES.
8700        02  DL-INITIAL             PIC X.
8800        02  FILLER                 PIC X(14) VALUE SPACES.
8900        02  DL-EMPLOYEE-NUMBER     PIC 9(9).
9000        02  FILLER                 PIC X(15) VALUE SPACES.
9100        02  DL-DEPARTMENT          PIC X(3).
9200        02  FILLER                 PIC X(10) VALUE SPACES.
9300        02  DL-SALARY              PIC  $ZZZ,ZZZ.
9400
9500    01  SUMMARY-LINE.
9600        02  FILLER                 PIC X(70) VALUE SPACES.
9700        02  SL-NUMBER-OF-EMPLOYEES PIC ZZZ9.
9800        02  FILLER                 PIC X(5) VALUE SPACES.
9900        02  FILLER                 PIC X(9) VALUE "EMPLOYEES".
10000       02  FILLER                 PIC X(7) VALUE SPACES.
10100       02  SL-SALARY-TOTAL        PIC $***,***,***.
```

Program 8.1 (continued)

```
10200
10300     01  PAGE-TOTAL-LINE.
10400         02  FILLER              PIC X(85) VALUE SPACES.
10500         02  FILLER              PIC X(10) VALUE "PAGE TOTAL".
10600         02  FILLER              PIC X(4) VALUE SPACES.
10700         02  PTL-PAGE-TOTAL      PIC $ZZZ,ZZZ.
10800
10900     PROCEDURE DIVISION.
11000
11100     1000-MAIN-LOGIC.
11200
11300         PERFORM 2000-INITIALIZATION.
11400         PERFORM 3000-CONTROL
11500             UNTIL END-OF-FILE.
11600         PERFORM 9700-TERMINATION.
11700         STOP RUN.
11800
11900     2000-INITIALIZATION.
12000
12100         OPEN INPUT ALPHABETIC-FILE
12200              OUTPUT ALPHABETIC-LIST.
12300         PERFORM 8000-WRITE-HEADINGS.
12400         PERFORM 4000-READ.
12500
12600     3000-CONTROL.
12700
12800         IF LINE-COUNT > LINES-PER-PAGE
12900             PERFORM 9500-PAGE-TOTAL-OUTPUT
13000             PERFORM 8000-WRITE-HEADINGS.
13100         PERFORM 5000-MOVE-INPUT-FIELDS.
13200         PERFORM 6000-CALCULATIONS.
13300         PERFORM 7000-WRITE-DETAIL-LINE.
13400         PERFORM 4000-READ.
13500
13600     4000-READ.
13700
13800         READ ALPHABETIC-FILE
13900             AT END MOVE "YES" TO EOF-FLAG.
14000
14100     5000-MOVE-INPUT-FIELDS.
14200
14300         MOVE IR-NAME            TO DL-NAME.
14400         MOVE IR-INITIAL         TO DL-INITIAL.
14500         MOVE IR-EMPLOYEE-NUMBER TO DL-EMPLOYEE-NUMBER.
14600         MOVE IR-SALARY          TO DL-SALARY.
14700         MOVE IR-DEPARTMENT      TO DL-DEPARTMENT.
14800
14900     6000-CALCULATIONS.
15000
15100         ADD 1 TO NUMBER-OF-EMPLOYEES.
15200         ADD IR-SALARY TO SALARY-TOTAL.
15300         ADD IR-SALARY TO PAGE-TOTAL.
15400
```

Program 8.1 *(continued)*

```
15500    7000-WRITE-DETAIL-LINE.
15600
15700        MOVE DETAIL-LINE TO PRINT-LINE.
15800        WRITE PRINT-LINE AFTER 2 LINES.
15900        ADD 2 TO LINE-COUNT.
16000
16100    8000-WRITE-HEADINGS.
16200
16300        ADD 1 TO PAGE-COUNT.
16400        MOVE PAGE-COUNT              TO MH-PAGE-NUMBER.
16500        WRITE PRINT-LINE FROM MAJOR-HEADING AFTER PAGE.
16600        WRITE PRINT-LINE FROM SUBHEADING AFTER 2 LINES.
16700        MOVE 3 TO LINE-COUNT.
16800
16900    9000-WRITE-SUMMARY-LINE.
17000
17100        MOVE NUMBER-OF-EMPLOYEES     TO SL-NUMBER-OF-EMPLOYEES.
17200        MOVE SALARY-TOTAL            TO SL-SALARY-TOTAL.
17300        MOVE SUMMARY-LINE            TO PRINT-LINE.
17400        WRITE PRINT-LINE AFTER 3 LINES.
17500
17600    9500-PAGE-TOTAL-OUTPUT.
17700
17800        MOVE PAGE-TOTAL TO PTL-PAGE-TOTAL.
17900        WRITE PRINT-LINE FROM PAGE-TOTAL-LINE AFTER 2.
18000        MOVE 0 TO PAGE-TOTAL.
18100
18200    9700-TERMINATION.
18300
18400        PERFORM  9500-PAGE-TOTAL-OUTPUT.
18500        PERFORM  9000-WRITE-SUMMARY-LINE.
18600        CLOSE ALPHABETIC-FILE
18700             ALPHABETIC-LIST.
```

Figure 8.4   Structure diagram for Program 8.1

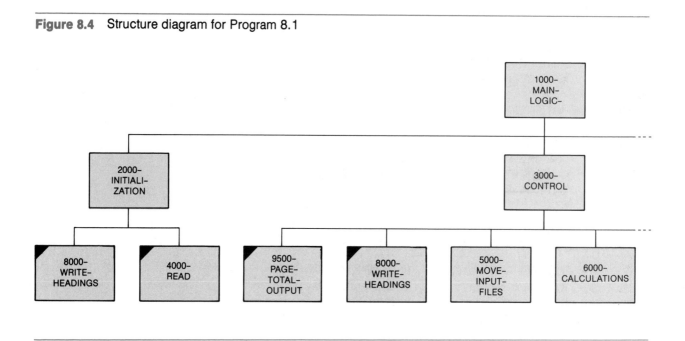

8.4   ADDITIONAL OUTPUT TECHNIQUES

The WRITE statement for the printer has some powerful options which were
not discussed in the earlier chapter and which are often useful in writing
reports. A general form of the WRITE statement is shown in Figure 8.5.

Figure 8.5   General form of the WRITE statement for the printer

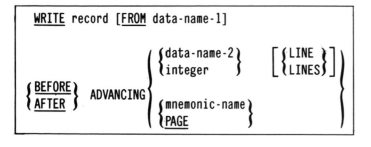

We have already discussed and illustrated the use of the *integer* and PAGE
options. The use of a *data-name-2* in the BEFORE/AFTER clause will cause the
system to advance a number of lines equal to the value of *data-name-2*. For
example, the code

```
MOVE 3 TO SPACING-COUNT.
WRITE PRINT-REC AFTER ADVANCING SPACING-COUNT.
```

is equivalent to

```
WRITE PRINT-REC AFTER ADVANCING 3.
```

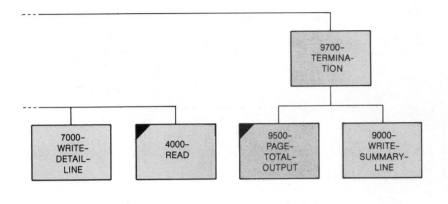

The use of a data-name in the BEFORE/AFTER clause gives the program considerable flexibility in the spacing of output lines without requiring extra output statements.

The flow of paper through a printer is controlled by a carriage control tape (Fig. 8.6). A carriage control tape is glued into a continuous loop and placed inside the printer mechanism, where a special device senses holes punched in various positions of the tape. A carriage control tape is divided into twelve channels. A hole punched in channel 1 typically denotes the top of a page of print; a hole punched in channel 12 denotes the bottom of a page. Typically, other channels are punched to correspond to positions on special preprinted forms (such as checks, invoices, or statements) that will be used for output operations. When the PAGE option is used, the printer begins spacing paper forward until the first channel punch is sensed on the carriage control tape.

By using the mnemonic option in the BEFORE/AFTER clause, the program can execute an advance to any desired channel punch. The mnemonic must be declared in the SPECIAL-NAMES paragraph of the ENVIRONMENT DIVISION. The general form of this paragraph is shown in Figure 8.7.

Figure 8.6 Carriage control tape

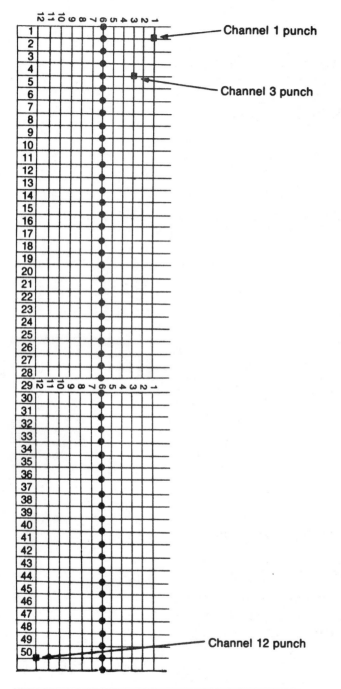

Figure 8.7 General form of the SPECIAL NAMES entry

```
SPECIAL-NAMES.
    function-name IS mnemonic-name. . .
```

The purpose of the *mnemonic-name* is to assign a meaningful name to the technical function to be performed. Mnemonic-names are governed by the same rules as other COBOL data-names; however, mnemonic-names should be as descriptive as possible of the function to be performed. Typical mnemonic-names would be:

```
TOP-OF-PAGE
BOTTOM-OF-PAGE
BEGINNING-OF-INVOICE-ITEMS
```

The exact form taken by function-names varies somewhat from one system to another. The following form is quite common:

Function-name	Meaning
C01	channel 1
C02	channel 2
C03	channel 3
.	.
.	.
.	.
C12	channel 12

For example, in order to associate the mnemonic TO-TOP-OF-PAGE with a channel 1 punch, TO-BEGINNING-OF-ADDRESS with channel 3, and TO-BOTTOM-OF-PAGE with channel 12, the following SPECIAL-NAMES entry would be used:

```
SPECIAL-NAMES.
    C01  IS TO-TOP-OF-PAGE
    C02  IS TO-BEGINNING-OF-ADDRESS
    C03  IS TO-BOTTOM-OF-PAGE.
```

The following WRITE statement then could be used to write a record at the top of a page:

```
WRITE PRINT-REC AFTER ADVANCING TO-TOP-OF-PAGE.
```

A skip to channel 1 will be executed by the above sentence before writing commences. In order to place a record in the portion of the page designated by the channel 3 punch, the following WRITE statement would be used:

```
WRITE PRINT-REC AFTER ADVANCING TO-BEGINNING-OF-ADDRESS.
```

A skip to channel 3 will be executed by the preceding sentence before writing commences.

WARNING! Don't rush to your computer center to try out this useful output feature. Find out first if your printer has a carriage control tape, and if so, what is on that tape. If a programmer executes a skip to a channel which has no corresponding punch on whatever carriage control tape happens to be mounted when the program is executed, the result may be "run away" paper. That is, paper will be ejected continuously while the printer is search-

ing the specific carriage control tape for the control punch. For this reason
the use of this feature is not encouraged in most student oriented computing
environments, though it can be quite valuable to the professional programmer.

8.5 INTERNATIONAL APPLICATIONS FEATURES

Reports often must be generated for us in countries which have different
conventions for writing numbers and different symbols for currency. The
SPECIAL-NAMES entry of the CONFIGURATION SECTION of the ENVIRONMENT DIVISION
can be used to modify the usual symbols used to denote the decimal point
and the currency symbol. This feature is useful in data processing applications involving European and other currencies which do not use the symbol
"$" for a currency symbol and/or the period for the decimal point. The
general form for these entries is shown in Figure 8.8.

Figure 8.8 General form of SPECIAL-NAMES entries for international applications

```
SPECIAL-NAMES.
  [CURRENCY SIGN IS literal]
  [DECIMAL-POINT IS COMMA].
```

The DECIMAL-POINT IS COMMA clause causes the role of the comma and the
period to be interchanged in specifying PICTUREs in the DATA DIVISION. This is
required for certain European countries in which a value such as 12,345,678.90
would be written as 12.345.678,90. If the DECIMAL-POINT IS COMMA clause is used,
PICTUREs such as 99.999.999,99 will cause the period to be used to denote
groups of digits and the comma to be inserted as a decimal point.

The CURRENCY SIGN IS clause enables the use of the specified literal in the
DATA DIVISION instead of the dollar sign. For example, to enable use of the
pound sign "£" as a currency symbol the entry

    CURRENCY SIGN IS "£".

would be used. With this entry, PICTURE codes such as

    £££,£££.99 and £Z,ZZZ,ZZZ.99

may be used in the DATA DIVISION. The system will use the specified symbol in
exactly the same way as a dollar sign for editing data. The literal used in the
CURRENCY SIGN clause may be any single character except 0 through 9, A, B, C,
D, L, P, R, S, V, X, Z, *, +, (, −,), /, =, comma, period, quotation mark or
space.

8.6 CONTROL BREAKS

Often, subtotals are required for related subsets of data within a report. For
example, suppose the data processed by Program 8.1 has been sorted into
order by department number. Program 8.2 then processes this data and
generates a report showing subtotals for each department.

The basic problem encountered in writing such a program is the recognition of breaks within the data (called *control breaks*). A control break occurs, for example, when a data record is read for an employee in a department whose number differs from the preceding employee's department number. At this point the program must produce the totals for the preceding department before processing the current data record. The technique used to detect a break requires a holding location. The content of this location is compared with the key field from the current record when each record is processed. The *key field* is the field used to organize the file; for example, in Program 8.2 the key field is the department identifier.

If the two values (content of holding location and key field) are the same, the current record belongs to the same group as the previous record. If the two values differ, the current record belongs to a different group and a control break is recognized. The control break processing routine, in addition to writing the required totals, must move the key field from the current record to the hold field so that the next control break can be determined. A basic problem occurs in using this scheme for the first record processed, as there is no preceding record with which to compare. This problem is solved by moving the value of the key field to the hold field after the first record is read and before it is processed. Of course, this action should be done only for the first record.

When end-of-file is encountered, a group of data records for the last group will have been processed, but no totals will have been produced for that group. It is therefore necessary to recognize a control break after end-of-file has been reached. This procedure is summarized in the pseudocode shown in Figure 8.9.

Figure 8.9 Generalized procedure for control break program

Main logic

    Open files
    Read input file
    Move key field to key field hold
    Do Process read until end of file
    Do Control break
    Close files
    Stop

Process read

    If key field not equal key field hold
        Do Control break
    End If
    Add appropriate data to subtotal
    Do other processing of data
    Write detail record
    Read input file

Control break

    Write subtotal record
    Move 0 to subtotal
    Move key field to key field hold

Figure 8.10 Printer spacing chart for control break program

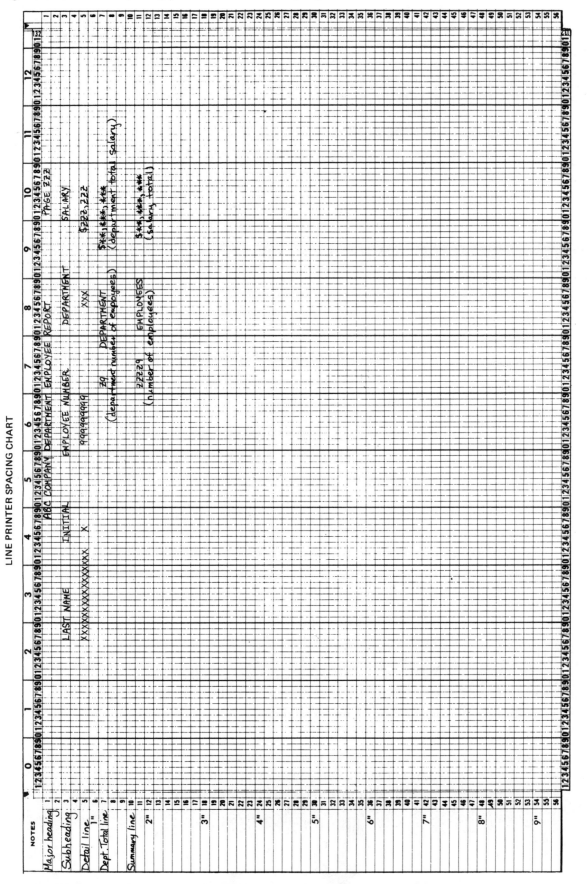

8.7 PROGRAM EXAMPLE

Problem Statement

The data file processed by Program 8.1 has been sorted into sequence by department identifier. Write a program to list the data records and print the total of salaries and number of employees for each department. The program must also print the grand total of all salaries and number of employees. Page headings and page numbers are required. The detail lines must be double spaced. The printer spacing chart for the required report is shown in Figure 8.10.

Problem Analysis

In this problem the key field is the department identifier. All data records for a department will occur in the data file in a continuous group. In order to produce the required department total for salaries and number of employees, we will use a field HOLD-DEPARTMENT, which will be initialized with the content of IR-DEPARTMENT (the key field on the input record). The first step in processing each data record is to compare IR-DEPARTMENT to HOLD-DEPARTMENT. If the two fields are not equal, the department totals that have been accumulated must be written, the accumulators for the department must be re-initialized and the content of IR-DEPARTMENT must be moved to HOLD-DEPARTMENT. These actions will be grouped together into a procedure that we will call *Department break*.

This program will require accumulators for subtotals of salary and number of employees by department (DEPT-TOTAL-SALARY and DEPARTMENT-NUMBER-OF-EMPLOYEES) and accumulators for the grand total of salaries and number of employees (SALARY-TOTAL and NUMBER-OF-EMPLOYEES).

With these considerations in mind we can now prepare a preliminary plan for the required program, using the general control break procedure in Figure 8.9 as a model. This preliminary plan is shown in Figure 8.11.

This plan does not take into consideration the page headings and page numbers that are required. These requirements will necessitate line counting, so we must define a field LINE-COUNT. An alternate procedure for producing page headings that can be used when page totals are not required is to initialize the line counter to a value indicating that the page is full. In this case we assume that the page contains 46 lines, so an appropriate initial value of LINE-COUNT would be 47. Using this approach, it is no longer necessary to write page headings as part of the initialization portion of the program. The program simply checks the line counter prior to writing each line of output. If the page is full (LINE-COUNT > 46) the headings are written. As the value of the line counter has been initialized to indicate a full page, this will cause the headings to be produced prior to writing the first detail line of the report as desired. Thereafter, page headings are written each time the page fills up with data.

It is necessary to check for full page prior to any output; thus, a page-full check should be performed as part of the control break processing as well. This change in handling of page headings does not affect other requirements of this procedure—the value of the line counter must be incremented each time output is written, and the page number (PAGE-COUNT) must be incremented each time page headings are written. This logic for pagination can now be added to the preliminary plan, resulting in a complete plan shown in Figure 8.12.

Figure 8.11   Preliminary plan for control break program

Main logic

    Open files
    Read employee file
    Move department identifier to hold department
    Do Control until end-of-file
    Do Department break
    Write summary line
    Close files
    Stop

Control

    If department identifier not equal hold department
        Do Department break
    End If
    Add 1 to department number of employees
    Add 1 to number of employees
    Add salary to department total salary
    Add salary to salary total
    Write detail line
    Read employee file

Department break

    Write department total line
    Move 0 to department number of employees
    Move 0 to department total salary
    Move department from input record to hold department

Figure 8.12   Completed plan for control break program

Main logic

    Open files
    Read employee file
    Move department identifier to hold department
    Do Control until end of file
    Do Department break
    Write summary line
    Close files
    Stop

Control

    If department identifier not equal hold department
        Do Department break
    End If
    Add 1 to department number of employees
    Add 1 to number of employees
    Add salary to department total salary
    Add salary to salary total

If page is full
    Do Write headings
End If
Write detail line
Increment line count
Read employee file

Department break

If page is full
    Do Write headings
End If
Write department total line
Increment line count
Move 0 to department number of employees
Move 0 to department total salary
Move department identifier to hold department

Write headings

Add 1 to page count
Write major heading
Write column heading
Initialize line count

Problem Solution

The solution to this problem is shown in Program 8.2 with structure diagram in Figure 8.13. The two major concepts illustrated in this program are the detection of control breaks and an alternate way to handle page headings.

Control breaks are detected by using the field HOLD–DEPARTMENT to store the previous value of IR–DEPARTMENT while a new record is read. The value of IR–DEPARTMENT is moved to HOLD–DEPARTMENT as part of the processing of the first record at line 13200. The first action taken in processing each record is to compare IR–DEPARTMENT to HOLD–DEPARTMENT (see line 14600). When the two fields are not equal, the procedure 6000–DEPARTMENT–BREAK is performed (line 14700). This procedure writes the subtotals (line 16900), re-initializes the accumulators for the subtotals (lines 17100-17200) and moves the current value of IR–DEPARTMENT to HOLD–DEPARTMENT.

Page headings are handled by initializing the value of LINE–COUNT to indicate a full page at line 4900. Prior to each output, the program checks for a full page (lines 15700, 16700). If the page is full, page headings are written. Because LINE–COUNT indicates that the page is full initially, page headings will be produced in advance of the first detail record. This technique makes it unnecessary to write page headings as part of the initialization procedure.

Program 8.2   Control break program

```
100      IDENTIFICATION DIVISION.
200
300      PROGRAM-ID. DEPARTMENT-REPORT.
400      AUTHOR. HORN.
500
600      ENVIRONMENT DIVISION.
700
800      CONFIGURATION SECTION.
900
1000     SOURCE-COMPUTER.
1100     OBJECT-COMPUTER.
1200
1300     INPUT-OUTPUT SECTION.
1400
1500     FILE-CONTROL.
1600
1700         SELECT EMPLOYEE-FILE ASSIGN TO DISK.
1800         SELECT DEPARTMENT-LIST  ASSIGN TO PRINTER.
1900
2000     DATA DIVISION.
2100
2200     FILE SECTION.
2300
2400     FD  EMPLOYEE-FILE
2500         LABEL RECORDS ARE STANDARD
2600         DATA RECORD IS INPUT-RECORD.
2700
2800     01  INPUT-RECORD.
2900         02  IR-NAME              PIC X(16).
3000         02  IR-INITIAL           PIC X.
3100         02  IR-EMPLOYEE-NUMBER    PIC 9(9).
3200         02  IR-DEPARTMENT        PIC X(3).
3300         02  IR-SALARY            PIC 9(6).
3400         02  FILLER               PIC X(45).
3500
3600     FD  DEPARTMENT-LIST
3700         LABEL RECORDS ARE OMITTED
3800         DATA RECORD IS PRINT-LINE.
3900
4000     01  PRINT-LINE               PIC X(132).
4100
4200     WORKING-STORAGE SECTION.
4300
4400     01  CONSTANTS.
4500         02  LINES-PER-PAGE       PIC 99 VALUE 46.
4600
4700     01  ACCUMULATED-TOTALS.
4800         03  PAGE-COUNT           PIC 999 VALUE ZERO.
4900         03  LINE-COUNT           PIC 999 VALUE 47.
5000         03  NUMBER-OF-EMPLOYEES  PIC 999 VALUE ZERO.
5100         03  SALARY-TOTAL         PIC 9(8) VALUE ZERO.
5200         03  DEPT-TOTAL-SALARY    PIC 9(8) VALUE ZERO.
5300         03  DEPARTMENT-NUMBER-OF-EMPLOYEES PIC 99 VALUE ZERO.
```

Program 8.2 (continued)

```
5400
5500      01  HOLD-FIELD.
5600          03  HOLD-DEPARTMENT          PIC X(3) VALUE SPACES.
5700
5800      01  EOF-FLAG                     PIC X(3) VALUE "NO".
5900              88  END-OF-FILE          VALUE "YES".
6000
6100      01  MAJOR-HEADING.
6200          02  FILLER                   PIC X(47) VALUE SPACES.
6300          02  FILLER                   PIC X(3) VALUE "ABC".
6400          02  FILLER                   PIC X VALUE SPACES.
6500          02  FILLER                   PIC X(7) VALUE "COMPANY".
6600          02  FILLER                   PIC X VALUE SPACES.
6700          02  FILLER                   PIC X(10) VALUE "DEPARTMENT".
6800          02  FILLER                   PIC X VALUE SPACES.
6900          02  FILLER                   PIC X(8) VALUE "EMPLOYEE".
7000          02  FILLER                   PIC X VALUE SPACES.
7100          02  FILLER                   PIC X(6) VALUE "REPORT".
7200          02  FILLER                   PIC X(15) VALUE SPACES.
7300          02  FILLER                   PIC X(5) VALUE "PAGE ".
7400          02  MH-PAGE-COUNTER          PIC ZZZ.
7500
7600      01  SUBHEADING.
7700          02  FILLER                   PIC X(26) VALUE SPACES.
7800          02  FILLER                   PIC X(9) VALUE "LAST NAME".
7900          02  FILLER                   PIC X(8) VALUE SPACES.
8000          02  FILLER                   PIC X(7) VALUE "INITIAL".
8100          02  FILLER                   PIC X(8) VALUE SPACES.
8200          02  FILLER                   PIC X(15) VALUE
8300                                       "EMPLOYEE NUMBER".
8400          02  FILLER                   PIC X(8) VALUE SPACES.
8500          02  FILLER                   PIC X(10) VALUE "DEPARTMENT".
8600          02  FILLER                   PIC X(8) VALUE SPACES.
8700          02  FILLER                   PIC X(6) VALUE "SALARY".
8800
8900      01  DETAIL-LINE.
9000          02  FILLER                   PIC X(26) VALUE SPACES.
9100          02  DL-NAME                  PIC X(16).
9200          02  FILLER                   PIC X(3) VALUE SPACES.
9300          02  DL-INITIAL               PIC X.
9400          02  FILLER                   PIC X(14) VALUE SPACES.
9500          02  DL-EMPLOYEE-NUMBER       PIC 9(9).
9600          02  FILLER                   PIC X(16) VALUE SPACES.
9700          02  DL-DEPARTMENT            PIC X(3).
9800          02  FILLER                   PIC X(10) VALUE SPACES.
9900          02  DL-SALARY                PIC $ZZZ,ZZZ.
10000
10100     01  DEPARTMENT-TOTAL-LINE.
10200         02  FILLER                   PIC X(70) VALUE SPACES.
10300         02  DTL-NUMBER-OF-EMPLOYEES PIC Z9.
10400         02  FILLER                   PIC X(5) VALUE SPACES.
10500         02  FILLER                   PIC X(9) VALUE "EMPLOYEES".
10600         02  FILLER                   PIC X(7) VALUE SPACES.
10700         02  DTL-TOTAL-SALARY         PIC $**,***,***.
10800
```

Program 8.2 (continued)

```
10900    01  SUMMARY-LINE.
11000        02  FILLER                 PIC X(70) VALUE SPACES.
11100        02  SL-NUMBER-OF-EMPLOYEES PIC ZZZ9.
11200        02  FILLER                 PIC X(5) VALUE SPACES.
11300        02  FILLER                 PIC X(9) VALUE "EMPLOYEES".
11400        02  FILLER                 PIC X(7) VALUE SPACES.
11500        02  SL-SALARY-TOTAL        PIC $***,***,***.
11600
11700    PROCEDURE DIVISION.
11800
11900    1000-MAIN-LOGIC.
12000
12100        PERFORM 2000-INITIALIZATION.
12200        PERFORM 3000-CONTROL
12300            UNTIL END-OF-FILE.
12400        PERFORM 9000-TERMINATION.
12500        STOP RUN.
12600
12700    2000-INITIALIZATION.
12800
12900        OPEN INPUT EMPLOYEE-FILE
13000             OUTPUT DEPARTMENT-LIST.
13100        PERFORM 4000-READ.
13200        MOVE IR-DEPARTMENT TO HOLD-DEPARTMENT.
13300
13400    3000-CONTROL.
13500
13600        PERFORM 5000-PROCESS.
13700        PERFORM 4000-READ.
13800
13900    4000-READ.
14000
14100        READ EMPLOYEE-FILE
14200            AT END MOVE "YES" TO EOF-FLAG.
14300
14400    5000-PROCESS.
14500
14600        IF IR-DEPARTMENT NOT = HOLD-DEPARTMENT
14700            PERFORM 6000-DEPARTMENT-BREAK.
14800        MOVE IR-NAME            TO DL-NAME.
14900        MOVE IR-INITIAL         TO DL-INITIAL.
15000        MOVE IR-EMPLOYEE-NUMBER TO DL-EMPLOYEE-NUMBER.
15100        MOVE IR-SALARY          TO DL-SALARY.
15200        MOVE IR-DEPARTMENT      TO DL-DEPARTMENT.
15300        ADD IR-SALARY TO DEPT-TOTAL-SALARY.
15400        ADD 1 TO DEPARTMENT-NUMBER-OF-EMPLOYEES.
15500        ADD IR-SALARY TO SALARY-TOTAL.
15600        ADD 1 TO NUMBER-OF-EMPLOYEES.
15700        IF LINE-COUNT > LINES-PER-PAGE
15800            PERFORM 7000-WRITE-HEADINGS.
15900        WRITE PRINT-LINE FROM DETAIL-LINE AFTER 2.
16000        ADD 2 TO LINE-COUNT.
16100
```

Program 8.2 (continued)

```
16200     6000-DEPARTMENT-BREAK.
16300
16400         MOVE DEPARTMENT-NUMBER-OF-EMPLOYEES TO
16500             DTL-NUMBER-OF-EMPLOYEES.
16600         MOVE DEPT-TOTAL-SALARY TO DTL-TOTAL-SALARY.
16700         IF LINE-COUNT > LINES-PER-PAGE
16800             PERFORM 7000-WRITE-HEADINGS.
16900         WRITE PRINT-LINE FROM DEPARTMENT-TOTAL-LINE AFTER 2.
17000         ADD 2 TO LINE-COUNT.
17100         MOVE 0 TO DEPARTMENT-NUMBER-OF-EMPLOYEES.
17200         MOVE 0 TO DEPT-TOTAL-SALARY.
17300         MOVE IR-DEPARTMENT TO HOLD-DEPARTMENT.
17400
17500     7000-WRITE-HEADINGS.
17600
17700         ADD 1 TO PAGE-COUNT.
17800         MOVE PAGE-COUNT TO MH-PAGE-COUNTER.
17900         WRITE PRINT-LINE FROM MAJOR-HEADING AFTER PAGE.
18000         WRITE PRINT-LINE FROM SUBHEADING AFTER 2.
18100         MOVE 3 TO LINE-COUNT.
18200
18300     8000-WRITE-SUMMARY-LINE.
18400
18500         MOVE NUMBER-OF-EMPLOYEES TO SL-NUMBER-OF-EMPLOYEES.
18600         MOVE SALARY-TOTAL TO SL-SALARY-TOTAL.
18700         WRITE PRINT-LINE FROM SUMMARY-LINE AFTER 3.
18800
18900     9000-TERMINATION.
19000
19100         PERFORM 6000-DEPARTMENT-BREAK.
19200         PERFORM 8000-WRITE-SUMMARY-LINE.
19300         CLOSE EMPLOYEE-FILE
19400             DEPARTMENT-LIST.
```

Figure 8.13   Structure diagram of control break program

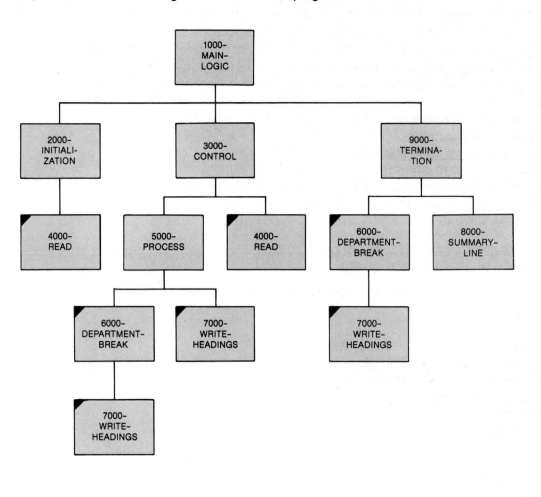

8.8   MULTILEVEL CONTROL BREAKS

Often reports require subtotals for more than one type of subset of the data. For example, suppose the department number of the data processed by Program 8.2 is coded with the division number of the company as the first digit of the department within the division. Division totals as well as department totals are produced by Program 8.3. This program requires the recognition of two levels of control breaks: a break in department number and a break in division number.

When two levels of subtotals are required, the file must be in sequence by the major key used as the basis for the largest groups within the file. Records within each major group must be in sequence by the minor key used as the basis for the smaller groups within each major group of data. In the example cited above, the major key is the division number and the minor key is the department number. In processing these records, a change in minor key field values must trigger the production of subtotals for the minor group of records—this change is called a *minor control break*. A change in the major key field values must trigger the production of subtotals for the last minor control group, as well as subtotals for the major subdivision of data. A change in values of the major key field is called a *major control break*. In terms of the division/department data, a change in department numbers where there is no change in division number must cause the production of totals for a department. A change in division numbers must cause the production of totals for the last department and then the totals for the division. At end-of-file, totals for the minor group followed by totals for the major group must be produced.

The recognition of major and minor control breaks requires the use of two hold fields—one for the major key field and one for the minor key field. When the first record is read, both hold fields are initialized. The first step in processing each data record is to check for control breaks. It is imperative that the program check first for the major break and, if a major break has not occurred, check for a minor break. This procedure is summarized in the generalized procedure shown in Figure 8.14.

Figure 8.14   Generalized procedure for two-level control break program

Main logic

    Open files
    Read input file
    Move major key field to major key field hold
    Move minor key field to minor key field hold
    Do Process read until end of file
    Do Minor control break
    Do Major control break
    Close files
    Stop

Process read

    If major key field not equal major key field hold
        Do Minor control break
        Do Major control break
    Else
        If minor key field not equal minor key field hold
            Do Minor control break
        End If
    End If
    Add appropriate data to subtotals
    Do other processing of data
    Write detail record
    Read input file

Minor control break

    Write minor subtotal record
    Move 0 to minor subtotal
    Move minor key field to minor key field hold

Major control break

    Write major subtotal record
    Move 0 to major subtotal
    Move major key field to major key field hold

The decision structure from the module *Process read* of Figure 8.14 is crucial to the correct detection of control breaks. A flowchart of this portion of the pseudocode is shown below:

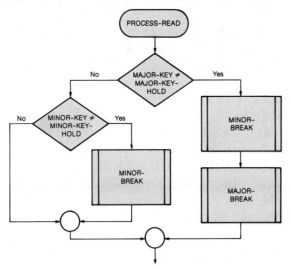

The program must check for a major control break prior to checking for a minor control break; but when a major control break is found, the minor break processing must be carried out before major break processing.

8.9   PROGRAM EXAMPLE

Problem Statement

Assume that the three-character department identifier in the data processed in Program 8.1 and 8.2 consists of two subfields: The first character represents a division within the company and the next two characters represent a department within the division. A report is required that will summarize employee data by department and by division. A printer spacing chart for the required report is shown in Figure 8.15.

Problem Analysis

This problem requires the use of two levels of control breaks—the major break based on the division identifier and the minor break based on the department identifier. The division identifier is the major key; the department identifier is the minor key. We have assumed that the file is in sequence by the three-character field, which has previously been referred to as a *department identifier*. As the division identifier is the leftmost character of the field, the data will be in the proper sequence required for this report, that is, the records for a division will be grouped together and within each division grouping the records for each department will occur as a group.

This program will require three sets of counters and accumulators—one set for the final totals (NUMBER-OF-EMPLOYEES and SALARY-TOTAL), another set for the major totals (DIVISION-NUMBER-OF-EMPLOYEES and DIVISION-TOTAL-SALARY), and a third set for the minor totals (DEPARTMENT-NUMBER-OF-EMPLOYEES and (DEPT-TOTAL-SALARY). The program will also require two hold fields—one for the major key (HOLD-DIVISION) and another for the minor key (HOLD-DEPARTMENT).

Figure 8.15 Printer spacing chart for two-level control

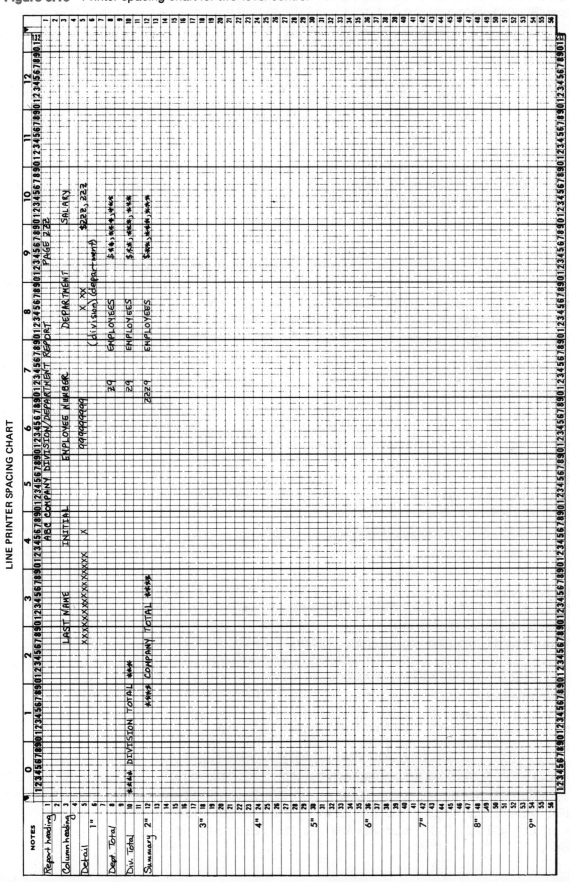

The plan for this program (shown in Figure 8.16) follows closely the general plan for two-level control break programs as shown in Figure 8.14. The technique to be used for page headings is similar to that used in Program 8.2; for simplicity, details are omitted from the plan.

Figure 8.16   Plan for two-level control break program

Main logic

    Open files
    Read employee file
    Move division identifier to hold division
    Move department identifier to hold department
    Do Control until end of file
    Do Department break
    Do Division break
    Write summary line
    Stop

Control

    If division identifier not equal hold division
        Do Department break
        Do Division break
    Else
        If department identifier not equal hold department
            Do Department break
        End If
    End If
    Add salary to salary total, department total salary, and division total salary
    Add 1 to number of employees, department number of employees and division number of employees
    Write detail line
    Read employee file

Department break

    Write department totals
    Move 0 to department salary total and department number of employees
    Move department identifier to hold department

Division break

    Write division totals
    Move 0 to division salary total and division number of employees
    Move division identifier to hold division

Problem Solution

The solution to this problem is shown in Program 8.3 with structure diagram in Figure 8.17. Note the technique used to handle two levels of control breaks. Both hold fields are initialized when the first record is read (see lines 15500 and 15600). The first step in processing each record is to check for control breaks (lines 16000-16500):

```
    IF IR-DIVISION NOT = HOLD-DIVISION
        PERFORM 6000-DEPARTMENT-BREAK
        PERFORM 6500-DIVISION-BREAK
    ELSE
        IF IR-DEPARTMENT NOT = HOLD-DEPARTMENT
            PERFORM 6000-DEPARTMENT-BREAK.
```

It is imperative that the program check for the major break before checking for the minor break because departments in two different divisions might have the same identifier. If there is a break in division identifiers, the program must write the department totals before writing the division totals. Note that the check for a break in department identifiers is made only if there is no break in division identifiers. This is imperative because, again, there might be departments in two different divisions with the same identifier.

Program 8.3   Two-level control break program

```
100       IDENTIFICATION DIVISION.
200
300       PROGRAM-ID. DIVISION-DEPARTMENT-REP.
400       AUTHOR. HORN.
500
600       ENVIRONMENT DIVISION.
700
800       CONFIGURATION SECTION.
900
1000      SOURCE-COMPUTER.
1100      OBJECT-COMPUTER.
1200
1300      INPUT-OUTPUT SECTION.
1400
1500      FILE-CONTROL.
1600
1700          SELECT EMPLOYEE-FILE ASSIGN TO DISK.
1800          SELECT DEPT-DIVISION-LIST ASSIGN TO PRINTER.
1900
2000      DATA DIVISION.
2100
2200      FILE SECTION.
2300
2400      FD  EMPLOYEE-FILE
2500          LABEL RECORDS ARE STANDARD
2600          DATA RECORD IS INPUT-RECORD.
2700
2800      01  INPUT-RECORD.
2900          02  IR-NAME             PIC X(16).
3000          02  IR-INITIAL          PIC X.
3100          02  IR-EMPLOYEE-NUMBER   PIC 9(9).
3200          02  IR-DIVISION         PIC X.
3300          02  IR-DEPARTMENT       PIC X(2).
3400          02  IR-SALARY           PIC 9(6).
3500          02  FILLER              PIC X(45).
3600
```

Program 8.3 (continued)

```
3700    FD  DEPT-DIVISION-LIST
3800        LABEL RECORDS ARE OMITTED
3900        DATA RECORD IS PRINT-LINE.
4000
4100    01  PRINT-LINE                  PIC X(132).
4200
4300    WORKING-STORAGE SECTION.
4400
4500    01  CONSTANTS.
4600        02  LINES-PER-PAGE          PIC 99 VALUE 46.
4700
4800    01  COUNTERS.
4900        03  PAGE-COUNT              PIC 999 VALUE ZERO.
5000        03  LINE-COUNT              PIC 999 VALUE 46.
5100            88  PAGE-FULL           VALUE 46 THRU 99.
5200
5300    01  ACCUMULATED-TOTALS.
5400        03  NUMBER-OF-EMPLOYEES            PIC 999 VALUE ZERO.
5500        03  SALARY-TOTAL                  PIC 9(8) VALUE ZERO.
5600        03  DEPARTMENT-NUMBER-OF-EMPLOYEES PIC 99 VALUE ZERO.
5700        03  DEPT-TOTAL-SALARY             PIC 9(8) VALUE ZERO.
5800        03  DIVISION-NUMBER-OF-EMPLOYEES  PIC 99 VALUE ZERO.
5900        03  DIVISION-TOTAL-SALARY         PIC 9(8) VALUE ZERO.
6000
6100    01  HOLD-FIELDS.
6200        03  HOLD-DEPARTMENT         PIC X(2) VALUE SPACES.
6300        03  HOLD-DIVISION           PIC X   VALUE SPACES.
6400
6500    01  EOF-FLAG                    PIC X(3) VALUE "NO".
6600        88  END-OF-FILE             VALUE "YES".
6700
6800    01  MAJOR-HEADING.
6900        02  FILLER                  PIC X(44) VALUE SPACES.
7000        02  FILLER                  PIC X(3) VALUE "ABC".
7100        02  FILLER                  PIC X VALUE SPACES.
7200        02  FILLER                  PIC X(7) VALUE "COMPANY".
7300        02  FILLER                  PIC X VALUE SPACES.
7400        02  FILLER                  PIC X(19) VALUE
7500            "DIVISION/DEPARTMENT".
7600        02  FILLER                  PIC X VALUE SPACES.
7700        02  FILLER                  PIC X(8) VALUE "EMPLOYEE".
7800        02  FILLER                  PIC X VALUE SPACES.
7900        02  FILLER                  PIC X(6) VALUE "REPORT".
8000        02  FILLER                  PIC X(10) VALUE SPACES.
8100        02  FILLER                  PIC X(5) VALUE "PAGE ".
8200        02  MH-PAGE-COUNTER         PIC ZZZ.
8300
8400    01  SUBHEADING.
8500        02  FILLER                  PIC X(26) VALUE SPACES.
8600        02  FILLER                  PIC X(9) VALUE "LAST NAME".
8700        02  FILLER                  PIC X(8) VALUE SPACES.
8800        02  FILLER                  PIC X(7) VALUE "INITIAL".
```

(handwritten annotation beside line 6200–6300): PIC X(2) VALUE "18".

```
8900        02 FILLER                PIC X(8) VALUE SPACES.
9000        02 FILLER                PIC X(15) VALUE
9100                                 "EMPLOYEE NUMBER".
9200        02 FILLER                PIC X(8) VALUE SPACES.
9300        02 FILLER                PIC X(10) VALUE "DEPARTMENT".
9400        02 FILLER                PIC X(8) VALUE SPACES.
9500        02 FILLER                PIC X(6) VALUE "SALARY".
9600
9700    01  DETAIL-LINE.
9800        02 FILLER                PIC X(26) VALUE SPACES.
9900        02 DL-NAME               PIC X(16).
10000       02 FILLER                PIC X(3) VALUE SPACES.
10100       02 DL-INITIAL            PIC X.
10200       02 FILLER                PIC X(14) VALUE SPACES.
10300       02 DL-EMPLOYEE-NUMBER    PIC 9(9).
10400       02 FILLER                PIC X(15) VALUE SPACES.
10500       02 DL-DIVISION           PIC X.
10600       02 FILLER                PIC X VALUE SPACES.
10700       02 DL-DEPARTMENT         PIC X(2).
10800       02 FILLER                PIC X(10) VALUE SPACES.
10900       02 DL-SALARY             PIC $ZZZ,ZZZ.
11000
11100   01  DEPARTMENT-TOTAL-LINE.
11200       02 FILLER                PIC X(70) VALUE SPACES.
11300       02 DTL-NUMBER-OF-EMPLOYEES PIC Z9.
11400       02 FILLER                PIC X(5) VALUE SPACES.
11500       02 FILLER                PIC X(9) VALUE "EMPLOYEES".
11600       02 FILLER                PIC X(7) VALUE SPACES.
11700       02 DTL-TOTAL-SALARY      PIC $**,***,***.
11800
11900   01  DIVISION-TOTAL-LINE.
12000       02 FILLER                PIC X(23) VALUE
12100           "**** DIVISION TOTAL ***".
12200       02 FILLER                PIC X(47) VALUE SPACES.
12300       02 DVT-NUMBER-OF-EMPLOYEES PIC Z9.
12400       02 FILLER                PIC X(5) VALUE SPACES.
12500       02 FILLER                PIC X(9) VALUE "EMPLOYEES".
12600       02 FILLER                PIC X(7) VALUE SPACES.
12700       02 DVT-TOTAL-SALARY      PIC $**,***,***.
12800
12900   01  SUMMARY-LINE.
13000       02 FILLER                PIC X(15) VALUE SPACES.
13100       02 FILLER                PIC X(23) VALUE
13200           "**** COMPANY TOTAL ****".
13300       02 FILLER                PIC X(30) VALUE SPACES.
13400       02 SL-NUMBER-OF-EMPLOYEES PIC ZZZ9.
13500       02 FILLER                PIC X(5) VALUE SPACES.
13600       02 FILLER                PIC X(9) VALUE "EMPLOYEES".
13700       02 FILLER                PIC X(7) VALUE SPACES.
13800       02 SL-SALARY-TOTAL       PIC $**,***,***.
13900
```

```
14000    PROCEDURE DIVISION.
14100
14200    1000-MAIN-LOGIC.
14300
14400        PERFORM 2000-INITIALIZATION.
14500        PERFORM 3000-CONTROL
14600            UNTIL END-OF-FILE.
14700        PERFORM 9000-TERMINATION.
14800        STOP RUN.
14900
15000    2000-INITIALIZATION.
15100
15200        OPEN INPUT EMPLOYEE-FILE
15300            OUTPUT DEPT-DIVISION-LIST.
15400        PERFORM 4000-READ.
15500        MOVE IR-DEPARTMENT TO HOLD-DEPARTMENT
15600        MOVE IR-DIVISION   TO HOLD-DIVISION.
15700
15800    3000-CONTROL.
15900
16000        IF IR-DIVISION NOT = HOLD-DIVISION
16100            PERFORM 6000-DEPARTMENT-BREAK
16200            PERFORM 6500-DIVISION-BREAK
16300        ELSE
16400            IF IR-DEPARTMENT NOT = HOLD-DEPARTMENT
16500                PERFORM 6000-DEPARTMENT-BREAK.
16600        PERFORM 5000-PROCESS.
16700        PERFORM 4000-READ.
16800
16900    4000-READ.
17000
17100        READ EMPLOYEE-FILE
17200            AT END MOVE "YES" TO EOF-FLAG.
17300
17400    5000-PROCESS.
17500
17600        MOVE IR-NAME            TO DL-NAME.
17700        MOVE IR-INITIAL         TO DL-INITIAL.
17800        MOVE IR-EMPLOYEE-NUMBER TO DL-EMPLOYEE-NUMBER.
17900        MOVE IR-SALARY          TO DL-SALARY.
18000        MOVE IR-DIVISION        TO DL-DIVISION.
18100        MOVE IR-DEPARTMENT      TO DL-DEPARTMENT.
18200        ADD IR-SALARY           TO DEPT-TOTAL-SALARY.
18300        ADD IR-SALARY           TO DIVISION-TOTAL-SALARY.
18400        ADD 1                   TO DEPARTMENT-NUMBER-OF-EMPLOYEES.
18500        ADD 1                   TO DIVISION-NUMBER-OF-EMPLOYEES.
18600        ADD IR-SALARY           TO SALARY-TOTAL.
18700        ADD 1                   TO NUMBER-OF-EMPLOYEES.
18800        IF PAGE-FULL
18900            PERFORM 7000-WRITE-HEADINGS.
19000        WRITE PRINT-LINE FROM DETAIL-LINE AFTER 2.
19100        ADD 2 TO LINE-COUNT.
19200
```

Program 8.3 (continued)

```
19300     6000-DEPARTMENT-BREAK.
19400
19500        MOVE DEPARTMENT-NUMBER-OF-EMPLOYEES TO
19600           DTL-NUMBER-OF-EMPLOYEES.
19700        MOVE DEPT-TOTAL-SALARY TO DTL-TOTAL-SALARY.
19800        IF PAGE-FULL
19900           PERFORM 7000-WRITE-HEADINGS.
20000        WRITE PRINT-LINE FROM DEPARTMENT-TOTAL-LINE AFTER 2.
20100        ADD 2 TO LINE-COUNT.
20200        MOVE 0 TO DEPARTMENT-NUMBER-OF-EMPLOYEES.
20300        MOVE 0 TO DEPT-TOTAL-SALARY.
20400        MOVE IR-DEPARTMENT TO HOLD-DEPARTMENT.
20500
20600     6500-DIVISION-BREAK.
20700
20800        MOVE DIVISION-TOTAL-SALARY TO DVT-TOTAL-SALARY.
20900        MOVE DIVISION-NUMBER-OF-EMPLOYEES TO DVT-NUMBER-OF-EMPLOYEES.
21000        IF PAGE-FULL
21100           PERFORM 7000-WRITE-HEADINGS.
21200        WRITE PRINT-LINE FROM   DIVISION-TOTAL-LINE AFTER 3.
21300        MOVE 0 TO DIVISION-NUMBER-OF-EMPLOYEES.
21400        MOVE 0 TO DIVISION-TOTAL-SALARY.
21500        MOVE IR-DIVISION TO HOLD-DIVISION.
21600
21700     7000-WRITE-HEADINGS.
21800
21900        ADD 1 TO PAGE-COUNT.
22000        MOVE PAGE-COUNT TO MH-PAGE-COUNTER.
22100        WRITE PRINT-LINE FROM MAJOR-HEADING AFTER PAGE.
22200        WRITE PRINT-LINE FROM SUBHEADING AFTER 2.
22300        MOVE 3 TO LINE-COUNT.
22400
22500     8000-WRITE-SUMMARY-LINE.
22600
22700        MOVE NUMBER-OF-EMPLOYEES TO SL-NUMBER-OF-EMPLOYEES.
22800        MOVE SALARY-TOTAL TO SL-SALARY-TOTAL.
22900        WRITE PRINT-LINE FROM SUMMARY-LINE AFTER 3.
23000
23100     9000-TERMINATION.
23200
23300        PERFORM 6000-DEPARTMENT-BREAK.
23400        PERFORM 6500-DIVISION-BREAK.
23500        PERFORM 8000-WRITE-SUMMARY-LINE.
23600        CLOSE EMPLOYEE-FILE
23700           DEPT-DIVISION-LIST.
```

Figure 8.17 Structure diagram for two-level control break program

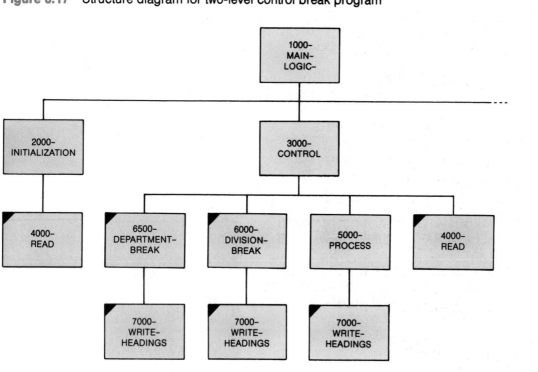

Note the sequence of actions taken by the program after end-of-file is detected (lines 23300-23500):

```
PERFORM 6000-DEPARTMENT-BREAK.
PERFORM 6500-DIVISION-BREAK.
PERFORM 8000-WRITE-SUMMARY-LINE.
```

The sequence in which these actions are taken is important because the line containing the totals for the last department must precede the line for the totals for the last division and all of these must come before the final totals.

Some programs may require three (or more) levels of totals and hence require as many levels of control break checks. In the case of three levels, we will call the most important key field the *major key*, the next most important the *intermediate key*, and the least important key field the *minor key*.

For example, suppose the data file described in Program 8.2 contained an additional field for plant and suppose each plant was organized into divisions and each division was organized into departments. The major key would be the plant identifier, the intermediate key would be the division identifier, and the minor key would be the department identifier. In order to recognize three levels of control breaks, the program will need three hold fields—one for each key. The overall logic for a three-level break program will resemble the two-level break procedure described in Figure 8.14. In this case, however, the first task of the process read module is to check for three conditions as shown in Figure 8.18.

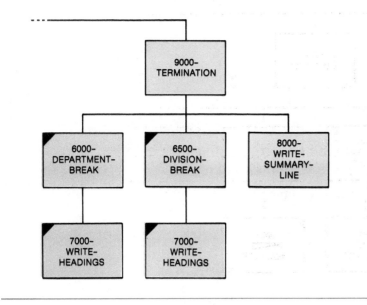

Figure 8.18 Decision structure for three-level control break program

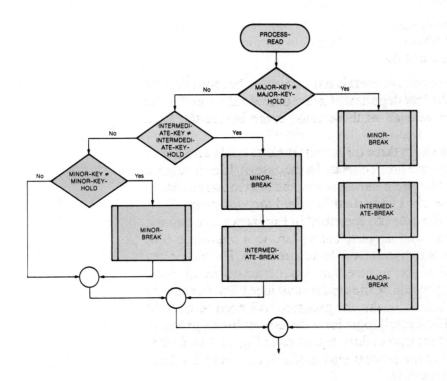

8.10 DEBUG CLINIC

Programs requiring line counting, page numbers, and subtotals are somewhat more complex than programs which have been encountered previously in this text. It is, therefore not uncommon for programmers to encounter logical errors during the debugging of such programs. The following list presents some of the most common problems and some suggestions as to the possible causes of the problems.

Logical Problem	Possible causes
No headings	Page heading paragraph not included
	PERFORM of page heading paragraph omitted
Headings on first page only	PERFORM of page heading paragraph not included in processing of body of report
	Line counter not incremented
Page headings occur on all pages but first	PERFORM of page heading paragraph not included in initialization
	Line counter not initialized properly
Page headings do not occur at top of every physical page of output	Line counter not incremented after each output
	Amount added to line counter not equal to number lines produced
	Number of lines per page used in program exceeds actual number of lines per page
Page headings occur in the middle of physical pages of output	Computer operator failed to align paper in printer properly
	Skipping to top of a new page is not a feature of the printer in use
	Skipping to top of a new page has been disallowed (this is sometimes done to save paper)
Page number is same on all pages	Page counter not incremented in page heading paragraph
Page totals are cumulative	Subtotal field not reinitialized to zero after production of subtotal output
Subtotal with value zero occurs before first detail output	Hold field has not been initialized for first input record
Subtotals occur after every detail output line	Hold field is not replaced with a new value in the control break routine

| No totals at end of report | Program does not perform control break routines as part of termination |
| A group includes an output line which should be included in the following group | Program is checking for control break after detail processing rather than before processing |

8.11 SELF-TEXT EXERCISES

1. Write DATA DIVISION entries required to define the folllowing file and its records:

   File-name: DATA-FILE

   Record names: DATA-REC-A, DATA-REC-B

   Record type A:

1-10	Bid-number
11-20	Project description
21-30	Bid amount
31	Record identification code ("A")

   Record type B:

1-10	Bid-number
11-20	Disbursement amount
21-30	Disbursement description
31	Record identification code ("B")

2. Write PROCEDURE DIVISION entries required to read DATA-FILE defined in Exercise 1 above.

3. Write SPECIAL-NAMES entries required to substitute the symbol "Q" for the dollar sign. Write a PICTURE code to edit a field defined as 9(6)V99.

4. In Program 8.1, the line counter is initialized to value 0. Each output operation forwards the counter. Before each output the counter is tested to see if the page is full. If the page is full a new page is initiated with headings and page number. Using this scheme, what would happen if the last line in the report fell on the last line of a page? What would happen if there were no records in the file?

5. In Program 8.2 an alternative method for handling line counting is used. The line counter is initialized to a value greater than the number of lines on a page. For example, if there are 46 lines on a page, the line counter is defined with initial value 47. The program then tests the line counter for full page before each output operation. Because of the initial value of the line count, page headings will be produced in advance of the first output operation and each time thereafter that the page becomes full. What advantages are there to this scheme? What would happen if

   1) there are no records in the file?
   2) the last line of the report falls on the last line of a page?

   Which method for line counting seems best?

   Is the method used in Program 8.2 compatible with page totals? Why or why not?

6. Should the number of lines per page be defined as a data item in WORKING-STORAGE? Why?

7. For Program 8.2, suppose we want to include the department number as a part of the output line showing each department total. Which of the following should be moved to the output record: IR-DEPARTMENT or HOLD-DEPARTMENT? Why?

8. Using the procedure shown in Figure 8.14 and 8.18 as guidelines, write a procedure for a three-level control break program.

8.12 PROGRAMMING EXERCISES

1. Write a program to determine the inventory value of stock items. Input consists of data records containing:

> Quantity
> Item stock number and name
> Unit cost

There may be more than one input record per item. For example, baseballs may have been purchased as follows: 5 baseballs at a unit cost of $2.00, and 4 baseballs at a unit cost of $2.25. The program should list the quantity, stock number and name, item weighted average unit cost, and total dollar value of each stock item in appropriately spaced columns. Headings on each page are required, as are page numbers. Also write the total value of all items in the inventory.

2. The XYZ Wholesale Supply Company has prepared records containing the following items:

> Department number
> Transaction date
> Amount of order

Write a program to list each record and produce totals for each department as well as overall totals. List the department number only once for each department's group of records. Use the following test data:

Department Number	Transaction Date	Amount of Order
100	1/10/86	6.75
100	1/10/86	14.85
100	1/11/86	7.00
100	1/13/86	19.50
102	1/10/86	7.95
102	1/11/86	9.95
102	1/11/86	18.50
103	1/12/86	19.70
103	1/13/86	6.50
104	1/11/86	4.50

Your output should be similar to

```
        XYZ WHOLESALE SUPPLY COMPANY

DEPARTMENT    TRANSACTION    AMOUNT OF
  NUMBER         DATE          ORDER
    100         1/10/86         6.75
                1/10/86        14.85
                1/11/86         7.00
                1/13/86        19.50
                TOTAL         $48.10*
```

```
102        1/10/86         7.95
           1/11/86         9.95
           1/11/86        18.50
           TOTAL         $36.40*

103        1/12/86        19.70
           1/13/86         6.50
           TOTAL         $26.20*

104        1/11/86        14.50
           TOTAL          $4.50*
           GRAND TOTAL  $115.20***
```

3. Modify the program written for Exercise 2 above to produce daily totals within each department. Assume that the data is in sequence by transaction date within each department group.

4. Write a program to alert top management of the XYZ Corporation when sales in its department are outside certain limits (abnormally high or abnormally low). Input records contain the department number, year, and total sales for that year. You may assume that the records are in ascending sequence by year and that all records for a given department are grouped together (the most recent year is the last record in the department group). If the most recent year's sales are more than 10 percent greater than the average for the entire period, then sales are high. If the most recent year's sales are less than 90 percent of the average for the period, then sales are low. Output should be one line per department consisting of department number, most recent year's sales, average sales and a flag HIGH or LOW if appropriate.

5. You have been hired as a programmer for the Harris Hardware Co. Harris makes nuts, bolts, and washers. At the end of each day, a record is prepared for each employee with the following format:

Positions

```
1-20    NAME
21-25   EMPLOYEE NO.
26-27   HOURS WORKED
28-30   RATE OF PAY
31-32   NUMBER OF DOZEN STAINLESS STEEL BOLTS MADE
33-34   NUMBER OF DOZEN STAINLESS STEEL NUTS MADE
35-36   NUMBER OF DOZEN STAINLESS STEEL WASHERS MADE
37-38   NUMBER OF DOZEN BRASS BOLTS MADE
39-40   NUMBER OF DOZEN BRASS NUTS MADE
41-42   NUMBER OF DOZEN BRASS WASHERS MADE
43-44   NUMBER OF DOZEN FIBER WASHERS MADE
45-80   BLANK
```

The cost of production *per item* is as follows:

	Nuts	Bolts	Washers
Stainless Steel	$0.07	$0.07	$0.07
Brass	$0.04	$0.05	$0.02
Fiber	—	—	$0.005

At the end of the week, all records for the week are processed. You may assume that prior to processing, the entire file has been sorted and all the records for each employee are together. There will be one to five records per employee. When each employee's records are processed, write out under appropriate headings his or her name, employee number, total production by category, total hours worked for the week, and pay for the week, counting any hours worked in one day in excess of eight hours as time and one half. When all records are processed, skip to a new page and give total production cost for each category as well as grand total cost of production for the week.

6. Write a program to perform an edit of the data described in Exercise 5 above. Your program should check for the following conditions:
   a. More than 5 records for one employee
   b. Record out of sequence
   c. HOURS-WORKED is blank or HOURS-WORKED > 18
   d. RATE-OF-PAY is blank
   e. All of the fields positions 31-44 are blank

   Write appropriate message when each condition is found.

7. Assume that the data described in Chapter 4, Section 14, Exercise 3 has been sorted into order by zone and selling price. Write a program to list the number of homes in each of the following categories for each zone:
   Selling price ≤ $40,000
   $40,000 < selling price ≤ $70,000
   $70,000 < selling price ≤ $95,000
   $95,000 < selling price

8. Assume that the data described in Chapter 6, Section 13, Exercise 2 has been sorted into sequence by account code. Write a program to list and summarize expenditures for each account.

TABLES AND PERFORM/VARYING

9

9.1 WHAT IS A TABLE?

A *table* is a sequence of consecutive storage locations (each of which is called an *element*) having a common name. The elements can be accessed using an element name and a specific subscript to point to the particular element to be referenced. For example, suppose we wish to store 75 values representing student grades. One approach would be to create individually named data items to store the values. Another approach would be to create a table and store the values in elements of the table. Such a table might be visualized as:

GRADE–TABLE								
GRADE (1)	GRADE (2)	GRADE (3)	GRADE (4)	GRADE (5)	GRADE (6)	GRADE (7)		GRADE (75)
0 4 5	0 9 2	0 7 0	0 9 6	0 5 2	0 9 3	1 0 0		0 8 0

The elements of the table are referenced by a name GRADE and a subscript value enclosed in parentheses.[1] The value of GRADE (1) is 45; the value of GRADE (75) is 80; and so on. The subscript points to a particular value in the table. A

---

1. Some compilers require that at least one space must precede a left parenthesis and one space must follow a right parenthesis. Also, a space must not follow a left parenthesis nor precede a right parenthesis. For example, the following table references are invalid for these compilers:

GRADE(1)   No space preceding left parenthesis
GRADE (1) Space following left parenthesis
GRADE (1) Space preceding right parenthesis

subscript must be either a constant or a data-name.[2] When a data-name is used, its value determines the particular element of the table being referenced. For example, the following are valid references:

GRADE (IND)   The value of IND at the time of execution will determine which element of GRADE is referenced.

GRADE (35)   The 35th element of GRADE is referenced.

The ability to use a variable as a subscript accounts for the utility of tables. For example, suppose we want to compute the sum of grades. If the grades had not been stored in a table, then a very long computational statement (involving 75 different data-names) would have to be used. However, with tables the sum can be accumulated using the following code:

```
        .
        .
        .
    MOVE 0 TO TOTAL-GRADE.
    MOVE 1 TO IND.
    PERFORM ADD-ROUTINE UNTIL IND > 75.
        .
        .
        .
ADD-ROUTINE.
    ADD GRADE (IND) TO TOTAL-GRADE.
    ADD 1 TO IND.
```

At the first repetition of ADD-ROUTINE, the value of IND will be 1, and the contents of GRADE (1) will be added to TOTAL-GRADE. Then the value of IND will become 2 and the contents of GRADE (2) will be added to TOTAL-GRADE, and so on. The process terminates when the value of IND exceeds 75 at which time all of the grades will have been added into TOTAL-GRADE.

9.2 THE OCCURS CLAUSE

The OCCURS clause is used in the DATA DIVISION to define a table. Figure 9.1 shows a general form for usage of the OCCURS clause. In the OCCURS clause *integer* specifies the number of elements to be contained in the table.

Figure 9.1   General form of the OCCURS clause

```
OCCURS integer TIMES
```

2. Some compilers permit any expression to be used as a subscript. For such compilers the following would be a valid table reference:

GRADE (IND + 3)   The expression IND + 3 will be evaluated to determine which element of GRADE is referenced.

The OCCURS clause cannot be used on an 01 level data item. For example, the following code would create the table for storing 75 grades:

```
01  GRADE-TABLE.
    02 GRADE PIC 999 OCCURS 75 TIMES.
```

The data-name GRADE-TABLE is a group data item; it is the overall name for the entire set of 75 data items. A data-name used with an OCCURS clause may be an elementary data item, as in the above example, or it may be a group data item. For example, suppose we wish to store the names and addresses of 100 people in such a way that one element of the table corresponds responds to the data being stored about one person. The following code could be used:

```
01  NAME-ADDRESS-TABLE.
    02 NAME-AND-ADDRESS OCCURS 100 TIMES.
       03 NAME    PIC X(20).
       03 ADDRESS PIC X(30).
```

In this case NAME-AND-ADDRESS is a group data item, each NAME-AND-ADDRESS is composed of two fields. The data stored for the fifth person then could be referenced by:

```
NAME-AND-ADDRESS (5)
```

When the OCCURS clause is used on a group data item, a subscript may be used not only on the group data item name but also on any subordinate field. In the above example it would also be valid to reference

```
NAME (5)
```

in order to obtain the name only, and

```
ADDRESS (5)
```

in order to obtain the address only. The data structure defined above may be visualized as follows:

NAME-ADDRESS-TABLE						
NAME-AND-ADDRESS (1)		NAME-AND-ADDRESS (2)			NAME-AND-ADDRESS (100)	
NAME (1)	ADDRESS (1)	NAME (2)	ADDRESS (2)		NAME (100)	ADDRESS (100)

Subscripts may be associated only with subordinate parts, not with the overall name of the data structure. For example: NAME-ADDRESS-TABLE (3) would be invalid, since NAME-ADDRESS-TABLE occurs exactly one time; it is a name for $100 \times (20 + 30) = 5000$ characters of data.

An alternative form for storing the above data would be

```
01  ALTERNATE-NAME-ADDRESS-TABLE.
    02 NAME    PIC X(20) OCCURS 100 TIMES.
    02 ADDRESS PIC X(30) OCCURS 100 TIMES.
```

This structure may be visualized as:

ALTERNATE–NAME–ADDRESS–TABLE						
NAME (1)	NAME (2)		NAME (100)	ADDRESS (1)	ADDRESS (2)		ADDRESS (100)

In this case both NAME (5) and ADDRESS (5) would have to be referenced to access all data stored for person number 5. This is less desirable than the other approach if both name and address are desired at the same time.

The subscript used in any reference to an element of a table must have a value in the range (one to the size of the table) specified in the OCCURS clause. Any reference involving a subscript having a value outside this range will result in an execution time error message. For example, for the NAME-ADDRESS-TABLE discussed above, the following references would be invalid:

```
NAME (0)      Zero is not in the range 1 to 100
NAME (101)    101 is too large
```

9.3 LOADING AND PROCESSING A TABLE

The OCCURS clause is required to define a table. Data can then be placed into the table. Usually it is not known exactly how many items are to be stored in a table, so the number of elements reserved in the OCCURS clause must be at least as large as the largest number of items anticipated. The program can use a counter to indicate the location into which the item is to be stored and to ensure that the maximum capacity of the table is not exceeded inadvertently. A program segment that could be used to store data into the NAME-ADDRESS-TABLE is shown below:

```
        .
        .
        .
        MOVE ZERO TO ERROR-FLAG.
        MOVE ZERO TO NUM-ELEMENTS.
        READ INPUT-FILE AT END MOVE "YES" TO EOF-FLAG.
        PERFORM STORE-AND-READ
            UNTIL EOF-FLAG = "YES" OR ERROR-FLAG = 1.
        .
        .
        .
    STORE-AND-READ.
        ADD 1 TO NUM-ELEMENTS.
        IF NUM-ELEMENTS > 100
            MOVE 1 TO ERROR-FLAG
        ELSE
            MOVE NAME-IN TO NAME (NUM-ELEMENTS)
            MOVE ADDRESS-IN TO ADDRESS (NUM-ELEMENTS)
            READ INPUT-FILE AT END MOVE "YES" TO EOF-FLAG.
```

In the above program segment the value contained in NUM-ELEMENTS after loading the data into the table reflects the actual number of elements contained in the table. Subsequent processing of the table would use this value for termination. For example, the following code could be used to produce a listing of the elements of NAME-ADDRESS-TABLE:

```
        MOVE ZERO TO TABLE-INDEX.
        PERFORM TABLE-OUTPUT
                UNTIL TABLE-INDEX = NUM-ELEMENTS.
        .
        .
        .
    TABLE-OUTPUT.
        ADD 1 TO TABLE-INDEX.
        MOVE NAME (TABLE-INDEX) TO NAME-OUT.
        MOVE ADDRESS (TABLE-INDEX) TO ADDRESS-OUT.
        WRITE OUTPUT-REC FROM NAME-AND-ADDRESS-OUT AFTER 1.
```

Numeric data contained in a table may be processed by any desired arithmetic statement. A subscript must be included to indicate which element of the table is to be operated on. Usually table elements are processed within a loop in order to perform similar operations on all or any of the elements.

Example

A table which represents the total sales for a store for each month in a year is defined in the DATA DIVISION by:

```
01  TOTAL-SALES-TABLE.
    03 TOTAL-SALES PIC 9(5)V99 OCCURS 12 TIMES.
```

This table can be visualized as shown below:

TOTAL-SALES-TABLE						
TOTAL-SALES (1)	TOTAL-SALES (2)	TOTAL-SALES (3)	TOTAL-SALES (4)	TOTAL-SALES (5)		TOTAL-SALES (12)
? ? ? ? ? ? ? ?	? ? ? ? ? ? ? ?	? ? ? ? ? ? ? ?	? ? ? ? ? ? ? ?	? ? ? ? ? ? ? ?	? ? ? ? ? ? ? ?	? ? ? ? ? ? ? ?

The question marks in the diagram indicate that the initial value in these locations is unknown. This table will be used for accumulation; therefore it is necessary to start each element at zero. To do this, it is necessary to move zero to TOTAL-SALES (1), TOTAL-SALES (2), and so on. This task can be accomplished by the following program segment:

```
        .
        .
        .
        PERFORM INITIALIZE-TABLE.
        .
        .
        .
    INITIALIZE-TABLE.
        MOVE 1 TO IND.
        PERFORM INITIALIZE-TABLE-ELEMENT
            UNTIL IND > 12.
    INITIALIZE-TABLE-ELEMENT.
        MOVE 0 TO TOTAL-SALES (IND).
        ADD 1 TO IND.
```

After the table has been initialized, the table elements can be used as accumulators. If MONTH-NO-IR and SALES-AMOUNT-IR are fields from an input record representing the number of the month and the amount of a sale, then the following program statement would accumulate the total sales by month:

```
ADD SALES-AMOUNT-IR TO TOTAL-SALES (MONTH-NO).
```

In this case MONTH-NO is used as a subscript to pick out the particular element of TOTAL-SALES-TABLE to be operated on.

9.4 OCCURS/DEPENDING ON

In cases where an entire table is not always utilized, it is advantageous to use the DEPENDING ON clause with the OCCURS. The DEPENDING ON clause specifies a data-name that will contain the number of table elements used. A general form of the OCCURS clause is given in Figure 9.2.

Figure 9.2   General form of OCCURS/DEPENDING ON

```
OCCURS integer-1 TO integer-2 TIMES
DEPENDING ON data-name
```

The content of *data-name* is treated as the upper limit of the table. Any reference to a table element using a subscript value larger than the content of *data-name* is treated as invalid. When the DEPENDING ON clause is included, you must specify the smallest number of table elements to be used *(integer-1)* and the maximum number of elements *(integer-2)*. It is an error for the content of *data-name* to be less than *integer-1* or greater than *integer-2*.

Example

Consider the table NAME-ADDRESS-TABLE defined above. An alternate way to create this table would be

```
01  NAME-ADDRESS-TABLE.
    02  NAME-AND-ADDRESS
            OCCURS 1 TO 100 TIMES
            DEPENDING ON NUM-ELEMENTS.
        03 NAME    PIC X(20).
        03 ADDRESS PIC X(30).
```

The data-name NUM-ELEMENTS is used in exactly the same way as before; it stores the location of the last table element in use. Sometimes the value of *data-name* is included as an input item rather than calculated by counting.

Example

Each record in a data file contains registration data for a student enrolled at XYZ College. Students may enroll for a maximum of ten courses. A field within the record specifies the number of courses in which the student is enrolled. The following DATA DIVISION entries could be used to define this record:

```
01   STUDENT-RECORD.
     03   STUDENT-NUM-SR PIC 9(9).
     03   STUDENT-NAME-SR PIC X(20).
     .
     .
     .
     03   NUM-COURSES-SR PIC 99.
     03   COURSE-ENROLLMENT-SR
              OCCURS 1 TO 10 TIMES
              DEPENDING ON NUM-COURSES-SR.
         05   COURSE-NUM-SR PIC 9(6).
         05   COURSE-NAME-SR PIC X(20).
```

This data structure can be visualized as shown in Figure 9.3. Note that the use of the DEPENDING ON clause does not affect the actual allocation of space for the table. In this case physical memory is allocated for ten table elements.

The advantage in using the DEPENDING ON clause is that the system will automatically check each subscript reference against the actual number of elements in use as opposed to the maximum number of elements allocated. Thus, in the example above, if the value of NUM-COURSES-SR is 4, a reference such as COURSE-NUM-SR (5) would be treated as invalid even though 5 is less than 10. It is strongly recommended that the programmer use the DEPENDING ON clause for any table that may be only partially used.

Figure 9.3   Layout of STUDENT-RECORD

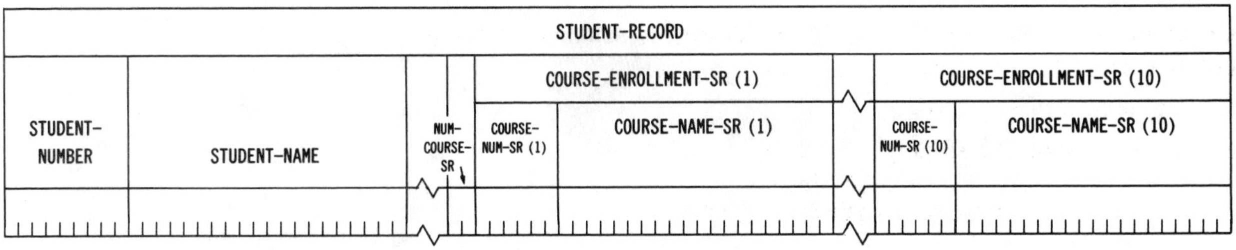

9.5   PERFORM WITH THE VARYING OPTION

The PERFORM statement with the VARYING option is used to initialize and move a counter automatically. For example:

```
PERFORM PARA VARYING INDX FROM 1 BY 1 UNTIL INDX > 10.
```

would cause the data-name INDX to have values of 1, 2, 3, . . . 9, 10 for successive executions of PARA. The execution of this statement proceeds as follows:

1) Move the initial value to the data-name (move 1 to INDX in this example).
2) If condition is *not* met, execute the paragraph; otherwise go on to the next statement (compare INDX to 10 in this example).
3) After execution of the paragraph add the increment to the data-name (add 1 to INDX in this example).
4) Go to Step 2.

Note that the incrementation of the variable is performed *before* the test is made; hence, the value of INDX after exit from the loop would be 11, the first value of INDX to satisfy the condition. Figure 9.4 illustrates the general form of the PERFORM statement with the VARYING option.

Figure 9.4   General form of PERFORM/VARYING

```
PERFORM paragraph-name              VARYING data-name
    FROM initial-value BY increment-value UNTIL condition
```

In the PERFORM/VARYING *initial-value* and *increment-value* may be a data-name or constant.[3]

A flowchart of the steps taken automatically in the execution of this version of the PERFORM statement will help you understand how it works (Fig. 9.5).

Figure 9.5   Flowchart form of PERFORM/VARYING

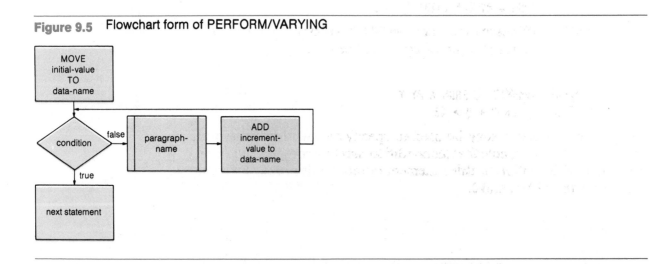

---

3. Some compilers will allow any arithmetic expression to be used to specify *initial-value* and *increment-value*.

For example, for the statement

```
PERFORM PARA VARYING INDX FROM 1 BY 1 UNTIL INDX > 10.
```

The corresponding flowchart would be

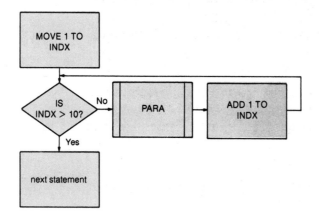

Examples

```
PERFORM PARA-A VARYING A FROM 10 BY -1 UNTIL A = 0.
```

The values of A for successive executions of PARA-A will be 10, 9, 8, ... 2, 1. The final value of A is 0, resulting in an exit from the loop.

```
PERFORM PARA-B
    VARYING B FROM 4 BY 0.5 UNTIL B > 6.
```

The values of B for successive executions of PARA-B will be 4, 4.5, 5, 5.5, 6. The final value of B is 6.5, resulting in an exit from the loop.

```
PERFORM PARA-C VARYING C FROM X BY Y
    UNTIL C > 13 OR C + Q > 43.
```

Note that a data-name may be used to specify an initial-value and an increment-value. Also, note that the condition may be a complex condition. The results of execution of this statement cannot be determined without knowing values of X, Y, and Q.

```
MOVE 10 TO Y.
PERFORM PARA-X
    VARYING X FROM Y BY 2 UNTIL X > 4.
```

In this example, PARA-X will not be executed since the condition is satisfied by the initial value of X.

The PERFORM statement with the VARYING option is quite useful for manipulating table elements. Compare the following coding examples:

Example

Without PERFORM/VARYING

```
          .
          .
          .
      MOVE 0 TO TOTAL-GRADE.
      MOVE 1 TO IND.
      PERFORM ADD-ROUTINE UNTIL IND > 75.
          .
          .
          .
  ADD-ROUTINE.
      ADD GRADE (IND) TO TOTAL-GRADE.
      ADD 1 TO IND.
```

With PERFORM/VARYING

```
          .
          .
          .
      MOVE 0 TO TOTAL-GRADE.
      PERFORM ADD-ROUTINE
          VARYING IND FROM 1 BY 1 UNTIL IND > 75.
          .
          .
          .
  ADD-ROUTINE.
      ADD GRADE (IND) TO TOTAL-GRADE.
```

The VARYING option offers a very useful technique for condensing all of the required steps for handling the table indexing variable into one statement.

Example

Without PERFORM/VARYING

```
          .
          .
          .
      PERFORM INITIALIZE-TABLE.
          .
          .
          .
  INITIALIZE-TABLE
      MOVE 1 TO IND.
      PERFORM INITIALIZE-TABLE-ELEMENT
          UNTIL IND > 12.
  INITIALIZE-TABLE-ELEMENT.
      MOVE 0 TO TOTAL-SALES (IND).
      ADD 1 TO IND.
```

With PERFORM/VARYING

```
      .
      .
      .
   PERFORM INITIALIZE-TABLE
       VARYING IND FROM 1 BY 1 UNTIL IND > 12.
      .
      .
      .
   INITIALIZE-TABLE.
       MOVE 0 TO TOTAL-SALES (IND).
```

Note the simplicity of the code which incorporates PERFORM/VARYING compared to the code without PERFORM/VARYING.

When using the PERFORM with the VARYING option, take care that the program does not enter an endless loop. The specified condition *must* occur for exiting from the loop; that is, the loop is repeated until the condition is found. For example, the following statements could cause an endless loop:

```
PERFORM PARA-D VARYING D FROM 1 BY 2 UNTIL D = 4.
```

The values of D will be 1, 3, 4, 5, ... Since D will never have the value 4 the loop will never terminate. The following statement, while syntactically correct, could cause an infinite loop or other execution time error depending on the values of table q:

```
PERFORM PARA-E VARYING E FROM 1 BY 1 UNTIL Q (E) = 0.
```

If an element of the array Q has value 0, the loop will terminate; otherwise, an execution time error will result. The above statement is useful for searching for a specified value in a table but it would be better to write:

```
PERFORM PARA-E VARYING E
    FROM 1 BY 1 UNTIL E > NUM-ELEMENTS OR Q (E) = 0.
```

Assuming that NUM-ELEMENTS is the number of elements of the table in use, the above statement will cause an exit when an element of the table Q having value 0 is found or when all the elements of Q have been compared. The search routine now can be written:

```
    PERFORM PARA-E VARYING E
        FROM 1 BY 1 UNTIL E > NUM-ELEMENTS OR Q (E) = 0.
    IF E > NUM-ELEMENTS
        PERFORM ELEMENT-NOT-FOUND
    ELSE
        PERFORM ELEMENT-FOUND.
       .
       .
       .
    PARA-E.
        EXIT.
```

This procedure assumes that the value of NUM-ELEMENTS is less than the table size. If it is possible for NUM-ELEMENTS to equal the table size, then it is also possible for the value of E to exceed the table size. In this case the reference to Q (E) will be invalid. This situation would arise when

- NUM-ELEMENTS is equal to table size
- There are no elements in the table with value zero.

In the light of these considerations it would be better to write the search routine as follows:

```
MOVE "NO" TO FOUND-FLAG.
PERFORM SEARCH-PROCEDURE
    VARYING E FROM 1 BY 1
        UNTIL E > NUM-ELEMENTS OR FOUND-FLAG = "YES".
IF FOUND-FLAG = "NO"
    PERFORM ELEMENT-NOT-FOUND
ELSE
    PERFORM ELEMENT-FOUND.
    .
    .
    .

SEARCH-PROCEDURE.
    IF Q (E) = 0
        MOVE "YES" TO FOUND-FLAG.
```

9.6 PERFORM WITH THE TIMES OPTION

Another form of the PERFORM statement can be used to execute a paragraph a number of times without varying a specific data-name. Figure 9.6 shows the general form of the PERFORM statement with the TIMES option:

Figure 9.6   General form of PERFORM/TIMES statement

PERFORM paragraph-name $\left\{ \begin{array}{c} \text{data-name} \\ \text{integer} \end{array} \right\}$ TIMES

The number of repetitions is specified using either an *integer*, as in

```
PERFORM PROCESS 10 TIMES.
```

or with a *data-name*, as in

```
PERFORM PROCESS N TIMES.
```

When a data-name is used, its value determines the number of repetitions. Thus, if the value of N is 10, the preceding two PERFORM statements are equivalent.

Example

A report is designed in such a way that five blank lines are needed at one point during the process of producing the report. The statement

```
PERFORM PRINT-BLANK-LINES 5 TIMES.
```

could be used where the procedure PRINT-BLANK-LINES could be defined as

```
PRINT-BLANK-LINES.
    MOVE SPACES TO PRINT-LINE.
    WRITE PRINT-LINE AFTER 1.
```

9.7　PROGRAM EXAMPLE

Problem Statement

A bank maintains a file as part of its data processing system which contains records recording the number of withdrawals customers have made from each account the customer has at the bank. In particular, each record contains the customer name and number of withdrawals. A report is needed by the bank's research officer that lists all records in the file. In addition, the report must contain the average number of withdrawals and a list of the accounts that have an excessive number of withdrawals. An account is considered to have an excessive number of withdrawals if the number of withdrawals exceeds four more than the average for all accounts. A printer spacing chart for the desired report is shown in Figure 9.7.

Problem Analysis

This problem calls for the program to pass through the data twice—once to produce the Customer Listing and a second time to produce the Excess Withdrawals report. A table can be used to store the customer data as it is being read during the production of the first report. Then the program can compute the average and, by processing the data stored in the table, the second report can be produced.

The program will, therefore, need a table. Each element of the table will contain a name and a number of withdrawals. For simplicity we shall assume that the bank has a maximum of 25 customers.

A preliminary plan for the report can now be written as:

Major logic
>   Open files
>   Read bank file
>   Do until end of file
>   Write detail line
>   Store customer data in table element
>   Read bank file
>   End Do
>   Do compute average
>   Do write excess withdrawal report
>   Close files
>   Stop

Because the number of customers in unknown to the program, it is necessary to use a field as a counter. Each time a record is processed, the counter can be incremented by one; the counter can also be used as a subscript to store the data into the appropriate table element. (The first record data will be stored in location 1, data from the second record will be stored in location 2, and so forth.) This field will then be used to determine the number of table elements

Figure 9.7   Printer spacing chart for Program 9.1

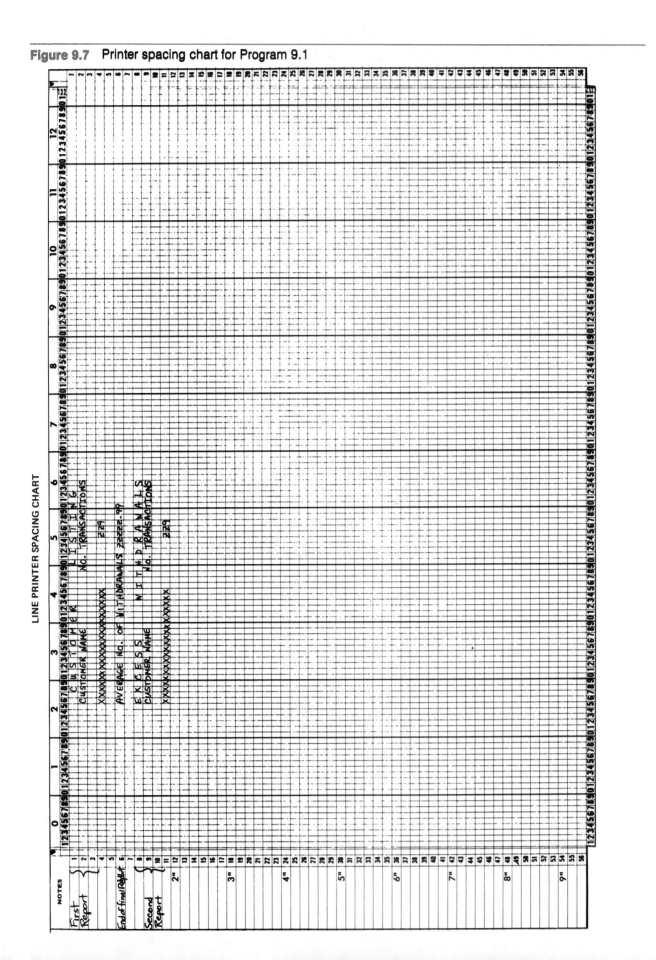

in use when the data is processed to compute the average and again when the second report is produced. Let us call this field KOUNT. The program will also need an accumulator initialized to zero to store the total of the data (TOTAL-WITHDRAWS) and a field to store the average (AVERAGE). Another data item (IND) will be needed as a subscript for the two parts of the program that will process the table.

The computation of AVERAGE will require two steps: compute TOTAL-WITHDRAWS and divide TOTAL-WITHDRAWS by KOUNT. Computing TOTAL-WITHDRAWS can be accomplished using a loop with the value of IND varying from 1 to KOUNT in increments of 1. During each repetition of the loop, data at location IND in the table is added to TOTAL-WITHDRAWS. When the loop terminates, TOTAL-WITHDRAWS will store the desired total.

The criterion for including data on the second report is that the number of withdrawals for that account exceeds AVERAGE +4. Only data that meets this condition will be listed.

With these considerations in mind we can write a final plan for the program as shown in Figure 9.8.

Figure 9.8 Plan for Program 9.1

Major logic

    Open files
    Read bank file
    Do Control until end of file
    Do Compute average
    Do Excess withdraw report
    Close files
    Stop

Control

    Add 1 to kount
    Write detail line
    Move data to table element (kount)
    Read bank file

Compute Average

    Do for values of ind from 1 to kount
        Add data (ind) to total withdraws
    End Do
    Average = total withdraws / kount
    Write average

Excess withdraw report

    Do for values of ind from 1 to kount
        If data (ind) > average + 4
            Write detail line
        End If
    End Do

Problem Solution

The program to solve this problem is shown in **Program 9.1**, with structure diagram in Figure 9.9. This program illustrates the use of a table to store data read from a data file. Note the use of the OCCURS/DEPENDING ON clause in the definition of the table at lines 8300-8400. This clause is not absolutely essential to the program, but it serves as an effective deterrent to attempts to process data in the table elements not used to store data from the file. If, in subsequent portions of the program a reference is made to the table with a subscript value larger than the value of KOUNT, an execution time error will result. Without the OCCURS/DEPENDING ON clause, the program could inadvertently process any one of the 25 elements of the table whether they stored data or not. This would show up as a logical error in the output produced by the program, but otherwise the program would continue execution.

The program would terminate with an invalid subscript error if the data file contained more than 25 records. As the program read the 26th record and incremented KOUNT to 26, the statement at line 12500 would result in a reference to the 26th element of the table, which does not exist. This problem could be corrected by revising 3000-CONTROL as follows:

```
3000-CONTROL.

    ADD 1 TO KOUNT.
    IF KOUNT < 26
        PERFORM 3500-DETAIL-LISTING
        MOVE NAME-IR    TO NAME (KOUNT)
        MOVE NUMBER-IR TO NUMBER-OR-WITHDRAWS (KOUNT)
        PERFORM 1500-READ
    ELSE
        WRITE PRINT-LINE FROM ERROR-MESSAGE AFTER 2
        CLOSE BANK-FILE
              REPORT-FILE
        STOP RUN.
```

An appropriate content for ERROR-MESSAGE would be

```
BANK FILE TOO LARGE-PROGRAM TERMINATED
```

It is important to avoid system diagnostic messages resulting from program errors insofar as is possible. A program should attempt to anticipate as many errors as possible and take care of writing its own error messages.

Program 9.1 Table program example

```
100      IDENTIFICATION DIVISION.
200
300      PROGRAM-ID. EXCESS-WITHDRAWALS.
400      AUTHOR. GARY GLEASON.
500
600      ENVIRONMENT DIVISION.
700
800      CONFIGURATION SECTION.
900
1000     SOURCE-COMPUTER.
1100     OBJECT-COMPUTER.
1200
1300     INPUT-OUTPUT SECTION.
```

Program 9.1 (continued)

```
1400
1500    FILE-CONTROL.
1600
1700        SELECT BANK-FILE ASSIGN TO DISK.
1800        SELECT REPORT-FILE ASSIGN TO PRINTER.
1900
2000    DATA DIVISION.
2100
2200    FILE SECTION.
2300
2400    FD  BANK-FILE
2500        LABEL RECORDS ARE STANDARD
2600        DATA RECORD IS INPUT-RECORD.
2700
2800    01  INPUT-RECORD.
2900        02 NAME-IR          PIC X(20).
3000        02 FILLER           PIC X(10).
3100        02 NUMBER-IR        PIC 999.
3200        02 FILLER           PIC X(47).
3300
3400    FD  REPORT-FILE
3500        LABEL RECORDS ARE OMITTED
3600        DATA RECORD IS PRINT-LINE.
3700
3800    01  PRINT-LINE          PIC X(132).
3900
4000    WORKING-STORAGE SECTION.
4100
4200    01  FLAGS.
4300        02 EOF-FLAG             PIC X(3) VALUE "NO".
4400
4500    01  SUBSCRIPT.
4600        02 IND                  PIC 99 VALUE ZERO.
4700
4800    01  COMPUTED-AMOUNTS.
4900        02 KOUNT                PIC 999 VALUE ZERO.
5000        02 TOTAL-WITHDRAWS      PIC 9(5) VALUE ZERO.
5100        02 AVERAGE              PIC 9(5)V99 VALUE ZERO.
5200
5300    01  HEADER-1-LINE.
5400        02 FILLER               PIC X(27) VALUE SPACES.
5500        02 FILLER               PIC X(15) VALUE "C U S T O M E R".
5600        02 FILLER               PIC X(7)  VALUE SPACES.
5700        02 FILLER               PIC X(13) VALUE "L I S T I N G".
5800
5900    01  HEADER-2-LINE.
6000        02 FILLER       PIC X(25) VALUE SPACES.
6100        02 FILLER       PIC X(11) VALUE "E X C E S S".
6200        02 FILLER       PIC X(7)  VALUE SPACES.
6300        02 FILLER       PIC X(21) VALUE "W I T H D R A W A L S".
6400
6500    01  HEADER-3-LINE.
6600        02 FILLER               PIC  X(25) VALUE SPACES.
6700        02 FILLER               PIC  X(13) VALUE "CUSTOMER NAME".
6800        02 FILLER               PIC  X(10) VALUE SPACES.
6900        02 FILLER               PIC  X(16) VALUE "NO. TRANSACTIONS".
7000
```

Program 9.1 (continued)

```
7100      01   AVERAGE-LINE.
7200           02 FILLER            PIC  X(25) VALUE SPACES.
7300           02 FILLER     PIC X(26) VALUE "AVERAGE NO. OF WITHDRAWALS".
7400           02 AVERAGE-OUT    PIC  Z(5).99.
7500
7600      01   DETAIL-LINE.
7700           02 FILLER            PIC X(25) VALUE SPACES.
7800           02 NAME-DL           PIC X(20).
7900           02 FILLER            PIC X(10) VALUE SPACES.
8000           02 NUMBER-DL         PIC  ZZ9.
8100
8200      01   TABLE-OF-WITHDRAWS.
8300           02   NAME-AND-NUMBER-OF-WITHDRAWS OCCURS 1 TO 25 TIMES
8400                DEPENDING ON KOUNT.
8500                03   NAME  PIC X(20).
8600                03   NUMBER-OF-WITHDRAWS PIC 999.
8700
8800      PROCEDURE DIVISION.
8900
9000      1000-MAJOR-LOGIC.
9100
9200           PERFORM 2000-INITIALIZATION.
9300           PERFORM 3000-CONTROL
9400               UNTIL EOF-FLAG = "YES".
9500           PERFORM 4000-COMPUTE-AVERAGE.
9600           PERFORM 5000-EXCESS-WITHDRAW-REPORT.
9700           PERFORM 9000-TERMINATION.
9800           STOP RUN.
9900
10000     1500-READ.
10100
10200          READ BANK-FILE
10300              AT END MOVE "YES" TO EOF-FLAG.
10400
10500     2000-INITIALIZATION.
10600
10700          OPEN INPUT BANK-FILE
10800               OUTPUT REPORT-FILE.
10900          PERFORM 2500-DETAIL-HEADING.
11000          PERFORM 1500-READ.
11100
11200     2500-DETAIL-HEADING.
11300
11400          WRITE PRINT-LINE FROM HEADER-1-LINE AFTER PAGE.
11500          WRITE PRINT-LINE FROM HEADER-3-LINE AFTER 1.
11600          MOVE SPACES TO PRINT-LINE.
11700          WRITE PRINT-LINE AFTER 1.
11800
11900     3000-CONTROL.
12000
12100          ADD 1 TO KOUNT.
12200          PERFORM 3500-DETAIL-LISTING.
12300          MOVE NAME-IR    TO NAME (KOUNT).
12400          MOVE NUMBER-IR  TO NUMBER-OF-WITHDRAWS (KOUNT).
12500          PERFORM 1500-READ.
```

Program 9.1 (continued)

```
12600
12700        3500-DETAIL-LISTING.
12800
12900           MOVE NAME-IR        TO NAME-DL.
13000           MOVE NUMBER-IR      TO NUMBER-DL.
13100           WRITE PRINT-LINE FROM DETAIL-LINE AFTER 1.
13200
13300        4000-COMPUTE-AVERAGE.
13400
13500           PERFORM 4500-COMPUTE-TOTAL
13600               VARYING IND FROM 1 BY 1 UNTIL IND > KOUNT.
13700           DIVIDE TOTAL-WITHDRAWS BY KOUNT GIVING AVERAGE.
13800           MOVE AVERAGE TO AVERAGE-OUT.
13900           WRITE PRINT-LINE FROM AVERAGE-LINE AFTER 2.
14000
14100        4500-COMPUTE-TOTAL.
14200
14300           ADD NUMBER-OF-WITHDRAWS (IND) TO TOTAL-WITHDRAWS.
14400
14500        5000-EXCESS-WITHDRAW-REPORT.
14600
14700           WRITE PRINT-LINE FROM HEADER-2-LINE AFTER PAGE.
14800           WRITE PRINT-LINE FROM HEADER-3-LINE AFTER 1.
14900           MOVE SPACES TO PRINT-LINE.
15000           WRITE PRINT-LINE AFTER 1.
15100           PERFORM 6000-DECISION-PRINT
15200               VARYING IND FROM 1 BY 1 UNTIL IND > KOUNT.
15300
15400        6000-DECISION-PRINT.
15500
15600           IF NUMBER-OF-WITHDRAWS (IND) > AVERAGE + 4
15700               MOVE NAME (IND) TO NAME-DL
15800               MOVE NUMBER-OF-WITHDRAWS (IND) TO NUMBER-DL
15900               WRITE PRINT-LINE FROM DETAIL-LINE AFTER  1.
16000
16100        9000-TERMINATION.
16200
16300           WRITE PRINT-LINE FROM AVERAGE-LINE AFTER 2.
16400           CLOSE BANK-FILE
16500                 REPORT-FILE.
```

Figure 9.9 Structure diagram of Program 9.1

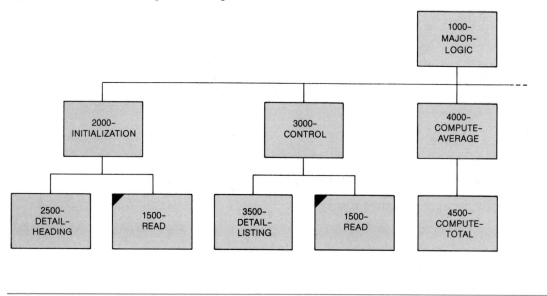

9.8 THE REDEFINES CLAUSE

In some instances there is a need to define the same data item with different names and differing characteristics. For example, suppose a product classification code contains eight digits, with the first two digits representing the division of the company which manufactures the item. For some purposes, it is useful to use one eight-digit numeric field; for others, it may be useful to have the field broken down into two fields. The REDEFINES clause is used in the DATA division to accomplish this:

```
03  PRODUCT-CLASSIFICATION-CODE PIC 9(8).
03  P-C-CODE REDEFINES PRODUCT-CLASSIFICATION-CODE.
    05 DIVISION-PC PIC 9(2).
    05 PRODUCT-PC  PIC 9(6).
```

Both PRODUCT-CLASSIFICATION-CODE and P-C-CODE refer to the same eight characters:

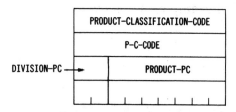

The REDEFINES clause is necessary because of the numeric nature of the data. At first glance the following code would seem to accomplish the same result:

```
03  PRODUCT-CLASSIFICATION-CODE.
    05  DIVISION-PC PIC 9(2).
    05  PRODUCT-PC  PIC 9(6).
```

However, the PRODUCT-CLASSIFICATION-CODE is a group item and hence an alphanumeric item, and cannot in general be used in computations or numeric edited output.

The general form of the REDEFINES clause is shown in Figure 9.10.

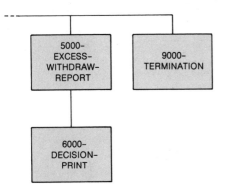

Figure 9.10   General form of the REDEFINES clause

```
level-number data-name-1 REDEFINES data-name-2
```

The *level-number* used on the REDEFINES entry must be the same as the level-number on *data-name-2* which is being "redefined." The REDEFINES clause may be used on a group data item as in the above example, or on an elementary data item as in the following example:

```
01  XYZ                PIC X(5).
01  ZYW REDEFINES XYZ PIC 9(5).
```

The above coding could be used when you want to reference the same field as both a numeric item and an alphanumeric item.

The REDEFINES clause is invalid if a data-name with a lower level number occurs between *data-name-2* and *data-name-1*. For example, the following code is invalid:

```
    03  FLDA PIC X(10)
02  FLDB.
    03  FLDC REDEFINES FLDA.
```

Data names with higher-level numbers may occur between *data-name-1* and *data-name-2*. For example, the following code could be used to define a data field as a six-digit numeric field and as three two-digit fields:

```
03  DATE-IN.
    05  MONTH-IN   PIC 99.
    05  DAY-IN     PIC 99.
    05  YEAR-IN    PIC 99.
03  DATE-NUM-IN REDEFINES DATE-IN PIC 9(6).
```

Note that the length of the item named by *data-name-1* must exactly equal the length of the item named in *data-name-2*. In the example above, DATE-IN and DATE-NUM-IN are each six characters in length.

9.9   TABLE LOOK-UP

The REDEFINES clause often is used in the creation of a table of constants to be processed by a program. Consider the following example: XYZ Manufacturing Corporation manufactures five types of widgets.

Code	Description
1	MIDGET
2	REGULAR
3	KING
4	SUPER
5	GIANT

A data record contains an item PRODUCT-CODE having value 1, 2, 3, 4 or 5; a program must output the corresponding verbal description.

One approach to the program is to create a table of constants as follows:

DESCRIPTION (1)	MIDGET
DESCRIPTION (2)	REGULAR
DESCRIPTION (3)	KING
DESCRIPTION (4)	SUPER
DESCRIPTION (5)	GIANT

The following code could be used to create this table:

```
01  DESCRIPTION-CONSTANTS.
    02  FILLER PIC X(7) VALUE "MIDGET".
    02  FILLER PIC X(7) VALUE "REGULAR".
    02  FILLER PIC X(7) VALUE "KING".
    02  FILLER PIC X(7) VALUE "SUPER".
    02  FILLER PIC X(7) VALUE "GIANT".
01  DESCRIPTION-TABLE REDEFINES DESCRIPTION-CONSTANTS.
    02  DESCRIPTION PIC X(7) OCCURS 5 TIMES.
```

The data layout created by the above may be visualized as:

DESCRIPTION-CONSTANTS				
DESCRIPTION-TABLE				
DESCRIPTION (1)	DESCRIPTION (2)	DESCRIPTION (3)	DESCRIPTION (4)	DESCRIPTION (5)
M I D G E T	R E G U L A R	K I N G	S U P E R	G I A N T

The data item PRODUCT-CODE from an input record can be used as a subscript to access the appropriate item from the table:

```
MOVE DESCRIPTION (PRODUCT-CODE) TO OUTPUT-DESCRIPTION.
```

If the value of PRODUCT-CODE is 1, 2, 3, 4 or 5, the above code will cause no problems; however, if some other value is contained in PRODUCT-CODE, the reference DESCRIPTION (PRODUCT-CODE) will produce an execution time error. A better statement for accessing the table would be:

```
IF PRODUCT-CODE = 0 OR PRODUCT-CODE > 5
    MOVE "INVALID" TO OUTPUT-DESCRIPTION
ELSE
    MOVE DESCRIPTION (PRODUCT-CODE) TO OUTPUT-DESCRIPTION.
```

In this example the look-up process was exceedingly simple, as there was a one-to-one correspondence between the PRODUCT-CODE and the table element containing the desired data DESCRIPTION (PRODUCT-CODE). If this correspondence does not exist, it may be necessary to search a table to find the desired element. The search may take the form of accessing elements of the table sequentially until the desired element is found, as in the following example: The XYZ Company uses a four digit inventory code for its five products:

Inventory Code	*Description*
1234	MIDGET
2314	REGULAR
8978	KING
8900	SUPER
7892	GIANT

The numeric data item INV-CODE is contained on an input-record. The program must output the corresponding word description.

The following code could be used to establish the table of constants:

```
01  INVENTORY-CONSTANTS.
    03  FILLER PIC X(11) VALUE "1234MIDGET".
    03  FILLER PIC X(11) VALUE "2314REGULAR".
    03  FILLER PIC X(11) VALUE "8978KING".
    03  FILLER PIC X(11) VALUE "8900SUPER".
    03  FILLER PIC X(11) VALUE "7892GIANT".
01  INVENTORY-TABLE REDEFINES INVENTORY-CONSTANTS.
    03  INVENTORY-ITEM OCCURS 5 TIMES.
        05  KODE PIC 9(4).
        05  DESCR PIC X(7).
```

This data defined above may be visualized as follows:

INVENTORY-CONSTANTS									
INVENTORY-TABLE									
INVENTORY-ITEM (1)		INVENTORY-ITEM (2)		INVENTORY-ITEM (3)		INVENTORY-ITEM (4)		INVENTORY-ITEM (5)	
KODE (1)	DESCR (1)	KODE (2)	DESCR (2)	KODE (3)	DESCR (3)	KODE (4)	DESCR (4)	KODE (5)	DESCR (5)
1234	MIDGET	2314	REGULAR	8978	KING	8900	SUPER	7892	GIANT

The program must search for an element KODE (IND), which is equal to INV-CODE. When such an element is found, the value of DESCR (IND) will contain the desired description. The following program segment could be used:

```
        MOVE "NO" TO FOUND-FLAG.
        PERFORM SEARCH-PROCEDURE
            VARYING INDX FROM 1 BY 1
            UNTIL   INDX > 5 OR FOUND-FLAG = "YES".
        IF FOUND-FLAG = "NO"
            MOVE "INVALID" TO OUTPUT-DESCRIPTION
        ELSE
            MOVE DESCR (INDX) TO OUTPUT-DESCRIPTION.
        .
        .
    SEARCH-PROCEDURE.
        IF KODE (INDX) = INV-KODE
            MOVE "YES" TO FOUND-FLAG.
```

9.10   COUNTING AND ACCUMULATION

Tables may be used for a variety of purposes. In previous examples, tables have been used to store both data and constants. Another usage for a table is in counting.

Example

A survey has been made of customer arrival times in the XYZ Department Store. One record has been prepared for each arrival, showing in coded form the hour during which the customer arrived. The following code was used in preparing the data records:

Hour	*Code*
9-10 A.M.	1
10-11 A.M.	2
11-12 A.M.	3
12-1 P.M.	4
1-2 P.M.	5
2-3 P.M.	6
3-4 P.M.	7
4-5 P.M.	8
5-6 P.M.	9

The output desired is a frequency distribution showing the number of customers who arrived during each hour.

A table of nine elements (to be utilized as counters) can be used to accumulate the desired counts. The elements of the table must be initialized to have value of zero. This process is complicated somewhat by the fact that the VALUE clause may not be used with an OCCURS clause in the DATA DIVISION; that is, the following code is invalid:

```
01  COUNTERS.
    03  KOUNT PIC 99 OCCURS 9 TIMES VALUE 0.
```

One approach to initialization is to use the REDEFINES option as though a table of constants were being created:

```
01  CONSTANTS.
    03  FILLER PIC X(18) VALUE ALL "0".
01  COUNTERS REDEFINES CONSTANTS.
    03  KOUNT PIC 99 OCCURS 9 TIMES.
```

For a large table this approach will become quite cumbersome and impractical. An alternative is to initialize the table in the PROCEDURE division prior to utilizing the variables for counting. For example:

```
        PERFORM INITIALIZE-KOUNT
                VARYING K FROM 1 BY 1 UNTIL K > 9.
    .
    .
    .
    INITIALIZE-KOUNT.
        MOVE ZERO TO KOUNT (K).
```

Once the table of counters has been initialized, the process of accumulating the required totals can begin. Suppose the data-name associated with the code on the data record is HOUR-CODE. The contents of this variable can be used to select which element of KOUNT is to be incremented. The basic code could be:

```
        ADD 1 TO KOUNT (HOUR-CODE).
```

If HOUR-CODE has value 1, KOUNT (1) will be incremented; if HOUR-CODE has value 2, one will be added to KOUNT (2), and so forth.

Tables also may be used for accumulation. For example, the XYZ Department store wants to determine which day of the week is on average its busiest day. A record for each date in the previous 52 weeks has been prepared with a code 1, 2, 3, . . . 7 showing the day of the week (DAY-CODE) and the amount of sales (SALES-AMOUNT) for that day.

A table containing seven elements can be used to accumulate the desired totals. Each element of the table must be initialized to have value zero; then as each data record is processed, the value of SALES-AMOUNT is added to the appropriate element of the table, as in the following code:

```
    .
    .
    .
    PERFORM INITIALIZATION
            VARYING K FROM 1 BY 1 UNTIL K > 7.
    PERFORM READ-AND-PROCESS
            UNTIL END-OF-FILE.
    .
    .
    .
INITIALIZATION.
    MOVE 0 TO TOTAL (K).
READ-AND-PROCESS.
    READ INPUT-FILE
        AT END MOVE "YES" TO EOF-FLAG.
    IF NOT END-OF-FILE
        ADD SALES-AMOUNT TO TOTAL (DAY-CODE).
```

9.11 TWO-LEVEL TABLES

All of the tables with which we have been dealing so far in this chapter have been one-level tables, i.e., they have been equivalent to linear lists of elements. In some situations we may need a data structure that is composed of a series of lists. Such a structure is called a *two-level table*. Elements of a two-level table require two subscripts in order to access a particular element.

For example, suppose we wish to store grades for four tests for up to 75 students. We could use a data structure such as:

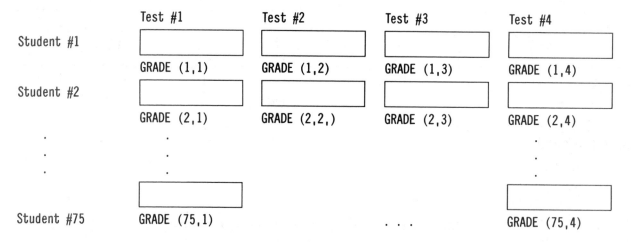

The elements of the table are referenced by the data-name GRADE and two subscripts. The first subscript refers to the student (the row). The second subscript refers to the test number for that student (the column).

Two usages of the OCCURS clause are required to create a two-level table. For example, the data structure could be created with the following DATA DIVISION entries:

```
01  NUM-STUDENTS PIC 99 VALUE 0.
01  GRADE-TABLE.
    02  STUDENT OCCURS 1 TO 75 TIMES DEPENDING ON NUM-STUDENTS.
        03  GRADE PIC 99 OCCURS 4 TIMES.
```

An alternate way to visualize this structure is as follows:

GRADE-TABLE													
STUDENT (1)				STUDENT (2)					STUDENT (75)			
GRADE (1,1)	GRADE (1,2)	GRADE (1,3)	GRADE (1,4)	GRADE (2,1)	GRADE (2,2)	GRADE (2,3)	GRADE (2,4)		GRADE (75,1)	GRADE (75,2)	GRADE (75,3)	GRADE (75,4)

Note that the data-name STUDENT may be subscripted. Thus, STUDENT (1) is a reference to all four grades of student number 1. However, STUDENT is a group item and, hence, is an alphanumeric field. Any reference to the data name GRADE must always include two subscripts.

The table could be expanded to store additional data such as the student's name and average grade. Consider the following code:

```
01  NUM-STUDENTS  PIC 99  VALUE 0.
01  STUDENT-DATA-TABLE.
    02  STUDENT OCCURS 1 TO 75 TIMES DEPENDING ON NUM-STUDENTS.
        03  NAME PIC X(20).
        03  GRADE PIC 99 OCCURS 4 TIMES.
        03  AVERAGE PIC 99.
```

The structure created by this code can be visualized as:

| STUDENT-DATA-TABLE | | | | | | | | | | | | | | | | | | | | |
| STUDENT (1) | | | | | | STUDENT (2) | | | | | | | STUDENT (75) | | | | | |
NAME (1)	GRADE (1,1)	GRADE (1,2)	GRADE (1,3)	GRADE (1,4)	AVERAGE (1)	NAME (2)	GRADE (2,1)	GRADE (2,2)	GRADE (2,3)	GRADE (2,4)	AVERAGE (2)		NAME (75)	GRADE (75,1)	GRADE (75,2)	GRADE (75,3)	GRADE (75,4)	AVERAGE (75)

Suppose the data record containing the students' names and grades has the following description:

```
01  DATA-RECORD.
    02  STUDENT-NAME PIC X(20).
    02  STUDENT-GRADE PIC 99 OCCURS 4 TIMES.
```

The following code would be used to input this data and store it into STUDENT-DATA-TABLE:

```
        .
        .
        .
    READ INPUT-FILE INTO DATA-RECORD
        AT END MOVE "YES" TO EOF FLAG.
    PERFORM STORE-AND-READ
        UNTIL END-OF-FILE OR NUM-STUDENTS = 75.
        .
        .
        .
STORE-AND-READ.
    ADD 1 TO NUM-STUDENTS.
    MOVE STUDENT-NAME TO NAME (NUM-STUDENTS).
    PERFORM GRADE-MOVE VARYING INX FROM 1 BY 1 UNTIL INX > 4.
    READ INPUT-FILE INTO DATA-RECORD
        AT END MOVE "YES" TO EOF-FLAG.
GRADE-MOVE.
    MOVE STUDENT-GRADE (INX) TO
        GRADE (NUM-STUDENTS, INX).
```

Assuming that the data has been stored, the following code could be used to compute the averages for each of the students:

```
    PERFORM AVERAGE-ROUTINE
        VARYING INX FROM 1 BY 1 UNTIL INX > NUM-STUDENTS.
        .
        .
        .
AVERAGE-ROUTINE.
    COMPUTE SUM-OF-GRADES = 0.
    PERFORM SUMMATION VARYING J FROM 1 BY 1 UNTIL J > 4.
    COMPUTE AVERAGE (INX) = SUM-OF-GRADES / 4.
SUMMATION.
    ADD GRADE (INX, J) TO SUM-OF-GRADES.
```

Two-level tables may be used for storing tables of constants which will be used by a program. Consider the example program in the next section.

9.12 PROGRAM EXAMPLE

Problem Statement

The following table shows the wholesale prices of various grades of petroleum products at four refineries:

	Refinery			
	1	2	3	4
Grade 1 Diesel	.71	.75	.78	.74
Grade 2 Regular	.84	.88	.83	.87
Grade 3 Unleaded	.97	.91	.92	.95

The number of gallons purchased, the refinery number and the type of fuel number have been stored on data records. A program which will look up the appropriate price per gallon and output the total amount of the purchase is needed. The printer spacing chart for the desired report is shown in Figure 9.11.

Problem Analysis

In this problem the price of gas depends on two factors—the grade and the refinery. Therefore a two-level table representing the prices of gas by grade (the first level) and refinery (the second level) will be useful. The program will then be able to use the grade number and refinery number from the input record directly to access the data in the table. In other respects this problem is very similar to other programs that process a data file to produce a report. A plan for this program is shown in Figure 9.12.

Figure 9.12 Plan for Program 9.2

Major logic

    Open files
    Read product file
    Do Process read until end of file
    Write summary line
    Close files
    Stop

Process read

    Compute fuel cost by multiplying price from table by gallons
    Accumulate totals
    Write detail line
    Read product file

Figure 9.11 Printer spacing chart for table look-up program

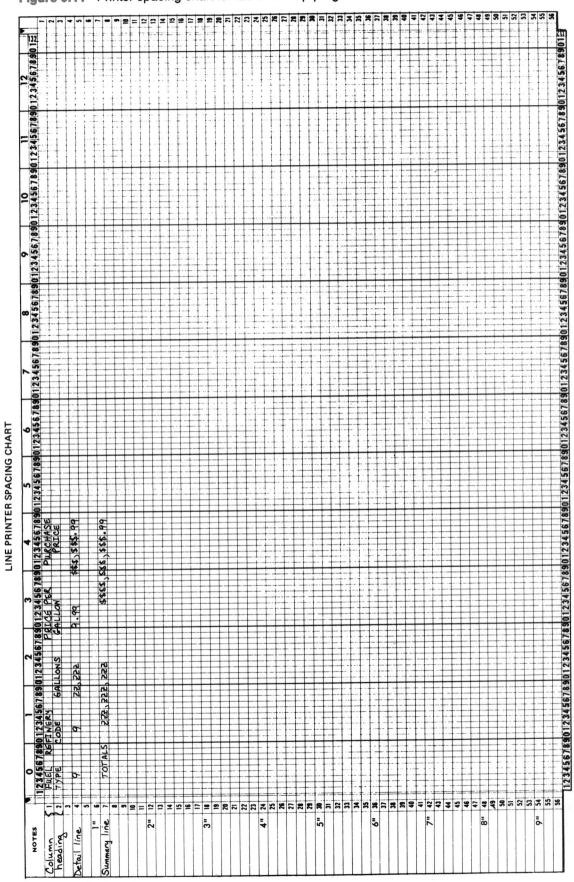

Problem Solution

A program for this problem is shown in Program 9.2 with structure diagram in Figure 9.13. This program illustrates the use of a two-level table of constants. The table is created at lines 5000 through 6800, using the REDEFINES clause at line 6600 to provide access to the constants created in the preceding data structure (FUEL-PRICE-TABLE defined in lines 5000-6500). This table can be visualized as shown below:

FUEL-PRICING-TABLE											
FUEL-PRICES											
DIESEL				REGULAR				UNLEADED			
FUEL-TYPE (1)				FUEL-TYPE (2)				FUEL-TYPE (3)			
PRICE (1,1)	PRICE (1,2)	PRICE (1,3)	PRICE (1,4)	PRICE (2,1)	PRICE (2,2)	PRICE (2,3)	PRICE (2,4)	PRICE (3,1)	PRICE (3,2)	PRICE (3,3)	PRICE (3,4)
0.71	0.75	0.78	0.74	0.84	0.88	0.83	0.87	0.97	0.91	0.92	0.95

At lines 13000 and 13200 the program uses data from the table for output and computation. The table reference is:

```
. . . PRICE (FUEL-TYPE-IR, REFINERY-CODE-IR) . . .
```

The first subscript corresponds to level one of the table (type of fuel) and the second subscript corresponds to level two of the table (refinery).

A potential problem arises if the value of FUEL-TYPE-IR is not in the range 1 to 3 or if the value of REFINERY-CODE-IR is not in the range 1 to 4. If either of these happens, the program will terminate at line 13000 with an out-of-range subscript error. In order to avoid this problem, the following modifications to the program can be made:

1) Modify the definition of the input record to include a named condition for FUEL-TYPE-IR and REFINERY-CODE-IR as shown below:

```
01  INPUT-RECORD.
    02  GALLONS-USED-IR      PIC 9(5).
    02  FUEL-TYPE-IR         PIC 9.
        88 VALID-FUEL-TYPE      VALUE 1 2 3.
    02  REFINERY-CODE-IR     PIC 9.
        88 VALID-REFINERY CODE  VALUE 1 THRU 4.
    02  FILLER               PIC X(77).
```

2) Modify lines 13000 through 13300 as follows:

```
IF VALID-FUEL-TYPE AND VALID-REFINERY-CODE
      MOVE PRICE (FUEL-TYPE-IR, REFINERY-CODE-IR)
          TO PRICE-PER-GALLON-DL
      MULTIPLY PRICE (FUEL-TYPE-IR, REFINERY-CODE-IR)
          BY GALLONS-IR GIVING FUEL-COST
ELSE
      MOVE ZERO TO PRICE-PER-GALLON-DL
                   FUEL-COST
      WRITE PRINT-LINE FROM ERROR-MESSAGE AFTER 2.
```

An appropriate content for ERROR-MESSAGE would be

```
INVALID DATA ON FOLLOWING RECORD
```

Note that the proposed modification does not terminate execution of the program, however, because zero is used as the fuel price the invalid data will not affect the final totals. If the modification is not made, the program could terminate with a system error message that might be difficult to understand. System error messages should be avoided if at all possible.

Program 9.2 Two-level table example

```
100     IDENTIFICATION DIVISION.
200
300     PROGRAM-ID. GAS-STATION.
400     AUTHOR. GARY GLEASON.
500
600     ENVIRONMENT DIVISION.
700
800     CONFIGURATION SECTION.
900
1000    SOURCE-COMPUTER.
1100    OBJECT-COMPUTER.
1200
1300    INPUT-OUTPUT SECTION.
1400
1500    FILE-CONTROL.
1600
1700        SELECT PRODUCT-FILE ASSIGN TO DISK.
1800        SELECT PURCHASE-FILE ASSIGN TO PRINTER.
1900
2000    DATA DIVISION.
2100
2200    FILE SECTION.
2300
2400    FD  PRODUCT-FILE
2500        LABEL RECORDS ARE STANDARD
2600        DATA RECORD IS INPUT-RECORD.
2700
2800    01  INPUT-RECORD.
2900        02 GALLONS-IR          PIC 9(5).
3000        02 FUEL-TYPE-IR        PIC 9.
3100        02 REFINERY-CODE-IR    PIC 9.
3200        02 FILLER              PIC X(77).
3300
3400    FD  PURCHASE-FILE
3500        LABEL RECORDS ARE OMITTED
3600        DATA RECORD IS PRINT-LINE.
3700
3800    01  PRINT-LINE          PIC X(132).
3900
4000    WORKING-STORAGE SECTION.
4100
4200    01  FLAGS.
4300        02  EOF-FLAG        PIC X(3) VALUE "NO".
4400
```

```
4500      01  TOTALS.
4600          02 FUEL-COST           PIC 9(6)V99 VALUE ZERO.
4700          02 TOTAL-GALLONS       PIC 9(9)    VALUE ZERO.
4800          02 TOTAL-COST          PIC 9(9)V99 VALUE ZERO.
4900
5000      01  FUEL-PRICING-TABLE.
5100          02  DIESEL.
5200              03  FILLER PIC 9V99 VALUE 0.71.
5300              03  FILLER PIC 9V99 VALUE 0.75.
5400              03  FILLER PIC 9V99 VALUE 0.78.
5500              03  FILLER PIC 9V99 VALUE 0.74.
5600          02  REGULAR.
5700              03  FILLER PIC 9V99 VALUE 0.84.
5800              03  FILLER PIC 9V99 VALUE 0.88.
5900              03  FILLER PIC 9V99 VALUE 0.83.
6000              03  FILLER PIC 9V99 VALUE 0.87.
6100          02  UN-LEADED.
6200              03  FILLER PIC 9V99 VALUE 0.97.
6300              03  FILLER PIC 9V99 VALUE 0.91.
6400              03  FILLER PIC 9V99 VALUE 0.92.
6500              03  FILLER PIC 9V99 VALUE 0.95.
6600      01  FUEL-PRICES REDEFINES FUEL-PRICING-TABLE.
6700          02  FUEL-TYPE OCCURS 3 TIMES.
6800              03  PRICE PIC 9V99 OCCURS 4 TIMES.
6900
7000      01  HEADLINE-1.
7100          02 FILLER              PIC X VALUE SPACES.
7200          02 FILLER              PIC X(14) VALUE "FUEL  REFINERY".
7300          02 FILLER              PIC X(12) VALUE SPACES.
7400          02 FILLER              PIC X(9) VALUE "PRICE PER".
7500          02 FILLER              PIC X(4) VALUE SPACES.
7600          02 FILLER              PIC X(8) VALUE "PURCHASE".
7700
7800      01  HEADLINE-2.
7900          02 FILLER              PIC X VALUE SPACES.
8000          02 FILLER              PIC X(12) VALUE "TYPE    CODE".
8100          02 FILLER              PIC X(4) VALUE SPACES.
8200          02 FILLER              PIC X(7) VALUE "GALLONS".
8300          02 FILLER              PIC X(4) VALUE SPACES.
8400          02 FILLER              PIC X(7) VALUE "GALLONS".
8500          02 FILLER              PIC X(8) VALUE SPACES.
8600          02 FILLER              PIC X(5) VALUE "PRICE".
8700
8800      01  DETAIL-LINE.
8900          02 FILLER              PIC X(3) VALUE SPACES.
9000          02 FUEL-TYPE-DL        PIC 9.
9100          02 FILLER              PIC X(7) VALUE SPACES.
9200          02 REFINERY-CODE-DL    PIC 9.
9300          02 FILLER              PIC X(5) VALUE SPACES.
9400          02 GALLONS-DL          PIC ZZ,ZZZ.
9500          02 FILLER              PIC X(6) VALUE SPACES.
9600          02 PRICE-PER-GALLON-DL PIC 9.99.
9700          02 FILLER              PIC X(5) VALUE SPACES.
9800          02 FUEL-COST-DL        PIC $$$$,$$$,$$$.99.
9900
10000     01  SUMMARY-LINE.
```

Program 9.2 (continued)

```
10100        02 FILLER                PIC X(12) VALUE "   TOTALS   ".
10200        02 TOTAL-GALLONS-SL      PIC ZZZ,ZZZ,ZZZ.
10300        02 FILLER                PIC X(10) VALUE SPACES.
10400        02 TOTAL-COST-SL         PIC $$$$,$$$,$$$.99.
10500
10600    PROCEDURE DIVISION.
10700
10800    1000-MAJOR-LOGIC.
10900
11000        PERFORM 2000-INITIALIZATION.
11100        PERFORM 3000-PROCESS-READ
11200            UNTIL EOF-FLAG = "YES".
11300        PERFORM 8000-WRITE-SUMMARY.
11400        PERFORM 9000-TERMINATION.
11500        STOP RUN.
11600
11700    2000-INITIALIZATION.
11800
11900        OPEN INPUT PRODUCT-FILE
12000             OUTPUT PURCHASE-FILE.
12100        WRITE PRINT-LINE FROM HEADLINE-1 AFTER PAGE.
12200        WRITE PRINT-LINE FROM HEADLINE-2 AFTER 1.
12300        PERFORM 4000-READ.
12400
12500    3000-PROCESS-READ.
12600
12700        MOVE FUEL-TYPE-IR     TO FUEL-TYPE-DL.
12800        MOVE REFINERY-CODE-IR TO REFINERY-CODE-DL.
12900        MOVE GALLONS-IR       TO GALLONS-DL.
13000        MOVE PRICE (FUEL-TYPE-IR, REFINERY-CODE-IR) TO
13100            PRICE-PER-GALLON-DL.
13200        MULTIPLY PRICE (FUEL-TYPE-IR, REFINERY-CODE-IR) BY
13300            GALLONS-IR GIVING FUEL-COST.
13400        MOVE FUEL-COST        TO FUEL-COST-DL.
13500        ADD  FUEL-COST        TO TOTAL-COST.
13600        ADD  GALLONS-IR       TO TOTAL-GALLONS.
13700        MOVE DETAIL-LINE TO PRINT-LINE.
13800        WRITE PRINT-LINE AFTER 1.
13900        PERFORM 4000-READ.
14000
14100    4000-READ.
14200
14300        READ PRODUCT-FILE
14400            AT END MOVE "YES" TO EOF-FLAG.
14500
14600    8000-WRITE-SUMMARY.
14700
14800        MOVE TOTAL-GALLONS TO TOTAL-GALLONS-SL.
14900        MOVE TOTAL-COST    TO TOTAL-COST-SL.
15000        WRITE PRINT-LINE FROM SUMMARY-LINE AFTER 2.
15100
15200    9000-TERMINATION.
15300
15400        CLOSE PRODUCT-FILE
15500             PURCHASE-FILE.
```

Figure 9.13   Structure diagram for Program 9.2

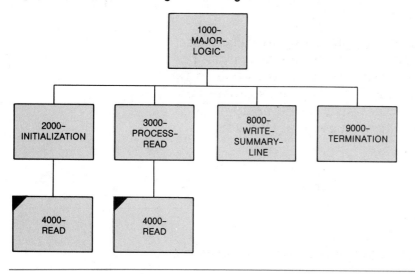

Figure 9.14   General form of the PERFORM/VARYING/AFTER statement

```
PERFORM   paragraph-name
   VARYING  data-name-1 FROM initial-value-1 BY increment-value-1 UNTIL condition-1
   [AFTER data-name-2 FROM initial-value-2 BY increment-value-2 UNTIL condition-2]
   [AFTER data-name-3 FROM initial-value-3 BY increment-value-3 UNTIL condition-3]
```

Figure 9.15   Flowchart of PERFORM/VARYING with one AFTER clause

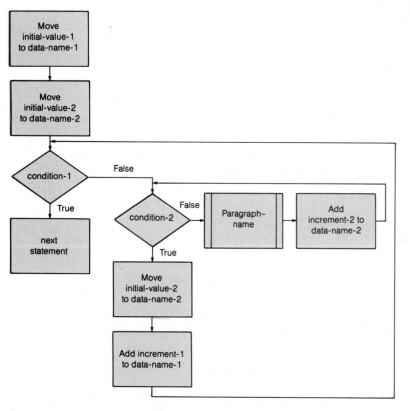

9.13   THE PERFORM/VARYING/AFTER STATEMENT

There are many instances, particularly when processing two-dimensional tables, when it is necessary to alter two variables over specified ranges. The PERFORM/VARYING/AFTER statement is an extension of the ideas utilized in PERFORM/VARYING and allows automatic control over two variables in one statement (Fig. 9.14). When one AFTER clause is used, *data-name-1* is varied through its range of values for each value of *data-name-2* (Fig. 9.15).

Example

Consider the statement:

```
PERFORM PARA-A
    VARYING X FROM 1 BY 1 UNTIL X > 4
    AFTER   Y FROM 1 BY 1 UNTIL Y > 3.
```

PARA-A would be executed $3 \times 4 = 12$ times with the following values of X and Y:

X	1	1	1	2	2	2	3	3	3	4	4	4
Y	1	2	3	1	2	3	1	2	3	1	2	3

For each new value of the first data-name X, the second data-name Y is reinitialized to its starting value and continues to be incremented until the second condition ($Y > 3$) is satisfied. The flowchart for this statement would be:

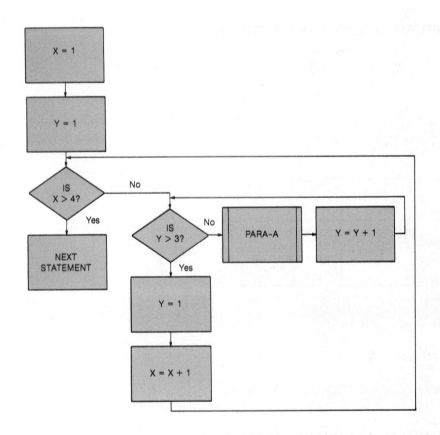

When two AFTER clauses are used, *data-name-3* is varied through its range of values for each value of *data-name-2* and *data-name-2* is varied through its range of values for each value of *data-name-1* (Fig. 9.16).

Example

Consider the statement:

```
PERFORM PARA-B
    VARYING X FROM 1 BY 1 UNTIL X > 3
    AFTER Y   FROM 1 BY 1 UNTIL Y > 4
    AFTER Z   FROM 1 BY 1 UNTIL Z > 2.
```

PARA-B would be executed $3 \times 4 \times 2 = 24$ times with the following values of X, Y and Z:

X	1 1 1 1 1 1 1 1 2 2 2 2 2 2 2 2 3 3 3 3 3 3 3 3
Y	1 1 2 2 3 3 4 4 1 1 2 2 3 3 4 4 1 1 2 2 3 3 4 4
Z	1 2 1 2 1 2 1 2 1 2 1 2 1 2 1 2 1 2 1 2 1 2 1 2

Figure 9.16   Flowchart of PERFORM/VARYING with two AFTER clauses

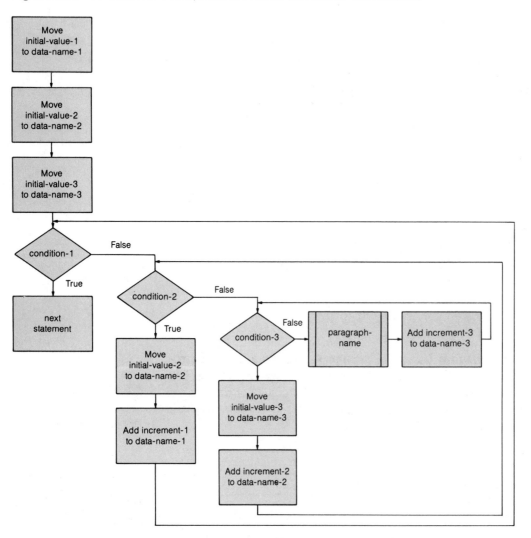

Example

A data file contains production data for each working day at Widgets Mfg., Inc. Each record contains the total number of units produced for each of the five production lines at the factory for a working day. At most, the file contains one year's data. For a program that will store this data into a table, the following DATA DIVISION entries could be used:

```
01  NUM-DAYS PIC 999 VALUE 0.
01  PRODUCTION-DATA.
    02  DAILY-DATA
        OCCURS 1 TO 366 TIMES
        DEPENDING ON NUM-DAYS.
        03  PRODUCTION PIC 9(5) OCCURS 5 TIMES.
```

Suppose the program has read and stored the data and that it is required to calculate the average daily production for all production lines. The following code could be used:

```
        .
        .

        .
    MOVE 0 TO PRODUCTION-TOTAL.
    PERFORM SUMMATION
        VARYING DAY-INDEX
          FROM 1 BY 1 UNTIL DAY-INDEX > NUM-DAYS
        AFTER LINE-INDEX
          FROM 1 BY 1 UNTIL LINE-INDEX > 5.
    COMPUTE AVERAGE-PRODUCTION =
        PRODUCTION-TOTAL / (NUM-DAYS * 5).
        .
        .

        .
SUMMATION.
    ADD PRODUCTION (DAY-INDEX, LINE-INDEX)
        TO PRODUCTION-TOTAL.
```

9.14 THREE-LEVEL TABLES

Tables of up to three levels may be created and processed by a COBOL program. A three-level table may be visualized as a series of two-level tables. For example, suppose an instructor has five classes, each class containing a maximum of 75 students each of whom takes five tests. A table to store this data could be defined as:

```
01  GRADE-TABLE.
    02  CLASS-ENTRY OCCURS 5 TIMES.
        03  STUDENT-ENTRY OCCURS 75 TIMES.
            04  TEST-ENTRY OCCURS 5 TIMES.
                05  GRADE PIC 99.
```

This structure may be visualized as shown in Figure 9.17

Figure 9.17 Representation of a three-level table

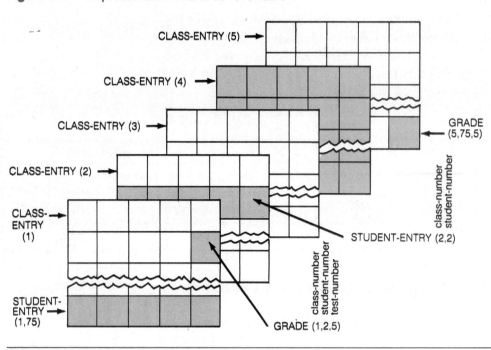

Figure 9.18 A three-level table

GRADE–TABLE																												
CLASS–ENTRY (1)																CLASS–ENTRY (5)												
STUDENT–ENTRY (1,1)					STUDENT–ENTRY (1,2)						STUDENT–ENTRY (1,75)						STUDENT–ENTRY (5,1)					STUDENT–ENTRY (5,75)					
TEST–ENTRY (1,1,1)	TEST–ENTRY (1,1,2)	TEST–ENTRY (1,1,3)	TEST–ENTRY (1,1,4)	TEST–ENTRY (1,1,5)	TEST–ENTRY (1,2,1)	TEST–ENTRY (1,2,2)	TEST–ENTRY (1,2,3)	TEST–ENTRY (1,2,4)	TEST–ENTRY (1,2,5)		TEST–ENTRY (1,75,1)	TEST–ENTRY (1,75,2)	TEST–ENTRY (1,75,3)	TEST–ENTRY (1,75,4)	TEST–ENTRY (1,75,5)		TEST–ENTRY (5,1,1)	TEST–ENTRY (5,1,2)	TEST–ENTRY (5,1,3)	TEST–ENTRY (5,1,4)	TEST–ENTRY (5,1,5)	TEST–ENTRY (5,75,1)	TEST–ENTRY (5,75,2)	TEST–ENTRY (5,75,3)	TEST–ENTRY (5,75,4)	TEST–ENTRY (5,75,5)	
GRADE (1,1,1)	GRADE (1,1,2)	GRADE (1,1,3)	GRADE (1,1,4)	GRADE (1,1,5)	GRADE (1,2,1)	GRADE (1,2,2)	GRADE (1,2,3)	GRADE (1,2,4)	GRADE (1,2,5)		GRADE (1,75,1)	GRADE (1,75,2)	GRADE (1,75,3)	GRADE (1,75,4)	GRADE (1,75,5)		GRADE (5,1,1)	GRADE (5,1,2)	GRADE (5,1,3)	GRADE (5,1,4)	GRADE (5,1,5)	GRADE (5,75,1)	GRADE (5,75,2)	GRADE (5,75,3)	GRADE (5,75,4)	GRADE (5,75,5)	

An alternate way to visualize this table is shown in Figure 9.18. Each CLASS–ENTRY is composed of a table of size 75×5; the entire structure contains $5 \times 75 \times 5 = 1875$ elements. References to CLASS–ENTRY require one subscript. References to STUDENT–ENTRY require two subscripts; the first indicates the class and the second indicates the student within the class. References to TEST–ENTRY and GRADE require three subscripts; the first indicates the class, the second indicates the student, and the third indicates the test.

Note that the order of subscripts from left to right corresponds to the order in which the OCCURS clauses are nested. It would be possible to create storage for this data in a number of different ways. So long as the subscripts used to reference the data correspond to the way in which the structure was created, the same processing steps can be accomplished. For example, suppose the following DATA DIVISION entry is made:

```
01  GRADE-TABLE-ALTERNATE.
    02  TEST-ENTRY OCCURS 5 TIMES.
        03  CLASS-ENTRY OCCURS 5 TIMES.
            04  STUDENT-ENTRY OCCURS 75 TIMES.
                05  GRADE PIC 99.
```

This structure can be visualized as:

GRADE-TABLE-ALTERNATE										
TEST-ENTRY (1)								TEST-ENTRY (5)		
CLASS-ENTRY (1,1)					CLASS-ENTRY (1,5)			CLASS-ENTRY (5,1)		
STUDENT-ENTRY-(1,1,1)	STUDENT-ENTRY (1,1,2)		STUDENT-ENTRY-(1,1,75)		STUDENT-ENTRY-(1,5,1)		STUDENT-ENTRY-(1,5,75)	STUDENT-ENTRY-(5,1,1)		STUDENT-ENTRY-(5,1,75)
GRADE (1,1,1)	GRADE (1,1,2)		GRADE (1,1,75)		GRADE (1,5,1)		GRADE (1,5,75)	GRADE (5,1,1)		GRADE (5,1,75)

Reference to GRADE (4, 1, 2) would mean test number 4, class number 1, student number 2.

The way in which a table should be created will be governed to some extent by the way data is organized on input and also by the type of processing to be performed. For example, suppose it is necessary to include a description of each class, the number of students in each class, and the name of each student in the data structure. The first way in which the data was defined can be modified easily to include this new data as shown below:

```
01  GRADE-TABLE-EXTENDED.
    02  CLASS-ENTRY OCCURS 5 TIMES.
        03  CLASS-DESCRIPTION PIC X(20).
        03  NUM-STUDENTS PIC 99.
        03  STUDENT-ENTRY OCCURS 75 TIMES.
            04  STUDENT-NAME PIC X(20).
            04  TEST-ENTRY OCCURS 5 TIMES.
                05  GRADE PIC 99.
```

Trying to modify GRADE-TABLE-ALTERNATE to include the new data would be difficult because it would be necessary to duplicate class and student information for each test.

Example

A company assigns a Christmas bonus based on type of employee (hourly or salaried), years with company (one to five) and job performance rating (one to four) according to the following tables:

	Hourly Job Performance						**Salaried** Job Performance			
	1	2	3	4			1	2	3	4
1	100	150	200	275		1	200	275	350	425
2	110	160	210	285		2	220	245	375	440
Years 3	140	190	230	295		Years 3	230	305	380	450
4	145	195	235	300		4	240	315	395	465
5	160	200	240	305		5	250	325	400	475

A data structure to store this data for a program which will look up the appropriate bonus value could be defined as:

```
01  BONUS-CONSTANTS.
    02  HOURLY-CONSTANTS.
        03  FILLER PIC X(12) VALUE "100150200275".
        03  FILLER PIC X(12) VALUE "110160210285".
        03  FILLER PIC X(12) VALUE "140190230295".
        03  FILLER PIC X(12) VALUE "145195235300".
        03  FILLER PIC X(12) VALUE "160200240305".
    02  SALARIED-CONSTANTS.
        03  FILLER PIC X(12) VALUE "200275350425".
        03  FILLER PIC X(12) VALUE "220245375440".
        03  FILLER PIC X(12) VALUE "230305380450".
        03  FILLER PIC X(12) VALUE "240315395465".
        03  FILLER PIC X(12) VALUE "250325400475".
01  BONUS-TABLE REDEFINES BONUS-CONSTANTS.
    02  EMPLOYEE-LEVEL-ENTRY OCCURS 2 TIMES.
        03  YEARS-WITH-CO-ENTRY OCCURS 5 TIMES.
            04  JOB-PERFORMANCE-ENTRY OCCURS 4 TIMES.
                05  BONUS-AMOUNT PIC 999.
```

Assume that the data-name EMPLOYEE-LEVEL contains a value 1 if the employee is hourly, and 2 if the employee is salaried. Also assume the JOB-PERFORMANCE contains a value 1 to 4 and that YEARS-WITH-CO contains the employee length of service. The following code could be used to compute CHRISTMAS-BONUS:

```
IF YEARS-WITH-CO < 1
    MOVE BONUS-AMOUNT (EMPLOYEE-LEVEL, 1, JOB-PERFORMANCE)
    TO CHRISTMAS-BONUS.
IF YEARS-WITH-CO > 5
    MOVE BONUS-AMOUNT (EMPLOYEE-LEVEL, 5, JOB-PERFORMANCE)
    TO CHRISTMAS-BONUS.
IF YEARS-WITH-CO > 0 AND YEARS-WITH-CO < 6
    MOVE BONUS-AMOUNT (EMPLOYEE-LEVEL, YEARS-WITH-CO, JOB-PERFORMANCE)
    TO CHRISTMAS-BONUS.
```

9.15   DEBUG CLINIC

Errors in utilizing tables most commonly result from problems with out-of-range subscript values. If a subscript value is outside the allowable range, an execution time error results. Typically the program terminates with an error message and perhaps a listing of information which the programmer can use to find the statement causing the problem. Frequently the programmer has to rerun the program with some diagnostic output to determine the values of appropriate data-names. Diagnostic output need consist only of the values of data-names and perhaps labels to help in evaluating the output produced. For example, suppose the cause of an execution time error has been traced to a statement such as:

```
COMPUTE TABL (X, Y) = . . .
        .
        .
        .
```

It would be useful to know the values of X and Y prior to the error. By inserting code such as the following, the programmer can determine these values:

```
        .
        .
        .
    PERFORM DIAGNOSTIC-OUTPUT.
    COMPUTE TABL (X, Y) = . . .
        .
        .
        .
DIAGNOSTIC-OUTPUT.
    MOVE X TO X-OUT.
    MOVE Y TO Y-OUT.
    WRITE PRINT-LINE FROM DIAGNOSTIC-LINE AFTER 1.
```

Once the cause of the problem has been found and eliminated, it is necessary to remove all executions of diagnostic output. It is not necessary to remove code from the DATA DIVISION or the diagnostic routine itself unless you want to optimize use of memory. Leaving these elements in a program may make the program easier to debug for some future programmer required to perform maintenance on the program.

9.16   DATA REPRESENTATION ON IBM SYSTEMS

In most computing systems more than one method for representing numeric data internally is used, and methods vary somewhat from system to system. In the discussion that follows, we shall restrict ourselves to a description of data representation used on IBM Systems 360/370/43xx/30xx and systems 34, and 36.

Although it is usually not absolutely necessary for the COBOL programmer to be aware of the different forms of data representation, there are some instances in which this knowledge enables the programmer to write programs which either are more efficient or use less memory, or both. This knowledge also may be required to process files produced as output by programs written in languages other than COBOL. On the IBM systems the following types of data representation are available:

Zoned decimal
Packed decimal
Binary
Single precision floating point
Double precision floating point

Zoned decimal data representation uses one byte (eight bits) to store each decimal digit. The first four bits for each byte are called the *zone* for the digit. The codes used are shown in Figure 9.19. Thus, a field containing three digits having value 370 would be represented as:

F3 F7 F0

The zone in the rightmost digit in the field is used to represent the sign. The following correspondence is used:

Zone	Meaning
F	unsigned (positive value)
C	signed positive
D	signed negative

For example, the value −23 would be represented as:

F2 D3

Figure 9.19   Representation of zoned decimal data

Digit	Binary representation	Hexadecimal representation
	Zone	Zone
	↓	↓
1	1111 0001	F1
2	1111 0010	F2
3	1111 0011	F3
4	1111 0100	F4
5	1111 0101	F5
6	1111 0110	F6
7	1111 0111	F7
8	1111 1000	F8
9	1111 1001	F9
0	1111 0000	F0

Packed decimal data representation uses each byte except the rightmost byte in the field to store *two* decimal digits. The rightmost four bits of the rightmost byte are used to store the sign using the codes described above. For example, the value 370 would be represented as:

Sign

37 0F

Note that the value 370, which requires three bytes when represented in zoned decimal, may be represented in just two bytes in pack decimal. The value of −23 would be represented as:

Sign

02 3D

In general, values larger than two digits in length occupy fewer bytes when represented in packed decimal than in zoned decimal. When computation is performed on zoned decimal data, the data must be transformed into packed decimal form. This transformation, of course, takes a certain amount of time, a consideration which could become significant if a large volume of computations are to be performed.

Binary data representation utilizes straight binary numeration to represent values. Either 16, 32, or 64 bits may be used for the data item. For example, the value 370 would be represented in 16 bits as:

00000001 01110010

Binary data is used for data items such as indices, which are not used for input or output and which can benefit from the very efficient manner in which the computer hardware performs computations with binary data.

Floating point data representation is similar in many respects to scientific notation. A data item is represented in memory by storing a sequence of significant digits and an exponent representing a power of the base. The following scheme is used:

exponent   fraction

↑
Assumed position of the decimal point

The value represented is then:

fraction $\times$ base^{exponent}

For example, assuming a base 10 system, the number 37,000,000 might be represented as

08 37 00 00

which would stand for

.370000 $\times$ 10^8 = 37,000,000

On IBM Systems, the actual base used is 16. Floating point data may be represented utilizing 32 bits (single precision). A single precision item utilizes the first 8 bits to represent the exponent and the remaining 24 bits to represent the fraction. A double precision item utilizes the first 8 bits for the exponent, just as for a single precision item, but the fraction is now longer (56 bits). The basic advantage to utilizing floating point data is that values with very large and very small magnitudes may be represented in a fixed space. The primary disadvantage is that only a limited number of significant digits can be represented. A COBOL programmer might wish to use floating point data when evaluating certain formulas that are primarily scientific in nature or when processing a file containing data items stored in this format.

9.17   THE USAGE CLAUSE

The USAGE clause used in the definition of an elementary data item in the DATA division specifies the type of data representation to be assumed for this data item. The general form for the USAGE clause is shown in Figure 9.20.
The details of internal representation of all data types are compiler dependent. DISPLAY is the default type for all numeric fields. Thus the definition

    03 FLDA PIC 99V9 USAGE IS DISPLAY.

is equivalent to

    03 FLDA PIC 99V9.

Figure 9.20   General form of the USAGE clause

```
           ┌ COMPUTATIONAL ┐
           │ COMP          │
USAGE IS   │               │
           │ DISPLAY       │
           └ INDEX         ┘
```

The type DISPLAY is used primarily for fields contained on input/output records.

A data item that has a USAGE of COMPUTATIONAL (or the equivalent COMP) is a numeric field typically used to store results of computations. Usually a field will be transformed from DISPLAY into COMPUTATIONAL any time an arithmetic operation is performed on the field. (The compiler inserts the code required to perform these transformations.) Defining fields used as counters, accumulators, and so on as USAGE COMPUTATIONAL makes the transformation unnecessary, thereby increasing the efficiency of the computer in executing the program.

USAGE type INDEX is used for data items to be used as subscripts for table references. The primary value of specifying a data item to have USAGE INDEX is to make table references more efficient. Data items specified as USAGE INDEX may be manipulated only by the PERFORM/VARYING statement and the SET statement. IBM compilers provide additional types of data in the USAGE clause as illustrated in Figure 9.21.

Figure 9.21   USAGE clause for IBM systems

```
           ┌ COMPUTATIONAL   ┐
           │ COMP            │
           │ COMPUTATIONAL-1 │
           │ COMP-1          │
           │ COMPUTATIONAL-2 │
USAGE IS   │ COMP-2          │
           │ COMPUTATIONAL-3 │
           │ COMP-3          │
           │ DISPLAY         │
           └ INDEX           ┘
```

Figure 9.22   Correspondence between USAGE and data representation for IBM systems

USAGE description	*Data representation*
DISPLAY	Zoned decimal
COMPUTATIONAL	Binary (no restrictions on manipulation)
COMPUTATIONAL-1	Single precision floating point
COMPUTATIONAL-2	Double precision floating point
COMPUTATIONAL-3	Packed decimal
INDEX	Binary (restrictions on manipulation)

The correspondence between the data types defined in the USAGE clause and the internal types defined in section 9.17 above is shown in Figure 9.22. COMPUTATIONAL-3 data may be specified for fields that are going to be used for computational purposes to reduce the amount of time required to convert from DISPLAY to COMPUTATIONAL-3 and back. For example, counters and accumulators that are used repeatedly in computation may be specified as COMPUTATIONAL-3.

Example

```
03  SUM PIC 9999V99 USAGE COMPUTATIONAL-3.
03  KOUNT PIC 9(5) USAGE COMPUTATIONAL-3.
```

Binary data is required in a COBOL program for subscript values. For example, the value of IND must be represented in binary when the statement MOVE DATA (IND) TO DATA-OUT is executed. If a data item used as a subscript is not a binary type item, the COBOL compiler generates code required to make the transformation, but this transformation takes time to perform. COMPUTATIONAL or INDEX data may be specified for fields that will be used as subscripts to reduce the time required to convert from DISPLAY to COMPUTATIONAL for each table reference.

Example

```
01  I PIC 99 USAGE COMPUTATIONAL.
    .
    .
    .
PROCEDURE DIVISION.
    .
    .
    .
    MOVE TABLE (I) TO AMOUNT-OUT.
```

The USAGE clause also may be required for describing records in files produced by other programs. For example, suppose we are given the following record description:

Record position	Description
1-16	Name
17-21	Year to date salary (packed decimal)
22-26	Year to date FICA (packed decimal)
27-35	Social security number

The record description that would be coded into the COBOL program would be:

```
01  INPUT-RECORD.
    02  NAME-IR PIC X(16).
    02  YTD-SAL-IR PIC 9999999V99 USAGE COMPUTATIONAL-3.
    02  YTD-FICA-IR PIC 9999999V99 USAGE COMPUTATIONAL-3.
    02  SS-NUM-IR PIC 9(9) USAGE DISPLAY.
```

Note that the field YTD-SAL occupies five bytes in the input record but is given a picture allowing for nine digits. When you use packed decimal data representation, a five-byte field can accommodate a number of this size. The use of USAGE DISPLAY to describe SS-NUM in the above example is for documentation purposes only; the record description would be used also by the program that first created the records in the file.

9.18   SELF—TEST EXERCISES

1. The following partial program contains a table for the description, part number, and price for the inventory of a small retail store. (Only a few items are listed, but the same principles would apply to a complete table or file on a mass storage device.)

```
01  INVENTORY-TABLE.
    03  FILLER PIC X(13) VALUE "AUDIO CABLE".
    03  FILLER PIC X(4) VALUE "1258".
    03  FILLER PIC 99V99 VALUE 4.00.
    03  FILLER PIC X(13) VALUE "EARPHONE".
    03  FILLER PIC X(4) VALUE "1296".
    03  FILLER PIC 99V99 VALUE 37.50.
    03  FILLER PIC X(13) VALUE "MICROPHONE".
    03  FILLER PIC X(4) VALUE "1459".
    03  FILLER PIC 99V99 VALUE 29.75.
    03  FILLER PIC X(13) VALUE "BATTERIES".
    03  FILLER PIC X(4) VALUE "1678".
    03  FILLER PIC 99V99 VALUE 2.35.
    03  FILLER PIC X(13) VALUE "CARRYING CASE".
    03  FILLER PIC X(4) VALUE "1789".
    03  FILLER PIC 99V99 VALUE 13.92.
    03  FILLER PIC X(13) VALUE "**NO MATCH**".
    03  FILLER PIC X(4) VALUE "9999".
    03  FILLER PIC 99V99 VALUE ZERO.
01  PARTS-TABLE REDEFINES INVENTORY-TABLE.
    02  PART OCCURS 6 TIMES.
        03  PART-DESCRIPTION PIC X(13).
        03  PART-NUMBER       PIC X(4).
        03  PART-PRICE        PIC 99V99.
```

   a. Write the PROCEDURE DIVISION for a program that could be used to change a price if the part number is known.

   b. Given a file with records containing part numbers and quantity ordered, write the PROCEDURE DIVISION for a program that will print billing invoices.

2. Draw a flowchart showing the execution of each of the following:

   a. PERFORM PARA-X
        VARYING J FROM 1 BY 1 UNTIL J > N.

   b. PERFORM PARA-Y
        VARYING L FROM 10 BY -1 UNTIL L = 0.

   c. PERFORM PARA-2
        VARYING K FROM 1 BY 1 UNTIL K = N
        AFTER M FROM 1 BY 1 UNTIL M = N.

   d. PERFORM PARA-W
        VARYING P FROM 2 BY 2 UNTIL P > N
        AFTER Q FROM 1 BY 3 UNTIL Q > N
        AFTER R FROM 1 BY 1 UNTIL R > N.

3. How many times will the specified paragraph be executed in each part of Exercise 2 if N has value 7? Show the values generated for the variables.

4. a. Consider the program example in Section 9.13 (Widget production data storage). Suppose that an output record is defined as:

```
01  DAILY-OUTPUT.
    03  DAY-DO PIC 999.
    03  DAILY-PRODUCTION-DO OCCURS 5 TIMES.
        05  FILLER PIC X(5).
        05  DAY-PRODUCTION-DO PIC Z(5).
```

Write PROCEDURE DIVISION code to write out the content of the table PRODUCTION-DATA.

   b. Write PROCEDURE DIVISION code to compute the average production by line for the table PRODUCTION-DATA.

   c. On some days the production lines must be closed because of malfunction of equipment. On these days, production is zero. Write PROCEDURE DIVISION code required to compute the number of days in which production is zero for each line.

5. Write PROCEDURE DIVISION code to compute the total of the elements of BONUS-TABLE defined in Section 9.14.

6. Given the array GRADE-TABLE-EXTENDED defined in Section 9.14, write PROCEDURE DIVISION code to compute the class average for each test and class.

7. True/False
   a. Standard COBOL permits use of expressions as subscripts.
   b. The VALUE clause may be used with the OCCURS clause in a DATA DIVISION entry.
   c. The use of the DEPENDING ON clause saves space since only the required amount of storage is allocated.
   d. The REDEFINES clause may be used only on an entry with the same level number as the data-name being redefined.
   e. In the PERFORM/VARYING statement, it is possible that the specified paragraph may never be executed.
   f. The maximum number of subscripts allowed in COBOL is three.

8. For an IBM system show the internal hexadecimal representation of a field with value +298 defined as:
   a. USAGE DISPLAY
   b. USAGE COMP
   c. USAGE COMP-3
   d. USAGE INDEX

9.19 PROGRAMMING EXERCISES

1. Records in a file consist of student names and one test grade per student. Load a table with this data. Compute the average grade. Count the number of grades above the average and number of grades below the average.

2. Write a program that will list the daily sales of soft drinks to retail dealers under the major headings: DEALER, ITEM, QUANTITY, UNIT PRICE and TOTAL. The QUANTITY and TOTAL columns should be summed for all dealers serviced that day. An input record includes the dealer's name, type of drink, and the number of cases. Using the OCCURS clause, set up a table of unit costs (constants) in storage for each type of drink. Use these values to compute

the total sales for each transaction as it is read. Types of drinks and unit costs are as follows:

Regulars   4.00 per case
Kings   5.00 per case
Cans   4.50 per case

3. Rewrite the program written for Chapter 5, Exercise 6 (page 144) using a table to store the digits of the account number.

4. Sales employees of ABC Furniture, Inc. are paid on a commission basis. The commission rate varies from item to item. A commission rate code, which is the last digit in the item stock number, is used to determine the percentage of the wholesale price to be paid as a commission rate:

Rate-code	Commission-rate
1	1.0%
2	3.5%
3	7.0%
4	10.5%
5	12.0%
6	15.75%

Data records containing the following fields are to be processed to produce an employee earnings report:

Employee number
Date of sale
Retail price
Wholesale price
Stock number

Assume that the records are sorted into sequence by employee number and date. Your program should list each item sold and the associated commission. Subtotals should be written for daily sales and commissions and each salesperson's total sales and commissions. Final totals of sales and commissions also should be written.

Use the following sample data:

Employee Number	Date of Sale	Retail Price	Wholesale Price	Stock Number
100	1/1/86	5.00	4.00	103
100	1/1/86	6.00	3.00	205
100	1/2/86	7.00	5.00	131
101	1/1/86	18.00	15.00	322
101	1/1/86	6.00	3.00	325
101	1/2/86	7.00	4.00	444
101	1/3/86	7.00	5.00	106
102	1/1/86	12.00	10.00	133

5. Modify the program for Exercise 4 above to calculate the average commission rate earned by each salesperson. Average commission rate is calculated by finding the sum of the commission rates and dividing by the number of sales.

6. Modify the program for Exercise 4 above to calculate the profit from each sale, total profit by salesperson, and total profits for the period. Profit is computed by subtracting the commission from the markup. Markup is the difference between retail price and wholesale price.

7. Modify the program written for Exercise 4 above to produce a report summarizing each salesperson's earnings. Print the report after the body of the existing output. Use tables to store each employee number and appropriate summary data. Assume that no more than 25 salespersons are employed.

8. Modify the program written for Exercise 4 above to produce a report summarizing sales by date. Print the report after the existing output. Use a table to accumulate sales for each date. Assume that no more than 31 different dates will be processed by the program.

9. Each record in a data file contains the following fields:

> Department number (1 to 9)
> Salesman number (1 to 25)
> Amount of sales

Write a program to compute the total sales for each salesperson and each department. The data is *not* sorted into sequence by department or salesperson. Assume that employee numbers are not uniquely assigned (e.g. Department 1 may have a Salesperson 1 and Department 2 may have a Salesperson 1, and so forth).

10. Each record in a data file contains the following fields:

> Department number (1 to 9)
> Salesperson number (1 to 25)
> Amount of sales for Monday
> Amount of sales for Tuesday
> Amount of sales for Wednesday
> Amount of sales for Thursday
> Amount of sales for Friday

Write a program to determine which salespersons have total weekly sales more than ten percent above the average weekly sales for all salespersons. Make the same assumptions regarding salesperson numbers as in Exercise 9 above.

11. Records in a data file contain a date and number of sales for that date. Write a program to produce a bar graph to represent this data. For example:

```
Date    Sales
1/1/86    3      ***
                 ***
1/2/86    4      ****
                 ****
1/3/86    0

1/4/86    7      *******
                 *******
```

12. Same as Exercise 11 above, except produce a vertical bar graph. Assume that the data file contains seven records. For example:

```
                              **
                              **
                              **
                              **
                      **      **
            **        **      **
            **        **      **
            **        **      **
          1/1/86    1/2/86  1/3/86  1/4/86
```

13. A field contains the results of a survey conducted by the marketing department of XYZ Corp. Each record contains the following fields:

> Age of respondent (1 to 99)
> Brand preference (1, 2, 3, or 4)

Write a program to summarize brand preference by age group. Your output should contain the number of respondents in each age group and the percentage of each age group that preferred each brand. The output should be similar to

Age	Number	Brand			
		1	2	3	4
1-10	17	20%	10%	5%	65%
11-20	80	30%	10%	0%	60%
.	.	.	.	.	.
.	.	.	.	.	.
.	.	.	.	.	.
91-100	1	100%	0%	0%	0%

14. Management at XYZ Burger Corporation would like a report showing the average daily sales at each of its 25 branch stores. Each store has an identifying number 1, 2, . . . 25. Input into your program consists of sales records containing the following data:

> Store-id-number
> Date
> Total sales

You may not assume that the data is sorted into any particular order.

15. Compute the overall average daily sales amount and the standard deviation of the average for the program in Exercise 14 above. Flag those stores with average sales that deviate by more than two standard deviations from the overall average. The standard deviation is computed as

$$\sqrt{\frac{\sum_{i=1}^{n} (x_i - \overline{x})^2}{n \cdot (n-1)}}$$

where x_i represents the data items; $\overline{x}$ represents the average for the data items; and n represents the number of items. In this problem, $\overline{x}$ represents the average daily sales for each store, $\overline{x}$ represents the overall average daily sales amount, and n represents the number of stores.

STRUCTURED COBOL PROGRAMMING ENVIRONMENT 10

10.1 SYSTEM DESIGN

In a large number of businesses, which rely on a data processing system for the timely and cost-effective supply of day-to-day information, the COBOL language and structured programming together form the basis for developing the software required by the system. A data processing system includes provision for

- origination and collection of data
- data storage and retrieval mechanisms
- reports and other forms of information that need to be produced
- dissemination of information (who gets what report at what time interval)
- methods for finding and correcting errors in data
- audit trails to assure correct processing of data
- backup plans to assure that the organization can continue to function in the event of computer malfunction or natural disaster
- security systems to prevent unauthorized access to data, information or programs
- hardware required to accomplish the data processing tasks
- initial and ongoing training of users
- day-to-day operation procedures
- types of documentation

Unless adequate plans and provisions are made for all of these areas, a data processing system will fail to meet the needs of the organization it is meant to serve.

The job of the programmer is affected in one way or another by decisions made about all these aspects of the system that forms the basic framework in which the programmer works. Programmers are also in a position to make recommendations regarding potential problems that they foresee and that may not have been adequately addressed in the overall plan. To the outside world, unfortunately, any problem in the data processing system is often attributed to the computer or to the programmer, whereas the blame often should be placed on poor planning in one or more of these areas. A good plan will help the data processing system function with few problems and will go far in improving the image of all data processing personnel, including the programming staff, in the eyes of the organization. A positive image is likely to be accompanied by such tangible benefits as job security and financial rewards.

In any medium-sized or large organization, the task of developing a data processing system is carried out by several people, each playing a specific role in the process. Three types of personnel are directly involved:

- systems analyst
- programming manager
- programmer

The job of the systems analyst is to build a comprehensive plan for a data processing system, and, once the plan is approved, to oversee implementation of the plan and assure that the ultimate system meets specifications. The roles of the systems analyst and the programming manager may be likened to those of the architect and general contractor for a building. The systems analyst, like the architect, is responsible for the conceptual design and plans. Just as the architect oversees the work of the general contractor, the systems analyst supervises the work of the programming staff, particularly during the testing phase when potential problems in the system are eliminated and the system is proved to meet the requirements. The programming manager's job may be compared to that of the general contractor; both are responsible for implementing the plans once they are made.

The role of the programmer may be likened to that of the subcontractor in a building project. Just as the general contractor employs specialized subcontractors to accomplish portions of a project, the programming manager assigns portions of the system to sometimes highly specialized programmers. For the completed system to function properly, the work of each programmer must integrate with that of other programmers assigned to the project. In order for this to be accomplished, very careful plans must be made. Every component of the system must be fully and precisely described so that the programmer responsible for each component knows what that component is expected to do. A system that is not well-described may result in programs that cannot be integrated into a complete system. When this happens, conflicting programs must be revised so that the desired system can be constructed. This revision, of course, is expensive and time-consuming and should be avoided whenever possible.

Thus, the system design and specifications not only have important implications for the ultimate utility of the system, they are also important in the system development process. A well-thought-out system not only will work better in the end, it is also likely to cost less to implement.

Two aspects of the system design are used most directly by the programmer: system flowcharts and program specification statements. They are the basic means by which the designer communicates with the programmers.

10.2   SYSTEM FLOWCHARTING

A system flowchart is a schematic representation of the data and processing steps in a data processing system. Unlike program flowcharts, no attempt is made to describe how the processing is to take place. The focus in a system flowchart is on data files (represented by blocks of different shapes, depending on the medium used to store the file), processing steps (represented by rectangles), and the flow of data to and from processing steps (represented by flow lines).

A list of the most common system flowchart symbols is shown in Figure 10.1. For example, the system flowchart shown in Figure 10.2 represents a system in which data from an on-line device is accepted by a program that generates information printed on the operator's screen and uses the data to update a data file stored on disk. The names used inside the blocks represent file names or program names. These are generally the file and program names used by the operating system for storage of these entities. Additional examples of system flowcharts are shown in Figures 10.5 and 10.6.

System flowcharts are useful to the systems analyst, programmers, and users in visualizing the flow of information within a data processing system. They are particularly useful in representing the sequences of processing steps when one step must be accomplished successfully before the next step can begin. Because of their utility, system flowcharts are used for documentation as well as for system design.

10.3   PROGRAM SPECIFICATIONS

The document of greatest importance to the programmer is the description of exactly what the program must accomplish. Program specification statements generally include a description of input and output files and their associated data records, a printer spacing or screen layout chart showing placement of required information and a description of what the program must accomplish. Depending on the complexity of the task at hand, the program specifications statement may or may not include a detailed description of the procedure to be used (in the form of code). This document is the programmer's basic reference for understanding the programming task at hand and designing the required program. Examples of program specification statements are contained in the following complete system specification. Clearly, a complete system design and specification document encompasses a great many different considerations essential to the completed system.

Typically, a completed design for a small system is a book containing several hundred pages. For a large system, the design will resemble a small library. Presented in the following pages is an abbreviated version of a system design for a data processing system for a hypothetical manufacturing company. Because this system is the basis for the program examples used in this text, understanding the system will help you appreciate the motivation behind each of the program examples and will help you visualize how the program fits with other components of the complete system.

Figure 10.1 System flowchart symbols

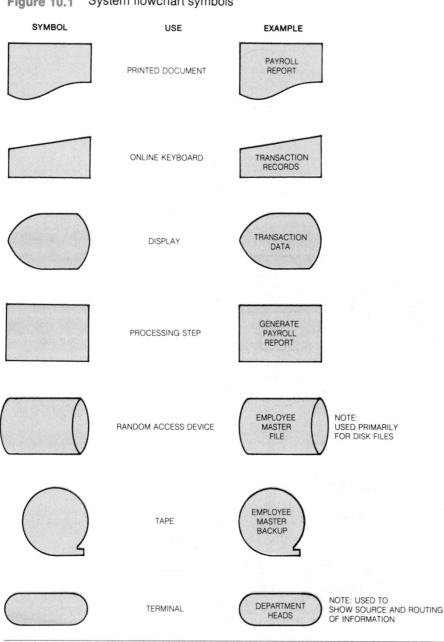

SYMBOL	USE	EXAMPLE	
	PRINTED DOCUMENT	PAYROLL REPORT	
	ONLINE KEYBOARD	TRANSACTION RECORDS	
	DISPLAY	TRANSACTION DATA	
	PROCESSING STEP	GENERATE PAYROLL REPORT	
	RANDOM ACCESS DEVICE	EMPLOYEE MASTER FILE	NOTE: USED PRIMARILY FOR DISK FILES
	TAPE	EMPLOYEE MASTER BACKUP	
	TERMINAL	DEPARTMENT HEADS	NOTE: USED TO SHOW SOURCE AND ROUTING OF INFORMATION

10.4 EXAMPLE OF A COMPLETE SYSTEM

Background

Amalgamated Custom Design, Inc., manufacturers customized T-shirts, jackets, hats, and other similar items. The company sells primarily to clubs, athletic teams, schools, and companies who desire custom printing on the products sold by Amalgamated. Amalgamated buys its plain (unprinted) products from a variety of sources. The company's production facilities are set up to process batches of similar items with the same design, such as a batch of jackets all with one design.

As orders are received, they are recorded in the Order Master File. An order is made up of one or more components; an order component corre-

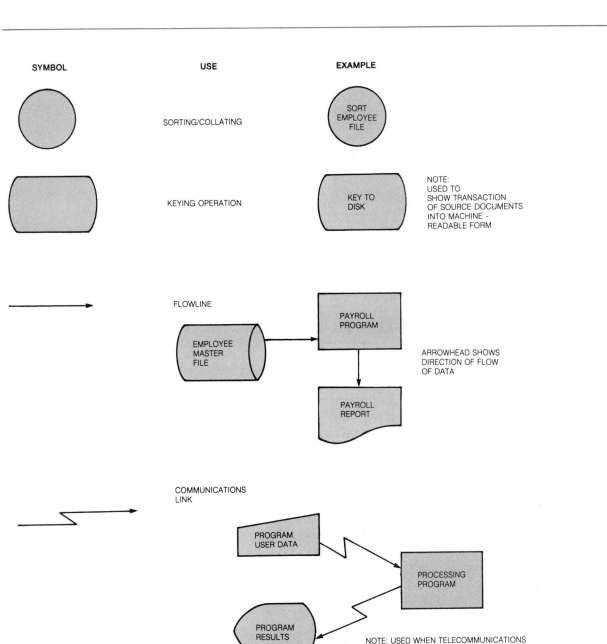

sponds to one line item on an order form for one specific product. An order component is submitted for production when there are sufficient raw materials on hand to manufacture the products required. Any order component that cannot be completed because of lack of sufficient raw materials is placed in a pending state and appropriate raw material orders are issued. When raw material is received, the pending order component is then submitted for production. The production supervisor examines each order component record, when it is submitted, to determine an estimated completion date for the batch of goods ordered. When the batch is completed, it is sent to the warehouse to await shipment. When all components of an order have been completed, shipping orders are issued.

Figure 10.2   System flowchart example

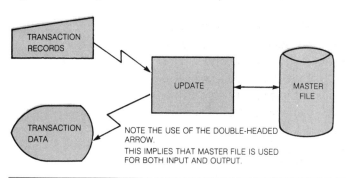

Computing Facilities

Amalgamated owns a small business computing system with both limited on-line and batch capabilities. Terminals are located in the main office and the production facility. The company's data processing system is made up of a mixture of batch and interactive components because of the limited number of terminals, the necessity of maintaining printed records of various types, and the relatively limited capacity of the computing system, which must be utilized efficiently. Batch programs are used for generating management reports, internal and external documents (like production orders, shipping orders and invoices), and related file updating. Interactive programs are used for data entry and information requests. The interactive programs are executed on demand from the appropriate terminal. During the day, the system is dedicated to these programs. In the evening, the batch portions of the system are processed.

Note that the characteristics of the company's computing system have a significant influence on the design of the data processing system. Under a different set of circumstances, it might be necessary to implement a system that is completely batch or completely interactive. The design described here is typical of that found in small or medium-sized businesses such as Amalgamated.

System Overview

The system is made up of three major subsystems:

- Raw Materials System
- Work in Progress System
- Order Control System

The Raw Materials System is used in submitting orders for production and in accounting for raw materials (unprinted products and other materials used in production). The Raw Materials Master File shows amounts of each raw material on hand, encumbered (needed to complete production orders but not yet used), and on order. The Raw Materials Master File is updated when materials are ordered, used, and received and when a production batch is submitted. The Raw Materials System also makes use of a Supplier Master File, which stores details of each supplier and is used in generating orders for supplies.

The Work in Progress System is used in determining the status of production of each batch of products. The Work in Progress Master File is updated when a batch is submitted and scheduled, and when production is completed.

The Order Control System is used to control orders from the time they are entered into the system until they are completed and goods are shipped. Orders are entered into the Order Master File when they are received. The system then determines if raw materials are available and either submits the order to the production facility or places the order component in a pending state until sufficient raw materials are available for production. When all order components have been completed, the Order Master File is updated and appropriate shipping orders are generated.

Figure 10.3 shows the states possible for an order from entry through shipping. Figure 10.4 shows states possible for order components.

Figure 10.3 Status chart of orders

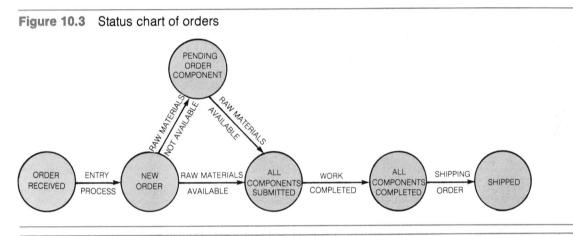

Figure 10.4 Status chart for order components

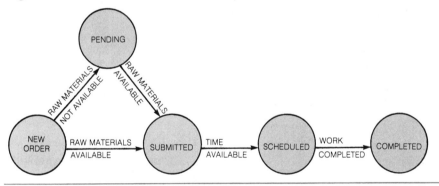

File Specifications

File Name: Raw Materials Master
Description: The Raw Materials Master File is used to account for raw materials in stock and on order and to determine whether sufficient stock is on hand to enable production of an order.
Organization: Indexed; keyed by item number
Record Content:
- item number   X(5)
- item description   X(10)
- unencumbered on hand   9(3)
- encumbered on hand   9(3)
- on order   9(3)
- item cost   999V99
- minimum order quantity   9(3)
- supplier number   X(5)

File Name:	Order Master File
Description:	The Order Master File is used to store orders as they are entered and to track orders during the production and shipping process.
Organization:	Sequential; in sequence by order number
Record Types:	• Order Master—there is one order master record for each order
	• Order Detail—there is one detail record for each component of the order

Order Master Record Content:		
• order number	X(5)
• customer number	9(9)
• customer name	X(20)
• customer address	X(20)
• number of order components	9(3)
• date of receipt	9(6)
• shipping date (blank until order is shipped)	9(6)

Order Detail Record Content:	
• order number	X(5)
• catalog number	X(5)
• quantity	9(3)
• number of order components	9(3)
• scheduled completion date	9(6)
• actual completion date	9(6)
• raw material requirements (from 1 to 5 raw material item numbers)	X(5)
• batch status—N new order	
P pending	
S submitted	
C completed	X
• customizing instructions	X(15)

File Name:	Work in Progress Master
Description:	The Work in Progress (WIP) Master File is used in scheduling and production of batches of products. A record is placed in the file when the batch is submitted for production. When the production supervisor schedules production for the batch, the file is updated to show estimated completion date. When production is completed, the file is updated again to show date of completion.
Organization:	Relative; randomized placement of records—key field is combined order number and catalog number (batch number).

Record Content:		
• order number ⎫	X(5)
• catalog number ⎬ batch number	X(5)
• quantity ⎭	9(3)
• number of order components	9(3)
• scheduled completion date (blank if not scheduled)	9(6)
• actual completion date (blank until completed)	9(6)
• raw material requirements (from 1 to 5 item numbers)	X(5) each

File Name:	Purchase Request File
Description:	The Purchase Request File is used to store purchase requests generated by New Order Processing.
Organization:	Sequential; sorted into sequence by supplier identification number and item number

Record Content:	• supplier ID number	X(5)
	• item number	X(5)
	• item description	X(10)
	• item cost	999V99
	• order quantity	9(3)

File Name:	Supplier Master File	
Description:	The Supplier Master File is used to generate purchase orders. It contains one record for each supplier with whom Amalgamated does business.	
Organization:	Sequential; in order by supplier identification number	
Record Content:	• supplier ID number	X(5)
	• supplier name	X(20)
	• supplier address	X(20)

File Name:	Order Transaction File	
Description:	Stores order transactions resulting from new orders being entered or orders being completed.	
Organization:	Sequential; sorted into sequence by order number	
Record Types:	• Order Master	Content of these records same as for Order Master File
	• Order Detail	
	• Component Completion	
	• Order Shipping	

Component Completion Record Content:	• order number	X(5)
	• catalog number	X(5)
	• completion date	9(6)
Order Shipping Record Content:	• order number	X(5)
	• shipping date	9(6)

Program Specifications

Title:	Raw Materials Update (Program 14.2)
Type:	Interactive
Purpose:	Updates the Raw Materials Master File from transactions regarding receipt and use of raw materials.

Title:	Work in Progress Update (Program 15.2)
Type:	Interactive/Menu Driven
Purpose:	Updates the Work in Progress Master File and Order Transaction Files. Options on Menu:

- L   List all scheduled batches
- U   List all unscheduled batches
- S   Schedule a batch
- C   Complete a batch (enables updating of WIP Master and places an appropriate record in Order Transaction File)
- A   Add a batch ⎫ used only for error correction and file
- D   Delete a batch ⎭ maintenance; records are added to the file as a result of New Order Processing described below

Title:	Order Entry (Program 11.3)
Type:	Interactive
Purpose:	Validates new order data and adds records to the Order Transaction File.

Title: Work in Progress Report (Program 10.1)
Type: Batch
Purpose: Produce report showing status of job components that are in production.

Title: Order Update (Program 11.3)
Type: Batch
Purpose: Updates Order Master File using records from the Order Transaction File to produce the New Order Master File.

Title: New Order Processing
Type: Batch
Purpose: Processes each component of a new order in the Order Master File. If sufficient raw materials are on hand, the batch is submitted for production (a record is added to the WIP Master and a written order is produced). If sufficient raw materials are not on hand, the batch is placed in a pending state and appropriate purchase request records are added to the Purchase Request File.

Title: Pending Order Processing
Type: Batch
Purpose: Processes all pending order components in the Order Master File. If sufficient raw materials are on hand, the batch is submitted for production (a record is added to the WIP Master and a written order is produced). The Order Master File is updated appropriately.

Title: Completed Order Processing
Type: Batch
Purpose: Generates shipping orders for those orders for which all components have been completed. Adds appropriate record to the Order Transaction File.

Title: Generate Purchase Orders (programs 12.1, 12.2, 12.2)
Type: Batch
Purpose: Summarizes purchase requests by supplier and generates purchase orders.

System Flowcharts

System flowcharts for this system are shown in Figures 10.5 and 10.6.

10.5 SURVEY OF PROGRAM DEVELOPMENT PRACTICES

Programming Team

In very small organizations, the roles of the systems analyst and the programmer may be combined into one job, typically called a *programmer-analyst*. In most organizations, however, system development involves both the systems analyst and the programming staff. A very small system might be assigned to a single programmer for implementation, but most systems require the services of several programmers.

In the past it was not uncommon for a programming manager to assign specific portions of a system to individual programmers for independent implementation, expecting that the system would function as a whole when each module was completed. Because the work of programmers working

Figure 10.5 System flowchart of interactive components

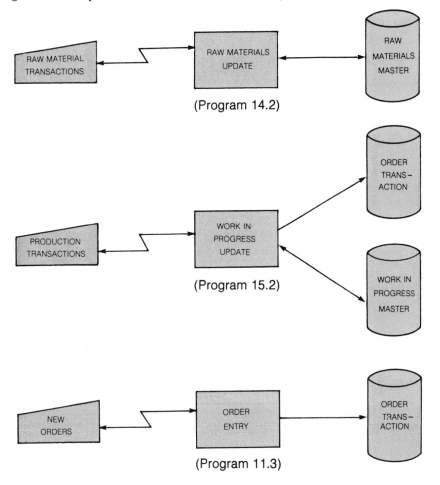

alone usually contained inconsistencies when their work was combined, this expectation was rarely met, and reworking of one or more components was often a necessity.

Current practice tends toward a closely coordinated team approach to program development. The programming manager assigns responsibility for the project to a team, usually with one member designated as the team leader. The team analyzes the project and collectively decides on a division of labor. Frequent meetings are held to clarify issues as they arise and to ensure coordinated effort. The programming team approach has a number of benefits:

- The team is able to capitalize on particular technical strengths of team members.
- The close coordination and review of each other's work ensures that the system will function correctly when finished.
- Team members learn from each other and thereby become better programmers in the long run.
- The team approach is good for morale, because team members are able to lend emotional support to each other.

The programming team approach, of course, is not without potential problems:

Figure 10.6   System flowchart of batch components

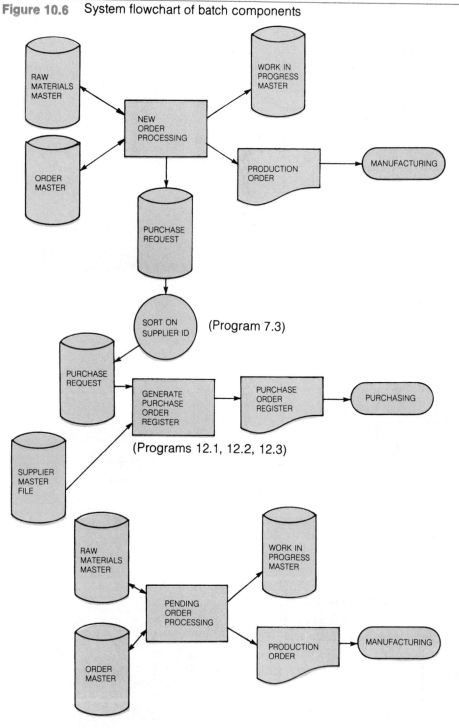

- The time spent in meetings and coordination may be excessive (and expensive).
- Team members may disagree on the best way to carry out the task, resulting in the necessity of spending time (and money) to resolve conflicts.
- Personality clashes among team members may be disruptive of the process.

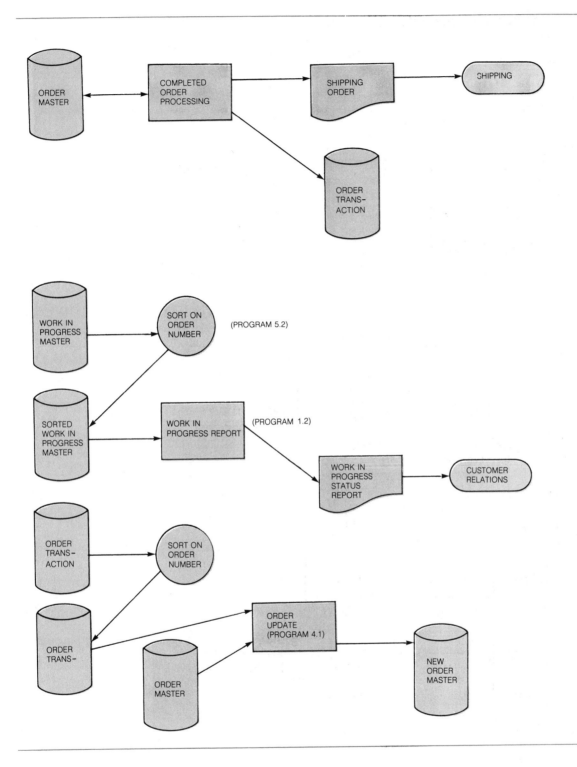

A well-chosen team with appropriate management and support is, however, a very efficient vehicle for implementing a system, and the technique is being used in a growing number of data processing installations today.

Structured Walk-Through
Another practice that lends itself naturally to the team approach is the *structured walk-through*. The idea is to prevent program errors before the program

is ever compiled and tested. In installations that use structured walk-throughs, the process usually contains the following steps:

1) A programmer codes a program.
2) Copies of the program code, together with appropriate documentation (pseudocode, HIPO charts, etc.), are distributed to each member of the team.
3) After allowing a suitable time interval (one to two days) for each person to review the program, the team meets as a group.
4) During the meeting, the programmer "walks through" the program, explaining the design, the purpose of each module and perhaps tracing the execution sequence for sample data.
5) The team then makes constructive criticism and, as a group, decides whether the program is ready to be compiled and tested or whether modifications need to be made.

This process is carried out while the program is in written form, not after the programmer has invested hours or days in entering the code and compiling the program. The purpose of the technique is to ensure that the program will work correctly the first time it's compiled. Although the technique works well in the programming team approach, it can be used in any environment. It is not necessary that the group members be involved directly with the project to be effective in locating logical errors and design flaws in a program.

A major problem with the structured walk-through technique is that the programmer must be able to accept criticism. Proponents of the method maintain that if programmers do not see a program as an extension of themselves, criticism of the program will not be seen as personal criticism. While this ideal of "ego-less" programming is appealing, most programmers do in fact have reasonably strong identification with the programs that they construct, and it is natural to resent criticism. Members of the review group must be very careful not to criticize the program but to make suggestions on how the program can be improved. The distinction between these two ideas is very fine, but it is crucial to the morale of the programmer whose work is being reviewed.

Another potential problem lies in the make-up of the review group. Programmers must not feel that they are on trial and that their supervisor is taking notes that will be used later for evaluation. For this reason, review groups normally are made up of the programmer's peers and exclude supervisory personnel. Also, to avoid the possibility of supervisory review, detailed written minutes of the meetings are not made. The purpose of the technique is to produce better programs, not to evaluate or judge the programmer. If the technique is seen by the programming staff as a means of evaluation, the effect on morale will be negative and the method could, in the end, be counterproductive.

Data Dictionary

The names assigned to a file and associated records and fields in a given COBOL program are, in general, an arbitrary choice of the programmer. The use of descriptive names to make the program readable and, hence, maintainable, is an important element of structured programming. In any system, there will usually be many programs that process a given file. If every program uses different names for the file and its records and fields, the process of maintaining these programs is complicated unnecessarily. Consider the job of the maintenance programmer assigned to change every program that processes a given file. Even though each program may function correctly in its own right and the names chosen may be descriptive and otherwise acceptable, it will be very confusing and will add a needless measure of complexity to force the maintenance programmer to contend with as many different names as there are programs. A much better approach is to establish a set of data names for each entity at the outset and require that each program in the system use these data names. This set of data names is commonly called a *data dictionary* and should be established before any program code is written. Each programmer working on the project must have access to the dictionary, and someone must assume responsibility for forcing compliance with the use of common data names. The data dictionary is commonly placed in the on-line system libraries to facilitate compliance with this standard.

Structured Implementation and Testing

The task of program testing involves verification that the program does indeed perform in accordance with the program specifications. For a simple program (and in most student environments), this task is usually undertaken in the following manner:

1) The programmer codes the program.
2) The program is compiled and corrected until there are no more syntax errors.
3) The programmer creates one or more sample data files. (These may have been provided as part of the assignment in a student environment.)
4) The program is executed.
5) If the output produced is consistent with the output expected from the given sample data, the program is accepted; otherwise, changes are made to the program and the process is completed.

While this procedure may be sufficient in some instances, it has too many flaws to be used with a large or complex program. One of the most glaring problems is that testing of the program does not begin until the entire coding process has been completed. It is well known that the number of errors and the difficulty of the debugging process tend to be related exponentially to the length and complexity of a program. For a large or complex program, the testing process should proceed in parallel with the implementation process; that is, the program should be tested at appropriate stages before all of the program modules are completely coded.

Two somewhat conflicting philosophies exist (both using the general name *structured implementation and testing*), which describe how this parallel testing process should be approached. One alternative is a *bottom-up* implementation and testing technique. In this technique, the lowest-level functioning modules are coded and tested independently. Then the next level of controlling modules are coded and tested with the verified low-level modules in place, and so on, proceeding ultimately to the highest level. By using this approach, the potential number and complexity of errors is limited at each stage of the process to the level just added to the program, thereby simplifying the debugging task. Although this is theoretically sound, some practical problems arise in following the procedure strictly:

- The task of testing functioning modules usually necessitates writing, debugging, and executing complete programs. The task of writing one program suddenly becomes the task of writing many (albeit simpler) programs.

- One will not know if the overall design is sound until the very last stage when all of the subordinate modules have been coded and tested. If there are problems at this top level, it is possible that the entire design will have to be reworked, invalidating much of the work that has gone on before.

An alternative to the bottom-up approach is the *top-down* approach. In this method, the program is implemented and tested in much the same way as it was designed–from the highest-level control modules to the lowest-level functioning modules. At each stage, modules that are yet to be coded are represented by *program stubs*. In COBOL, this typically means that the paragraph in question is represented by the paragraph name and the EXIT statement, although sometimes temporary output or assignment statements may also be used. Using the top-down approach, the programmer has at each stage a working prototype of the completed program. This technique enables the testing of the overall design first, so that, if changes are necessary, there has been little wasted effort. As with bottom-up testing, the potential number and complexity of errors is limited at each stage in the testing process, because the preceding stage has already been verified. On the other hand, it may be impossible to implement a meaningful program without some details supplied by lower-level modules. This is particularly true when a lower-level module passes a control variable to a higher-level module. The higher-level module cannot function correctly without appropriate values for that control data item.

Most programmers tend to use a pragmatic combination of the top-down and bottom-up approaches and vary their technique depending on the nature of the program at hand. For example, it may be practical to code and test input, output and certain computational modules separately in a bottom-up approach. At that point, however, it may be advantageous to turn to a top-down approach, using a skeleton structure with the now debugged and tested low-level modules in place.

In any case, programmers working on large or complex programs do not use the student program implementation and testing model outlined earlier. To use such a model would invite potential program debugging problems of great magnitude and complexity. The purpose of structured implementation and testing is to encounter and correct problems a few at a time and in areas of the program that can be readily isolated. Either a top-down or a bottom-up approach, or some combination of the two, will ultimately simplify the testing process and help to ensure a correctly functioning program when the programmer's work is finished.

10.6 PROGRAM EXAMPLE

Problem Statement

Write a program to produce the Work in Progress report for the Amalgamated Custom Design system described in Section 10.4. The program processes the Work in Progress Master file, which is a sequential file sorted into order number sequence as shown in the system flowchart of Figure 10.6. Each record in the file contains the following fields:

- Order number
- Catalog number
- Number of order components
- Scheduled completion date (spaces if not yet scheduled)
- Actual completion date (spaces if not yet completed)

When a batch is submitted for production, a record is placed in the Work in Progress Master File. When work is begun, the file is updated with a scheduled completion date. When work is completed, the file is updated again to show the actual completion date.

The report must show the status of each order component and contain a summary of the components of each order, as shown in the printer spacing chart in Figure 10.7.

Problem Analysis

This program will require a control break based on the order number, therefore a hold field (HOLD-ORDER-NUMBER) will be required. The summary line requires the number of components that have been submitted for production. This value can be calculated by counting each component as it is processed. This will require a counter (NUMBER-COMPONENTS-WIP), which will be set to zero initially and after each control break. The summary line also requires the number of components in the order. This value is contained on each order component record. In order to print this value on the summary line, a hold field (HOLD-COMPONENTS) will be required. This field will be handled essentially the same way as the hold field for the order number—the value of number of components from the first record in the order number group will be moved to the hold field and, after the summary line is written, the value of number of components from the first record of the new group will be moved to the hold field. Note that the number of components in the order has the same value on each order component record for the order. Pseudocode for the required program is shown in Figure 10.8.

Problem Solution

The required program is shown in Program 10.1 with structure diagram in Figure 10.10. This program is a control break program with the page headings similar to programs described in Chapter 8. Two new features of COBOL are illustrated in this program. The FD entry for WIP-MASTER-FILE is written in a fuller form (see lines 2400-2900) than has been used in previous programs in this text. A complete general syntax of the FD is shown in Figure 10.9.

Figure 10.7   Printer spacing chart for Work in Progress Report

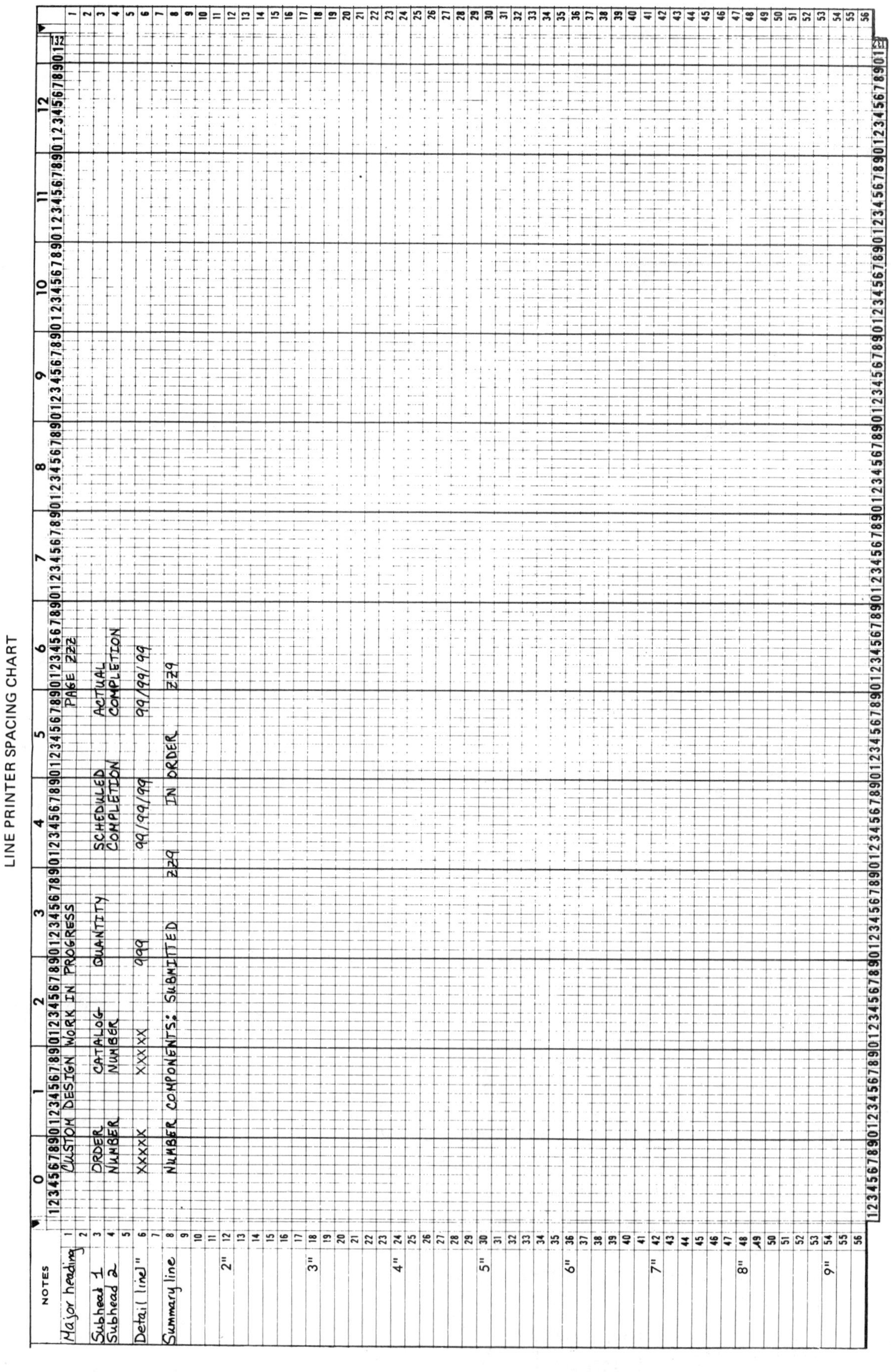

Figure 10.8 Pseudocode for Program 10.1

```
Open files
Read data file
Initialize hold fields
Do until end of file
     If new order
          Write summary record
          Increment line count
          Initialize number components
          Initialize hold feilds
     End If
     If page is full
          Write headings
          Initialize line count
     End If
     Move data from input area to output
     Increment number components
     Write detail record
     Increment line count
     Read data record
End Do
Write summary record
Close files
Stop
```

Figure 10.9 General form of the FD entry

$$
\begin{aligned}
&[\underline{FD}\ \text{file-name} \\
&\quad \left[\ \underline{BLOCK}\ \text{CONTAINS}\ [\text{integer-1}\ \underline{TO}]\ \text{integer-2}\ \left\{\begin{matrix}\underline{RECORDS}\\ CHARACTERS\end{matrix}\right\}\ \right] \\
&\quad [\ \underline{RECORD}\ \text{CONTAINS}\ [\text{integer-3}\ \underline{TO}]\ \text{integer-4}\ CHARACTERS] \\
&\quad \underline{LABEL}\ \left\{\begin{matrix}\underline{RECORD}\ IS\\ \underline{RECORDS}\ ARE\end{matrix}\right\}\left\{\begin{matrix}\underline{STANDARD}\\ \underline{OMITTED}\end{matrix}\right\} \\
&\quad \left[\ \underline{VALUE}\ \underline{OF}\ \text{implementor-name-1}\ IS\ \left\{\begin{matrix}\text{data-name-1}\\ \text{literal-1}\end{matrix}\right\}\right. \\
&\qquad\quad \left[\ \text{implementor-name-2}\ IS\ \left\{\begin{matrix}\text{data-name-2}\\ \text{literal-2}\end{matrix}\right\}\right]\ \cdots\ \Big] \\
&\quad \left[\ \underline{DATA}\ \left\{\begin{matrix}\underline{RECORD}\ IS\\ \underline{RECORDS}\ ARE\end{matrix}\right\}\ \text{data-name-3}\ [\ \text{data-name-4}\ ]\ \cdots\ \right]
\end{aligned}
$$

The RECORD CONTAINS clause specifies the number of characters contained on a record. This clause is optional and generally used for documentation purposes only, as the length of the record specified for the file in the record description is used by the system as the record length, regardless of the entry in the RECORD CONTAINS clause. The BLOCK CONTAINS clause is used to describe the blocking factor in use when the file was created. One use of the VALUE OF clause is to specify the name of the file as it is known to the operating system. The syntax of this statement is highly dependent on the compiler in use. The general form of this clause is:

$$
\underline{VALUE}\ \underline{OF}\ \text{implementor-name}\ IS\ \left\{\begin{matrix}\text{data-name}\\ \text{literal}\end{matrix}\right\}
$$

In the system used to compile Program 10.1, *Implementor-name* is TITLE and the literal "WORKINPROCESS1" is used to assign this name to the file WIP-MASTER-FILE. The system you are using may or may not make use of this clause. In many operating systems, the external file name is specified using job control statements. Check the documentation for your system before making use of this feature.

A second new feature of COBOL illustrated in this program is the BLANK WHEN ZERO clause. This is used at lines 9900 and 10100 to suppress printing of data when the item has value zero. Regardless of the edit picture used to describe a field, if the BLANK WHEN ZERO clause is present, spaces will be inserted in the field when the value being moved into the field has value zero.

Example

```
MOVE FLDA TO FLDB

  0 0 0                         └─┴─┴─┴─┘
     ^

FLDA PIC 99V9              FLDB PIC 99.9 BLANK WHEN ZERO

  0 0 1                      0 0 . 1
     ^

FLDA PIC 99V9              FLDB PIC 99.9 BLANK WHEN ZERO
```

Program 10.1   Work in progress report program

```
100      IDENTIFICATION DIVISION.
200
300      PROGRAM-ID. WIP-REPORT.
400      AUTHOR. GLEASON.
500
600      ENVIRONMENT DIVISION.
700
800      CONFIGURATION SECTION.
900
1000     SOURCE-COMPUTER.
1100     OBJECT-COMPUTER.
1200
1300     INPUT-OUTPUT SECTION.
1400
1500     FILE-CONTROL.
1600
1700         SELECT WIP-MASTER-FILE ASSIGN TO DISK.
1800         SELECT OUTPUT-FILE     ASSIGN TO PRINTER.
1900
2000     DATA DIVISION.
2100
2200     FILE SECTION.
2300
2400     FD  WIP-MASTER-FILE
2500         RECORD CONTAINS 84 CHARACTERS
2600         BLOCK CONTAINS 30 RECORDS
2700         VALUE OF TITLE IS "WORKINPROCESS1"
2800         LABEL RECORDS ARE STANDARD
2900         DATA RECORD IS INPUT-RECORD.
```

Program 10.1 *(continued)*

```
3000
3100    01   INPUT-RECORD           PIC X(84).
3200
3300    FD   OUTPUT-FILE
3400         LABEL RECORDS ARE OMITTED
3500         DATA RECORD IS PRINT-LINE.
3600
3700    01   PRINT-LINE             PIC X(132).
3800
3900    WORKING-STORAGE SECTION.
4000
4100    01   EOF-AND-HOLD-FIELDS.
4200         03  EOF-FLAG              PIC XXX VALUE "NO ".
4300         03  HOLD-ORDER-NUMBER     PIC X(5) VALUE SPACES.
4400         03  HOLD-COMPONENTS       PIC 999 VALUE ZERO.
4500
4600    01   COUNTERS.
4700         03  PAGE-COUNT            PIC 999 VALUE ZERO.
4800         03  NUMBER-COMPONENTS-WIP PIC 999 VALUE ZERO.
4900         03  LINE-COUNT            PIC 999 VALUE 16.
5000             88  PAGE-FULL      VALUE 16 THRU 999.
5100
5200    01   MAJOR-HEADING.
5300
5400         02  FILLER       PIC X(5) VALUE SPACES.
5500         02  FILLER   PIC X(29) VALUE "CUSTOM DESIGN WORK IN PROCESS".
5600         02  FILLER       PIC X(22) VALUE SPACES.
5700         02  FILLER       PIC X(5) VALUE "PAGE ".
5800         02  MH-PAGE-COUNTER PIC ZZZ.
5900
6000    01   SUBHEAD-1.
6100         03  FILLER     PIC X(5) VALUE SPACES.
6200         03  FILLER     PIC X(5) VALUE "ORDER".
6300         03  FILLER     PIC X(6) VALUE SPACES.
6400         03  FILLER     PIC X(7) VALUE "CATALOG".
6500         03  FILLER     PIC X(5) VALUE SPACES.
6600         03  FILLER     PIC X(8) VALUE "QUANTITY".
6700         03  FILLER     PIC X(5) VALUE SPACES.
6800         03  FILLER     PIC X(9) VALUE "SCHEDULED".
6900         03  FILLER     PIC X(6) VALUE SPACES.
7000         03  FILLER     PIC X(6) VALUE "ACTUAL".
7100
7200    01   SUBHEAD-2.
7300         03  FILLER     PIC X(5) VALUE SPACES.
7400         03  FILLER     PIC X(6) VALUE "NUMBER".
7500         03  FILLER     PIC X(5) VALUE SPACES.
7600         03  FILLER     PIC X(6) VALUE "NUMBER".
7700         03  FILLER     PIC X(19) VALUE SPACES.
7800         03  FILLER     PIC X(10) VALUE "COMPLETION".
7900         03  FILLER     PIC X(5) VALUE SPACES.
8000         03  FILLER     PIC X(10) VALUE "COMPLETION".
8100
8200    01   WIP-MASTER-RECORD.
8300         03  ORDER-NUMBER-WMR           PIC X(5).
8400         03  CATALOG-NUMBER-WMR         PIC X(5).
8500         03  QUANTITY-WMR               PIC 9(3).
```

Program 10.1 (continued)

```
8600        03 NUMBER-COMPONENTS-WMR          PIC 9(3).
8700        03 SCHEDULED-COMPLETION-DATE-WMR  PIC 9(6).
8800        03 ACTUAL-COMPLETION-DATE-WMR     PIC 9(6).
8900        03 RAW-MAT-WMR                    PIC X(5) OCCURS 5 TIMES .
9000
9100    01  DETAIL-LINE.
9200        03 FILLER      PIC X(5) VALUE SPACES.
9300        03 ORDER-NUMBER-DL               PIC X(5).
9400        03 FILLER      PIC X(6) VALUE SPACES.
9500        03 CATALOG-NUMBER-DL             PIC X(5).
9600        03 FILLER      PIC X(7) VALUE SPACES.
9700        03 QUANTITY-DL                   PIC 9(3).
9800        03 FILLER      PIC X(10) VALUE SPACES.
9900        03 SCHEDULED-COMPLETION-DATE-DL PIC 99/99/99 BLANK WHEN ZERO.
10000       03 FILLER      PIC X(7) VALUE SPACES.
10100       03 ACTUAL-COMPLETION-DATE-DL    PIC 99/99/99 BLANK WHEN ZERO.
10200
10300   01  CONTROL-BREAK-SUMMARY.
10400       03 FILLER   PIC X(5) VALUE SPACES.
10500       03 FILLER   PIC X(28) VALUE "NUMBER COMPONENTS: SUBMITTED".
10600       03 FILLER   PIC X(5) VALUE SPACES.
10700       03 NUMBER-COMPONENTS-WIP-CBS    PIC ZZ9.
10800       03 FILLER   PIC X(5) VALUE SPACES.
10900       03 FILLER   PIC X(8) VALUE "IN ORDER".
11000       03 FILLER   PIC X(5) VALUE SPACES.
11100       03 COMPONENTS-IN-ORDER-CBS PIC ZZZ9.
11200
11300   PROCEDURE DIVISION.
11400
11500   1000-MAIN-LOGIC.
11600
11700       PERFORM 2000-INITIALIZATION.
11800       PERFORM 3000-CONTROL
11900           UNTIL EOF-FLAG = "YES".
12000       PERFORM 6500-ORDER-NUMBER-BREAK.
12100       PERFORM 9000-TERMINATION.
12200       STOP RUN.
12300
12400   2000-INITIALIZATION.
12500
12600       OPEN INPUT WIP-MASTER-FILE
12700            OUTPUT OUTPUT-FILE.
12800       PERFORM 4000-READ.
12900       MOVE ORDER-NUMBER-WMR TO HOLD-ORDER-NUMBER.
13000       MOVE NUMBER-COMPONENTS-WMR TO HOLD-COMPONENTS.
13100
13200   3000-CONTROL.
13300
13400       PERFORM 4050-CONTROL-BREAK-CHECK.
13500       PERFORM 5000-CHECK-FULL-PAGE.
13600       PERFORM 5100-MOVE-FIELDS.
13700       PERFORM 5200-ADD-ORDER-COMPONENTS.
13800       PERFORM 5300-WRITE-DETAIL.
13900       PERFORM 4000-READ.
14000
```

Program 10.1 (continued)

```
14100        4000-READ.
14200
14300            READ WIP-MASTER-FILE
14400                INTO WIP-MASTER-RECORD
14500                    AT END MOVE "YES" TO EOF-FLAG.
14600
14700        4050-CONTROL-BREAK-CHECK.
14800
14900            IF ORDER-NUMBER-WMR NOT = HOLD-ORDER-NUMBER
15000                PERFORM 6500-ORDER-NUMBER-BREAK.
15100
15200        5000-CHECK-FULL-PAGE.
15300
15400            IF PAGE-FULL
15500                PERFORM 7000-WRITE-HEADINGS.
15600
15700        5100-MOVE-FIELDS.
15800
15900            MOVE ORDER-NUMBER-WMR TO ORDER-NUMBER-DL.
16000            MOVE CATALOG-NUMBER-WMR TO CATALOG-NUMBER-DL.
16100            MOVE QUANTITY-WMR TO QUANTITY-DL.
16200            MOVE SCHEDULED-COMPLETION-DATE-WMR TO
16300                SCHEDULED-COMPLETION-DATE-DL.
16400            MOVE ACTUAL-COMPLETION-DATE-WMR TO
16500                ACTUAL-COMPLETION-DATE-DL.
16600
16700        5200-ADD-ORDER-COMPONENTS.
16800
16900            ADD 1 TO NUMBER-COMPONENTS-WIP.
17000
17100        5300-WRITE-DETAIL.
17200
17300            MOVE DETAIL-LINE TO PRINT-LINE.
17400            WRITE PRINT-LINE AFTER 2.
17500            ADD 1 TO LINE-COUNT.
17600
17700        6500-ORDER-NUMBER-BREAK.
17800
17900            MOVE NUMBER-COMPONENTS-WIP TO NUMBER-COMPONENTS-WIP-CBS.
18000            MOVE HOLD-COMPONENTS TO COMPONENTS-IN-ORDER-CBS.
18100            WRITE PRINT-LINE FROM CONTROL-BREAK-SUMMARY AFTER 2.
18200            ADD 2 TO LINE-COUNT.
18300            IF PAGE-FULL
18400                PERFORM 7000-WRITE-HEADINGS
18500            ELSE
18600                MOVE SPACES TO PRINT-LINE
18700                WRITE PRINT-LINE AFTER 2
18800                ADD 2 TO LINE-COUNT.
18900            MOVE 0 TO NUMBER-COMPONENTS-WIP.
19000            MOVE NUMBER-COMPONENTS-WMR TO HOLD-COMPONENTS.
19100            MOVE ORDER-NUMBER-WMR TO HOLD-ORDER-NUMBER.
19200
```

```
19300      7000-WRITE-HEADINGS.
19400
19500          ADD 1 TO PAGE-COUNT.
19600          MOVE PAGE-COUNT TO MH-PAGE-COUNTER.
19700          WRITE PRINT-LINE FROM MAJOR-HEADING AFTER PAGE.
19800          WRITE PRINT-LINE FROM SUBHEAD-1 AFTER 2.
19900          WRITE PRINT-LINE FROM SUBHEAD-2 AFTER 1.
20000          MOVE SPACES TO PRINT-LINE.
20100          WRITE PRINT-LINE AFTER 1.
20200          MOVE 5 TO LINE-COUNT.
20300
20400      9000-TERMINATION.
20500
20600          CLOSE WIP-MASTER-FILE
20700                OUTPUT-FILE.
```

Program 10.1 (continued)

Figure 10.10   Structure diagram for Program 10.1

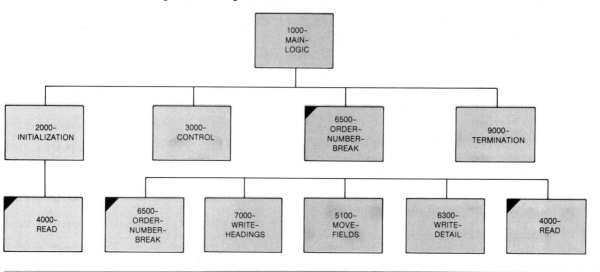

10.7 LIBRARIES AND THE COPY STATEMENT

The data dictionary is an important concept when more than one program must be written to process the same data. Adherence to the data names defined in the data dictionary by all programs processing the same data will greatly enhance the maintainability of the programs in the system.

COBOL contains provisions for the establishment of libraries that can contain COBOL source code. The compiler is then able to insert elements from the library directly into COBOL source programs. The result is the same as if a programmer had written the inserted code, but, of course, that programmer was relieved of the necessity by the existence of the code in the library. This library facility can be used to implement the data dictionary. If file and record descriptions are placed in the library, any program requiring access to file simply causes the required statements to be inserted into the program, and at that point all of the data names will be defined to the standard established for the system.

The mechanism for placing text into a library is dependent on the operating system in use. Refer to the system reference manuals for specific instructions in this regard. Some systems maintain only one library (called the "Source Statement Library" in IBM's DOS operating system) whereas others permit the establishment of several libraries, each with a user defined name. Entries in the library consist of sequences of COBOL code identified by a *text-name*.

The content of a library entry can be inserted into a COBOL program using the COPY statement. A general form of the COPY statement is shown in Figure 10.11.

Figure 10.11   General form of the COPY statement

When the COPY statement is used, the content of the specified text is placed in the COBOL program, replacing the COPY statement itself. On some compilers, the COPY statement is also shown for documentation. The *library-name* option is used only if the named library feature is part of the operating system in use. The COPY statement may be placed anywhere in the program, although it is most often used in the DATA and, to a lesser extent, in the PROCEDURE DIVISIONs. A basic limitation of the COPY statement is that the text inserted in the program cannot contain a COPY statement.

For example, let us assume that the following code has been entered into the library AMALGAMATED-PRODUCTION-SYSTEM, using the *text-name* WORK -IN-PROG-REC-DESC:

```
01   WIP-MASTER-RECORD.
     03   ORDER-NUMBER-WMR              PIC X(5).
     03   CATALOG-NUMBER-WMR            PIC X(5).
     03   QUANTITY-WMR                  PIC 9(3).
     03   NUMBER-COMPONENTS-WMR         PIC 9(3).
     03   SCHEDULED-COMPLETION-DATE-WMR PIC 9(6).
     03   ACTUAL-COMPLETION-DATE-WMR    PIC 9(6).
     03   RAW-MAT-WMR                   PIC X(5) OCCURS 5 TIMES.
```

In Program 10.1, it would be possible to use the statement

```
COPY WORK-IN-PROG-RECORD-DESC OF AMALGAMATED-PRODUCTION-SYSTEM.
```

at line 8200, omitting lines 8300 through 8900 from the source program. The result would be indistinguishable from the code shown in Program 10.1.

Another possible use for this facility is to place PROCEDURE DIVISION modules in the library. This may reduce the work required when the same procedure is needed by several different programs in the system. The system is easier to maintain if each program uses exactly the same logic to carry out the same procedure. Use of the library can help to ensure this consistency.

One definite advantage of using the library is that if code in any of the library entries must be changed, the change can be made only once; each of the affected programs can then be recompiled and the change is propagated throughout the system in a relatively painless fashion. This is certainly a much more efficient method than inserting the new code separately into each affected program. The only disadvantage of this technique is that someone must keep track of which programs are affected and, during the conversion process, which programs have been converted and which have not. One useful technique is to place comment statements specifying a version number in each library entry. These comments are copied harmlessly into each COBOL program. However, it is possible to examine the revision number in the source code to know where that program stands in the revision process.

10.8 STRUCTURED DESIGN AND DOCUMENTATION TECHNIQUES

Documentation is defined as any document that aids in understanding a program. A primary form of documentation is a listing of the program itself. One of the goals of structured programming is to reduce reliance on other forms of documentation by making the source program as readable and easy to follow as possible. For short programs this may be sufficient, but for longer or more complex programs, other forms of documentation may be desirable.

Simple programs may be coded as they are being designed by the programmer. The programmer typically is able to visualize the program modules and their relationships without a formal design document. As programs become longer and more complex, it may be necessary to write down the design using one of a variety of techniques. The written design may then be analyzed and rewritten as necessary to produce an optimum program design. Often, several people who must communicate with one another are involved in the design process; this makes the design document a necessity.

Program design documents are used, rather than coded programs, for this design phase because the design document is less work to produce and, hence, to modify than a complete program. Typically, many details of the complete program are omitted in the design document. The emphasis is on specifying program modules, their functions and relationships. The design document is useful not only before a program is written, but also afterwards, to document the structure of the program. The design documents described in this section are usually included with the program listing and sample outputs as part of the documentation package for a program.

Structure Diagram
Structure diagrams offer a method for exhibiting the hierarchical structure of a program. Each module is represented as a block in the diagram; the module name is written in the block. If one module is executed via a PERFORM statement from another, a line connecting the two blocks is drawn.

Flowcharting
Program flowcharting is one of the oldest design and documentation techniques. The processing steps and the program flow of control are represented visually, using the standard symbols shown in Figure 1.10. Program flowcharts are used less than other techniques for program design because they tend to be quite cumbersome and they tend to focus an processing steps rather than the overall program design. Program flowcharts are useful for visualizing program flow within a module, but are not very useful for analyzing the relationships among program modules, which is the fundamental issue in program design.

Data Flow Diagram

A data flow diagram is a means for analyzing

- the sequence of processing steps that will be required to accomplish a particular task
- the data required for each step

Processing steps are represented as a circle with a description of the step placed inside the circle. Arrows connect the circles to show the sequencing of the steps. A description of the data required for that step is placed on the arrow leading to the processing step.

Consider the data flow diagram shown in Figure 10.12, which describes the familiar process of preparing a payroll report from records containing hours, rate of pay, and so forth. Data descriptions do not reflect the physical form of the data (data file, record or computed value). The processing steps do not reflect the nature of the program module that will accomplish the required task. The emphasis in a data flow diagram is on the transformations that the data will undergo, not on the logic required to make those transformations.

Two symbols used in data flow diagrams are worthy of special note. The symbol ⊕ indicates that one path or the other in the flow diagram will be taken. In the diagram of Figure 10.12, employees without overtime will be processed by "Compute Regular Pay"; employees with overtime will be processed by "Compute Overtime Pay." The symbol * indicates that the data from several sources are to be combined in a given processing step. In the diagram of Figure 10.12, amounts calculated from "Compute Regular Pay" and "Compute Overtime Pay" are collected for processing at the step "Prepare Output Record."

Data flow diagrams provide a convenient method for analyzing the processing and data transformations in systems involving manual steps or a number of related computer programs. In using data flow diagrams, it is important to include appropriate amounts of detail. If too little detail is shown, the diagram contributes little to the reader's understanding of the system. If too much detail is shown, the reader is overwhelmed and again the diagram fails to communicate knowledge of the system in question. Deciding what is appropriate detail is a judgement made with knowledge of the intended audience.

Figure 10.12   Data flow diagram example

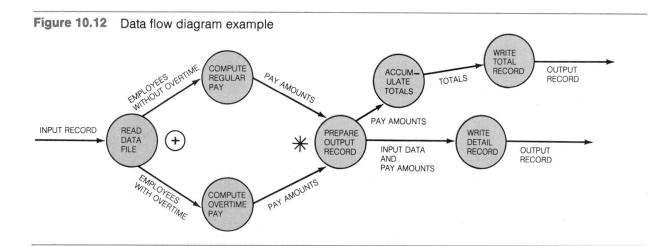

Pseudocode

Pseudocode is a means of describing the processing steps required for accomplishing the goals of a program in an informal language—one that lacks the rigorous syntax of a formal computer language like COBOL. Because the language is informal and the purpose of pseudocode is to communicate the program design and function at a relatively high level, much of the detail required by an actual program may be summarized in the pseudocode. Pseudocode enables the programmer to focus on the algorithms required for the solution of the problem at hand without getting too involved with the details of implementation required in the actual program.

There is no generally agreed upon syntax used for pseudocode. All programmers adopt a style suited to their way of approaching a programming task. Although the syntax is informal, the program must be understandable to another programmer and preferably a nonprogrammer as well. The principal of utilizing only the four basic control structures (sequence, decision, iteration, and case) must not be violated, but the manner used to describe these structures may vary in any way desired to the programmer. Often a program undergoes various transformations at the pseudocode stage, each transformation yielding a version of the program showing more detail than the previous one. This is the essence of the practice of top-down program design. (See Section 3.2 Top-Down Program Design.) Figure 10.8 illustrates the use of pseudocode in the design of Program 10.1.

The pseudocode used in this instance presents a different way of expressing a procedure. In previous examples, modules of the program have been described in the pseudocode. In this figure the entire procedure has been expressed as one module. Both types of pseudocode are equally valid; the decision as to which to use depends only on the preference of the programmer. When a program is relatively short, the form shown in Figure 10.8 is often used. As programs get more involved, it may be advantageous to segment the pseudocode into modules.

In using pseudocode, the programmer must strike a balance between showing too much detail, which makes the pseudocode as troublesome and unwieldy as the COBOL program, and too little detail, which leaves out significant portions of the program logic.

Ideally, the pseudocode is detailed enough to assure that coding of the program will proceed smoothly and is brief enough to afford the reader an overall view of the program's function without becoming enmeshed in detail. This latter characteristic is particularly important when pseudocode is used as a form of documentation.

HIPO

HIPO is an acronym for *H*ierarchy, *I*nput, *P*rocessing, *O*utput. It is a formal technique (generally associated with IBM) for specifying program design. The technique consists of three parts:

1) H (*H*ierarchy) refers to a structure diagram of essentially the type described earlier in this section. In this context, the structure diagram is called a VTOC, for *V*isual *T*able *of* *C*ontents.
2) IPO (*I*nput *P*rocessng *O*utput) refers to a form used to specify each program module in terms of data required (its input), the processing that will take place, and the results (its output).
3) Pseudocode for each program module.

IPO specifications and pseudocode for a portion of Program 10.1 are shown in Figure 10.13. The hierarchy chart for Program 10.1 is shown in Figure 10.10. These two documents form a complete HIPO documentation of Program 10.1.

Many data processing managers require HIPO design and documentation technique as the standard for all programs developed at their installations.

The method is well defined and orderly, and includes sufficient detail to facilitate coding of a program. Including the hierarchy chart makes it easier for others to understand the overall control structure of the program.

The only problem with using this method is that it generates large amounts of material, much of which is redundant. Critics of this method believe that the time, energy, and money devoted to the religious adherence to these formats could be saved by using less formal methods that convey the same information with a much smaller expenditure of resources.

Figure 10.13 IPO specifications for a portion of Program 10.2 (Courtesy of IBM). Reprinted by permission from "IBM HIPO Worksheet GX20-1970."© 1970 by International Business Machines Corporation

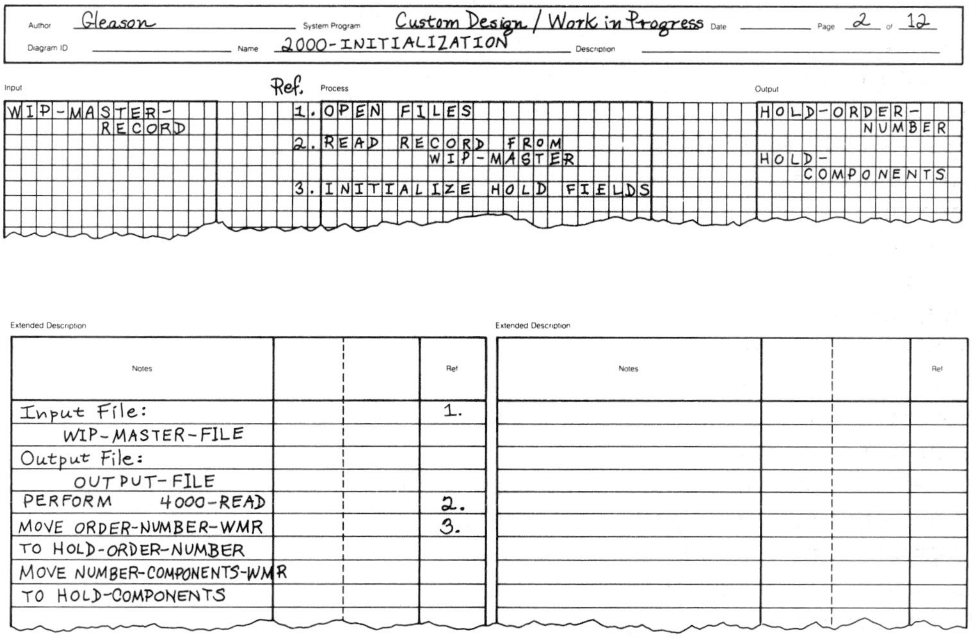
Author Gleason System Program Custom Design / Work in Progress Date Page 2 of 12
Diagram ID Name 2000-INITIALIZATION Description

Input	Ref.	Process	Output
WIP-MASTER-RECORD	1.	OPEN FILES	HOLD-ORDER-NUMBER
	2.	READ RECORD FROM WIP-MASTER	HOLD-COMPONENTS
	3.	INITIALIZE HOLD FIELDS	

Extended Description

Notes		Ref
Input File:		1.
WIP-MASTER-FILE		
Output File:		
OUTPUT-FILE		
PERFORM 4000-READ		2.
MOVE ORDER-NUMBER-WMR		3.
TO HOLD-ORDER-NUMBER		
MOVE NUMBER-COMPONENTS-WMR		
TO HOLD-COMPONENTS		

Nassi-Shneiderman Charts

A Nassi-Shneiderman chart (named for Isaac Nassi and Ben Shneiderman) resembles a program flowchart in many respects. Both are graphic representations of the program logic. But, unlike traditional program flowcharts, Nassi-Shneiderman charts can be used only to represent the basic control structures required in structured programming. An example of a Nassi-Shneiderman chart for Program 10.1 is shown in Figure 10.14. The left-hand margin of the chart is used to record module names. Rectangles in the body of the chart surround pseudocode specifications of the module content. Decisions are shown graphically by splitting the blocks in the body of the chart into two parts, one part representing actions to be taken if the question is answered "yes," the other part if the question is answered "no."

Nassi-Shneiderman charts offer a convenient graphic representation of a program closely related to the structure and form taken by the actual program code. Short programs lend themselves to Nassi-Shneiderman charts more than do long programs. Critics of the charts point out that the graphic portion of the chart really contributes little clarity and that the

Figure 10.14   Nassi-Shneiderman chart for Program 10.1

Main Logic
Perform Initialization
Perform Control Until EOF-FLAG = 'YES'
Perform Order Number Break
Perform Termination
Stop Run

Initiali-zation	Open Files
	Perform Read
	Initialize HOLD Fields

Control	Perform Control-Break Check
	Perform Check Full Page
	Perform Move Fields
	Perform Add Order Components
	Perform Write Detail
	Perform Read

Read	Read WIP-MASTER-FILE
	End of File? — Yes / No
	Move 'YES' To EOF-FLAG

Control-Break Check	ORDER-NUMBER-WMR ≠ HOLD-ORDER-NUMBER — Yes / No
	Perform Order-Number Break

Check Full Page	Page full? — Yes / No
	Perform Write Headings

Move Fields	Move Data from Input Fields To Output Record

Add Order Components	Add 1 To NUMBER-COMPONENTS-WIF

Write Detail	Write Detail Line
	Increment LINE-COUNT

Order-Number Break	Write Control-Break Summary Line
	Increment LINE-COUNT
	Initialize NUMBER-COMPONENTS-WIF
	Initialize HOLD Fields

Write Headings	Increment PAGE-COUNT
	Write Headings
	Initialize LINE-COUNT

Termin-ation	Close Files

pseudocode alone is sufficient. A major problem with any graphic form of program documentation is that it does not lend itself to creation or manipulation by electronic means (such as word processors or editors). Any program change requiring a corresponding change in the documentation must be accomplished by hand, which tends to be expensive and to open the possibility of typographical errors.

Chapin Charts

Chapin charts (named for their inventor, Ned Chapin) are an alternative form of graphic representation of program logic, representing something of a compromise between traditional program flowcharts and Nassi-Shneiderman charts. Like traditional program flowcharts, each module in a Chapin chart is drawn separately. As in Nassi-Shneiderman charts, the decision structure is represented as a yes/no division beneath the question. Chapin borrowed the oval terminal symbol from traditional program flowcharts and used it to denote the module entry point, program termination, and performance of a module. Like the Nassi-Shneiderman chart, the Chapin chart uses a rectangular grid to surround each program statement.

A Chapin chart for Program 10.1 is shown in Figure 10.15. The advantages and disadvantages of Chapin charts resemble those of Nassi-Shneiderman charts.

At this time, there is no single form of structured design and documentation technique that is universally accepted as the best. In many installations, certain forms have been adopted as local standards; all programs and systems developed at that location must conform to those specifications. Probably the most widely accepted forms are pseudocode and structure diagrams. Other forms are used less often but still find defenders in various segments of the data processing community.

10.9 STRUCTURED PROGRAMMING THEORY: COHESION AND COUPLING

In the past decade, a great deal of theoretical work has been done in structured programming. One widely used concept is that of *cohesion*. Cohesion means what its definition would imply, namely "that which binds together" or "what makes it stick." Module cohesion refers to the logical "glue" that binds the parts of the module together. There are several types of cohesion, which have been ranked according to their desirability, as shown in Figure 10.16.

Functional cohesion is the highest-level and most desirable type of cohesion. A module that exhibits strong functional cohesion performs a single well-defined task, which can generally be described in two or three words. Typical examples of modules exhibiting functional cohesion include

```
CALCULATE-GROSS-PAY
WRITE-HEADING-LINE
VALIDATE-EMPLOYEE-NUMBER
LOOKUP-BONUS-AMOUNT
```

Modules with functional cohesion tend to be homogeneous–all parts of the module contribute materially to the task at hand. They tend to be easy to understand and, hence, relatively easy to debug and maintain. Functional cohesion is the goal for designing all program modules.

Figure 10.15   Chapin chart for Program 10.1

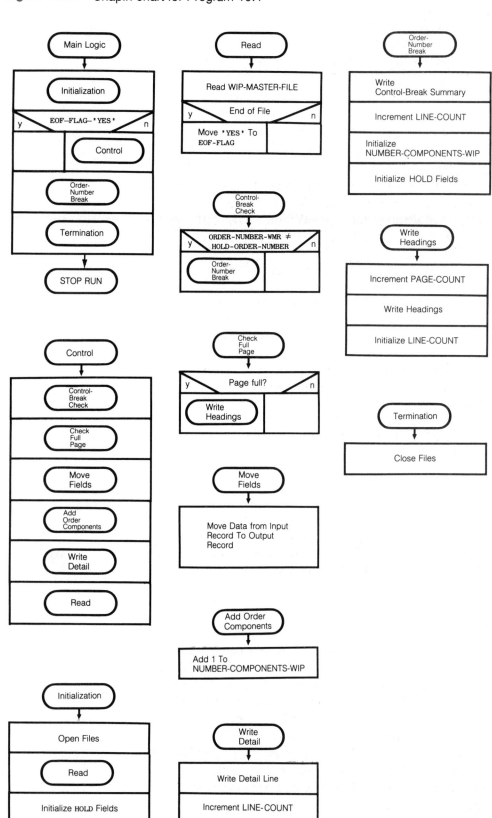

Figure 10.16   Levels of module cohesion

Cohesion Type	*Desirability*
Function	high
Sequence	↑
Data	│
Procedure	│
Time	│
Logic	↓
Coincidence	low

Sequential cohesion implies that the module is made up of elements that must be performed in a designated sequence. Very often the name of the module would (or should) incorporate the word AND indicating that several tasks are being carried out in sequence. Typical examples include

```
PROCESS-DATA-AND-READ-NEXT-REC
VALIDATE-HRS-COMPUTE-OVERTIME
```

Modules exhibiting sequential cohesion, though less desirable than those exhibiting functional cohesion, may be unavoidable in actual coding of a COBOL program because some programming tasks are essentially sequential in nature.

Data-related cohesion refers to a module that performs several tasks on the same or related data items. For example, a module titled

```
VALIDATE-DATA-RECORD
```

in which each field in the record is validated, exhibits data-related cohesion. Other examples are

```
MOVE-INPUT-DATA-TO-OUTPUT-REC
PROCESS-INPUT-DATA
```

Procedural cohesion refers to a module that relates strongly to the control structure of the program. For example, a module titled LOOP-CONTROL signifies that the main purpose of the module is to enter a loop and continue its execution. Other module names that are indicative of procedural cohesion include

```
CHOOSE-APPROPRIATE-ACTION
LOOP-UNTIL-TERMINATION
```

Modules exhibiting procedural cohesion can result from over-reliance on flowcharting as a program design technique. When decisions with regard to modularization are made by arbitrarily partitioning the flowchart using the control structure as the only criterion, the resulting modules are likely to exhibit procedural cohesion. For example, consider the flowchart shown in Figure 10.17. Module 1 and Module 2 as shown would exhibit procedural cohesion: Module 1 is based on decision structure; Module 2 is based on an iteration structure. It is preferable to partition the program into modules based on the function to be performed by the module rather than on the control structure that happens to be required.

Figure 10.17 Modular decomposition example

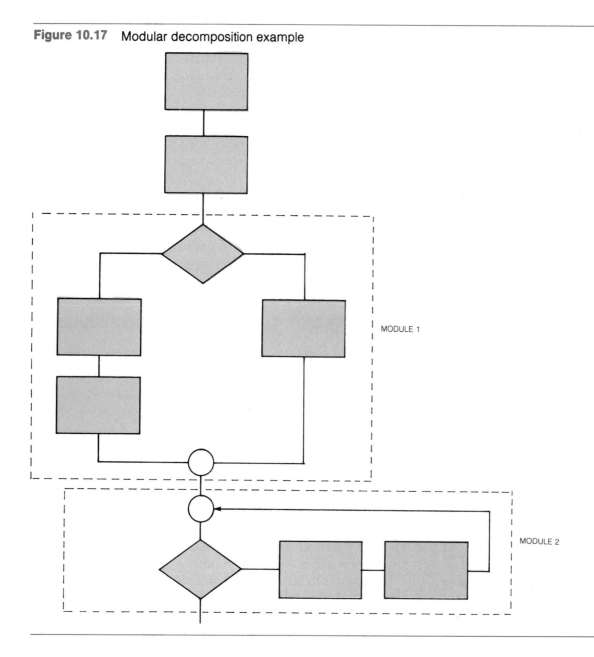

Time-related cohesion implies that the components are related to the time in the execution of the program at which they will be executed. Typical examples include

`INITIALIZATION-ROUTINE`

and

`TERMINATION.`

All of the components of `INITIALIZATION-ROUTINE` must be executed before a processing loop is entered; `TERMINATION` consists of tasks to be performed after the loop has been completed. Although temporal cohesion ranks relatively low in terms of desirability, modules of this type are, in practice, generally unavoidable in actual coding of structured COBOL programs.

Logical cohesion characterizes a module that consists of a sequence of tasks related in some way but generally spanning several functional areas.

For example, a module that reads a data record from each of several files, one that validates data items from several sources, or one that handles all error messages from a variety of sources would tend to exhibit logical cohesion. Although the tasks performed by modules such as these are related in some fashion, they are less cohesive than other module types because they are composed of several more specific functions.

The least cohesive type of module exhibits coincidental cohesion. This implies that the module contains unrelated tasks that have arbitrarily been grouped together into a module. They result from poor planning or (at times) arbitrary limitations on module size or the number of modules in a program. Modules of this type should be avoided completely in a structured program. Although functional cohesion is the goal for all program modules and should form the basis for program design, the actual coding of a structured COBOL program will usually result in some modules with a weaker type of cohesion. It is always possible to avoid modules with coincidental cohesion, but it is not always possible to avoid modules with other less desirable forms of cohesion.

A useful exercise is to examine an existing COBOL program and attempt to categorize the cohesion of each module. This exercise will point out the looseness of the categories described above. It is possible for two persons to classify modules in different ways; the definitions of cohesive types are not specific enough to enable categorizations that can be agreed upon by all. The types of cohesion should be treated as theoretical categories, and the general dictum that in "good" programs the modules should exhibit high levels of cohesion should be treated as a goal in the design and coding phases of the program development cycle.

Module Coupling

The concept of module coupling relates to the types of connections that exist among modules. In general, the more that one module must "know" about another in order for the interface between them to work properly, the more tightly connected the modules are. In general, the goal is to produce modules that are as loosely coupled as possible. The ideal is to be able to consider a module to be a "black box" that performs its function on demand without requiring that the user be aware of the internal workings of the box. Loosely coupled modules are desirable because they tend to enhance maintainability of the program. The problem with tightly coupled modules is that a change in one module is likely to require changes in other modules to make the program work properly. Often these required changes are obscure and may not be evident until a revised program fails to function properly.

It is possible to identify several types of module coupling:

- content
- control
- data

Content coupling, which is the strongest form of coupling, results when one module refers to the contents of another module. In a COBOL program, content coupling can occur when one paragraph of a multiparagraph module is executed by another module. For example, consider the program segment shown in Figure 10.18.

Figure 10.18   Example of content coupling

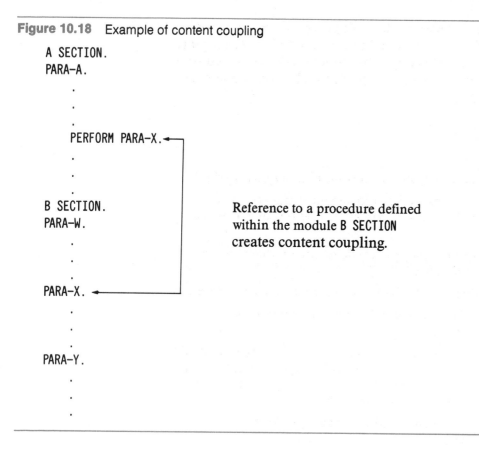

```
A SECTION.
PARA-A.
        .
        .
        .
        .
        PERFORM PARA-X.

        .
        .
        .
B SECTION.
PARA-W.
        .
        .
        .
PARA-X.
        .
        .
        .
PARA-Y.
        .
        .
        .
```

Reference to a procedure defined
within the module B SECTION
creates content coupling.

B SECTION contains several paragraphs that are normally treated as a single program module. A reference to any of these paragraphs (such as that shown in Figure 10.18) creates a connection between the modules based on a procedure name defined inside B SECTION. Another way in which content coupling can occur insidiously is when control passes from one module to another by default. This can happen when, because of a flaw in the control structure, a program allows control to pass from one paragraph to the one that happens to follow it.

In general, elimination of most uses of the GO TO statement in structured COBOL has eliminated most of the cases of content coupling between modules, which is quite common in nonstructured programs. Content coupling can and should be avoided in designing and coding a structured COBOL program.

Control coupling is a somewhat weaker form of coupling in which a control variable is passed between two modules. A control variable is one used to determine what action to take in some situation. An end-of-file flag is a common example of a control variable. Its purpose is to record the fact that an end-of-file condition has been encountered and to pass this information to another module, which takes appropriate action. Control coupling connects the module that tests the variable and the module that sets the variable.

Data coupling is a still weaker form of coupling in which modules are connected by access to a common set of data items. Two modules that process the same input record or the same table of constants are connected by data coupling.

In practice, control coupling and data coupling are very common in COBOL programs; content coupling should be avoided. Control coupling should be used only where necessary. The unnecessary use of control variables results in unnecessarily tightly coupled modules, which may cause problems during maintenance.

10.10 SELF-TEST EXERCISES

1. In what way is the programmer's job related to the overall system design?

2. How are the roles of the systems analyst, programming manager, and programmer like those of the architect, contractor, and subcontractor of a building project?

3. Compare the system flowchart and program flowchart. In what ways are they similar; how are they different?

4. In a system flowchart, what is meant by the use of the double-headed arrow?

5. What is the purpose of the program specification statement? What information is usually included?

6. With respect to the Amalgamated Custom Design production system, what motivated the implementation of some portions of the system as interactive systems and other portions as batch? In this system, what general types of programs are interactive and what types are batch?

7. Briefly explain the major advantages and disadvantages of the programming team approach.

8. What is the primary purpose of the structured walk-through? Describe the major disadvantage of the technique.

9. What is "ego-less" programming?

10. What is the primary purpose of the data dictionary concept? How can it be implemented in a COBOL environment?

11. How does structured implementation and testing differ from the usual student implementation and testing technique?

12. Why do most programmers use a combination of top-down and bottom-up techniques for structured implementation and testing?

13. What is a "program stub?"

14. What is the purpose of the COPY statement? What are considerations for its use at your installation?

15. Examine each of the modules of Program 10.1 and classify the type of cohesion that appears to be exhibited.

16. Explain the "black-box" concept of program design.

17. Give an example of control coupling in Program 10.1.

18. Document a program you have written with each of the following:

    flowchart
    structure diagram
    pseudocode
    Nassi-Shneiderman chart
    Chapin chart

10.11 PROGRAMMING EXERCISES

1. The first record in a file contains the current date, and subsequent records each contain a name and a date of birth. The output is to include the number of people contained in the file, the name of the oldest person and his or her date of birth, and the name of the youngest person and his or her date of birth.

2. The first record in a file contains the current date. Each succeeding record contains (among other items) the date of the last time an item was sold, the number of items on hand, the cost per item, and the regular selling price. A store plans to have a sale on slow moving items. The purpose of the program is to produce a report showing recommended sale prices as follows:

   If the item has not been sold in the last 30 days, discount is 10%.
   If the item has not been sold in the last 60 days, discount is 20%.
   If the item has not been sold in the last 90 days, discount is 40%.

   Any item that has sold in the last 30 days is not placed on sale. If there is only one of any item left in stock, it is to be discounted only five percent. Sale prices may not be lower than cost.

3. Revise the program in Section 6.13, Exercise 6 to use a date record for the current date.

4. Write a program to calculate the depreciation expense and book value for an asset. Depreciation should be calculated using the following three methods:
   a. *Straight Line Method*

      The amount of depreciation per year is:

      $$\frac{\text{cost - salvage value}}{\text{number of years}}$$

   For example, for an asset which cost \$22,000 and has a salvage value of \$2,000 and a life expectancy of five years, the depreciation amount is:

   $(22,000 - 2,000) / 5 = 4,000$

   The new book value is computed by subtracting the depreciation amount from the current book value. The resulting table would be:

Year	Depreciation expense	Book value
1	4,000	18,000
2	4,000	14,000
3	4,000	10,000
4	4,000	6,000
5	4,000	2,000

   b. *Sum of Years Digits Method*

      The amount of depreciation for the *i*th year is:

      $(\text{cost} - \text{salvage value}) * P_i$
      where P_i is a factor computed in the following way:

      1) Compute the sum:
         $S = 1 + 2 + 3 + \ldots + n$ where n represents the number of years
      2) Compute $P_i = (n + 1 - i) / S$ for $i = 1, 2, 3 \ldots n$.

         For example, if cost = 22,000 and n = 5, we find
         $S = 1 + 2 + 3 + 4 + 5 = 15$
         and
         $P_1 = (5 + 1 - 1) / 15 = 1 / 3$
         $P_2 = (5 + 1 - 2) / 15 = 4/15$

Thus the depreciation amount for the first year is

(22,000 − 2,000) * 1/3 = 6,666

For the second year the amount is

(22,000 − 2,000) * 4/15 = 5,333

The resulting table would be

Year	Depreciation expense	Book value
1	6,666	15,333
2	5,333	10,000
3	4,000	6,000
4	2,666	3,333
5	1,333	2,000

c. *Declining Balance Method*

The depreciation value is computed by multiplying the old book value by a constant fraction M. The value of M is defined by

$M = P / n$

where P is a proportion chosen by the accountant and n represents the number of years. For example, suppose cost = \$22,000, $n = 5$ and $P = 150\%$ (there is no salvage value using this method). Then,

$M = 150\% / 5 = 30\%$

depreciation = 22,000 * .30 = 6,600

new book value = 22,000 − 6,600 = 15,400

The resulting table would be

Year	Depreciation expense	Book value
1	6,600	15,400
2	4,620	10,780
3	3,234	7,546
4	2,263	5,282
5	1,584	3,697

5. A file contains records pertaining to the amount and analysis of the milk given by cows at a dairy. Each record contains the following items:

> Cow i.d. number
> Date
> Amount of milk
> Butterfat content of milk (percentage)

Write a program to compute the mean and standard deviation for the butterfat content of the milk. The mean is computed by finding the sum of all the observations and dividing by the number of observations:

$$m = \frac{\sum x_i}{n}$$

The standard deviation (represented by σ) is computed using the formula:

$$\sigma = \sqrt{\frac{\sum (x_i - m)^2}{n}}$$

Your program should flag the output for each cow which has an average butterfat content greater than $m + 2\sigma$ or less than $m - 2\sigma$.

6. XYZ Pharmacy, Inc. maintains a system designed to give their customers a statement at the end of each year showing all medicines purchased during the year. Design such a system, making appropriate assumptions regarding what data will be collected and what files will be maintained.

7. An insurance company maintains a file which has records containing (among other things):

>   Policy number
>   Amount of claim
>   Date of accident
>   Sex of driver
>   Age of driver

Write a program to compute the frequency of claims and average claim amount for each cell of the following table:

Age	M	F
18-21		
22-25		
26-30		
31-35		
36-50		
51-65		
Over 65		

8. Modify the program written for Exercise 7 above to print the proportion of claims computed by dividing the number of claims for drivers in a particular age/sex group by the total number of policy holders in this age/sex group. Assume that your program has access to the master policy file to calculate the required totals for all policy holders.

References

Chapin, N., et al. "Structured Programming Simplified," *Computer Decisions*. Vol. 6, no.6 (June 1974), pp.28-31.

Nassi, I., and B. Shneiderman, "Flowchart Techniques for Structured Programming." *ACM SIGPLAN Notices*. Vol. 8, no. 8 (August 1973), pp. 12-26.

Yourdon, E., and L.L. Constantine, *Structured Design*, Englewood Cliffs, N.J.:   Prentice-Hall, Inc., 1979.

INTERACTIVE PROGRAMS AND CHARACTER STRING MANIPULATION 11

11.1 INTERACTIVE VS. BATCH ENVIRONMENTS

In many computer systems, the user's primary means of communication with the system is through a computer terminal. The user enters data at the terminal and the computer responds with appropriate messages. Such systems are referred to as *interactive* systems, as the user and computer system engage in a very immediate form of interaction. In other systems, data and programs are prepared in isolation from the computer, using some machine-readable medium. (Punched cards are a prime example, but other machine-readable mediums include off-line optical scanners, written forms, and floppy disks prepared off-line.) When all of the data has been prepared (or when the entire program has been encoded into machine-readable form) the data, program, and operating system instructions are submitted for processing. Systems of this type are generally referred to as *batch* processing systems. Data is accumulated over time and processed as a batch rather than immediately as it is collected, which is characteristic of an interactive system.

When using an interactive system for program development, the user's primary tool is an operating system program called an *editor*. An editor allows the user to create and update files. The first step in developing a COBOL program is to build a file containing the COBOL program statements. The editor usually contains provisions for listing files, adding records to files, changing all or part of existing records, and deleting records from files. The COBOL programmer makes use of this facility to list the program and to add, change, or delete portions of the program. When satisfied with the program, the programmer then enters appropriate operating system instructions to compile the program. If the compilation is successful, the output produced by the program is generally directed either to the terminal or to an auxiliary printer associated with the terminal. If the compilation is not successful because of syntax errors, the programmer may display the error messages produced by the compiler at the terminal. It is then necessary to use the editor to make necessary revisions to the program. Specific details on use of terminals, operating system instructions, and editor instructions vary greatly from one computing system to another; secure detailed information appropriate to the system available for use before attempting to enter a COBOL program.

Regardless of the type of system used to prepare the program, a processing program may be classed as batch or interactive depending on the mode of usage designed into the program. If the program is designed to process data files that are in place at the time the program begins execution, the program may be classed as a batch-oriented program. Such programs can typically be scheduled to run at any time convenient for the computing system and usually are assigned a low priority because response time is not an important factor to the user. On the other hand, if the program is designed to allow the user to enter data at the terminal and produce responses at the terminal, then the program is primarily interactive in nature. Such programs are typically run by the user when there is data to be processed, or they may run continuously to capture and process data as it occurs. In any case, interactive programs must be assigned a high priority within the system, because system response time is a crucial factor in the usability of the software. Remember, the way in which the program is developed has no bearing on the way in which a program processes data. Most program development systems have both interactive and batch components, depending on the needs of the user and the capabilities of the hardware.

11.2 DESIGN AND IMPLEMENTATION OF INTERACTIVE PROGRAMS

In writing a program that is interactive in nature, a programmer must realize that methods of reading data entered at the terminal and writing information to the terminal differ from one system to another. In some systems, the terminal is treated as a data file similar to files assigned to other devices. In such systems, a terminal file is defined in SELECT and FD entries and the usual READ and WRITE instructions are used. In other systems, input from the terminal is handled by the ACCEPT statement, and output to the terminal is produced by the DISPLAY statement. In early implementation of COBOL, which were generally found on batch-oriented systems, the ACCEPT and DISPLAY verbs were used only to communicate with the computer operator. With the advent of interactive systems, ACCEPT and DISPLAY have been adapted not only to perform their original function, but also to allow communications with a program user at a terminal. This adaptation is not universal, however. Check the documentation for your system before attempting to use ACCEPT and DISPLAY in the manner outlined below.

Figure 11.1   General form of the ACCEPT statement

The general form of the ACCEPT statement is shown in Figure 11.1 Depending on the system in use, the ACCEPT statement without the FROM option may automatically cause the system to input data from the terminal being used to execute the program. On other systems, it is necessary to define a mnemonic in the SPECIAL-NAMES paragraph of the IDENTIFICATION DIVISION to identify the specific device to be used in the operation. For example, an appropriate SPECIAL-NAMES entry would be:

```
SPECIAL-NAMES.
     CONSOLE IS OPERATORS-INPUT-DEVICE.
```

With this mnemonic declared, an appropriate ACCEPT statement would be:

```
ACCEPT DATA-IN FROM OPERATORS-INPUT-DEVICE.
```

When an ACCEPT statement is executed, a message is written at the console, alerting the user that the program is waiting for him or her to enter some data. Execution of the program is suspended until the user completes the input operation.

Suppose the data-item NUMBER-IN is defined as

```
03 NUMBER-IN PIC 9(4).
```

and the program statement

```
ACCEPT NUMBER-IN.
```

is executed. After displaying an appropriate message, the system will wait until the user enters data at the terminal. The characters entered by the user will be stored in NUMBER-IN and execution will proceed with the next statement.

It is important that the user enter the data expected by the program. The characters entered by the user are stored in the designated memory location in order from left to right. If too few characters are entered, the remaining rightmost characters may be padded with blanks or zeros, or the system may respond with a message requesting more data. If too many characters are entered, excess characters on the right are ignored.

Example

```
03 NUMBER-IN PIC 9(4).
          .
          .
          .
     ACCEPT NUMBER-IN.
```

If the user enters 1234, the value stored in NUMBER-IN will be

| 1 | 2 | 3 | 4 |

If the user enters 12345, the value stored in NUMBER-IN will be

| 1 | 2 | 3 | 4 |

because excess digits on the right are truncated. If the user enters 123, the value stored in NUMBER-IN will be left-justified. The rightmost positions may contain invalid data.

| 1 | 2 | 3 | ? |

Some systems will request that the user enter more data which will be used to fill out the remaining position in NUMBER-IN.

Example

```
01  DATA-REC.
    03  NAME-DR PIC X(10).
    03  SS-NUM-DR PIC 9(9).
        .
        .
        .
    ACCEPT DATA-REC.
```

The expected number of characters is 19—the length of the group item DATA-REC. The first 10 characters entered will be stored in NAME-DR; the next 9 characters will be stored in SS-NUM-DR.

The ACCEPT statement may also be used in a batch-oriented computing system to allow the system operator to enter small amounts of data. In such systems, this statement is used only for small amounts of data because of the low speed that is typical of an operator's console and because it takes up the operator's time. It can be useful, however, to allow the operator to enter a data item such as the current date for a report or to allow the operator to select among various functions that a program might perform. Also, a program might, for security reasons, ask the operator to enter his or her name and the time of the run.

Corresponding to the input statement ACCEPT, which allows the user to enter data at a terminal, is the output statement DISPLAY, which causes output at the terminal. The general form of the DISPLAY statement is shown in Figure 11.2.

Any sequence of literals or data items may be written on the terminal using the DISPLAY statement. For example:

```
DISPLAY WS-DATA.
```

would cause the contents of WS-DATA to be written. The statement

```
DISPLAY "ENTER CURRENT DATE".
```

could be followed by

```
ACCEPT DATE-IN.
```

The written message produced by the DISPLAY statement serves to guide the operator's response to the item required by the ACCEPT statement.

Figure 11.2 General form of the DISPLAY statement

```
DISPLAY  {literal  }  [UPON  {hardware-name}]
         {data-name}         {mnemonic name}
```

Example

```
DISPLAY "ENTER NAME AND SOCIAL SECURITY NUMBER"
ACCEPT DATA-REC.
DISPLAY "NAME ", NAME-DR, " SS-NO. ", SS-NUM-DR.
```

This example illustrates the use of the DISPLAY statement to prompt the user for the data and echo the input received. Suppose INPUT-REC is defined as in the example above and the user enters the following data:

```
JOHN JONES123456789
```

The expected output from the second DISPLAY statement is

```
NAME JOHN JONES SS-NO. 123456789
```

The use of an echo such as this is important to ensure that the data entered by the user is correct, and, if not, to give the user a chance to correct the data.

In batch-oriented systems, the DISPLAY statement may be used to direct messages to the system operator's console. It may be used to prompt the operator regarding data requested by an ACCEPT statement. It may also be used to write messages regarding errors or exceptional conditions encountered during the execution of the program.

Typically, error messages regarding data being processed are displayed on the operator's console only on small computing systems that run one program at a time. On larger systems that may execute many programs at one time, error messages are usually written on the printer or on a disk file that is examined after completion of the program.

11.3 PROGRAM EXAMPLE

Write an interactive program to allow the user to create a file composed of records containing a name and a social security number. Include a provision for the user to check and correct data before it is written to the file.

Problem Analysis

We will assume that the system uses ACCEPT and DISPLAY to communicate with interactive users. The program must include prompts directing the user to enter data. Before data is written to the file, the program must display the data that has been entered and allow the user to verify the correctness of the data. This will be handled by displaying a question and accepting a response from the user. If the response indicates that the data is correct, the record is written on the file; if the response indicates incorrect data, the user enters the data again. This procedure is repeated until an acceptable data record has been entered.

As there is no AT END clause on the ACCEPT statement, there is no "automatic" technique to determine when the end of the file being entered by the user has been reached. This is, of course, a necessary task as the file being created must be closed when all data has been written on it, in order for the file to become permanent. The task of determining when there is no more data will be handled by requiring the user to enter the character "END" in the name field when all data has been entered. Thus, the procedure used to enter a data record must be repeated until either the name field contains "END" or a valid record has been entered. A plan for this program is shown in Figure 11.3.

Figure 11.3   Plan for interactive file builder program

Main Logic

```
     Open output file
     Do Get data until answer = "Y" or name = "END"
     Do until name = "END"
          Write data record
          Move "N" to answer
          Do Get data until answer = "Y" or name = "END"
     End Do
     Close file
     Stop
```

Get data

```
     Get name
     If name not = "END"
          Get social security number
          Write record data or user device
          Get answer
     End if
```

Problem Solution

A solution to this problem is shown in Program 11.1 with structure diagram in Figure 11.4. The program creates a file DATA-FILE assigned to disk. Note the nonstandard SELECT statement at line 1800. In the system used to compile and execute this program, the external name for the file is specified as part of the system name in the SELECT entry for the file. The user enters records one field at a time at the terminal (lines 5600-6000). The program echos the data (line 6100) and gives the user the opportunity to reject the data or accept it for entry onto the file (line 6200-6300). Note the use of a special value contained in the field NAME-DR used to end the data entry/file building process. When the user enters the characters "END" as the content of NAME-DR, the program closes the output file, making the data permanent (see lines 4400-4600). The general approach used in this program is useful for building the data files required for most programming exercises in this text.

11.4   MENU-DRIVEN PROGRAMS

An important aspect of interactive programs is how easy they are to use—their "user friendliness." The program's human interface is its instructions and menus. The program user needs instructions on how to use the program, what data is required, what options are available, what codes to use, and so forth. These instructions are, of course, included in the written documentation (usually called a "user's guide"), written by the programmer or other member of the data processing staff. It is also very useful to include at least some of these instructions in the program itself so that users do not have to rely solely on the written documentation.

User instructions take a variety of distinct forms. Often one or more screens of information will be displayed when execution of the program is initiated. Line 5200 of Program 11.1 is an example of such initial information generated at the beginning of the program. Prompts may be displayed on the screen when specific data or codes must be entered. Lines 5600 and 5900 of Program 11.1 are examples of such prompts. A third type of user information is the *menu*. Menus are used when a program allows the user to select certain options. After a menu is displayed, the user enters a code (selected from the menu) that corresponds to the action he/she desires to carry out. Menus usually have additional options including "Help," which causes the program to display information to help the user and "Quit," which enables the user to terminate the program. The program repeats the menu display/user response/program action sequence until the user selects "Quit."

Program 11.1   Interactive file creation program

```
000100 IDENTIFICATION DIVISION.
000200*
000300 PROGRAM-ID. FILE-BUILDER.
000400 AUTHOR. HORN.
000500*REMARKS. INTERACTIVE FILE CREATION PROGRAM.
000600*
000700 ENVIRONMENT DIVISION.
000800*
000900 CONFIGURATION SECTION.
001000*
001100 SOURCE-COMPUTER.
001200 OBJECT-COMPUTER.
001300*
001400 INPUT-OUTPUT SECTION.
001500*
001600 FILE-CONTROL.
001700*
001800       SELECT DATA-FILE ASSIGN TO OUTPUT "DATA/FIL".
001900*
002000 DATA DIVISION.
002100*
002200 FILE SECTION.
002300*
002400 FD    DATA-FILE
002500       LABEL RECORDS ARE STANDARD
002600       DATA RECORD IS DATA-REC.
002700*
002800 01    DATA-REC.
002900       03  NAME-DR         PIC X(10).
003000       03  SS-NUM-DR       PIC 9(9).
003100*
003200 WORKING-STORAGE SECTION.
003300*
003400 01 CONTROL-FIELDS.
003500       02  ANSWER          PIC X VALUE "N".
003600*
003700 PROCEDURE DIVISION.
003800*
003900 1000-MAIN-LOGIC.
004000*
```

```
004100          PERFORM 2000-INITIALIZATION.
004200          PERFORM 3000-GET-DATA
004300               UNTIL ANSWER = "Y" OR NAME-DR = "END".
004400          PERFORM 4000-BUILD-FILE
004500               UNTIL NAME-DR = "END".
004600          PERFORM 5000-TERMINATION.
004700          STOP RUN.
004800*
004900 2000-INITIALIZATION.
005000*
005100          OPEN OUTPUT DATA-FILE.
005200          DISPLAY "ENTER END IN NAME FIELD TO TERMINATE PROGRAM".
005300*
005400 3000-GET-DATA.
005500*
005600          DISPLAY "ENTER NAME".
005700          ACCEPT NAME-DR.
005800          IF NAME-DR NOT = "END"
005900               DISPLAY "ENTER SOCIAL SECURITY NUMBER"
006000               ACCEPT SS-NUM-DR
006100               DISPLAY "NAME " NAME-DR " SS NUM. "  SS-NUM-DR
006200               DISPLAY "IS DATA CORRECT?"
006300               ACCEPT ANSWER.
006400*
006500 4000-BUILD-FILE.
006600*
006700          WRITE DATA-REC.
006800          MOVE "N" TO ANSWER.
006900          PERFORM 3000-GET-DATA
007000               UNTIL ANSWER = "Y" OR NAME-DR = "END".
007100*
007200 5000-TERMINATION.
007300*
007400          CLOSE DATA-FILE.
```

Program 11.1 (continued)

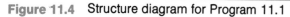

Figure 11.4 Structure diagram for Program 11.1

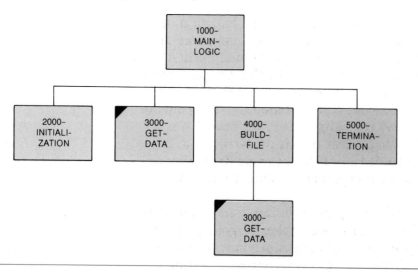

11.5 PROGRAM EXAMPLE

Problem Statement

Revise Program 11.1 to allow the user to create DATA-FILE or to list DATA-FILE. Include a menu to allow the user to choose the task which he or she desires to carry out.

Problem Analysis

A preliminary plan for the program is shown below; this basic plan is shared by all menu driven programs:

```
Do until quit
      Display menu
      Accept user choice
      Carry out program action
End Do
Stop
```

The required menu will have four options which can be selected in any sequence:

Code	Function
C	Create file
L	List file
H	Help
Q	Quit

The process of creating a file will be handled as in Program 11.1. Listing the file will employ the logic used any time a sequential file is processed from beginning to end. The "HELP" command will result in a display of information regarding how to use the program. Any invalid choice will result in an error message and the menu will be displayed again. The program plan can now be written as shown in Figure 11.5.

Problem Solution

The required program is shown in Program 11.2 with structure diagram in Figure 11.6. Note that the program segment containing the paragraphs 4000-CREATE-FILE, 4100-GET-DATA and 4200-BUILD-FILE are virtually identical to the corresponding paragraphs in Program 11.1. In this program these paragraphs are required to carry out the program action CREATE-FILE. The paragraphs 5000-LIST-FILE and 5100-WRITE-READ are required to carry out the program action LIST-FILE. The only paragraph in the program that is not completely coded is 6000-HELP. The content of this paragraph should be chosen with knowledge of the intended user of the program. Inexperienced users generally require more detailed explanations than do more knowledgeable users.

In practice, menus may contain many more choices than the one contained in Program 11.2 and, in particularly complex programs, the first action the program takes in response to a particular choice may be to display another menu (called a *submenu*) containing options related to that choice.

Any menu-driven program or program module will use the same logic as shown in Program 11.2, regardless of the size or complexity of the program.

In general, the number of choices offered in any menu should be reasonably small and clearly defined so that the user has no difficulty in deciding which action to choose. The art of designing good interactive programs requires attention to human psychology as well as to the technical requirements of the task at hand. Very often, as part of the program development process, the menu and instruction portions of programs are field-tested and refined repeatedly, based on the reactions of the test subjects. Careful attention to these details may make the difference between a program that contributes positively to overall productivity of an organization and one that makes a negative contribution.

Figure 11.5   Plan for Program 11.2

Main logic

```
Do until quit
     Display menu
     Get choice
     If choice is create file
          Do create file
     Else
          If choice is list file
               Do list file
          Else
               If choice is help
                    Do help
               Else
                    If choice is invalid
                         Do error display
                    End If
               End If
          End If
     End If
End Do
Stop
```

Program 11.2   Menu-driven file utility program

```
000100 IDENTIFICATION DIVISION.
000200*
000300 PROGRAM-ID. FILE-UTILITY.
000400 AUTHOR. HORN.
000500*REMARKS. MENU DRIVEN FILE UTILITY PROGRAM.
000600*
000700 ENVIRONMENT DIVISION.
000800*
000900 CONFIGURATION SECTION.
001000*
```

```
001100 SOURCE-COMPUTER.
001200 OBJECT-COMPUTER.
001300*
001400 INPUT-OUTPUT SECTION.
001500*
001600 FILE-CONTROL.
001700*
001800      SELECT DATA-FILE ASSIGN TO INPUT-OUTPUT "DATA/FIL".
001900      SELECT PRINT-FILE ASSIGN TO PRINT "PRINTER".
002000*
002100 DATA DIVISION.
002200*
002300 FILE SECTION.
002400*
002500 FD   DATA-FILE
002600      LABEL RECORDS ARE STANDARD
002700      DATA RECORD IS DATA-REC.
002800*
002900 01   DATA-REC.
003000      03   NAME-DR              PIC X(10).
003100      03   SS-NUM-DR            PIC 9(9).
003200*
003300 FD   PRINT-FILE
003400      DATA RECORD IS PRINT-REC.
003500*
003600 01   PRINT-REC                 PIC X(132).
003700*
003800 WORKING-STORAGE SECTION.
003900*
004000 01   CONTROL-FIELDS.
004100      02 ANSWER                 PIC X VALUE "N".
004200      02 CHOICE                 PIC X VALUE SPACE.
004300         88   CREATE-FILE             VALUE "C".
004400         88   LIST-FILE               VALUE "L".
004500         88   HELP                    VALUE "H".
004600         88   QUIT                    VALUE "Q".
004700*
004800 01   FLAGS.
004900      02   EOF-FLAG             PIC XXX VALUE "NO".
005000*
005100 PROCEDURE DIVISION.
005200*
005300 1000-MAIN-LOGIC.
005400*
005500      PERFORM 2000-PROGRAM-ACTION
005600          UNTIL QUIT.
005700      STOP RUN.
005800*
005900 2000-PROGRAM-ACTION.
006000*
006100      PERFORM 3000-MENU-DISPLAY.
006200      PERFORM 3100-GET-CHOICE.
```

```
006300        IF CREATE-FILE                         Program 11.2 (continued)
006400            PERFORM 4000-CREATE-FILE
006500        ELSE
006600            IF LIST-FILE
006700                PERFORM 5000-LIST-FILE
006800            ELSE
006900              IF HELP
007000                  PERFORM 6000-HELP
007100              ELSE
007200                IF QUIT
007300                    NEXT SENTENCE
007400                ELSE
007500                    PERFORM 7000-ERROR-DISPLAY.
007600*
007700 3000-MENU-DISPLAY.
007800*
007900        DISPLAY "CODE    MEANING".
008000        DISPLAY "C       CREATE DATA FILE".
008100        DISPLAY "L       LIST    DATA FILE".
008200        DISPLAY "H       HELP".
008300        DISPLAY "Q       QUIT".
008400*
008500 3100-GET-CHOICE.
008600*
008700        DISPLAY "ENTER CODE FOR DESIRED FUNCTION".
008800        ACCEPT CHOICE.
008900*
009000 4000-CREATE-FILE.
009100*
009200        OPEN OUTPUT DATA-FILE.
009300        DISPLAY
009400        "ENTER END IN NAME FIELD WHEN ALL DATA HAS BEEN ENTERED".
009500        PERFORM 4100-GET-DATA
009600            UNTIL ANSWER = "Y" OR NAME-DR = "END".
009700        PERFORM 4200-BUILD-FILE
009800            UNTIL NAME-DR = "END".
009900        CLOSE DATA-FILE.
010000*
010100 4100-GET-DATA.
010200*
010300        DISPLAY "ENTER NAME".
010400        ACCEPT NAME-DR.
010500        IF NAME-DR NOT = "END"
010600            DISPLAY "ENTER SOCIAL SECURITY NUMBER"
010700            ACCEPT SS-NUM-DR
010800            DISPLAY "NAME " NAME-DR " SS NO. " SS-NUM-DR
010900            DISPLAY "IS DATA CORRECT?"
011000            ACCEPT ANSWER.
011100*
011200 4200-BUILD-FILE.
011300*
011400        WRITE DATA-REC.
011500        MOVE "N" TO ANSWER.
011600        PERFORM 4100-GET-DATA
011700            UNTIL ANSWER = "Y" OR NAME-DR = "END".
011800*
```

Program 11.2 (continued)

```
011900 5000-LIST-FILE.
012000*
012100     OPEN INPUT DATA-FILE
012200          OUTPUT PRINT-FILE.
012300     MOVE "NO" TO EOF-FLAG.
012400     READ DATA-FILE
012500          AT END MOVE "YES" TO EOF-FLAG.
012600     PERFORM 5100-WRITE-READ
012700          UNTIL EOF-FLAG = "YES".
012800     CLOSE DATA-FILE
012900          PRINT-FILE.
013000*
013100 5100-WRITE-READ.
013200*
013300     WRITE PRINT-REC FROM DATA-REC AFTER 1.
013400     READ DATA-FILE
013500          AT END MOVE "YES" TO EOF-FLAG.
013600
013700
013800*
013900 6000-HELP.
014000*
014100     EXIT.
014200*IN THIS MODULE DETAILED EXPLANATIONS OF EACH OF THE
014300*CHOICES WOULD BE PRESENTED
014400*
014500 7000-ERROR-DISPLAY.
014600*
014700     DISPLAY "INVALID CHOICE CODE".
```

Figure 11.6 Structure diagram for Program 11.2

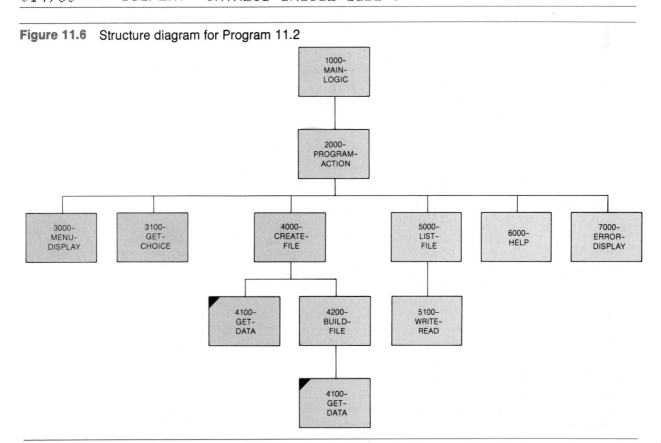

11.6   FORMATTED SCREENS

Interactive program use can be greatly facilitated by the use of formatted screens. A formatted screen is one in which certain information is displayed constantly during the time in which a user is entering data or commands. The ordinary mode of operation for most terminals involves *scrolling*. Text is displayed from top to bottom on the screen. When the screen is full, new text is displayed at the bottom of the screen, the top line is removed, and other lines on the screen are moved towards the top. The trouble with this method of using the screen is that important information may be lost when it is scrolled off. Status information, instructions, previously entered data and so forth may be needed at all times during an operation. The solution to this problem is to change the operation of the terminal to a nonscrolling mode. Required information can then be written at desired locations on the screen and remain there. The screen format may contain provisions for predefining fields into which data are entered. These fields may be high-lighted by reverse video or other means. When the user has finished entering data in one field, the cursor may automatically advance to the next field under program control. In other implementations, the user may control the cursor (by cursor control keys or a "mouse") but be able to enter data only in predefined fields.

Unfortunately, there is no standard method for implementing formatted screens in a COBOL environment. In some systems, the ACCEPT and DISPLAY verbs are enhanced with nonstandard options to control the location and format of data and text being written to the screen or entered at the terminal. In other systems, special control codes are written to the terminal screen using the ordinary READ and WRITE verbs. In still other systems, it is necessary to write a special program to be executed at the terminal to perform the formatting operations; the COBOL program running on the host computer is not involved in the formatting operations at all. Because of this lack of standardization, use the manufacturers reference manuals to determine how to format screens on the system you are using.

A great deal of the software for microcomputers depends heavily on formatted screens. For example, Apple Corporation's Macintosh™ makes extensive use of screens displaying menus and featuring fields called *windows* that have a predefined, specific use.[1] In all likelihood, interactive programs of the future will have to make use of similar features because they contribute significantly to the program's "user friendliness" and to its potential for acceptance and use by people with little experience. or training.

At the present time, most COBOL compilers do not provide good facilities for screen formatting. The facilities that are provided are specific to the particular compiler: they may be excellent, but they are not standard COBOL.

11.7   THE STRING STATEMENT

There are many instances, particularly in an interactive program, when it is necessary to bring data items that have been defined separately together into

---

1. Macintosh is a trademark licensed to Apple Computer, Inc.

one field. An example would be to convert the contents of the two data items defined as

```
03  FIRST-NAME    PIC X(20).
03  LAST-NAME     PIC X(20).
```

into a single string of characters to be contained in a field called NAME with the first and last names separated by a single space. Suppose the content of the data items FIRST- NAME and LAST-NAME are as shown below:

```
 M A R Y
FIRST—NAME PIC X(20)
```

```
 S M I T H
LAST—NAME PIC X(20)
```

The desired transformation would be a field with content:

```
 M A R Y   S M I T H
NAME PIC X(17)
```

The STRING statement offers the COBOL programmer a very convenient means for performing such transformations. A general form of the STRING statement is shown in Figure 11.7.

The items specified before the DELIMITED phrase are sending fields; the item specified by *data-name-3* is the receiving field. Data is transferred from the sending fields to the receiving field as with the alphanumeric MOVE, except that filling the receiving field with blanks is not performed. The DELIMITED BY clause specifies the condition for termination of transfer of characters from the sending field. The content of *data-name-2* or *literal-2* must be a single character. Transfer of data terminates when that character is found in the sending field. Specification of SIZE in the DELIMITED BY clause will cause transfer of all characters of the sending item.

Figure 11.7   General form of the STRING statement

```
STRING  { data-name-1 }  . . .  DELIMITED BY  { data-name-2 }  } . . .
        { literal-1    }                      { literal-2    }  }
                                              { SIZE         }

        INTO data-name-3
        [ON OVERFLOW statement]
```

Example

```
STRING FLD-A FLD-B DELIMITED BY SPACE
       INTO FLD-C.
```

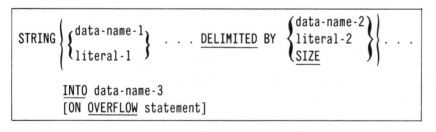

```
 A B C D                    1 2 3   4 5 6 7 8
FLD—A  PIC X(8)            FLD—B  PIC X(10)
   From      From
   FLDA-A    FLD-B    These characters not replaced

 A B C D 1 2 3 ? ? ? ?
FLD—C  PIC X(10).
```

First the characters "ABCD" are moved from FLD-A into FLD-C. When the space is encountered in FLD-A, characters from FLD-B are transferred into FLD-C. Transfer of characters from FLD-B terminates after the first three characters because the fourth character is a space. Note that the remaining characters of FLD-C retain their format content.

Example

```
STRING ITEM-1 DELIMITED BY SIZE
       ITEM-2 DELIMITED BY "-"
       INTO ITEM-3.
```

A B C		1 2 - 3 4
ITEM-1 PIC X(5)		ITEM-2 PIC X(5)

From ITEM-1   From ITEM-2   ↙This character not replaced

A B C 1 2 ?
ITEM-3 PIC X(8)

All of the characters from ITEM-1 are moved to ITEM-3 because ITEM-1 is delimited by SIZE. The first two characters from ITEM-2 are moved into ITEM-3. Transfer of characters terminates when the delimiting character "-" is encountered in ITEM-2.

Example

```
STRING FIRST-NAME DELIMITED BY SPACE
       " "         DELIMITED BY SIZE
       LAST-NAME   DELIMITED BY SPACE
       INTO NAME.
```

M A R Y
FIRST-NAME   PIC X(20)

S M I T H
LAST-NAME   PIC X(20)

From FIRST-NAME   From Literal   From LAST-NAME   These characters not changed.

M A R Y S M I T H ? ? ? ? ? ? ?
NAME   PIC X(17)

Note that it is necessary to ensure that the receiving field contains spaces before execution of the STRING statement because the trailing characters are not modified.

If the delimiting character is not found in a sending field, all of the characters in the field are transferred to the receiving field.

Example

```
STRING FLD-X "-" FLD-Y DELIMITED BY CHAR
       INTO FLD-Z.
```

```
 *
 └┘
CHAR PIC X

 ┌─┬─┬─┬─┬─┐
 │A│B│C│D│ │
 └─┴─┴─┴─┴─┘
FLD-X PIC X(5)

 ┌─┬─┬─┬─┬─┐
 │1│2│*│3│ │
 └─┴─┴─┴─┴─┘
FLD-Y PIC X(5)
```

From   From   From
FLD-X   Literal   FLD-Y   These characters not changed.

```
 ┌─┬─┬─┬─┬─┬─┬─┬─┬─┬─┐
 │A│B│C│D│ │-│1│2│?│?│
 └─┴─┴─┴─┴─┴─┴─┴─┴─┴─┘
FLD-Z PIC X(10)
```

The content of CHAR is used as the delimiting character for FLD-X, FLD-Y and the literal "-". All characters of FLD-X and the literal are transferred to FLD-Z since neither contains the delimiting character.

Transfer of characters terminates either when all of the characters in the sending fields have been transferred or when there is no more room in the receiving field. The ON OVERFLOW clause can be used to take action in the latter case—when the receiving field is full and there are more characters in the sending fields to be transferred.

Example

```
STRING FLD-Q FLD-R DELIMITED BY SIZE
       INTO FLD-S
       ON OVERFLOW PERFORM ERROR-MSG.

 ┌─┬─┬─┐                ┌─┬─┬─┐
 │1│2│3│                │A│B│C│
 └─┴─┴─┘                └─┴─┴─┘
FLD-Q PIC 999          FLD-R PIC XXX
```

From FLD-Q   From FLD-R

```
 ┌─┬─┬─┬─┐
 │1│2│3│A│
 └─┴─┴─┴─┘
FLD-S PIC X(4)
```

In this case, FLD-S is too short to contain all characters from the receiving fields, resulting in an overflow situation. The paragraph ERROR-MSG would be executed. If the ON OVERFLOW clause had been omitted, the content of FLD-S would be as shown and the program would continue with the next statement.

11.8   THE UNSTRING STATEMENT

The UNSTRING statement performs the inverse function of the STRING statement. The STRING statement brings many separate items together into one fields; the UNSTRING statement enables the program to separate the content of one field into many different items. For example, suppose you want to separate the characters in a field such as

```
 ┌─┬─┬─┬─┬─┬─┬─┬─┬─┬─┬─┬─┬─┬─┬─┬─┬─┐
 │M│A│R│Y│ │S│M│I│T│H│ │ │ │ │ │ │ │
 └─┴─┴─┴─┴─┴─┴─┴─┴─┴─┴─┴─┴─┴─┴─┴─┴─┘
NAME    PIC X(17)
```

into two items such as

```
 M A R Y
└──┴──┴──┴──┴──┴──┴──┴──┴──┴──┴──┴──┴──┴──┴──┴──┴──┴──┴──┘
FIRST-NAME    PIC X(20)
```

```
 S M I T H
└──┴──┴──┴──┴──┴──┴──┴──┴──┴──┴──┴──┴──┴──┴──┴──┴──┴──┴──┘
LAST-NAME     PIC X(20)
```

The UNSTRING statement will enable the program to make this transformation. A general form for the UNSTRING statement is shown in Figure 11.8.

Figure 11.8   General form of the UNSTRING statement

```
UNSTRING data-name-1

  ⎡                           ⎧data-name-2⎫⎤
  ⎣DELIMITED BY [ALL]         ⎩literal    ⎭⎦

  INTO data-name-3. . .
  [ON OVERFLOW statement]
```

Data-name-1 is the sending field; *data-name-3* and those following are receiving fields. Characters are transferred from the sending field to the receiving fields from left to right. If the DELIMITED BY clause is omitted, characters are moved into the first receiving field until the field is filled, then characters are moved into the second receiving field, and so forth. Transfer of characters terminates when all of the characters in the sending field have been transferred or when all of the receiving fields have been filled.

Example

```
UNSTRING FLD-A INTO FLD-B FLD-C.
```

```
 A B C D E F G H
└──┴──┴──┴──┴──┴──┴──┴──┘
FLD-A PIC X(8)
```

```
 A B C
└──┴──┴──┘
FLD-B PIC X(3)
```

```
 D E F G
└──┴──┴──┴──┘
FLD-C PIC X(4)
```

The DELIMITED BY clause enables the programmer to specify a character or characters to be used to terminate transfer of characters into a receiving field. When the delimiter is found in the sending field, transfer of characters to the receiving field ceases. If other receiving fields are present, transfer of characters resumes with the leftmost character following the delimiter.

Example

```
UNSTRING FLD-E
      DELIMITED BY "-"
      INTO FLD-F, FLD-G, FLD-H.
```

```
 1 2 3 - 4 5 - 6 7 8 9
FLD-E PIC X(11)

 1 2 3
FLD-F PIC 999

 4 5
FLD-G PIC 99

 6 7 8 9
FLD-H PIC 9999
```

Transfer of data into FLD-F ceases when the first "–" is encountered in FLD-E. In like fashion, transfer into FLD-G is terminated by a second "–".

Example

```
UNSTRING NAME
        DELIMITED BY SPACE
        INTO FIRST-NAME LAST-NAME.

 M A R Y   S M I T H
NAME PIC X(17)

 M A R Y
FIRST-NAME PIC X(20)

 S M I T H
LAST-NAME PIC X(20)
```

Note that receiving fields are padded on the right with blanks if the number of characters received is less than the field width.

If two or more delimiters appear in adjacent positions of the sending field, the affected receiving field will be either blank filled (if an alphanumeric item) or zero filled (if a numeric item).

Example

```
UNSTRING INPUT-STRING
        DELIMITED BY ","
        INTO NUM-1, NUM-2, NUM-3.

 1 2 3 , , 4 5
INPUT-STRING PIC X(10)

 1 2 3
NUM-1 PIC 999

 0 0 0
NUM-2 PIC 999

 4 5
NUM-3 PIC 999
```

The first occurrence of the comma terminates transfer of characters into NUM-1. The second occurrence of a comma terminates transfer of data into NUM-2; as no data was transferred and the field is numeric, it is zeroed out. Note that NUM-3 receives data as an alphanumeric data item rather than a numeric item; the program should ensure that each item has valid data in it before any further processing takes place.

If the ALL option is used in the DELIMITED BY clause, all adjacent delimiters are treated as one delimiter.

Example

```
UNSTRING NAME
    DELIMITED BY ALL SPACES
    INTO FIRST-NAME LAST-NAME.
```

```
J O H N     D O E
```
NAME PIC X(17)

```
J O H N
```
FIRST-NAME PIC X(20)

```
D O E
```
LAST-NAME PIC X(20).

The three adjacent spaces in positions 5 through 7 of NAME are treated as one delimiter. Transfer of data into LAST-NAME begins at position 8.

The ON OVERFLOW clause can be used to take action when there are additional characters in the sending field, when all receiving fields have been filled, or when all characters in the sending field have been used and additional receiving fields have not been filled.

Example

```
UNSTRING FLD-A INTO FLD-B FLD-C
    ON OVERFLOW PERFORM ERROR-MSG.
```

```
A B C               A               B
```
FLD-A PIC X(3)   FLD-B PIC X   FLD-C PIC X

Since FLD-A has an additional character which is not examined, an overflow condition results in the execution of ERROR-MSG.

Example

```
UNSTRING FLD-D
    DELIMITED BY SPACE
    INTO FLD-E FLD-F
    ON OVERFLOW MOVE "YES" TO ERROR-FLAG.
```

```
A B C D
```
FLD-D PIC X(4)

```
A B C
```
FLD-E PIC X(3)

```
 ? ? ? ? ?
└─┴─┴─┴─┴─┘
FLD-F PIC X(5)
```

Since the sending field does not contain an instance of the delimiter, transfer of data into FLD-F cannot begin, hence an overflow condition occurs.

11.9   THE INSPECT STATEMENT

The INSPECT statement allows a program to process individual characters in a data item by replacing some certain characters with other characters. A general form for the INSPECT statement is shown in Figure 11.9.

The INSPECT statement will cause some (or all) of the characters in *data-name-1* to be replaced. *Literal-1* or *data-name-2* specifies the character(s) to be replaced. *Literal-2* or *data-name-3* specifies the replacement character(s).

The LEADING option will cause leftmost occurrences of specified characters to be replaced.

Figure 11.9   General form for the INSPECT statement

```
                                    ⎧ALL    ⎫ ⎧literal-1  ⎫    ⎧literal-2  ⎫
INSPECT data-name-1 REPLACING       ⎨LEADING⎬ ⎨           ⎬ BY ⎨           ⎬
                                    ⎩FIRST  ⎭ ⎩data-name-2⎭    ⎩data-name-3⎭
```

Example

Suppose you wish to insert asterisks in place of leading zeros in a field. The following code could be used:

```
INSPECT DATA-FIELD REPLACING LEADING "0" BY "*".
```

Before execution

```
 0 0 0 4 3 0 5 7
└─┴─┴─┴─┴─┴─┴─┴─┘
DATA-FIELD
```

After execution

```
 * * * 4 3 0 5 7
└─┴─┴─┴─┴─┴─┴─┴─┘
DATA-FIELD
```

The next zero is not replaced because it is not a leading zero. If no characters satisfying the condition LEADING "0" had been found, content of the field would not be changed.

The ALL option will cause all occurrences of specified characters to be replaced.

Example

```
INSPECT FLD-OUT REPLACING ALL " " BY ",".
```

Before execution

```
 1 2 3   4 5   6 7 8 9
└─┴─┴─┴─┴─┴─┴─┴─┴─┴─┴─┘
FLD-OUT
```

After execution

$\underline{|1_{\,}2_{\,}3_{\,}|_{\,}4_{\,}5_{\,}|_{\,}6_{\,}7_{\,}8_{\,}9_{\,}|}$
FLD-OUT

The FIRST option will replace the first (leftmost) occurrence of a specified character by another character. All other occurrences of the character will be unaffected.

Example

INSPECT ITEM-A REPLACING FIRST "*" BY "$".

Before execution

$\underline{|_{\,}*_{\,}*_{\,}*_{\,}*_{\,}1_{\,}2_{\,}._{\,}3_{\,}0_{\,}|}$
ITEM-A

After execution

$\underline{|_{\,}\$_{\,}*_{\,}*_{\,}*_{\,}1_{\,}2_{\,}._{\,}3_{\,}0_{\,}|}$
ITEM-A

The INSPECT statement actually has many more options than shown in Figure 11.9. The following sections, which are reprinted from the COBOL ANSI-74 standard, contain a complete description of the INSPECT statement.

Function

The INSPECT statement provides the ability to tally (Format 1), replace (Format 2), or tally and replace (Format 3) occurrences of single characters or groups of characters in a data item.

General Format

Format 1

INSPECT identifier-1 TALLYING

$$\left\{ \text{, identifier-2 } \underline{\text{FOR}} \left\{ \left\{ \begin{matrix} \underline{\text{ALL}} \\ \underline{\text{LEADING}} \\ \underline{\text{CHARACTERS}} \end{matrix} \right\} \left\{ \begin{matrix} \text{identifier-3} \\ \text{literal-1} \end{matrix} \right\} \right\} \left[\left\{ \begin{matrix} \underline{\text{BEFORE}} \\ \underline{\text{AFTER}} \end{matrix} \right\} \text{INITIAL} \left\{ \begin{matrix} \text{identifier-4} \\ \text{literal-2} \end{matrix} \right\} \right] \right\} \cdots \right\} \cdots$$

Format 2

INSPECT identifier-1 REPLACING

$$\left\{ \begin{matrix} \underline{\text{CHARACTERS}} \ \underline{\text{BY}} \left\{ \begin{matrix} \text{identifier-6} \\ \text{literal-4} \end{matrix} \right\} \left[\left\{ \begin{matrix} \underline{\text{BEFORE}} \\ \underline{\text{AFTER}} \end{matrix} \right\} \text{INITIAL} \left\{ \begin{matrix} \text{identifier-7} \\ \text{literal-5} \end{matrix} \right\} \right] \\ \left\{ \left\{ \begin{matrix} \underline{\text{ALL}} \\ \underline{\text{LEADING}} \\ \underline{\text{FIRST}} \end{matrix} \right\} \left\{ \text{, } \left\{ \begin{matrix} \text{identifier-5} \\ \text{literal-3} \end{matrix} \right\} \ \underline{\text{BY}} \left\{ \begin{matrix} \text{identifier-6} \\ \text{literal-4} \end{matrix} \right\} \left[\left\{ \begin{matrix} \underline{\text{BEFORE}} \\ \underline{\text{AFTER}} \end{matrix} \right\} \text{INITIAL} \left\{ \begin{matrix} \text{identifier-4} \\ \text{literal-5} \end{matrix} \right\} \right] \right\} \cdots \right\} \end{matrix} \right\} \cdots$$

Format 3

INSPECT identifier-1 TALLYING

$$\left\{ \text{, identifier-2 } \underline{\text{FOR}} \right\} \left\{ , \begin{Bmatrix} \underline{\text{ALL}} \\ \underline{\text{LEADING}} \\ \underline{\text{CHARACTERS}} \end{Bmatrix} \begin{Bmatrix} \text{identifier-6} \\ \text{literal-1} \end{Bmatrix} \left[\begin{Bmatrix} \underline{\text{BEFORE}} \\ \underline{\text{AFTER}} \end{Bmatrix} \text{INITIAL} \begin{Bmatrix} \text{identifier-4} \\ \text{literal-2} \end{Bmatrix} \right] \right\} \cdots \right\} \cdots$$

REPLACING

$$\left\{ \begin{matrix} \underline{\text{CHARACTERS BY}} \begin{Bmatrix} \text{identifier-6} \\ \text{literal-4} \end{Bmatrix} \left[\begin{Bmatrix} \underline{\text{BEFORE}} \\ \underline{\text{AFTER}} \end{Bmatrix} \text{INITIAL} \begin{Bmatrix} \text{identifier-7} \\ \text{literal-5} \end{Bmatrix} \right] \\ \left\{ , \begin{Bmatrix} \underline{\text{ALL}} \\ \underline{\text{LEADING}} \\ \underline{\text{FIRST}} \end{Bmatrix} \right\} , \begin{Bmatrix} \text{identifier-5} \\ \text{literal-3} \end{Bmatrix} \underline{\text{BY}} \begin{Bmatrix} \text{identifier-6} \\ \text{literal-4} \end{Bmatrix} \left[\begin{Bmatrix} \underline{\text{BEFORE}} \\ \underline{\text{AFTER}} \end{Bmatrix} \text{INITIAL} \begin{Bmatrix} \text{identifier-7} \\ \text{literal-5} \end{Bmatrix} \right] \right\} \cdots \end{matrix} \right\} \cdots$$

Syntax Rules

All Formats

1) Identifier-1 must reference either a group item or any category of elementary item, described (either implicitly or explicitly) as usage is DISPLAY.

2) Identifier-3 . . . identifier-n must reference either an elementary alphabetic, alphanumeric or numeric item described (either implicitly or explicitly) as usage is DISPLAY.

3) Each literal must be non-numeric and may be any figurative constant, except ALL.

4) In Level 1, literal-1, literal-2, literal-3, literal-4, and literal-5 and the data items referenced by identifier-3, identifier-4, identifier-5, identifier-6 and identifier-7 must be one character in length. Except as specifically noted in syntax and general rules, this restriction on length does not apply to Level 2.

Formats 1 and 3 Only

5) Identifier-2 must reference an elementary numeric data item.

6) If either literal-1 or literal-2 is a figurative constant, the figurative constant refers to an implicit one-character data item.

Formats 2 and 3 Only

7) The size of the data referenced by literal-4 or identifier-6 must be equal to the size of the data referenced by literal-3 or identifier-5. When a figurative constant is used as literal-4, the size of the figurative constant is equal to the size of literal-3 or the size of the data item referenced by identifier-5.

8) When the CHARACTERS phrase is used, literal-4, literal-5, or the size of the data item referenced by identifier-6, identifier-7 must be one character in length.

9) When a figurative constant is used as literal-3, the data referenced by literal-4 or identifier-6 must be one character in length.

General Rules

1) Inspection (which includes the comparison cycle, the establishment of boundaries for the BEFORE or AFTER phrase, and the mechanism for tallying and/or replacing) begins at the leftmost character position of the data item referenced by identifier-1, regardless of its class, and proceeds from left to right to the rightmost character position as described in general rules 4 through 6.

2) For use in the INSPECT statement, the contents of the data item referenced by identifier-1, identifier-3, identifier-4, identifier-5, identifier-6 or identifier-7 will be treated as follows:

   a) If any of identifier-1, identifier-3, identifier-4, identifier-5, identifier-6 or identifier-7 are described as alphanumeric, the INSPECT statement treats the contents of each identifier as a character-string.

   b) If any of identifier-1, identifier-3, identifier-4, identifier-5, identifier-6 or identifier-7 are described as alphanumeric edited, numeric edited or unsigned numeric, the data item is inspected as though it had been redefined as alphanumeric (see general rule 2a) and the INSPECT statement had been written to reference the redefined data item.

   c) If any of identifier-1, identifier-3, identifier-4, identifier-5, identifier-6 or identifier-7 are described as signed numeric, the data item is inspected as though it had been moved to an unsigned numeric data item of the same length and then the rules in general rule 2b had been applied.

3) In general, rules 4 through 11, all references to literal-1, literal-2, literal-3, literal-4, and literal-5 apply equally to the contents of the data item referenced by identifier-3, identifier-4, identifier-5, identifier-6, and identifier-7, respectively.

4) During inspection of the contents of the data item referenced by identifier-1, each properly matched occurrence of literal-1 is tallied (Formats 1 and 3) and/or each properly matched occurrence of literal-3 is replaced by literal-4 (Formats 2 and 3).

5) The comparison operation to determine the occurrences of literal-1 to be tallied and/or occurrences of literal-3 to be replaced, occurs as follows:

   a) The operands of the TALLYING and REPLACING phrases are considered in the order they are specified in the INSPECT statement from left to right. The first literal-1, literal-3 is compared to an equal number of contiguous characters, starting with the leftmost character position in the data item referenced by identifier-1. Literal-1, literal-3 and that portion of the contents of the data item referenced by identifier-1 match, if and only if, they are equal, character for character.

   b) If no match occurs in the comparison of the first literal-1, literal-3, the comparison is repeated with each successive literal-1, literal-3, if any, until a match is found or there is no next successive literal-1, literal-3. When there is no next successive literal-1, literal-3, the character position in the data item referenced by identifier-1 immediately to the right of the leftmost character position considered in the last comparison cycle is considered as the leftmost character position, and the comparison cycle begins again with the first literal-1, literal-3.

c) Whenever a match occurs, tallying and/or replacing takes place as described in general rules 8 through 10 below. The character position in the data item referenced by identifier-1 immediately to the right of the rightmost character position that participated in the match is now considered to be the leftmost character position of the data item referenced by identifier-1, and the comparison cycle starts again with the first literal-1, literal-3.

d) The comparison operation continues until the rightmost character position in the data item referenced by identifier-1, has participated in a match or has been considered as the leftmost character position. When this occurs, inspection is terminated.

e) If the CHARACTERS phrase is specified, an implied one-character operand participates in the cycle described in general rules 5a through 5d above, except that no comparison to the contents of the data item referenced by identifier-1 participating in the current comparison cycle.

6) The comparison operation defined in general rule 5 is affected by the BEFORE and AFTER phrases as follows:

a) If the BEFORE or AFTER phrase is not specified, literal-1, literal-3 or the implied operand of the CHARACTERS phrase participates in the comparison operation as described in general rule 5.

b) If the BEFORE phrase is specified, the associated literal-1, literal-3 or the implied operand of the CHARACTERS phrase participates only in those comparison cycles that involve that portion of the contents of the data item referenced by identifier-1 from its leftmost character position up to, but not including, the first occurrence of literal-2, literal-5 within the contents of the data item referenced by identifier-1. The position of this first occurrence is determined before the first cycle of the comparison operation described in general rule 5 is begun. If, on any comparison cycle, literal-1, literal-3 or the implied operand of the CHARACTERS phrase is not eligible to participate, it is considered not to match the contents of the data item referenced by identifier-1. If there is no occurrence of literal-2, literal-5 within the contents of the data item referenced by identifier-1, its associated literal-1, literal-3, or the implied operand of the CHARACTERS phrase participates in the comparison operation as though the BEFORE phrase had not been specified.

c) If the AFTER phrase is specified, the associated literal-1, literal-3 or the implied operand of the CHARACTERS phrase may participate only in those comparison cycles which involve that portion of the contents of the data item referenced by identifier-1 from the character position immediately to the right of the rightmost character position of the first occurrence of literal-2, literal-5 within the contents of the data item referenced by identifier-1, and the rightmost character position of the data item referenced by identifier-1. The position of the first occurrence is determined before the first cycle of the comparison operation described in general rule 5 is begun. If, on any comparison cycle, literal-1, literal-3 or the implied operand of the CHARACTERS phrase is not eligible to participate, it is considered not to match the contents of the data item referenced by identifier-1. If there is no occurrence of literal-2, literal-5 within the contents of the data item referenced by indentifier-1, its associated literal-1, literal-3 or the implied operand of the CHARACTERS phrase never is eligible to participate in the comparison operation.

Format 1

7) The content of the data item referenced by identifier-2 is not initialized by the execution of the INSPECT statement.
8) The rules for tallying are as follows:
   a) If the ALL phrase is specified, the contents of the data item referenced by identifier-2 is incremented by one (1) for each occurrence of literal-1 matched within the contents of the data item referenced by identifier-1.
   b) If the LEADING phrase is specified, the contents of the data item referenced by identifier-2 is incremented by one (1) for each contiguous occurrence of literal-1 matched within the contents of the data item referenced by identifier-1, provided that the leftmost such occurrence is at the point where comparison began in the first comparison cycle in which literal-1 was eligible to participate.
   c) If the CHARACTERS phrase is specified, the contents of the data item referenced by identifier-2 is incremented by one (1) for each character matched—in the sense of general rule 5e—within the contents of the data item referenced by identifier-1.

Format 2

9) The required words ALL, LEADING and FIRST are adjectives that apply to each succeeding BY phrase until the next adjective appears.
10) The rules for replacement are as follows:
   a) When the CHARACTERS phrase is specified, each character matched (in the sense of general rule 5e) in the contents of the data item referenced by identifier-1 is replaced by literal-4.
   b) When the adjective ALL is specified, each occurrence of literal-3 matched in the contents of the data item referenced by identifier-1 is replaced by literal-4.
   c) When the adjective LEADING is specified, each contiguous occurrence of literal-3 matched in the contents of the data item reference by identifier-1 is replaced by literal-4, provided that the leftmost occurrence is at the point where comparison began in the first comparison cycle in which literal-3 was eligible to participate.
   d) When the adjective FIRST is specified, the leftmost occurrence of literal-3 matched within the contents of the data item referenced by identifier-1 is replaced by identifier-4.

Format 3

11) A Format 3 INSPECT statement is interpreted and executed as though two successive INSPECT statements specifying the same identifier-1 had been written, with one statement being a Format 1 statement with TALLYING phrases identical to those specified in the Format 3 statement and the other statement being a Format 2 statement with

REPLACING phrases identical to those specified in the Format 3 statement. The general rules given for matching and counting apply to the Format 1 statement; the general rules given for matching and replacing apply to the Format 2 statement. Below are six examples of the INSPECT statement.

Example

INSPECT word TALLYING count FOR LEADING "L" BEFORE INITIAL "A", count-1 FOR LEADING "A" BEFORE INITIAL "L".

Where word = LARGE, count = 1, count-1 = 0.
Where word = ANALYST, count = 0, count-1 = 1.

INSPECT word TALLYING count FOR ALL "L", REPLACING LEADING "A" BY "E" AFTER INITIAL "L".

Where word= CALLAR, count=2, word=CALLAR.
Where word = SALAMI, count = 1, word = SALEMI.
Where word = LATTER, count = 1, word = LETTER.

INSPECT word REPLACING ALL "A" BY "G" BEFORE INITIAL "X".

Where word = ARXAX, word =GRXAX.
Where word = HANDAX, word = HGNDGX.

INSPECT word TALLYING count FOR CHARACTERS AFTER INITIAL "J" REPLACING ALL "A" BY "B".

Where word = ADJECTIVE, count = 6, word = BDJECTIVE.
Where word = JACK, count = 3, word = JBCK.
Where word = JUJMAB, count = 5, word = JUJMBB.

INSPECT word REPLACING ALL "X" BY "Y", "B" BY "Z", "W" BY "Q" AFTER INITIAL "R".

Where word = RXXBOWY, word = RYYZOQY.
Where word = YZACDWBR, word = YZACDWZR.
Where word = RAWRRXEB, word = RAQRYEZ.

INSPECT word REPLACING CHARACTERS BY "B" BEFORE INITIAL "A".

word before: 1 2 X Z A B C D
word after: B B B B A B C D

11.10 AN EXAMPLE—DATA VALIDATION AND FILE CREATION

One of the primary responsibilities of a system designer is to take steps to help ensure the integrity of the data in the system. There is nothing more frustrating and irritating than a system into which invalid data is difficult or impossible to correct. A recent survey of computer users showed that invalid data is the most common source of user dissatisfaction with data processing systems. To help ensure that invalid data does not enter a system, the data entry program must contain logic to detect invalid data and to allow the data entry person to correct the data before it is stored.

Validity checking may be performed on the characters that make up a field, on the value of the field itself, and on the relationships among the fields within the record. Typically, certain fields can be identified as containing only numeric or alphabetic characters. If the data entered by the user contains characters of an inappropriate type, the data can be rejected as invalid. If the field contains valid characters, it may be possible to perform a range check to determine if the value of the item is outside known boundaries. If the item is too large, too small or otherwise contains an inappropriate value, the data can be rejected. For alphanumeric fields, it is usually important that the data be left-justified within the field, i.e., that the first character in the field begins in the leftmost character of the field. The program can check the leftmost characters of such fields and reject those with leading spaces.

A collection of otherwise valid data fields may not constitute a valid data record. The data entry person may have inadvertently entered data from parts of two or more separate records into one or have made erroneous key strokes in entering the data. Errors of this type are common if the persons's attention is distracted during the data entry process. There may be ways in which a program can check on the consistency among the values contained in fields within a record and reject a record determined to be invalid. A second technique is to display data entered by the user and ask if the record is valid. After reviewing the data, the user may spot errors made in the data entry process. The program should then provide a means for the user to correct individual fields of the entire record.

11.11   PROGRAM EXAMPLE

Problem Statement

Write a program to add new customer orders for the Amalgamated Custom Design system described in Section 10.4. As shown in Figure 10.5, the program is interactive. Data is entered at a terminal and stored in the Order Transaction File.

Two types of records are created when an order is processed: the master record contains data regarding the customer, and detail records contain data about each component of the order. The program must perform validity checking at the character, field, and record levels.

Problem Analysis

Character and field checking are performed as each field is entered; the record check is performed after all fields have been entered but before the record is added to the file. Unless all validity checks are passed at all levels, the record is not added to the file. In this program, the procedure used to carry out validity checking at the record level is to display the content of the record to the user and ask if the data is correct. If the data is not correct, the user is given the option of correcting individual fields in the case of the master record or re-entering the entire record in the case of the detail record. The program logic that requires the user to re-enter the entire record is more straightforward than one permitting the user to change individual fields; the simpler approach is acceptable if there are relatively few fields within the record.

The procedure used to carry out validity checking at the character and field levels is summarized in the following pseudocode:

```
            Move "NO" to valid field
            Do until valid field = "YES"
                Display prompt
                Accept data
                If data is valid
                    Move "YES" to valid field
                Else
                    Display error message
                End If
            End Do
```

Problem Solution

The required origin is shown in Program 11.3 with structure diagram shown
in Figure 11.11. The types of validity checks carried out in this program are
summarized in Figure 11.10. Note the use of the INSPECT statement shaded in
Program 11.3. It is used to determine the number of spaces in some fields and
the number of leading spaces in other fields. The INSPECT statement is a
powerful tool for performing through data validation.

Program 11.3 Order entry program

```
000100 IDENTIFICATION DIVISION.
000200*
000300 PROGRAM-ID. ORDER-ENTRY.
000400 AUTHOR. HORN.
000500*REMARKS.   INTERACTIVE ORDER ENTRY WITH DATA VALIDATION
000600*            FOR AMALGAMATED CUSTOM DESIGN SYSTEM.
000700*
000800 ENVIRONMENT DIVISION.
000900*
001000 CONFIGURATION SECTION.
001100*
001200 SOURCE-COMPUTER.
001300 OBJECT-COMPUTER.
001400*
001500 INPUT-OUTPUT SECTION.
001600*
001700 FILE-CONTROL.
001800*
001900     SELECT ORDER-TRANSACTION-FILE ASSIGN TO OUTPUT "ORDTRANS".
002000*
002100 DATA DIVISION.
002200*
002300 FILE SECTION.
002400*
002500 FD  ORDER-TRANSACTION-FILE
002600     LABEL RECORDS ARE STANDARD
002700     DATA RECORD IS TRANS-RECORD.
002800*
002900 01  TRANS-RECORD.
003000     05 FILLER   PIC X(80).
003100*
```

```
003200 WORKING-STORAGE SECTION.                              Program 11.3 (continued)
003300*
003400 01   FLAGS.
003500      03   MORE-ORDERS                  PIC XXX VALUE "YES".
003600      03   VALID-FIELD                  PIC XXX VALUE "NO ".
003700      03   VALID-RECORD                 PIC XXX VALUE "NO ".
003800*
003900 01   COUNTERS.
004000      03   NUM-DETAIL                   PIC 99   VALUE 0.
004100      03   NUM-SPACES                   PIC 99   VALUE 0.
004200      03   NUM-RAW                      PIC 99   VALUE 0.
004300*
004400 01   ORDER-MASTER-RECORD.
004500      03   DATA-AREA-OMR.
004600           05   ORDER-NUMBER-OMR        PIC X(5).
004700           05   CUS-NUMBER-OMR          PIC 9(9).
004800           05   CUS-NAME-OMR            PIC X(20).
004900           05   CUS-ADDR-OMR.
005000                10   STREET-OMR         PIC X(10).
005100                10   CITY-OMR           PIC X(10).
005200                10   STATE-OMR          PIC XX.
005300                10   ZIP-OMR            PIC 9(5).
005400           05   NUM-COMPONENTS-OMR      PIC 999.
005500           05   RECEIPT-DATE-OMR.
005600                10   MON-OMR            PIC 99.
005700                10   DAY-OMR            PIC 99.
005800                10   YEAR-OMR           PIC 99.
005900      03   CONSTANT-AREA-OMR.
006000           05   FILLER                  PIC X(9) VALUE SPACES.
006100           05   FILLER                  PIC X VALUE "M".
006200*
006300 01   ORDER-DETAIL-RECORD.
006400      03   DATA-AREA-ODR.
006500           05   ORDER-NUMBER-ODR        PIC X(5).
006600           05   CATALOG-NUMBER-ODR      PIC X(5).
006700           05   NUM-COMPONENTS-ODR      PIC 999.
006800           05   QUANTITY-ODR            PIC 999.
006900           05   RAW-MATERIALS-ODR.
007000                10   RAW-MAT-ENTRY PIC X(5) OCCURS 5 TIMES.
007100           05   BATCH-STATUS-ODR        PIC X.
007200           05   CUST-INST-ODR           PIC X(20).
007300      03   CONSTANT-AREA-ODR.
007400           05   FILLER                  PIC X(17) VALUE SPACES.
007500           05   FILLER                  PIC X VALUE "D".
007600*
007700 01   CONTROL-FIELDS.
007800      02 FIELD-NUMBER                   PIC 99 VALUE ZERO.
007900      02 NUM-RAW-MAT                    PIC 9 VALUE ZERO.
008000*
008100 01   INPUT-FIELDS.
008200      02 ONE-RAW-MAT                    PIC X(5) VALUE SPACES.
008300*
```

Program 11.3 (continued)

```
008400 PROCEDURE DIVISION.
008500*
008600 1000-MAIN-LOGIC.
008700*
008800     PERFORM 2000-INITIALIZATION.
008900     PERFORM 3000-PROCESS-ORDERS
009000         UNTIL MORE-ORDERS = "NO ".
009100     PERFORM 9000-TERMINATION.
009200     STOP RUN.
009300*
009400 2000-INITIALIZATION.
009500*
009600     OPEN OUTPUT ORDER-TRANSACTION-FILE.
009700     DISPLAY "AMALGAMATED CUSTOM DESIGN, INC.".
009800     DISPLAY "ORDER ENTRY".
009900*
010000 3000-PROCESS-ORDERS.
010100*
010200     PERFORM 4000-CREATE-MASTER.
010300     PERFORM 4200-CREATE-DETAIL
010400         VARYING NUM-DETAIL FROM 1 BY 1
010500             UNTIL NUM-DETAIL > NUM-COMPONENTS-OMR.
010600     PERFORM 4300-MORE-ORDERS.
010700*
010800 4000-CREATE-MASTER.
010900*
011000     MOVE "NO " TO VALID-RECORD.
011100     PERFORM 4100-GET-MASTER
011200         UNTIL VALID-RECORD = "YES".
011300     WRITE TRANS-RECORD FROM ORDER-MASTER-RECORD.
011400*
011500 4100-GET-MASTER.
011600*
011700     MOVE "NO " TO VALID-FIELD.
011800     PERFORM 4110-GET-ORDER-NUMBER
011900         UNTIL VALID-FIELD = "YES".
012000     MOVE "NO " TO VALID-FIELD.
012100     PERFORM 4120-GET-CUS-NUM
012200         UNTIL VALID-FIELD = "YES".
012300     MOVE "NO " TO VALID-FIELD.
012400     PERFORM 4130-GET-CUS-NAME
012500         UNTIL VALID-FIELD = "YES".
012600     MOVE "NO " TO VALID-FIELD.
012700     PERFORM 4140-GET-ADDR
012800         UNTIL VALID-FIELD = "YES".
012900     MOVE "NO " TO VALID-FIELD.
013000     PERFORM 4150-GET-NUM-COMP
013100         UNTIL VALID-FIELD = "YES".
013200     MOVE "NO " TO VALID-FIELD.
013300     PERFORM 4160-GET-DATE
013400         UNTIL VALID-FIELD = "YES".
013500     PERFORM 4170-VALID-RECORD-CHECK
013600         UNTIL VALID-FIELD = "YES".
013700*
```

Program 11.3 *(continued)*

```
013800 4110-GET-ORDER-NUMBER.
013900*
014000     DISPLAY "ENTER ORDER NUMBER".
014100     ACCEPT ORDER-NUMBER-OMR.
014200     MOVE 0 TO NUM-SPACES.
014300     INSPECT ORDER-NUMBER-OMR
014400         TALLYING NUM-SPACES FOR ALL SPACES.
014500     IF NUM-SPACES = 0
014600         MOVE "YES" TO VALID-FIELD
014700     ELSE
014800         DISPLAY "INVALID ORDER NUMBER".
014900*
015000 4120-GET-CUS-NUM.
015100*
015200     DISPLAY "ENTER CUSTOMER NUMBER".
015300     ACCEPT CUS-NUMBER-OMR.
015400     IF CUS-NUMBER-OMR NUMERIC
015500         MOVE "YES" TO VALID-FIELD
015600     ELSE
015700         DISPLAY "INVALID CUSTOMER NUMBER".
015800*
015900 4130-GET-CUS-NAME.
016000*
016100     DISPLAY "ENTER CUSTOMER NAME".
016200     ACCEPT CUS-NAME-OMR.
016300     MOVE 0 TO NUM-SPACES.
016400     INSPECT CUS-NAME-OMR
016500         TALLYING NUM-SPACES FOR LEADING SPACES.
016600     IF NUM-SPACES NOT = 0
016700         DISPLAY "INVALID CUSTOMER NAME"
016800     ELSE
016900         MOVE "YES" TO VALID-FIELD.
017000*
017100 4140-GET-ADDR.
017200*
017300     MOVE "NO " TO VALID-FIELD.
017400     PERFORM 4141-GET-STREET
017500         UNTIL VALID-FIELD = "YES".
017600     MOVE "NO " TO VALID-FIELD.
017700     PERFORM 4142-GET-CITY
017800         UNTIL VALID-FIELD = "YES".
017900     MOVE "NO " TO VALID-FIELD.
018000     PERFORM 4143-GET-STATE
018100         UNTIL VALID-FIELD = "YES".
018200     MOVE "NO " TO VALID-FIELD.
018300     PERFORM 4144-GET-ZIP
018400         UNTIL VALID-FIELD = "YES".
018500*
018600 4141-GET-STREET.
018700*
018800     DISPLAY "ENTER CUSTOMER STREET ADDRESS".
018900     ACCEPT STREET-OMR.
019000     MOVE 0 TO NUM-SPACES.
```

```
019100        INSPECT STREET-OMR
019200            TALLYING NUM-SPACES FOR LEADING SPACES.
019300     IF  NUM-SPACES = 0
019400        MOVE "YES" TO VALID-FIELD
019500     ELSE
019600        DISPLAY "INVALID ADDRESS".
019700*
019800 4142-GET-CITY.
019900*
020000     DISPLAY "ENTER CITY".
020100     ACCEPT CITY-OMR.
020200     MOVE 0 TO NUM-SPACES.
020300        INSPECT CITY-OMR
020400            TALLYING NUM-SPACES FOR LEADING SPACES.
020500     IF NUM-SPACES = 0 AND CITY-OMR ALPHABETIC
020600        MOVE "YES" TO VALID-FIELD
020700     ELSE
020800        DISPLAY "INVALID CITY NAME".
020900*
021000 4143-GET-STATE.
021100*
021200     DISPLAY "ENTER TWO CHARACTER STATE ABBREVIATION".
021300     ACCEPT STATE-OMR.
021400     MOVE 0 TO NUM-SPACES.
021500        INSPECT STATE-OMR
021600            TALLYING NUM-SPACES FOR ALL SPACES.
021700     IF STATE-OMR ALPHABETIC AND NUM-SPACES = 0
021800        MOVE "YES" TO VALID-FIELD
021900     ELSE
022000        DISPLAY "INVALID STATE".
022100*
022200 4144-GET-ZIP.
022300*
022400     DISPLAY "ENTER ZIP CODE".
022500     ACCEPT ZIP-OMR.
022600     IF ZIP-OMR NUMERIC
022700        MOVE "YES" TO VALID-FIELD
022800     ELSE
022900        DISPLAY "INVALID ZIP CODE".
023000*
023100 4150-GET-NUM-COMP.
023200*
023300     DISPLAY "ENTER NUMBER OF ORDER COMPONENTS".
023400     ACCEPT NUM-COMPONENTS-OMR.
023500     IF NUM-COMPONENTS-OMR NOT NUMERIC
023600        DISPLAY "INVALID VALUE"
023700     ELSE
023800        IF NUM-COMPONENTS-OMR = 0
023900           DISPLAY "VALUE MUST BE GREATER THAN ZERO"
024000        ELSE
024100           MOVE "YES" TO VALID-FIELD.
024200*
```

Program 11.3 (continued)

```
024300 4160-GET-DATE.
024400*
024500     DISPLAY "ENTER DATE ORDER RECIEVED IN FORM mmddyy".
024600     ACCEPT RECEIPT-DATE-OMR.
024700     IF RECEIPT-DATE-OMR NOT NUMERIC
024800         DISPLAY "INVALID DATE"
024900     ELSE
025000         IF MON-OMR < 1 OR MON-OMR > 12
025100             DISPLAY "INVALID MONTH"
025200         ELSE
025300             IF DAY-OMR < 1 OR DAY-OMR > 31
025400                 DISPLAY "INVALID DAY"
025500             ELSE
025600                 MOVE "YES" TO VALID-FIELD.
025700*
025800 4170-VALID-RECORD-CHECK.
025900*
026000     DISPLAY "RECAPITULATION OF ORDER INFORMATION".
026100     DISPLAY "FIELD".
026200     DISPLAY "NUMBER".
026300     DISPLAY "_____".
026400     DISPLAY "   1     ORDER NUMBER ", ORDER-NUMBER-OMR.
026500     DISPLAY "   2     CUSTOMER NUMBER ", CUS-NUMBER-OMR.
026600     DISPLAY "   3     CUSTOMER NAME ", CUS-NAME-OMR.
026700     DISPLAY "   4     ADDRESS ", CUS-ADDR-OMR.
026800     DISPLAY "   5     NUMBER COMPONENTS ", NUM-COMPONENTS-OMR.
026900     DISPLAY "   6     RECEIPT DATE ", RECEIPT-DATE-OMR.
027000     DISPLAY "_____".
027100     DISPLAY "DOES ALL DATA APPEAR TO BE CORRECT?".
027200     ACCEPT VALID-RECORD.
027300     IF VALID-RECORD = "YES"
027400         DISPLAY "ORDER MASTER DATA ADDED TO FILE"
027500     ELSE
027600         PERFORM 4171-CORRECT-DATA.
027700*
027800 4171-CORRECT-DATA.
027900*
028000     DISPLAY "ENTER NUMBER OF FIELD YOU WISH TO CORRECT".
028100     ACCEPT FIELD-NUMBER.        .
028200     MOVE "NO " TO VALID-FIELD.
028300     IF FIELD-NUMBER = 1
028400         PERFORM 4110-GET-ORDER-NUMBER
028500             UNTIL VALID-FIELD = "YES".
028600     IF FIELD-NUMBER = 2
028700         PERFORM 4120-GET-CUS-NUM
028800             UNTIL VALID-FIELD = "YES".
028900     IF FIELD-NUMBER = 3
029000         PERFORM 4130-GET-CUS-NAME
029100             UNTIL VALID-FIELD = "YES".
029200     IF FIELD-NUMBER = 4
029300         PERFORM 4140-GET-ADDR
029400             UNTIL VALID-FIELD = "YES".
029500     IF FIELD-NUMBER = 5
029600         PERFORM 4150-GET-NUM-COMP
029700             UNTIL VALID-FIELD = "YES".
```

Program 11.3 (continued)

```
029800        IF FIELD-NUMBER = 6
029900            PERFORM 4160-GET-DATE
030000                UNTIL VALID-FIELD = "YES".
030100        IF FIELD-NUMBER < 1 OR FIELD-NUMBER > 6
030200            DISPLAY "INVALID FIELD NUMBER".
030300*
030400 4200-CREATE-DETAIL.
030500*
030600        MOVE ORDER-NUMBER-OMR TO ORDER-NUMBER-ODR.
030700        MOVE NUM-COMPONENTS-OMR TO NUM-COMPONENTS-ODR.
030800        MOVE "N" TO BATCH-STATUS-ODR.
030900        MOVE "NO " TO VALID-RECORD.
031000        PERFORM 4210-GET-DETAIL
031100            UNTIL VALID-RECORD = "YES".
031200        WRITE TRANS-RECORD FROM ORDER-DETAIL-RECORD.
031300*
031400 4210-GET-DETAIL.
031500*
031600        DISPLAY "ORDER NUMBER : ", ORDER-NUMBER-ODR.
031700        DISPLAY "COMPONENT NUMBER : ", NUM-DETAIL.
031800        MOVE "NO " TO VALID-FIELD.
031900        PERFORM 4211-GET-CAT-NUM
032000            UNTIL VALID-FIELD = "YES".
032100        MOVE "NO " TO VALID-FIELD.
032200        PERFORM 4212-GET-QTY
032300            UNTIL VALID-FIELD = "YES".
032400        MOVE "NO " TO VALID-FIELD.
032500        PERFORM 4213-GET-NUM-RAW-MAT
032600            UNTIL VALID-FIELD = "YES".
032700        MOVE SPACES TO RAW-MATERIALS-ODR.
032800        PERFORM 4214-GET-RAW-MAT
032900            VARYING NUM-RAW FROM 1 BY 1
033000                UNTIL NUM-RAW > NUM-RAW-MAT.
033100        DISPLAY "ENTER CUSTOMIZING INSTRUCTIONS IF ANY".
033200        ACCEPT CUST-INST-ODR.
033300        PERFORM 4216-DISPLAY-DETAIL.
033400        DISPLAY "DOES THE DATA APPEAR TO BE CORRECT?".
033500        ACCEPT VALID-RECORD.
033600        IF VALID-RECORD = "YES"
033700            DISPLAY "COMPONENT DATA ADDED TO THE FILE"
033800        ELSE
033900            DISPLAY "REENTER DATA FOR THIS COMPONENT".
034000*
034100 4211-GET-CAT-NUM.
034200*
034300        DISPLAY "ENTER CATALOG NUMBER".
034400        ACCEPT CATALOG-NUMBER-ODR.
034500        MOVE 0 TO NUM-SPACES.
034600        INSPECT CATALOG-NUMBER-ODR
034700            TALLYING NUM-SPACES FOR ALL SPACES.
034800        IF NUM-SPACES = 0
034900            MOVE "YES" TO VALID-FIELD
035000        ELSE
035100            DISPLAY "INVALID CATALOG NUMBER".
035200*
```

Program 11.3 (continued)

```
035300 4212-GET-QTY.
035400*
035500     DISPLAY "ENTER QUANTITY".
035600     ACCEPT QUANTITY-ODR.
035700     IF QUANTITY-ODR NOT NUMERIC
035800         DISPLAY "INVALID QUANTITY"
035900     ELSE
036000         IF QUANTITY-ODR = 0
036100             DISPLAY "QUANTITY MUST BE GREATER THAN ZERO"
036200         ELSE
036300             MOVE "YES" TO VALID-FIELD.
036400*
036500 4213-GET-NUM-RAW-MAT.
036600*
036700     DISPLAY "ENTER NUMBER OF RAW MATERIALS".
036800     ACCEPT NUM-RAW-MAT.
036900     IF NUM-RAW-MAT NOT NUMERIC
037000         DISPLAY "INVALID VALUE"
037100     ELSE
037200         IF NUM-RAW-MAT = 0
037300             DISPLAY "VALUE MUST BE GREATER THAN ZERO"
037400         ELSE
037500             IF NUM-RAW-MAT > 5
037600                 DISPLAY "VALUE MUST BE LESS THAN SIX"
037700             ELSE
037800                 MOVE "YES" TO VALID-FIELD.
037900*
038000 4214-GET-RAW-MAT.
038100*
038200     MOVE "NO " TO VALID-FIELD.
038300     PERFORM 4215-GET-ONE-RAW-MAT
038400         UNTIL VALID-FIELD = "YES".
038500     MOVE ONE-RAW-MAT TO RAW-MAT-ENTRY (NUM-RAW).
038600*
038700 4215-GET-ONE-RAW-MAT.
038800*
038900     DISPLAY "ENTER RAW MATERIAL NO. ", NUM-RAW.
039000     ACCEPT ONE-RAW-MAT.
039100     MOVE 0 TO NUM-SPACES.
039200     INSPECT ONE-RAW-MAT
039300         TALLYING NUM-SPACES FOR ALL SPACES.
039400     IF NUM-SPACES = 0
039500         MOVE "YES" TO VALID-FIELD
039600     ELSE
039700         DISPLAY "INVALID RAW MATERIAL NUMBER".
039800*
039900 4216-DISPLAY-DETAIL.
040000*
040100     DISPLAY "_____".
040200     DISPLAY "ORDER NUMBER : ", ORDER-NUMBER-ODR.
040300
040400     DISPLAY "COMPONENT NUMBER : ", NUM-DETAIL, " OF ".
040500     DISPLAY "                         ", NUM-COMPONENTS-ODR,
040600                                         " COMPONENTS".
```

```
040700          DISPLAY "_____".
040800          DISPLAY "CATALOG NUMBER : ", CATALOG-NUMBER-ODR.
040900          DISPLAY "QUANTITY : ", QUANTITY-ODR.
041000          DISPLAY "RAW MATERIALS : ", RAW-MATERIALS-ODR.
041100          DISPLAY "CUSTOMIZING : ", CUST-INST-ODR.
041200          DISPLAY "_____".
041300*
041400 4300-MORE-ORDERS.
041500*
041600          DISPLAY "ARE THERE MORE ORDERS?"
041700          ACCEPT MORE-ORDERS.
041800*
041900 9000-TERMINATION.
042000*
```

Figure 11.10	Types of validity checks found in Program 11.3	
Field Name	*Types of Checks*	*Module Name*
ORDER-NUMBER	must contain no spaces	4110-GET-ORDER-NUMBER
CUS-NUMBER	numeric characters	4120-GET-CUS-NUM
CUS-NAME	left-justification	4130-GET-CUS-NAME
STREET	left-justification	4141-GET-STREET
CITY	alphabetic characters left-justification no periods or abbreviations	4142-GET-CITY
STATE	alphabetic characters must contain no spaces	4143-GET-STATE
ZIP	numeric characters	4144-GET-ZIP
NUM-COMPONENTS	numeric characters greater than 0	4150-GET-NUM-COMP
DATE	numeric characters month in range 1 to 12 day in range 1 to 31	4160-GET-DATE
FIELD-NUMBER	must be in range 1 to 6	4171-CORRECT-DATA
CATALOG-NUMBER	must contain no spaces	4211-GET-CAT-NUM
QUANTITY	numeric characters value greater than 0	4212-GET-QTY
NUM-RAW-MAT	numeric characters value in range 1 to 5	4213-GET-NUM-RAW-MAT
ONE-RAW-MAT	must contain no spaces	4215-GET-ONE-RAW-MAT

Figure 11.11   Partial structure diagram of Program 11.3

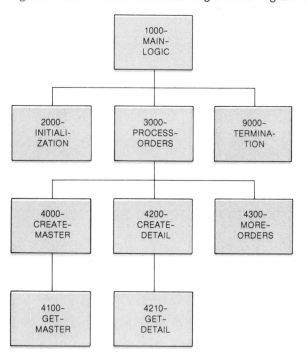

11.12   DEBUG CLINIC

As programs become longer and more complex, the job of providing adequate test data becomes more demanding. In fact, it may be necessary to test programs with more than one set of data records to make sure the program will function properly in all sets of circumstances. A common practice is to test each program at least three times: once with no data (that is, with an input file that contains no data records); again with "good" data (data that results in no error conditions); and finally with "bad" data (data that tests the program's ability to handle error conditions). The development of a set of data records that provides a thorough test of the program's logic should be started in the program development cycle. This task is one that beginning programmers often do not perform adequately because it can be tedious and time-consuming; however, the success or failure of a programming project often hinges as much on thorough testing of the finished product as it does on imaginative program design or meticulous coding. Testing a program is usually divided into two phases:

1) The programmer executes the program using the data designed to verify that the program performs correctly (called *alpha* testing).
2) Representative users test the program with actual data (called *beta* testing).

A program should be thoroughly alpha tested before beta testing begins. Very often, beta testing will reveal errors that went undetected when the programmer tested the program. Placing a program into production before it has been adequately tested surely will be embarrassing for the programmer and perhaps expensive for the organization. The old engineering maxim "there is never time to do it right but always time to do it over" often applies to programming.

11.13 SELF-TEST EXERCISES

1. In general terms, distinguish between a batch system and an interactive system.

2. What are some problems that must be considered in designing an interactive program that are not present in a batch program?

3. How are ACCEPT and DISPLAY used in a batch system? How can they be used in an interactive system?

4. List three distinctive types of user instructions typically supplied by an interactive program.

5. How is a submenu related to a main menu?

6. Why are formatted screens useful in an interactive program?

7. What COBOL verbs are used to communicate with an interactive user in your system?

8. What methods exist in your system to provide for a formatted screen?

9. Given the fields shown below, show the result of each STRING statement.

```
 A B - C
ITEM-A  PIC X(4).

 1 2 * 3 4
ITEM-B  PIC X(5).

 A - 1 2 *
ITEM-C  PIC X(5).


ITEM-R  PIC X(10)   VALUE SPACES.
```
   a. STRING ITM-A ITM-B ITM-C
            DELIMITED BY "-"
            INTO ITM-R.
   b. STRING ITEM-B DELIMITED BY "*"
            ITEM-C ITEM-A DELIMITED BY "-"
            INTO ITEM-R.
   c. STRING ITEM-C DELIMITED BY SIZE
            ITEM-A DELIMITED BY "C"
            ITEM-B DELIMITED BY "*"
            INTO ITEM-R.
   d. STRING ITEM-A DELIMITED BY "*"
            ITEM-B DELIMITED BY "-"
            INTO ITEM-R.

10. Given the fields shown below, show the result of each UNSTRING statement

```
 A B C - D E * 1 2 3 - - X Y * Z W
FLD-Z PIC X(17)


FLD-A PIC X(4)
```

```
 ⌞_⌞_⌞_⌞_⌞
 FLD-B PIC X(5)

 ⌞_⌞_⌞_⌞_⌞_⌞
 FLD-C PIC X(6)
```
a. UNSTRING FLD-Z
            INTO FLD-A FLD-B FLD-C.
b. UNSTRING FLD-Z
            DELIMITED BY "*".
            INTO FLD-A, FLD-B FLD-C.
c. UNSTRING FLD-Z
            DELIMITED BY "-"
            INTO FLD-A FLD-B FLD-C.
d. UNSTRING FLD-Z
            DELIMITED BY ALL "-"
            INTO FLD-A FLD-B FLD-C.
e. UNSTRING FLD-Z
            DELIMITED BY "-"
            INTO FLD-A FLD-B.

11. A field NAME-IN contains a name in the form

    first-name middle-initial last-name

where one or more spaces separates each group of characters. The output
required is a field NAME-OUT in the form:

    last-name, first-name middle-initial

Write PROCEDURE DIVISION code to transform NAME-IN into NAME-OUT. For
example:

```
 J O H N   A   D O E
 ‾‾‾‾‾‾‾‾‾‾‾‾‾‾‾‾‾‾‾‾‾‾‾‾‾‾‾‾‾
 NAME-IN PIC X(20)

 D O E ,   J O H N   A .
 ‾‾‾‾‾‾‾‾‾‾‾‾‾‾‾‾‾‾‾‾‾‾‾‾‾‾‾‾‾
 NAME-OUT PIC X(20)
```

12. Write PROCEDURE DIVISION code to transform a nine-digit social security number
into the form:

    ddd-dd-dddd.

13. Show the result of each INSPECT statement

```
 A B 1 A B A
 ‾‾‾‾‾‾‾‾‾‾‾‾
 ITEM-A PIC X(6)
```
a. INSPECT ITEM-A REPLACING ALL "A" BY "B".
b. INSPECT ITEM-A REPLACING LEADING "A" BY " ".
c. INSPECT ITEM-A REPLACING FIRST "B" BY " ".

11.14 PROGRAMMING EXERCISES

1. Write an interactive menu-driven program to allow a user to create or list the
   Supplier Master File used by Amalgamated Custom Design. Your program
   should validate data placed in the file as appropriate.

2. Modify Program 11.1 to perform validation of the data entered and to give
   the user an alternative means of terminating the data entry process. *Hint:* give
   the user a prompt such as "More Data? (Y/N)."

3. The master file for ABC Automotive Parts Distributed, Inc., inventory system contains the following fields:

Position	Description
1-6	Part number
7-20	Part description
21-29	Vendor number
30-35	Wholesale price (2 decimal places)
36-42	Retail price (2 decimal places)
43-46	Number on hand

   Write an interactive program to allow a user to create this file.

4. Write an interactive program to allow a user to perform any of the following operations, using the master file described in Exercise 3:

   - create the file
   - list the file on screen
   - list the file on printer

5. Write an interactive program that would allow a user to perform any of the following operations, using the master file described in Exercise 3:

   - Display all relevant information for a part number entered by the user
   - Display a list of parts supplied by a vendor, where the user enters any Desired vendor number

   Note that in either case there may be no information to display. Make sure that your program writes appropriate error messages.

6. Write an interactive data entry/data validation program to create a transaction file for an inventory system designed for ABC Automotive Parts Distributors, Inc. Each record in the file contains the following fields:

Position	Description
1-6	Part number
7	Transaction code
8-13	Transaction date (*mmddyy* format)
14-16	Transaction quantity
17-30	Part description
31-39	Vendor number
40-45	Wholesale price (2 decimal places)
46-52	Retail price (2 decimal places)
53-60	Invoice number
61-80	Not used

   The following are valid transaction codes:

Codes	Meaning
S	Sale
R	Receipt
N	New item
D	Delete item
C	Change in one or more fields

   Fields required are dependent on the type of transaction, as shown by the following table:

Field	Transaction Code				
	S	R	N	D	C
Transaction code	✔	✔	✔	✔	✔
Part number	✔	✔	✔	✔	✔
Transaction date	✔	✔	1	1	1
Transaction quantity	✔	✔			
Part description			✔		2
Vendor number			✔		2
Wholesale price			✔		2
Retail price			✔		2
Invoice number	✔	✔			

Note: ✔ required
    1 Current date
    2 Field is optional

Additional considerations:

- Transaction quantity may be negative.
- Unused fields must be blank on output record.

7. Write a program to produce personalized form letters for use in a promotional scheme for Widgets, Inc. The company is sponsoring a contest which requires that the contestants return his or her letter to be eligible to win. The format of the letter can be discerned from the following sample letter addressed to John K. Doe, 123 Maple Street., Anywhere, FL, 32534. (Screened portions of the letter must be changed for each recipient.)

Widgets Inc.
1000 Boulevard
Somewhere, FL 10000

John K. Doe
123 Maple Street
Anywhere, FL 32534

Dear John:

How would you like to add $10,000 to the Doe bank account? You could make this deposit to an Anywhere bank by returning this letter to Widgets, Inc. in the enclosed envelope.

    Imagine the envy of your neighbors on Maple Street when they learn of your good fortune! Nothing to buy. Enter today.

Yours truly,
Widgets, Inc.

Record Layout

Positions	Description
1-10	Last name
11-20	First name
21-21	Middle initial
22-35	Street address
36-45	City
46-47	State
48-52	Zip

Use the following sample data:

Name	*Address*			
Doe John K	123 Maple Street	Anywhere	FL	32555
Smith Mary A	1000 Oak Ave	Somewhere	FL	32544
Brown Susan S	14 Main Rd	Overthere	AL	52055
Jones Jim	1421 Broadway	New York	NY	10000

SEARCH PROCEDURES

12.1 ORIGINATION OF TABLE DATA

Data that is to be stored in table form may originate either from within the program itself or from a data file. When table data is relatively stable, it may be useful to create the table by defining constants within the program. For example, a table of the number of days in each month, a list of the names of the days of the week, and a table showing the association between the two-character abbreviations for a state name and the full state name are examples of tables that normally would be created as constants within a program. In the unlikely event that changes must be made in any of these items, the program must be recompiled.

When table data is subject to change, however, it is preferable to store the data in a file and have the program load the data as an initialization step. In this way, changes to the table data can be made without recompiling the program. Tax tables, tables showing associations between product codes and product names or price, and lists of vendors are examples of table data that is somewhat volatile and should be loaded from a data file rather than built into a program as constants.

Example

Suppose you need to compute the differences in days between two dates. This computation is often needed in banking and other accounting applications. (The existence of leap years complicates matters somewhat, so for the moment we shall assume that leap years do not exist.) One method for making this computation is to compute the *Julian* date for each date and then subtract. The Julian date is defined as the number of days up to and including the specified date from a certain point (the beginning of the year or the beginning of the century). For example, with respect to the beginning of the year, the Julian date for January 1 is 1, for February 1 is 32, for December 31 is 365. With respect to the beginning of the century, the Julian date for January 1, 1900, is 1 and for January 1, 1985 is 31,026, which can be computed by $85 \times 365 + 1$. Thus, to compute the difference between two dates such as February 1, 1984, and January 6, 1985, compute the Julian date with respect to the century for each of these dates and subtract. The Julian date for February 1, 1984, is $84 \times 365 + 31 + 1 = 30,692$; the Julian date for January 6, 1985, is $85 \times 365 + 6 = 31,031$; the difference is $31,031 - 30,692 = 339$ days.

To compute the Julian date with respect to the beginning of a year, add up the number of days that have elapsed in preceding months and then add the day of the present month. For example, to compute the Julian date of March 6, it is necessary to add the number of days in January (31) and February (28), and then add 6, which represents the number of days up to and including March 6. A table like that shown in Figure 12.1, which contains the total number of days that have accumulated from the beginning of the year to the beginning of each month, will be useful in carrying out this computation.

For example, in computing the Julian date for March 6, the program will access the third element of the table and add 6:

```
DAYS-PREVIOUS-ENTRY (3) + 6 = 59 + 6 = 65.
```

Of course, this computation must be adjusted if the year in question is a leap year. The adjustment is reasonably straightforward and we shall leave leaping year consideration as an exercise. Note that in this example the values are constant; barring a change in the calendar, they will not change, so it is perfectly safe to build these values into the programs as a table of constants.

Figure 12.1 The Julian date of the day preceding the beginning of each month

```
01   DAY-CONSTANTS.
     03  FILLER PIC 999 VALUE 0.
     03  FILLER PIC 999 VALUE 31.
     03  FILLER PIC 999 VALUE 59.
     03  FILLER PIC 999 VALUE 90.
     03  FILLER PIC 999 VALUE 120.
     03  FILLER PIC 999 VALUE 151.
     03  FILLER PIC 999 VALUE 181.
     03  FILLER PIC 999 VALUE 212.
     03  FILLER PIC 999 VALUE 243.
     03  FILLER PIC 999 VALUE 273.
     03  FILLER PIC 999 VALUE 304.
     03  FILLER PIC 999 VALUE 334.
01   DAYS-PREVIOUS-TABLE REDEFINES DAY-CONSTANTS.
     03  DAYS-PREVIOUS-ENTRY PIC 999 OCCURS 12 TIMES.
```

Example

ABC Hamburger, Inc., is a company that franchises hamburger stands all over the world. Each product sold at an ABC Hamburger Store is identified by a three-character code. This code is used in all data reported to the company by franchises; however, management reports need to have a verbal description of the item rather than the code. Stores generally sell about twenty different items at any given time. From time to time items are discontinued and new items are introduced.

In any program that must print a description of the item, the use of a table to store the association between the code and the description will be quite useful. Because the table contents do change from time to time, it is much more efficient to load the table contents from a data file. In this way, changes in products do not necessitate recompilations of programs that must refer to the information.

A COBOL program to load this table data is shown in Figure 12.2. Note the use of the field NUMBER-OF-PRODUCTS. Although this item is not used in the loading process, it will be very important in subsequent uses of the table.

Figure 12.2 Table loading program

```
100     IDENTIFICATION DIVISION.
200
300     PROGRAM-ID. TABLE-LOAD.
400     AUTHOR. HORN.
500
600     ENVIRONMENT DIVISION.
700
800     CONFIGURATION SECTION.
900
1000    SOURCE-COMPUTER.
1100    OBJECT-COMPUTER.
1200
1300    INPUT-OUTPUT SECTION.
1400
1500    FILE-CONTROL.
1600
1700        SELECT PRODUCT-ID-FILE ASSIGN TO DISK.
1800
1900    DATA DIVISION.
2000
2100    FILE SECTION.
2200
2300    FD  PRODUCT-ID-FILE
2400        RECORD CONTAINS 84 CHARACTERS
2500        BLOCK CONTAINS 30 RECORDS
2600        LABEL RECORDS ARE STANDARD
2700        VALUE OF TITLE IS "PRODUCT/IDENTIFICATION/FILE"
2800        DATA RECORD IS PRODUCT-ID-RECORD.
2900
3000    01  PRODUCT-ID-RECORD.
3100        03 PRODUCT-CODE-PI          PIC XXX.
3200        03 PRODUCT-DESCRIPTION-PI    PIC X(20).
3300        03 FILLER                    PIC X(61).
3400
3500    WORKING-STORAGE SECTION.
3600
3700    01  FLAGS.
3800        02 EOF-PI-FLAG              PIC XXX VALUE "NO".
3900
4000    01  INDEXES.
4100        02 INDX                     PIC 99  VALUE ZERO.
4200
```

```
4300      01  COUNTERS.
4400          02  NUMBER-OF-PRODUCTS      PIC 99  VALUE ZERO.
4500
4600      01  CONSTANTS.
4700          02  TABLE-SIZE             PIC 99 VALUE 40.
4800
4900      01  PRODUCT-TABLE.
5000          03 PRODUCT-ENTRY OCCURS 40 TIMES.
5100             05 PRODUCT-CODE-ENTRY       PIC XXX.
5200             05 PRODUCT-DESCRIPTION-ENTRY PIC X(20).
5300
5400      PROCEDURE DIVISION.
5500
5600      1000-MAIN-PROCESSING.
5700
5800          PERFORM 2000-TABLE-INITIALIZATION.
5900          STOP RUN.
6000
6100      2000-TABLE-INITIALIZATION.
6200
6300          OPEN INPUT PRODUCT-ID-FILE.
6400          READ PRODUCT-ID-FILE
6500              AT END MOVE "YES" TO EOF-PI-FLAG.
6600          PERFORM 3000-TABLE-LOAD
6700              VARYING INDX FROM 1 BY 1
6800                  UNTIL INDX > TABLE-SIZE OR EOF-PI-FLAG = "YES".
6900          CLOSE PRODUCT-ID-FILE.
7000
7100      3000-TABLE-LOAD.
7200
7300          MOVE PRODUCT-ID-RECORD TO PRODUCT-ENTRY (INDX).
7400          ADD 1 TO NUMBER-OF-PRODUCTS.
7500          READ PRODUCT-ID-FILE
7600              AT END MOVE "YES" TO EOF-PI-FLAG.
```

12.2   DIRECT ACCESS TO TABLE DATA

Occasionally it is possible to create a table that can be accessed by the program directly, that is, by directly specifying the subscript of the desired table element. This is the case with the table shown in Figure 12.1. The COBOL code required to compute the difference between two dates specified in the form of *mmddyy* can be coded as shown in Figure 12.3.

The reference DAY-PREVIOUS-ENTRY (MONTH-1) constitutes a direct access to the table. The content of the data name MONTH-1 represents the position in the table that contains the desired data.

Technically, any table contains two elements: *arguments* and *values*. An argument is the data item used to access the table; a value is the data item associated with the argument in the table. The basic task of accessing data within a table is to locate the value associated with a given argument.

In the example of Figure 12.1, the arguments are 1, 2, 3, ... 12; the values are 0, 31, 59, ... 334. In the example of Figure 12.2, the arguments are the product codes, and the values are the product descriptions.

Figure 12.3   Date difference computation

```
COMPUTE-DATE-DIFFERENCE.
    COMPUTE JULIAN-1 =
        365 * YEAR-1 +
        DAYS-PREVIOUS-ENTRY (MONTH-1) +
        DAY-1.
    COMPUTE JULIAN-2 =
        365 * YEAR-2 +
        DAYS-PREVIOUS-ENTRY (MONTH-2) +
        DAY-2.
    COMPUTE DIFFERENCE = JULIAN-2 - JULIAN-1.
```

In the example of Figure 12.1, there is a one-to-one correspondence between the argument and the position of the value associated with that argument. The value associated with argument 1 is stored in the first position of the table, the value associated with argument 2 is stored in the second position, and so on. This one-to-one correspondence enables direct access to the table entries and makes the explicit storage of the arguments within the table unnecessary. Note that in Figure 12.2, the values are such that this direct access technique is not appropriate. In Figure 12.2, the arguments are stored *along with* the values in such a way that the content of the first argument is associated with the first value, the second argument with the second value, and so on.

We shall refer to these stored arguments as *table arguments* to distinguish them from a specific argument which is used to access the table at any given time. This specific argument is an *actual argument*.

In order to access the data in the table for a given actual argument, it is necessary to find out which table argument matches it. The location associated with the table argument is the location of the required value. For example, suppose the actual argument value is $3\,A\,2$, and suppose the third element of the table contains

PRODUCT- CODE- ENTRY (3)	PRODUCT-DESCRIPTION-ENTRY (3)
3 A 2	R E G U L A R H A M B U R G E R

Since the content of PRODUCT-CODE-ENTRY (3) is equal to "3A2", the required value is contained in

PRODUCT-DESCRIPTION-ENTRY (3)

The process of locating a desired table element when direct access is not possible is called *searching*. Various search techniques are described in the remaining sections of this chapter.

12.3   SEQUENTIAL SEARCH

The most primitive search technique is the exhaustive search of a table. In an exhaustive search, the actual argument is compared to each table argument until either a matching table argument is found or the end of the table is reached. There are two possible outcomes in any search procedure: either the desired element is found or it is not present in the table.

In the case of the exhaustive search procedure, an element is found when a match is made; if the end of the table is reached before a match is made, the element is not present in the table. It is necessary to arrive at a method to communicate the result of a search to the calling procedure. One method is to use a control field with three possible values:

```
CONTINUE
FOUND
NOT PRESENT
```

The control field is initialized to have value CONTINUE. The search procedure resets the field to FOUND or NOT PRESENT when appropriate; execution of the search procedure is repeated so long as the value of the data item is CONTINUE. Pseudocode for the exhaustive search procedure using this approach is shown in Figure 12.4.

Figure 12.4 Exhaustive search procedure

```
Move "CONTINUE" to search flag
Move 1 to pointer
Do while search flag = "CONTINUE"
      If table argument (pointer) = actual argument
            Move "FOUND" to search flag
      Else
            Add 1 to pointer
            If pointer > table limit
                  Move "NOT PRESENT" to search flag
            End If
      End If
End Do
If search flag = "FOUND"
      Use data in table value (pointer) as appropriate
Else
      Take action appropriate when data is not present in table
End If
```

If the table arguments are in ascending or descending sequence, it is possible to improve on the Exhaustive Search Procedure. Note that the procedure of Figure 12.4 requires that each element of the table be examined in the case that an actual argument is not present in the table. If the table arguments are in ascending sequence, it is possible to conclude that the actual argument was not found in the table the first time that a table argument of greater value is encountered. Pseudocode for this modification is shown in Figure 12.5. When this procedure is appropriate, the *average* number of comparisons required to determine that an actual argument is not present is reduced to one-half of the number of the elements in the table. The number of repetitions of the loop required to locate an element that is present in the table is not changed.

Figure 12.5   Sequential search of a sequenced table

```
Move "CONTINUE" to search flag
Move 1 to pointer
Do while search flag = "CONTINUE"
     If table argument (pointer) = actual argument
          Move "FOUND" to search flag
     Else
          Add 1 to pointer
          If pointer > table limit
               Move "NOT PRESENT" to search flag
          Else
               If table argument (pointer) > actual argument
                    Move "NOT PRESENT" to search flag
               End If
          End If
     End If
End Do
If search flag = "FOUND"
     Use data in table value (pointer) as appropriate
Else
     Take action appropriate when data is not present in table
End If
```

12.4   PROGRAM EXAMPLE

Problem Statement

Write a program to create a purchase order register for the Amalgamated Custom Design system. Prepared input to the program comes from the PURCHASE-REQUEST-FILE, which contains one record for each item to be purchased. The PURCHASE-REQUEST-RECORD contains the supplier identification number for each item. Other information about the supplier is supplied by SUPPLIER-MASTER-FILE, which contains one record for each supplier. A printer spacing chart for the required report is shown in Figure 12.6.

Problem Analysis

This program must look up each supplier identification number to determine the supplier name and address for writing a detail line of the required report. In order to facilitate this process, we can load the entire SUPPLIER-MASTER-FILE into a table (assuming, of course, that it is relatively short and that enough memory is available). The file is in sequence by supplier identification number, so that the program can use the sequential search of a sequenced table procedure shown in Figure 12.5. A plan for the program is shown in Figure 12.7.

Problem Solution

The required program is shown in Program 12.1 with structure diagram shown in Figure 12.8. The program loads the content of SUPPLIER-MASTER-FILE

Figure 12.6   Printer spacing chart for purchase order report

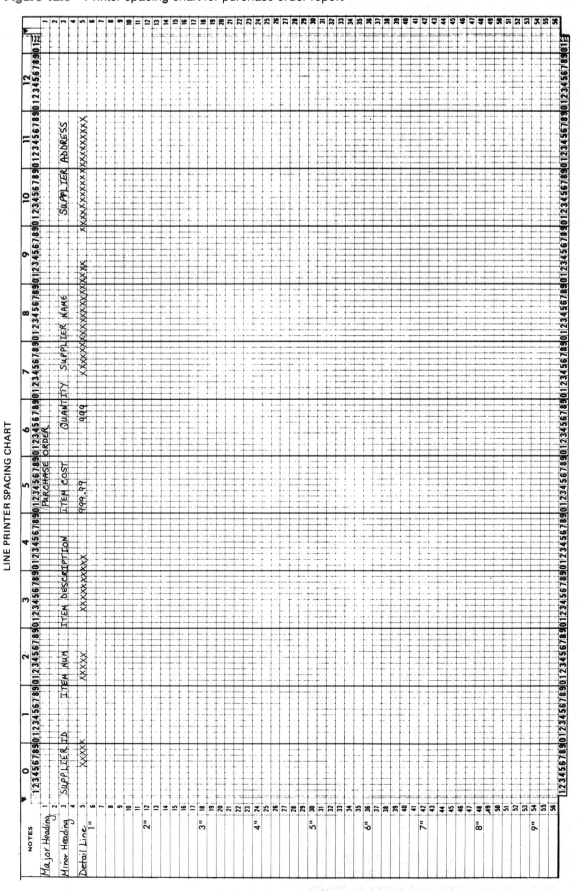

into SUPPLIER-TABLE (see lines 12400-13300) before processing any data from
PURCHASE-REQUEST-FILE. In this way, the data is readily available as each
record in PURCHASE-REQUEST-FILE is processed.

As each PURCHASE-REQUEST-RECORD is processed, the paragraph 5100-SEARCH
(see lines 18500-19700) is used to locate the table argument that is equal to
the actual argument SUPPLIER-ID-NUMBER-PRR (from PURCHASE-REQUEST-RECORD).
If the value is located, the associated table values are used in creating the
required output record (see lines 16400-17900). If the item is not located, the
paragraph 6100-NOT-PRESENT is executed (see line 18100). For simplicity, the
paragraph 6100-NOT-PRESENT takes no action; in a real application, this
paragraph would be responsible for writing appropriate error messages. The
paragraph 5100-SEARCH is a straightforward implementation of the sequential search procedure described in Figure 12.5.

Figure 12.7   Plan for sequential search program

Main logic

    Load supplier master file data into table
    Open purchase request file
    Read purchase request file
    Do Search read until end of file
    Close files
    Stop

Search read

    Look up supplier id number in table
    If found
        Move data to detail line
        Write detail line
    Else
        Write error message
    End If
    Read purchase request file

Program 12.1   Sequential search example

```
100     IDENTIFICATION DIVISION.
200
300     PROGRAM-ID. SEQUENTIAL-SEARCH.
400     AUTHOR. GARY.
500
600     ENVIRONMENT DIVISION.
700
800     CONFIGURATION SECTION.
900
1000    SOURCE-COMPUTER.
1100    OBJECT-COMPUTER.
1200
1300    INPUT-OUTPUT SECTION.
1400
1500    FILE-CONTROL.
1600
1700        SELECT PURCHASE-REQUEST-FILE ASSIGN TO DISK.
1800        SELECT SUPPLIER-MASTER-FILE ASSIGN TO DISK.
1900        SELECT PRINTED-DETAIL-FILE ASSIGN TO PRINTER.
```

Program 12.1 (continued)

```
2000
2100    DATA DIVISION.
2200
2300    FILE SECTION.
2400
2500    FD  PURCHASE-REQUEST-FILE
2600        RECORD CONTAINS 84 CHARACTERS
2700        BLOCK CONTAINS 30 RECORDS
2800        VALUE OF TITLE IS "PURCHASEREQ"
2900        DATA RECORD IS INPUT-RECORD.
3000
3100    01  PURCHASE-REQUEST-RECORD.
3200        03  SUPPLIER-ID-NUMBER-PRR          PIC X(5).
3300        03  ITEM-NUMBER-PRR                 PIC X(5).
3400        03  ITEM-DESCRIPTION-PRR            PIC X(10).
3500        03  ITEM-COST-PRR                   PIC 999V99.
3600        03  ORDER-QUANTITY-PRR              PIC 9(3).
3700        03  FILLER                          PIC X(56).
3800
3900    FD  SUPPLIER-MASTER-FILE
4000        RECORD CONTAINS 84 CHARACTERS
4100        BLOCK  CONTAINS 30 RECORDS
4200        VALUE OF TITLE IS "SUPPLIERINFO"
4300        DATA RECORD IS SUPPLIER-MASTER-RECORD.
4400
4500    01  SUPPLIER-MASTER-RECORD.
4600        03 SUPPLIER-ID-NUMBER-SMR           PIC X(5).
4700        03 SUPPLIER-NAME-SMR                PIC X(20).
4800        03 SUPPLIER-ADDRESS-SMR             PIC X(20).
4900        03 FILLER                           PIC X(39).
5000
5100    FD  PRINTED-DETAIL-FILE
5200        LABEL RECORDS ARE STANDARD
5300        DATA RECORD IS OUTPUT-RECORD.
5400
5500    01  OUTPUT-RECORD            PIC X(132).
5600
5700    WORKING-STORAGE SECTION.
5800
5900    01  FLAGS.
6000        02 ERROR-FLAG               PIC X(3) VALUE "NO".
6100        02 SEARCH-FLAG              PIC X(11) VALUE "CONTINUE".
6200        02 EOF-FLAG-SMF             PIC X(3) VALUE "NO".
6300        02 EOF-FLAG-PRR             PIC X(3) VALUE "NO".
6400
6500    01  INDEXES.
6600        02 X                        PIC 999 VALUE ZERO.
6700
6800    01  COUNTERS.
6900        02 NUM-ELEMENTS             PIC 999 VALUE ZERO.
7000
7100    01  SUPPLIER-TABLE.
7200        02  SUPPLIER-ENTRY OCCURS 1 TO 100 TIMES
7300                DEPENDING ON NUM-ELEMENTS.
```

Program 12.1 (continued)

```
7400            03  SUPPLIER-ID-NUMBER      PIC X(5).
7500            03  SUPPLIER-NAME           PIC X(20).
7600            03  SUPPLIER-ADDRESS        PIC X(20).
7700
7800    01  MAJOR-HEADING.
7900        02  FILLER              PIC X(50) VALUE SPACES.
8000        02  FILLER              PIC X(14) VALUE "PURCHASE ORDER".
8100
8200    01  MINOR-HEADING.
8300        02  FILLER              PIC X(11) VALUE "SUPPLIER ID".
8400        02  FILLER              PIC X(6) VALUE SPACES.
8500        02  FILLER              PIC X(8) VALUE "ITEM NUM".
8600        02  FILLER              PIC X(4) VALUE SPACES.
8700        02  FILLER              PIC X(16) VALUE "ITEM DESCRIPTION".
8800        02  FILLER              PIC X(4) VALUE SPACES.
8900        02  FILLER              PIC X(9) VALUE "ITEM COST".
9000        02  FILLER              PIC X(6) VALUE SPACES.
9100        02  FILLER              PIC X(8) VALUE "QUANTITY".
9200        02  FILLER              PIC X(2) VALUE SPACES.
9300        02  FILLER              PIC X(13) VALUE "SUPPLIER NAME".
9400        02  FILLER              PIC X(14) VALUE SPACES.
9500        02  FILLER              PIC X(16) VALUE "SUPPLIER ADDRESS".
9600
9700    01  DETAIL-LINE.
9800        02  FILLER              PIC X(5) VALUE SPACES.
9900        02  DL-SUPPLIER-ID-NUMBER  PIC X(5).
10000       02  FILLER              PIC X(10) VALUE SPACES.
10100       02  DL-ITEM-NUMBER      PIC X(5).
10200       02  FILLER              PIC X(8) VALUE SPACES.
10300       02  DL-ITEM-DESCRIPTION PIC X(10).
10400       02  FILLER              PIC X(7) VALUE SPACES.
10500       02  DL-ITEM-COST        PIC 999.99.
10600       02  FILLER              PIC X(10) VALUE SPACES.
10700       02  DL-ORDER-QUANTITY   PIC 9(3).
10800       02  FILLER              PIC X(5) VALUE SPACES.
10900       02  DL-SUPPLIER-NAME    PIC X(20).
11000       02  FILLER              PIC X(5) VALUE SPACES.
11100       02  DL-SUPPLIER-ADDRESS PIC X(20).
11200
11300   PROCEDURE DIVISION.
11400
11500   1000-MAIN-LOGIC.
11600
11700       PERFORM 2000-READ-LOAD-TABLE.
11800       PERFORM 3000-INITIALIZATION.
11900       PERFORM 4000-SEARCH-READ
12000           UNTIL EOF-FLAG-PRR = "YES".
12100       PERFORM 9000-TERMINATION.
12200       STOP RUN.
12300
12400   2000-READ-LOAD-TABLE.
12500
12600       MOVE ZERO TO ERROR-FLAG.
12700       MOVE ZERO TO NUM-ELEMENTS.
```

Program 12.1 (continued)

```
12800          OPEN INPUT SUPPLIER-MASTER-FILE.
12900          READ SUPPLIER-MASTER-FILE
13000              AT END MOVE "YES" TO EOF-FLAG-SMF.
13100          PERFORM 2100-STOR-READ
13200              UNTIL EOF-FLAG-SMF = "YES" OR ERROR-FLAG = "YES".
13300          CLOSE SUPPLIER-MASTER-FILE.
13400
13500      2100-STOR-READ.
13600
13700          ADD 1 TO NUM-ELEMENTS.
13800          IF NUM-ELEMENTS > 100
13900              MOVE "YES" TO ERROR-FLAG
14000          ELSE
14100              MOVE SUPPLIER-MASTER-RECORD
14200                  TO SUPPLIER-ENTRY (NUM-ELEMENTS).
14300              READ SUPPLIER-MASTER-FILE
14400                  AT END MOVE "YES" TO EOF-FLAG-SMF.
14500
14600      3000-INITIALIZATION.
14700
14800          OPEN INPUT PURCHASE-REQUEST-FILE
14900               OUTPUT PRINTED-DETAIL-FILE.
15000          READ PURCHASE-REQUEST-FILE
15100              AT END MOVE "YES" TO EOF-FLAG-PRR.
15200          MOVE MAJOR-HEADING TO OUTPUT-RECORD.
15300          WRITE OUTPUT-RECORD AFTER PAGE.
15400          MOVE MINOR-HEADING TO OUTPUT-RECORD.
15500          WRITE OUTPUT-RECORD AFTER 2.
15600                              .
15700      4000-SEARCH-READ.
15800
15900          MOVE "CONTINUE" TO SEARCH-FLAG.
16000          MOVE 1 TO X.
16100          PERFORM 5100-SEARCH
16200              UNTIL SEARCH-FLAG NOT EQUAL "CONTINUE".
16300          IF SEARCH-FLAG = "FOUND"
16400              MOVE SUPPLIER-ID-NUMBER-PRR
16500                  TO DL-SUPPLIER-ID-NUMBER
16600              MOVE ITEM-NUMBER-PRR
16700                  TO DL-ITEM-NUMBER
16800              MOVE ITEM-DESCRIPTION-PRR
16900                  TO DL-ITEM-DESCRIPTION
17000              MOVE ITEM-COST-PRR
17100                  TO DL-ITEM-COST
17200              MOVE ORDER-QUANTITY-PRR
17300                  TO DL-ORDER-QUANTITY
17400              MOVE SUPPLIER-NAME (X)
17500                  TO DL-SUPPLIER-NAME
17600              MOVE SUPPLIER-ADDRESS (X)
17700                  TO DL-SUPPLIER-ADDRESS
17800              MOVE DETAIL-LINE TO OUTPUT-RECORD
17900              WRITE OUTPUT-RECORD AFTER 2
18000          ELSE
18100              PERFORM 6100-NOT-PRESENT.
```

```
18200        READ PURCHASE-REQUEST-FILE
18300            AT END MOVE "YES" TO EOF-FLAG-PRR.
18400
18500    5100-SEARCH.
18600
18700        IF SUPPLIER-ID-NUMBER (X) = SUPPLIER-ID-NUMBER-PRR
18800            MOVE "FOUND" TO SEARCH-FLAG
18900        ELSE
19000            ADD 1 TO X
19100            IF X > NUM-ELEMENTS
19200                MOVE "NOT PRESENT" TO SEARCH-FLAG
19300            ELSE
19400                IF SUPPLIER-ID-NUMBER (X) > SUPPLIER-ID-NUMBER-PRR
19500                    MOVE "NOT PRESENT" TO SEARCH-FLAG
19600                ELSE
19700                    NEXT SENTENCE.
19800
19900    6100-NOT-PRESENT.
20000
20100        EXIT.
20200
20300    9000-TERMINATION.
20400
20500        CLOSE PURCHASE-REQUEST-FILE
20600              PRINTED-DETAIL-FILE.
```

Program 12.1 (continued)

Figure 12.8 Structure diagram for Program 12.1

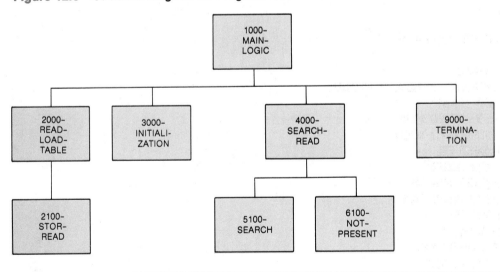

12.5 BINARY SEARCH

The procedure shown in Figure 12.5 makes use of the sequencing of the table arguments in determining that an element is not present, but makes no use of the sequencing in locating an element that is present. The binary search procedure described in this section makes use of the sequential nature of the table to reduce not only the average number of comparisons required to determine that an element is *not* present, but also to reduce the number of comparisons required to locate an element that *is* present in the table.

The idea behind the binary search is employed intuitively by people playing a game in which they have to guess a number. In response to each guess, the player who knows the number responds "higher" or "lower" or "you got it," depending on the value of the target number and the value of the guess. The optimum strategy for players of this game is to begin at the middle of the range. For example, if the range is known to be from 1 to 100, the initial guess would be 50. If the response to this guess is "higher," the player knows that the target value is in the range 51 to 100; if the response is "lower," the target value is in the range 1 to 49. In either case, the next guess should be at the halfway point in the range. With successive guesses, the width of the range containing the unknown value is reduced by one-half until finally the target value is found.

In order to apply this idea to searching for an element in a table, we shall need two pointers, HIGH and LOW, which will point to the upper and lower limits of the segment of the table containing the desired value. At each repetition of the search procedure, the midpoint of this range (MID) is computed. (The fraction resulting from the computation MID = (HIGH + LOW)/2 is dropped.) The actual argument is then compared to the table argument at location MID. If the arguments are equal, the search terminates. If the actual argument is less than the table argument at MID, the procedure is repeated with the value of MID replacing the value of HIGH; if the actual argument is greater than the table argument at location MID, the procedure is repeated, with the value of MID replacing the value of LOW. Pseudocode for this procedure is shown Figure 12.9; examples of the execution of this procedure are shown in Figures 12.10 and 12.11.

The maximum number of repetitions required for termination of this procedure is dependent on the size of the table, as shown in Figure 12.12. In general, it can be shown that, in the worst case, the number of repetitions required for termination of a binary search of a table of n elements is the smallest integer greater than $\log_2 n$. For example, if $n = 8$, $\log_2 8 = 3$ (since $2^3 = 8$). The smallest integer greater than 3 is 4; therefore if $n = 8$, 4 repetitions would be required in the worst possible case for termination of the binary search.

For a given actual argument, of course, the procedure may terminate in fewer repetitions than the maximum number required. The average behavior will be a little better than the worst case behavior, but not dramatically so, as with the procedure for sequential search of a sequenced table.

Example

Program 12.2 is the same as Program 12.1, except that a binary search is implemented rather than a sequential search. The paragraph 5100-SEARCH of Program 12.1 is replaced by 5200-SEARCH (see lines 19200-19800). The paragraph 5200-SEARCH is a straightforward implementation of the binary search procedure of Figure 12.9.

Figure 12.9   Binary search procedure

```
Low = 0
High = table limit + 1
Move "CONTINUE" to search flag
Do while search flag = "CONTINUE"
      Mid = (low + high) / 2
      If table argument (mid) = actual argument
            Move "FOUND" to search flag
      Else
            If table argument (mid) > actual argument
                  Move mid to low
            Else
                  Move mid to high
            End If
            If high − low = 1
                  Move "NOT PRESENT" to search flag
            End If
      End If
End Do
If search flag = "FOUND"
      Use data in table value (mid) as appropriate
Else
      Take action appropriate when data is not present in table
End If
```

Figure 12.10   Binary search example for data present in table

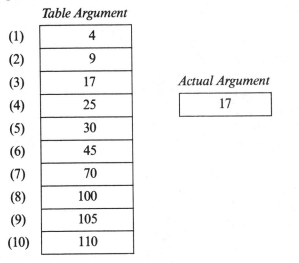

Table Argument

(1)	4
(2)	9
(3)	17
(4)	25
(5)	30
(6)	45
(7)	70
(8)	100
(9)	105
(10)	110

Actual Argument

17

	Values of			
Repetition	LOW	HIGH	MID	Comments
1	0	11	5	17 < TABLE-ARGUMENT (5)
2	0	5	2	17 > TABLE-ARGUMENT (2)
3	2	5	3	17 = TABLE-ARGUMENT (3)
				Search is completed

Figure 12.11   Binary search example for data not present in table

Table Argument

(1)	4
(2)	9
(3)	17
(4)	25
(5)	30
(6)	45
(7)	70
(8)	100
(9)	105
(10)	110

Actual Argument

104

Repetition	*LOW*	*Values of HIGH*	*MID*	*Comments*
1	0	11	5	104 > TABLE–ARGUMENT (5)
2	5	11	8	104 > TABLE–ARGUMENT (8)
3	8	11	9	104 < TABLE–ARGUMENT (9)
4	8	9	8	104 > TABLE–ARGUMENT (8)
				HIGH – LOW = 1 therefore element is not in table

Figure 12.12   Worst case behavior for the binary search

Table Size n	*Maximum Repetitions*	$LOG_2 n$	*Table Size* n	*Maximum Repetitions*	$LOG_2 n$
1	1	0	19	5	4.24793
2	2	1	.	.	.
3	2	1.58496	.	.	.
4	3	2	.	.	.
5	3	2.32193	29	5	4.85798
6	3	2.58496	30	5	4.90689
7	3	2.80736	31	5	4.9542
8	4	3	32	6	5
9	4	3.16993	33	6	5.04439
10	4	3.32193	34	6	5.08746
11	4	3.45943	35	6	5.12928
12	4	3.58496	.	.	.
13	4	3.70044	.	.	.
14	4	3.80736	.	.	.
15	4	3.90689	61	6	5.93074
16	5	4	62	6	5.9542
17	5	4.08746	63	6	5.97728
18	5	4.16993	64	7	6

Program 12.2   Binary search example

```
100       IDENTIFICATION DIVISION.
200
300       PROGRAM-ID. BINARY-SEARCH.
400       AUTHOR. GARY.
500
600       ENVIRONMENT DIVISION.
700
800       CONFIGURATION SECTION.
900
1000      SOURCE-COMPUTER.
1100      OBJECT-COMPUTER.
1200
1300      INPUT-OUTPUT SECTION.
1400
1500      FILE-CONTROL.
1600
1700          SELECT PURCHASE-REQUEST-FILE ASSIGN TO DISK.
1800          SELECT SUPPLIER-MASTER-FILE ASSIGN TO DISK.
1900          SELECT PRINTED-DETAIL-FILE ASSIGN TO PRINTER.
2000
2100      DATA DIVISION.
2200
2300      FILE SECTION.
2400
2500      FD  PURCHASE-REQUEST-FILE
2600          RECORD CONTAINS 84 CHARACTERS
2700          BLOCK CONTAINS 30 RECORDS
2800          VALUE OF TITLE IS "PURCHASEREQ"
2900          DATA RECORD IS INPUT-RECORD.
3000
3100      01  PURCHASE-REQUEST-RECORD.
3200          03  SUPPLIER-ID-NUMBER-PRR        PIC X(5).
3300          03  ITEM-NUMBER-PRR              PIC X(5).
3400          03  ITEM-DESCRIPTION-PRR          PIC X(10).
3500          03  ITEM-COST-PRR                PIC 999V99.
3600          03  ORDER-QUANTITY-PRR            PIC 9(3).
3700          03  FILLER                       PIC X(56).
3800
3900      FD  SUPPLIER-MASTER-FILE
4000          RECORD CONTAINS 84 CHARACTERS
4100          BLOCK  CONTAINS 30 RECORDS
4200          VALUE OF TITLE IS "SUPPLIERINFO"
4300          DATA RECORD IS SUPPLIER-MASTER-RECORD.
4400
4500      01  SUPPLIER-MASTER-RECORD.
4600          03 SUPPLIER-ID-NUMBER-SMR         PIC X(5).
4700          03 SUPPLIER-NAME-SMR             PIC X(20).
4800          03 SUPPLIER-ADDRESS-SMR          PIC X(20).
4900          03 FILLER                        PIC X(39).
5000
```

Program 12.2 (continued)

```
5100    FD  PRINTED-DETAIL-FILE
5200        LABEL RECORDS ARE STANDARD
5300        DATA RECORD IS OUTPUT-RECORD.
5400
5500    01  OUTPUT-RECORD                   PIC X(132).
5600
5700    WORKING-STORAGE SECTION.
5800
5900    01  FLAGS.
6000        02  ERROR-FLAG          PIC X(3) VALUE "NO".
6100        02  SEARCH-FLAG         PIC X(11) VALUE "CONTINUE".
6200        02  EOF-FLAG-SMF        PIC X(3) VALUE "NO".
6300        02  EOF-FLAG-PRR        PIC X(3) VALUE "NO".
6400
6500    01  POINTERS.
6600        02  MID                 PIC 999 VALUE ZERO.
6700        02  HIGH                PIC 999 VALUE ZERO.
6800        02  LOW                 PIC 999 VALUE ZERO.
6900
7000    01  COUNTERS.
7100        02  NUM-ELEMENTS        PIC 999 VALUE ZERO.
7200
7300    01  CONSTANTS.
7400        02  TABLE-SIZE          PIC 999 VALUE 100.
7500
7600    01  SUPPLIER-TABLE.
7700        02  SUPPLIER-ENTRY OCCURS 1 TO 100 TIMES
7800                DEPENDING ON NUM-ELEMENTS.
7900            03  SUPPLIER-ID-NUMBER   PIC X(5).
8000            03  SUPPLIER-NAME        PIC X(20).
8100            03  SUPPLIER-ADDRESS     PIC X(20).
8200
8300    01  MAJOR-HEADING.
8400
8500        02  FILLER          PIC X(50) VALUE SPACES.
8600        02  FILLER          PIC X(14) VALUE "PURCHASE ORDER".
8700
8800    01  MINOR-HEADING.
8900        02  FILLER          PIC X(11) VALUE "SUPPLIER ID".
9000        02  FILLER          PIC X(6) VALUE SPACES.
9100        02  FILLER          PIC X(8) VALUE "ITEM NUM".
9200        02  FILLER          PIC X(4) VALUE SPACES.
9300        02  FILLER          PIC X(16) VALUE "ITEM DESCRIPTION".
9400        02  FILLER          PIC X(2) VALUE SPACES.
9500        02  FILLER          PIC X(9) VALUE "ITEM-COST".
9600        02  FILLER          PIC X(6) VALUE SPACES.
9700        02  FILLER          PIC X(8) VALUE "QUANTITY".
9800        02  FILLER          PIC X(2) VALUE SPACES.
9900        02  FILLER          PIC X(13) VALUE "SUPPLIER NAME".
10000       02  FILLER          PIC X(14) VALUE  SPACES.
10100       02  FILLER          PIC X(16) VALUE "SUPPLIER ADDRESS".
10200
```

Program 12.2 (continued)

```
10300    01  DETAIL-LINE.
10400        02  FILLER                 PIC X(5) VALUE SPACES.
10500        02  DL-SUPPLIER-ID-NUMBER  PIC X(5).
10600        02  FILLER                 PIC X(10) VALUE SPACES.
10700        02  DL-ITEM-NUMBER         PIC X(5).
10800        02  FILLER                 PIC X(8) VALUE SPACES.
10900        02  DL-ITEM-DESCRIPTION    PIC X(10).
11000        02  FILLER                 PIC X(7) VALUE SPACES.
11100        02  DL-ITEM-COST           PIC 999.99.
11200        02  FILLER                 PIC X(10) VALUE SPACES.
11300        02  DL-ORDER-QUANTITY      PIC 9(3).
11400        02  FILLER                 PIC X(5) VALUE SPACES.
11500        02  DL-SUPPLIER-NAME       PIC X(20).
11600        02  FILLER                 PIC X(5) VALUE SPACES.
11700        02  DL-SUPPLIER-ADDRESS    PIC X(20).
11800
11900    PROCEDURE DIVISION.
12000
12100    1000-MAIN-LOGIC.
12200
12300        PERFORM 2000-READ-LOAD-TABLE.
12400        PERFORM 3000-INITIALIZATION.
12500        PERFORM 4000-SEARCH-READ
12600            UNTIL EOF-FLAG-PRR = "YES".
12700        PERFORM 9000-TERMINATION.
12800        STOP RUN.
12900
13000    2000-READ-LOAD-TABLE.
13100
13200        MOVE ZERO TO ERROR-FLAG.
13300        MOVE ZERO TO NUM-ELEMENTS.
13400        OPEN INPUT SUPPLIER-MASTER-FILE.
13500        READ SUPPLIER-MASTER-FILE
13600            AT END MOVE "YES" TO EOF-FLAG-SMF.
13700        PERFORM 2100-STOR-READ
13800            UNTIL EOF-FLAG-SMF = "YES" OR ERROR-FLAG = "YES".
13900        CLOSE SUPPLIER-MASTER-FILE.
14000
14100    2100-STOR-READ.
14200
14300        ADD 1 TO NUM-ELEMENTS.
14400        IF NUM-ELEMENTS > TABLE-SIZE
14500            MOVE "YES" TO ERROR-FLAG
14600        ELSE
14700            MOVE SUPPLIER-MASTER-RECORD
14800                TO SUPPLIER-ENTRY (NUM-ELEMENTS).
14900            READ SUPPLIER-MASTER-FILE
15000                AT END MOVE "YES" TO EOF-FLAG-SMF.
15100
```

```
15200    3000-INITIALIZATION.
15300
15400        OPEN INPUT PURCHASE-REQUEST-FILE
15500             OUTPUT PRINTED-DETAIL-FILE.
15600        READ PURCHASE-REQUEST-FILE
15700            AT END MOVE "YES" TO EOF-FLAG-PRR.
15800        MOVE MAJOR-HEADING TO OUTPUT-RECORD.
15900        WRITE OUTPUT-RECORD AFTER PAGE.
16000        MOVE MINOR-HEADING TO OUTPUT-RECORD.
16100        WRITE OUTPUT-RECORD AFTER 2.
16200
16300    4000-SEARCH-READ.
16400
16500        MOVE 0 TO LOW.
16600        ADD 1 NUM-ELEMENTS GIVING HIGH.
16700        MOVE "CONTINUE" TO SEARCH-FLAG.
16800        PERFORM 5200-SEARCH
16900            UNTIL SEARCH-FLAG NOT EQUAL "CONTINUE".
17000        IF SEARCH-FLAG = "FOUND"
17100            MOVE SUPPLIER-ID-NUMBER-PRR
17200                TO DL-SUPPLIER-ID-NUMBER
17300            MOVE ITEM-NUMBER-PRR
17400                TO DL-ITEM-NUMBER
17500            MOVE ITEM-DESCRIPTION-PRR
17600                TO DL-ITEM-DESCRIPTION
17700            MOVE ITEM-COST-PRR
17800                TO DL-ITEM-COST
17900            MOVE ORDER-QUANTITY-PRR
18000                TO DL-ORDER-QUANTITY
18100            MOVE SUPPLIER-NAME (MID)
18200                TO DL-SUPPLIER-NAME
18300            MOVE SUPPLIER-ADDRESS (MID)
18400                TO DL-SUPPLIER-ADDRESS
18500            MOVE DETAIL-LINE TO OUTPUT-RECORD
18600            WRITE OUTPUT-RECORD AFTER 2
18700        ELSE
18800            PERFORM 6100-NOT-PRESENT.
18900        READ PURCHASE-REQUEST-FILE
19000            AT END MOVE "YES" TO EOF-FLAG-PRR.
19100
19200    5200-SEARCH.
19300
19400        COMPUTE MID = (LOW + HIGH) / 2.
19500        IF SUPPLIER-ID-NUMBER (MID) = SUPPLIER-ID-NUMBER-PRR
19600            MOVE "FOUND" TO SEARCH-FLAG
19700        ELSE
19800            PERFORM 5800-CONT-SEARCH.
19900
20000    5800-CONT-SEARCH.
20100
20200        IF SUPPLIER-ID-NUMBER (MID) < SUPPLIER-ID-NUMBER-PRR
20300            MOVE MID TO LOW
20400        ELSE
20500            MOVE MID TO HIGH.
20600        IF HIGH - LOW = 1
20700            MOVE "NOT PRESENT" TO SEARCH-FLAG.
```

Program 12.2 (continued)

```
20800
20900    6100-NOT-PRESENT.
21000
21100       EXIT.
21200
21300    9000-TERMINATION.
21400
21500       CLOSE PURCHASE-REQUEST-FILE
21600             PRINTED-DETAIL-FILE.
```

12.6 RANDOMIZED TABLES

Although the binary search technique is very good for sequenced tables, the expected number of comparisons required to locate a desired entry is still greater than one, which is, of course, the ideal. A carefully constructed randomized table makes it possible to approach this ideal, even when the nature of the table arguments makes a direct-access technique impossible.

The idea behind a randomized table is to place the table argument and its associated table values in a location computed from the table argument. The computational formula used for this purpose is called a *hash* function. The table arguments and values will generally be scattered throughout the table space in a random fashion. In order to access the table, the hash function is applied to the actual argument. If the actual argument matches the table argument at the computed location, the procedure terminates.

A problem that arises in the implementation of this procedure is the possible existence of two or more table arguments (called *synonyms*) that yield the same location value when the hash function is applied. In the loading process an instance of this sort is called a *collision*. Collisions are unavoidable because the hash function usually does not yield a one-to-one correspondence between table arguments and table locations. A collision can be handled by placing the table argument in another unused table location determined systematically from the location originally computed. A common technique is to search the table sequentially until an unused table element is found and then place the table argument and associated value in that location.

The existence of synonyms makes the search procedure somewhat more complicated. If the table argument is not equal to the actual argument at the location "predicted" by the hash function, it is necessary to use the same procedure that was used to handle collisions until either a table argument is found that matches the actual argument or an unused element is found. In the latter instance, we conclude that the desired argument is not present in the table.

In order to optimize access time with a randomized table, it is important to keep the number of synonyms to a minimum. Two considerations are important in this regard: table size and hash function. The table size must be larger than the amount of data to be stored. It has been shown experimentally that the number of collisions begins to increase dramatically when the table is two-thirds full. Even if the table space is quite large, a poorly chosen hash function can reduce the efficiency of this technique. A good hash function must scatter the table elements in a random fashion throughout the table space. A function that tends to favor one area or that results in tight clusters of elements in one or more areas is not desirable.

A great deal of research has been done on hash functions. Although there is no universally "best" function, the following procedure is quite good in a variety of situations: for a table of size n, compute the remainder after dividing the argument by n. The hash function value is the remainder plus one.

It can be shown that this function results in best performance when n is a prime number. (A prime number is one that is divisible only by one and itself. The first few primes are 2, 3, 5, 7, 11, 13, 17, 19, 23, 29, 31, and so on. Note that this function always yields values in the range 1, 2, ... n, since the possible values of the reminders are 0, 1, 2, ... $(n-1)$. For example, suppose the table size is 17 and we want to compute the hash function for argument 45. First compute the remainder after dividing 45 by 17:

$$
\begin{array}{r}
2 \text{ r } 11 \\
17\overline{)45} \\
\underline{34} \\
11
\end{array}
$$

Then add 1: $11 + 1 = 12$. Twelve is the hash function value for argument 45.

A procedure for loading data into a randomized table is shown in Figure 12.13. Note that it is necessary for the program to be able to determine whether a table element is in use or not. This can be accomplished by initializing the entire table space to some constant (for example, SPACES or ZEROES) before beginning the loading process. Note also that the table is in a sense circular: the element following the last table element is the first one. This is necessary in order to handle collisions with the last element in the table.

Figure 12.13 Loading a randomized table

```
L = hash function (argument)
Move "CONTINUE" to search flag
Do while search flag = "CONTINUE"
      If table location L is unused
            Move data to table location L
            Move "FINISH" to search flag
      Else
            L = L + 1
            If L > table limit
                  L = 1
            End If
      End If
End Do
```

A procedure for searching for data in a randomized table is shown in Figure 12.14. Note that this procedure is quite similar to the loading procedure, with the added facility for locating a TABLE-ARGUMENT equal to an ACTUAL-ARGUMENT.

Figure 12.14 Searching a randomized table

```
L = hash function (actual argument)
Move "CONTINUE" to search flag
Do while search flag = "CONTINUE"
      If table argument at location L = actual argument
            Move "FOUND" to search flag
      Else
            If table location L is unused
                  Move "NOT PRESENT" to search flag
            Else
                  L = L + 1
                  If L > table limit
                        L = 1
                  End If
            End If
      End If
End Do
If search flag = "FOUND"
      Use data from table value (L) as appropriate
Else
      Take action appropriate when data is not present in table
End If
```

Example

Program 12.3 performs the same functions as programs 12.1 and 12.2, except that the randomized table is used. The paragraph 2000–READ–LOAD–TABLE of Program 12.2 is modified to perform two paragraphs: 2110–INITIALIZE–TABLE (lines 15100-15300) and 2200–LOAD–TABLE (lines 15500-16400). The purpose of 2100–INITIALIZE–TABLE is to mark all of the positions of the table as unused by moving spaces to each element. The paragraph 2200–LOAD–TABLE is an implementation of the procedure shown in Figure 12.13. In this case, the table limit is 97 (a prime number).

A paragraph 5200–SEARCH of Program 12.2 is replaced by paragraph 5300–SEARCH (lines 21800-23000). 5300–SEARCH is a direct implementation of the procedure shown in Figure 12.14.

Program 12.3 Randomized search example

```
100      IDENTIFICATION DIVISION.
200
300      PROGRAM-ID. RANDOMIZE-SEARCH.
400      AUTHOR. GARY.
500
600      ENVIRONMENT DIVISION.
700
800      CONFIGURATION SECTION.
900
```

Program 12.3 (continued)

```
1000      SOURCE-COMPUTER.
1100      OBJECT-COMPUTER.
1200
1300      INPUT-OUTPUT SECTION.
1400
1500      FILE-CONTROL.
1600
1700          SELECT PURCHASE-REQUEST-FILE ASSIGN TO DISK.
1800          SELECT SUPPLIER-MASTER-FILE ASSIGN TO DISK.
1900          SELECT PRINTED-DETAIL-FILE ASSIGN TO PRINTER.
2000
2100      DATA DIVISION.
2200
2300      FILE SECTION.
2400
2500      FD  PURCHASE-REQUEST-FILE
2600          RECORD CONTAINS 84 CHARACTERS
2700          BLOCK CONTAINS 30 RECORDS
2800          VALUE OF TITLE IS "PURCHASEREQ"
2900          DATA RECORD IS INPUT-RECORD.
3000
3100      01  PURCHASE-REQUEST-RECORD.
3200          03  SUPPLIER-ID-NUMBER-PRR            PIC X(5).
3300          03  SUPPLIER-ID-NUMBER-PRR-NUM
3400              REDEFINES SUPPLIER-ID-NUMBER-PRR  PIC 9(5).
3500          03  ITEM-NUMBER-PRR                   PIC X(5).
3600          03  ITEM-DESCRIPTION-PRR              PIC X(10).
3700          03  ITEM-COST-PRR                     PIC 999V99.
3800          03  ORDER-QUANTITY-PRR                PIC 9(3).
3900          03  FILLER                            PIC X(56).
4000
4100      FD  SUPPLIER-MASTER-FILE
4200          RECORD CONTAINS 84 CHARACTERS
4300          BLOCK  CONTAINS 30 RECORDS
4400          VALUE OF TITLE IS "SUPPLIERINFO"
4500          DATA RECORD IS SUPPLIER-MASTER-RECORD.
4600
4700      01  SUPPLIER-MASTER-RECORD.
4800          03 SUPPLIER-ID-NUMBER-SMR             PIC X(5).
4900          03 SUPPLIER-ID-NUMBER-SMR-NUM
5000             REDEFINES SUPPLIER-ID-NUMBER-SMR   PIC 9(5).
5100          03 SUPPLIER-NAME-SMR                  PIC X(20).
5200          03 SUPPLIER-ADDRESS-SMR               PIC X(20).
5300          03 FILLER                             PIC X(39).
5400
5500      FD  PRINTED-DETAIL-FILE
5600          LABEL RECORDS ARE STANDARD
5700          DATA RECORD IS OUTPUT-RECORD.
5800
5900      01  OUTPUT-RECORD                         PIC X(132).
6000
```

```
6100       WORKING-STORAGE SECTION.
6200
6300    01  FLAGS.
6400        02 ERROR-FLAG          PIC X(3) VALUE "NO".
6500        02 SEARCH-FLAG         PIC X(11) VALUE "CONTINUE".
6600        02 EOF-FLAG-SMF        PIC X(3) VALUE "NO".
6700        02 EOF-FLAG-PRR        PIC X(3) VALUE "NO".
6800
6900    01  COMPUTED-VALUES.
7000        02 QUOT                PIC 9999 VALUE ZERO.
7100
7200    01  INDEXES.
7300        02 INDX               PIC 99    VALUE ZERO.
7400        02 X                  PIC 999   VALUE ZERO.
7500
7600    01  POINTERS.
7700        02 MID                PIC 999   VALUE ZERO.
7800        02 HIGH               PIC 999   VALUE ZERO.
7900        02 LOW                PIC 999   VALUE ZERO.
8000
8100    01  COUNTERS.
8200        02 NUM-ELEMENTS        PIC 999 VALUE ZERO.
8300
8400    01  CONSTANTS.
8500        02 TABLE-SIZE          PIC 99 VALUE 97.
8600
8700    01  SUPPLIER-TABLE.
8800        02  SUPPLIER-ENTRY OCCURS 97 TIMES.
8900            03  SUPPLIER-ID-NUMBER   PIC X(5).
9000            03  SUPPLIER-NAME        PIC X(20).
9100            03  SUPPLIER-ADDRESS     PIC X(20).
9200
9300    01  MAJOR-HEADING.
9400        02  FILLER             PIC X(50) VALUE SPACES.
9500        02  FILLER             PIC X(14) VALUE "PURCHASE ORDER".
9600
9700    01  MINOR-HEADING.
9800        02 FILLER              PIC X(11) VALUE "SUPPLIER".
9900        02 FILLER              PIC X(6) VALUE SPACES.
10000       02 FILLER              PIC X(8) VALUE "ITEM NUM".
10100       02 FILLER              PIC X(4) VALUE SPACES.
10200       02 FILLER              PIC X(16) VALUE "ITEM DESCRIPTION".
10300       02 FILLER              PIC X(4) VALUE SPACES.
10400       02 FILLER              PIC X(9) VALUE "ITEM COST".
10500       02 FILLER              PIC X(6) VALUE SPACES.
10600       02 FILLER              PIC X(8) VALUE "QUANTITY".
10700       02 FILLER              PIC X(2) VALUE SPACES.
10800       02 FILLER              PIC X(13) VALUE "SUPPLIER NAME".
10900       02 FILLER              PIC X(14) VALUE  SPACES.
11000       02 FILLER              PIC X(16) VALUE "SUPPLIER ADDRESS".
11100
```

Program 12.3 (continued)

```
11200     01  DETAIL-LINE.
11300         02  FILLER                   PIC X(5) VALUE SPACES.
11400         02  DL-SUPPLIER-ID-NUMBER    PIC X(5).
11500         02  FILLER                   PIC X(10) VALUE SPACES.
11600         02  DL-ITEM-NUMBER           PIC X(5).
11700         02  FILLER                   PIC X(8) VALUE SPACES.
11800         02  DL-ITEM-DESCRIPTION      PIC X(10).
11900         02  FILLER                   PIC X(7) VALUE SPACES.
12000         02  DL-ITEM-COST             PIC 999.99.
12100         02  FILLER                   PIC X(10) VALUE SPACES.
12200         02  DL-ORDER-QUANTITY        PIC 9(3).
12300         02  FILLER                   PIC X(5) VALUE SPACES.
12400         02  DL-SUPPLIER-NAME         PIC X(20).
12500         02  FILLER                   PIC X(5) VALUE SPACES.
12600         02  DL-SUPPLIER-ADDRESS      PIC X(20).
12700
12800     PROCEDURE DIVISION.
12900
13000     1000-MAIN-LOGIC.
13100
13200         PERFORM 2000-READ-LOAD-TABLE.
13300         PERFORM 3000-INITIALIZATION.
13400         PERFORM 4000-SEARCH-READ
13500             UNTIL EOF-FLAG-PRR = "YES".
13600         PERFORM 9000-TERMINATION.
13700         STOP RUN.
13800
13900     2000-READ-LOAD-TABLE.
14000
14100         PERFORM 2100-INITIALIZE-TABLE
14200             VARYING INDX FROM 1 BY 1
14300                 UNTIL INDX > TABLE-SIZE.
14400         OPEN INPUT SUPPLIER-MASTER-FILE.
14500         READ SUPPLIER-MASTER-FILE
14600             AT END MOVE "YES" TO EOF-FLAG-SMF.
14700         PERFORM 2200-LOAD-TABLE
14800             UNTIL EOF-FLAG-SMF = "YES".
14900         CLOSE SUPPLIER-MASTER-FILE.
15000
15100     2100-INITIALIZE-TABLE.
15200
15300         MOVE SPACES TO SUPPLIER-ENTRY (INDX).
15400
15500     2200-LOAD-TABLE.
15600
15700         DIVIDE SUPPLIER-ID-NUMBER-SMR-NUM BY TABLE-SIZE
15800             GIVING QUOT REMAINDER INDX.
15900         ADD 1 TO INDX.
16000         MOVE "CONTINUE" TO SEARCH-FLAG.
16100         PERFORM 2300-PLACE-ELEMENT-IN-TABLE
16200             UNTIL SEARCH-FLAG NOT = "CONTINUE".
16300         READ SUPPLIER-MASTER-FILE
16400             AT END MOVE "YES" TO EOF-FLAG-SMF.
16500
```

Program 12.3 *(continued)*

```
16600        2300-PLACE-ELEMENT-IN-TABLE.
16700
16800            IF SUPPLIER-ID-NUMBER (INDX) = SPACES
16900                MOVE SUPPLIER-MASTER-RECORD
17000                    TO SUPPLIER-ENTRY (INDX)
17100                MOVE "FINISH" TO SEARCH-FLAG
17200            ELSE
17300                ADD 1 TO INDX
17400                    IF INDX > TABLE-SIZE
17500                        MOVE 1 TO INDX
17600                    ELSE
17700                        NEXT SENTENCE.
17800
17900        3000-INITIALIZATION.
18000
18100            OPEN INPUT PURCHASE-REQUEST-FILE
18200                OUTPUT PRINTED-DETAIL-FILE.
18300            READ PURCHASE-REQUEST-FILE
18400                AT END MOVE "YES" TO EOF-FLAG-PRR.
18500            MOVE MAJOR-HEADING TO OUTPUT-RECORD.
18600            WRITE OUTPUT-RECORD AFTER PAGE.
18700            MOVE MINOR-HEADING TO OUTPUT-RECORD.
18800            WRITE OUTPUT-RECORD AFTER 2.
18900
19000        4000-SEARCH-READ.
19100
19200            DIVIDE SUPPLIER-ID-NUMBER-PRR-NUM BY TABLE-SIZE
19300                GIVING QUOT REMAINDER X.
19400            ADD 1 TO X.
19500            MOVE "CONTINUE" TO SEARCH-FLAG.
19600            PERFORM 5300-SEARCH UNTIL SEARCH-FLAG NOT EQUAL "CONTINUE".
19700            IF SEARCH-FLAG = "FOUND"
19800                MOVE SUPPLIER-ID-NUMBER-PRR
19900                    TO DL-SUPPLIER-ID-NUMBER
20000                MOVE ITEM-NUMBER-PRR
20100                    TO DL-ITEM-NUMBER
20200                MOVE ITEM-DESCRIPTION-PRR
20300                    TO DL-ITEM-DESCRIPTION
20400                MOVE ITEM-COST-PRR
20500                    TO DL-ITEM-COST
20600                MOVE ORDER-QUANTITY-PRR
20700                    TO DL-ORDER-QUANTITY
20800                MOVE SUPPLIER-NAME (X)
20900                    TO DL-SUPPLIER-NAME
21000                MOVE SUPPLIER-ADDRESS (X)
21100                    TO DL-SUPPLIER-ADDRESS
21200                MOVE DETAIL-LINE TO OUTPUT-RECORD
21300                WRITE OUTPUT-RECORD AFTER 2
21400            ELSE
21500                PERFORM 6100-NOT-PRESENT.
21600            READ PURCHASE-REQUEST-FILE AT END MOVE "YES" TO EOF-FLAG-PRR.
21700
```

Program 12.3 (continued)

```
21800      5300-SEARCH.
21900
22000          IF SUPPLIER-ID-NUMBER (X) = SUPPLIER-ID-NUMBER-PRR
22100             MOVE "FOUND" TO SEARCH-FLAG
22200          ELSE
22300            IF SUPPLIER-ID-NUMBER (X) = SPACES
22400               MOVE "NOT PRESENT" TO SEARCH-FLAG
22500            ELSE
22600              ADD 1 TO X
22700                  IF X > TABLE-SIZE
22800                     MOVE 1 TO X
22900                  ELSE
23000                      NEXT SENTENCE.
23100
23200      6100-NOT-PRESENT.
23300
23400          EXIT.
23500
23600      9000-TERMINATION.
23700
23800          CLOSE PURCHASE-REQUEST-FILE
23900                PRINTED-DETAIL-FILE.
```

12.7   COMPARISON OF TABLE ORGANIZATION AND SEARCH TECHNIQUES

Five table organization and search techniques have been described in this chapter:

1) Direct Access
2) Exhaustive Search
3) Sequential Search of a Sequenced Table
4) Binary Search
5) Randomized Tables

These methods can be compared in terms of their relative capabilities and efficiency. In general, a programmer should use the most efficient method appropriate for a given program. Figure 12.15 gives a summary of relevant information with respect to each of these methods and can be used to help make the best decision. Figure 12.16 shows a graph of the average behavior expected of the five techniques in determining that an argument is not present in the table.

Analysis of Figures 12.15 and 12.16 leads to the following conclusions:

1) The Direct Access technique is the most efficient and is the method of choice when it is appropriate.
2) If data is sequenced and must remain so, the binary search is the most efficient method in all respects and is the method of choice.
3) If sufficient memory is available and fast table access is important, a randomized table is the best method.
4) Exhaustive search is the least efficient method and should be used only if no other method is appropriate.

Figure 12.15   Comparison of table organization/search techniques for a table of n elements

Method	Worst Case Number Repetitions		Expected Average Number of Repetitions		Considerations
	Find an argument	Argument not present	Find an argument	Argument not present	
Direct Access	1	1	1	1	Requires a one-to-one correspondence between table arguments and positions.
Exhaustive Search	n	n	n/2	n	Least efficient technique but requires minimum storage and no sequencing of data.
Sequential Search	n	n	n/2	n/2	Requires sequenced table arguments.
Binary Search	smallest integer greater than $\log_2 n$	smallest integer greater than $\log_2 n$	less than $\log_2 n$	less than $\log_2 n$	Requires sequenced table arguments.
Randomized Table	n*	n*	close to 1	close to 1	Requires more table space than actual table size. Efficiency depends on fullness and hash function. Sequence of data is destroyed.

* Worst case behavior will result when the table is full

12.8   SEARCH, SEARCH ALL, AND SET STATEMENTS

Many versions of COBOL include the SEARCH ALL and SEARCH statements to perform searching. In order to use these statements, you must include the INDEXED and KEY clauses in the OCCURS clause, which is used to define the table. The general form of the OCCURS clause with these options is shown in Figure 12.17.

The data names specified in the KEY clause must be data fields within the table itself. The table must be organized into ASCENDING or DESCENDING sequence based on the key fields. The *index-name* used in the INDEXED clause will be used by the SEARCH statement in its search of the table. The *index-name* must not be defined elsewhere in the program, since further definition of this *index-name* will be handled by the compiler automatically.

Figure 12.18 shows a table of product numbers (the table arguments) and product descriptions (the table values) set up for application of a SEARCH verb.

The SEARCH ALL statement is used to perform a search of the table entries until a desired condition has been satisfied. The general form of the SEARCH ALL statement is shown in Figure 12.19. Although the ANSI specifications for

Figure 12.16 Expected average number of repetitions in determining that an argument is not present

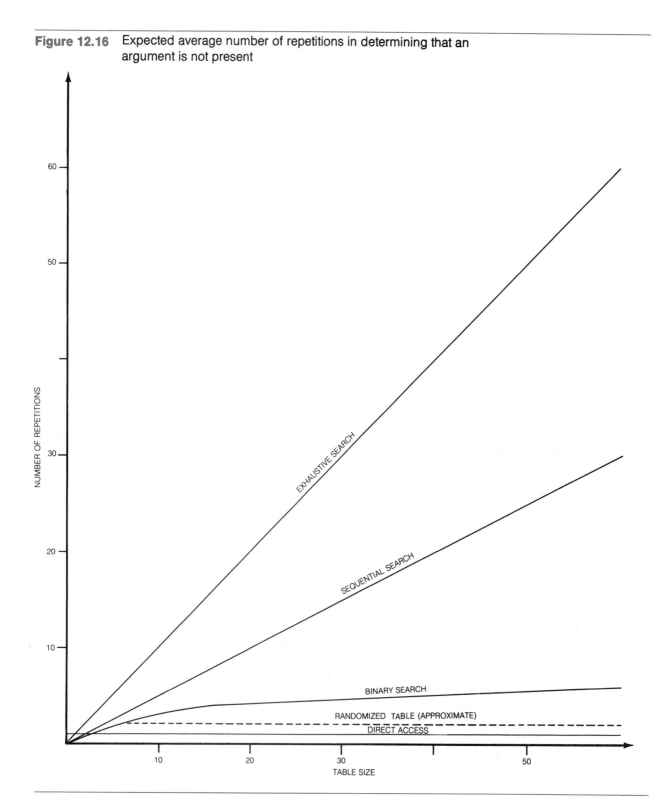

COBOL do not specify the type of procedure to be used in implementing SEARCH ALL, most compilers use a binary search which is the most efficient procedure available.

The conditions specified in the WHEN clause are tested for successive values of the table index. When the condition is satisfied, the statement following the condition is executed. The condition must *not* be complex; it

Figure 12.17 General form of the OCCURS clause with the KEY clause

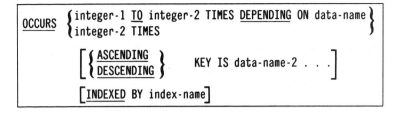

Figure 12.18 Definition of PRODUCT-TABLE for application of SEARCH verb

```
01  TABLE-CONSTANTS.
    03  FILLER PIC X(5) VALUE "0134A".
    03  FILLER PIC X(20) VALUE "JACKET, SPORT".
    03  FILLER PIC X(5) VALUE "3142X".
    03  FILLER PIC X(20) VALUE "MEN'S SHIRT".
        .
        .
        .
01  PRODUCT-TABLE REDEFINES TABLE-CONSTANTS.
    03  PRODUCT-TABLE-ENTRY OCCURS 50 TIMES
            ASCENDING KEY IS TABLE-PRODUCT-NO
            INDEXED BY TABLE-INDEX.
        05  TABLE-PRODUCT-NO        PIC X(5).
        05  TABLE-PRODUCT-DESCRIPTION PIC X(20).
```

Figure 12.19 General form of the SEARCH ALL statement

```
SEARCH ALL      data-name-1   [AT END statement-1]
    WHEN       {data-name-2   {IS EQUAL TO}  value-1}
               {               {IS =       }         }
               {condition-name-1                     }

        [      {data-name-3   {IS EQUAL TO}  value-2}]  . . .
        [ AND  {               {IS =       }         }]
        [      {condition-name-2                     }]

        {statement-2   }
        {NEXT SENTENCE }
```

must test for equality of the key field to some value. If the system searches the
entire table without finding the condition to be satisfied, the statement in the
AT END clause is executed. The programmer need not initialize or modify the
table index variable; the SEARCH ALL statement performs these tasks
automatically. For example, the search procedure to locate data in
PRODUCT-TABLE, defined in Figure 12.18, could be coded as follows:

```
SEARCH ALL PRODUCT-TABLE-ENTRY
    AT END MOVE "INVALID PRODUCT"
          TO PRODUCT-DESCRIPTION
    WHEN PRODUCT-NO = TABLE-PRODUCT-NO (TABLE-INDEX)
          MOVE TABLE-PRODUCT-DESCRIPTION (TABLE-INDEX)
          TO PRODUCT-DESCRIPTION.
```

A flowchart showing how the general SEARCH ALL statement is executed is shown in Figure 12.20, and the SEARCH ALL example is illustrated in Figure 12.21.

It is convenient to use the table index (the variable specified in the INDEXED BY clause) when referencing elements of the table for purposes of placing data in the table or modifying data in the table. However, the index name cannot be modified by the usual arithmetic operation statements used for other COBOL data names. An index name may be initialized only by the SET statement, which has the general form shown in Figure 12.22. An index name is defined in an INDEXED BY clause or by specifyng USAGE IS INDEX.

The value may be an integer constant, another index name or a data name having an integer value. For example, the index name TABLE-INDEX in the previous example could be initialized to value 1 by the statement:

```
SET TABLE-INDEX TO 1.
```

An index variable may be incremented (or decremented) by the SET statement, the general form of which is shown in Figure 3.25.

For example, the statement

```
SET TABLE-INDEX UP BY 1.
```

would cause the value 1 to be added to TABLE-INDEX. The statement

```
SET TABLE-INDEX DOWN BY 2.
```

would cause 2 to be subtracted from TABLE-INDEX.

Figure 12.20   Flowchart of SEARCH ALL

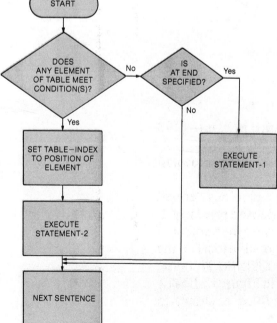

Figure 12.21 Flowchart of SEARCH ALL example

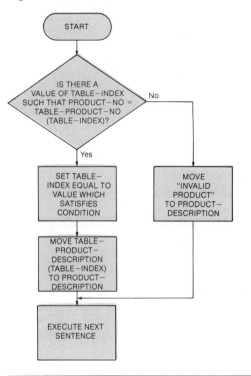

Figure 12.22 General form of the SET/TO statement

```
SET index-name. . .TO value.
```

Figure 12.23 General form of the SET UP/DOWN statement

```
SET index-name. . . { UP BY  }  value.
                     { DOWN BY }
```

Example

Suppose that 50 product numbers and descriptions defined in Figure 12.18 are to be loaded into the table from a file, rather than being coded as constants into the DATA division of the program. The program segment shown in Figure 12.24 will perform this task.

It is improbable that this table would contain such a precisely defined number of entries, however, as products are added and deleted regularly. It would be unfortunate to have to recompile a program because the number of products changed, and indeed this is not necessary. It is possible to set up the table to contain a variable number of entries using the DEPENDING ON clause. The table in Figure 12.18 could now be defined as shown in Figure 12.25. The routine to load the data into the table must next be modified, as shown in Figure 12.26.

Figure 12.24   Loading PRODUCT—TABLE from a data file

```
3000-LOAD-TABLE SECTION.
3010-LOAD-CONTROL.
    SET TABLE-INDEX TO 0.
    OPEN INPUT PRODUCT-TABLE-FILE.
    READ PRODUCT-TABLE-FILE
        AT END MOVE "YES" TO EOF-FLAG.
    PERFORM 3020-LOAD-READ UNTIL
        EOF-FLAG = "YES" OR TABLE-INDEX = 50.
    IF EOF-FLAG NOT = "YES" OR TABLE-INDEX < 50
        PERFORM 3030-LOAD-ERROR.
    GO TO 3040-LOAD-EXIT.
3020-LOAD-READ.
    SET TABLE-INDEX UP BY 1.
    MOVE PRODUCT-TABLE-RECORD TO
        PRODUCT-TABLE-ENTRY (TABLE-INDEX).
    READ PRODUCT-TABLE-FILE
        AT END MOVE "YES" TO EOF-FLAG.
3030-LOAD-ERROR.
    EXIT.
3040-LOAD-EXIT.
    EXIT.
```

Figure 12.25   Alternate definition of PRODUCT—TABLE

```
01   NUMBER-OF-PRODUCTS PIC 999 VALUE 0.
01   PRODUCT-TABLE.
     03   PRODUCT-TABLE-ENTRY
          OCCURS 1 TO 999 TIMES
              DEPENDING ON NUMBER-OF-PRODUCTS
          ASCENDING KEY IS TABLE-PRODUCT-NO
          INDEXED BY TABLE-INDEX.
```

The general form of the SEARCH statement is shown in Figure 12.27. The SEARCH statement is similar in many respects to the SEARCH ALL statement; however, there is one essential difference. The SEARCH ALL statement includes a provision to initialize the index automatically, while the SEARCH statement does not include this feature. When using the SEARCH verb, the programmer must initialize the index prior to execution of the SEARCH statement. Another difference between the SEARCH ALL and SEARCH statements is that, in SEARCH statements, conditions may be simple or complex and may involve inequalities as well as equality. As with the SEARCH ALL statement, the SEARCH statement provides for automatic incrementing of the index and automatic execution statements in the AT END clause if the value of the index exceeds the number of elements in the table. Figure 12.28 illustrates a flowchart of the execution of the SEARCH statement.

Figure 12.26 Alternate PRODUCT—TABLE load procedure

```
3100-LOAD-TABLE SECTION.
3110-LOAD-CONTROL.
    SET TABLE-INDEX TO 0.
    OPEN INPUT PRODUCT-TABLE-FILE.
    READ PRODUCT-TABLE-FILE
        AT END MOVE "YES" TO EOF-FLAG.
    PERFORM 3120-LOAD-READ UNTIL
        EOF-FLAG = "YES" OR NUMBER-OF-PRODUCTS = 999.
    IF EOF-FLAG NOT = "YES"
        PERFORM 3130-LOAD-ERROR.
    GO TO 3140-LOAD-EXIT.
3120-LOAD-READ.
    SET TABLE-INDEX UP BY 1.
    ADD 1 TO NUMBER-OF-PRODUCTS.
    MOVE PRODUCT-TABLE-RECORD TO
        PRODUCT-TABLE-ENTRY (TABLE-INDEX).
    READ PRODUCT-TABLE-FILE
        AT END MOVE "YES" TO EOF-FLAG.
3130-LOAD-ERROR.
    EXIT.
3140-LOAD-EXIT.
    EXIT.
```

Figure 12.27 General form of the SEARCH statement

```
SEARCH data-name    [AT END statement-1]
   {WHEN condition-1 { statement-2  }} . . .
                     { NEXT SENTENCE }
```

Figure 12.28 Flowchart of the SEARCH statement

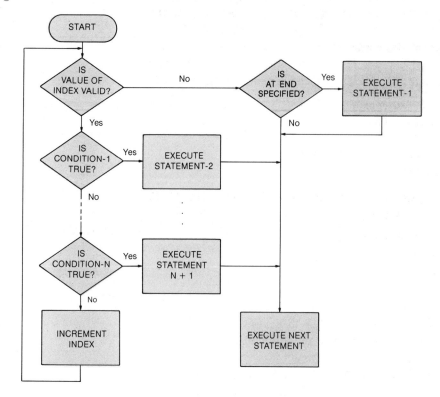

Figure 12.29 Deduction table

Miles Driven	Deduction Amount
Under 3,000	$ 8
3,000 under 4,000	14
4,000 under 5,000	19
5,000 under 6,000	23
6,000 under 7,000	27
7,000 under 8,000	31
8,000 under 9,000	35
9,000 under 10,000 . . .	39
10,000 under 11,000 . . .	43
11,000 under 12,000 . . .	48
12,000 under 13,000 . . .	51
13,000 under 14,000 . . .	56
14,000 under 15,000 . . .	60
15,000 under 16,000 . . .	64
16,000 under 17,000 . . .	68
17,000 under 18,000 . . .	72
18,000 under 19,000 . . .	76
19,000 under 20,000 . . .	81
20,000*	83

*For over 20,000 miles, use table amounts for total miles driven. For example, for 25,000 miles, add the deduction for 5,000 to the deduction for 20,000 miles.

For example, let's use the SEARCH statement to look up the tax deduction permitted by the IRS for gasoline tax at five cents per gallon (Figure 12.29).

The code required to set up the table is:

```
01   TAX-TABLE.
     02   TAX-ENTRY OCCURS 18 TIMES
          ASCENDING KEY IS BREAK-MILEAGE
          INDEXED BY TAX-TABLE-INDEX.
          03   LOW-MILEAGE   PIC 9(5).
          03   BREAK-MILEAGE PIC 9(5).
          03   DEDUCTION-AMT PIC 9(3).
```

The code required to compute the deduction allow (MILEAGE-DEDUCTION) for the number of miles driven (MILEAGE) is:

```
DIVIDE MILEAGE BY 20000 GIVING MULTIPLIER
     REMAINDER LOOK-UP-FACTOR.
SET TAX-TABLE-INDEX TO 1.
SEARCH TAX-ENTRY
     WHEN LOOK-UP-FACTOR > LOW-MILEAGE (TAX-TABLE-INDEX)
          OR LOOK-UP-FACTOR = LOW-MILEAGE (TAX-TABLE-INDEX)
          AND LOOK-UP-FACTOR < BREAK-MILEAGE (TAX-TABLE-INDEX)
     COMPUTE MILEAGE-DEDUCTION =
          MULTIPLIER * 83 + DEDUCTION-AMT (TAX-TABLE-INDEX).
```

Note that when MILEAGE is less than 20,000, the value of MULTIPLIER will be zero, so the value of MILEAGE-DEDUCTION will be computed as 0 * 83 plus the appropriate value from the TAX-TABLE. When MILEAGE has a value greater than 20,000, an appropriate multiple of 83 will be added to the value from the TAX-TABLE.

12.9   DEBUG CLINIC

Some COBOL compilers permit the use of a standard debugging facility that can be of considerable value in providing diagnostic output. When the debug facility is available, the programmer places a D in position 7 of any program line that is a part of the diagnostic procedure. The compiler ordinarily will omit any line coded with a D in position 7; in order to include such lines in the compiled program, the clause WITH DEBUGGING MODE must be included in the SOURCE-COMPUTER paragraph of the ENVIRONMENT DIVISION (see Figure 12.30). If this clause is omitted, lines of the program that contain a D in position 7 are treated as comments; they are included in the program listing but not translated into the object program. If the clause is included, debug lines are translated as a part of the object program. Without the debug facility, it is necessary to remove references to diagnostic output from a program after the program is debugged. Using the debug facility enables the programmer to include or omit diagnostic output from a program by changing only the SOURCE-COMPUTER paragraph.

Figure 12.30 Debug example

COBOL CODING FORM

PROGRAM | REQUESTED BY | PAGE 1 OF 2
PROGRAMMER | DATE | IDENT. 73 80

```
PAGE LINE
NO.  NO.  A   B
     01      IDENTIFICATION DIVISION.
     02       .
     03       .
     04       .
     05      ENVIRONMENT DIVISION.
     06      CONFIGURATION SECTION.
     07      SOURCE-COMPUTER. computer-name WITH DEBUG MODE.
     08       .
     09       .
     10       .
     11      DATA DIVISION.
     12       .
     13       .
     14       .
     15    D 01  DIAGNOSTIC-LINE.
     16    D        03 FILLER PIC X(3) VALUE "X =".
     17    D        03 X-OUT  PIC 9(5).
     18    D        03 FILLER PIC X(3) VALUE "Y =".
     19    D        03 Y-OUT  PIC 9(5).
     20       .
```

Boyd & Fraser Publishing Co.

COBOL CODING FORM

PROGRAM | REQUESTED BY | PAGE 2 OF 2
PROGRAMMER | DATE | IDENT. 73 80

```
PAGE LINE
NO.  NO.  A   B
     01      PROCEDURE DIVISION.
     02       .
     03       .
     04       .
     05    D        PERFORM DIAGNOSTIC-OUTPUT.
     06             COMPUTE TABL (X, Y) = . . .
     07       .
     08       .
     09       .
     10    D DIAGNOSTIC-OUTPUT.
     11    D        MOVE X TO X-OUT.
     12    D        MOVE Y TO Y-OUT.
     13    D        WRITE PRINT-LINE FROM DIAGNOSTIC-LINE AFTER 1.
     14       .
     15       .
     16       .
```

12.10 SELF-TEST EXERCISES

1. For a year to be a leap year, two conditions must be met:
   a. The year must be divisible by 4.
   b. If the year is divisible by 100, it must also be divisible by 400.

   Modify the code of Figure 12.3 to take leap years into consideration.
   Hint: On the average, a year has 365¼ days.

2. Revise the code of Program 12.1 to use
   a. the SEARCH ALL statement
   b. the SEARCH statement

3. Write pseudocode for a binary search to locate data in the table of Figure 12.29.

4. Construct tables similar to those of Figures 12.10 and 12.11, showing the steps involved in locating ACTUAL-ARGUMENT 115 and 3.

5. A randomized table containing 7 elements is to be formed containing the following data:

   6, 19, 23, 20

   Show the placement of the data in the table. How does the placement change if data is loaded in the following order:

   20, 6, 19, 23

6. For each of the five techniques shown in Figure 12.15, compare the expected average number of repetitions to find that an argument is not present for $n = 10, 50, 100, 500, 1000, 5,000, 10,000$. Comment on the sequential search and binary search techniques as the value of n increases.

7. Compare the relative advantages and disadvantages of the five table organization and access techniques described in this chapter.

8. Which table organization and access technique would be most appropriate in each of the following situations? Defend your answers.
   a. A table of part numbers and associated unit prices has been established. An inquiry supplies the part number and the program looks up the unit price. Some numbers are referenced constantly, while others are rarely used.
   b. A 50-element table has been established associating the two-character abbreviation with the state name (sample entry TX TEXAS). The program must supply the full state name in response to the code.
   c. A table associating UPC (Universal Product Code) and a product description and unit price has been established. The table is to be used in an on-line inquiry system such as a supermarket check-out system, in which the optimum response time is a critical factor. The computer contains more than enough memory to accommodate program and table.

9. What will happen if the procedure described in Figure 12.14 is used when the table is full?

10. a. Write a COBOL procedure to load a sequenced table from a data file. Relevant DATA DIVISION entries are:

```
SELECT TABLE-FILE ASSIGN TO DISK.
        .
        .
        .
FD TABLE-FILE
   LABEL RECORDS ARE STANDARD.
01  TABLE-RECORD.
    05  TABLE-ARGUMENT-TR PIC 9(6).
    05  TABLE-VALUE-TR    PIC X(20).
        .
        .
        .
01  TABLE-DATA.
    05  TABLE-ENTRY OCCURS 1 TO 100 TIMES
                DEPENDING ON NUM-ENTRY.
        10  TABLE-ARGUMENT PIC 9(6).
        10  TABLE-VALUE    PIC X(20).
01  NUM-ENTRY PIC 999 VALUE 0.
```

    b. Modify the table definition given above to permit the use of the SEARCH ALL statement, assuming that the table is organized in ascending sequence.

    c. Write a COBOL procedure using a SEARCH ALL statement to locate the TABLE-VALUE corresponding to the content of ACTUAL-ARGUMENT. If the value exists, move it to OUTPUT-VALUE; otherwise, move spaces to OUTPUT-VALUE.

12.11 PROGRAMMING EXERCISES

1. Write a program to load the table of Figure 12.19 from a data file and process a representative sample of actual mileage values. Write versions of your program using each of the following access techniques:

> Sequential Search
> Binary Search
> SEARCH verb

Compare the execution time for each program.

Note: it may take a fairly large sample data file to be able to observe differences in execution time. If you are unable to see differences in execution time at first, increase the size of the sample data file.

2. Write a program to create a randomized table of 100 different values of your choice for a sequence of table sizes. Keep track of the number of collisions encountered when the size of the table equals 103, 113, 131, 151, 163, 173, 181, 191, 193. What happens to the number of collisions as the table size increases? Is there a point at which the decline becomes pronounced?

3. In the ABC Hamburgers, Inc., accounting system (see Section 12.1), a program is needed to summarize sales by product type for each store. The output should be one page for each store with a line for each item, containing:

> Product code
> Product description
> Units sold
> Gross revenue generated by product

A summary line containing total revenue for each store is also required. Two data files are to be processed:

PRODUCT-ID-FILE (see Figure 12.2)

and

SALES-FILE

Each record in SALES-FILE contains the following fields:

Store identification (5 digits)
Product code (3 characters)
Units sold
Selling price each

The sales file is in sequence by store identification number, but *not* by product code.

Write a program to produce this report. Use the table access method of your choice.

4. ABC Hamburgers, Inc., management requires a report showing the status of each account in its accounts receivable system. A data file is available with records containing the following fields:

Account identification
Balance due (may be credit balance or zero)
Date of last payment (zero if new account)

An account is considered current if the balance due is positive and a payment has been made within the last 30 days. An account is considered in arrears if the balance due is positive and the last payment was made more than 30 days previously. A new account is considered current if the balance due is zero or a credit, or if the balance due is positive and the date of first purchase is within 30 days of the current date. The report should list each account and flag those that are in arrears. For those that are in arrears, the report should list one of the following messages, depending on the age of the account.

31 TO 60 DAYS
61 TO 90 DAYS
91 TO 120 DAYS
MORE THAN 120 DAYS

5. Write a program for XYZ College registration system to generate trial schedules for students. Registration records listing section numbers that the student desires to take are submitted. Each registration record contains the following data:

Student number (9 digits)
Student name (20 characters)
Section requests (3 digits each)

(From 1 to 10 section requests may be included on each record.) The program must list trial schedule, including for each section the following data:

Student name
Student number
Section number
Course number
Course description
Hours
Days
Credits

Two files are available:

> Section master file
> Course master file

Each record in the Section Master File contains the following entries;

> Section number (3 digits)
> Course number (6 digits)
> Days
> Times

The file is in sequence by section number. Each record in the Course Master File contains:

> Course number (6 characters)
> Course description (20 characters)
> Credits (2 digits)

The file is in sequence by course number. The program should load each of these files into appropriate tables. For each section in which a student desires enrollment, the program must reference the tables in order to look up the required information.

6. A program is required to produce student grade summary reports. Two files are available:
   1) TABLE-FILE contains (in course number sequence) the course number, department number, course name and number of credits.
   2) STUDENT-GRADE contains grades for each course a student has taken and in sequence by student number. Each record contains:

   > STUDENT-ID (9 digits)
   > COURSE-NUMBER (7 characters)
   > GRADE (1 character)
   > TERM-DATE (4 characters)

   Your report should list each course taken, credits and grade. It should also compute and print each student's Grade Point Average (GPA). (Use the scheme employed at your college to compute GPA.) Four versions of this program are required:
   1) Use a sequential search of a sequenced table to perform table look-up.
   2) Use a binary search to perform table look-up.
   3) Use a hash table technique to perform table look-up.
   4) Use a SEARCH or SEARCH ALL statement to perform table look-up.

SEQUENTIAL FILE MAINTENANCE 13

13.1 OVERVIEW OF FILE-ORIENTED SYSTEMS

Most data processing systems make extensive use of files for data storage. Indeed, the success or failure of a system often may be traced to the skill with which the files are designed and maintained. The choice of file organization and content is one of the most basic choices to be made in designing a system. Systems are designed around two basic types of files: master and transaction. Master files, in general, contain basic data about each entity in the system (a part, a person, an order, etc.) Transaction files contain data about changes or other activity as they relate to the entities in the system. For example, in a personnel system, the transaction file would store specific data about leave taken, hours worked, address changes, and so on. Transaction files may be regarded as relatively temporary storage vehicles, whereas a master file may be thought of as relatively permanent storage for summaries of the transactions that have occurred.

File Maintenance

Two basic problems must be solved in any data processing system: file maintenance and information reporting. Reporting information involves access to one or more files that contain data of interest. The program (or other access mechanism) lists, counts, accumulates, selects, computes, and produces the desired information. Most of the COBOL programs you have written thus far have probably been of this type.

The file maintenance task, on the other hand, involves manipulating data stored in the system's files. Programs that perform file maintenance must take into consideration the following types of activities that may need to be performed:

- addition—records must be added to the file.
- deletion—records must be removed from the file.
- change—one or more fields within a record must be changed.

Some people distinguish between file maintenance and file updating. File maintenance is the periodic nonroutine process of adding and deleting records and correcting errors by changing fields within records. File updating is the routine processing of transactions that cause changes in one or more fields in a record. For purposes of this text, updating will be treated as a specific type of maintenance—changing the content of a field. The logic required to perform this task is the same whether changes are made routinely or nonroutinely.

Both master files and transaction files must be maintained. In maintaining a master file relating to the employees of a company, for example, it is necessary to be able to add records as new employees are hired, remove records when employees leave, and change any item of information contained in any employee's record to reflect changes in the employee's job, place of residence, income-tax withholding status and so on. Transaction files must also be maintained. The most common type of maintenance is to add records to the file, but it may also be necessary to delete a transaction or change an existing transaction if an error is found.

File maintenance may be performed in two distinctly different computing environments: batch and interactive. In a batch environment, transactions are accumulated over a period of time and then used to update appropriate files. In an interactive environment, transactions are usually processed immediately to update the relevant files.

In interactive systems, transaction files may not be maintained, or they may be maintained for archival purposes only. Many systems (like Amalgamated Custom Design's system) use a mixture of interactive and batch concepts. Some maintenance is performed in an interactive manner (e.g., Raw Materials Master, Work in Progress Master), while other maintenance is performed in a batch mode (e.g., New Order Processing, Order Update).

Backups

Regardless of the type of computing environment, one problem must be confronted in any system design: How can the system recover in the event of user operation error, equipment malfunction, sabotage, or natural disaster? Detailed plans need to be made for all of these contingencies. One tool that is often used in these plans is the *backup* file, a copy of a file. The backup file may be stored in the same or different medium and at the same or different location. Quite often, levels of backups are maintained: recently created backups are stored at the computer center site, and older backups are stored in a separate location. Because they are compact and relatively inexpensive, tapes are often used for backups, even when original files are stored on disk.

The goal in planning for system malfunction is to be able to re-establish the system in its former state in a reasonable amount of time (and, it is to be hoped, at reasonable expense).

In a batch system, it is usually possible to load the most recently available version of the master files, re-create transaction files for transactions that have occurred since the last time the (backup) master file was updated, and run appropriate programs to perform the update.

In an interactive system, the process of re-creating transactions is made more difficult by the fact that the transactions are entered at keyboards and, often, there is no written record of the transaction. Usually these types of systems keep track of all transactions as they enter the system in a file that may be referred to as a *transaction log.* If something happens to destroy the current versions of the master file, the transaction log may be used to re-create all the changes that users have made since the backup was created. (The only transactions that are lost in such a system are transactions that have been entered by the user but not yet recorded by the system on the transaction log.)

Backups for both master and transaction files serve other purposes in data processing systems. Not only do they permit recovery in case of emergency, they also provide a record of the status of the system at specified intervals and a permanent record of all data the system has processed. This is very important in establishing an *audit trail* for auditors, who must certify that the system is indeed performing its functions correctly. Backups of this type are also important to enable programmers to determine the nature and source of errors in the system—and can be used to test new versions of the system prior to actual implementation.

Access Methods

Files may be accessed sequentially or randomly. In sequential access, records in the file may be processed in sequential order from first to last. The files you have been working with up until now have been accessed sequentially. In random access, records are made available for processing on demand; that is, the program may process any record in the file as needed, without having to process other records. Random access files are a very powerful tool, particularly in an interactive computing environment, because file updates can be performed very conveniently at the same time that transactions are entered. Sequential access to data is useful when the entire file must be processed from start to finish. In a batch system, file maintenance is often accomplished by sorting the transactions into the same sequence as the master file and processing records alternately from both files, proceeding sequentially from first to last.

Activity

A very important consideration in designing a file maintenance system is the amount of activity that is anticipated. Activity may be defined as the ratio of transaction records to master file records in a given time period. For example, suppose a master file contains 100 records and suppose there will be an average of 200 transactions per day to be processed. The activity ratio is $^{200}/_{100} = 2$. In other words, there will be on the average twice as many transactions as master file records. In another instance, one might anticipate 50 transactions per day in a system with 100 records in its master file. In this case, the activity ratio is $^{50}/_{100} = .5$: there will be half as many transactions as there are master file records.

The concept of activity is important because it may help in choosing whether to update a file randomly or sequentially. Updating randomly will create a heavier workload on the system than sequential updates because random access takes more time to execute than sequential access. Thus, *other things being equal*, it may be advantageous to use sequential updates in a system with high activity and random updates when activity is expected to be low. "Other things being equal," of course, covers a lot of ground. There are situations in which random updating is justified, even when activity is high, because random updating makes the updated record immediately available for further processing—a requirement in many interactive systems. Even when immediate updates are desirable, the overhead involved in random access may tax the abilities of a computer system, making immediate updating not feasible for that system.

Volatility

Activity includes transactions of all types—adding, changing, deleting. A related idea, *volatility,* is concerned only with adding and deleting records. Volatility is the ratio of additions and deletions to the number of records in the file. For example, if 50 additions and/or deletions are expected for a file initially containing 100 records, the volatility ratio is $^{50}/_{100} = .5$. A very static file has very few or no additions and deletions and an expected volatility ratio of close to zero.

Volatility affects the choice of file update technique. If random updating is being performed on a highly volatile file, the size of the file changes quite rapidly as records are added and removed. This process places demands on the secondary storage space and the operating system, which may adversely affect the performance of the system. Using sequential updating of a highly volatile file enables a more systematic, controlled expansion and contraction of the file space and thereby places less of a burden on the computing system resources.

COBOL offers three distinct file organization techniques:

- sequential
- indexed
- relative.

Each of these techniques offers advantages and limitations that make the choice of file organization a critical matter in the design of a data processing system. This chapter will cover sequential files; Chapter 14 treats indexed files, and Chapter 15 covers relative files.

13.2 ADVANTAGES AND LIMITATIONS OF SEQUENTIAL FILES

A *sequential* file is a file organization technique that enables access to the records from the first record to the second record, and so on to the end of the file. Each READ or WRITE to a sequential file causes the next record in the file to be read or written. Historically, sequential files were the first method used to store data for access by computers. The one-after-the-other access technique was motivated by the magnetic tapes that were used (and, of course, still are used) for data storage.

Because of the physical nature of the tape, sequential storage and access is the only practical technique available. When a disk is used for storage of a sequential file, the sequential access mechanism is maintained by the operating system. Insofar as the program is concerned, the physical medium used for storage of a file is immaterial; the important aspect of the file is the capability for sequential access that is enforced when a file is declared to be sequential.

Sequential files are, of course, limited by the fact that only the next record is available for processing. In order to access the fifth record in the file, it is necessary to read the first four, whether or not any processing is to be done on these records. However, sequential file organization does have some advantages over other file organization techniques when sequential access to the data is required by the program:

1) A sequential file can be reassigned from tape to disk, or vice versa, without affecting the logic of the program. Other file organization techniques generally require the random access capabilities of a disk.

2) Sequential file organization is usually simpler than other organization techniques and usually does not require the space for tables and directories needed by other file organization techniques.

3) Virtually all system software and every programming language has capabilities for handling sequential files; the same is not always true for other file organization techniques.

4) Processing time is usually faster with a sequential file than with files organized in other ways. This may become a critical concern with smaller computing systems or when large amounts of data must be stored and processed.

Even though other file organization techniques offer greater flexibility in access techniques, sequential files remain a very useful method for data storage and access.

13.3 REVIEW OF SEQUENTIAL FILE OPEN AND CLOSE

The OPEN statement causes the operating system to make a file available for processing. A file must be opened before any input or output operation can be performed on it. A sequential file can be opened in one of four modes: INPUT, OUTPUT, I-O and EXTEND (Figure 13.1).

Figure 13.1 General form of the OPEN statement

```
        ⎧  INPUT file-name    ⎡⎧ REVERSED       ⎫⎤ . . . ⎫
        ⎪                     ⎣⎩ WITH NO REWIND ⎭⎦        ⎪
OPEN   ⎨   OUTPUT file-name    [WITH NO REWIND]   . . .   ⎬
        ⎪  I-O file-name . . .                            ⎪
        ⎩  EXTEND file-name . . .                         ⎭
```

When a file is opened in INPUT mode, the records from the file are made available to the program one at a time from first to last. The file must exist on the device specified in the SELECT statement for the file. Two options exist for tape files opened in INPUT mode: WITH NO REWIND and REVERSED. Ordinarily, a tape reel is rewound from the take-up reel onto its original reel and positioned at the first record in the file when the file is opened. The WITH NO REWIND clause can be used when a reel of tape contains more than one file and you want to open the second file, or subsequent files, on that tape. When the first file is closed, the tape must not be rewound; the reel must be left in position for the next file to be opened. The REVERSED option will cause the file to be positioned at its last record and read in reverse order from last to first. These options are ignored if the file is assigned to a disk. The REVERSED and NO REWIND options are not included in all COBOL compilers.

When a file is opened in OUTPUT mode, the file is assumed to have no data records in it. If records already were present in the file, opening it for OUTPUT would destroy them. WRITE statements cause records to be placed in the file sequentially from first to last. The WITH NO REWIND clause has the same effect in the OUTPUT mode as it does in the INPUT mode.

When a file is opened in I-0 (Input-Output) mode, it is assumed to exist and may be processed by READ and REWRITE statements. The REWRITE statement will cause the content of a record that has been read (and perhaps changed by the processing program) to be rewritten, destroying the content of the original. This mode can be used for disk files only; it is not valid for tape files.

When a file is opened in EXTEND mode, the operating system locates the last record in the file; any record written in the file will follow that record. EXTEND mode may not be implemented on all compilers.

The CLOSE statement terminates processing of a file. The file must be open at the time of execution of a CLOSE statement. After a file has been closed, no further input or output operations may be executed. A general form of the CLOSE statements is shown in Figure 13.2.

Figure 13.2   General form of the CLOSE statement

```
CLOSE file-name  [WITH {NO REWIND}] ...
                        {LOCK     }
```

When a file is assigned to tape, the NO REWIND clause will prevent the reel of tape from being repositioned at the beginning of the file. Otherwise, rewinding is automatically performed as part of the CLOSE operation if the NO REWIND clause is omitted.

The LOCK option will prevent the current program (or any subsequent program in the job) from reopening the file. The LOCK option should be invoked if it would be an error for any further processing of the file to take place. In some operating systems the LOCK phrase has the additional function of causing the file to become permanent, if the file is being created by this program. For these operating systems, a file will be purged from the disk at the end of the program unless the LOCK option is used.

13.4   MERGING

Often it is necessary to merge two sequentially organized files of similar data to create one file in proper sequence that contains all the data from the original two files. Both files must be sorted into the same sequence based on the same key field. A procedure to perform this task is illustrated in Figure 13.3. Data from TRANSACTION-FILE is to be merged with OLD-MASTER-FILE to create NEW-MASTER-FILE.

In order to maintain sequence in the output file, one record from each of the two input files is read. The record with the smaller key field value is written to the output file, and the next record is read from the appropriate file. This process is repeated until end-of-file is reached on both the TRANSACTION-FILE and the OLD-MASTER-FILE.

The key field for each file is used to enable the program to continue processing until end-of-file has been reached on both files. When end-of-file is reached on either of the input files, a high value is moved to the key field for that file. This value is chosen to be the largest value that can be stored in the key field. Processing continues until both key fields have the high value. This method makes it unnecessary to have separate logic within the program to handle the remaining records on one file when end-of-file has been reached on the other.

For example, if end-of-file is reached on the old master file, the value of *old master key* will become the high value. As this is the largest value that can be contained in the field, all values of *transaction key* must be less than *old master key,* which will result in the transaction record being selected for output each time. When end-of-file is finally reached on TRANSACTION-FILE, the value of *transaction key* will become the high value and the procedure will terminate.

Note that it is possible to create a new file with records having key fields with equal values. This condition may or may not be an error, depending on the particular application.

The following modification to the procedure in Figure 13.3 could check for equal values in key fields:

```
Do until transaction key = high value and old master key = high value
    If transaction key = old master key
        Write error message
    Else
        If . . .
            .
            .
            .
```

13.5   CHANGE

Records stored in a file will need to be changed (updated) from time to time. One approach to file updating is to submit change transactions in essentially the same format as the records to be updated, but to have blanks in fields that do not require changes and new data in all fields that require change. It is desirable for the program that performs the update function to accept any number of changes for a given record; the changes all may be placed on the same change record or on different change records.

Figure 13.3   Pseudocode for merge procedure

```
Open files
Read transaction file
      At end move high value to transaction key
Read old master file
      At end move high value to old master key
Do until transaction key = high value and old master key = high value
      If transaction key < old master key
            Write new master record from transaction record
            Read transaction file
                  At end move high value to transaction key
      Else
            Write new master record from old master record
            Read old master file
                  At end move high value to old master key
      End If
End Do
Close Files
Stop
```

Figure 13.4   Pseudocode for file updating (change transactions only)

```
Open files
Read transaction file
      At end move high value to transaction key
Read old master file
      At end move high value to old master key
Do until transaction key = high value and old master key = high value
      If transaction key < old master key
            Write error message
            Read transaction file
                  At end move high value to transaction key
      Else
            If transaction key = old master key
                  Do update procedure
                  Read transaction file
                        At end move high value to old master key
            Else
                  Write new master record from old master record
                  Read old master file
                        At end move high value to old master key
            End If
      End If
End Do
Close files
Stop
```

Figure 13.5 Pseudocode for record deletion

```
Open files
Read transaction file
     At end move high value to transaction key
Read old master file
     At end move high value to old master key
Do until transaction key = high value and old master key = high value
     If transaction key = old master key
          Read old master file
               At end move high value to old master key
          Read transaction file
               At end move high value to transaction key
     Else
          If transaction key > old master key
               Write new master record from old master record
               Read old master file
                    At end move high value to old master key
          Else
               Write error message
               Read transaction file
                    At end move high value to transaction key
          End If
     End If
End Do
Close files
Stop
```

The logic required to perform the update function can be treated as an extension of the procedure outlined in Figure 13.3. The procedure would be rewritten as shown in Figure 13.4.

The update procedure would scan the transaction record for nonblank fields. The content of each nonblank field would replace the appropriate field in the old master record. After the update procedure is executed, the next transaction record is read. The updated old master record is written onto the new file only when a transaction record containing a larger key field has been read.

Another approach to transaction processing makes use of a code in the transaction record that will be used by the program to determine what action to take. This is the method used in Program 13.1. The transaction code option affects only the update procedure itself; the logic of Figure 13.4 remains unchanged.

13.6 DELETE

It is often necessary to delete unneeded records from a file. For a personnel file, the employee may have quit or been fired; for an inventory file, the item may no longer be stocked. When an entirely new updated file is being produced, a record is deleted simply by not writing that record onto the new master file.

For example, suppose a transaction file consists of records to be deleted from the old master file. Pseudocode for a program that will delete these records from the new master file is shown in Figure 13.5. A record is deleted by this procedure, which skips over both the transaction record and the matching old master record; this is accomplished by reading the next record from each of these files and not writing the matching old master record to the new master file. Note that if the value of the transaction key field is less than the old master key field, then that transaction must be an error. In this case, it is impossible to find a record in the old master file that will match the transaction, as the file is assumed to be in ascending sequence and all subsequent key field values will be even larger.

13.7 COMPLETE FILE MAINTENANCE PROCESS

The procedures in Figures 13.3, 13.4, and 13.5 are suitable when the transaction file contains only one type of transaction—add, change, or delete. In most instances, it is desirable to be able to perform all three types of transactions using one procedure. In the most general case, it is possible that records may be added and one or more fields changed and then deleted in the same batch of transactions. The procedure shown in Figure 13.6 can be used for this purpose. There are two major differences between the procedure in Figure 13.6 and the procedure in Figure 13.5. In Figure 13.6:

1) Data either from the old master file or, for new records, from the transaction file is moved to the new master record when the record is read. All changes are then made to the new master record. When a break is found in the transactions, the new master record is written.

2) A flag (*read flag*) is used to determine if it is appropriate to read the next record from the old master file. When a record is added, data from the transaction record is moved to the new master record and the *read flag* is set to "NO". The current old master file record remains the next record from that file to be processed. When it is appropriate to get the next old master file record for processing, *read flag* is tested. If its value is "NO", reading the next record from the old master file is bypassed.

The procedure in Figure 13.6 makes use of the key fields for end-of-file detection in the same way as previous procedures; the details are omitted from the pseudocode for clarity.

The procedure of Figure 13.6 makes use of the Case structure, which can be very useful in describing such complex procedures. The Case structure is appropriate when exactly one condition of a series of possibilities will hold. The general form of the Case structure and some alternate ways to represent the same logic is shown in Figure 13.7.

Figure 13.6 Pseudocode for complete file update procedure

```
Open files
Read transaction file
Read old master file
Move "YES" to read flag
Move old master record to new master record
Do until transaction key = high value and new master key = high value
    If transaction key > new master key
        Write new master record
        If read flag = "YES"
            Read old master file
        End If
        Move old master record to new master record
        Move "YES" to read flag
    Else
        If transaction key = new master key
            Case
                Transaction is add
                    Write error message 1
                    Read transaction file
                Transaction is delete
                    Read transaction file
                    If read flag = "YES"
                        Read old master file
                    End If
                    Move old master record to new master record
                    Move "YES" to read flag
                Transaction is change
                    Do update procedure
                    Read transaction file
            End Case
        Else
            Case
                Transaction is add
                    Move transaction record to new master record
                    Move "NO" to read flag
                Transaction is delete
                    Write error message 2
                Transaction is change
                    Write error message 3
            End Case
            Read transaction file
        End If
    End If
End Do
Close files
Stop
```

Figure 13.7   General form of the case structure

General Form   *If/Else Equivalent*

Case   If condition-1
      Condition-1   Action-1-1
            Action-1-1   .
                  .   .
                  .   Else
                  .   If condition-2
      Condition-2   Action-2-1
            Action-2-1   .
                  .   .
                  .   Else
                  .   .
                  .   .
      .   .
      .   If condition-n
      Condition-n   Action-n-1
            Action-n-1   .
                  .   .
                  .   .
                  .   End If
End Case   .
                                                                           .
                                                                           .
                                                                     End If
                                                              End If

Flowchart Equivalent

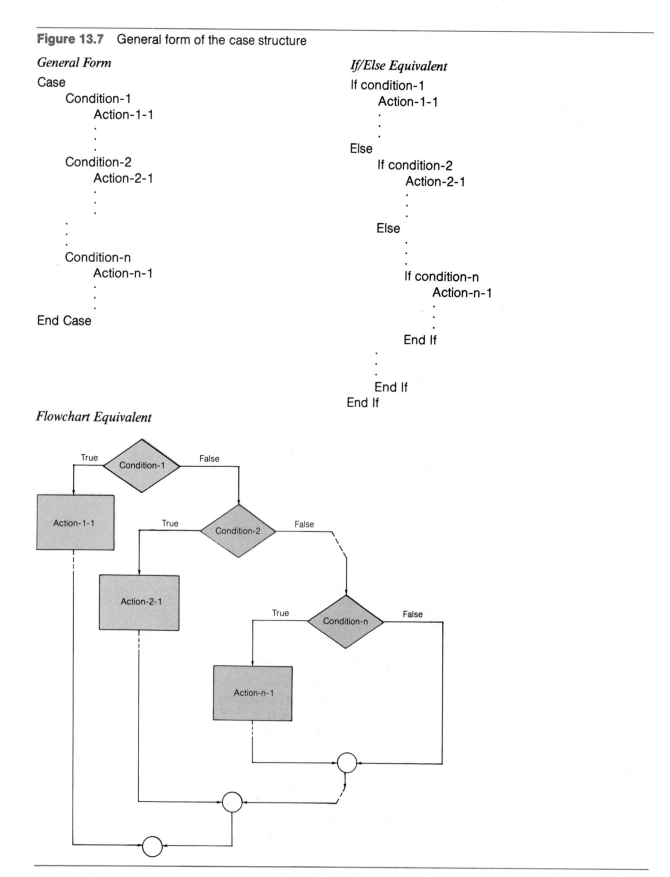

The Case structure is not one of the fundamental structures required for structured programming, as exactly the same function can be achieved by using nested IF/ELSE statements. Case structure is, however, a convenient means of representing the concept of selection among a variety of mutually exclusive alternatives.

Implementation of the Case structure in COBOL 74 requires nested IF/ELSE statements. The standard for COBOL 85 contains an EVALUATE statement that can be used to implement the Case structure in a very straight-forward way.

13.8 PROGRAM EXAMPLE

Problem Statement

Write a program to update ORDER-MASTER-FILE used in the Amalgamated Custom Design data processing system described in Section 10.4. The program must process ORDER-MASTER-FILE and ORDER-TRANSACTION-FILE to produce NEW-MASTER-FILE.

Problem Analysis

The ORDER-MASTER-FILE is a sequential file containing one master record for each order (record code "M") and detail records for each order component (record code "D"). The file ORDER-TRANSACTION-FILE contains new order records (record codes "M" and "D") and transaction records, generated when an order component is completed (record code "0") and when an order is shipped (record code "S"). (There is no provision for deleting records from the file.)

Transactions are placed in the ORDER-TRANSACTION-FILE when new orders are processed.

The completion of an order component and shipping of an order are recorded by placing an appropriate transaction record in ORDER-TRANSACTION-FILE. The logic required for this program follows the general plan of the procedure shown in Figure 13.6, with the omission of delete transactions.

Problem Solution

The required program is shown in Program 13.1 with structure diagram in Figure 13.8. Program 13.1 follows the general logical scheme shown in Figure 13.6, with the following exception: a block of records relating to a specific order (the master record and related detail records) is read and stored for subsequent processing (see 2200-READ-OLD-MASTER at lines 16400-17100). When all transactions relating to an order have been processed, the entire block of records is written onto NEW-MASTER-FILE (see lines 19300-19500). Tables are used to store the block of records (see lines 12300-13500). This method is made necessary by the fact that the detail records relating to order components are not in sequence. When a type "0" transaction is processed, the program uses a sequential search procedure (see lines 25600-26400) to locate the detail record required. Note that any number of additions and changes may be made; a block of records relating to an order is held in memory until there is a change in order numbers before a record is written onto the NEW-MASTER-FILE.

Program 13.1 Order update program

```
100       IDENTIFICATION DIVISION.
200
300       PROGRAM-ID. SEQUENTIAL-UPDATE.
400       AUTHOR. GARY.
500
600       ENVIRONMENT DIVISION.
700
800       CONFIGURATION SECTION.
900
1000      SOURCE-COMPUTER.
1100      OBJECT-COMPUTER.
1200
1300      INPUT-OUTPUT SECTION.
1400
1500      FILE-CONTROL.
1600
1700          SELECT ORDER-MASTER-FILE ASSIGN TO DISK.
1800          SELECT ORDER-TRANSACTION-FILE ASSIGN TO DISK.
1900          SELECT NEW-MASTER-FILE ASSIGN TO DISK.
2000          SELECT PRINT ASSIGN TO PRINTER.
2100
2200      DATA DIVISION.
2300
2400      FILE SECTION.
2500
2600      FD  PRINT
2700          LABEL RECORDS ARE OMITTED
2800          RECORD CONTAINS 132 CHARACTERS
2900          DATA RECORD IS PRINT-LINE.
3000
3100      01  PRINT-LINE            PIC X(132).
3200
3300      FD  ORDER-MASTER-FILE
3400          RECORD CONTAINS 84 CHARACTERS
3500          BLOCK CONTAINS 30 RECORDS
3600          VALUE OF TITLE IS "ORDER/MASTER"
3700          LABEL RECORDS ARE STANDARD
3800          DATA RECORD IS ORDER-MASTER-RECORD.
3900
4000      01  ORDER-MASTER-RECORD.
4100          02 FILLER             PIC X(69).
4200          02 RECORD-CODE-MASTER  PIC X.
4300          02 FILLER             PIC X(14).
4400
4500      FD  ORDER-TRANSACTION-FILE
4600          RECORD CONTAINS 84 CHARACTERS
4700          BLOCK CONTAINS 30 RECORDS
4800          VALUE OF TITLE IS "ORDER/TRANSACTION"
4900          LABEL RECORDS ARE STANDARD
5000          DATA RECORD IS ORDER-TRANSACTION-RECORD.
5100
```

Program 13.1 (continued)

```
5200    01  ORDER-TRANSACTION-RECORD.
5300        02  ORDER-NUMBER-OTR          PIC 9(5).
5400        02  FILLER                    PIC X(64).
5500        02  RECORD-CODE-TRANSACTION   PIC X.
5600        02  FILLER                    PIC X(14).
5700
5800    FD  NEW-MASTER-FILE
5900        RECORD CONTAINS 84 CHARACTERS
6000        BLOCK CONTAINS 30 RECORDS
6100        VALUE OF TITLE IS "ORDER/MASTER/NEW"
6200        LABEL RECORDS ARE STANDARD
6300        DATA RECORD IS NEW-MASTER-RECORD.
6400
6500    01  NEW-MASTER-RECORD         PIC X(84).
6600
6700    WORKING-STORAGE SECTION.
6800
6900    01  FLAGS.
7000        02  SEARCH-FLAG           PIC X(11) VALUE "CONTINUE".
7100        02  READ-FLAG             PIC XXX VALUE "YES".
7200
7300    01  INDEXES.
7400        02  INDX                  PIC 99 VALUE ZERO.
7500
7600    01  OLD-ORDER-RECORD.
7700        02  OLD-ORDER-MASTER-RECORD.
7800            03  ORDER-NUMBER-OMR          PIC 9(5).
7900            03  CUSTOMER-NUMBER-OMR       PIC 9(9).
8000            03  CUSTOMER-NAME-OMR         PIC X(20).
8100            03  CUSTOMER-ADDRESS-OMR      PIC X(20).
8200            03  NUM-ORDER-COMPS-OMR       PIC 9(3).
8300            03  DATE-OF-RECEIPT-OMR       PIC 9(6).
8400            03  SHIPPING-DATE-OMR         PIC 9(6).
8500            03  RECORD-CODE-OMR           PIC X.
8600            03  FILLER                    PIC X(14).
8700        02  OLD-ORDER-DETAIL-RECORD
8800            OCCURS 9 TIMES.
8900            03  ORDER-NUMBER-ODR          PIC 9(5).
9000            03  CATALOG-NUMBER-ODR        PIC X(5).
9100            03  QUANTITY-ODR              PIC 9(3).
9200            03  NUM-ORDER-COMPS           PIC 9(3).
9300            03  SCHEDULED-COMPLETION-DATE-ODR  PIC 9(6).
9400            03  ACTUAL-COMPLETION-DATE-ODR     PIC 9(6).
9500            03  RAW-MATERIAL-REQ-ODR PIC X(5) OCCURS 5 TIMES.
9600            03  BATCH-STATUS-ODR          PIC X.
9700            03  CUSTOMIZING-INSTRUCTIONS-ODR   PIC X(15).
9800            03  RECORD-CODE-ODR           PIC X.
9900            03  FILLER                    PIC X(14).
10000
10100   01  COMP-TRANS-COMPLETION-RECORD.
10200       03  ORDER-NUMBER-OTCR         PIC 9(5).
10300       03  CATALOG-NUMBER-OTCR       PIC X(5).
10400       03  COMPLETION-DATE-OTCR      PIC 9(6).
10500       03  FILLER                    PIC X(68).
10600
```

Program 13.1 (continued)

```
10700        01  ORDER-TRAN-SHIPPING-RECORD.
10800            03 ORDER-NUMBER-OTSR              PIC 9(5).
10900            03 SHIPPING-DATE-OTSR             PIC 9(6).
11000            03 FILLER                         PIC X(73).
11100
11200        01  NEW-ORDER-RECORD.
11300            02  NEW-ORDER-MASTER-RECORD.
11400                03 ORDER-NUMBER-NOMR          PIC 9(5).
11500                03 CUSTOMER-NUMBER-NOMR       PIC 9(9).
11600                03 CUSTOMER-NAME-NOMR         PIC X(20).
11700                03 CUSTOMER-ADDRESS-NOMR      PIC X(20).
11800                03 NUM-ORDER-COMPS-NOMR       PIC 9(3).
11900                03 DATE-OF-RECEIPT-NOMR       PIC 9(6).
12000                03 SHIPPING-DATE-NOMR         PIC 9(6).
12100                03 RECORD-CODE-NOMR           PIC X.
12200                03 FILLER                     PIC X(14).
12300            02  NEW-ORDER-DETAIL-RECORD
12400                OCCURS 9 TIMES.
12500                03 ORDER-NUMBER-NODR          PIC 9(5).
12600                03 CATALOG-NUMBER-NODR        PIC X(5).
12700                03 QUANTITY-NODR              PIC 9(3).
12800                03 NUM-ORDER-COMPS-NODR       PIC 9(3).
12900                03 SCHEDULED-COMP-DATE-NODR   PIC 9(6).
13000                03 ACTUAL-COMP-DATE-NODR      PIC 9(6).
13100                03 RAW-MATERIAL-REQ-NODR PIC X(5) OCCURS 5 TIMES.
13200                03 BATCH-STATUS-NODR          PIC X.
13300                03 CUSTOMIZING-INSTRUCTIONS-NODR  PIC X(15).
13400                03 RECORD-CODE-NODR           PIC X.
13500                03 FILLER                     PIC X(14).
13600
13700        PROCEDURE DIVISION.
13800
13900        1000-MAIN-LOGIC.
14000
14100            PERFORM 2000-INITIALIZATION.
14200            PERFORM 3000-UPDATE
14300                UNTIL ORDER-NUMBER-OTR = 99999
14400                    AND ORDER-NUMBER-NOMR = 99999.
14500            PERFORM 9900-TERMINATION.
14600            STOP RUN.
14700
14800        2000-INITIALIZATION.
14900
15000            OPEN INPUT ORDER-TRANSACTION-FILE
15100                       ORDER-MASTER-FILE
15200                 OUTPUT NEW-MASTER-FILE
15300                        PRINT.
15400            PERFORM 2100-READ-TRANSACTION.
15500            PERFORM 2200-READ-OLD-MASTER-FILE.
15600            MOVE OLD-ORDER-RECORD TO NEW-ORDER-RECORD.
15700            MOVE "YES" TO READ-FLAG.
15800
15900        2100-READ-TRANSACTION.
16000
16100            READ ORDER-TRANSACTION-FILE
16200                AT END MOVE 99999 TO ORDER-NUMBER-OTR.
```

Program 13.1 (continued)

```
16300
16400    2200-READ-OLD-MASTER-FILE.
16500
16600        READ ORDER-MASTER-FILE
16700            AT END MOVE 99999 TO ORDER-NUMBER-OMR.
16800        IF ORDER-NUMBER-OMR NOT = HIGH-VALUE
16900            MOVE ORDER-MASTER-RECORD TO OLD-ORDER-MASTER-RECORD
17000            PERFORM 2400-READ-OMF VARYING INDX FROM 1 BY 1
17100                    UNTIL INDX > NUM-ORDER-COMPS-OMR.
17200
17300    2400-READ-OMF.
17400
17500        READ ORDER-MASTER-FILE
17600            AT END MOVE 99999 TO ORDER-NUMBER-OMR.
17700        MOVE ORDER-MASTER-RECORD TO
17800            OLD-ORDER-DETAIL-RECORD (INDX).
17900
18000    3000-UPDATE.
18100
18200        IF ORDER-NUMBER-OTR > ORDER-NUMBER-NOMR
18300            PERFORM 4000-GOOD-NEW-MASTER
18400        ELSE
18500          IF ORDER-NUMBER-OTR = ORDER-NUMBER-NOMR
18600                PERFORM 4200-UPDATE-IF-VALID
18700            ELSE
18800                PERFORM 4400-ADD-IF-VALID.
18900
19000    4000-GOOD-NEW-MASTER.
19100
19200        WRITE NEW-MASTER-RECORD FROM NEW-ORDER-MASTER-RECORD.
19300        PERFORM 4100-WRITE-NEW-MASTER
19400            VARYING INDX FROM 1 BY 1
19500                UNTIL INDX > NUM-ORDER-COMPS-NOMR.
19600        IF READ-FLAG = "YES" AND ORDER-NUMBER-OMR NOT = 99999
19700            PERFORM 2200-READ-OLD-MASTER-FILE.
19800        MOVE OLD-ORDER-RECORD TO NEW-ORDER-RECORD.
19900        MOVE "YES" TO READ-FLAG.
20000
20100    4100-WRITE-NEW-MASTER.
20200
20300        WRITE NEW-MASTER-RECORD FROM NEW-ORDER-DETAIL-RECORD (INDX).
20400
20500    4200-UPDATE-IF-VALID.
20600
20700        IF RECORD-CODE-TRANSACTION = "M"
20800            PERFORM 9000-WRITE-ERROR-MESSAGE-1
20900        ELSE
21000          IF RECORD-CODE-TRANSACTION = "C"
21100                PERFORM 8000-COMP-COMPLETION
21200            ELSE
21300              IF RECORD-CODE-TRANSACTION = "O"
21400                  PERFORM 8100-ORDER-SHIPPING
21500                ELSE
21600                    PERFORM 9200-WRITE-ERROR-MESSAGE-3.
21700        PERFORM 2100-READ-TRANSACTION.
21800
```

Program 13.1 (continued)

```
21900        4400-ADD-IF-VALID.
22000
22100            IF RECORD-CODE-TRANSACTION = "M"
22200               MOVE ORDER-TRANSACTION-RECORD TO
22300                   NEW-ORDER-MASTER-RECORD
22400               PERFORM 4410-READ-STORE
22500                   VARYING INDX FROM 1 BY 1
22600                       UNTIL INDX > NUM-ORDER-COMPS-NOMR
22700               MOVE "NO" TO READ-FLAG
22800            ELSE
22900               IF RECORD-CODE-TRANSACTION = "C"
23000                   PERFORM 9100-WRITE-ERROR-MESSAGE-2
23100               ELSE
23200                   PERFORM 9400-WRITE-ERROR-MESSAGE-5.
23300            PERFORM 2100-READ-TRANSACTION.
23400
23500        4410-READ-STORE.
23600
23700            PERFORM 2100-READ-TRANSACTION.
23800            MOVE ORDER-TRANSACTION-RECORD TO
23900                   NEW-ORDER-DETAIL-RECORD (INDX).
24000
24100        8000-COMP-COMPLETION.
24200
24300            MOVE ORDER-TRANSACTION-RECORD TO
24400                   COMP-TRANS-COMPLETION-RECORD.
24500            MOVE 1 TO INDX.
24600            MOVE "CONTINUE" TO SEARCH-FLAG.
24700            PERFORM 8010-SEARCH-PROCEDURE
24800               UNTIL SEARCH-FLAG NOT = "CONTINUE".
24900            IF SEARCH-FLAG = "FOUND"
25000               MOVE "C" TO BATCH-STATUS-NODR (INDX)
25100               MOVE COMPLETION-DATE-OTCR TO
25200                   ACTUAL-COMP-DATE-NODR (INDX)
25300            ELSE
25400               PERFORM 9300-WRITE-ERROR-MESSAGE-4.
25500
25600        8010-SEARCH-PROCEDURE.
25700
25800            IF CATALOG-NUMBER-NODR (INDX) =
25900               CATALOG-NUMBER-OTCR
26000               MOVE "FOUND" TO SEARCH-FLAG
26100            ELSE
26200               ADD 1 TO INDX
26300               IF INDX > NUM-ORDER-COMPS-NOMR
26400                   MOVE "NOT PRESENT" TO SEARCH-FLAG.
26500
26600        8100-ORDER-SHIPPING.
26700
26800            MOVE ORDER-TRANSACTION-RECORD TO
26900                   ORDER-TRAN-SHIPPING-RECORD.
27000            MOVE SHIPPING-DATE-OTSR TO SHIPPING-DATE-NOMR.
27100
```

Program 13.1 (continued)

```
27200    9000-WRITE-ERROR-MESSAGE-1.
27300
27400        MOVE "ERROR1" TO PRINT-LINE.
27500        WRITE PRINT-LINE AFTER 1.
27600
27700    9100-WRITE-ERROR-MESSAGE-2.
27800
27900        MOVE "ERROR2" TO PRINT-LINE.
28000        WRITE PRINT-LINE AFTER 1.
28100
28200    9200-WRITE-ERROR-MESSAGE-3.
28300
28400        MOVE "ERROR3" TO PRINT-LINE.
28500        WRITE  PRINT-LINE AFTER 1.
28600
28700    9300-WRITE-ERROR-MESSAGE-4.
28800
28900        MOVE "ERROR4" TO PRINT-LINE.
29000        WRITE PRINT-LINE AFTER 1.
29100
29200    9400-WRITE-ERROR-MESSAGE-5.
29300
29400        MOVE "ERROR5" TO PRINT-LINE.
29500        WRITE PRINT-LINE AFTER 1.
29600
29700    9900-TERMINATION.
29800
29900        CLOSE ORDER-TRANSACTION-FILE
30000             PRINT
30100             ORDER-MASTER-FILE
30200             NEW-MASTER-FILE WITH LOCK.
```

Figure 13.8   Structure diagram of Program 13.1

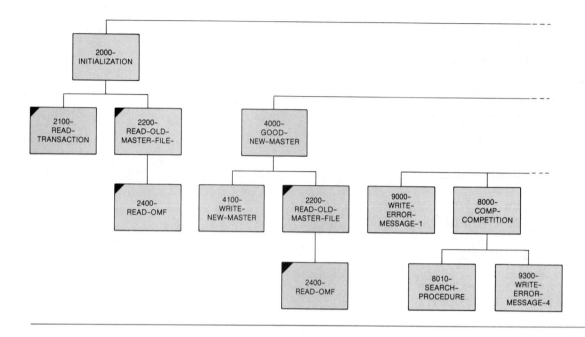

13.9   ADDING RECORDS WITH EXTEND

In order to add records to an existing disk or tape file, it is necessary to open the file in EXTEND mode. For example, to add records to a file MASTER-FILE, you would use:

    OPEN EXTEND MASTER-FILE.

EXTEND mode causes the operating system to locate the last record in the file and place any additional records to be written in the file following that record. A program to add records to MASTER-FILE is shown in Figure 13.9.

If a file opened in EXTEND mode does not exist, the effect of EXTEND is the same as opening the file in OUTPUT mode: the file is created and records are placed in the file in sequential order.

In using EXTEND mode, you cannot merge the new records with the existing records in the file. The file MASTER-FILE will not be in proper sequence (see Figure 13.9). It would be necessary to sort the file using either a system utility program or the COBOL SORT facility (see Chapter 7) in order to perform any further processing of the file.

13.10   UPDATING A SEQUENTIAL FILE IN PLACE

As noted earlier, a tape file cannot be updated in place; a completely new file must be produced each time an update operation is performed. Files that are stored on mass storage, however, may be updated in place. New records can be added to the file, and existing records can be changed or even deleted without requiring that an entirely new file be created.

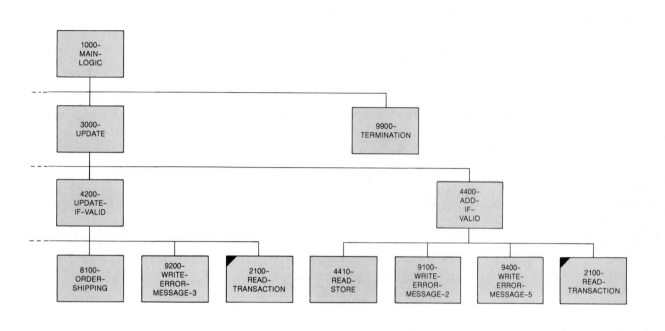

Adding records to an existing file is accomplished using EXTEND mode. Changing existing records and deleting records is accomplished by opening the file in I–0 mode and using the REWRITE verb. When the file is opened in I–0 mode, as in

```
OPEN I-0 MASTER-FILE.
```

records may be read from the file using the verb READ and written on the file using REWRITE. The REWRITE statement can be used only after a READ operation. It causes the record that was read to be rewritten onto the file; the new copy of the record replaces the old one. The general form of the REWRITE statement is shown in Figure 13.10.

Figure 13.10 General form of the REWRITE statement

```
REWRITE record-name [FROM data-name]
```

For example, in order to rewrite a record onto MASTER-FILE, the statement

```
REWRITE MASTER-RECORD.
```

can be used. The REWRITE statement may be executed only once for a given record; it will replace the last record read from the file.

The basic procedure used to change an existing record in a file is to make changes to the record based on transactions. After all transactions regarding a particular record are processed, the changed record is rewritten

Figure 13.9 Extend program example

```
000100 IDENTIFICATION DIVISION.
000200*
000300 PROGRAM-ID. EXTEND-EXAMPLE.
000400*
000500 ENVIRONMENT DIVISION.
000600*
000700 CONFIGURATION SECTION.
000800*
000900 SOURCE-COMPUTER.
001000 OBJECT-COMPUTER.
001100*
001200 INPUT-OUTPUT SECTION.
001300*
001400 FILE-CONTROL.
001500*
001600       SELECT MASTER-FILE ASSIGN TO OUTPUT "MASTER/DAT".
001700*
001800 DATA DIVISION.
001900*
002000 FILE SECTION.
002100*
002200 FD   MASTER-FILE
002300       LABEL RECORDS ARE STANDARD
002400       DATA RECORD IS MASTER-RECORD.
002500*
002600 01   MASTER-RECORD PIC X(80).
002700*
002800 WORKING-STORAGE SECTION.
002900*
003000 01   CONTROL-FIELDS.
003100       02 MORE-DATA     PIC X VALUE "Y".
003200*
003300 PROCEDURE DIVISION.
003400*
003500 1000-MAIN-CONTROL.
003600*
003700       OPEN EXTEND MASTER-FILE.
003800       PERFORM 2000-GET-RECORD.
003900       PERFORM 3000-WRITE-GET
004000           UNTIL MORE-DATA = "N".
004100       CLOSE MASTER-FILE.
004200       STOP RUN.
004300*
004400 2000-GET-RECORD.
004500*
004600       DISPLAY "ENTER MASTER RECORD".
004700       ACCEPT MASTER-RECORD.
004800*
```

```
004900 3000-WRITE-GET.
005000*
005100     WRITE MASTER-RECORD.
005200     DISPLAY "MORE DATA (Y/N)".
005300     ACCEPT MORE-DATA.
005400     IF MORE-DATA = "Y"
005500         PERFORM 2000-GET-RECORD.
```

onto the file using the REWRITE statement. This approach is used in the procedure shown in Figure 13.11.

In order to delete records from a file, it is necessary to add a deletion code to the record. When the deletion code has a predetermined value, the record is considered to have been deleted; if the code has any other value, the record is considered to be active. The routine that reads records from the file must bypass all deleted records. Records from the file are read until either a nondeleted record is found or the end-of-file is reached.

Figure 13.11 Pseudocode for in-place update of a sequential file

```
Open files
Read transaction file
Do Read master file procedure
    Case
        Transaction key = master key
            Case
                Transaction is change
                    Do update procedure
                    Read transaction file
                Transaction is delete
                    Move "DELETE" to deletion code
                    Rewrite master record
                    Read transaction file
                    Do Read master file procedure
            End Case
        Transaction key < master key
            Write error message: "Invalid transaction"
            Read transaction file
        Transaction key > master key
            Rewrite master record
            Do Read master file procedure
    End Case
End Do
Close files
Stop
```

Note: All changes are made to the master record before it is rewritten onto the master file. This procedure will accomodate multiple change transactions for one master record.

Pseudocode for the procedure to read a record from MASTER-FILE is as follows:

Read master file procedure
    Read master file
    Do until end of file or active record
        Read master file
    End Do

This method for deleting records has some advantages over physically removing records from a file. The record remains in the file and is, therefore, accessible by any program processing the file. A report showing all deleted records can be produced at any time. A record can be changed back to active status by changing the value of the deletion code. However, there are some disadvantages. Eventually the file may become full of deleted records, causing the file to take up too much space on the disk. Because any program processing the file must read (and ignore) deleted records as well as active records, the performance of the computing system for programs processing the file may be degraded. When a file becomes full of deleted records, it is necessary to create a second file that contains only active records and omits those that have been deleted. A backup of the old version of the file can be maintained (usually on tape) should it be necessary to access any of the records in the original version of the file.

13.11 THE MERGE STATEMENT

The process of merging two sets of data, each of which is already in sequence, has been described in Section 13.4. The COBOL sort facility has a MERGE statement available to perform this task. The general form of the MERGE statement is shown in Figure 13.12. Many of the considerations regarding use of the SORT statement are true for the MERGE statement. For example, the MERGE statement requires the use of a sort-work-file, which is used the same way in the MERGE as in the SORT. In fact, MERGE is actually a version of the SORT, with some restrictions in its syntax. The major differences are as follows:

1) The verb MERGE replaces the verb SORT.
2) The USING clause must be included; there is no provision for an INPUT PROCEDURE.
3) At least two files must be listed in the USING clause. More can be named, if desired.

Example

Suppose that two files called DATA-FILE-A and DATA-FILE-B are in ascending sequence. The key field in each case is an account number. Suppose further that a sort work-file called SORT-WORK has been declared and that the sort work record has been given an appropriate description. If the content of DATA-FILE-A is to be merged into DATA-FILE-B, creating a new file called DATA-FILE-C, the following code would be used:

```
MERGE SORT-WORK
    ON ASCENDING KEY ACCOUNT-NUM-SWR
    USING DATA-FILE-A DATA-FILE-B
    GIVING DATA-FILE-C.
```

If DATA-FILE-B were to be merged into DATA-FILE-A, the following code would be used:

```
MERGE SORT-WORK
    ON ASCENDING KEY ACCOUNT-NUM-SWR
    USING DATA-FILE-A DATA-FILE-B
    GIVING DATA-FILE-A.
```

Figure 13.12 General form of the MERGE statement

The MERGE procedure assumes that its input files are in the required sequence. If either of the files is out of sequence, the procedure will generally terminate execution of the program with an appropriate error message.

It should be noted that the SORT verb could be substituted for MERGE in the preceding example with little effect on the outcome; the only difference would be that the SORT procedure would not terminate if records that were out of sequence were encountered. What, then, is the advantage of using MERGE rather than SORT? If it is known that existing files are in sequence, MERGE may be preferable to SORT. MERGE tends to be faster than SORT and uses less mass storage space for work areas.

The amount of execution time and mass storage space required for execution of a SORT statement is not insignificant. Because of the assumptions about the sequencing of the data, MERGE should be executed in much less time (and with the least possible use of work areas) than SORT, even for the same data files.

13.12 DEBUG CLINIC

When writing programs dealing extensively with files, the programmer may be confronted with system error messages produced during execution of the program if an error is made. Failing to open the file prior to an input or output operation, attempting an input operation on a file opened in output mode, and attempting a REWRITE operation when a file is not opened in I-0 mode, are a few examples of errors that will produce execution-time error messages and cause termination of the program.

COBOL provides a way for the programmer to monitor the results of all input/output verbs. To make use of this facility, a FILE STATUS clause is added to the SELECT entry as shown in Figure 13.13.

Figure 13.13 General form of the SELECT entry for sequential files

```
SELECT file-name
    ASSIGN TO system-name
    [FILE STATUS IS data-name.].
```

The data name declared as a FILE STATUS item is automatically updated to show the result of each input/output operation related to the file. The FILE STATUS item must be two characters in length and must be defined in the DATA DIVISION. For example, to define a FILE STATUS item for a MASTER FILE, the SELECT entry could be written as:

```
SELECT MASTER-FILE
    ASSIGN TO DISK
    FILE STATUS IS MASTER-STATUS.
```

The field MASTER-STATUS would be defined in WORKING-STORAGE as:

```
01  MASTER-STATUS.
    02  M-STATUS-1 PIC 9.
    02  M-STATUS-2 PIC 9.
```

Defining the FILE STATUS item as a group item subdivided into two fields, each of length one, is useful because each digit of the FILE STATUS item is a code with a specified meaning (Figure 13.14).

Figure 13.14 Meaning of FILE STATUS codes for sequential files

Status-key 1	Status-key 2	Meaning
0	0	Successful completion
1	0	At end
3	0	Permanent error
3	4	Boundary violation
9	–	Differs among compilers

For example, if the value of MASTER-STATUS was "00" after an OPEN, READ or WRITE statement, the file was opened or a record was read or written without incident. If the value of MASTER-STATUS was "10" after a READ, the end-of-file was encountered. The meaning of other settings of the FILE STATUS item may differ among systems; check with your COBOL system manual. The FILE STATUS item can be processed by a program as any other item; for example, it can be tested:

```
IF MASTER-STATUS NOT = "00"
```

The FILE STATUS item can be made a part of diagnostic output, as in:

```
READ MASTER-FILE
    AT END MOVE "YES" TO EOF-FLAG.
MOVE MASTER-STATUS TO M-STATUS-OUT.
WRITE OUTPUT-LINE FROM DIAGNOSTIC-LINE AFTER 1.
```

The use of the FILE STATUS item in diagnostic output is particularly helpful in debugging programs when system error messages are not specific enough to enable you to determine the cause of the problem.

13.13 APPLICATIONS OF SEQUENTIAL FILES

Although there are many limitations to the use of sequential file organization in data processing systems, this technique remains useful in several situations. If the file will be stored on and processed from tape, sequential organization is the only available choice. In batch-oriented systems, master files and transaction files may be given sequential organization when random access is not needed by the logic of the system design. Note that it is usually necessary to sort sequential files into sequence before they can be processed. A transaction file must be in sequence using the same key field as the related master file before updating is performed. In interactive systems, sequential files are appropriate for transaction log files (containing records of all transactions entered by users), which are maintained for re-creation of the master file in case of system problems. Sequential files are also useful for backups of active files regardless of the organization of the active file. The program that re-creates the active file also re-creates the appropriate file organization.

Sequential file organization is not appropriate when a file must be *completely* updated interactively. (If only change and delete are needed, sequential organization may be used.) Sequential files are not appropriate when random access to data is needed. Even when random access is not needed by any component of the system but programs require access to the records in the file in different sequences (necessitating repeated sorting of the file), other file organization techniques should be considered.

Because sequential file organization is simple and flexible, it is the method of choice in many situations; however, each system must be evaluated carefully. Over-reliance on sequentially organized files may lead to systems that spend too much time in sorting and that are inflexible and cumbersome.

13.14   SELF-TEST EXERCISES

1. What input/output statements are valid when a file is opened as INPUT, OUTPUT, I-0, and EXTEND?

2. Define each of the following terms:
   a. rewind
   b. key field
   c. audit trail
   d. file status
   e. backup
   f. activity
   g. volatility

3. Are there any circumstances in which placement of a large value, such as 99999, in a key field when end-of-file is reached would be invalid? How would the method be modified if the key field were alphanumeric?

4. Write the pseudocode for a program required to merge three files, FILE-A, FILE-B, FILE-C, with respective record key fields KEY-A, KEY-B, KEY-C. The output file is NEW-FILE.

5. What are two types of file access methods supported in COBOL? What are the advantages and disadvantages of each method?

6. How does the expected activity in a system affect the choice of file update technique?

7. How does the expected volatility in a file affect the choice of file update technique?

8. Is it possible for the volatility ratio to exceed the activity ratio? Why or why not?

9. Describe two distinct approaches to entering change records. What are the advantages and limitations of each?

10. Under what circumstances should a sequential file be used in a system? When would a sequential file be inappropriate?

11. Why are backup files often given sequential organization?

12. What are the main differences between batch and interactive file-update procedures?

13. What are the primary limitations on updating a sequential file in place? When is this technique appropriate?

14. In the procedure in Figure 13.6, what purpose is served by the item *read flag?*

15. In Program 13.1, what would be appropriate content for error messages written in paragraphs 9000 to 9400?

13.15   PROGRAMMING EXERCISES

1. Write a program to update the TABLE-FILE used in programming Exercise 6, Section 11, in Chapter 12. The update program should allow the user to perform the following functions:

Function	Transaction Code
Add a course	A
Change department number	CD
Change course name	CN
Change number credits	CC
Delete course	D

The update program should process the old TABLE-FILE and a TRANSACTION-FILE to produce a NEW-TABLE-FILE. Include a listing of all files.

2. Write a program to create a student master file for ABC College. Each record should contain the following fields:

> Student number
> Name
> Address
> Major (2 character code)
> Date of first enrollment (*mmddyy*)
> Date of last enrollment (*mmddyy*)
> Credit hours currently enrolled
> Cumulative G.P.A.

3. Write a program to process a transaction file containing records for new students. Your program should update the master file created in Exercise 2.

4. Write a program that uses a transaction file to update the student master file created in Exercise 2. Records in the transaction file have the same layout as records in the master file with the addition of a transaction code.

Function	Transaction Code
New student	NS
Change name	CN
Change address	CA
Change major	CM
Change date of first enrollment	CF
Change date of last enrollment	CL
Change credit hours completed	CC
Change credit hours currently enrolled	CE
Change GPA	CG
Delete student	DS

5. A student grade file contains records, in sequence by student number, with the following fields:

> Student number
> Section number
> Course number
> Credit hours
> Grade (A, B, C, D, F, or W)

Write a program to process the student grade file to update fields of the master student file created in Exercise 2. Use an update-in-place technique.

6. Write a program to update a master file with records defined as follows:

Picture	*Description*
X(5)	Store identifier
X(3)	Department identifier
9(9)	Customer number
9(6)	Date of sale—*mmddyy*
99	Quantity
9(9)	Inventory number of item sold
9999V99	Wholesale price/item
9999V99	Retail price/item
XX	Status code: Paid by cash (CA)
	Paid by VISA (VS)
	Paid by MasterCard (MC)
	Credit purchase (CR)
X	Tax code: Sale is taxable (T)
	Sale is nontaxable (N)

INDEXED FILES 14

14.1 ADVANTAGES AND LIMITATIONS OF INDEXED FILES

The only way to access records stored in a sequential file is one after another—that is, sequentially. Sequential access always means the processing of each record in a file from first to last, one after the other. Although this step-by-step process may be suitable for many purposes, there are some applications in which the computer must access records randomly. For example, it may be desirable to update a file *without* having the transactions sorted into sequential order. As each transaction is processed, the associated master file record must be read (i.e., the master file must be read randomly). *Random access* is the ability to access any record regardless of its position in the file and without accessing previous records. A type of file organization technique that permits random access is *indexed* organization, available to COBOL programmers in most computer systems.

An indexed file is a sequential file similar in many ways to those discussed in Chapter 13. In fact, an indexed file can be used in place of any sequential file, if desired. However, indexed files give us a very powerful added capability—the ability to process records from the file randomly. In random processing, the program specifies a value and the READ statement immediately returns the record from the file that has a key field with that value. Records not only may be read from the file but also may be changed and placed directly back into the file. Unlike the technique used in sequential processing, with random processing records also may be deleted or added to the file without the program having to create an entirely new file.

In a sense, storing records in an indexed file is like storing pages in a looseleaf notebook with external tabs on each page showing page numbers. The user can retrieve any page from the notebook at will by using the appropriate tab. In a similar way, a program can retrieve any desired record from an indexed file by specifying the key field value. The user of the looseleaf notebook can retrieve any desired record, make changes and reinsert it into the notebook. In much the same way, a program can perform similar operations on data records contained in an indexed file. The notebook user has the option of throwing pages away at will; in a similar way, records can be deleted from an indexed file.

The implementation of indexed files differs in many details among various computing systems. Typically, however, the system maintains at least one *index*, a table of pointers to records within the file. To access a record, the system looks up the key field value in the index and uses the pointer (which may be the actual physical address of the record) to read the desired record from the file. In some systems more than one index is maintained, which requires the look-up operation to proceed from a master index through one or more subindexes to find the record in the file. These indexes may be stored in the computer's memory or as part of the disk file itself. Using the looseleaf notebook analogy, the index corresponds roughly to the tabs on each page; it gives the system the ability to access records on demand.

Records within an indexed file generally are stored in sequential order to permit rapid and efficient sequential retrieval of the records. Thus, when the file is created initially, the records stored in the file *must* be in sequential order. All required indexes are built by the operating system at the time the file is created. Adding records to and deleting records from the file are done in ways that do not destroy the sequential ordering of the records in the file. This is because typically there will be associated with the file an *overflow area*, a disk area into which added records are placed. In order to maintain the sequential nature of the file, appropriate pointers are constructed to indicate the sequential position within the file for added records. Deleted records generally are removed from the file by setting a code, rather than by physically removing the data.

If a great many records have been added to or deleted from an indexed file, the overflow area may be filled up entirely with the new records, while the deleted records still are occupying physical space within the file. At this point it becomes necessary to reorganize the file by physically removing the deleted records and inserting the added records into their appropriate physical position. This operation typically is provided for by an operating system *utility* program designed for this task. Utility programs are provided for the user as a part of the operating system.

The primary advantages of indexed files are their provisions for both sequential and random access to data. Indexed files also enable in-place file updating, including add, change, and delete—a facility not available for sequential files. On the other hand, there are some disadvantages that must be considered. Indexed files must be assigned to a mass storage device (typically disk) with random access capabilities; this precludes use of magnetic tape for an indexed file. Sequential files, on the other hand, may be assigned to any mass storage device (disk or tape). There is considerable system overhead in the storage space required for an indexed file. As noted above, indexes and an overflow area must be allocated, in addition to space for data. This overhead reduces the amount of data that can be stored on a given device. Sequential files, on the other hand, require little additional storage other than actual data areas. The sequential processing time for an indexed file tends to be slower than for a sequential file. This is particularly true when the file has been updated with many new records that have been placed in overflow areas. The operating system takes care of locating desired records in the file, but many disk access operations may be required. Access time for a sequential file, however, tends to be as fast as possible, usually requiring only one disk access for reading each block of data. In some systems, indexed files require periodic reorganization to clear out overflow areas and purge the file of deleted records; this operation is not required for sequential files. Indexed files are not universally supported in all programming languages and other system software. Thus, an indexed file created by a COBOL program may not be available for processing by a program written in another programming language or by a file management utility program. Sequential files, on the other hand, may generally be processed by programs written in any language and by any system utility.

When choosing a file organization technique for a file in a given system, the systems analyst or programmer must carefully weigh the relative merits of all available options for file organization. Random access and in-place update capabilities are not achieved without cost.

Figure 14.1 SELECT entry for creation of an indexed file

```
SELECT    file-name ASSIGN TO system-name
          ORGANIZATION IS INDEXED
          ACCESS IS SEQUENTIAL
          RECORD KEY IS data-name.
```

14.2 FILE CREATION

To create an indexed file, the SELECT sentence for that file must contain entries shown in Figure 14.1. The ACCESS clause specifies SEQUENTIAL, as the records placed in the file will be in sequential order. The ORGANIZATION clause specifies the type of file organization—in this case INDEXED. If the ORGANIZATION clause were omitted, the file would be assumed to have standard sequential organization. The RECORD KEY clause specifies the name of the field within the record defined for the file that will be used for creating and accessing the file. The records must be in ascending sequence based on the value contained in this key field. There must not be any records with the same field value. For example, note the SELECT entry for the file RAW-MATERIAL-MASTER-FILE defined in Program 14.1 at lines 1800-2100.

The WRITE statement for an indexed file must be of the form shown in Figure 14.2. The statement in the INVALID KEY clause is executed when an attempt is made to write to the file a record that has an invalid key field value. When an indexed file is created, the INVALID KEY condition will be encountered when the key fields of the records are not in ascending sequence or when an attempt is made to place two records with the same key field value into the file. In Program 14.1, the WRITE statement at lines 7900-8100

```
WRITE RAW-MATERIAL-MASTER-RECORD
    INVALID KEY
        PERFORM 8000-ERROR.
```

will cause the paragraph 8000-ERROR to be executed if the record keys are duplicated or out of sequence. For the sake of simplicity, this paragraph has been left empty in Program 14.1. In any real application, however, an appropriate error message (such as KEY IS DUPLICATED) would be placed in this paragraph. When an INVALID KEY condition is encountered, the record that caused the condition is not written onto the file.

Figure 14.2   WRITE statement for indexed file

```
WRITE record-name [FROM data-name]
    INVALID KEY statement
```

14.3   PROGRAM EXAMPLE

Problem Statement

Write a program for the Amalgamated Custom Design system to convert a sequential file containing data for the Raw Materials Master File into an indexed file containing the same data.

Problem Analysis

Recall that the raw material master file contains one record for each item stocked by the company for use in the production of its finished products. The file is accessed:

1) When new orders are processed, to determine which order components can be submitted for production (New Order Processing)
2) When the Order Master File is processed, to determine whether there are order components that can be scheduled (Pending Order Processing)
3) When raw materials are received or used (Raw Materials Update— Program 14.2)

In all of these programs, the data being processed is not in sequence by item number. In the cases of New Order Processing and Pending Order Processing, the Order Master File that is in sequence by order number is the primary file. The Raw Materials Master File must be accessed several times for each order to determine whether there are sufficient raw materials on hand to submit a production order for a specific order component. If there are sufficient raw materials on hand, the Raw Materials Master File must be updated to show that some of the raw materials have been encumbered. New Order Processing also updates the Raw Materials Master if a purchase request is generated for an item. In the case of the Raw Material Update, transactions are processed interactively when shipments are used in production, and when shipments are received from suppliers.

Because of these requirements—random access and in-place update capabilities—the Raw Materials Master File is implemented as an indexed file. The required program is used to convert an ordinary sequential file into an indexed file. This program would be useful during the start-up of the system—the sequential file can be created by the system editor or from a tape file.

The procedure required for the program is relatively simple, as shown in the following plan:

Open files
Read input file
Do until end of file
    Move input data to raw material master record
    Write raw material master record
    Read input file
End Do
Close files
Stop

Problem Solution

The required program is shown in Program 14.1, with structure diagram in Figure 14.3. INPUT-FILE is an ordinary sequential file created through the system editor. RAW-MATERIAL-MASTER-FILE is an indexed file accessed sequentially with record key ITEM-NUMBER-RMMR, as shown in the SELECT entry for the file at lines 1800-2100. Note that the definition of ITEM-NUMBER-RMMR at line 3500 indicates that it is alphanumeric, as its picture code is X(5). This corresponds to the requirement in most systems that a key field must be defined as alphanumeric (even though the field might actually contain numeric data).

As noted above, the WRITE statement used for an indexed file must contain the INVALID KEY clause (see lines 8000-8100). In this case, the paragraph 8000-ERROR will be executed if the data in INPUT-FILE contains records with duplicate or out of sequence key field values.

Program 14.1   Indexed file creation

```
100     IDENTIFICATION DIVISION.
200
300     PROGRAM-ID. INDEXED-CREATE.
400     AUTHOR. GARY.
500
600     ENVIRONMENT DIVISION.
700
800     CONFIGURATION SECTION.
900
1000    SOURCE-COMPUTER.
1100    OBJECT-COMPUTER.
1200
1300    INPUT-OUTPUT SECTION.
1400
1500    FILE-CONTROL.
1600
1700        SELECT INPUT-FILE            ASSIGN TO DISK.
1800        SELECT RAW-MATERIAL-MASTER-FILE ASSIGN TO DISK
1900            ACCESS IS SEQUENTIAL
2000            ORGANIZATION IS INDEXED
2100            RECORD KEY IS ITEM-NUMBER-RMMR.
```

Program 14.1 (continued)

```
2200
2300    DATA DIVISION.
2400
2500
2600    FILE SECTION.
2700
2800    FD   RAW-MATERIAL-MASTER-FILE
2900         RECORD CONTAINS 37 CHARACTERS
3000         VALUE OF TITLE IS "RAW/MATERIAL/MASTER"
3100         LABEL RECORDS ARE STANDARD
3200         DATA RECORD IS RAW-MATERIAL-MASTER-RECORD.
3300
3400    01   RAW-MATERIAL-MASTER-RECORD.
3500         03   ITEM-NUMBER-RMMR                PIC X(5).
3600         03   ITEM-DESCRIPTION-RMMR           PIC X(10).
3700         03   UNENCUMBERED-ON-HAND-RMMR       PIC 9(3).
3800         03   ENCUMBERED-ON-HAND-RMMR         PIC 9(3).
3900         03   ON-ORDER-RMMR                   PIC 9(3).
4000         03   ITEM-COST-RMMR                  PIC 9(3)V99.
4100         03   MINIMUM-ORDER-QUANTITY-RMMR     PIC 9(3).
4200         03   SUPPLIER-ID-NUMBER-RMMR         PIC X(5).
4300
4400    FD   INPUT-FILE
4500         RECORD CONTAINS 84 CHARACTERS
4600         BLOCK CONTAINS 30 RECORDS
4700         LABEL RECORDS ARE STANDARD
4800         VALUE OF TITLE IS "RAW/MATERIAL"
4900         DATA RECORD IS INPUT-RECORD.
5000
5100    01   INPUT-RECORD                         PIC X(84).
5200
5300    WORKING-STORAGE SECTION.
5400
5500    01 FLAGS.
5600       03 EOF-FLAG              PIC X(3) VALUE "NO".
5700          88 END-OF-FILE        VALUE "YES".
5800
5900    PROCEDURE DIVISION.
6000
6100    1000-MAJOR-LOGIC.
6200
6300       PERFORM 2000-INITIALIZATION.
6400       PERFORM 3000-CREATE-MASTER-FILE
6500          UNTIL END-OF-FILE.
6600       PERFORM 9000-TERMINATION.
6700       STOP RUN.
6800
6900    2000-INITIALIZATION.
7000
7100       OPEN INPUT INPUT-FILE
7200            OUTPUT RAW-MATERIAL-MASTER-FILE.
7300       READ INPUT-FILE
7400          AT END MOVE "YES" TO EOF-FLAG.
7500
```

```
7600    3000-CREATE-MASTER-FILE.
7700
7800        MOVE INPUT-RECORD TO RAW-MATERIAL-MASTER-RECORD.
7900        WRITE RAW-MATERIAL-MASTER-RECORD
8000            INVALID KEY
8100                PERFORM 8000-ERROR.
8200        READ INPUT-FILE
8300            AT END MOVE "YES" TO EOF-FLAG.
8400
8500    8000-ERROR.
8600
8700        EXIT.
8800
8900    9000-TERMINATION.
9000
9100        CLOSE RAW-MATERIAL-MASTER-FILE
9200                INPUT-FILE.
```

Program 14.1 (continued)

Figure 14.3 Structure diagram for Program 14.1

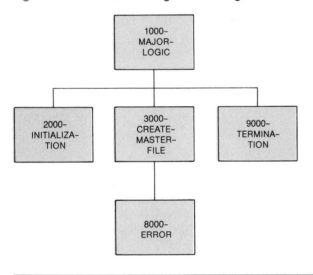

14.4 ACCESSING DATA RECORDS

When an indexed file is used as an input file in a program, the records may be accessed either sequentially or randomly. Sequential accessing of records in an indexed file is like processing a sequential file. Records are read from the beginning to the end of the file. The READ statement must include an AT END clause to specify the action to be taken when end of file is found. Sequential processing of an indexed file and the creation of an indexed file use the same SELECT entry. For example, the program shown in Figure 14.4 could be used to list the records contained in RAW-MATERIAL-MASTER-FILE created by Program 14.1.

Figure 14.4 Indexed file listing program

```
100      IDENTIFICATION DIVISION.
200
300      PROGRAM-ID. INDEXED-LIST.
400      AUTHOR. HORN.
500
600      ENVIRONMENT DIVISION.
700
800      CONFIGURATION SECTION.
900
1000     SOURCE-COMPUTER.
1100     OBJECT-COMPUTER.
1200
1300     INPUT-OUTPUT SECTION.
1400
1500     FILE-CONTROL.
1600
1700         SELECT PRINT-FILE                ASSIGN TO PRINTER.
1800         SELECT RAW-MATERIAL-MASTER-FILE ASSIGN TO DISK
1900             ACCESS IS SEQUENTIAL
2000             ORGANIZATION IS INDEXED
2100             RECORD KEY IS ITEM-NUMBER-RMMR.
2200
2300     DATA DIVISION.
2400
2500     FILE SECTION.
2600
2700     FD   RAW-MATERIAL-MASTER-FILE
2800          RECORD CONTAINS 37 CHARACTERS
2900          VALUE OF TITLE IS "RAW/MATERIAL/MASTER"
3000          LABEL RECORDS ARE STANDARD
3100          DATA RECORD IS RAW-MATERIAL-MASTER-RECORD.
3200
3300     01   RAW-MATERIAL-MASTER-RECORD.
3400          03   ITEM-NUMBER-RMMR              PIC X(5).
3500          03   ITEM-DESCRIPTION-RMMR         PIC X(10).
3600          03   UNENCUMBERED-ON-HAND-RMMR     PIC 9(3).
3700          03   ENCUMBERED-ON-HAND-RMMR       PIC 9(3).
3800          03   ON-ORDER-RMMR                 PIC 9(3).
3900          03   ITEM-COST-RMMR                PIC 9(3)V99.
4000          03   MINIMUM-ORDER-QUANTITY-RMMR   PIC 9(3).
4100          03   SUPPLIER-ID-NUMBER-RMMR       PIC X(5).
4200
4300     FD   PRINT-FILE
4400          RECORD CONTAINS 132 CHARACTERS
4500          DATA RECORD IS PRINT-RECORD.
4600
4700     01   PRINT-RECORD              PIC X(132).
4800
4900     WORKING-STORAGE SECTION.
5000
5100     01   FLAGS.
5200          03 EOF-FLAG               PIC X(3) VALUE "NO".
5300
```

```
5400      PROCEDURE DIVISION.
5500
5600      1000-MAJOR-LOGIC.
5700
5800          PERFORM 2000-INITIALIZATION.
5900          PERFORM 3000-LISTING
6000              UNTIL EOF-FLAG = "YES".
6100          PERFORM 9000-TERMINATION.
6200          STOP RUN.
6300
6400      2000-INITIALIZATION.
6500
6600          OPEN OUTPUT PRINT-FILE
6700               INPUT  RAW-MATERIAL-MASTER-FILE.
6800          READ RAW-MATERIAL-MASTER-FILE
6900              AT END MOVE "YES" TO EOF-FLAG.
7000
7100      3000-LISTING.
7200
7300          WRITE PRINT-RECORD FROM RAW-MATERIAL-MASTER-RECORD
7400              AFTER ADVANCING 1 LINE.
7500          READ RAW-MATERIAL-MASTER-FILE
7600              AT END MOVE "YES" TO EOF-FLAG.
7700
7800      9000-TERMINATION.
7900
8000          CLOSE RAW-MATERIAL-MASTER-FILE
8100                PRINT-FILE.
```

Note that except for the SELECT entry (lines 1800-2100), the program is similar to a file listing program for a sequential file.

To get the computer to read records from an indexed file in random sequence, you must use the SELECT entry shown in Figure 14.5.

Figure 14.5 SELECT entry for random access to an indexed file

```
SELECT   file-name ASSIGN TO system-name
         ORGANIZATION IS INDEXED
         ACCESS IS RANDOM
         RECORD KEY IS data-name
```

The ACCESS clause specifies RANDOM, as the records will be read only on demand rather than sequentially. As with sequential processing, the RECORD KEY clause specifies the field that has been used as the basis for organizing the file. In order to access a record from the file, the program must place a value in the field specified as the RECORD KEY and then execute a READ statement of the form shown in Figure 14.6. If such a record exists, the data is returned to the program and processing continues normally. If such a record does not exist or if the record has been deleted, an INVALID KEY condition will be detected and reported.

Figure 14.6   General form of READ statement for random access to an indexed file

```
READ file-name [INTO data-name]
    INVALID KEY statement
```

The general form for a READ statement for randomly accessing a file is shown in Figure 14.6. If an INVALID KEY condition is detected, the statement in the INVALID KEY clause will be executed.

Consider Program 14.2 in the next section. The purpose of this program is to update the indexed file RAW-MATERIAL-MASTER-FILE, which is used in the Amalgamated Custom Design system. RAW-MATERIAL-MASTER-FILE is defined in the SELECT entry at lines 1800-2100. The RECORD KEY is the field ITEM-NUMBER-RMMR. The random READ statement is used when an update transaction is processed (see the paragraph 6600-UPDATE-USED at lines 21700-22700. In this procedure, the item number of the record to be updated is placed into ITEM-NUMBER-RMMR by the statement (line 22000):

```
READ TRANSACTION-FILE INTO ITEM-NUMBER-RMMR.
```

Then, the following random READ statement is used to read the record associated with this item number from the file (lines 22200-22300):

```
READ RAW-MATERIAL-MASTER-FILE
    INVALID KEY MOVE "NO" TO VALID-TRANSACTION-FLAG.
```

If the record exists, data from the record is read and placed in the record defined for the file. If the record does not exist, the statement in the INVALID KEY clause is executed.

The random READ is also used in the routine for adding a record to the file (see the paragraph 6000-ADD-NEW-RECORD at lines 15800-16800). In this case, if a record is found, it means that an attempt is being made to add a record that already exists; if a record is not found (the INVALID KEY condition is true), it means that a record with that item number is not present in the file and processing of the transaction can proceed.

14.5   UPDATING AN INDEXED FILE

When a complete update is performed on a sequential file, it is necessary to create an entirely new file with the changes inserted at appropriate points. Indexed files may be updated in place; records may be added, changed, or deleted in an existing file without the program having to create a new file. Moreover, because an indexed file can be accessed randomly, the transaction records do not have to be in any particular sequence. As each transaction record is read, the appropriate master file record will be read, the changes will be made to it, and the record will be rewritten onto the master file.

The SELECT sentence for an indexed file to be updated randomly will be the same as for a file to be processed randomly. A file to be updated will be processed as both an input file (when a record is read from the file) and an output file (when the updated record is written onto the file). For this reason, the file must be opened in I–0 mode. The same READ statement used to access data from a file randomly is also used when the file is opened in I–0 mode. The INVALID KEY clause must be present. The statement required to rewrite the changed record onto the file has the form shown in Figure 14.7.

Figure 14.7   General form of the REWRITE statement for an indexed file

```
REWRITE record-name [FROM data-name]
    INVALID KEY statement
```

In order to use the REWRITE statement, a record first must have been accessed via a READ statement. The key field value of the present record is compared against the key field value of the last record read from the file. If the two key field values are not equal, then the INVALID KEY condition is true. Therefore, it is important that the program does not modify the key field value between the point at which the record is read and when it is rewritten onto the file. Program 14.2 illustrates the updating process. In this program, the REWRITE verb is used for transactions that involve changing values for existing fields in the master file (lines 21400-21500).

```
REWRITE RAW-MATERIAL-MASTER-RECORD
    INVALID KEY PERFORM 8100-ERROR-2.
```

The INVALID KEY clause is used to write an error message of the form INTERNAL LOGIC ERROR. The INVALID KEY clause will be executed only if the content of the key field has changed between the time a record was read and the point at which the REWRITE statement is executed. The purpose of this error message— which, if everything is done properly, will never be printed—is primarily to warn the programmer during testing that the key field value has changed.

14.6   ADDING AND DELETING RECORDS

In order to add records to an indexed file or delete records from an indexed file, ACCESS must be random, and the file must be opened in I–0 mode. The WRITE statement shown in Figure 14.2 is used to write new records in the file. The INVALID KEY condition occurs when an attempt is made to write a record with a key field that duplicates the key field of a record already present in the file. The DELETE statement, which has the general form shown in Figure 14.8, is used to delete records from an indexed file.

Figure 14.8   General form of the DELETE statement

```
DELETE file-name RECORD
    [INVALID KEY statement]
```

If the file is being processed in sequential access mode, the DELETE statement will cause deletion of the last record read from the file. The INVALID KEY clause cannot be specified in this case.

If the file is being processed in random access mode, the content of the record key is used to determine the record to be deleted from the file. The INVALID KEY condition occurs if the file does not contain a record with a record key equal to that contained in the record key field.

In order for the records to be deleted from a file, the file must be opened in I–O mode, as deletion actually causes the system to read the file (to determine if a record exists) and to write a new value into a code field to indicate that the record is deleted.

14.7 A COMPLETE FILE UPDATE EXAMPLE

Problem Statement

Write an interactive program to update the Raw Material Master File that is part of the Amalgamated Custom Design system. The Raw Material Master File is an indexed file. Transactions will be entered interactively by the program user. Transactions of the following types must be processed:

Transaction Code	Meaning	Action
A	Add	Add new record to Raw Material Master File.
D	Delete	Delete record from Raw Material Master File.
R	Receipt	Update unencumbered number on hand and number on order.
U	Use	Update encumbered number on hand.

Problem Analysis

The required program will be menu driven. In order to facilitate control of the program, we will add another option Q for "quit". This option will be selected when the user has entered all transactions during a given session. When this option is selected, the program closes the Raw Material Master File thereby making the changes permanent. A preliminary plan for the program is shown below:

```
Open files
Display menu
Read transaction code
Do until transaction code = "Q"
      Perform required update
      Read transaction code
End Do
Close files
Stop
```

This plan indicates that the menu is displayed only one time (at the beginning of the execution of the program). In case the user forgets the available options, it is useful to include a menu option allowing for the menu to be displayed again. We shall call this a "Help" option and use the transaction code H. An alternative to this procedure is to display the menu after each transaction, which can become annoying to the user entering data. With this modification in mind, we can now revise the plan for the program as shown below:

```
Open files
Display menu
Read transaction code
Do until transaction code = "Q"
     If transaction code = "A"
          Add new record
     End If
     If transaction code = "D"
          Delete record
     End If
     If transaction code = "R"
          Update receipt
     End If
     If transaction code = "U"
          Update used
     End If
     If invalid transaction code
          Write error message
     End If
     If transaction code = "H"
          Display menu
     End If
     Read transaction code
End Do
Close files
Stop
```

The procedure for adding a new record can be summarized as follows:

Add new record

```
     Read record key field
     Move "NO" to valid transaction flag
     Read raw material master file
          Invalid key move "YES" to valid transaction flag
     If valid transaction flag = "YES"
          Add record to file
     Else
          Write error message
     End If
```

The user first enters the key-field value of the record to be added. The program attempts to read the record with this key-field value from the file. If this record does not exist (hence the invalid key condition will be met) the record does not duplicate an existing record and, therefore, the process of entering data and writing the new record can be carried out. If a record does exist, this transaction cannot be continued further.

The procedure for deleting a record is much simpler as shown below:

Delete record

> Read record key field
> Delete raw material master file record
> > Invalid key write error message

If a record does not exist with the key-field value entered by the user, the invalid key condition will be true when the delete statement is executed, resulting in an error message being written.

The procedure for updating individual fields within a record requires that the user first enter the key-field value of the record. The program attempts to read this record from the master file. If it does not exist, the transaction is invalid and the procedure terminates, otherwise the user enters the transaction value (number items received or used). The program then adds or subtracts the transaction value to/from the value of number on hand in the master file record. Then the master file record is *rewritten* in the master file. The new record content replaces the old. This procedure may be summarized as follows:

Update receipt/used

> Read record key field
> Move "YES" to valid transaction flag
> Read raw material master file
> > Invalid key move "NO" to valid transaction flag
> If valid transaction flag = "YES"
> > Read transaction value
> > Update number on hand
> > Rewrite raw material master record
> Else
> > Write error message
> End If

Problem Solution

The required program is shown in Program 14.2, with structure diagram in Figure 14.9. The access method used for transactions in this program differs from other interactive programs that have been included thus far in the text. In many systems, COBOL programs use ACCEPT and DISPLAY to communicate with an interactive terminal. However, on some systems, ACCEPT and DISPLAY are used to communicate with the system operator's console only. In such systems, it is necessary to establish a file and assign it to the interactive device (see line 1700 in Program 14.2). The file is opened in I-0 mode (see line 12200) to enable both input and output operations to be performed. The program then uses ordinary READ and WRITE statements (instead of the ACCEPT and DISPLAY statements used previously) to perform input and output operations. In this case, the AT END clause is not included on the READ statement since there is no way for the system to determine when the end of file has been encountered. For this reason a menu option "Q" is included to terminate processing (see line 6300). Note also that there is no AFTER clause included on the WRITE statement, since there is no vertical spacing mechanism associated with the terminal display.

Three additional error messages not included in the program plan outlined above are required in the actual program. For example, in the procedure described for adding a new record, the program first attempts to read a record from the file (lines 16300-16400). If it does not exist, then the transaction processing continues. After new data has been entered, the program writes the master file record (lines 18600-18700). This write statement must include an INVALID KEY clause, as the file is being accessed randomly. At this point the invalid key condition will hold if the new record duplicates an existing one. As the program has just ascertained that no record exists with this key-field value, this condition should never occur. However, due to logical error in the program, the condition might occur, hence the message written as "INTERNAL LOGIC ERROR 7". A similar explanation accounts for the messages "INTERNAL LOGIC ERROR 5" and "INTERNAL LOGIC ERROR 2".

Program 14.2 Indexed file creation

```
100     IDENTIFICATION DIVISION.
200
300     PROGRAM-ID. INDEXED-UPDATE.
400     AUTHOR. WAYNE.
500
600     ENVIRONMENT DIVISION.
700
800     CONFIGURATION SECTION.
900
1000    SOURCE-COMPUTER.
1100    OBJECT-COMPUTER.
1200
1300    INPUT-OUTPUT SECTION.
1400
1500    FILE-CONTROL.
1600
1700        SELECT TRANSACTION-FILE          ASSIGN TO REMOTE.
1800        SELECT RAW-MATERIAL-MASTER-FILE ASSIGN TO DISK
1900            ACCESS IS RANDOM
2000            ORGANIZATION IS INDEXED
2100            RECORD KEY IS ITEM-NUMBER-RMMR.
2200
2300    DATA DIVISION.
2400
2500    FILE SECTION.
2600
2700    FD  RAW-MATERIAL-MASTER-FILE
2800        RECORD CONTAINS 37 CHARACTERS
2900        VALUE OF TITLE IS "RAW/MATERIAL/MASTER"
3000        LABEL RECORDS ARE STANDARD
3100        DATA RECORD IS RAW-MATERIAL-MASTER-RECORD.
3200
```

Program 14.2 (continued)

```
3300    01   RAW-MATERIAL-MASTER-RECORD.
3400         03   ITEM-NUMBER-RMMR              PIC X(5).
3500         03   ITEM-DESCRIPTION-RMMR         PIC X(10).
3600         03   UNENCUMBERED-ON-HAND.
3700             05   UNENCUMBERED-ON-HAND-RMMR  PIC 9(3).
3800         03   ENCUMBERED-ON-HAND.
3900             05   ENCUMBERED-ON-HAND-RMMR   PIC 9(3).
4000         03   ON-ORDER.
4100             05   ON-ORDER-RMMR             PIC 9(3).
4200         03   ITEM-COST.
4300             05   ITEM-COST-RMMR            PIC 9(3)V99.
4400         03   MINIMUM-ORDER-QUANTITY.
4500             05   MINIMUM-ORDER-QUANTITY-RMMR PIC 9(3).
4600         03   SUPPLIER-ID-NUMBER-RMMR       PIC X(5).
4700
4800    FD   TRANSACTION-FILE
4900         RECORD CONTAINS 80 CHARACTERS
5000         DATA RECORD IS TRANSACTION-RECORD.
5100
5200    01   TRANSACTION-RECORD               PIC X(80).
5300
5400    WORKING-STORAGE SECTION.
5500
5600    01  MAIN-MENU-CONSTANTS.
5700        03 LINE-1-MM PIC X(80) VALUE "    MAIN MENU".
5800        03 LINE-2-MM PIC X(80) VALUE "_____       ".
5900        03 LINE-3-MM PIC X(80) VALUE "A  ADD RECORD".
6000        03 LINE-4-MM PIC X(80) VALUE "D  DELETE A RECORD".
6100        03 LINE-5-MM PIC X(80) VALUE "R  RECEIPT OF MATERIAL".
6200        03 LINE-6-MM PIC X(80) VALUE "U  USE OF MATERIAL".
6300        03 LINE-7-MM PIC X(80) VALUE "Q  QUIT".
6400        03 LINE-8-MM PIC X(80) VALUE "H  HELP".
6500        03 LINE-9-MM PIC X(80) VALUE "_____".
6600
6700    01  MAIN-MENU REDEFINES MAIN-MENU-CONSTANTS.
6800        03 LINE-MM   OCCURS 9 TIMES PIC X(80).
6900
7000    01  PROMPTS.
7100        03 PROMPT-USED                  PIC X(80)
7200                    VALUE "ENTER NUMBER USED".
7300        03 PROMPT-RECEIVED              PIC X(80)
7400                    VALUE "ENTER NUMBER RECEIVED".
7500        03 PROMPT-ITEM-NUMBER           PIC X(80)
7600                    VALUE "ENTER ITEM NUMBER".
7700        03 PROMPT-ITEM-DESCRIPTION      PIC X(80)
7800                    VALUE "ENTER ITEM DESCRIPTION".
7900        03 PROMPT-UNENCUMBERED-ON-HAND PIC X(80)
8000                    VALUE "ENTER UNENCUMBERED ON HAND".
8100        03 PROMPT-ENCUMBERED-ON-HAND    PIC X(80)
8200                    VALUE "ENTER ENCUMBERED ON HAND".
8300        03 PROMPT-ON-ORDER              PIC X(80)
8400                    VALUE "ENTER NUMBER ON ORDER".
8500        03 PROMPT-ITEM-COST             PIC X(80)
8600                    VALUE "ENTER ITEM COST".
```

Program 14.2 (continued)

```
8700            03 PROMPT-MINIMUM-ORDER-QTY     PIC X(80)
8800                    VALUE "ENTER MINIMUM ORDER QUANTITY".
8900            03 PROMPT-SUPPLIER-ID          PIC X(80)
9000                     VALUE "ENTER SUPPLIER ID NUMBER".
9100            03 PROMPT-ENTER-TRANS-CODE     PIC X(80)
9200              VALUE "ENTER TRANSACTION CODE: A ,D, U, R, Q, or H".
9300
9400      01  INDEXES.
9500            03 INDX                  PIC 99 VALUE 0.
9600
9700      01  NUMBER-RECEIVED.
9800            03 NUMBER-RECEIVED-WS     PIC 999 VALUE 0.
9900
10000     01  NUMBER-USED.
10100           03 NUMBER-USED-WS        PIC 999 VALUE 0.
10200
10300     01  CONTROL-FIELDS.
10400           03 TRANSACTION-CODE       PIC X VALUE "Q".
10500             88 VALID-TRANS-CODE   VALUE "A" "D" "U" "R" "Q" "H".
10600
10700     01  FLAGS.
10800           03 VALID-TRANSACTION-FLAG   PIC XXX VALUE "YES".
10900
11000     PROCEDURE DIVISION.
11100
11200     1000-MAJOR-LOGIC.
11300
11400         PERFORM 2000-INITIALIZATION.
11500         PERFORM 3000-UPDATE-MASTER-FILE
11600              UNTIL TRANSACTION-CODE = "Q".
11700         PERFORM 9000-TERMINATION.
11800         STOP RUN.
11900
12000     2000-INITIALIZATION.
12100
12200         OPEN I-O TRANSACTION-FILE
12300                  RAW-MATERIAL-MASTER-FILE.
12400         PERFORM 4000-DISPLAY-MENU.
12500         PERFORM 5000-ACCEPT-TRANSACTION-CODE.
12600
12700     3000-UPDATE-MASTER-FILE.
12800
12900         IF TRANSACTION-CODE = "A"
13000            PERFORM 6000-ADD-NEW-RECORD.
13100         IF TRANSACTION-CODE = "D"
13200            PERFORM 6200-DELETE-RECORD.
13300         IF TRANSACTION-CODE = "R"
13400            PERFORM 6400-UPDATE-RECEIPT.
13500         IF TRANSACTION-CODE = "U"
13600            PERFORM 6600-UPDATE-USED.
13700         IF NOT VALID-TRANS-CODE
13800            PERFORM 8000-ERROR-1.
13900         IF TRANSACTION-CODE = "H"
14000            PERFORM 4000-DISPLAY-MENU.
14100         PERFORM 5000-ACCEPT-TRANSACTION-CODE.
```

Program 14.2 (continued)

```
14200
14300      4000-DISPLAY-MENU.
14400
14500          PERFORM 4010-DISPLAY-MENU-LINES
14600              VARYING INDX FROM 1 BY 1 UNTIL INDX > 9.
14700
14800      4010-DISPLAY-MENU-LINES.
14900
15000          MOVE LINE-MM (INDX) TO TRANSACTION-RECORD.
15100          WRITE TRANSACTION-RECORD.
15200
15300      5000-ACCEPT-TRANSACTION-CODE.
15400
15500          WRITE TRANSACTION-RECORD FROM PROMPT-ENTER-TRANS-CODE.
15600          READ TRANSACTION-FILE INTO TRANSACTION-CODE.
15700
15800      6000-ADD-NEW-RECORD.
15900
16000          WRITE TRANSACTION-RECORD FROM PROMPT-ITEM-NUMBER.
16100          READ TRANSACTION-FILE INTO ITEM-NUMBER-RMMR.
16200          MOVE "NO" TO VALID-TRANSACTION-FLAG.
16300          READ RAW-MATERIAL-MASTER-FILE
16400              INVALID KEY MOVE "YES" TO VALID-TRANSACTION-FLAG.
16500          IF VALID-TRANSACTION-FLAG = "YES"
16600              PERFORM 6010-ADD-RECORD
16700          ELSE
16800              PERFORM 8200-ERROR-3.
16900
17000      6010-ADD-RECORD.
17100
17200          WRITE TRANSACTION-RECORD FROM PROMPT-ITEM-DESCRIPTION.
17300          READ TRANSACTION-FILE INTO ITEM-DESCRIPTION-RMMR.
17400          WRITE TRANSACTION-RECORD FROM PROMPT-UNENCUMBERED-ON-HAND.
17500          READ TRANSACTION-FILE INTO UNENCUMBERED-ON-HAND.
17600          WRITE TRANSACTION-RECORD FROM PROMPT-ENCUMBERED-ON-HAND.
17700          READ TRANSACTION-FILE INTO ENCUMBERED-ON-HAND.
17800          WRITE TRANSACTION-RECORD FROM PROMPT-ON-ORDER.
17900          READ TRANSACTION-FILE INTO ON-ORDER.
18000          WRITE TRANSACTION-RECORD FROM PROMPT-ITEM-COST.
18100          READ TRANSACTION-FILE INTO ITEM-COST.
18200          WRITE TRANSACTION-RECORD FROM PROMPT-MINIMUM-ORDER-QTY.
18300          READ TRANSACTION-FILE INTO MINIMUM-ORDER-QUANTITY.
18400          WRITE TRANSACTION-RECORD FROM PROMPT-SUPPLIER-ID.
18500          READ TRANSACTION-FILE INTO SUPPLIER-ID-NUMBER-RMMR.
18600          WRITE RAW-MATERIAL-MASTER-RECORD
18700              INVALID KEY PERFORM 8600-ERROR-7.
18800
18900      6200-DELETE-RECORD.
19000
19100          WRITE TRANSACTION-RECORD FROM PROMPT-ITEM-NUMBER.
19200          READ TRANSACTION-FILE INTO ITEM-NUMBER-RMMR.
19300          DELETE RAW-MATERIAL-MASTER-FILE RECORD
19400              INVALID KEY PERFORM 8300-ERROR-4.
```

Program 14.2 (continued)

```
19500
19600      6400-UPDATE-RECEIPT.
19700
19800          WRITE TRANSACTION-RECORD FROM PROMPT-ITEM-NUMBER.
19900          READ TRANSACTION-FILE INTO ITEM-NUMBER-RMMR.
20000          MOVE "YES" TO VALID-TRANSACTION-FLAG.
20100          READ RAW-MATERIAL-MASTER-FILE
20200              INVALID KEY MOVE "NO" TO VALID-TRANSACTION-FLAG.
20300          IF VALID-TRANSACTION-FLAG = "YES"
20400              PERFORM 6410-GET-RECEIPT
20500          ELSE
20600              PERFORM 8000-ERROR-1.
20700
20800      6410-GET-RECEIPT.
20900
21000          WRITE TRANSACTION-RECORD FROM PROMPT-RECEIVED.
21100          READ TRANSACTION-FILE INTO NUMBER-RECEIVED.
21200          ADD NUMBER-RECEIVED-WS TO UNENCUMBERED-ON-HAND-RMMR.
21300          SUBTRACT NUMBER-RECEIVED-WS FROM ON-ORDER-RMMR.
21400          REWRITE RAW-MATERIAL-MASTER-RECORD
21500              INVALID KEY PERFORM 8100-ERROR-2.
21600
21700      6600-UPDATE-USED.
21800
21900          WRITE TRANSACTION-RECORD FROM PROMPT-ITEM-NUMBER.
22000          READ TRANSACTION-FILE INTO ITEM-NUMBER-RMMR.
22100          MOVE "YES" TO VALID-TRANSACTION-FLAG.
22200          READ RAW-MATERIAL-MASTER-FILE
22300              INVALID KEY MOVE "NO" TO VALID-TRANSACTION-FLAG.
22400          IF VALID-TRANSACTION-FLAG = "YES"
22500              PERFORM 6610-GET-USED
22600          ELSE
22700              PERFORM 8500-ERROR-6.
22800
22900      6610-GET-USED.
23000
23100          WRITE TRANSACTION-RECORD FROM PROMPT-USED.
23200          READ TRANSACTION-FILE INTO NUMBER-USED.
23300          SUBTRACT NUMBER-USED-WS FROM ENCUMBERED-ON-HAND-RMMR.
23400          REWRITE RAW-MATERIAL-MASTER-RECORD
23500              INVALID KEY PERFORM 8400-ERROR-5.
23600
23700      8000-ERROR-1.
23800
23900          MOVE "INVALID TRANSACTION CODE" TO TRANSACTION-RECORD.
24000          WRITE TRANSACTION-RECORD.
24100
24200      8100-ERROR-2.
24300
24400          MOVE "INTERNAL LOGIC ERROR 2" TO TRANSACTION-RECORD.
24500          WRITE TRANSACTION-RECORD.
24600
```

```
24700     8200-ERROR-3.
24800
24900         MOVE "ATTEMPT TO ADD RECORD WITH EXISTING ITEM NUMBER"
25000             TO TRANSACTION-RECORD.
25100         WRITE TRANSACTION-RECORD.
25200
25300     8300-ERROR-4.
25400
25500         MOVE "RECORD NOT IN FILE" TO TRANSACTION-RECORD.
25600         WRITE TRANSACTION-RECORD.
25700
25800     8400-ERROR-5.
25900
26000         MOVE "INTERNAL LOGIC ERROR 5" TO TRANSACTION-RECORD.
26100         WRITE TRANSACTION-RECORD.
```

Program 14.2 (continued)

Figure 14.9 Structure diagram of Program 14.2

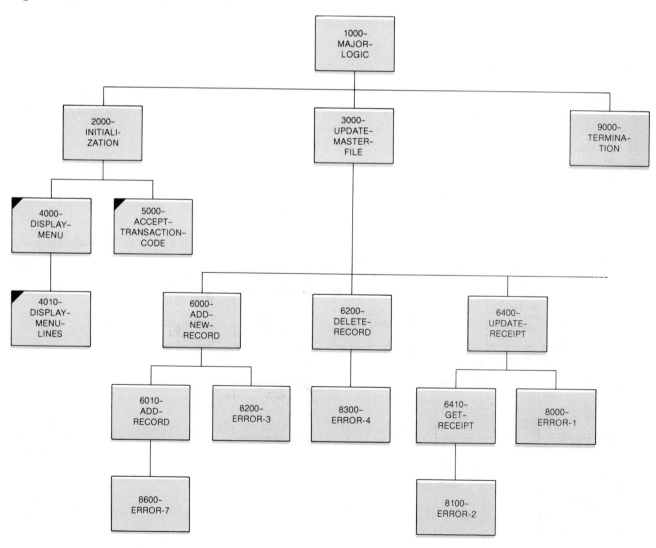

Program 14.2 (continued)

```
26200
26300       8500-ERROR-6.
26400
26500           MOVE "INVALID ITEM NUMBER" TO TRANSACTION-RECORD.
26600           WRITE TRANSACTION-RECORD.
26700
26800       8600-ERROR-7.
26900
27000           MOVE "INTERNAL LOGIC ERROR 7" TO TRANSACTION-RECORD.
27100           WRITE TRANSACTION-RECORD.
27200
27300       9000-TERMINATION.
27400
27500           CLOSE RAW-MATERIAL-MASTER-FILE
27600                 TRANSACTION-FILE.
```

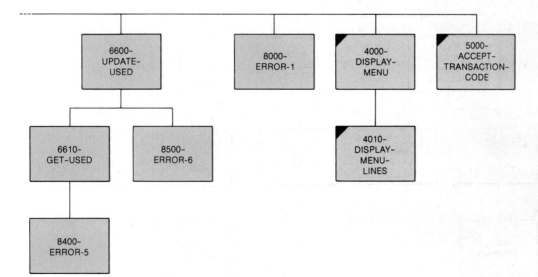

14.8 DYNAMIC ACCESS

In addition to sequential and random access methods discussed previously, COBOL permits dynamic access to an indexed file. Dynamic access permits both sequential access and random access to the same file in the same program. The general form of the SELECT entry for dynamic access is shown in Figure 14.10.

Figure 14.10 General form of SELECT entry for dynamic access to an indexed file

```
SELECT   file-name ASSIGN TO system-name
         ORGANIZATION IS INDEXED
         ACCESS MODE IS DYNAMIC
         RECORD KEY IS data-name.
```

When an indexed file is accessed dynamically and opened in either INPUT or I-0 mode, records are read sequentially from the file using the Format-1 READ statement with the NEXT RECORD option, as shown in Figure 14.11. In order to read records randomly from a file, a Format-2 READ statement is required.

When a Format-1 READ statement is executed, the next available record is read from the file; if the file has just been opened, then the first record is read. When a Format-2 READ statement is executed, the value contained in the key field specified for the file is used to determine the record to be read. If a Format-1 READ statement is executed after a Format-2 statement, the record immediately following the record by the Format-2 statement will be read. This feature can be used to continue the processing of an indexed file in a sequential manner after reading a specified record.

Figure 14.11 General form of READ statements

```
Format-1   (for sequential access)
READ       file-name [NEXT] RECORD
           [INTO data-name]
           [AT END statement]

Format-2   (for random access)
READ       file-name RECORD
           [INTO data-name]
           [KEY IS data-name]
           [INVALID KEY statement
```

For example, suppose we want to process all the records in the RAW-MATERIAL-MASTER-FILE described in Program 14.2, beginning with item number 11111. The SELECT statement would be written as

```
SELECT RAW-MATERIAL-MASTER-FILE
    ASSIGN TO DISK
    ORGANIZATION IS INDEXED
    ACCESS IS DYNAMIC
    RECORD KEY IS ITEM-NUMBER-RMMR.
```

The program would initially execute a procedure like the following:

```
MOVE "11111" TO ITEM-NUMBER-RMMR.
MOVE "YES" TO RECORD-PRESENT-FLAG.
READ RAW-MATERIAL-MASTER-FILE
    INVALID KEY MOVE "NO" TO RECORD-PRESENT-FLAG.
```

This procedure will read the required record if it is present in the file. Then a procedure like the following could process the remainder of the records in the file:

```
MOVE "NO" TO EOF-FLAG.
IF RECORD-PRESENT-FLAG = "YES"
    PERFORM PROCESS-READ UNTIL EOF-FLAG = "YES".
PROCESS-READ.
    PERFORM PROCESS-RECORD.
    READ RAW-MATERIAL-MASTER-FILE
        NEXT RECORD
        AT END MOVE "YES" TO EOF-FLAG.
```

In this example, a Format-1 READ statement is used for sequential access to the data after the Format-2 READ statement has read the initial record. Note that the NEXT clause is required when both Format-1 and Format-2 READ statements are present.

Some versions of COBOL support the START statement, which can be used to begin processing of an indexed file accessed in dynamic mode at a specified record. The general form of the START statement is shown in Figure 14.12. The START statement will cause subsequent access to the file to begin with a record whose key-field value satisfies the relation specified in the KEY IS clause. The data-name specified in the KEY IS clause will normally be the RECORD KEY field specified for the file. For example, suppose INVENTORY-FILE has been established as an indexed file with key field INVENTORY-NUMBER-IR, with length 4. In order to begin processing this file with the record *following* the record with inventory number equal to 5000, the following could be used:

```
MOVE "5000" TO INVENTORY-NUMBER-IR.
START INVENTORY-FILE KEY > INVENTORY-NUMBER-IR
    INVALID KEY PERFORM 3000-ERROR.
```

Figure 14.12 General form of the START statement

```
                                 ┌   ⎧ EQUAL TO        ⎫              ┐
                                 │   ⎪ =               ⎪              │
                                 │   ⎪ GREATER THAN    ⎪              │
START file-name          KEY IS  │   ⎨ >               ⎬  data-name   │
                                 │   ⎪ NOT LESS THAN   ⎪              │
                                 └   ⎩ NOT <           ⎭              ┘
                         [INVALID KEY statement]
```

The INVALID KEY condition will result if there is no record in the file satisfying the condition (i.e., no record with key-field value greater than 5000).

If the KEY IS clause is omitted, the current content of the RECORD KEY is used for comparison and the "equal to" relation is assumed. For example, to begin processing of the file with record 5000, either of the following two coding sequences could be used:

```
MOVE "5000" TO INVENTORY-NUMBER-IR.
START INVENTORY-FILE
    KEY IS EQUAL TO INVENTORY-NUMBER-IR
    INVALID PERFORM 3000-ERROR.
```

or

```
MOVE "5000" TO INVENTORY-NUMBER-IR.
START INVENTORY-FILE
    INVALID KEY PERFORM 3000-ERROR.
```

The NOT LESS THAN option is useful to begin processing of a file at a specified record if it exists or, if it does not, at the next record. For example, to begin the processing of INVENTORY-FILE at record 5000, or if record 5000 is not in the file with the first record with key field greater than 5000, the following code could be used:

```
MOVE "5000" TO INVENTORY-NUMBER-IR.
START INVENTORY-FILE
    KEY NOT LESS THAN INVENTORY-NUMBER-IR
    INVALID KEY PERFORM 3000-ERROR.
```

14.9 ACCESS METHOD AND OPEN MODES

An indexed file may be accessed by three methods (SEQUENTIAL, RANDOM, and DYNAMIC) and opened in three modes (INPUT, OUTPUT, I-O). The combination of access method and open mode governs the types of input/output statements that may be used.

Sequential Access

INPUT mode permits the statements READ (Format-1) and START to be used. This combination is used to read all or part of a file sequentially.

OUTPUT mode permits the WRITE statement. This combination is used to create an indexed file.

I-0 mode permits use of READ (Format-1), REWRITE, START, and DELETE statements. This combination is used for sequentially updating an indexed file. Note that new records cannot be added, because the WRITE statement cannot be used.

Random Access

INPUT mode permits the Format-2 READ statement only. This combination is used to access data records in the file randomly; no changes to the file can be made.

OUTPUT mode permits the WRITE statement only. This combination is used to add records to a file randomly.

I-0 mode permits the use of READ (Format-2), WRITE, REWRITE, START, and DELETE statements. This combination is used to perform random updating of an indexed file; it permits addition, deletion, and changing of records.

Dynamic Access

INPUT mode permits the Format-1 READ for sequential access, the Format-2 READ for random access, and the START statement. This combination is used to process sequential segments of an indexed file.

OUTPUT mode permits the WRITE statement only. This combination can be used only to add records to an indexed file; dynamic access always implies that the file is in existence.

I-0 mode permits the use of Format-1 READ (for sequential access), Format-2 READ (for random access), WRITE, REWRITE, START, and DELETE statements. This combination allows the program the greatest possible flexibility in processing an indexed file.

Choosing the Best Combination

In general, a programmer should choose that combination of access method and open mode that permits only the type of operation on a file required by the particular program. This practice will result in fewer potential errors in the long run, and it is in keeping with a widely held belief that restricting operations on a file to the minimum required to perform a given task enhances the overall security of the data processing system.

14.10 MULTIPLE RECORD KEYS

In our previous discussion of indexed files, we have included only one record key (called the *prime key*). All access to the file was governed by the content of that field. It is possible to specify alternate record key fields to provide other ways to access data in the file when the file is first created. The record keys declared when the file is created define all the record keys that can be used by other programs that need access to that file.

For example, the prime key for the file mentioned in Section 14.7 is INVENTORY-NUMBER-IR. By placing an appropriate value in this field, the program is able to read the corresponding record from the file. But suppose the record associated with a particular part description must be accessed. To enable the program to access the desired record, the part description field must be declared to be an ALTERNATE KEY by including the appropriate clause in the SELECT sentence. The general form of the SELECT entry for indexed files is shown in Figure 14.13.

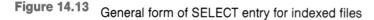

Figure 14.13   General form of SELECT entry for indexed files

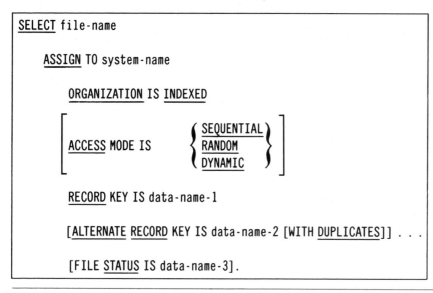

The ALTERNATE KEY clause provides a major option: if duplicate values of the alternate key are permitted, the WITH DUPLICATES clause is included. If each record in the file must have a unique value in the alternate key field (in the same way as each record must have a unique value in the prime key field), the clause is omitted. For example, to permit access to the file INVENTORY-FILE by both inventory number and part description, the SELECT entry could be written as

```
SELECT INVENTORY-FILE
    ASSIGN TO DISK
    ORGANIZATION IS INDEXED
    ACCESS IS DYNAMIC
    RECORD KEY IS INVENTORY-NUMBER-IR
    ALTERNATE RECORD KEY IS PART-DESCRIPTION-IR WITH DUPLICATES.
```

This example assumes that more than one record may have the same part description. More than one alternate record key is permitted on most COBOL systems. For example, the following SELECT would provide access by part supplier as well as inventory number and part description.

```
SELECT INVENTORY-FILE
    ASSIGN TO DISK
    ORGANIZATION IS INDEXED
    ACCESS IS DYNAMIC
    RECORD KEY IS INVENTORY-NUMBER-IR
    ALTERNATE RECORD KEY IS PART-DESCRIPTION-IR WITH DUPLICATES
    ALTERNATE RECORD KEY IS PART-SUPPLIER-IR WITH DUPLICATES.
```

In the two SELECT entries above, the WITH DUPLICATES clause was included for each alternate key because this is the most common situation in data organization: there is a single unique identifying number or name associated with a record and other nonunique numbers or names associated with the record, as well.

Often all records associated with a given nonunique identifier need to be found. In this example, a list of all inventory items supplied by a given supplier or all inventory items with a given description could be produced. To accomplish this, a START statement is used to locate the first desired record and sequential READs to locate the remainder. Because this method of access is used, DYNAMIC access must be specified in the SELECT entry, as shown in the above examples.

For example, the following program segment could be used to list all parts supplied by "ABC SUPPLY".

```
LIST-BY-SUPPLIER.
    MOVE "ABC SUPPLY" TO PART-SUPPLIER-IR.
    MOVE "CONTINUE" TO LIST-FLAG.
    START INVENTORY-FILE
        KEY = PART-SUPPLIER-IR
        INVALID KEY
            MOVE "FINISH" TO LIST-FLAG.
    IF LIST-FLAG = "FINISH"
        DISPLAY "NO RECORDS FOR ABC SUPPLY"
    PERFORM READ-LIST
        UNTIL LIST-FLAG = "FINISH".
READ-LIST.
    READ INVENTORY-FILE NEXT RECORD
        AT END MOVE "FINISH" TO LIST-FLAG.
    IF LIST-FLAG NOT = "FINISH" AND
        PART-SUPPLIER-IR = "ABC SUPPLY"
            DISPLAY INVENTORY-RECORD
        ELSE
            MOVE "FINISH" TO LIST-FLAG.
```

The START statement establishes a *key of reference* to be used in subsequent sequential READ statements. The first READ statement reads the record located by the START statement; subsequent repetitions of the READ statement read other records in sequence, using the established key of reference. Because of the START statement in this example, the key of reference is PART-SUPPLIER-IR and the records will be returned in sequence based on this field rather than on the actual physical sequence of the records in the file. In this context, "NEXT RECORD" should be construed as the record following in the sequence of data records if the file were sorted on this key. In previous examples, the key of reference has always been the prime key; now we are able to specify other fields as well.

Example

Write a program segment to list all inventory items whose part descriptions begin with WASHER. (This type of processing would be particularly valuable in an interactive environment where the user is not quite sure of the part desired and wishes to examine some likely alternatives.)

```
LIST-PARTS-BY-NAME.
    MOVE "WASHER" TO TEST-VALUE.
    INSPECT TEST-VALUE REPLACING ALL " " BY HIGH-VALUE.
    MOVE "WASHER" TO PART-DESCRIPTION-IR.
    START INVENTORY-FILE
        KEY IS NOT LESS THAN PART-DESCRIPTION-IR
        INVALID KEY
            MOVE "FINISH" TO LIST-FLAG.
    IF LIST-FLAG = "FINISH"
        DISPLAY "NO RECORDS IN FILE".
    PERFORM READ-LIST
        UNTIL LIST-FLAG = "FINISH".
READ-LIST.
    READ INVENTORY-FILE NEXT RECORD
        AT END MOVE "FINISH" TO LIST-FLAG.
    IF LIST-FLAG NOT = "FINISH"
        AND PART-DESCRIPTION-IR < TEST-VALUE
        DISPLAY INVENTORY-RECORD
    ELSE
        MOVE "FINISH" TO LIST-FLAG.
```

In this example, all records with part description fields having values ranging from "WASHER" to "WASHERZZZ . . .Z" will be DISPLAYed.

It is also possible to access a file randomly, using either the prime key, as we have done previously, or any of the alternate keys. This is accomplished by using a Format-2 READ statement including the KEY IS clause (see Figure 14.11). If the KEY IS clause is omitted, the content of the prime key is used to access the file. By specifying one of the alternate keys as the data name in the KEY IS clause, the record corresponding to that key field value will be read. If there is more than one record in the file with the same key field value (remember that duplicates may be allowed for alternate record keys), the record read will be the first record placed in the file with the specified key field value.

For example, suppose we wish to read the first record associated with the supplier "ABC SUPPLY" from the file INVENTORY-FILE described above. This can be accomplished by the following statements:

```
MOVE "ABC SUPPLY" TO PART-SUPPLIER-IR.
READ INVENTORY-FILE
    KEY IS PART-SUPPLIER-IR
    INVALID KEY
        PERFORM SUPPLIER-NOT-FOUND.
```

Execution of a Format-2 READ statement sets the key of reference in much the same way as a START statement. If the file is open in DYNAMIC mode, subsequent Format-1 READ statements would access the next record based on the key of reference (PART-SUPPLIER-IR in this example). Using this feature, it is possible to rewrite the routine to list all records associated with the supplier "ABC SUPPLY", as follows:

```
LIST-BY-SUPPLIER-2.
    MOVE "ABC SUPPLY" TO PART-SUPPLIER-IR.
    MOVE "CONTINUE" TO LIST-FLAG.
    READ INVENTORY-FILE
        KEY IS PART-SUPPLIER-IR
        INVALID KEY
            MOVE "FINISH" TO LIST-FLAG.
    IF LIST-FLAG = "FINISH"
        DISPLAY "NO RECORDS FOR ABC SUPPLY".
    PERFORM LIST-READ
        UNTIL LIST-FLAG = "FINISH".
LIST-READ.
    DISPLAY INVENTORY-RECORD.
    READ INVENTORY-FILE NEXT RECORD
        AT END
            MOVE "FINISH" TO LIST-FLAG.
    IF LIST-FLAG NOT = "FINISH" AND
        PART-SUPPLIER-IR NOT = "ABC SUPPLY"
            MOVE "FINISH" TO LIST-FLAG.
```

14.11 DEBUG CLINIC

The use of a FILE STATUS item can help ease the task of debugging a program which processes an indexed file. The FILE STATUS item is updated automatically after each input/output operation. The value contained in the item shows the status of the input/output operation. In order to make use of a FILE STATUS item, you must include FILE STATUS entry in the SELECT sentence for the file, as shown in Figure 14.13.

A FILE STATUS item must be defined as a two-character field in WORKING-STORAGE. The meaning ascribed to each possible setting of the FILE STATUS item is shown in Figure 14.14.

Figure 14.14 Meaning of a FILE STATUS item for indexed input/output

First Character	Second Character	Meaning
0	0	Successful Completion
0	2	Successful Completion, Duplicate Key
1	0	At End
2	1	Sequence Error
2	2	Duplicate Key
2	3	No Record Found
2	4	Boundary Violation
3	0	Permanent Error
9	–	Implementor Defined

There are two ways in which these codes can be of importance to the programmer. Perhaps the most common use is in interpreting system error messages when a program terminates abnormally. For example, a program that is creating an indexed file should terminate if a sequence error is encountered in the data being written to the file. The error message produced may include a reference to the file status value, which in this case would be 21.

A second way in which the file status item can be used is for the program to assume control of error conditions relating to file processing statement. This is possible by the inclusion of a DECLARATIVES SECTION and appropriate USE statements that serve to "trap" the ordinary error-handling procedure and give control of the process back to the program.

If a DECLARATIVES section is to be used, it must precede all other components of the PROCEDURE DIVISION. A general form for coding a DECLARATIVES section is shown in Figure 14.15. The DECLARATIVES section begins with a header

```
DECLARATIVES.
```

and ends with

```
END DECLARATIVES.
```

Figure 14.15   General form of PROCEDURE DIVISION with a DECLARATIVES section

```
PROCEDURE DIVISION.
DECLARATIVES.
section-name SECTION.
    declarative-sentence.
⎡paragraph-name.      ⎤
⎣   sentence . . .⎦      . . .
END DECLARATIVES.
section-name SECTION.
⎡paragraph-name.      ⎤
⎣   sentence . . .⎦      . . .
```

The DECLARATIVES must contain at least one named SECTION. Following the section header is a *declarative-sentence* that begins with "USE" and that determines when the procedure being specified will be executed. Readers familiar with the Report Writer will recall that DECLARATIVES are useful for intervening in the "normal" sequence of events in that context as well. Following the *declarative-sentence* may be one or more paragraphs containing COBOL code; these paragraphs are, however, optional. A typical general form for the USE statement as related to input/output operations is shown in Figure 14.16.

Figure 14.16   General form of the USE statement

```
USE AFTER ERROR PROCEDURE ON file-name. . .
```

If an appropriate DECLARATIVES section is included in a program, exceptional conditions such as end-of-file and sequence error will cause execution of the DECLARATIVES section code. If this code permits or if the DECLARATIVES section contains no executable code, control returns to the statement following the I-0 statement that caused the original exceptional condition. At this point, the program can test the file status code and take whatever action may be appropriate under the circumstances. For example, suppose the file INVENTORY-FILE is defined as follows:

```
SELECT INVENTORY-FILE
    ASSIGN TO DISK
    ORGANIZATION IS INDEXED
    ACCESS IS SEQUENTIAL
    RECORD KEY IS INVENTORY-NUMBER-IR
    FILE STATUS IS INV-STATUS.
```

A PROCEDURE DIVISION and relevant INPUT/OUTPUT statements for a program that will create this file are shown below:

```
PROCEDURE DIVISION.
DECLARATIVES.
ERROR-TRAP SECTION.
    USE AFTER ERROR PROCEDURE ON INVENTORY-FILE.
END DECLARATIVES.
PROCESSING SECTION.
1000-MAIN-PROCESS.
    .
    .

    .
    OPEN OUTPUT INVENTORY-FILE.
    IF INV-STATUS NOT = "00"
        DISPLAY "ERROR IN OPENING INVENTORY-FILE"
        DISPLAY "STATUS = " INV-STATUS
        PERFORM 9000-TERMINATION.
    .
    .

    .
2000-WRITE-READ.
    WRITE INVENTORY-RECORD.
    IF INV-STATUS = "00" OR
        INV-STATUS = "02"
        NEXT SENTENCE
    ELSE
        DISPLAY "ERROR IN WRITING INVENTORY-FILE"
        DISPLAY "STATUS = " INV-STATUS
        PERFORM 9000-TERMINATION.
    .
    .
    .
```

When using declaratives to trap errors for a file, it is not necessary to include an INVALID KEY clause on any input/output statement addressing that file. This technique does, however, place an added burden on the programmer to take appropriate action when error conditions do occur. If the program does not handle the conditions correctly, errors that are quite difficult to diagnose will result. On a more positive note, this technique can make systems appear to be more "user friendly" by shielding the user from the more esoteric system-produced error messages. This technique is highly recommended for interactive systems because, in many instances, the user can take corrective action in the event of exceptional conditions; otherwise, the program would usually be terminated by the operating system.

14.12 APPLICATIONS OF INDEXED FILES

Indexed files are very useful in designing a system when

1) random access to the data is required
2) sequential access to the data is required or desirable
3) complete in-place update capabilities (add, change, delete) are required

The choice of key fields is critical when an indexed file is designed. If multiple access paths are desired, the specification of multiple records keys should be considered. In an extreme situation, every field within the record could be declared as a key field. The general problem with multiple key fields and the basic reason that this facility should be used judiciously is the overhead required by alternate key fields. Additional space must be reserved for the pointers that permit access by alternate keys. Speed of access may also be critical, particularly in smaller systems. For example, in most systems, an indexed file is maintained in physical sequence based on the prime key, yielding very efficient sequential access to the data. (Only records that have been added are not physically located in the proper sequence.) Attempting to gain sequential access by any of the alternate keys requires the system to read records in other than the physical sequence. This is likely to be much more time-consuming than the corresponding operation using the prime key.

When considering indexed organization for a file, the systems analyst should be aware of the activity and volatility expected for the file. Recall that *activity* refers to the relative frequency of file access operations, and *volatility* is related to the occurrence of record additions and deletions. Activity is an important consideration because, in general, random access to a file requires more system resources than does sequential access. A large indexed file with high activity may take much more of the system's capacity than is necessary or feasible. In such situations, it may be advisable or necessary, because of system constraints, to revise the system design to maintain the file as a sequential file. Generally this is possible, but it will require sorting files in order to use them and may rule out interactive transaction processing for the file.

The expected volatility of a file is an important consideration because additions are usually placed in an overflow area and deleted records are flagged as deleted but still occupy space in the system. As the number of record additions increases, the amount of time required to access records in the file increases as well. As noted earlier, it is necessary in some systems to reorganize the file periodically to physically remove deleted records and to merge new records into the file in physical sequence.

If the file is highly volatile, and especially if it is also large, these considerations place a considerable burden on the system's resources, which may preclude use of an indexed file. In this case, it may be necessary to redesign the system and use sequential organization and sequential update techniques (or a relative file), which place less of a load on the system.

In any system permitting in-place updating of files, the maintenance of transaction logs and backups for relevant files is especially important. Sources of problems that may affect the integrity of data in the system are myriad and impossible to control to any great extent. When problems arise that destroy the integrity of a data file, it is necessary to re-create the data based on the backup file and the transaction log. In some large systems, this will be taken care of as a function of the operating system, but in most systems this function must be designed into each application system. For example, in Program 14.2, every transaction that has an effect on the indexed master file should be written on a transaction log file. In this way, by running a program that processes the transactions contained in the transaction log file against the backup version of the master file, an up-to-date version of the master file can be re-created.

Indexed files are very powerful and permit great latitude in the design of a data processing system. In addition to considering the logical needs of the system being designed, however, it is important for the systems analyst to consider:

- the expected activity
- the expected volatility
- the need to create backups and transaction logs
- the need to process the file by other systems that may not support indexed files
- the need for periodic reorganization of indexed files (in some systems)
- the storage capacity of the disk or other available random access storage device
- the capacity of the computing system vis-à-vis the requirements of processing indexed files

In some instances, these system considerations will make alternate choices for file organization techniques mandatory.

14.13   SELF-TEST EXERCISES

1. Complete the following table by entering valid input/output statements for
   each combination of file access method and open mode:

OPEN MODE

	INPUT	OUTPUT	I/O
SEQUENTIAL			
RANDOM			
DYNAMIC			

FILE ACCESS METHOD

2. What combination of access method and open mode would be best for the
   indexed file described in each of the following operations:
   a. creating an indexed file
   b. making a sequential organized file of transactions to update an indexed
      file
   c. processing a sequentially organized file of transactions to update an
      indexed file
   d. deleting records randomly from an indexed file
   e. reading data randomly from an indexed file
   f. adding records randomly to an indexed file
   g. sequentially listing a portion of the records in an indexed file
   h. updating (add/delete/change) records in an indexed file with the same
      program

3. Distinguish between the WRITE and REWRITE statements. What purpose is
   served by each?

4. Distinguish between Format-1 READ and Format-2 READ. What purpose is
   served by each?

5. Can an indexed file be created under dynamic access? Explain.

6. Write code required to begin sequential processing of an indexed file, beginning with the record with key-field value 200 or the next available record.

7. A Format-2 READ statement for an indexed file has resulted in a FILE STATUS
   item value 23. Were the statements in the INVALID KEY clause of the statement
   executed? Why or why not?

8. An indexed file containing inventory data must be created from a sequential file. The IDENTIFICATION, ENVIRONMENT, and DATA DIVISION are given below. Write the PROCEDURE DIVISION to create the indexed file and produce a listing of the file.

```
IDENTIFICATION DIVISION.
PROGRAM-ID.  EXERCISE 8 SECTION 14.12.
AUTHOR.  YOUR NAME.
ENVIRONMENT DIVISION.
CONFIGURATION SECTION.
SOURCE-COMPUTER.
OBJECT-COMPUTER.
INPUT-OUTPUT SECTION.
FILE-CONTROL.
    SELECT INPUT-FILE ASSIGN TO DISK.
    SELECT INVENTORY-FILE ASSIGN TO DISK
        ORGANIZATION IS INDEXED
        ACCESS IS SEQUENTIAL
        RECORD KEY IS INVENTORY-NUMBER-IRR.
    SELECT PRINT ASSIGN TO PRINTER.
DATA DIVISION.
FILE SECTION.
FD  INPUT-FILE
    LABEL RECORDS ARE STANDARD
    DATA RECORD IS INPUT-RECORD.
01  INPUT-RECORD.
    02  INVENTORY-NUMBER-IR          PIC X(5).
    02  DESCRIPTION-IR               PIC X(20).
    02  QUANTITY-ON-HAND-IR          PIC 9(5).
    02  REORDER-POINT-IR             PIC 9(5).
    02  REORDER-AMOUNT-IR            PIC 9(5).
    02  UNIT-SELLING-PRICE-IR        PIC 9(4)V99.
    02  UNIT-COST-PRICE-IR           PIC 9(4)V99.
FD  INVENTORY FILE
    LABEL RECORDS ARE STANDARD
    DATA RECORD IS INVENTORY-RECORD.
01  INVENTORY-RECORD.
    02  INVENTORY-NUMBER-IRR         PIC X(5).
    02  DESCRIPTION-IRR              PIC X(20).
    02  QUANTITY-ON-HAND-IRR         PIC 9(5).
    02  REORDER-POINT-IRR            PIC 9(5).
    02  REORDER-AMOUNT-IRR           PIC 9(5).
    02  UNIT-SELLING-PRICE-IRR       PIC 9(4)V99.
    02  UNIT-COST-PRICE-IRR          PIC 9(4)V99.
FD  PRINT
    LABEL RECORDS ARE OMITTED
    DATA RECORD IS PRINT-LINE.
01  PRINT-LINE    PIC X(132).
WORKING-STORAGE SECTION.
01  FLAGS.
    03  EOF-FLAG  PIC XXX VALUE "NO".
```

9. Write the PROCEDURE DIVISION to create a listing of the file INVENTORY-FILE created in Exercise 8.

10. A transaction file contains sales records for the inventory system described in Exercise 8. Each record in the file contains an inventory number and the

number of parts sold. A program is required to update the file INVENTORY-MASTER based on the sales data. The IDENTIFICATION, ENVIRONMENT, and DATA DIVISIONS for the program are given below. Write the PROCEDURE DIVISION.

```
IDENTIFICATION DIVISION.
PROGRAM-ID  EXERCISE 10 SECTION 14.12.
AUTHOR.    YOUR NAME.
ENVIRONMENT DIVISION.
CONFIGURATION SECTION.
SOURCE-COMPUTER.
OBJECT-COMPUTER.
INPUT-OUTPUT SECTION.
FILE-CONTROL.
    SELECT SALES-FILE ASSIGN TO DISK.
    SELECT INVENTORY-FILE ASSIGN TO DISK
        ORGANIZATION IS INDEXED
        ACCESS IS RANDOM
        RECORD KEY IS INVENTORY-NUMBER-IRR.
    SELECT PRINT ASSIGN TO PRINTER.
DATA DIVISION.
FILE SECTION.
FD  SALES-FILE
    LABEL RECORDS ARE STANDARD
    DATA RECORD IS SALES-RECORD.
01  SALES-RECORD.
    02  INVENTORY-NUMBER-SR          PIC X(5).
    02  NUMBER-SOLD-SR               PIC 999.
FD  INVENTORY-FILE.
    LABEL RECORDS ARE STANDARD
    DATA RECORD IS INVENTORY-RECORD.
01  INVENTORY-RECORD.
    02  INVENTORY-NUMBER-IRR         PIC X(5).
    02  DESCRIPTION-IRR              PIC X(20).
    02  QUANTITY-ON-HAND-IRR         PIC 9(5).
    02  REORDER-POINT-IRR            PIC 9(5).
    02  REORDER-AMOUNT-IRR           PIC 9(5).
    02  UNIT-SELLING-PRICE-IRR       PIC 9(4)V99.
    02  UNIT-COST-PRICE-IRR          PIC 9(4)V99.
FD  PRINT
    LABEL RECORDS ARE OMITTED
    DATA RECORD IS PRINT-LINE.
01  PRINT-LINE    PIC X(132).
WORKING-STORAGE SECTION.
01  FLAGS.
    03  EOF-FLAG  PIC XXX VALUES "NO".
```

11. Write the SELECT entry and PROCEDURE DIVISION for a program that would process all records in INVENTORY-FILE (described in Exercise 10) that follow the record with inventory number "05000".

12. Write the PROCEDURE DIVISION for a program to update the file INVENTORY-FILE described above. The transaction file contains records in essentially the same format as the records in the file to be updated, with the addition of a transaction code. The update program processes each transaction, taking appropriate action on records in the file to be updated. The following transaction codes are used:

Code	Meaning
CD	change description
CQ	change quantity on hand
CP	change reorder point
CA	change reorder amount
CS	change unit selling price
CC	change unit cost
AQ	add to quantity on hand
SQ	subtract from quantity on hand
AR	add record to file
DR	delete record from file

The IDENTIFICATION, ENVIRONMENT and DATA DIVISIONs are shown below.

```
        IDENTIFICATION DIVISION.
        PROGRAM-ID.  EXERCISE 12 SECTION 14.12.
        AUTHOR.  YOUR NAME.
        ENVIRONMENT DIVISION.
        CONFIGURATION SECTION.
        SOURCE-COMPUTER.
        OBJECT-COMPUTER.
        INPUT-OUTPUT SECTION.
        FILE-CONTROL.
            SELECT TRANSACTIONS ASSIGN TO DISK.
            SELECT INVENTORY-FILE ASSIGN TO DISK
                ORGANIZATION IS INDEXED
                ACCESS IS RANDOM
                RECORD KEY IS INVENTORY-NUMBER-IR.
            SELECT PRINT ASSIGN TO PRINTER.
        DATA DIVISION.
        FILE SECTION.
        FD  TRANSACTIONS
            LABEL RECORDS ARE STANDARD
            DATA RECORD IS TRANSACTION-RECORD.
        01  TRANSACTION-RECORD.
            03  INVENTORY-NUMBER-TR          PIC X(5).
            03  DESCRIPTION-TR               PIC X(20).
            03  QUANTITY-ON-HAND-TR          PIC 9(5).
            03  REORDER-POINT-TR             PIC 9(5).
            03  REORDER-AMOUNT-TR            PIC 9(5).
            03  UNIT-SELLING-PRICE-TR       PIC 9(4)V99.
            03  UNIT-COST-PRICE-TR          PIC 9(4)V99.
            03  TRANSACTION-CODE-TR         PIC XX.
                88  CHANGE-DESCRIPTION           VALUE "CD".
                88  CHANGE-QUANTITY-ON-HAND      VALUE "CQ".
                88  CHANGE-REORDER-POINT         VALUE "CP".
                88  CHANGE-REORDER-AMOUNT        VALUE "CA".
                88  CHANGE-UNIT-SELLING-PRICE    VALUE "CS".
                88  CHANGE-UNIT-COST             VALUE "CC".
                88  ADD-TO-QTY-ON-HAND           VALUE "AQ".
                88  SUBTRACT-FROM-QTY-ON-HAND    VALUE "SQ".
                88  ADD-RECORD                   VALUE "DR".
                88  DELETE-RECORD                VALUE "DR".
                88  VALID-TRANSACTION-CODE       VALUE
                    "CD", "CQ", "CP", "CA", "CS",
                    "CC", "AQ", "SQ", "AR", "DR".
```

```
FD  INVENTORY-FILE
    LABEL RECORDS ARE STANDARD
    DATA RECORD IS INVENTORY-RECORD.
01  INVENTORY-RECORD.
    03  INVENTORY-NUMBER-IR        PIC X(5).
    03  DESCRIPTION-IR             PIC X(20).
    03  QUANTITY-ON-HAND-IR        PIC 9(5).
    03  REORDER-POINT-IR           PIC 9(5).
    03  REORDER-AMOUNT-IR          PIC 9(4)V99.
    03  UNIT-SELLING-PRICE-IR      PIC 9(4)V99.
    03  UNIT-COST-PRICE-IR         PIC 9(4)V99.
FD  PRINT
    LABEL RECORDS ARE OMITTED
    DATA RECORD IS PRINT-RECORD.
01  PRINT-RECORD  PIC X(132).
WORKING-STORAGE SECTION.
01  FLAGS.
    03  EOF-FLAG  PIC X(3)  VALUE "NO".
        88  END-OF-TRANSACTIONS  VALUE "YES".
    03  RECORD-FOUND-FLAG  PIC X(3)  VALUE "YES".
        88  RECORD-FOUND  VALUE "YES".
```

13. A personnel file, which will be accessed by employee Social Security number (prime key), employee name, department number, and zip code (alternate keys), is to be created as an indexed file. Write the SELECT entry for the program that will create the file.

14. For the personnel file of Exercise 13, write the SELECT entry and a PROCEDURE DIVISION for a program that will create a listing of all employees in Department 3.

14.14 PROGRAMMING EXERCISES

1. Write a program to create an indexed file with records in the following format:

Picture	Description
X(5)	Store identifier
X(3)	Department identifier
9(6)V99	Year-to-date total cash sales
9(6)V99	Year-to-date total VISA sales
9(6)V99	Year-to-date total MasterCard sales
9(6)V99	Year-to-date total credit sales
9(6)V99	Year-to-date total taxable sales
9(6)V99	Year-to-date total nontaxable sales
9(6)V99	Year-to-date total wholesale sales
9(6)V99	Year-to-date total retail sales

Use the eight-character field containing the store identifier and the department identifier as the key field for the file.

2. Write a program to use the data file described below to update the file created in Exercise 1.

Picture	Description
X(5)	Store identifier
X(3)	Department identifier
9(9)	Customer number
9(6)	Date of sale—mmddyy
99	Quantity
9(9)	Inventory number of item sold
9999V99	Wholesale price/item
9999V99	Retail price/item
XX	Status code: paid by cash (CA)
	paid by VISA (VS)
	paid by MasterCard (MC)
	credit purchase (CR)
X	Tax code: Sale is taxable (T)
	Sale is nontaxable (N)

3. Write a program to create a report summarizing the data contained in the file created in Exercise 1. Include totals for each store and the entire company.

4. Write a program to produce a report listing those departments showing a profit that is zero or negative.

5. XYZ College requires a student records system. At the heart of the system will be a Student Master File. The file will be indexed using the student Social Security number as the prime key. Each record in the Master File will contain the following fields:

   Student Social Security number
   Name
   Address
   Declared major (2-character code)
   Birthdate
   Sex code
   Credit hours completed
   Grade point average
   Credit hours in progress
   Credit hours in progress
   Date of first registration
   Date of last registration

   Write a program to create the Student Master File with data of your choosing.

6. Write a program to update the Student Master File created in Exercise 5. Include provisions to:

   Add a new student
   Delete a student
   Change any field

7. Write an interactive program to process registration information for XYZ College. The program must update appropriate fields in the Student Master File record for each student registering for a course and must create a sequential file REGISTRATION-DETAIL containing one record for each course registration. (If a student registers for 2 courses, REGISTRATION-DETAIL will contain 2 records.) Each REGISTRATION-DETAIL record should contain the following fields:

> Course number
> Section number
> Student Social Security number
> Registration date
> Credit hours
> Grade (blank until course is completed)

8. Assume that the file REGISTRATION-DETAIL has been updated with grades at the end of the term and is in sequence by student Social Security number. Write a program to update the Student Master File.

9. Modify the program written for Exercise 5 to allow access to records by declared major. Write an interactive program to allow a user to enter a major and secure a listing of all students with that declared major.

10. Write a program to purge inactive student records from the Student Master File described in Exercise 5. Students are classified as inactive if they have not registered for courses in the previous five years. Any record removed from the Student Master File should be added to a sequential Inactive Student File.

11. The following problems relate to Exercise 1, Section 15, Chapter 13.
    a. Write a program to transform TABLE-FILE into an indexed file.
    b. Revise the program to update the indexed TABLE-FILE.

RELATIVE FILES 15

15.1 CAPABILITIES OF RELATIVE FILES

Random access to data is a very powerful tool for designing data processing systems. The random access features of indexed files open up possibilities that do not exist with sequential files alone. COBOL systems provide another file type that supports random access—relative files. A relative file is a sequence of records that can be accessed by a record number. The program can access the first record or the fifteenth record or the eighth record or, indeed, any record within the file by specifying the number of the desired record and executing an appropriate READ or WRITE/REWRITE statement. The operating system takes care of locating the record within the file (for a READ) or placing the record in the file (for a WRITE or REWRITE).

In many respects, a relative file resembles a table. In both cases, access to the content is gained by specifying the location of the desired element in the structure. Of course, a relative file is physically located in mass storage, whereas a table is located in memory. Because of this difference, the access speed is dramatically different; it may differ by a factor of 1000 or more. This difference in speed must be considered when deciding whether a table or relative file is to be used in a particular application. If sufficient memory is available, a table is much more efficient, but if the amount of data exceeds memory size, a relative file offers roughly the same capabilities except for speed.

For situations in which the key field for a file is restricted, a relative file can enable very efficient direct access to records within a data file. For example, suppose an organization uses three-digit employee numbers. It would be possible to use the employee number as the address of the employee record within the data file. Thus, employee 203 would be placed in the 203rd record in the file. Because there are 999 possible employee numbers, the file would need to contain 999 records. This method is analogous to the direct table look-up method described in Chapter 12.

Usually, however, key-field values are not this small. An employee number is typically the employee Social Security number—a nine-digit number. An attempt to use the direct method described above would require a file containing 1,000,000,000 records, which would far exceed the capacity of any mass storage device currently available. Moreover, only the records associated with actual employees would be used; the vast majority would contain no data. Clearly, the direct access method will not work except in very restricted circumstances.

Relative files can be very useful, however, if the records are randomly placed in the file. This method is similar to the hash table method, in which a record's address is determined using a hash function. Some people call this method *direct file organization*.

The hash function computes an address based on the record key. A very common hash function is the division/remainder method: divide the key-field value by the number of records in the file. Take the remainder and add 1. For example, if the file contained 59 records, the address record for 203 would be computed as follows:

$$\begin{array}{r} 3 \\ 59\overline{)203} \\ \underline{177} \\ 26 \end{array}$$

The record address is 26 + 1 = 27. Of course, this method can result in *synonyms*—records that have different key fields yielding the same address.

One method of handling synonyms is to examine following records until an unused record is located (when loading data) or until the desired record is located (when searching for data). The event of finding a used position while searching for a place to put data is a *collision*.

As with the hash table technique, this method has been shown to work best when the file size is a prime number. When the file is more than two-thirds full, the number of collisions rises dramatically. This results in a severe degradation in the performance of the program, because multiple reads must be executed to locate a single record. Within these constraints, the randomized placement of records in a relative file offers a good alternative to indexed files for many applications that require random access data files.

15.2 FILE CREATION—SEQUENTIAL ACCESS

As with indexed files, relative files must first be created in a sequential mode. After the file exists, random access to the file is permitted. When using a randomization technique, it is necessary to write a program that creates a relative file made up of records containing null values. For example, all numeric fields may be initialized to zero and all alphanumeric fields to spaces. The size of the file is fixed at the time the file is initially created. Once the file has been created with "dummy" records, another program is required to load actual data into the file, using a randomization technique. This program will use random access to write records into the file at desired locations.

The general form of the SELECT entry for a relative file is shown in Figure 15.1. Note that the ACCESS MODE may be SEQUENTIAL, RANDOM, or DYNAMIC, as needed.

The program to create the initial version of the file will need SEQUENTIAL access because records will be written onto the file sequentially from first to last. As with indexed files, RANDOM access implies that the program will specify the desired record before an input/output statement, and DYNAMIC access implies that random and sequential access statements are permitted for the file.

Figure 15.1   General form of the SELECT entry for a relative file

```
SELECT file-name
ASSIGN TO system-name
  ORGANIZATION IS RELATIVE
  ┌                     ⎧SEQUENTIAL [RELATIVE KEY IS data-name-1]⎫ ⎤
  │ ACCESS MODE IS ⎨ ⎰RANDOM ⎱ RELATIVE KEY IS data-name-1       ⎬ │
  └                     ⎩ ⎱DYNAMIC⎰                              ⎭ ⎦
[FILE STATUS IS data-name-2].
```

The mechanism for specifying the record to be read or written is contained in the RELATIVE KEY clause. The *data-name* specified here must contain the address of the desired record before a random access input/output statement can be executed. This *data-name* must be defined as an unsigned integer by the program, typically as a WORKING-STORAGE item.

Note that for ACCESS MODE IS SEQUENTIAL, the RELATIVE KEY clause is optional and would, in most instances, be omitted. The only time a RELATIVE KEY clause is needed for SEQUENTIAL access is when a START statement will be used in the program. In this case, the desired record number is placed in the relative key field prior to execution of the START. We shall say more about the RELATIVE KEY clause in the following section. A typical SELECT entry for a program that would create an initial version of a relative file is:

```
SELECT file-name
    ASSIGN TO system-name
    ORGANIZATION IS RELATIVE
    ACCESS MODE IS SEQUENTIAL.
```

The ACCESS MODE clause in this case is actually optional; if the ACCESS MODE clause is omitted, SEQUENTIAL access is assumed.

The general form for input/output statements for sequential access to a relative file is shown in Figure 15.2. A sequential access relative file may be opened in INPUT, OUTPUT or I-0 mode. If the file is being created, it would be opened as OUTPUT. The only valid input/output statement for an OUTPUT file is WRITE. The same method is used to secure a sequential listing of all files, whether sequential, indexed or relative: by opening the file as INPUT and using the sequential READ statement. Opening the file in I-0 mode will enable all input/output statements except WRITE. (See Section 4 of this chapter for more details.)

Note that the WRITE statement must include the INVALID KEY clause unless a USE procedure for the file has been specified (see Chapter 14, Section 10). The invalid key condition will be true when an attempt is made to write beyond the physical limits of a file.

Figure 15.2   Sequential access input/output statements for relative files

```
READ file-name [NEXT] RECORD [INTO data-name] AT END statement
WRITE record-name [FROM data-name] INVALID KEY statement


      ┌ INPUT  file-name . . . ┐
OPEN  ┤ OUTPUT file-name . . . ├ . . .
      └ I-O    file-name . . . ┘
```

If a RELATIVE KEY clause is specified in the SELECT, the value of the relative key field will be updated as a result of each execution of a WRITE statement. Thus, the value contained in the relative key field will always be the number of the record just written—for example, 1 after the first record, 2 after the second record, and so on.

The sequential READ statement for a relative file has the same considerations as sequential READs for other file types. The NEXT clause is required only for sequential access when the access mode is DYNAMIC.

15.3   PROGRAM EXAMPLE

Problem Statement

Write a program to carry out the initial file creation for the Work In Progress Master File, which is part of the Amalgamated Custom Design system described in Chapter 10, Section 4.

Problem Analysis

Recall that this is a relative file with randomized placement of records using the key field designated as the batch number. The initial version of the file consists of 97 records, all of which contain spaces. Because the number of records chosen is a prime number considerably larger than the number of records anticipated to be contained in the file, the randomization procedure and the retrieval procedures will be as efficient as possible.

Problem Solution

The required program is shown in Program 15.1, with a structure diagram in Figure 15.3. The SELECT statement specifies that WIP-MASTER-FILE is a RELATIVE file with SEQUENTIAL access (see lines 1800-2000). The file is opened in OUTPUT mode (line 5000). The procedure 2000-WRITE-WIP-RECORD is executed 97 times (line 5200) thereby creating an initial version of the file containing 97 records. Note that the WRITE statement at lines 5800-5900 must contain the INVALID KEY clause. In this case the INVALID KEY condition would arise only if there was no room on the device for all of the records of the file. Note also that the file is closed WITH LOCK (see line 5300). On the system used for this program, the WITH LOCK clause is needed to make the file permanent. This clause may or may not be required on your system.

Program 15.1   Initial file creation for Work in Progress Master File

```
100
200        IDENTIFICATION DIVISION.
300
400        PROGRAM-ID. WIP-CREATE.
500        AUTHOR. WAYNE.
600
700        ENVIRONMENT DIVISION.
800
900        CONFIGURATION SECTION.
1000
1100       SOURCE-COMPUTER.
1200       OBJECT-COMPUTER.
1300
1400       INPUT-OUTPUT SECTION.
1500
1600       FILE-CONTROL.
1700
1800           SELECT WIP-MASTER-FILE ASSIGN TO DISK
1900               ORGANIZATION IS RELATIVE
2000               ACCESS IS SEQUENTIAL.
2100
2200       DATA DIVISION.
2300
2400       FILE SECTION.
2500
2600       FD  WIP-MASTER-FILE
2700           RECORD CONTAINS 84 CHARACTERS
2800           BLOCK CONTAINS 30 RECORDS
2900           LABEL RECORDS ARE STANDARD
3000           VALUE OF TITLE IS "WIP/MASTER/FILE"
3100           DATA RECORD IS WIP-MASTER-RECORD.
3200
3300       01  WIP-MASTER-RECORD.
3400           03 BATCH-NUMBER-WMR              PIC 9(10).
3500           03 BATCH-NUMBER-WMR-A REDEFINES BATCH-NUMBER-WMR.
3600              05 ORDER-NUMBER-WMR           PIC 9(5).
3700              05 CATALOG-NUMBER-WMR         PIC 9(5).
3800           03 QUANTITY-WMR                  PIC 9(3).
3900           03 NUMBER-COMPONENTS-WMR         PIC 9(3).
4000           03 SCHEDULED-COMPLETION-DATE-WMR PIC 9(6).
4100           03 ACTUAL-COMPLETION-DATE-WMR    PIC 9(6).
4200           03 RAW-MATERIALS-WMR      PIC X(5) OCCURS 5 TIMES.
4300           03 DELETION-CODE-WMR             PIC X.
4400           03 FILLER                        PIC X(30).
4500
4600       PROCEDURE DIVISION.
4700
4800       1000-MAIN-PROCEDURE.
4900
5000           OPEN OUTPUT WIP-MASTER-FILE.
5100           MOVE SPACES TO WIP-MASTER-RECORD.
5200           PERFORM 2000-WRITE-WIP-MASTER-RECORD 97 TIMES.
5300           CLOSE WIP-MASTER-FILE WITH LOCK.
5400           STOP RUN.
```

Program 15.1 (continued)

```
5500
5600     2000-WRITE-WIP-MASTER-RECORD.
5700
5800        WRITE WIP-MASTER-RECORD
5900            INVALID KEY PERFORM 8000-ERROR-EXIT.
6000
6100     8000-ERROR-EXIT.
6200
6300        EXIT.
```

Figure 15.3   Structure diagram for Program 15.1

15.4   UPDATING PROCEDURES—RANDOM ACCESS

Once a relative file has been created, it can be accessed randomly for purposes of retrieving and modifying data. When using the randomizing technique, placing a data record in the file is, technically, modifying one of the dummy records previously placed in the file; this requires random access. Random access to a relative file is possible if ACCESS MODE IS RANDOM or ACCESS MODE IS DYNAMIC is included in the SELECT entry for the file. The clause ACCESS MODE IS DYNAMIC will permit both sequential and random access to the file.

The general form for input/output statements required for random access to a relative file is shown in Figure 15.4. The READ statement is valid if the file is opened in INPUT or I-0 mode. In order to READ a record randomly, the program must place the number of the desired record into the relative key field defined in the SELECT entry for the file. The READ statement will then access that record in the file. If there is no record associated with the address contained in the relative key field, the INVALID KEY condition exists. The INVALID KEY clause is required unless appropriate DECLARATIVE/USE entries are provided.

Figure 15.4 General form for relative file random access input/output statements

```
READ file-name RECORD [INTO data-name] INVALID KEY statement

REWRITE record-name [FROM data-name] INVALID KEY statement

       (INPUT file-name . . . )
OPEN  {OUTPUT file-name . . .}  . . .
       (I-O file-name . . .    )
```

Example

Suppose a file has been defined by the following SELECT entry:

```
SELECT DATA-MASTER
    ASSIGN TO DISK
    ORGANIZATION IS RELATIVE
    ACCESS IS RANDOM
    RELATIVE KEY IS DATA-ADDRESS.
```

Assuming that the file is open in INPUT or I-0 mode, the following code would be used to read the fourth record from the file:

```
MOVE 4 TO DATA-ADDRESS.
READ DATA-MASTER
    INVALID KEY PERFORM ERROR-EXIT.
```

Remember that the relative key field must be defined in the DATA DIVISION as an unsigned integer. In this example, an appropriate definition would be

```
01  DATA-ADDRESS        PIC 999.
```

The length of the field must, of course, be governed by the total number of records in the file.

The REWRITE statement is used to replace the content of a record whose address is specified in the relative key field. The file must be open in I-0 mode to permit execution of the REWRITE statement. The reason for this is that, in executing the REWRITE, the system first reads the file to determine whether the record exists. If it does, then the new content is written into the appropriate position within the file. If the desired record does not exist, the INVALID KEY condition occurs and the action specified in the statement is taken. The INVALID KEY clause is required unless appropriate DECLARATIVE/USE entries for the file have been included.

Example

Suppose the content of the twenty-third record of the file DATA-MASTER must be changed. Assuming that the file is open in I-0 mode, the following code could be used:

```
MOVE NEW-DATA TO DATA-MASTER-RECORD.
MOVE 23 TO DATA-ADDRESS.
REWRITE DATA-MASTER-RECORD
    INVALID KEY PERFORM ERROR-EXIT-2.
```

This code could, of course, be rewritten using the FROM option as follows:

```
MOVE 23 TO DATA-ADDRESS
REWRITE DATA-MASTER-RECORD
    FROM NEW-DATA
    INVALID KEY PERFORM ERROR-EXIT-2.
```

Technically, the WRITE statement is also permitted in random access to a relative file. The WRITE statement can be used to add records to a file; the number of the record must be placed in the relative key field prior to execution of the WRITE. If a record with that number does not exist, it will be added to the file; if a record does exist, an INVALID KEY condition results. The size of a randomized file cannot be changed unless the physical position for each record in the file is recomputed, because the file size is a critical component of the hash function. Therefore, use of the random WRITE statement for a randomized file would result in the destruction of the structure of the file. New records are placed into the file using the REWRITE to replace one of the dummy records with actual data.

The procedure for placing records in a randomized file is described in pseudocode in Figure 15.5. The procedure begins by calculating the expected address using the appropriate hash function. The corresponding record is read from the file. If the record contains no data (i.e., it is a dummy record), the program can REWRITE the dummy record with actual data. If, on the other hand, the record contains data (a collision has occurred), the procedure increments the address by one and the process is repeated. Remember that the file is essentially circular: the record following the last one in the file is the first one, so if the address becomes larger than the file size, it is reset to one.

Figure 15.5 Adding records to a randomized file

```
Record address = hash function (key field)
Move "CONTINUE" to found flag
Do while found flag = "CONTINUE"
        Read data file
        If record contains data
                Add 1 to record address
                If record address > file size
                        Move 1 to record address
                End If
        Else
                Move "FINISH" to found flag
        End If
End Do
Move actual data to data file record
Rewrite data file record
```

Pseudocode for a procedure to change the content of existing records is shown in Figure 15.6. We assume that transaction data is available to update a data record. The procedure for locating a record terminates when the key field from the record just read matches the transaction key. If a dummy record is read before the desired record is located, the desired record is not present in the file. If the record read is neither the desired record nor a dummy record, the address is incremented so the next record can be read. The procedure terminates when either the desired record is found or when it is determined that the desired record is not present, at which time appropriate action is taken. If the matching record is found, changes are made to the appropriate fields in the record and the record is rewritten to the file.

Figure 15.6   Changing a record in a randomized file

```
Record address = hash function (transaction key)
Move "CONTINUE" to found flag
Do while found flag = "CONTINUE"
        Read data file
        If record does not contain data
                Move "NOT PRESENT" to found flag
        Else
                If key field = transaction key
                        Move "FOUND" to found flag
                Else
                        Add 1 to record address
                        If record address > file size
                                Move 1 to record address
                        End If
                End If
        End If
End Do
If found flag = "FOUND"
        Move transaction data to appropriate fields in data record
        Rewrite data record
Else
        Take action appropriate for invalid transaction
End If
```

Deleting records from a randomized file is accomplished by performing a logical deletion rather than a physical deletion. To accomplish this, it is necessary to include a code within the record to mark it as active or deleted. Deleting a record then requires only that the deletion code be changed for that record. All programs that access the data file must check the deletion code field to determine whether the record is active before making use of the data. A deleted record can also be reused for a new data record if needed. A procedure for deleting records is shown in Figure 15.7. Note that this procedure is essentially similar to the one required to change a record. Deleting a record becomes a specialized type of change.

Figure 15.7 Deleting records from a randomized file

```
Record address = hash function (transaction key)
Move "CONTINUE" to found flag
Do while found flag = "CONTINUE"
      Read data file
      If record does not contain data
            Move "NOT PRESENT" to found flag
      Else
            If key field = transaction key
                  Move "FOUND" to found flag
            Else
                  Add 1 to record address
                  If record address > file size
                        Move 1 to record address
                  End if
            End if
      End If
End Do
If found flag = "FOUND"
      Reset deletion code field
      Rewrite data record
Else
      Take action appropriate for invalid transaction
End If
```

15.5 PROGRAM EXAMPLE

Problem Statement

Write a general file update and maintenance program for the Work In Progress Master File that was initialized by Program 15.1. The program must be interactive and menu driven with the capability of generating output either on the screen or the printer.

Problem Analysis

The Work In Progress Master File must be updated when a completion date for a batch is scheduled and when a batch is actually completed. Records are automatically added to the file when an order enters the system, however as this program must be a general maintenance program, we must implement a procedure to allow the user not only to update records but also to add and delete records as needed. The following transaction codes are appropriate:

Transaction Code	Action
L	List scheduled order components on terminal or printer.
U	List unscheduled order components on terminal or printer.
S	Update scheduled completion date.
C	Update actual completion date; add appropriate transaction record to Order Transaction File.
A	Add a record to Work In Progress Master File; used for performing error correction and file maintenance only since the system will automatically place records in the file when an order is entered into the system (see Section 10.4).
D	Delete an order component from the file; used for file maintenance only.
H	Help; display menu.
Q	Quit; terminate execution of the program.

The logic required for adding, changing, and deleting records in a randomized relative file has been described in Figures 15.5, 15.6, and 15.7. The required program will implement these general procedures as needed to process the user's transactions.

Problem Solution

The required program is shown in Program 15.2 with a partial structure diagram in Figure 15.8.

Program 15.2 contains procedures for locating a record if it is present in the file (see 5000-SEARCH, beginning at line 35100) and locating a position for adding a record to the file (see 5100-FIND-LOC-NEW-REC, beginning at line 37400). The primary distinction between these procedures is that the procedure 5000-SEARCH terminates when an unused record in the file has been located or when the record has been located (see lines 35600-35700), whereas the procedure 5100-FIND-LOC-NEW-REC terminates when either an unused or deleted record has been located (see lines 37900-38000). The latter procedure does not contain provision for locating a record in the file, since 5100-FIND-LOC-NEW-REC is executed only after it has been determined that the record to be added is not present in the file (see lines 19300-20500).

Note that deletion of records is accomplished by REWRITE after the appropriate value has been moved to the deletion code field (see lines 23600-23700). Although the DELETE verb is available for RELATIVE files, its use in this context would destroy the structure of the file. (The DELETE verb is discussed in Section 4 of this chapter.)

An interesting feature of Program 15.2 is the optional printout for transaction codes L and U. If a printed output is not desired, the PRINT-FILE is not opened or, of course, closed. The data item PRINT-OPEN-FLAG, which initially has value "NO" (see line 7800), is used to "remember" whether the file has been opened (see lines 25800-26000) and whether or not the file should be closed (see lines 44900-45000).

Program 15.2   Work in progress update program

```
100      IDENTIFICATION DIVISION.
200
300      PROGRAM-ID. WIP-UPDATE.
400      AUTHOR. WAYNE.
500
600      ENVIRONMENT DIVISION.
700
800      CONFIGURATION SECTION.
900
1000     SOURCE-COMPUTER.
1100     OBJECT-COMPUTER.
1200
1300     INPUT-OUTPUT SECTION.
1400
1500     FILE-CONTROL.
1600
1700         SELECT WIP-MASTER-FILE      ASSIGN TO DISK
1800             ORGANIZATION IS RELATIVE
1900             ACCESS IS DYNAMIC
2000             RELATIVE KEY IS WIP-KEY.
2100         SELECT TRANSACTION-FILE     ASSIGN TO REMOTE.
2200         SELECT ORDER-TRANSACTION-FILE ASSIGN TO DISK.
2300         SELECT PRINT-FILE           ASSIGN TO PRINTER.
2400
2500     DATA DIVISION.
2600
2700     FILE SECTION.
2800
2900     FD  TRANSACTION-FILE
3000         DATA RECORD IS TRANSACTION-RECORD.
3100
3200     01  TRANSACTION-RECORD             PIC X(80).
3300
3400     FD  PRINT-FILE
3500         LABEL RECORDS ARE OMITTED
3600         DATA RECORD IS PRINT-RECORD.
3700
3800     01  PRINT-RECORD                   PIC X(132).
3900
4000     FD  WIP-MASTER-FILE
4100         RECORD CONTAINS 84 CHARACTERS
4200         BLOCK CONTAINS 30 RECORDS
4300         LABEL RECORDS ARE STANDARD
4400         VALUE OF TITLE IS "WIP/MASTER/FILE"
4500         DATA RECORD IS WIP-MASTER-RECORD.
4600
4700     01  WIP-MASTER-RECORD.
4800         03 BATCH-NUMBER-WMR            PIC 9(10).
4900         03 BATCH-NUMBER-WMR-A REDEFINES BATCH-NUMBER-WMR.
5000            05 ORDER-NUMBER-WMR         PIC 9(5).
5100            05 CATALOG-NUMBER-WMR       PIC 9(5).
5200         03 QUANTITY.
5300            05 QUANTITY-WMR             PIC 9(3).
```

Program 15.2 (continued)

```
5400          03 NUMBER-COMPONENTS.
5500             05 NUMBER-COMPONENTS-WMR       PIC 9(3).
5600          03 SCHEDULED-COMPLETION-DATE.
5700             05 SCHEDULED-COMPLETION-DATE-WMR PIC 9(6).
5800          03 ACTUAL-COMPLETION-DATE.
5900             05 ACTUAL-COMPLETION-DATE-WMR   PIC 9(6).
6000          03 RAW-MATERIALS.
6100             05 RAW-MATERIALS-WMR     PIC X(5) OCCURS 5 TIMES.
6200          03 DELETION-CODE-WMR             PIC X.
6300          03 FILLER                        PIC X(30).
6400
6500     FD  ORDER-TRANSACTION-FILE
6600         RECORD CONTAINS 84 CHARACTERS
6700         BLOCK CONTAINS 30 RECORDS
6800         LABEL RECORDS ARE STANDARD
6900         VALUE OF TITLE IS "ORDER/TRANSACTION"
7000         DATA RECORD IS ORDER-RECORD.
7100     01  ORDER-RECORD                      PIC X(84).
7200
7300     WORKING-STORAGE SECTION.
7400
7500     01  FLAGS.
7600          02 EOF-FLAG                 PIC X(3)  VALUE "NO".
7700          02 SEARCH-FLAG              PIC X(13) VALUE "CONTINUE".
7800          02 PRINT-OPEN-FLAG          PIC X(3)  VALUE "NO".
7900
8000     01  CONTROL-FIELDS.
8100          02 TRANSACTION-CODE         PIC X.
8200          88 VALID-TRANSACTION-CODE VALUES ARE "L" "U" "S" "C"
8300                                             "A" "D" "H" "Q".
8400     01  PROMPTS.
8500          03 PROMPT-TRANSACTION-CODE  PIC X(80) VALUE
8600             "ENTER TRANSACTION CODE: L, U, S, C, A, D, H, or Q".
8700          03 PROMPT-BATCH-NUMBER      PIC X(80) VALUE
8800             "ENTER BATCH NUMBER".
8900          03 PROMPT-QUANTITY          PIC X(80) VALUE
9000             "ENTER QUANTITY".
9100          03 PROMPT-NUMBER-COMPONENTS PIC X(80) VALUE
9200             "ENTER NUMBER COMPONENTS IN ORDER".
9300          03 PROMPT-SCHEDULED         PIC X(80) VALUE
9400             "ENTER SCHEDULED COMPLETION DATE".
9500          03 PROMPT-ACTUAL            PIC X(80) VALUE
9600             "ENTER ACTUAL COMPLETION DATE".
9700          03 PROMPT-RAW-MATERIAL      PIC X(80) VALUE
9800             "ENTER RAW MATERIAL REQUIREMENTS".
9900          03 PROMPT-OUTPUT-TYPE       PIC X(80) VALUE
10000            "ENTER OUTPUT TYPE: P(rint) or D(isplay)".
10100
10200    01  MAIN-MENU-CONSTANTS.
10300         03 FILLER PIC X(80) VALUE "       MAIN MENU".
10400         03 FILLER PIC X(80) VALUE "_____".
10500         03 FILLER PIC X(80) VALUE "L  LIST SCHEDULED BATCHES".
10600         03 FILLER PIC X(80) VALUE "U  LIST UNSCHEDULED BATCHES".
10700         03 FILLER PIC X(80) VALUE "S  SCHEDULE A BATCH".
10800         03 FILLER PIC X(80) VALUE "C  BATCH COMPLETION".
```

Program 15.2 (continued)

```
10900        03 FILLER PIC X(80) VALUE "A  ADD A BATCH".
11000        03 FILLER PIC X(80) VALUE "D  DELETE A BATCH".
11100        03 FILLER PIC X(80) VALUE "H  HELP".
11200        03 FILLER PIC X(80) VALUE "Q  QUIT".
11300        03 FILLER PIC X(80) VALUE "_____".
11400
11500    01  MAIN-MENU REDEFINES MAIN-MENU-CONSTANTS.
11600        03 MAIN-MENU-LINE OCCURS 11 TIMES PIC X(80).
11700
11800    01  ORDER-COMPLETION-TRANS.
11900        03 BATCH-NUMBER-OCT      PIC 9(10).
12000        03 COMPLETION-DATE-OCT   PIC 9(6).
12100        03 FILLER                PIC X(53) VALUE SPACES.
12200        03 FILLER                PIC X VALUE "C".
12300
12400    01  OUTPUT-FIELD.
12500        02 OUTPUT-TYPE           PIC X    VALUE "P".
12600
12700    01  INDEXES.
12800        02  INDX                 PIC 999 VALUE ZERO.
12900
13000    01  CALCULLATED-VALUES.
13100        02 WIP-KEY               PIC 99  VALUE ZERO.
13200        02 QUOTIENT              PIC 99  VALUE ZERO.
13300
13400    01  CONSTANTS.
13500        02 FILE-SIZE             PIC 99  VALUE 97.
13600
13700    01  INPUT-FIELD.
13800        02 BATCH-NUMBER-TRANS-A.
13900           03 BATCH-NUMBER-TRANS PIC 9(10).
14000
14100    PROCEDURE DIVISION.
14200
14300    1000-MAIN-PROCEDURE.
14400
14500        PERFORM 2000-INITIALIZATION.
14600        PERFORM 4000-FILE-UPDATE
14700           UNTIL TRANSACTION-CODE = "Q".
14800        PERFORM 9000-TERMINATION.
14900        STOP RUN.
15000
15100    2000-INITIALIZATION.
15200
15300        OPEN I-O         WIP-MASTER-FILE
15400                         TRANSACTION-FILE
15500           EXTEND        ORDER-TRANSACTION-FILE.
15600        PERFORM 3000-MENU-DISPLAY.
15700        PERFORM 3100-ACCEPT-TRANSACTION-CODE.
15800
15900    3000-MENU-DISPLAY.
16000
16100        PERFORM 3010-DISPLAY-MENU-LINES
16200             VARYING INDX FROM 1 BY 1 UNTIL INDX > 11.
16300
```

Program 15.2 (continued)

```
16400       3010-DISPLAY-MENU-LINES.
16500
16600           WRITE TRANSACTION-RECORD FROM MAIN-MENU-LINE (INDX).
16700
16800       3100-ACCEPT-TRANSACTION-CODE.
16900
17000           WRITE TRANSACTION-RECORD FROM PROMPT-TRANSACTION-CODE.
17100           READ TRANSACTION-FILE INTO TRANSACTION-CODE.
17200
17300       4000-FILE-UPDATE.
17400
17500           IF TRANSACTION-CODE = "A"
17600               PERFORM 4100-ADD-RECORD.
17700           IF TRANSACTION-CODE = "D"
17800               PERFORM 4200-DELETE-RECORD.
17900           IF TRANSACTION-CODE = "L"
18000               PERFORM 4300-LIST-SCHEDULED-BATCHES.
18100           IF TRANSACTION-CODE = "U"
18200               PERFORM 4400-LIST-UNSCHEDULED-BATCHES.
18300           IF TRANSACTION-CODE = "S"
18400               PERFORM 4500-SCHEDULE-BATCH.
18500           IF TRANSACTION-CODE = "C"
18600               PERFORM 4600-COMPLETE-BATCH.
18700           IF TRANSACTION-CODE = "H"
18800               PERFORM 3000-MENU-DISPLAY.
18900           IF NOT VALID-TRANSACTION-CODE
19000               PERFORM 8000-ERROR-1.
19100           PERFORM 3100-ACCEPT-TRANSACTION-CODE.
19200
19300       4100-ADD-RECORD.
19400
19500           MOVE PROMPT-BATCH-NUMBER TO TRANSACTION-RECORD.
19600           WRITE TRANSACTION-RECORD.
19700           READ TRANSACTION-FILE INTO BATCH-NUMBER-TRANS-A.
19800           PERFORM 5000-SEARCH.
19900           IF SEARCH-FLAG = "NOT PRESENT"
20000               PERFORM 5100-FIND-LOC-NEW-REC
20100               PERFORM 4110-GET-MOVE-DATA
20200               REWRITE WIP-MASTER-RECORD
20300                       INVALID KEY PERFORM 8100-ERROR-2
20400           ELSE
20500               PERFORM 8200-ERROR-3.
20600
20700       4110-GET-MOVE-DATA.
20800
20900           MOVE  PROMPT-QUANTITY TO TRANSACTION-RECORD.
21000           WRITE TRANSACTION-RECORD.
21100           READ TRANSACTION-FILE INTO QUANTITY.
21200           MOVE PROMPT-NUMBER-COMPONENTS TO TRANSACTION-RECORD.
21300           WRITE TRANSACTION-RECORD.
21400           READ TRANSACTION-FILE INTO NUMBER-COMPONENTS.
21500           MOVE PROMPT-SCHEDULED TO TRANSACTION-RECORD.
21600           WRITE TRANSACTION-RECORD.
21700           READ TRANSACTION-FILE INTO SCHEDULED-COMPLETION-DATE.
21800           MOVE PROMPT-ACTUAL TO TRANSACTION-RECORD.
```

Program 15.2 *(continued)*

```
21900        WRITE TRANSACTION-RECORD.
22000        READ TRANSACTION-FILE INTO ACTUAL-COMPLETION-DATE.
22100        MOVE PROMPT-RAW-MATERIAL TO TRANSACTION-RECORD.
22200        WRITE TRANSACTION-RECORD.
22300        READ TRANSACTION-FILE INTO RAW-MATERIALS.
22400        MOVE SPACES TO DELETION-CODE-WMR.
22500        MOVE BATCH-NUMBER-TRANS TO BATCH-NUMBER-WMR.
22600
22700    4200-DELETE-RECORD.
22800
22900        WRITE TRANSACTION-RECORD FROM PROMPT-BATCH-NUMBER.
23000        READ TRANSACTION-FILE INTO BATCH-NUMBER-TRANS-A.
23100        PERFORM 5000-SEARCH.
23200        IF SEARCH-FLAG = "NOT PRESENT"
23300            PERFORM 8400-ERROR-5
23400        ELSE
23500            MOVE "D" TO DELETION-CODE-WMR
23600            REWRITE WIP-MASTER-RECORD
23700                    INVALID KEY PERFORM 8500-ERROR-6.
23800
23900    4300-LIST-SCHEDULED-BATCHES.
24000
24100        PERFORM 4310-INITIALIZE-FOR-LIST.
24200        IF OUTPUT-TYPE = "P"
24300            MOVE "SCHEDULED ORDER COMPONENTS" TO PRINT-RECORD
24400            WRITE PRINT-RECORD AFTER PAGE
24500        ELSE
24600            MOVE "SCHEDULED ORDER COMPONENTS" TO
24700                    TRANSACTION-RECORD
24800            WRITE TRANSACTION-RECORD.
24900        PERFORM 4320-LIST-SCH-READ UNTIL EOF-FLAG = "YES".
25000
25100    4310-INITIALIZE-FOR-LIST.
25200
25300        WRITE TRANSACTION-RECORD FROM PROMPT-OUTPUT-TYPE.
25400        READ TRANSACTION-FILE INTO OUTPUT-TYPE.
25500        MOVE 1 TO WIP-KEY.
25600        START WIP-MASTER-FILE KEY = WIP-KEY
25700                INVALID KEY PERFORM 8900-ERROR-10.
25800        IF OUTPUT-TYPE = "P" AND PRINT-OPEN-FLAG = "NO"
25900            OPEN OUTPUT PRINT-FILE
26000            MOVE "YES" TO PRINT-OPEN-FLAG.
26100        MOVE "NO" TO EOF-FLAG.
26200        READ WIP-MASTER-FILE NEXT RECORD
26300            AT END MOVE "YES" TO EOF-FLAG.
26400
26500    4320-LIST-SCH-READ.
26600
26700        IF BATCH-NUMBER-WMR-A NOT = SPACES AND
26800            SCHEDULED-COMPLETION-DATE-WMR NOT = ZERO AND
26900            DELETION-CODE-WMR NOT = "D"
```

Program 15.2 (continued)

```
27000              IF OUTPUT-TYPE = "P"
27100                  WRITE PRINT-RECORD FROM WIP-MASTER-RECORD
27200                              AFTER 1
27300              ELSE
27400                  IF OUTPUT-TYPE = "D"
27500                      WRITE TRANSACTION-RECORD FROM
27600                          WIP-MASTER-RECORD.
27700          READ WIP-MASTER-FILE NEXT RECORD
27800              AT END MOVE "YES" TO EOF-FLAG.
27900
28000      4400-LIST-UNSCHEDULED-BATCHES.
28100
28200          PERFORM 4310-INITIALIZE-FOR-LIST.
28300          IF OUTPUT-TYPE = "P"
28400              MOVE "UNSCHEDULED ORDER COMPONENTS" TO
28500                      PRINT-RECORD
28600              WRITE PRINT-RECORD AFTER 1
28700          ELSE
28800              IF OUTPUT-TYPE = "D"
28900                  MOVE "UNSCHEDULED ORDER COMPONENTS" TO
29000                          TRANSACTION-RECORD
29100                  WRITE TRANSACTION-RECORD.
29200          PERFORM 4420-LIST-UNSCH-READ UNTIL EOF-FLAG = "YES".
29300
29400      4420-LIST-UNSCH-READ.
29500
29600          IF BATCH-NUMBER-WMR-A NOT = SPACES AND
29700              SCHEDULED-COMPLETION-DATE-WMR = ZERO AND
29800              DELETION-CODE-WMR NOT = "D"
29900              IF OUTPUT-TYPE = "P"
30000                  WRITE PRINT-RECORD FROM WIP-MASTER-RECORD
30100                          AFTER 1
30200              ELSE
30300                  IF OUTPUT-TYPE = "D"
30400                      WRITE TRANSACTION-RECORD FROM
30500                          WIP-MASTER-RECORD.
30600          READ WIP-MASTER-FILE NEXT RECORD
30700              AT END MOVE "YES" TO EOF-FLAG.
30800
30900      4500-SCHEDULE-BATCH.
31000
31100          WRITE TRANSACTION-RECORD FROM PROMPT-BATCH-NUMBER.
31200          READ TRANSACTION-FILE.
31300          PERFORM 5000-SEARCH.
31400          IF SEARCH-FLAG = "NOT PRESENT"
31500              PERFORM 8400-ERROR-5
31600          ELSE
31700              PERFORM 4510-HANDLE-SCHEDULE.
31800
```

Program 15.2 (continued)

```
31900        4510-HANDLE-SCHEDULE.
32000
32100            WRITE TRANSACTION-RECORD FROM PROMPT-SCHEDULED.
32200            READ TRANSACTION-FILE INTO SCHEDULED-COMPLETION-DATE.
32300            REWRITE WIP-MASTER-RECORD
32400                        INVALID KEY PERFORM 8600-ERROR-7.
32500
32600        4600-COMPLETE-BATCH.
32700
32800            WRITE TRANSACTION-RECORD FROM PROMPT-BATCH-NUMBER.
32900            READ TRANSACTION-FILE INTO BATCH-NUMBER-TRANS-A.
33000            PERFORM 5000-SEARCH.
33100            IF SEARCH-FLAG = "NOT PRESENT"
33200                PERFORM 8400-ERROR-5
33300            ELSE
33400                PERFORM 4610-HANDLE-COMPLETION.
33500
33600        4610-HANDLE-COMPLETION.
33700
33800            WRITE TRANSACTION-RECORD FROM PROMPT-ACTUAL.
33900            READ TRANSACTION-FILE INTO ACTUAL-COMPLETION-DATE.
34000            REWRITE WIP-MASTER-RECORD
34100                INVALID KEY PERFORM 8700-ERROR-8.
34200            PERFORM 4620-ADD-RECORD-TO-ORDER-TRANS.
34300
34400        4620-ADD-RECORD-TO-ORDER-TRANS.
34500
34600            MOVE BATCH-NUMBER-TRANS TO BATCH-NUMBER-OCT.
34700            MOVE ACTUAL-COMPLETION-DATE-WMR TO
34800                COMPLETION-DATE-OCT.
34900            WRITE ORDER-RECORD FROM ORDER-COMPLETION-TRANS.
35000
35100        5000-SEARCH.
35200
35300            DIVIDE BATCH-NUMBER-TRANS BY FILE-SIZE
35400                GIVING QUOTIENT REMAINDER WIP-KEY.
35500            MOVE "CONTINUE" TO SEARCH-FLAG.
35600            PERFORM 5010-READ-COMPARE
35700                UNTIL SEARCH-FLAG NOT = "CONTINUE".
35800
35900        5010-READ-COMPARE.
36000
36100            READ WIP-MASTER-FILE
36200                INVALID KEY PERFORM 8300-ERROR-4.
36300            IF BATCH-NUMBER-WMR = BATCH-NUMBER-TRANS
36400              AND DELETION-CODE-WMR NOT = "D"
36500                MOVE "FOUND" TO SEARCH-FLAG
36600            ELSE
36700                IF BATCH-NUMBER-WMR-A = SPACES
36800                    MOVE "NOT PRESENT" TO SEARCH-FLAG
36900                ELSE
37000                    ADD 1 TO WIP-KEY
37100                    IF WIP-KEY > FILE-SIZE
37200                        MOVE 1 TO WIP-KEY.
37300
```

Program 15.2 (continued)

```
37400    5100-FIND-LOC-NEW-REC.
37500
37600        MOVE "CONTINUE" TO SEARCH-FLAG.
37700        DIVIDE BATCH-NUMBER-TRANS BY FILE-SIZE
37800            GIVING QUOTIENT REMAINDER WIP-KEY.
37900        PERFORM 5110-READ-COMPARE
38000            UNTIL SEARCH-FLAG NOT = "CONTINUE".
38100
38200    5110-READ-COMPARE.
38300
38400        READ WIP-MASTER-FILE
38500            INVALID KEY PERFORM 8800-ERROR-9.
38600        IF BATCH-NUMBER-WMR-A = SPACES OR
38700           DELETION-CODE-WMR  = "D"
38800            MOVE "FINISH" TO SEARCH-FLAG
38900        ELSE
39000           ADD 1 TO WIP-KEY
39100           IF WIP-KEY > FILE-SIZE
39200             MOVE 1 TO WIP-KEY.
39300
39400    8000-ERROR-1.
39500
39600        MOVE "INVALID TRANSACTION CODE" TO TRANSACTION-RECORD.
39700        WRITE TRANSACTION-RECORD.
39800
39900    8100-ERROR-2.
40000
40100        MOVE "INTERNAL LOGIC ERROR 2" TO TRANSACTION-RECORD.
40200        WRITE TRANSACTION-RECORD.
40300
40400    8200-ERROR-3.
40500
40600        MOVE "RECORD PRESENT IN FILE" TO TRANSACTION-RECORD.
40700        WRITE TRANSACTION-RECORD.
40800
40900    8300-ERROR-4.
41000
41100        MOVE "INTERNAL LOGIC ERROR 4" TO TRANSACTION-RECORD.
41200        WRITE TRANSACTION-RECORD.
41300
41400    8400-ERROR-5.
41500
41600        MOVE "RECORD NOT FOUND" TO TRANSACTION-RECORD.
41700        WRITE TRANSACTION-RECORD.
41800
41900    8500-ERROR-6.
42000
42100        MOVE "INTERNAL LOGIC ERROR 6" TO TRANSACTION-RECORD.
42200        WRITE TRANSACTION-RECORD.
42300
42400    8600-ERROR-7.
42500
42600        MOVE "INTERNAL LOGIC ERROR 7" TO TRANSACTION-RECORD.
42700        WRITE TRANSACTION-RECORD.
42800
```

```
42900     8700-ERROR-8.
43000
43100         MOVE "INTERNAL LOGIC ERROR 8" TO TRANSACTION-RECORD.
43200         WRITE TRANSACTION-RECORD.
43300
43400     8800-ERROR-9.
43500
43600         MOVE "INTERNAL LOGIC ERROR 9" TO TRANSACTION-RECORD.
43700         WRITE TRANSACTION-RECORD.
43800
43900     8900-ERROR-10.
44000
44100         MOVE "INTERNAL LOGIC ERROR 10" TO TRANSACTION-RECORD.
44200         WRITE TRANSACTION-RECORD.
44300
44400     9000-TERMINATION.
44500
44600         CLOSE WIP-MASTER-FILE WITH LOCK
44700              ORDER-TRANSACTION-FILE WITH LOCK
44800              TRANSACTION-FILE.
44900         IF PRINT-OPEN-FLAG = "YES"
45000              CLOSE PRINT-FILE.
```

Program 15.2 (continued)

Figure 15.8   Partial structure diagram for Program 15.2

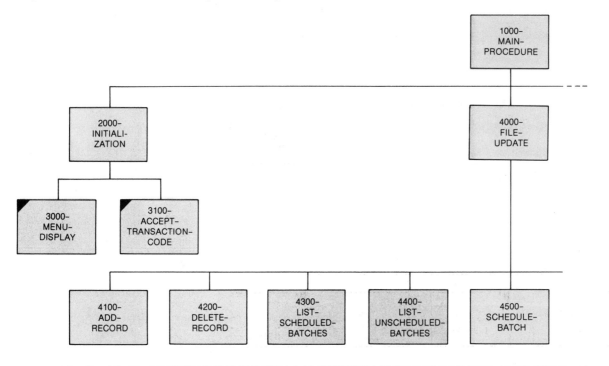

15.6   OTHER INPUT/OUTPUT STATEMENTS

When a COBOL relative file is used to store a randomized set of records, only the input/output statements described in the preceding sections are required:

Sequential WRITE
Random READ
REWRITE

Other input/output statements that are available include:

Sequential READ
Random WRITE
DELETE
START

The sequential READ is valid if the file is specified as SEQUENTIAL or DYNAMIC access and open in INPUT or I-O mode. When DYNAMIC access is used, the NEXT clause must be included in the READ statement to specify a sequential READ (see Figure 15.2). The sequential READ enables *next record* access to records within the file.

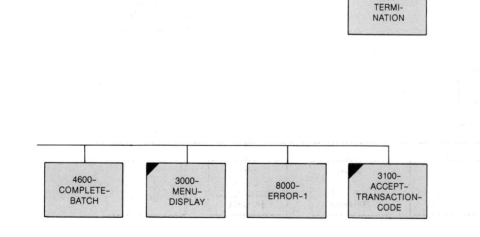

Consider the problem of clearing a randomized file of deleted records. As the number of deleted records increases, the performance of the system degrades because the number of collisions increases during each file access. At some point it will become advantageous to make a new version of the file with all deleted records omitted. In order to perform this function, a program will be needed to read each record from the old file (sequentially) and place each active record in its appropriate position in the new file. Pseudocode for this operation is shown in Figure 15.9. Note that this same procedure would be required to increase the physical size of a randomized file, since the placement of the record in the file depends on the file size.

A COBOL relative file is also useful for storing a table that contains too many elements to store in memory. Recall that a relative file bears a strong resemblance to a table; the relative key takes the place of a subscript as the method of specifying the desired element. Suppose, for example, we wish to use a relative file to store a table in which the table arguments are in ascending sequence. The program could search the file sequentially (using ACCESS MODE IS SEQUENTIAL and sequential READ), or the more efficient binary search procedure could be used (using ACCESS MODE IS RANDOM and random READ). In the latter case, the relative key value would be computed before each READ in the same way that the subscript for the table entry was computed for a binary search.

Figure 15.9   Removing deleted records from a randomized file

```
Open files
Read next record from data file
Do while not end of data file
     If active record
          Record address = hash function (record key)
          Move "CONTINUE" to found flag
          Do while found flag = "CONTINUE"
               Read new data file
               If record does not contain data
                    Move "FINISH" to found flag
               Else
                    Add 1 to record address
                    If record address greater than file size
                         Move 1 to record address
                    End If
               End If
          End Do
          Move data record to new data record
          Rewrite new data record
     End If
     Read next record from data file
End Do
Close files
Stop
```

Notes: Data file is accessed sequentially
         New data file is accessed randomly

In this type of application of relative files, the random WRITE with general form shown in Figure 15.10 and the DELETE verb shown in Figure 15.11 may be useful. Prior to execution of either of these statements, the record number of the desired record must be placed in the relative key field specified for the file. The random WRITE could be used to add records onto the end of a relative file. This operation is analogous to opening a sequential file in EXTEND mode and writing records into the file; new records are placed in the file following existing records.

Figure 15.10   General form of the random WRITE statement for relative files

```
WRITE record-name
    [FROM data-name]
    INVALID KEY statement
```

Figure 15.11   General form of the DELETE statement for relative files

```
DELETE file-name RECORD INVALID KEY statement
```

For example, if a relative file contained 100 records and 10 records need to be added to the file. the following code could be used:

```
MOVE 100 TO RELATIVE-KEY.
PERFORM WRITE-PROCESS 10 TIMES.
    .
    .
    .
WRITE-PROCESS.
    ADD 1 TO RELATIVE-KEY.
    READ NEW-DATA-FILE AT END MOVE "YES" TO EOF.
    WRITE DATA-RECORD
        FROM NEW-DATA-RECORD
        INVALID KEY PERFORM ERROR-EXIT.
```

The INVALID KEY condition occurs if the file already contains a record that has the number found in the relative key field.

The DELETE statement may be used to remove records from a relative file. For example, if record number 4 needed to be removed from a relative file, the following code could be used:

```
MOVE 4 TO RELATIVE-KEY.
DELETE DATA-FILE RECORD
    INVALID KEY PERFORM ERROR-EXIT.
```

The INVALID KEY condition exists if a record with the appropriate address is not found in the file. In this example, the INVALID KEY condition is true if the file contains only three records or if record 4 had been deleted. Note that the DELETE statement does *not* cause a change in the record number of remaining records in the file. For example, in this example, the record that was previously number 5 will remain record number 5.

The START statement (see Figure 15.12) is useful to begin sequential processing of a relative file at any desired point. The *data-name* used in the statement must be the relative key for the file. If the KEY clause is omitted, the IS EQUAL TO phrase is implied. For example, in order to begin processing of a relative file DATA-FILE with the fourth record, the following code could be used:

```
MOVE 4 TO RELATIVE-KEY.
START DATA-FILE KEY IS = RELATIVE-KEY
    INVALID KEY
        PERFORM ERROR-EXIT.
```

Figure 15.12 General form of the START statement for a relative file

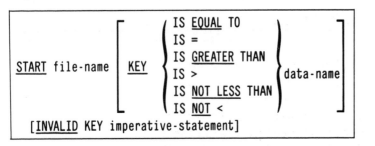

The INVALID KEY condition is true if no record in the file exists that meets the prescribed condition (if, for example, record 4 had been deleted). The file must be open in INPUT or I-0 mode. Access mode must be SEQUENTIAL or DYNAMIC.

Program 15.2 contains an example of the use of DYNAMIC access mode to enable both sequential and random access to the Work In Progress Master File. For purposes of updating, adding and deleting records, random access is needed. In order to list desired records (transaction codes L and U), the file must be searched completely. This is accomplished by using the START statement with the value of the relative key set to 1 (see lines 25600-25700). The sequential READ statement with the AT END clause is then used to read records from the file (see lines 26200-26300, 27700-27800, 30600-30700).

15.7 DEBUG CLINIC

Associated with each relative file is a two-character file status item that contains information about the status of an input/output operation. The program can gain access to this item if the FILE STATUS clause is included in the SELECT entry for the file. Definitions of possible settings of the file status item are shown in Figure 15.13. The use of the file status item is similar in relative, sequential and indexed files (see Section 12, Chapter 13, and Section 11, Chapter 14).

Figure 15.13   FILE STATUS item settings for relative files

Setting	Meaning
00	Successful completion
10	End of file
22	Duplicate key
23	No record found
24	Boundary violation
30	Permanent error
9x	Implementor defined
	(See local documentation)

15.8   COMPARISON WITH OTHER FILE TYPES

The choice of file organization and content is one of the most crucial decisions of all in the design of a data processing system. The choice must be made only after careful consideration of both the present and potential future needs of the user and the capabilities and limitations of the various file organization techniques. When random access is needed for a file, there is often a choice of indexed or relative files. In general, an indexed file should be chosen if both random and sequential access to data in sequence are required. Indexed files have some drawbacks. Access speed is often relatively slow, as many mass storage operations may be required for one record to be read. A relative file is a good choice if the key field can be used as a record address. A randomized relative file is a good choice if sequential access to the data is not needed. In both cases, the number of mass storage operations is reduced to one for direct access, or close to one, on the average, for a randomized file. For storage and access of table data in mass storage rather than in memory, a relative file is the method of choice, as it permits easy implementation of any desired search procedure and easy methods for performing file maintenance. In general, the choice of a relative file over an indexed file may make the program more efficient in execution time. Both relative and indexed files demand extra space on the mass storage medium, and both types of files must be assigned to a device capable of random access. If space is at a premium, or if tape must be used for file storage, the only type of file organization available is sequential.

Relative files are quite often under-utilized in data processing systems because they are comparatively new (this implementation was first described in the ANSI 74 Standard) and their capabilities are not fully understood by a large percentage of practicing programmers and analysts. If properly used, relative files can contribute efficiency to data processing systems that is not possible with other file organization techniques.

15.9 SELF-TEST EXERCISES

1. List valid input/output statements for each file access and open mode for relative files.

OPEN *Mode*

	INPUT	OUTPUT	I/O
SEQUENTIAL			
RANDOM			
DYNAMIC			

Access Type

2. Suppose a randomized set of records is contained in the relative file DATA-FILE. Write pseudocode for a program to list all deleted records.

3. How would a system be designed to warn an operator or systems programmer when a randomized relative file should be reorganized?

4. Can the DELETE verb be used to remove records from a randomized file? Why?

5. How are new records added to a randomized file? Can the random WRITE be used for this purpose?

6. Revise the procedures of Figures 15.5 and 15.6 to take into account deleted records.

7. How could an indexed file be used to store table data? What would be the most efficient look-up procedure for this technique?

8. Why would a programmer or analyst choose relative organization for a file?

9. List the major disadvantages of relative files.

10. Each record in a relative file contains the fields TABLE-ARGUMENT and TABLE-VALUE. Using a binary search, write pseudocode for a procedure to locate the value associated with ACTUAL-ARGUMENT.

11. Suggest an alternative method for handling error messages in Program 15.2, one that reduces the number of paragraphs in the program.

12. Would it be possible to delete the procedure in Program 15.2 that is used to locate a position for a new record after it is determined that the record is not present in the file? What would be the consequences of doing this?

15.10 PROGRAMMING EXERCISES

1. The following problems relate to Exercise 1 in Section 15, Chapter 13:
   a. Write a program to transform TABLE-FILE into a relative file with randomized placement of records.
   b. Revise the program to update the relative TABLE-FILE.

2. Revise the program written for Exercise 6 in Section 10, Chapter 12, to process the relative TABLE-FILE created in Exercise 1 above.

3. Revise the program written for Exercise 1 in Section 10, Chapter 12, to use a randomized relative file to store the table of deduction amounts.

4. Revise the program written for Exercise 2 in Section 10, Chapter 12, to use a randomized relative file in place of a table. Compare execution times for the new program with those of the original program. How do you explain the differences?

5. Do the same task as described in Exercise 4 above, but change the file organization to indexed. Compare execution times and explain differences.

6. Revise the programs written for Exercises 1 and 2 in Section 14, Chapter 14, to use a relative file with randomized placement of records.

7. Write a program to create a randomized relative file for the student master file described in Exercise 2 of Section 15, Chapter 13.

8. Write a program to update the file created in Exercise 7 above, using the codes described in Exercise 4 of Section 15, Chapter 13.

SUBPROGRAMS 16

16.1 THE SUBPROGRAM CONCEPT

A *subprogram* is a program that is executed by another program. Subprograms cannot be executed on their own; they must be combined with a *calling program* that exercises control of the execution sequence by calling for the execution of subprograms as needed. Subprograms are typically compiled separately from the calling program; hence, the overall structure of a COBOL subprogram will resemble any other program in many respects. For example, a subprogram is organized into four DIVISIONs, as is a calling program; the syntax used to specify entries in each DIVISION is in general the same for all programs. Each program unit (calling program or subprogram) typically requires a separate execution of the COBOL compiler, although some compilers will accept multiple program units during one execution.

After a subprogram is compiled, it is typically stored in a library, where it is accessible to any program that needs to execute the procedure contained in the subprogram. Some operating systems execute a linking function prior to creating and storing an executable program. *Linking* means that the calling program and any required subprograms are located and assigned memory locations that do not conflict. Typically these are contiguous, as shown in Figure 16.1, but this is not necessarily the case. Also, the linking function resolves addressing references from one program unit to another, so that when a reference in the calling program to a subprogram is made during execution, the correct address is in place. The completely linked program forms an executable set of program units, called a *load module*. The load module is usually stored in a library and is ready for immediate execution. Other operating systems determine the location for referenced subprograms during the execution process. That is, when the calling program references a subprogram, the operating system searches the library of subprograms and, if the subprogram is available, memory space is found for the subprogram, and addressing conflicts are resolved. Check with local documentation to determine which type of system you are using.

Figure 16.1   Linking example

After Compilation

Program units exist as separate modules.

After Linking

Program units have been relocated and assigned nonconflicting memory locations.

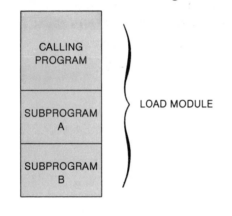

Subprograms are likely to be written for tasks that are needed by more than one program. The procedure is written, compiled, and debugged only once. It can then be made available to all programs requiring that that task be performed. For example, suppose a payroll system is being developed. The analyst identifies several programs in the system that will need to compute federal withholding tax. Rather than reproduce the required logic in each program, it would be advantageous to develop a subprogram to carry out this task.

Subprograms are also useful to enhance the maintainability of a system. If the rules for computing federal withholding tax change (which they do from time to time), it is sufficient to rewrite the subprogram and then relink the program units to create an updated run unit. In systems that load subprograms during execution time, it is sufficient to change only the subprogram. The revised version of the procedure will then be made available to the programs automatically.

16.2   WRITING SUBPROGRAMS

Communication of data is usually required between a calling program and a subprogram. The subprogram carries out its operations using data supplied to it by the calling program and/or returns values to the calling program.

A subprogram has three distinct features that are not found in other programs:

1. A LINKAGE SECTION in the DATA DIVISION, in which descriptions of the data that will be passed between the calling program and the subprogram are placed.
2. A USING clause on the PROCEDURE DIVISION entry, in which specific items to be passed between the calling program and subprogram are listed.
3. An EXIT PROGRAM statement, which serves to return control from the subprogram to the calling program.

The general form for the DATA DIVISION with a LINKAGE SECTION is shown in Figure 16.2. The LINKAGE SECTION contains data descriptions of items described in the CALL statement (in the calling program) and the USING clause (in the subprogram). The data items are described in the LINKAGE SECTION using essentially the same syntax as for items in the WORKING–STORAGE SECTION with the following exception: in the LINKAGE SECTION, the VALUE clause can be used only for 88-level items, because the value of data items being described is defined in the calling program or computed in the subprogram.

Figure 16.2 General form of the DATA DIVISION with LINKAGE SECTION

```
DATA DIVISION.
  ┌FILE SECTION.              ┐
  └file-section-entries . . . ┘

  ┌WORKING—STORAGE SECTION.        ┐
  └record-description-entry . . .  ┘

  ┌LINKAGE SECTION.                ┐
  └record-description-entry . . .  ┘

  ┌REPORT SECTION.            ┐
  └report-section-entries . . .┘
```

No space is actually allocated for items defined in the LINKAGE SECTION. The data names defined here enable the subprogram to reference data actually defined in the calling program. The LINKAGE SECTION may contain a sequence of elementary data items or record descriptions (group data items), as necessary. The length of each item must match the length defined for the associated data item in the main program.

The general form of the PROCEDURE DIVISION entry with a USING clause is shown in Figure 16.3. The data names included in the list must be defined in the LINKAGE SECTION of the subprogram as 01-level or 77-level items.[1] The USING

---

1. A 77-level item can be included only in WORKING–STORAGE. It must be an elementary data item. In the past it was common to use 77-level items as indexes, counters, accumulators, etc. Present COBOL standards usually preclude the use of 77-level items, although they continue to be supported by the compiler. Future standards for COBOL will probably not support 77-level items.

clause is necessary to pass data between the calling program and the subprogram.

The general form of the EXIT PROGRAM statement is shown in Figure 16.4. When the EXIT PROGRAM statement is executed, control returns to the calling program. EXIT PROGRAM must not be combined with any other statement and must be the only sentence in a paragraph.

Figure 16.3   General form of the PROCEDURE DIVISION entry for subprograms

```
PROCEDURE DIVISION [USING data-name . . .].
```

Figure 16.4   General form of the EXIT PROGRAM statement

```
paragraph-name.
    EXIT PROGRAM.
```

Example

Programs often require dates in the form

  month-name day, year

rather than the year, month, day form provided by the operating system when an ACCEPT/FROM DATE statement is executed.

The statement ACCEPT DATE-IN FROM DATE will return a six-digit numeric value in DATE-IN in the form *yymmdd*. Thus, August 6, 1986, would be returned as

Year Month Day

8 6 0 8 0 6

```
01  DATE-IN.
    03  YEAR-IN   PIC 99.
    03  MONTH-IN  PIC 99.
    03  DAY-IN    PIC 99.
```

Although the logic required to transform this data into the desired form is relatively straightforward and can easily be reproduced in any program, the need for making this transformation occurs in many programs. Therefore, writing a subprogram to do this task would be very beneficial.

Program 16.1 is a subprogram to carry out this transformation. In this example, the LINKAGE SECTION contains only one entry—DATE-STRING—but, in general, a LINKAGE SECTION can contain any number of entries. Note the USING clause in the PROCEDURE DIVISION entry. The content of DATE-STRING will be passed back to the calling program when the EXIT PROGRAM statement is executed. In this example, control passes from 1000-MAIN-PROCESSING to 1100-DATE-TRANSLATION-EXIT automatically. This is acceptable for this simple example, but in reality it is a form of content coupling that should be avoided in a structured program (see Chapter 10, Section 9). If there were other paragraphs in the subprogram, it would be necessary to use the statement GO TO 1100-DATE-TRANSLATION-EXIT as the last statement in 1000-MAIN PROCESSING in order to transfer control to the EXIT PROGRAM sentence. Note also the PROGRAM-ID entry. In most systems, this entry is the name of the program module that must be referenced when the subprogram is executed by a calling program.

Program 16.1 Date transformation subprogram

```
100      IDENTIFICATION DIVISION.
200
300      PROGRAM-ID. DATETRAN.
400      AUTHOR. HORN.
500
600      ENVIRONMENT DIVISION.
700
800      CONFIGURATION SECTION.
900
1000     SOURCE-COMPUTER.
1100     OBJECT-COMPUTER.
1200
1300     DATA DIVISION.
1400
1500     WORKING-STORAGE SECTION.
1600
1700     01  MONTH-NAME-CONSTANTS.
1800         03 FILLER PIC X(9) VALUE "JANUARY".
1900         03 FILLER PIC X(9) VALUE "FEBRUARY".
2000         03 FILLER PIC X(9) VALUE "MARCH".
2100         03 FILLER PIC X(9) VALUE "APRIL".
2200         03 FILLER PIC X(9) VALUE "MAY".
2300         03 FILLER PIC X(9) VALUE "JUNE".
2400         03 FILLER PIC X(9) VALUE "JULY".
2500         03 FILLER PIC X(9) VALUE "AUGUST".
2600         03 FILLER PIC X(9) VALUE "SEPTEMBER".
2700         03 FILLER PIC X(9) VALUE "OCTOBER".
2800         03 FILLER PIC X(9) VALUE "NOVEMBER".
2900         03 FILLER PIC X(9) VALUE "DECEMBER".
3000
3100     01  MONTH-NAME-TABLE REDEFINES MONTH-NAME-CONSTANTS.
3200         03 MONTH-NAME PIC X(9) OCCURS 12 TIMES.
3300
3400     01  DATE-IN.
3500         03 YEAR-IN    PIC 99.
3600         03 MONTH-IN   PIC 99.
3700         03 DAY-IN     PIC 99.
3800
3900     01  CALCULATED-VALUES.
4000         03 YEAR-NUMBER   PIC 9999.
4100         03 DAY-NUMBER    PIC ZZ.
4200         03 CENTURY       PIC 9999 VALUE 1900.
4300
4400     LINKAGE SECTION.
4500
4600     01  DATE-STRING   PIC X(18).
4700
4800     PROCEDURE DIVISION USING DATE-STRING.
```

Program 16.1 (continued)

```
4900
5000     1000-MAIN-PROCESING.
5100
5200         ACCEPT DATE-IN FROM DATE.
5300         MOVE DATE-IN TO DAY-NUMBER.
5400         ADD CENTURY YEAR-IN GIVING YEAR-NUMBER.
5500         MOVE SPACES TO DATE-STRING.
5600         STRING
5700           MONTH-NAME (MONTH-IN) DELIMITED BY SPACE
5800           " " DAY-NUMBER "," YEAR-NUMBER DELIMITED BY SIZE
5900           INTO DATE-STRING.
6000
6100     1100-DATE-TRANSLATION-EXIT.
6200
6300         EXIT PROGRAM.
```

16.3   THE CALL STATEMENT

The CALL statement, which has the general form shown in Figure 16.5, is used to execute a subprogram. The CALL statement includes the name of the subprogram as a literal and a list of data items that are passed to the subprogram. It is imperative that the items in this list match the number and size of items specified in the subprogram's PROCEDURE DIVISION USING clause and defined in the subprogram's LINKAGE SECTION.

For example, to execute the subprogram DATETRAN shown in Program 16.1, the statement

```
CALL "DATETRAN" USING DATE-OUT.
```

could be used. In this instance, the item DATE-OUT must be defined in the calling program so that it is consistent with the definition of the corresponding item in the subprogram. It is not necessary that the list of items in the CALL statement be 01-level or 77-level items, but this is permitted if appropriate. Thus, a description such as

```
03 DATE-OUT PIC X(18).
```

would suffice for this CALL.

A subprogram can be executed as many times as desired from a calling program with the same or a different list of items in the statement. It is also possible for a subprogram to CALL another subprogram: the CALL statement is valid in any program module. In no case, however, may a subprogram call itself or call another subprogram that would result in its execution.

In systems that load subprograms during execution, the CALL statement may be able to use a *data-name* in place of the literal containing the subprogram name. For example, in such systems the following statements would be valid:

```
MOVE "DATETRAN" TO SUBPROG-NAME.
CALL SUBPROG-NAME USING DATE-OUT.
```

This option is not available on systems that create a complete load module before the program is executed, since the content of the *data-name* used in the CALL statement is not defined prior to execution.

Figure 16.5 General form of the CALL statement

```
CALL "program-name" [USING data-name . . .]
```

16.4 PROGRAM EXAMPLE

In Chapter 12, a program that produced a Purchase Order Register as part of the Amalgamated Custom Design data processing system was developed. Program 12.1 utilizes a sequential look-up procedure to locate data (name and address) for suppliers in a table that was loaded from a file (SUPPLIER-MASTER-FILE). In Program 16.2, a revision of Program 12.1, the look-up procedure is carried out in a subprogram rather than in an internal procedure. The subprogram, which is called SEQSEARCH, is shown in Program 16.3.

In Program 16.2, the subprogram is invoked by the CALL statement at lines 12800-13000. Five arguments are passed to the subprogram:

```
SUPPLIER-TABLE
NUM-ELEMENTS
SEARCH-FLAG
X
SUPPLIER-ID-NUM-ARG
```

Note that it was necessary in the subprogram to define a new data item (SUPPLIER-ID-NUM-ARG) with an 01-level in order to obey the dictum that all fields in the USING clause be defined with 01-levels or 77-levels.

In Program 16.3, all the arguments are defined in the LINKAGE SECTION and listed in the USING clause of the PROCEDURE DIVISION entry. In these two programs, the same data names have been used in both the calling program and the subprogram. Although this practice aids in readability, it is not required by COBOL syntax. Each program is compiled separately. The only communication between the two programs is via the list of data items in the USING clauses. Note that the sequence of items and the description of the items match exactly in the two programs. This *is* a requirement. If each item does not match its counterpart, or if the descriptions of the items are not the same, the results of executing the program unit are unpredictable and, in all likelihood, will result in a system error message of some type; certainly the results of the execution will be invalid.

Program 16.2 Sequential search example with subprogram

```
100     IDENTIFICATION DIVISION.
200
300     PROGRAM-ID. SEC-SEARCH-SUB.
400     AUTHOR. WAYNE.
500
600     ENVIRONMENT DIVISION.
700
800     CONFIGURATION SECTION.
```

Program 16.2 (continued)

```
900
1000    SOURCE-COMPUTER.
1100    OBJECT-COMPUTER.
1200
1300    INPUT-OUTPUT SECTION.
1400
1500    FILE-CONTROL.
1600
1700        SELECT PURCHASE-REQUEST-FILE ASSIGN TO DISK.
1800        SELECT SUPPLIER-MASTER-FILE ASSIGN TO DISK.
1900        SELECT PRINTED-DETAIL-FILE ASSIGN TO PRINTER.
2000
2100    DATA DIVISION.
2200
2300    FILE SECTION.
2400
2500    FD  PURCHASE-REQUEST-FILE
2600        RECORD CONTAINS 84 CHARACTERS
2700        BLOCK CONTAINS 30 RECORDS
2800        LABEL RECORDS ARE STANDARD
2900        VALUE OF TITLE IS "PURCHASEREQ"
3000        DATA RECORD IS INPUT-RECORD.
3100
3200    01  PURCHASE-REQUEST-RECORD.
3300        03  SUPPLIER-ID-NUMBER-PRR          PIC X(5).
3400        03  ITEM-NUMBER-PRR                 PIC X(5).
3500        03  ITEM-DESCRIPTION-PRR            PIC X(10).
3600        03  ITEM-COST-PRR                   PIC 999V99.
3700        03  ORDER-QUANTITY-PRR              PIC 9(3).
3800        03  FILLER                          PIC X(56).
3900
4000    FD  SUPPLIER-MASTER-FILE
4100        RECORD CONTAINS 84 CHARACTERS
4200        BLOCK  CONTAINS 30 RECORDS
4300        LABEL RECORDS ARE STANDARD
4400        VALUE OF TITLE IS "SUPPLIERINFO"
4500        DATA RECORD IS SUPPLIER-MASTER-RECORD.
4600
4700    01  SUPPLIER-MASTER-RECORD.
4800        03 SUPPLIER-ID-NUMBER-SMR           PIC X(5).
4900        03 SUPPLIER-NAME-SMR                PIC X(20).
5000        03 SUPPLIER-ADDRESS-SMR             PIC X(20).
5100        03 FILLER                           PIC X(39).
5200
5300    FD  PRINTED-DETAIL-FILE
5400        LABEL RECORDS ARE OMITTED
5500        DATA RECORD IS OUTPUT-RECORD.
5600
5700    01  OUTPUT-RECORD                       PIC X(132).
5800
5900    WORKING-STORAGE SECTION.
6000
6100    01  SUPPLIER-ID-NUMBER-ARG      PIC X(5).
6200
6300    01  NUM-ELEMENTS                PIC 999 VALUE ZERO.
```

```
6400
6500     01  SEARCH-FLAG              PIC X(11) VALUE "CONTINUE".
6600
6700     01  X                        PIC 999 VALUE ZERO.
6800
6900     01  FLAGS.
7000         02 ERROR-FLAG            PIC 9 VALUE ZERO.
7100         02 EOF-FLAG-SMF          PIC X(3) VALUE "NO".
7200         02 EOF-FLAG-PRR          PIC X(3) VALUE "NO".
7300
7400     01  SUPPLIER-TABLE.
7500         02  SUPPLIER-ENTRY OCCURS 1 TO 100 TIMES
7600                 DEPENDING ON NUM-ELEMENTS.
7700             03  SUPPLIER-ID-NUMBER    PIC X(5).
7800             03  SUPPLIER-NAME         PIC X(20).
7900             03  SUPPLIER-ADDRESS      PIC X(20).
8000
8100     01  MAJOR-HEADING.
8200         02  FILLER               PIC X(50) VALUE SPACES.
8300         02  FILLER               PIC X(14) VALUE "PURCHASE ORDER".
8400
8500     01  MINOR-HEADING.
8600         02 FILLER                PIC X(11) VALUE "SUPPLIER ID".
8700         02 FILLER                PIC X(6) VALUE SPACES.
8800         02 FILLER                PIC X(8) VALUE "ITEM NUM".
8900         02 FILLER                PIC X(4) VALUE SPACES.
9000         02 FILLER                PIC X(16) VALUE "ITEM DESCRIPTION".
9100         02 FILLER                PIC X(4) VALUE SPACES.
9200         02 FILLER                PIC X(9) VALUE "ITEM COST".
9300         02 FILLER                PIC X(6) VALUE SPACES.
9400         02 FILLER                PIC X(8) VALUE "QUANTITY".
9500         02 FILLER                PIC X(2) VALUE SPACES.
9600         02 FILLER                PIC X(13) VALUE "SUPPLIER NAME".
9700         02 FILLER                PIC X(14) VALUE SPACES.
9800         02 FILLER                PIC X(16) VALUE "SUPPLIER ADDRESS".
9900
10000    01  DETAIL-LINE.
10100        02  FILLER               PIC X(5) VALUE SPACES.
10200        02  DL-SUPPLIER-ID-NUMBER PIC X(5).
10300        02  FILLER               PIC X(10) VALUE SPACES.
10400        02  DL-ITEM-NUMBER       PIC X(5).
10500        02  FILLER               PIC X(8) VALUE SPACES.
10600        02  DL-ITEM-DESCRIPTION  PIC X(10).
10700        02  FILLER               PIC X(7) VALUE SPACES.
10800        02  DL-ITEM-COST         PIC 999.99.
10900        02  FILLER               PIC X(10) VALUE SPACES.
11000        02  DL-ORDER-QUANTITY    PIC 9(3).
11100        02  FILLER               PIC X(5) VALUE SPACES.
11200        02  DL-SUPPLIER-NAME     PIC X(20).
11300        02  FILLER               PIC X(5) VALUE SPACES.
11400        02  DL-SUPPLIER-ADDRESS  PIC X(20).
11500
11600    PROCEDURE DIVISION.
11700
```

```
11800    1000-MAIN-LOGIC.                              Program 16.2 (continued)
11900
12000        PERFORM 2000-READ-LOAD-TABLE.
12100        PERFORM 3000-INITIALIZATION.
12200        PERFORM 4000-SEARCH-READ
12300            UNTIL EOF-FLAG-PRR = "YES".
12400        PERFORM 9000-TERMINATION.
12500        STOP RUN.
12600
12700    2000-READ-LOAD-TABLE.
12800
12900        MOVE ZERO TO ERROR-FLAG.
13000        MOVE ZERO TO NUM-ELEMENTS.
13100        OPEN INPUT SUPPLIER-MASTER-FILE.
13200        READ SUPPLIER-MASTER-FILE
13300            AT END MOVE "YES" TO EOF-FLAG-SMF.
13400        PERFORM 2100-STOR-READ
13500            UNTIL EOF-FLAG-SMF = "YES" OR ERROR-FLAG = 1.
13600        CLOSE SUPPLIER-MASTER-FILE.
13700
13800    2100-STOR-READ.
13900
14000        ADD 1 TO NUM-ELEMENTS.
14100        IF NUM-ELEMENTS > 100
14200            MOVE 1 TO ERROR-FLAG
14300        ELSE
14400            MOVE SUPPLIER-MASTER-RECORD
14500                TO SUPPLIER-ENTRY (NUM-ELEMENTS).
14600            READ SUPPLIER-MASTER-FILE
14700                AT END MOVE "YES" TO EOF-FLAG-SMF.
14800
14900    3000-INITIALIZATION.
15000
15100        OPEN INPUT PURCHASE-REQUEST-FILE
15200             OUTPUT PRINTED-DETAIL-FILE.
15300        READ PURCHASE-REQUEST-FILE
15400            AT END MOVE "YES" TO EOF-FLAG-PRR.
15500        MOVE MAJOR-HEADING TO OUTPUT-RECORD.
15600        WRITE OUTPUT-RECORD AFTER PAGE.
15700        MOVE MINOR-HEADING TO OUTPUT-RECORD.
15800        WRITE OUTPUT-RECORD AFTER 2.
15900
16000    4000-SEARCH-READ.
16100
16200        MOVE SUPPLIER-ID-NUMBER-PRR TO SUPPLIER-ID-NUMBER-ARG.
16300        CALL "SEQSEARCH"
16400            USING SUPPLIER-TABLE  NUM-ELEMENTS  SEARCH-FLAG  X,
16500                SUPPLIER-ID-NUMBER-ARG.
16600        IF SEARCH-FLAG = "FOUND"
16700            MOVE SUPPLIER-ID-NUMBER-PRR
16800                TO DL-SUPPLIER-ID-NUMBER
16900            MOVE ITEM-NUMBER-PRR
17000                TO DL-ITEM-NUMBER
17100            MOVE ITEM-DESCRIPTION-PRR
17200                TO DL-ITEM-DESCRIPTION
```

Program 16.2 (continued)

```
17300           MOVE ITEM-COST-PRR
17400               TO DL-ITEM-COST
17500           MOVE ORDER-QUANTITY-PRR
17600               TO DL-ORDER-QUANTITY
17700           MOVE SUPPLIER-NAME (X)
17800               TO DL-SUPPLIER-NAME
17900           MOVE SUPPLIER-ADDRESS (X)
18000               TO DL-SUPPLIER-ADDRESS
18100           MOVE DETAIL-LINE TO OUTPUT-RECORD
18200           WRITE OUTPUT-RECORD AFTER 2
18300        ELSE
18400           PERFORM 6100-NOT-PRESENT.
18500        READ PURCHASE-REQUEST-FILE
18600            AT END MOVE "YES" TO EOF-FLAG-PRR.
18700
18800   6100-NOT-PRESENT.
18900
19000        EXIT.
19100
19200   9000-TERMINATION.
19300
19400        CLOSE PURCHASE-REQUEST-FILE
19500              PRINTED-DETAIL-FILE.
```

Program 16.3 Sequential search subprogram

```
300     IDENTIFICATION DIVISION.
400
500     PROGRAM-ID. SEQSEARCH.
600     AUTHOR. WAYNE.
700
800     ENVIRONMENT DIVISION.
900
1000    CONFIGURATION SECTION.
1050
1100    SOURCE-COMPUTER.
1200    OBJECT-COMPUTER.
1300
1500    DATA DIVISION.
1600
1700    LINKAGE SECTION.
1750
1800    01  X                          PIC 999.
1900    01  SUPPLIER-ID-NUMBER-ARG      PIC X(5).
2000    01  SEARCH-FLAG                 PIC X(11).
2100    01  NUM-ELEMENTS                PIC 999.
2150
2200    01  SUPPLIER-TABLE.
2300        02  SUPPLIER-ENTRY OCCURS 1 TO 100 TIMES
2400                DEPENDING ON NUM-ELEMENTS.
2500            03  SUPPLIER-ID-NUMBER  PIC X(5).
2600            03  SUPPLIER-NAME       PIC X(20).
2700            03  SUPPLIER-ADDRESS    PIC X(20).
```

Program 16.3 (continued)

```
2800
3000     PROCEDURE DIVISION
3050
3100         USING SUPPLIER-TABLE  NUM-ELEMENTS  SEARCH-FLAG
3200             X  SUPPLIER-ID-NUMBER-ARG.
3300
3400     1000-SEARCH-CONTROL.
3450
3500         MOVE "CONTINUE" TO SEARCH-FLAG.
3600         MOVE 1 TO X.
3700         PERFORM 2000-SEARCH UNTIL SEARCH-FLAG NOT EQUAL "CONTINUE".
3800         GO TO 9000-SEARCH-EXIT.
3850
3900     2000-SEARCH.
3950
4000         IF SUPPLIER-ID-NUMBER (X) = SUPPLIER-ID-NUMBER-ARG
4100             MOVE "FOUND" TO SEARCH-FLAG
4200         ELSE
4300             ADD 1 TO X
4400             IF X > NUM-ELEMENTS
4500                 MOVE "NOT PRESENT" TO SEARCH-FLAG
4600             ELSE
4700                 IF SUPPLIER-ID-NUMBER (X) > SUPPLIER-ID-NUMBER-ARG
4800                     MOVE "NOT PRESENT" TO SEARCH-FLAG
4900                 ELSE
5000                     NEXT SENTENCE.
5050
5100     9000-SEARCH-EXIT.
5150
5200         EXIT PROGRAM.
```

16.5 IMPLICATIONS FOR PROGRAM DEVELOPMENT

Subprograms are an important tool in system development. An obvious benefit is that programmers can develop subprograms for procedures that will be needed by several different programs in the system. Writing and testing the subprograms need only be carried out one time, thereby saving the time and effort that would otherwise be required to incorporate the procedure into each program in which it is required.

Subprograms are also useful in developing large programs (even when the procedure may be needed only once in the entire system) because subprograms can be developed, coded, compiled, and tested independently of other program units. Thus, it is often possible to break up a large program into a series of semi-independent subprograms. Testing a subprogram with data usually requires that a calling program (sometimes called a *main program*) be written to pass data to the subprogram and to receive and interpret the output of the subprogram, but such developmental programs are relatively easy to write. Of course, they are ultimately discarded when the subprograms are combined into a complete working program. One advantage of this "bottom-up" program development approach is that the debugging and testing task is carried out in incremental steps. If the specifications for each of the subprograms have been correctly written, and if each subprogram has been thoroughly tested to verify that it performs the functions defined for it in the specifications, the task of combining the subprograms into a whole program is greatly simplified. After this kind of testing, problems that may become evident can usually be traced to the main program, which controls execution of the subprograms, because the logic in the subprograms has already been tested.

There are also some quite pragmatic benefits from this approach to program development. Once the subprogram specifications have been written, different programmers may proceed with coding and testing concurrently, reducing the time period required for developing the program. The load placed on the computing system is reduced somewhat because many small compilations, instead of a smaller number of large ones, will be performed over a period of time. These benefits are not gained without some cost, however. The total number of hours of programmer effort required to complete a project may increase because of the need to write specifications for subprograms, the necessity for writing developmental main programs to test each subprogram, and the need to coordinate the efforts of several programmers working on the same project. Some of this time may, of course, be recouped when the entire program is finally assembled for testing. If all has gone well, the final product should be relatively bug-free and require a minimum amount of time for testing and implementation.

16.6 SELF-TEST EXERCISES

1. Define the following terms:
   a. subprogram
   b. calling program
   c. program unit
   d. load module
   e. linking

2. Describe two ways in which program units are converted into executable programs.

3. Which DIVISION may be omitted in a subprogram?

4. What are three features found in subprograms that are not found in other programs?

5. What restriction is placed on data items defined in the LINKAGE SECTION?

6. What restrictions are placed on items listed in a PROCEDURE DIVISION USING clause?

7. Where is the name of a subprogram defined?

8. What are some advantages of subprograms for program development and maintenance?

9. How is linking handled on your system?

10. Is it possible for a subprogram to execute another subprogram? What restrictions are there in this regard?

11. Write a subprogram to accept a date in the form *mmddyy*, and convert it to the Julian date equivalent. The Julian date is the day of the year; the Julian date for January 1 is 1, for February 1 is 32, and for December 31 is 365 or 366 (depending on whether it is a leap year). (See Chapter 12, Section 13, Exercise 1.)

12. Write a subprogram to accept one data item, FULL-NAME, which contains a string of characters in the form

> last-name first-name middle-initial

and returns three items

> LAST—NAME, FIRST—NAME, MIDDLE—INITIAL

For example, if the content of FULL-NAME were

> D,O,E, ,J,O,H,N, ,E, , , , , , , , , , ,
> FULL—NAME PIC X(20)

the required items would be

> D,O,E, , , , , , , ,
> LAST—NAME PIC X(10)

> J,O,H,N, , , , , , ,
> FIRST—NAME PIC X(10)

> E,
> MIDDLE—INITIAL PIC X

16.7 PROGRAMMING ASSIGNMENTS

1. The statement

> ACCEPT data-name FROM TIME

places an eight-digit numeric value into the specified *data-name*. The value is composed of hours (2 digits), minutes (2 digits), seconds (2 digits) and hundredths of a second (2 digits). Hours are expressed on a 24-hour-clock basis, like this:

12-hour-clock time	*Value of TIME*
1:30 A.M.	01300000
12:00 P.M.	12000000
2:56 P.M.	14560000

Write and test a subprogram to convert the value of time and return to the calling program a string of characters like those shown above. Round off the value of minutes to the nearest minute.

2. Consider the sales file described in Chapter 8, Section 12, Exercise 2. A program needs to summarize this data by department and by date, i.e., two reports will be generated, a Department Report in which data is summarized by department identifier, and a Daily Summary Report in which data is summarized by date. Write the program, using subprograms where possible to simplify the program development task.

3. Revise the program written for Chapter 12, Section 10, Exercise 1, using subroutines to carry out the search procedures.

4. Revise the program written for Chapter 7, Section 17, Exercise 3, using a subprogram to produce the required lists.

5. Revise the program written for Chapter 14, Section 14, Exercise 9, using a subprogram to produce the required output.

DATA BASE MANAGEMENT SYSTEMS 17

17.1 WHAT IS A DATA BASE MANAGEMENT SYSTEM?

The total of all data collected and stored in a computing system is often referred to as a *data base*. Traditionally, data processing systems have organized the data base as a collection of distinct files, each of which is designed around the needs of a specific portion of the system. Thus, the data base for a typical small business contains files relating to employees, inventory, accounts receivable and payable, orders for goods, and so on. The Amalgamated Custom Design data processing system described in Chapter 10 is a small example of a traditional data processing system organized in this fashion.

In recent years, traditional data processing systems have gradually given way to systems organized around a *data base management system* (usually referred to as *DBMS*). A data base management system is designed to facilitate the organization and retrieval of data and to solve problems faced by users of traditional file-oriented data processing systems.

As data bases have become larger and more complex, the task of organizing the data in a coherent and logical fashion has grown increasingly difficult. The root of the problem lies in the fact that actual description and organization of the data is spread through hundreds of programs that process and maintain the data. A data base management system forces a single well-defined description of the data base. In this description, the logical relationships among the data items are explicitly defined and the methods of access to the data are specified.

Traditional systems often became so large and complex that no one fully understood all of the data and its relationships. A DBMS provides a tool for simplifying and understanding the data base, which is a first step toward utilizing its full potential.

In traditional file-oriented systems, the task of ensuring the accuracy and completeness of the data within the data base becomes a task of herculean proportions. These systems tend to be developed in a piecemeal fashion over a period of time, often using many different programmers and analysts. The tasks of data validation and verification are spread throughout the entire system. Unfortunately, each program tends to use different standards and techniques, resulting in wide variations in reliability among data items in the system.

In traditional systems, it is not uncommon to find some items reproduced many times throughout a system. It is also not uncommon to find that updates to such fields are not propagated properly. A data base management system typically provides for standardized data validation techniques specified at the same time the data is defined. The DBMS ensures that the specified validation is performed whenever that item is updated.

In addition, a DBMS strives to eliminate redundancy within the data base. Any data item is stored only once, and then appropriate relationships are defined to link that item with other related items in the data base. In traditional systems, the problem of finding some like items updated and some not is prevalent; the problem is alleviated in a DBMS.

Data processing systems are not static. In most situations they are continually being revised and modified to reflect the changes within the organization they serve. A problem in traditional systems is that any reorganization of the physical data–new data that must be processed, changes in existing data items, and new organization for a file, for example–necessitates rewriting all affected programs. In a data base management system, each program is provided with a logical view of the data that is divorced from the physical organization of the data. Thus, changes in physical makeup of the data have no effect on the programs unless there is a corresponding change in the logical requirements for the program.

As users have become more sophisticated about data processing and computers, they have increased informational demands on systems. In a typical traditional system, a user initiates a request to the data processing department for new information. If the request is feasible and judged to be cost effective, the analyst and programmer develop a program to meet the need. Unfortunately, this a time-consuming and expensive process. Often, the user's need for information has changed long before the data processing department can get around to fulfilling the request.

There are two ways that the need for timely production of information is addressed in a DBMS. A data base management system provides for report generating facilities, which can greatly reduce the turnaround time required to produce new reports of a routine nature. The data base management system also typically provides query systems designed for nonprofessional users with ad hoc informational needs. A query system usually operates in an on-line environment, allowing the user to phrase questions in an Englishlike language and responding with information from the data base.

As traditional systems become larger and interactive components are incorporated into them, security of the data becomes an increasing problem. The data needs to be protected from access by unauthorized users and from inadvertent or deliberate sabotage. Traditional systems generally incorporate features to help solve this problem, but unfortunately, each program in the system has to have some component of the protection system built in. Ensuring an effective system with so many components becomes difficult, if not impossible. Data base management systems provide a centralized mechanism for ensuring that access to the data and the ability to change data is restricted to those programs and users authorized to do so. This mechanism is usually defined at the time the data is defined. Thus, data base management systems are designed to perform the following functions, each of which represents a need not satisfied in traditional systems:

- provide for a single description of the whole data base
- ensure accuracy and completeness of the data
- insulate programs from the physical makeup of the data
- facilitate production of routine reports
- process ad hoc inquiries in a timely manner
- provide for data security

The net effect of the DBMS is to provide a coherent model of the data base, centralized controls over the quality of the data contained in it, and useful techniques for retrieving the data to meet the informational needs of users.

17.2   ORIGIN OF DBMS

Data base management systems are the product of a long evolution of developments designed to help increase the effectiveness of data processing systems. One of the first of these developments was the use of the operating system as an interface between the program and the actual data. Program requests for data are intercepted by the operating system, which contains procedures for actually performing the input and output operation. The diagram in Figure 17.1 illustrates this first stage of evolution. The advantage of this over the earlier system, which incorporated actual logic into each program to perform the physical manipulation of the input/output device, was to simplify each program and to provide for the sharing of data resources among programs being executed concurrently.

At the next stage of development, the operating system began to provide tools for the organization of and manipulation of data. Multiple types of file organization that enable random as well as sequential access to data were developed at this time. Various utility programs for performing limited manipulation on data, such as copying data from one file to another and sorting it, were included with operating systems or were available for purchase. Report generators such as language Report Program Generator (RPG) and the report writer facility in COBOL were introduced. All of these facilitated the task of organizing and manipulating data.

Data base management systems represent a final stage in this evolution. A component of the DBMS usually referred to as the Data Base Manager acts as an interface between requests for data and the traditional operating system with its file organization techniques. In a typical operation, a request for data from a program written in a traditional language (such as COBOL), from a report generator, or from an ad hoc query written in a query language, is processed by the Data Base Manager. The Data Base Manager accesses the Data Description to determine where the data is located. The Data Base Manager then issues requests (which will be serviced by the operating system in the traditional fashion) for data to be read from one or more files within the data base. A similar procedure is used to update data within the data base. The Data Base Manager accepts the new data, determines the location of all data items within the data base that are affected, and initiates the required write operations that will be carried out by the operating system.

The DBMS adds an additional software interface between the user and the physical data. This interface allows users to concern themselves with the logical makeup of the data and relationships among various data items. The DBMS performs the function of mapping this logical view of the data onto its physical organization. This capability, plus the ad hoc query and report generators that are also supplied, improves the quality and usefulness of computer data processing systems.

Figure 17.1   Evolution of DBMS

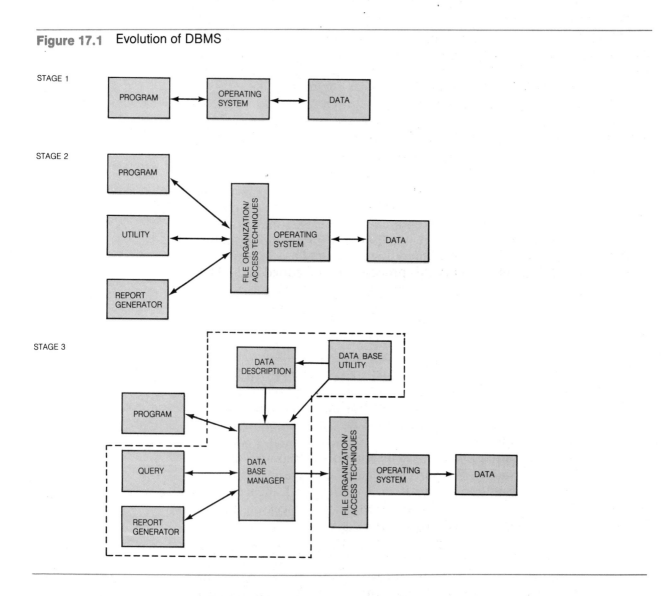

17.3   COMPONENTS OF A DBMS

A data base management system is made up of a number of different but related components. Users of a DBMS most often start with the system's

Data Definition Facility. This facility includes a data definition language (which usually looks like an enhanced version of the COBOL DATA DIVISION) and a data definition processor. The user codes the description of the data base in the data definition language and submits it to the data definition processor, which acts as a compiler to generate the internal data description. This internal description, usually referred to as a *schema*, is the description used by the Data Base Manager in all access to the data base. The Data Base Manager is typically a program that is always active in the system. It uses the schema as a "road map" to determine how the data is organized, what operations are allowed, how the data is to be validated, and how to respond to inquiries for data. The data definition language is also used to generate and store *subschemas*–portions of the schema that will be referenced by user programs. A program requiring access to the data base copies a subschema from a library, much as the COPY statement in traditional program development settings copies COBOL code into a program.

After the data base has been defined and its schema is in place, the Data Manipulation Facility can be used. The purpose of this facility is to provide access to the data. The Data Manipulation Facility consists of some type of Data Manipulation Language and the Data Base Manager. Data Manipulation Languages are usually implemented as enhanced versions of existing programming languages. Thus, if COBOL is used to access the data base, additional nonstandard verbs and other facilities are added to the language, and an appropriate compiler is provided.

A very important component of the system is the Data Base Query Facility. It consists of a Data Base Query Language and a processor to respond to queries. In some systems, this processor is embedded in the Data Base Manager; in others, it exists as a separate program acting as an interface between the user and the Data Base Manager. In any case, the query language is normally used in an interactive manner, with users phrasing inquiries in a relatively "natural" language and receiving responses in the form of data or help in phrasing queries in acceptable fashion. The Data Base Query Facility is (or should be) designed to be as user friendly as possible; certainly it should not require extensive technical expertise to use. The Query Facility is meant for the casual user who has immediate needs for data and not for routine data processing applications, which continue to be handled by traditional means.

Many data base management systems support a Report Generator Facility. This facility consists of Report Generator Language and a compiler to translate programs written in the Report Generator Language. This facility is designed for use by the professional data processing staff to increase its productivity in generating routine reports.

All data base management systems supply utilities to be used by the Data Base Administrator (the staff person charged with maintaining the data base). Typically, these utilities contain an initializer, which is required to allocate space and initialize tables and parameters when a data base is created; a system to maintain a journal of all transactions processed by the system, to be used in the case of malfunction and to provide an audit trail; and statistical report generators, which the administrator uses to monitor the performance of the system and to evaluate the need to modify portions of the system in order to improve performance.

17.4   ALTERNATIVE DESIGN PHILOSOPHIES

One of the most powerful features of data base management systems is the ability to reflect the logical relations among data elements in the definition of the data base. There are three common methods for organizing data to reflect these relationships:

- hierarchical
- network
- relational

In a *hierarchial* organization, data is viewed as a tree structure in which an element higher in the tree is considered to be the "owner" of subordinate elements. For example, consider a set of data relating to doctors, patients, and office calls that is maintained in a group medical practice. There are several doctors, each doctor sees many patients, and each patient makes numerous office calls. A hierarchical arrangement of this data is shown in Figure 17.2.

Figure 17.2   Hierarchical organization example

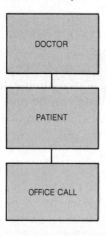

Data is organized in order to answer particular questions. The kinds of questions that can be answered easily depends on the structuring–the ownership properties–of the data. The hierarchical organization of data is useful for answering questions such as "What patients see Dr. X?" and "How many times has patient Y seen Dr. X?" Essentially, the hierarchical model is useful for reflecting one-to-one or one-to-many relationships.

The hierarchical model is less useful in reflecting many-to-one relationships, often found in data. For example, suppose a patient sees more than one doctor in the clinic. In the hierarchical model, the patient would be represented several times, once in each doctor's set of records; this makes the task of responding to the query "Which doctors see patient Y?" quite complex.

An alternative to the hierarchical model is the *network* model. In this model, each basic entity is linked to others using pointers that represent the relationships in the data. For example, the relationships among the doctor, patient, and office call data could be visualized as shown in Figure 17.3.

Figure 17.3   Network organization example

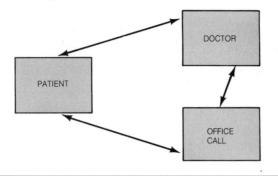

In this example, each patient is associated with one or more doctors and each doctor is associated with one or more patients. Each patient is related to a group of office calls, which in turn are linked to the appropriate doctor. A network approach is useful for reflecting the many-to-one as well as the one-to-many types of relationships commonly encountered in data. Using pointers enables access to required data without exhaustive search of the data base. On the other hand, the complexity of the linkage among the data elements makes this approach the most complex in implementation and use.

A third type of organization is called *relational*. In this approach, the data is viewed as a series of tables, each of which specifies a relation. Each row of the table is identified by one or more key fields. Other elements of the table are functionally dependent on the key fields. For example, suppose we have the data records shown in Figure 17.4 reflecting activity in the doctor/patient/office-call data base described above. This data can be organized into a series of relations, as shown in Figure 17.5. The primary purpose of the multiple tables is to provide for logical access to all the relationships contained in the data and to remove redundancy as much as possible. The primary advantage of the relational model is its simplicity. The disadvantages stem from the amount of processing that may be required to answer queries not implicit in the relations used. For example, responding to the query "What is the name of Doctor Number 1?" is quite easy, as the doctor number/name relation is contained in the data base. Responding to the query "Which doctor does patient number 1 see?" or "Which patients does doctor number 1 see?" are more difficult, because responding to either of these queries necessitates an exhaustive search of the office call/patient number/doctor number relation. The current trend in data base management systems is towards the relational approach because of its relative symplicity and because current computing systems finally have sufficient power to handle the large computational overhead required.

Figure 17.4   Sample doctor/patient/office call data base

Doctor Number	Doctor Name	Patient Number	Patient Name	Office Call		
				Number	Date	Charge
1	X	1	Y	1	1/2/86	50.00
1	X	1	Y	3	1/3/86	35.00
1	X	3	Z	4	1/3/86	40.00
2	A	1	Y	2	1/2/86	30.00
2	A	2	W	5	1/3/86	60.00

Figure 17.5   Relational organization of doctor/patient/office call data

Doctor Number	Name		Patient Number	Name
1	X		1	Y
2	A		2	W
			3	Z

Office Call Number	Patient Number	Doctor Number	Date	Charge
1	1	1	1/2/86	50.00
2	1	2	1/2/86	30.00
3	1	1	1/3/86	35.00
4	3	1	1/3/86	40.00
5	2	2	1/3/86	60.00

17.5   SURVEY OF EXISTING SYSTEMS

Data base management systems have been implemented on the full range of computing equipment from micros to mainframes. They were first developed for mainframe systems; later they were adapted for use on mini- and finally on microcomputing systems. The capabilities of DBMS vary widely from system to system within the general framework outlined in Section 17.3. Figure 17.6 lists some widely used DBMS for mainframe and mini systems; Figure 17.7 lists some DBMS used on micro systems. Along with wide variation in capabilities, there is an almost equally wide variation in cost. A mainframe DBMS may cost $50,000 or more, whereas a micro DBMS may cost under $1,000. Many systems sold for microcomputers, which at first glance might be considered a "data base management system," should more precisely be called "file management systems" because the system does not have a multi-file capability. Such systems are capable of extensive manipulation of data within one file, but not of linking data among several different files. Examples of file management systems are shown in Figure 17.8. When considering the purchase of a piece of software for a micro system, the buyer must determine whether the software is a file management system or a true data base management system.

Selecting an appropriate DBMS for a given application is very important, but it is not an easy task. A great deal of time and effort must be expended to create the data base and build applications around the system. Unfortunately, DBMSs are largely nonstandard. Converting from one DBMS to another usually requires the user to start over from the beginning; very little of the effort expended on the existing system can be transferred to the new system. Thus, making a good choice of DBMS is quite important, because users are normally locked into the choice for a long period of time. Unfortunately, because of the wide range of features and capabilities, choosing among available alternatives may be quite complex. The user should strive to choose a system that will not only meet current needs, but will also expand to meet anticipated (and unanticipated) future needs.

Figure 17.6 DBMS for mainframe and mini systems

Name	Supplier	Type
DMS II	Burroughs	Network
DMS-170	Control Data	Network
DBMS/10	DEC	Network
IMS 2	IBM	Hierarchical
DBMS 110	Univac	Network
Oracle	Oracle Corp	Relational
IDMS	Cullinane	Network
System 2000	MRI	Hierarchical
Prime DBMS	Prime	Network

Figure 17.7 DBMS for microcomputers

Name	Supplier	Type
Condor/20	Condor Computer Corp.	Relational
dBASE II	Ashton-Tate	Relational
dBASE III		
MDBS III	Micro Data Base Systems	Network
DataStar	MicroPro International	Network
Pearl	Relational Systems International Corp.	Relational
10 BASE	Fox Research, Inc	Relational

Figure 17.8 File management systems for microcomputer systems

Name	Supplier
PFS:File	Software Publishing
Profile II	Radio Shack
Main Street Filer	Main Street Software
Easy Filer	Sorcim/Information Unlimited Software
File-it!	Relational Database Systems Inc.
Ultrafile	Continental Software
VisiFile	VisiCorp

17.6 SELF-TEST EXERCISES

1. Define the following terms
   a. data base
   b. data base management system
   c. report generator
   d. Data Base Manager
   e. Data Definition Language
   f. schema
   g. subschema
   h. Data Manipulation Language
   i. query facility

2. What are some problems in file-oriented data processing systems that are addressed by data base management systems?

3. Describe how a typical request for data is handled by a DBMS.

4. Distinguish between a Data Base Manager and a Data Base Administrator.

5. What utilities are usually provided with a DBMS?

6. Briefly distinguish among hierarchical, network, and relational data base management systems.

7. Distinguish between a data base management system and a file management system.

REPORT WRITER A

The report writer module allows the programmer to specify report features including headings, subtotals, and final totals without writing the detailed PROCEDURE DIVISION logic required to produce these elements. The required PROCEDURE DIVISION logic is generated by the COBOL compiler; the programmer is freed from the tedious task of coding and debugging routines for the line counting, page numbering, data movement, and control breaks. The report writer is not available on all COBOL compilers; the reader should check locally available documentation before attempting to write programs using report writer.

The report writer contains facilities to automatically generate the following report elements:

1. Report heading—produced automatically once at the beginning of the report
2. Page heading—produced automatically at the beginning of each page
3. Detail line—as many different types of detail lines as may be required may be specified; production is under the control of the programmer
4. Control heading—produced automatically once at the beginning of processing of each control group
5. Control footing—produced automatically at the end of processing of each control group
6. Page footing—produced automatically at the end of each page
7. Report footing—produced automatically at the end of the report

Additionally, the report writer contains facilities for generating subtotals, line and page counting, generating output lines without MOVE or WRITE statements, and a variety of other features to facilitate the programmer's task in writing report type programs. The report writer does not assume the complete task of controlling the program; the programmer must still open files, control the processing of records, and close files upon completion of processing. The report writer does include three additional and very powerful PROCEDURE DIVISION verbs:

1. INITIATE—used to begin the production of the report
2. GENERATE—used to produce detail, control break and page related lines
3. TERMINATE—used to end the production of the report

Use of these verbs causes the "automatic" features of the report writer module to be carried out during execution of the program.

A.1 PROGRAM EXAMPLE

Program 8.1 of Chapter 8 is rewritten using the report writer and shown as Program A.1. The report produced by this program makes use of the following elements:

- Report heading
- Page heading
- Detail line
- Page footing (page totals)
- Control footing (final totals)

Let us examine the program required to produce this report.

Program A.1   Alphabetic employee report program with Report Writer

```
100      IDENTIFICATION DIVISION.
200
300      PROGRAM-ID. BASIC-REPORT.
400
500      ENVIRONMENT DIVISION.
600
700      CONFIGURATION SECTION.
800
900      SOURCE-COMPUTER.
1000     OBJECT-COMPUTER.
1100
1200     INPUT-OUTPUT SECTION.
1300
1400     FILE-CONTROL.
1500
1600         SELECT ALPHABETIC-FILE ASSIGN TO DISK.
1700         SELECT ALPHABETIC-LIST ASSIGN TO PRINTER.
1800
1900     DATA DIVISION.
2000
2100     FILE SECTION.
2200
2300     FD  ALPHABETIC-FILE
2400         LABEL RECORDS ARE STANDARD
2500         DATA RECORD IS INPUT-RECORD.
2600
```

Program A.1 (continued)

```
2700      01   INPUT-RECORD.
2800           02  IR-NAME              PIC X(16).
2900           02  IR-INITIAL           PIC X.
3000           02  IR-EMPLOYEE-NUMBER    PIC X(9).
3100           02  IR-DEPARTMENT         PIC X(3).
3200           02  IR-SALARY            PIC 9(6).
3300           02  FILLER               PIC X(45).
3400
3500      FD   ALPHABETIC-LIST
3600           LABEL RECORDS ARE OMITTED
3700           REPORT IS EMPLOYEE-REPORT.
3800
3900      WORKING-STORAGE SECTION.
4000
4100      01   FLAGS.
4200           03  EOF-FLAG             PIC X(3) VALUE "NO".
4300           88 END-OF-FILE           VALUE "YES".
4400
4500      01   TOTALS.
4600           02  PAGE-TOTAL           PIC 9(6)V99 VALUE ZERO.
4700           02  NUMBER-OF-EMPLOYEES  PIC 9(4) VALUE ZERO.
4800
4900      REPORT SECTION.
5000
5100      RD   EMPLOYEE-REPORT
5200           CONTROL IS FINAL
5300           PAGE LIMIT IS 45 LINES
5400           HEADING 1
5500           FIRST DETAIL 5
5600           LAST DETAIL 43
5700           FOOTING    45.
5800
5900      01   TYPE IS REPORT HEADING
6000           LINE NUMBER IS 1.
6100           02  COLUMN NUMBER IS 48
6200               PIC IS X(11)
6300               VALUE IS "ABC COMPANY".
6400           02  COLUMN NUMBER IS 61
6500               PIC X(10)
6600               VALUE IS "ALPHABETIC".
6700           02  COLUMN 72
6800               PIC X(8)
6900               VALUE "EMPLOYEE".
7000           02  COLUMN 81 PIC X(6) VALUE "REPORT".
7100
7200      01   COLUMN-HEAD
7300           TYPE IS PAGE HEADING
7400           LINE NUMBER IS 3.
7500           02 COLUMN 27 PIC X(9)  VALUE "LAST NAME".
7600           02 COLUMN 44 PIC X(7)  VALUE "INITIAL".
7700           02 COLUMN 59 PIC X(15) VALUE "EMPLOYEE NUMBER".
7800           02 COLUMN 82 PIC X(10) VALUE "DEPARTMENT".
7900           02 COLUMN 100 PIC X(6) VALUE "SALARY".
8000           02 COLUMN 103 PIC X(4) VALUE "PAGE".
```

Program A.1 (continued)

```
8100        02 COLUMN 108 PIC ZZ SOURCE IS PAGE-COUNTER.
8200
8300    01  DETAIL-LINE
8400        TYPE IS DETAIL
8500        LINE NUMBER IS PLUS 2.
8600        02 COLUMN 27 PIC X(16) SOURCE IS IR-NAME.
8700        02 COLUMN 44 PIC X SOURCE IS IR-INITIAL.
8800        02 COLUMN 59 PIC X(9) SOURCE IS IR-EMPLOYEE-NUMBER.
8900        02 COLUMN 84 PIC X(3) SOURCE IS IR-DEPARTMENT.
9000        02 COLUMN 97 PIC $ZZZ,ZZZ SOURCE IS IR-SALARY.
9100
9200    01  TYPE IS PAGE FOOTING
9300        LINE IS PLUS 2.
9400        02 PF-PAGE-TOTAL
9500           COLUMN 89 PIC $ZZZ,ZZZ.99
9600           SOURCE IS PAGE-TOTAL.
9700
9800    01  TYPE IS CONTROL FOOTING FINAL
9900        LINE IS PLUS 2.
10000       02  COLUMN 71 PIC ZZZ9
10100          SOURCE IS NUMBER-OF-EMPLOYEES.
10200       02  COLUMN 80 PIC X(9) VALUE "EMPLOYEES".
10300       02  COLUMN 96 PIC $***,***,999
10400          SUM IR-SALARY.
10500
10600   PROCEDURE DIVISION.
10700
10800   DECLARATIVES.
10900
11000   1000-END-OF-PAGE SECTION.
11100
11200       USE BEFORE REPORTING COLUMN-HEAD.
11300
11400   1100-INITIALIZE-PAGE-TOTAL.
11500
11600       MOVE ZERO TO PAGE-TOTAL.
11700
11800   END DECLARATIVES.
11900
12000   2000-MAIN SECTION.
12100
12200   2100-MAIN-LOGIC.
12300
12400       PERFORM 3000-INITIALIZATION.
12500       PERFORM 4000-CONTROL UNTIL END-OF-FILE.
12600       PERFORM 9000-TERMINATION.
12700       STOP RUN.
12800
12900   3000-INITIALIZATION.
13000
13100       OPEN INPUT ALPHABETIC-FILE
13200            OUTPUT ALPHABETIC-LIST.
13300       INITIATE EMPLOYEE-REPORT.
13400       PERFORM 6000-READ.
13500
```

Program A.1 *(continued)*

```
13600     4000-CONTROL.
13700
13800        ADD 1 TO NUMBER-OF-EMPLOYEES.
13900        ADD IR-SALARY TO PAGE-TOTAL.
14000        GENERATE DETAIL-LINE.
14100        PERFORM 6000-READ.
14200
14300     6000-READ.
14400
14500        READ ALPHABETIC-FILE
14600           AT END MOVE "YES" TO EOF-FLAG.
14700
14800     9000-TERMINATION.
14900
15000        TERMINATE EMPLOYEE-REPORT.
15100        CLOSE ALPHABETIC-FILE
15200              ALPHABETIC-LIST.
```

Comparison of programs 8.1 and A.1 will reveal major differences in the DATA and PROCEDURE Divisions.

The program involves two files—ALPHABETIC-FILE and ALPHABETIC-LIST—defined in SELECT statements (lines 1600-1700) and in FD entries (lines 2300-3700). The FD entry for Alphabetic-List (lines 3400-3500) makes use of the REPORT clause:

```
FD  ALPHABETIC-LIST
    LABEL RECORDS ARE OMITTED
    REPORT IS EMPLOYEE-REPORT.
```

The REPORT clause specifies the report name and serves to link the file to the RD entry of the REPORT SECTION which follows.

The WORKING-STORAGE SECTION of the DATA DIVISION (lines 3900-4700) contains far fewer entries in Program A.1 compared to Program 8.2. The specification of an end of file flag is still required (lines 4100-4300). (Recall that the reading and processing of files is still controlled by the programmer in the usual way.) Also required are accumulators that are not under automatic control of the report writer logic. In this case accumulators PAGE-TOTAL and NUMBER-OF-EMPLOYEES must be defined (lines 4600-4700). (Note that is not necessary to initialize PAGE-TOTAL to zero, as this task will be accomplished within the PROCEDURE DIVISION.) The accumulator for the final total is defined later and will be handled as part of the automatic functions provided by report writer.

The REPORT SECTION of the DATA DIVISION is used to give an overall description of the report (the RD entry at lines 5100-5700) and to describe the different types of lines to be included in the report (as 01 entries following the RD entry at lines 5900-10400). The overall syntax of the REPORT SECTION is similar to that of the FILE SECTION with the RD entry taking the place of the FD entry and line descriptions taking the place of record descriptions.

The RD entry at lines 5100-5700 contains the report name and numerous clauses specifying information pertaining to the entire report as shown on the next page.

```
RD  EMPLOYEE-REPORT
    CONTROL IS FINAL
    PAGE LIMIT IS 45 LINES
    HEADING 1
    FIRST DETAIL 5
    LAST DETAIL 43
    FOOTING 45.
```

The report name (EMPLOYEE-REPORT) must match the name specified in the
REPORT clause of the FD entry of the associated file. The CONTROL IS clause
specifies the level(s) of control breaks to be recognized in the report. CONTROL
IS FINAL specifies that the only control break desired is to be the end of the
report. If other levels of subtotals had been desired, the names of the control
files would be specified here. (A more complete discussion of this feature is
presented in Section A.3.) The PAGE LIMIT clause specifies the total number of
lines on a report page. The HEADING clause specifies the line number for the
page headings. The FIRST DETAIL and LAST DETAIL clauses specify the line number for the first and last detail lines, respectively. The FOOTING clause specifies
the line number for page footing output.

The 01 entries following the RD entry specify the lines of the report and
differentiate them by type. The first 01 entry (lines 5900-6000) specifies the
report heading as follows:

```
01  TYPE IS REPORT HEADING
    LINE NUMBER IS 1.
```

The 02 entries which follow (lines 6100-7000) specify the content of the report
heading:

```
02  COLUMN NUMBER IS 48
    PIC IS X(11)
    VALUE IS "ABC COMPANY".
02  COLUMN NUMBER IS 61
    PIC X(10)
    VALUE IS "ALPHABETIC".
02  COLUMN 72
    PIC X(8)
    VALUE IS "EMPLOYEE".
02  COLUMN 81 PIC X(6) VALUE "REPORT".
```

Note that most entries in the REPORT SECTION do not have to have a data-name
associated with them; even the data-name FILLER is not required. Note also
the use of the LINE NUMBER and COLUMN NUMBER clauses. The LINE NUMBER clause
specifies the line number on the page for the placement of the line; the COLUMN
NUMBER clause specifies the column number in the line for the placement of
the item being described. Compare the above specifications for the heading
line to the specification of essentially the same line of output in Program 8.1.
In Program 8.1 this heading also includes the page number and was reproduced on each page of the report. In Program A.1 this heading is produced
only once—at the beginning of the report—and hence page numbers have
been included in the column heading line which will be produced at the top
of each page.

The page headings are defined in the next series of entries (lines 7200-
8100):

```
01  COLUMN-HEAD
    TYPE IS PAGE HEADING
    LINE NUMBER IS 3.
    02  COLUMN 27 PIC X(9) VALUE "LAST NAME".
    02  COLUMN 44 PIC X(7) VALUE "INITIAL".
    02  COLUMN 59 PIC X(15) VALUE "EMPLOYEE-NUMBER".
    02  COLUMN 82 PIC X(10) VALUE "DEPARTMENT".
    02  COLUMN 100 PIC X(6) VALUE "SALARY".
    02  COLUMN 103 PIC X(4) VALUE "PAGE".
    02  COLUMN 108 PIC ZZ SOURCE IS PAGE-COUNTER.
```

In the above 01 entry the data-name COLUMN-HEAD is required because it will be referenced later in the PROCEDURE DIVISION. Note the use of the SOURCE IS clause in the last 02 entry above. The SOURCE IS clause takes the place of a MOVE instruction. When this line of output is generated, the content of the field designated in a SOURCE IS clause is moved automatically to the specified field on the output record. Note that it is not even necessary to designate a data-name for the receiving field. In this case the field designated in the SOURCE IS clause is PAGE-COUNTER which is a field automatically defined and incremented by the report writer.

The next series of entries specify the detail line of the report (lines 8300−9000).

```
01  DETAIL-LINE
    TYPE IS DETAIL
    LINE NUMBER IS PLUS 2.
    02  COLUMN 27 PIC X(16) SOURCE IS IR-NAME.
    02  COLUMN 44 PIC X SOURCE IS IR-INITIAL.
    02  COLUMN 59 PIC X(9) SOURCE IS IR-EMPLOYEE-NUMBER.
    02  COLUMN 84 PIC X(3) SOURCE IS IR-DEPARTMENT.
    02  COLUMN 97 PIC $ZZZ,ZZZ SOURCE IS IR-SALARY.
```

The data-name for a type DETAIL line is not optional as with other lines because it is necessary to reference this line by name from the PROCEDURE DIVISION. (The GENERATE statement must include a data-name.) Note the use of the clause

```
LINE NUMBER IS PLUS 2
```

in the definition of the detail line. This entry specifies where the next detail line is to be placed (in this case double spacing is specified). Recall that the position of the first detail line is specified in the RD entry.

The next series of entries specify the page footing (lines 9200-9600).

```
01  TYPE IS PAGE FOOTING
    LINE IS PLUS 2.
    02  PF-PAGE-TOTAL
        COLUMN 89 PIC $ZZZ,ZZZ.99
        SOURCE IS PAGE-TOTAL.
```

This line will automatically be produced when a page is full and before page headings on the next page.

The last series of entries in the REPORT SECTION define the line containing final totals (lines 9800-10400):

```
01  TYPE IS CONTROL FOOTING FINAL
    LINE IS PLUS 2.
    02  COLUMN 71 PIC ZZZ9
        SOURCE IS NUMBER-OF-EMPLOYEES.
    02  COLUMN 80 PIC X(9) VALUE "EMPLOYEES".
    02  COLUMN 96 PIC $**,***,999
        SUM IR-SALARY.
```

Note the use of the SUM clause in the last entry for this line. This clause causes the sum of the values of the specified field to be computed automatically and, when the line is generated, the value of the sum is moved to the designated receiving field in the output record. Only lines of type CONTROL FOOTING can contain an element specified with the SUM clause. (One might inquire why this line is declared to be type CONTROL FOOTING rather than type REPORT FOOTING, as both are produced one time at the end of the report. The necessity of including a SUM clause governed the choice of line types.)

Comparison of the PROCEDURE DIVISION of Programs 8.1 and A.1 will reveal the extent of the programming effort saved by use of the report writer features. Note the absence of routine MOVE statements, manipulation of the PAGE-COUNTER and LINE-COUNTER, and WRITE statements. All of this logic will be generated by report writer.

In Program A.1 it is necessary to include DECLARATIVES prior to the description of the program logic. DECLARATIVES generally are used to specify actions that are to be performed automatically by the program when certain conditions are encountered. In this case a DECLARATIVES procedure is required to zero out the field PAGE-TOTAL for each new page. The DECLARATIVES specifications from lines 10800-11300 are shown below:

```
DECLARATIVES.
1000-END-OF-PAGE SECTION.
    USE BEFORE REPORTING COLUMN-HEAD.
1100-INITIALIZE-PAGE-TOTAL.
    MOVE ZERO TO PAGE-TOTAL.
END DECLARATIVES.
```

DECLARATIVES are terminated by the sentence END DECLARATIVES, and are composed of any number of SECTION's. The SECTION header describes when the procedure described in that SECTION is to be executed. The USE statement describes the relevant condition. In this case,

```
USE BEFORE REPORTING COLUMN-HEAD.
```

means that the procedure is to be executed automatically prior to producing the line COLUMN-HEAD. (Any named line from the report could be included in a USE specification.) Note that if the DECLARATIVES procedure had been omitted, the page total would have become a running total. There is no other way in the program to zero out this field because production of the line is controlled "automatically" by report writer.

The main portion of the PROCEDURE DIVISION logic resembles that of any other COBOL program as shown below:

```
2000-MAIN SECTION.
2100-MAIN-LOGIC.
    PERFORM 3000-INITIALIZATION.
    PERFORM 4000-CONTROL UNTIL END-OF-FILE.
    PERFORM 9000-TERMINATION.
    STOP RUN.
```

```
3000-INITIALIZATION.
    OPEN INPUT ALPHABETIC-FILE
        OUTPUT ALPHABETIC-LIST.
    INITIATE EMPLOYEE-REPORT.
    PERFORM 6000-READ.
4000-CONTROL.
    ADD 1 TO NUMBER-OF-EMPLOYEES.
    ADD IR-SALARY TO PAGE-TOTAL.
    GENERATE DETAIL-LINE.
    PERFORM 6000-READ.
6000-READ.
    READ ALPHABETIC-FILE
        AT END MOVE "YES" TO EOF-FLAG.
9000-TERMINATION.
    TERMINATE EMPLOYEE-REPORT.
    CLOSE ALPHABETIC-FILE
          ALPHABETIC-LIST.
```

The section header is required following DECLARATIVES. The paragraph 2100-MAIN-LOGIC controls execution of other paragraphs as in any structured program. The paragraph 3000-INITIALIZATION serves to OPEN the required files, INITIATE the report and cause the first record to be read. As a result of the INITIATE verb

1. All accumulators automatically controlled by report writer are set to zero (in this program the field used to accumulate the sum of the values is IR-SALARY)
2. PAGE-COUNTER is set to 1
3. LINE-COUNTER is set ot 0 (LINE-COUNTER is an automatically allocated and controlled data-name similar to PAGE-COUNTER).

The paragraph 4000—CONTROL causes processing of the data record just read, the production of the relevant report lines (via the GENERATE statement), and the reading of the next record. In this case, processing the data record entails incrementing the accumulator NUMBER-OF-EMPLOYEES and adding IR-SALARY to PAGE-TOTAL. (Recall that the SUM clause can only be used in conjunction with CONTROL FOOTING lines, hence accumulating PAGE-TOTAL must be accomplished "manually".) The effect of the GENERATE statement is dependent on the current stage of program execution. If this is the first execution of the GENERATE statement the following actions take place.

1. Produce report heading
2. Execute DECLARATIVES procedure
3. Produce COLUMN-HEADING
4. Produce DETAIL-LINE
5. Increment LINE-COUNTER

On subsequent executions of the GENERATE statement the following actions take place:

1. If LINE-COUNTER > last detail line number
   Produce page footing
   Execute DECLARATIVES procedure
   Increment PAGE-COUNTER
   Produce COLUMN-HEADING
   Initialize LINE-COUNTER

  2. Produce DETAIL-LINE

  3. Increment LINE-COUNTER

The paragraph 9000-TERMINATION is executed after all records from the file ALPHABETIC-FILE have been processed. The paragraph terminates production of the report (via the TERMINATE statement), closes the files, and stops execution of the program. The TERMINATE statement causes CONTROL FOOTING FINAL type lines to be produced followed by production of REPORT FOOTING lines (if any—in this example there were none).

A.2 GENERAL FORMS

Complete explanation of all facets of report writer is beyond the scope of this appendix. General forms of all elements of ANSI-74 COBOL including report writer are shown in Appendix C. Following is a description of some of the more useful features of report writer.

Figure A.1   General form of the REPORT SECTION entry

```
REPORT SECTION.
RD   report name
     [{CONTROL IS  }{          data-name-1 . . .     }]
     [{CONTROLS ARE}{FINAL [data-name-1] . . .}]
     [      [{LIMIT IS   }          { LINE }]]
     [ PAGE [{LIMITS ARE }integer-1 { LINES}]]
     [HEADING integer-2]
     [FIRST DETAIL integer-3]
     [LAST DETAIL integer-4]
     [FOOTING integer-5].
report-group-description-entry. . . .
```

The REPORT SECTION

The general form of the REPORT SECTION is shown in Figure A.1. Of particular importance is the CONTROL clause of the RD entry. In this entry a list of data names is specified that form the basis for detection of control breaks and the generation of subtotals. For example, in order to produce subtotals for departments in Program A.1, the RD entry would be

```
RD  DEPARTMENT-REPORT
    CONTROL IS IR-DEPARTMENT
       .
       .
       .
```

In order to produce both department subtotals and final totals, the RD entry would be (see Program A.2)

```
RD  DEPARTMENT-REPORT
    CONTROLS ARE FINAL
            IR-DEPARTMENT
```

.
.
.

The order of listing of data-names in the CONTROL IS clause determines the relative ordering of control breaks from highest to lowest level. Lower level breaks occur more frequently than higher level breaks. For example, in order to produce both department and division subtotals as in Program 8.3, the following RD entry would be used:

```
RD  DIVISION-REPORT
    CONTROLS ARE FINAL
                 IR-DIVISION
                 IR-DEPARTMENT
```

.
.
.

Figure A.2 General form of 01 entry for report writer

```
01  [data-name-1]

    [LINE NUMBER IS {integer-1       }]
                    {PLUS integer-2  }

              ( {REPORT HEADING}                       )
              ( {RH            }                       )
              ( {PAGE HEADING}                         )
              ( {PH          }                         )
    TYPE IS   ( {CONTROL HEADING} {data-name-2}        )
              ( {CH             } {FINAL      }        )
              ( {DETAIL}                               )
              ( {DE    }                               )
              ( {CONTROL FOOTING} {data-name-3}        )
              ( {CF             } {FINAL      }        )
              ( {PAGE FOOTING}                         )
              ( {PF          }                         )
              ( {REPORT FOOTING}                       )
              ( {RF            }                       )
```

The Report Group Description

The general form of the 01 level report group description is shown in Figure A.2. Following the RD entry, 01 level descriptors are required to specify the various elements of the report. Of particular importance is the CONTROL FOOTING entry, which is used to generate control breaks for each of the control fields specified in the CONTROL clause of the RD entry. For example, to generate department subtotals for the report of Program A.1 an 01 entry such as the following would be required:

```
01  LINE NUMBER IS PLUS 2
    TYPE IS CONTROL FOOTING IR-DEPARTMENT.
```

Figure A.3   General form for subordinate group descriptions for report writer

Format 1

```
level-number     [data-name-1]

                 [LINE NUMBER IS { integer-1        } ]
                                 { PLUS integer-2    }
```

Format 2

```
level-number     [data-name-1]
                 [GROUP INDICATE]
                 [COLUMN NUMBER IS integer-1]

                 { PICTURE }
                 { PIC     }  IS picture-codes

                 ( SOURCE IS data-name-2 )
                 { VALUE IS literal      }
                 ( SUM data-name-3 . . . )
```

Each level of control break required a separate 01 report group description entry. The content of the line is produced when a change in the control field is encountered.

The general forms of subordinate report group descriptions are shown in Figure A.3. Format 1-type descriptions may be used to create multiple report lines of a particular type. Format 2-type descriptions are used to specify elementary data items for a line. For example, suppose we wish to create two lines of output per page heading so that the output from the Program A.1 would more closely resemble that of Program 8.1. The following code could be used:

```
01  TYPE IS PAGE HEADING.
    02  LINE NUMBER IS 1.
        03  COLUMN 48 PIC X(11) VALUE "ABC COMPANY".
        03  COLUMN 61 PIC X(10) VALUE "ALPHABETIC".
        03  COLUMN 72 PIC X(8) VALUE "EMPLOYEE".
        03  COLUMN 81 PIC X(6) VALUE "REPORT".
        03  COLUMN 95 PIC X(4) VALUE "PAGE".
        03  COLUMN 100 PIC ZZZ SOURCE IS PAGE-NUMBER.
    02  LINE NUMBER IS PLUS 2.
        03  COLUMN 27 PIC X(9) VALUE "LAST NAME".
        03  COLUMN 44 PIC X(7) VALUE "INITIAL".
        03  COLUMN 59 PIC X(15) VALUE "EMPLOYEE NUMBER".
        03  COLUMN 82 PIC X(10) VALUE "DEPARTMENT".
        03  COLUMN 100 PIC X(6) VALUE "SALARY".
```

With the above code page headings would consist of two lines at line numbers 1 and 3 on each page.

The GROUP INDICATE clause can be used only on specification of lines of type DETAIL. When the clause is present, the content of the field is printed for the first record of each control group and for the first record at the top of a new page. See, for example, line 8000 of Program A.2. Without this clause the department number would be printed with each record producing output similar to that of Program 8.2.

The SUM clause causes the automatic accumulation of the sum of specified data items. The clause can only be used in the specification of lines of type CONTROL FOOTING. The value of the accumulator is reset to zero each time the content is printed hence this feature is well suited to the automatic generation of subtotals as shown in Program A.2.

A.3 CONTROL BREAK EXAMPLE

Program A.2 uses report writer to produce essentially the same report as that of Program 8.2. The output consists of a detailed listing of the input file with totals for each department as well as final totals. Report writer elements found in Program A.2 include

- Multiple-line page heading
- Detail line
- Control heading based on department number
- Control footing based on department number
- Control footing final

As with Program A.1, most of the desired output can be handled "automatically" by features of report writer. However, the process of counting elements of each control group makes the use of DECLARATIVES necessary to zero out the counter DEPT-NUMBER-OF-EMPLOYEES. The appropriate time to perform this task would normally be after the value of the field has been printed and before processing the next record. Unfortunately the USE statement contains only the option BEFORE REPORTING; there is no direct way to cause the desired action after the control footing line as been produced. The problem is solved in the following fashion: We introduce a line of type CONTROL HEADING into the report. Lines of this type are produced automatically at the beginning of processing of each control group. In our case the timing of the production of the line is more important than its content (which is merely a sequence of spaces). We use DECLARATIVES to execute a procedure prior to production of this line. In the procedure we zero out the counter thus forcing the counter to be reset to zero at the beginning of processing of each control group. When the GENERATE statement (line 13200) is executed the following actions take place:

1. If LINE-COUNTER > last detail line number
   Increment PAGE-COUNTER
   Produce page headings
   Initialize LINE-COUNTER
2. If control break has occured
   Produce DEPARTMENT-SUMMARY-LINE
   Zero out salary accumulator on this line
   Execute DECLARATIVES procedure
   Produce DEPARTMENT-HEADING-LINE
   Increment LINE-COUNTER
3. Produce DETAIL-LINE
4. Add IR-SALARY to appropriate accumulators
5. Increment LINE-COUNTER

Because of the timing of the production of DEPARTMENT-HEADING-LINE, we are able to use the BEFORE REPORTING feature of the USE statement to cause the desired actions to be taken at the appropriate time—after the totals have been produced and before processing of the next record.

Careful analysis of the examples and explanations in this appendix should enable the reader to get started using report writer. A useful exercise would be to rewrite any program from Chapter 8 using report writer. Report writer has a great many restrictions, which the programmer may inadvertently violate in his/her initial programming efforts. If problems are encountered, the COBOL reference manual for the user's system should be consulted.

Program A.2   Control break program with report writer

```
100     IDENTIFICATION DIVISION.
200
300     PROGRAM-ID. CONTROL-BREAK-REPORT.
400
500     ENVIRONMENT DIVISION.
600
700     CONFIGURATION SECTION.
800
900     SOURCE-COMPUTER.
1000    OBJECT-COMPUTER.
1100
1200    INPUT-OUTPUT SECTION.
1300
1400    FILE-CONTROL.
1500
1600        SELECT EMPLOYEE-FILE ASSIGN TO DISK.
1700        SELECT DEPARTMENT-LIST ASSIGN TO PRINTER.
1800
1900    DATA DIVISION.
2000
2100    FILE SECTION.
2200
2300    FD  EMPLOYEE-FILE
2400        LABEL RECORDS ARE STANDARD
2500        DATA RECORD IS INPUT-RECORD.
2600
2700    01  INPUT-RECORD.
2800        02 IR-NAME              PIC X(16).
2900        02 IR-INITIAL           PIC X.
3000        02 IR-EMPLOYEE-NUMBER    PIC X(9).
3100        02 IR-DEPARTMENT        PIC X(3).
3200        02 IR-SALARY            PIC 9(6).
3300        02 FILLER               PIC X(45).
3400
3500    FD  DEPARTMENT-LIST
3600        LABEL RECORDS ARE OMITTED
3700        REPORT IS EMPLOYEE-REPORT.
3800
3900    WORKING-STORAGE SECTION.
```

Program A.2 (continued)

```
4000
4100    01  FLAGS.
4200        02  EOF-FLAG              PIC X(3) VALUE "NO".
4300        88 END-OF-FILE           VALUE "YES".
4400
4500    01  TOTALS.
4600        02  TOTAL-NUMBER-OF-EMPLOYEES   PIC 9(4) VALUE ZERO.
4700        02  DEPT-NUMBER-OF-EMPLOYEES    PIC 9(4) VALUE ZERO.
4800
4900    REPORT SECTION.
5000
5100    RD  EMPLOYEE-REPORT
5200        CONTROLS ARE FINAL
5300                    IR-DEPARTMENT
5400        PAGE LIMIT IS 45 LINES
5500        HEADING 1
5600        FIRST DETAIL 5
5700        LAST DETAIL 45.
5800
5900    01  TYPE IS PAGE HEADING.
6000        02 LINE NUMBER IS 1.
6100            03 COLUMN 48 PIC X(11) VALUE "ABC COMPANY".
6200            03 COLUMN 61 PIC X(10) VALUE "DEPARTMANT".
6300            03 COLUMN 72 PIC X(8)  VALUE "EMPLOYEE".
6400            03 COLUMN 81 PIC X(6)  VALUE "REPORT".
6500            03 COLUMN 103 PIC X(4) VALUE "PAGE".
6600            03 COLUMN 108 PIC ZZ SOURCE IS PAGE-COUNTER.
6700        02 LINE NUMBER IS PLUS 2.
6800            03 COLUMN 27 PIC X(9)  VALUE "LAST NAME".
6900            03 COLUMN 44 PIC X(7)  VALUE "INITIAL".
7000            03 COLUMN 59 PIC X(15) VALUE "EMPLOYEE NUMBER".
7100            03 COLUMN 82 PIC X(10) VALUE "DEPARTMENT".
7200            03 COLUMN 100 PIC X(6) VALUE "SALARY".
7300
7400    01  DETAIL-LINE
7500        TYPE IS DETAIL
7600        LINE NUMBER IS PLUS 2.
7700        02 COLUMN 27 PIC X(16) SOURCE IS IR-NAME.
7800        02 COLUMN 44 PIC X SOURCE IS IR-INITIAL.
7900        02 COLUMN 59 PIC X(9) SOURCE IS IR-EMPLOYEE-NUMBER.
8000        02 COLUMN 84 PIC X(3) SOURCE IS IR-DEPARTMENT GROUP INDICATE.
8100        02 COLUMN 97 PIC $ZZZ,ZZZ SOURCE IS IR-SALARY.
8200
8300    01  DEPARTMENT-HEADING-LINE
8400        TYPE IS CONTROL HEADING IR-DEPARTMENT
8500        LINE IS PLUS 1.
8600        02 COLUMN 1 PIC X VALUE SPACES.
8700
8800    01  DEPARTMENT-SUMMARY-LINE
8900        TYPE IS CONTROL FOOTING IR-DEPARTMENT
9000        LINE IS PLUS 2.
9100        02 COLUMN 71 PIC Z9 SOURCE IS DEPT-NUMBER-OF-EMPLOYEES.
9200        02 COLUMN 77
9300           PIC X(9)
9400           VALUE "EMPLOYEES".
```

```
9500        02 COLUMN 94
9600           PIC $**,***,***
9700           SUM IR-SALARY.
9800
9900    01  TYPE IS CONTROL FOOTING FINAL
10000       LINE IS PLUS 2.
10100       02  COLUMN 71 PIC ZZZ9
10200           SOURCE IS TOTAL-NUMBER-OF-EMPLOYEES.
10300       02  COLUMN 80 PIC X(9) VALUE "EMPLOYEES".
10400       02  COLUMN 96 PIC $**,***,***
10500           SUM IR-SALARY.
10600
10700    PROCEDURE DIVISION.
10800
10900    DECLARATIVES.
11000
11100    1000-INITIALIZE SECTION.
11200
11300        USE BEFORE REPORTING DEPARTMENT-HEADING-LINE.
11400
11500    1100-INIT-DEPT-NUM-EMPLOYEES.
11600
11700        MOVE ZERO TO DEPT-NUMBER-OF-EMPLOYEES.
11800
11900    END DECLARATIVES.
12000
12100    2000-MAIN SECTION.
12200
12300    3000-MAIN-LOGIC.
12400
12500        PERFORM 4000-INITIALIZATION.
12600        PERFORM 5000-CONTROL UNTIL END-OF-FILE.
12700        PERFORM 9000-TERMINATION.
12800        STOP RUN.
12900
13000    4000-INITIALIZATION.
13100
13200        OPEN INPUT EMPLOYEE-FILE
13300             OUTPUT DEPARTMENT-LIST.
13400        INITIATE EMPLOYEE-REPORT.
13500        PERFORM 6000-READ.
13600
13700    5000-CONTROL.
13800
13900        GENERATE DETAIL-LINE.
14000        ADD 1 TO TOTAL-NUMBER-OF-EMPLOYEES.
14100        ADD 1 TO DEPT-NUMBER-OF-EMPLOYEES.
14200        PERFORM 6000-READ.
14300
14400    6000-READ.
14500
14600        READ EMPLOYEE-FILE
14700            AT END MOVE "YES" TO EOF-FLAG.
14800
14900    9000-TERMINATION.
```

Program A.2 (continued)

```
15000
15100        TERMINATE EMPLOYEE-REPORT.
15200        CLOSE EMPLOYEE-FILE
15300            DEPARTMENT-LIST.
```

THE ANSI 85 STANDARD B

B.1 INTRODUCTION

For several years, the Technical Committee X3J4 of the American National Standards Institute (ANSI) has been working on a revision of the ANSI 74 COBOL Standard. The new standard was to have been released in 1981 and would therefore have been referred to as the ANSI 81 Standard. Because of delay brought about by dissension within the COBOL community and by legal problems, the proposal was not released on schedule. As of this writing, the standard has been released, but copies of it are unavailable. Therefore, this text focuses on the proposed standard.

Part of the problem with the proposed standard is that fairly drastic changes in the language are proposed—changes that many users contend would force existing COBOL programs to be rewritten in order to be compatible with the new compiler. The document *Draft Proposed Revised X3.23 American National Standard Programming Language COBOL* (Technical Committee X3J4 Programming Language COBOL, June 1983) lists 106 substantive changes that would not affect existing programs and 50 substantive changes that potentially would affect existing programs. The general outline of the major proposed changes is fairly clear. The remainder of this appendix contains a list of the most important proposed changes.

B.2 CHANGES IN THE ANSI 85 STANDARD

Scope Delimiters for Conditional Statements

The ANSI 74 Standard COBOL recognizes the period as the end of a conditional statement, making it impossible to construct sentences out of successive conditional statements. The proposed standard includes reserved words that act as delimiters for conditional statements:

```
END-ADD          END-MULTIPLY      END-START
END-CALL         END-PERFORM       END-STRING
END-COMPUTE      END-READ          END-SUBTRACT
END-DELETE       END-RECEIVE       END-UNSTRING
END-DIVIDE       END-RETURN        END-WRITE
END-EVALUATE     END-REWRITE
END-IF           END-SEARCH
```

Thus, in the proposed language, it is possible to construct a sentence containing several conditional statements, as in

```
IF A = B
    READ INPUT-FILE
        AT END MOVE "YES" TO EOF
    END-READ
    PERFORM COMPUTATION-PROCEDURE-1
ELSE
    MULTIPLY A BY B GIVING C
        ON SIZE ERROR MOVE "YES" TO ERROR-FLAG
    END-MULTIPLY
    PERFORM COMPUTATION-PROCEDURE-2
END-IF
    .
    .
    .
```

Additional Reserved Words

In addition to the reserved words listed above, the following words are added to the reserved word list:

```
ALPHABET              CONTINUE          OTHER
ALPHABETIC-LOWER      CONVERTING        PACKED-DECIMAL
ALPHABETIC-UPPER      DAY-OF-WEEK       PADDING
ALPHANUMERIC          EVALUATE          PURGE
ALPHANUMERIC-EDITED   EXTERNAL          REFERENCE
ANY                   FALSE             REPLACE
BINARY                GLOBAL            STANDARD-2
CLASS                 INITIALIZE        TEST
COMMON                NUMERIC-EDITED    THEN
CONTENT               ORDER             TRUE
```

Alternative Action Specifications for Conditional Statements

Many statements in the ANSI 74 Standard contain provision for taking action when some condition is found (SIZE ERROR, AT END, INVALID KEY, etc.) but no provision for taking action when this condition is *not* found. The proposed language contains the following new clauses:

Clause	Statements
NOT ON SIZE ERROR	ADD
	COMPUTE
	MULTIPLY
	SUBTRACT
	DIVIDE

```
NOT AT END            READ
                      RETURN
NOT INVALID KEY       READ
                      WRITE
                      REWRITE
                      START
                      DELETE
NOT END-OF-PAGE       WRITE
NOT ON OVERFLOW       STRING
                      UNSTRING
```

For example, in the proposed language, the following would be a valid statement:

```
ADD A, B, GIVING C
    ON SIZE ERROR
        MOVE "YES" TO ERROR-FLAG
    NOT ON SIZE ERROR
        MOVE "NO" TO ERROR-FLAG
```

Changes to Character Set

Lower-case letters may be used in alphanumeric constants. The comma, semicolon, and space may be used interchangeably in the program.

Optional Entries

The ENVIRONMENT DIVISION and all of its sections are optional. the LABEL RECORDS clause is optional, if omitted STANDARD is assumed. The word FILLER may be omitted in DATA DIVISION entries. The PROCEDURE DIVISION is optional. THe EXIT PROGRAM statement is optional in subprograms.

Text Editing

The REPLACE statement causes replacement of specified text by other characters within the COBOL program.

Deleted COBOL Elements

The following elements have been deleted:

1) MEMORY SIZE clause of the OBJECT-COMPUTER paragraph
2) ENTER statement
3) REVERSED phrase of the OPEN statement

Additional I-O Status Values

Numerous additional values have been added to the list of I-0 status values, which will add considerable potential for detection and correction of file-related errors from within the program.

Automatic Closing of Files

The STOP RUN and CANCEL statements will cause all open files to be closed.

Additional Files in Open Mode Extend

Relative and indexed as well as sequential files can be OPENed in EXTEND mode.

Evaluate Statement

The EVALUATE statement makes implementation of the Case Structure easier.

Example

```
EVALUATE TRANSACTION-CODE
    WHEN "D"     PERFORM DELETE-PROCEDURE
    WHEN "C"     PERFORM CHANGE-PROCEDURE
    WHEN "A"     PERFORM ADD-PROCEDURE
END-EVALUATE
```

GENERAL FORM OF COBOL ELEMENTS **C**

GENERAL FORMAT FOR IDENTIFICATION DIVISION

IDENTIFICATION DIVISION.

PROGRAM-ID. program-name.

[AUTHOR. [comment-entry] ...]

[INSTALLATION. [comment-entry] ...]

[DATE-WRITTEN. [comment-entry] ...]

[DATE-COMPILED. [comment-entry] ...]

[SECURITY. [comment-entry] ...]

GENERAL FORMAT FOR ENVIRONMENT DIVISION

ENVIRONMENT DIVISION.

CONFIGURATION SECTION.

SOURCE-COMPUTER. computer-name [WITH DEBUGGING MODE] .

OBJECT-COMPUTER. computer-name

$$\left[, \text{ MEMORY SIZE integer } \left\{ \begin{array}{l} \text{WORDS} \\ \text{CHARACTERS} \\ \text{MODULES} \end{array} \right\} \right]$$

[, PROGRAM COLLATING SEQUENCE IS alphabet-name]

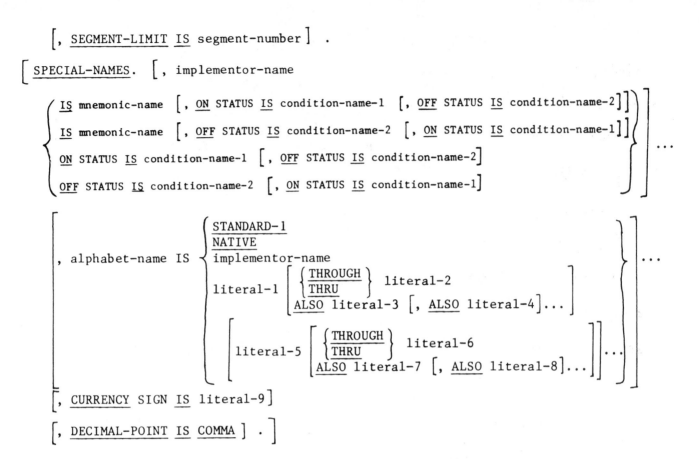

```
[, SEGMENT-LIMIT IS segment-number] .

[SPECIAL-NAMES. [, implementor-name

    ⎧ IS mnemonic-name [, ON STATUS IS condition-name-1 [, OFF STATUS IS condition-name-2]]⎫ ⎤
    ⎪ IS mnemonic-name [, OFF STATUS IS condition-name-2 [, ON STATUS IS condition-name-1]]⎪ ⎥ ...
    ⎨ ON STATUS IS condition-name-1 [, OFF STATUS IS condition-name-2]                       ⎬ ⎥
    ⎩ OFF STATUS IS condition-name-2 [, ON STATUS IS condition-name-1]                       ⎭ ⎦

    ⎡                    ⎧ STANDARD-1                                                    ⎫ ⎤
    ⎢                    ⎪ NATIVE                                                        ⎪ ⎥
    ⎢                    ⎪ implementor-name                                              ⎪ ⎥
    ⎢                    ⎪         ⎡ ⎧THROUGH⎫ literal-2                               ⎤ ⎪ ⎥
    ⎢ , alphabet-name IS ⎨ literal-1 ⎢ ⎩THRU  ⎭                                       ⎥ ⎬ ... ⎥
    ⎢                    ⎪         ⎣ ALSO literal-3 [, ALSO literal-4]...              ⎦ ⎪ ⎥
    ⎢                    ⎪         ⎡         ⎡ ⎧THROUGH⎫ literal-6                   ⎤⎤ ⎪ ⎥
    ⎢                    ⎪         ⎢ literal-5 ⎢ ⎩THRU  ⎭                           ⎥⎥...⎪ ⎥
    ⎢                    ⎩         ⎣         ⎣ ALSO literal-7 [, ALSO literal-8]... ⎦⎦ ⎭ ⎥
    ⎢ , CURRENCY SIGN IS literal-9⎤                                                         ⎥
    ⎣ , DECIMAL-POINT IS COMMA ] . ⎦
```

GENERAL FORMAT FOR ENVIRONMENT DIVISION

```
[INPUT-OUTPUT SECTION.

FILE-CONTROL.

    {file-control-entry} ...

[I-O-CONTROL.

    ⎡ ; RERUN ⎡ ON ⎧file-name-1       ⎫⎤
    ⎢         ⎣    ⎩implementor-name  ⎭⎦
    ⎢              ⎧⎧ [END OF] ⎧REEL⎫⎫             ⎫
    ⎢              ⎪⎨          ⎩UNIT⎭⎬ OF file-name-2⎪
    ⎢       EVERY  ⎨⎩integer-1 RECORDS⎭             ⎬ ...
    ⎢              ⎪ integer-2 CLOCK-UNITS          ⎪
    ⎣              ⎩ condition-name                 ⎭

    ⎡         ⎡RECORD    ⎤                                   ⎤
    ⎢ ; SAME  ⎢SORT      ⎥ AREA FOR file-name-3 {, file-name-4} ...⎥ ...
    ⎣         ⎣SORT-MERGE⎦                                   ⎦

    ⎡ ; MULTIPLE FILE TAPE CONTAINS file-name-5 [POSITION integer-3]

         [, file-name-6 [POSITION integer-4]] ... ] ...   .]]
```

GENERAL FORMAT FOR FILE CONTROL ENTRY

FORMAT 1:

<u>SELECT</u> [OPTIONAL] file-name

    <u>ASSIGN</u> TO implementor-name-1 [, implementor-name-2] ...

    $\left[\text{; } \underline{\text{RESERVE}} \text{ integer-1} \begin{bmatrix} \text{AREA} \\ \text{AREAS} \end{bmatrix}\right]$

    $\left[\text{; } \underline{\text{ORGANIZATION}} \text{ IS } \underline{\text{SEQUENTIAL}}\right]$

    $\left[\text{; } \underline{\text{ACCESS}} \text{ MODE IS } \underline{\text{SEQUENTIAL}}\right]$

    $\left[\text{; FILE } \underline{\text{STATUS}} \text{ IS data-name-1}\right]$.

FORMAT 2:

<u>SELECT</u> file-name

    <u>ASSIGN</u> TO implementor-name-1 [, implementor-name-2] ...

    $\left[\text{; } \underline{\text{RESERVE}} \text{ integer-1} \begin{bmatrix} \text{AREA} \\ \text{AREAS} \end{bmatrix}\right]$

    ; <u>ORGANIZATION</u> IS <u>RELATIVE</u>

    $\left[\text{; } \underline{\text{ACCESS}} \text{ MODE IS } \left\{ \begin{array}{l} \underline{\text{SEQUENTIAL}} \quad [, \underline{\text{RELATIVE}} \text{ KEY IS data-name-1}] \\ \left\{ \begin{array}{l} \underline{\text{RANDOM}} \\ \underline{\text{DYNAMIC}} \end{array} \right\} \quad , \underline{\text{RELATIVE}} \text{ KEY IS data-name-1} \end{array} \right\}\right]$

    $\left[\text{; FILE } \underline{\text{STATUS}} \text{ IS data-name-2}\right]$.

FORMAT 3:

<u>SELECT</u> file-name

    <u>ASSIGN</u> TO implementor-name-1 [, implementor-name-2] ...

    $\left[\text{; } \underline{\text{RESERVE}} \text{ integer-1} \begin{bmatrix} \text{AREA} \\ \text{AREAS} \end{bmatrix}\right]$

    ; <u>ORGANIZATION</u> IS <u>INDEXED</u>

    $\left[\text{; } \underline{\text{ACCESS}} \text{ MODE IS } \left\{ \begin{array}{l} \underline{\text{SEQUENTIAL}} \\ \underline{\text{RANDOM}} \\ \underline{\text{DYNAMIC}} \end{array} \right\}\right]$

    ; <u>RECORD</u> KEY IS data-name-1

    $\left[\text{; } \underline{\text{ALTERNATE}} \text{ } \underline{\text{RECORD}} \text{ KEY IS data-name-2} \left[\text{WITH } \underline{\text{DUPLICATES}}\right]\right]$ ...

    $\left[\text{; FILE } \underline{\text{STATUS}} \text{ IS data-name-3}\right]$.

FORMAT 4:

SELECT file-name ASSIGN TO implementor-name-1 [, implementor-name-2] ...

GENERAL FORMAT FOR DATA DIVISION

DATA DIVISION.

[FILE SECTION.

[FD file-name

    [; BLOCK CONTAINS [integer-1 TO] integer-2 $\left\{ \begin{array}{l} \text{RECORDS} \\ \text{CHARACTERS} \end{array} \right\}$]

    [; RECORD CONTAINS [integer-3 TO] integer-4 CHARACTERS]

    ; LABEL $\left\{ \begin{array}{l} \text{RECORD IS} \\ \text{RECORDS ARE} \end{array} \right\}$ $\left\{ \begin{array}{l} \text{STANDARD} \\ \text{OMITTED} \end{array} \right\}$

    [; VALUE OF implementor-name-1 IS $\left\{ \begin{array}{l} \text{data-name-1} \\ \text{literal-1} \end{array} \right\}$

        [, implementor-name-2 IS $\left\{ \begin{array}{l} \text{data-name-2} \\ \text{literal-2} \end{array} \right\}$] ...]

    [; DATA $\left\{ \begin{array}{l} \text{RECORD IS} \\ \text{RECORDS ARE} \end{array} \right\}$ data-name-3 [, data-name-4] ...]

    [; LINAGE IS $\left\{ \begin{array}{l} \text{data-name-5} \\ \text{integer-5} \end{array} \right\}$ LINES [, WITH FOOTING AT $\left\{ \begin{array}{l} \text{data-name-6} \\ \text{integer-6} \end{array} \right\}$]

        [, LINES AT TOP $\left\{ \begin{array}{l} \text{data-name-7} \\ \text{integer-7} \end{array} \right\}$] [, LINES AT BOTTOM $\left\{ \begin{array}{l} \text{data-name-8} \\ \text{integer-8} \end{array} \right\}$]]

    [; CODE-SET IS alphabet-name]

    [; $\left\{ \begin{array}{l} \text{REPORT IS} \\ \text{REPORTS ARE} \end{array} \right\}$ report-name-1 [, report-name-2] ...] .

[record-description-entry] ...] ...

[SD file-name

    [; RECORD CONTAINS [integer-1 TO] integer-2 CHARACTERS]

    [; DATA $\left\{ \begin{array}{l} \text{RECORD IS} \\ \text{RECORDS ARE} \end{array} \right\}$ data-name-1 [, data-name-2] ...] .

{record-description-entry} ...] ...]

$\Big[$ WORKING-STORAGE SECTION.

$\begin{bmatrix} \text{77-level-description-entry} \\ \text{record-description-entry} \end{bmatrix} \ \cdots \ \Big]$

$\Big[$ LINKAGE SECTION.

$\begin{bmatrix} \text{77-level-description-entry} \\ \text{record-description-entry} \end{bmatrix} \ \cdots \ \Big]$

$\Big[$ COMMUNICATION SECTION.

[communication-description-entry

[record-description-entry] ...] ... $\Big]$

$\Big[$ REPORT SECTION.

[RD   report-name

$\qquad \Big[; \ \underline{\text{CODE}} \ \text{literal-1} \Big]$

$\qquad \Big[; \ \begin{Bmatrix} \underline{\text{CONTROL}} \ \text{IS} \\ \underline{\text{CONTROLS}} \ \text{ARE} \end{Bmatrix} \ \begin{Bmatrix} \text{data-name-1} \ [, \ \text{data-name-2}] \ \cdots \\ \underline{\text{FINAL}} \ [, \ \text{data-name-1} \ [, \ \text{data-name-2}] \ \cdots] \end{Bmatrix} \Big]$

$\qquad \Big[; \ \underline{\text{PAGE}} \ \begin{bmatrix} \text{LIMIT IS} \\ \text{LIMITS ARE} \end{bmatrix} \ \text{integer-1} \ \begin{bmatrix} \text{LINE} \\ \text{LINES} \end{bmatrix} \ [, \ \underline{\text{HEADING}} \ \text{integer-2}]$

$\qquad\qquad [, \ \underline{\text{FIRST}} \ \underline{\text{DETAIL}} \ \text{integer-3}] \ [, \ \underline{\text{LAST}} \ \underline{\text{DETAIL}} \ \text{integer-4}]$

$\qquad\qquad [, \ \underline{\text{FOOTING}} \ \text{integer-5}] \ \Big] \ .$

{report-group-description-entry } ...] ... $\Big]$

GENERAL FORMAT FOR DATA DESCRIPTION ENTRY

FORMAT 1:

level-number $\left\{\begin{array}{l}\text{data-name-1}\\ \underline{\text{FILLER}}\end{array}\right\}$

$\left[\text{; }\underline{\text{REDEFINES}}\text{ data-name-2}\right]$

$\left[\text{; }\left\{\begin{array}{l}\underline{\text{PICTURE}}\\ \underline{\text{PIC}}\end{array}\right\}\text{ IS character-string}\right]$

$\left[\text{; }\left[\underline{\text{USAGE}}\text{ IS}\right]\left\{\begin{array}{l}\underline{\text{COMPUTATIONAL}}\\ \underline{\text{COMP}}\\ \underline{\text{DISPLAY}}\\ \underline{\text{INDEX}}\end{array}\right\}\right]$

$\left[\text{; }\left[\underline{\text{SIGN}}\text{ IS}\right]\left\{\begin{array}{l}\underline{\text{LEADING}}\\ \underline{\text{TRAILING}}\end{array}\right\}\left[\underline{\text{SEPARATE}}\text{ CHARACTER}\right]\right]$

$\left[\text{; }\underline{\text{OCCURS}}\left\{\begin{array}{l}\text{integer-1 }\underline{\text{TO}}\text{ integer-2 TIMES }\underline{\text{DEPENDING}}\text{ ON data-name-3}\\ \text{integer-2 TIMES}\end{array}\right\}\right.$

$\left[\left\{\begin{array}{l}\underline{\text{ASCENDING}}\\ \underline{\text{DESCENDING}}\end{array}\right\}\text{ KEY IS data-name-4 }\left[\text{, data-name-5}\right]\text{ ... }\right]\text{ ...}$

$\left.\left[\underline{\text{INDEXED}}\text{ BY index-name-1 }\left[\text{, index-name-2}\right]\text{ ... }\right]\right]$

$\left[\text{; }\left\{\begin{array}{l}\underline{\text{SYNCHRONIZED}}\\ \underline{\text{SYNC}}\end{array}\right\}\left[\begin{array}{l}\underline{\text{LEFT}}\\ \underline{\text{RIGHT}}\end{array}\right]\right]$

$\left[\text{; }\left\{\begin{array}{l}\underline{\text{JUSTIFIED}}\\ \underline{\text{JUST}}\end{array}\right\}\text{ RIGHT}\right]$

$\left[\text{; }\underline{\text{BLANK}}\text{ WHEN }\underline{\text{ZERO}}\right]$

$\left[\text{; }\underline{\text{VALUE}}\text{ IS literal}\right]\text{ .}$

FORMAT 2:

66 data-name-1; $\underline{\text{RENAMES}}$ data-name-2 $\left[\left\{\begin{array}{l}\underline{\text{THROUGH}}\\ \underline{\text{THRU}}\end{array}\right\}\text{ data-name-3}\right]$

FORMAT 3:

88 condition-name; $\left\{\begin{array}{l}\underline{\text{VALUE}}\text{ IS}\\ \underline{\text{VALUES}}\text{ ARE}\end{array}\right\}$ literal-1 $\left[\left\{\begin{array}{l}\underline{\text{THROUGH}}\\ \underline{\text{THRU}}\end{array}\right\}\text{ literal-2}\right.$

$\left[\text{, literal-3 }\left[\left\{\begin{array}{l}\underline{\text{THROUGH}}\\ \underline{\text{THRU}}\end{array}\right\}\text{ literal-4}\right]\right]\text{ ... }\right.\text{ .}$

GENERAL FORMAT FOR COMMUNICATION DESCRIPTION ENTRY

FORMAT 1:

CD cd-name;

$$\text{FOR} \left[\text{INITIAL} \right] \text{INPUT} \begin{bmatrix} \left[; \text{SYMBOLIC \underline{QUEUE} IS data-name-1} \right] \\ \qquad \left[; \text{SYMBOLIC \underline{SUB-QUEUE-1} IS data-name-2} \right] \\ \qquad \left[; \text{SYMBOLIC \underline{SUB-QUEUE-2} IS data-name-3} \right] \\ \qquad \left[; \text{SYMBOLIC \underline{SUB-QUEUE-3} IS data-name-4} \right] \\ \qquad \left[; \underline{\text{MESSAGE}} \ \underline{\text{DATE}} \text{ IS data-name-5} \right] \\ \qquad \left[; \underline{\text{MESSAGE}} \ \underline{\text{TIME}} \text{ IS data-name-6} \right] \\ \qquad \left[; \text{SYMBOLIC \underline{SOURCE} IS data-name-7} \right] \\ \qquad \left[; \underline{\text{TEXT}} \ \underline{\text{LENGTH}} \text{ IS data-name-8} \right] \\ \qquad \left[; \underline{\text{END}} \ \underline{\text{KEY}} \text{ IS data-name-9} \right] \\ \qquad \left[; \underline{\text{STATUS}} \ \underline{\text{KEY}} \text{ IS data-name-10} \right] \\ \qquad \left[; \text{MESSAGE \underline{COUNT} IS data-name-11} \right] \\ \left[\text{data-name-1, data-name-2, ..., data-name-11} \right] \end{bmatrix}$$

FORMAT 2:

CD cd-name; FOR <u>OUTPUT</u>

[; <u>DESTINATION</u> <u>COUNT</u> IS data-name-1]

[; <u>TEXT</u> <u>LENGTH</u> IS data-name-2]

[; <u>STATUS</u> <u>KEY</u> IS data-name-3]

[; <u>DESTINATION</u> <u>TABLE</u> <u>OCCURS</u> integer-2 TIMES

      [; <u>INDEXED</u> BY index-name-1 [, index-name-2]...]]

[; <u>ERROR</u> <u>KEY</u> IS data-name-4]

[; SYMBOLIC <u>DESTINATION</u> IS data-name-5] .

GENERAL FORMAT FOR REPORT GROUP DESCRIPTION ENTRY

FORMAT 1:

01 [data-name-1]

    [; <u>LINE</u> NUMBER IS $\left\{\begin{array}{l}\text{integer-1} \; [\text{ON } \underline{\text{NEXT}} \; \underline{\text{PAGE}}] \\ \underline{\text{PLUS}} \text{ integer-2}\end{array}\right\}$]

    [; <u>NEXT</u> <u>GROUP</u> IS $\left\{\begin{array}{l}\text{integer-3} \\ \underline{\text{PLUS}} \text{ integer-4} \\ \underline{\text{NEXT}} \; \underline{\text{PAGE}}\end{array}\right\}$]

    ; <u>TYPE</u> IS $\left\{\begin{array}{l}\left\{\begin{array}{l}\underline{\text{REPORT}} \; \underline{\text{HEADING}} \\ \underline{\text{RH}}\end{array}\right\} \\ \left\{\begin{array}{l}\underline{\text{PAGE}} \; \underline{\text{HEADING}} \\ \underline{\text{PH}}\end{array}\right\} \\ \left\{\begin{array}{l}\underline{\text{CONTROL}} \; \underline{\text{HEADING}} \\ \underline{\text{CH}}\end{array}\right\} \left\{\begin{array}{l}\text{data-name-2} \\ \underline{\text{FINAL}}\end{array}\right\} \\ \left\{\begin{array}{l}\underline{\text{DETAIL}} \\ \underline{\text{DE}}\end{array}\right\} \\ \left\{\begin{array}{l}\underline{\text{CONTROL}} \; \underline{\text{FOOTING}} \\ \underline{\text{CF}}\end{array}\right\} \left\{\begin{array}{l}\text{data-name-3} \\ \underline{\text{FINAL}}\end{array}\right\} \\ \left\{\begin{array}{l}\underline{\text{PAGE}} \; \underline{\text{FOOTING}} \\ \underline{\text{PF}}\end{array}\right\} \\ \left\{\begin{array}{l}\underline{\text{REPORT}} \; \underline{\text{FOOTING}} \\ \underline{\text{RF}}\end{array}\right\}\end{array}\right\}$

    [; [<u>USAGE</u> IS] <u>DISPLAY</u>] .

FORMAT 2:

level-number [data-name-1]

    [; <u>LINE</u> NUMBER IS $\left\{\begin{array}{l}\text{integer-1} \; [\text{ON } \underline{\text{NEXT}} \; \underline{\text{PAGE}}] \\ \underline{\text{PLUS}} \text{ integer-2}\end{array}\right\}$]

    [; [<u>USAGE</u> IS] <u>DISPLAY</u>] .

FORMAT 3:

level-number [data-name-1]

    [; <u>BLANK</u> WHEN <u>ZERO</u>]

    [; <u>GROUP</u> INDICATE]

    [; $\left\{\begin{array}{l}\underline{\text{JUSTIFIED}} \\ \underline{\text{JUST}}\end{array}\right\}$ RIGHT]

    [; <u>LINE</u> NUMBER IS $\left\{\begin{array}{l}\text{integer-1} \; [\text{ON } \underline{\text{NEXT}} \; \underline{\text{PAGE}}] \\ \underline{\text{PLUS}} \text{ integer-2}\end{array}\right\}$]

$$\left[\; ; \underline{\text{COLUMN}} \text{ NUMBER IS integer-3}\right]$$

$$; \left\{\begin{matrix} \underline{\text{PICTURE}} \\ \underline{\text{PIC}} \end{matrix}\right\} \text{ IS character-string}$$

$$\left\{\begin{matrix} ; \underline{\text{SOURCE}} \text{ IS identifier-1} \\ ; \underline{\text{VALUE}} \text{ IS literal} \\ \{; \underline{\text{SUM}} \text{ identifier-2 } \left[, \text{ identifier-3}\right] \ldots \\ \left[\underline{\text{UPON}} \text{ data-name-2 } \left[, \text{ data-name-3}\right] \ldots \right]\} \ldots \\ \left[\underline{\text{RESET}} \text{ ON } \left\{\begin{matrix}\text{data-name-4} \\ \underline{\text{FINAL}}\end{matrix}\right\}\right] \end{matrix}\right\}$$

$$\left[\; ; \left[\underline{\text{USAGE}} \text{ IS}\right] \; \underline{\text{DISPLAY}}\right] \; .$$

GENERAL FORMAT FOR PROCEDURE DIVISION

FORMAT 1:

$\underline{\text{PROCEDURE}}$ $\underline{\text{DIVISION}}$ $\left[\underline{\text{USING}} \text{ data-name-1 } \left[, \text{ data-name-2}\right] \ldots \right]$.

$\left[\underline{\text{DECLARATIVES}}.\right.$

$\{$ section-name $\underline{\text{SECTION}}$ [segment-number] . declarative-sentence

[paragraph-name. [sentence] ...] ... $\}$ ...

$\underline{\text{END}}$ $\underline{\text{DECLARATIVES}}.\left.\right]$

$\{$ section-name $\underline{\text{SECTION}}$ [segment-number] .

[paragraph-name. [sentence] ...] ... $\}$ ...

FORMAT 2:

$\underline{\text{PROCEDURE}}$ $\underline{\text{DIVISION}}$ $\left[\underline{\text{USING}} \text{ data-name-1 } \left[, \text{ data-name-2}\right] \ldots \right]$.

$\{$ paragraph-name. [sentence] ... $\}$ ...

GENERAL FORMAT FOR VERBS

ACCEPT identifier [FROM mnemonic-name]

ACCEPT identifier FROM $\left\{ \begin{array}{l} \underline{DATE} \\ \underline{DAY} \\ \underline{TIME} \end{array} \right\}$

ACCEPT cd-name MESSAGE COUNT

ADD $\left\{ \begin{array}{l} identifier-1 \\ literal-1 \end{array} \right\}$ $\left[\begin{array}{l} , identifier-2 \\ , literal-2 \end{array} \right]$ ... TO identifier-m [ROUNDED]

    [, identifier-n [ROUNDED]] ... [; ON SIZE ERROR imperative-statement]

ADD $\left\{ \begin{array}{l} identifier-1 \\ literal-1 \end{array} \right\}$, $\left\{ \begin{array}{l} identifier-2 \\ literal-2 \end{array} \right\}$ $\left[\begin{array}{l} , identifier-3 \\ , literal-3 \end{array} \right]$ ...

    GIVING identifier-m [ROUNDED] [, identifier-n [ROUNDED]] ...

    [; ON SIZE ERROR imperative-statement]

ADD $\left\{ \begin{array}{l} \underline{CORRESPONDING} \\ \underline{CORR} \end{array} \right\}$ identifier-1 TO identifier-2 [ROUNDED]

    [; ON SIZE ERROR imperative-statement]

ALTER procedure-name-1 TO [PROCEED TO] procedure-name-2

    [, procedure-name-3 TO [PROCEED TO] procedure-name-4] ...

CALL $\left\{ \begin{array}{l} identifier-1 \\ literal-1 \end{array} \right\}$ [USING data-name-1 [, data-name-2] ...]

    [; ON OVERFLOW imperative-statement]

CANCEL $\left\{ \begin{array}{l} identifier-1 \\ literal-1 \end{array} \right\}$ $\left[\begin{array}{l} , identifier-2 \\ , literal-2 \end{array} \right]$ ...

CLOSE file-name-1 $\left[\begin{array}{l} \left\{ \begin{array}{l} \underline{REEL} \\ \underline{UNIT} \end{array} \right\} \left[\begin{array}{l} WITH \underline{NO} \underline{REWIND} \\ FOR \underline{REMOVAL} \end{array} \right] \\ WITH \left\{ \begin{array}{l} \underline{NO} \underline{REWIND} \\ \underline{LOCK} \end{array} \right\} \end{array} \right]$

$\left[, file-name-2 \left[\begin{array}{l} \left\{ \begin{array}{l} \underline{REEL} \\ \underline{UNIT} \end{array} \right\} \left[\begin{array}{l} WITH \underline{NO} \underline{REWIND} \\ FOR \underline{REMOVAL} \end{array} \right] \\ WITH \left\{ \begin{array}{l} \underline{NO} \underline{REWIND} \\ \underline{LOCK} \end{array} \right\} \end{array} \right] \right]$ ...

CLOSE file-name-1 [WITH LOCK] [, file-name-2 [WITH LOCK]] ...

COMPUTE identifier-1 $\big[$ROUNDED$\big]$ $\big[$, identifier-2 $\big[$ROUNDED$\big]\big]$ ...

     = arithmetic-expression $\big[$; ON SIZE ERROR imperative-statement$\big]$

DELETE file-name RECORD $\big[$; INVALID KEY imperative-statement$\big]$

DISABLE $\left\{\begin{array}{l}\text{INPUT}\\\text{OUTPUT}\end{array}\right.$ $\big[$TERMINAL$\big]\Big\}$ cd-name WITH KEY $\left\{\begin{array}{l}\text{identifier-1}\\\text{literal-1}\end{array}\right\}$

DISPLAY $\left\{\begin{array}{l}\text{identifier-1}\\\text{literal-1}\end{array}\right\}$ $\left[\begin{array}{l}\text{, identifier-2}\\\text{, literal-2}\end{array}\right]$ ... $\big[$UPON mnemonic-name$\big]$

DIVIDE $\left\{\begin{array}{l}\text{identifier-1}\\\text{literal-1}\end{array}\right\}$ INTO identifier-2 $\big[$ROUNDED$\big]$

     $\big[$, identifier-3 $\big[$ROUNDED$\big]\big]$ ... $\big[$; ON SIZE ERROR imperative-statement$\big]$

DIVIDE $\left\{\begin{array}{l}\text{identifier-1}\\\text{literal-1}\end{array}\right\}$ INTO $\left\{\begin{array}{l}\text{identifier-2}\\\text{literal-2}\end{array}\right\}$ GIVING identifier-3 $\big[$ROUNDED$\big]$

     $\big[$, identifier-4 $\big[$ROUNDED$\big]\big]$ ... $\big[$; ON SIZE ERROR imperative-statement$\big]$

DIVIDE $\left\{\begin{array}{l}\text{identifier-1}\\\text{literal-1}\end{array}\right\}$ BY $\left\{\begin{array}{l}\text{identifier-2}\\\text{literal-2}\end{array}\right\}$ GIVING identifier-3 $\big[$ROUNDED$\big]$

     $\big[$, identifier-4 $\big[$ROUNDED$\big]\big]$ ... $\big[$; ON SIZE ERROR imperative-statement$\big]$

DIVIDE $\left\{\begin{array}{l}\text{identifier-1}\\\text{literal-1}\end{array}\right\}$ INTO $\left\{\begin{array}{l}\text{identifier-2}\\\text{literal-2}\end{array}\right\}$ GIVING identifier-3 $\big[$ROUNDED$\big]$

     REMAINDER identifier-4 $\big[$; ON SIZE ERROR imperative-statement$\big]$

DIVIDE $\left\{\begin{array}{l}\text{identifier-1}\\\text{literal-1}\end{array}\right\}$ BY $\left\{\begin{array}{l}\text{identifier-2}\\\text{literal-2}\end{array}\right\}$ GIVING identifier-3 $\big[$ROUNDED$\big]$

     REMAINDER identifier-4 $\big[$; ON SIZE ERROR imperative-statement$\big]$

ENABLE $\left\{\begin{array}{l}\text{INPUT}\\\text{OUTPUT}\end{array}\right.$ $\big[$TERMINAL$\big]\Big\}$ cd-name WITH KEY $\left\{\begin{array}{l}\text{identifier-1}\\\text{literal-1}\end{array}\right\}$

ENTER language-name $\big[$routine-name$\big]$.

EXIT $\big[$PROGRAM$\big]$.

GENERATE $\left\{\begin{array}{l}\text{data-name}\\\text{report-name}\end{array}\right\}$

GO TO $\big[$procedure-name-1$\big]$

GO TO procedure-name-1 $\big[$, procedure-name-2$\big]$ ... , procedure-name-n

     DEPENDING ON identifier

IF condition; $\left\{\begin{array}{l}\text{statement-1}\\\text{NEXT SENTENCE}\end{array}\right\}$ $\left\{\begin{array}{l}\text{; ELSE statement-2}\\\text{; ELSE NEXT SENTENCE}\end{array}\right\}$

INITIATE report-name-1 $\big[$, report-name-2$\big]$ ...

<u>INSPECT</u> identifier-1 <u>TALLYING</u>

$$\left\{ , \text{identifier-2 } \underline{FOR} \left\{ , \left\{ \begin{matrix} \underline{ALL} \\ \underline{LEADING} \\ \underline{CHARACTERS} \end{matrix} \right\} \left\{ \begin{matrix} \text{identifier-3} \\ \text{literal-1} \end{matrix} \right\} \left[\left\{ \begin{matrix} \underline{BEFORE} \\ \underline{AFTER} \end{matrix} \right\} \text{ INITIAL } \left\{ \begin{matrix} \text{identifier-4} \\ \text{literal-2} \end{matrix} \right\} \right] \right\} \cdots \right\} \cdots$$

<u>INSPECT</u> identifier-1 <u>REPLACING</u>

$$\left\{ \begin{matrix} \underline{CHARACTERS} \underline{BY} \left\{ \begin{matrix} \text{identifier-6} \\ \text{literal-4} \end{matrix} \right\} \left[\left\{ \begin{matrix} \underline{BEFORE} \\ \underline{AFTER} \end{matrix} \right\} \text{ INITIAL } \left\{ \begin{matrix} \text{identifier-7} \\ \text{literal-5} \end{matrix} \right\} \right] \\ \left\{ , \left\{ \begin{matrix} \underline{ALL} \\ \underline{LEADING} \\ \underline{FIRST} \end{matrix} \right\} \left\{ , \left\{ \begin{matrix} \text{identifier-5} \\ \text{literal-3} \end{matrix} \right\} \underline{BY} \left\{ \begin{matrix} \text{identifier-6} \\ \text{literal-4} \end{matrix} \right\} \left[\left\{ \begin{matrix} \underline{BEFORE} \\ \underline{AFTER} \end{matrix} \right\} \text{ INITIAL } \left\{ \begin{matrix} \text{identifier-7} \\ \text{literal-5} \end{matrix} \right\} \right] \right\} \cdots \right\} \cdots \end{matrix} \right\}$$

<u>INSPECT</u> identifier-1 <u>TALLYING</u>

$$\left\{ , \text{identifier-2 } \underline{FOR} \left\{ , \left\{ \begin{matrix} \underline{ALL} \\ \underline{LEADING} \\ \underline{CHARACTERS} \end{matrix} \right\} \left\{ \begin{matrix} \text{identifier-3} \\ \text{literal-1} \end{matrix} \right\} \left[\left\{ \begin{matrix} \underline{BEFORE} \\ \underline{AFTER} \end{matrix} \right\} \text{ INITIAL } \left\{ \begin{matrix} \text{identifier-4} \\ \text{literal-2} \end{matrix} \right\} \right] \right\} \cdots \right\} \cdots$$

    <u>REPLACING</u>

$$\left\{ \begin{matrix} \underline{CHARACTERS} \underline{BY} \left\{ \begin{matrix} \text{identifier-6} \\ \text{literal-4} \end{matrix} \right\} \left[\left\{ \begin{matrix} \underline{BEFORE} \\ \underline{AFTER} \end{matrix} \right\} \text{ INITIAL } \left\{ \begin{matrix} \text{identifier-7} \\ \text{literal-5} \end{matrix} \right\} \right] \\ \left\{ , \left\{ \begin{matrix} \underline{ALL} \\ \underline{LEADING} \\ \underline{FIRST} \end{matrix} \right\} \left\{ , \left\{ \begin{matrix} \text{identifier-5} \\ \text{literal-3} \end{matrix} \right\} \underline{BY} \left\{ \begin{matrix} \text{identifier-6} \\ \text{literal-4} \end{matrix} \right\} \left[\left\{ \begin{matrix} \underline{BEFORE} \\ \underline{AFTER} \end{matrix} \right\} \text{ INITIAL } \left\{ \begin{matrix} \text{identifier-7} \\ \text{literal-5} \end{matrix} \right\} \right] \right\} \cdots \right\} \cdots \end{matrix} \right\}$$

<u>MERGE</u> file-name-1 ON $\left\{ \begin{matrix} \underline{ASCENDING} \\ \underline{DESCENDING} \end{matrix} \right\}$ KEY data-name-1 [, data-name-2] ...

       $\left[\text{ON} \left\{ \begin{matrix} \underline{ASCENDING} \\ \underline{DESCENDING} \end{matrix} \right\} \text{KEY data-name-3 } [, \text{data-name-4}] \ldots \right] \ldots$

    $\left[\text{COLLATING } \underline{SEQUENCE} \text{ IS alphabet-name} \right]$

     <u>USING</u> file-name-2, file-name-3 [, file-name-4] ...

$$\left\{ \begin{matrix} \underline{OUTPUT} \underline{PROCEDURE} \text{ IS section-name-1 } \left[\left\{ \begin{matrix} \underline{THROUGH} \\ \underline{THRU} \end{matrix} \right\} \text{ section-name-2} \right] \\ \underline{GIVING} \text{ file-name-5} \end{matrix} \right\}$$

<u>MOVE</u> $\left\{ \begin{matrix} \text{identifier-1} \\ \text{literal} \end{matrix} \right\}$ <u>TO</u> identifier-2 [, identifier-3] ...

<u>MOVE</u> $\left\{ \begin{matrix} \underline{CORRESPONDING} \\ \underline{CORR} \end{matrix} \right\}$ identifier-1 <u>TO</u> identifier-2

<u>MULTIPLY</u> $\left\{ \begin{matrix} \text{identifier-1} \\ \text{literal-1} \end{matrix} \right\}$ <u>BY</u> identifier-2 [<u>ROUNDED</u>]

   [, identifier-3 [<u>ROUNDED</u>]] ... [; ON <u>SIZE</u> <u>ERROR</u> imperative-statement]

$$\text{\underline{MULTIPLY}} \begin{Bmatrix} \text{identifier-1} \\ \text{literal-1} \end{Bmatrix} \text{\underline{BY}} \begin{Bmatrix} \text{identifier-2} \\ \text{literal-2} \end{Bmatrix} \text{\underline{GIVING} identifier-3} \left[\text{\underline{ROUNDED}} \right]$$

$$\left[, \text{ identifier-4} \left[\text{\underline{ROUNDED}} \right] \right] \ldots \left[; \text{ ON \underline{SIZE} \underline{ERROR} imperative-statement} \right]$$

$$\text{\underline{OPEN}} \begin{Bmatrix} \text{\underline{INPUT} file-name-1} \left[\begin{matrix} \text{\underline{REVERSED}} \\ \text{WITH \underline{NO} REWIND} \end{matrix} \right] \left[, \text{ file-name-2} \left[\begin{matrix} \text{\underline{REVERSED}} \\ \text{WITH \underline{NO} REWIND} \end{matrix} \right] \right] \ldots \\ \text{\underline{OUTPUT} file-name-3} \left[\text{WITH \underline{NO} REWIND} \right] \left[, \text{ file-name-4} \left[\text{WITH \underline{NO} REWIND} \right] \right] \ldots \\ \text{\underline{I-O} file-name-5} \left[, \text{ file-name-6} \right] \ldots \\ \text{\underline{EXTEND} file-name-7} \left[, \text{ file-name-8} \right] \ldots \end{Bmatrix} \ldots$$

$$\text{\underline{OPEN}} \begin{Bmatrix} \text{\underline{INPUT} file-name-1} \left[, \text{ file-name-2} \right] \ldots \\ \text{\underline{OUTPUT} file-name-3} \left[, \text{ file-name-4} \right] \ldots \\ \text{\underline{I-O} file-name-5} \left[, \text{ file-name-6} \right] \ldots \end{Bmatrix} \ldots$$

$$\text{\underline{PERFORM} procedure-name-1} \left[\begin{Bmatrix} \text{\underline{THROUGH}} \\ \text{\underline{THRU}} \end{Bmatrix} \text{procedure-name-2} \right]$$

$$\text{\underline{PERFORM} procedure-name-1} \left[\begin{Bmatrix} \text{\underline{THROUGH}} \\ \text{\underline{THRU}} \end{Bmatrix} \text{procedure-name-2} \right] \begin{Bmatrix} \text{identifier-1} \\ \text{integer-1} \end{Bmatrix} \text{\underline{TIMES}}$$

$$\text{\underline{PERFORM} procedure-name-1} \left[\begin{Bmatrix} \text{\underline{THROUGH}} \\ \text{\underline{THRU}} \end{Bmatrix} \text{procedure-name-2} \right] \text{\underline{UNTIL} condition-1}$$

$$\text{\underline{PERFORM} procedure-name-1} \left[\begin{Bmatrix} \text{\underline{THROUGH}} \\ \text{\underline{THRU}} \end{Bmatrix} \text{procedure-name-2} \right]$$

$$\text{\underline{VARYING}} \begin{Bmatrix} \text{identifier-2} \\ \text{index-name-1} \end{Bmatrix} \text{\underline{FROM}} \begin{Bmatrix} \text{identifier-3} \\ \text{index-name-2} \\ \text{literal-1} \end{Bmatrix}$$

$$\text{\underline{BY}} \begin{Bmatrix} \text{identifier-4} \\ \text{literal-3} \end{Bmatrix} \text{\underline{UNTIL} condition-1}$$

$$\left[\text{\underline{AFTER}} \begin{Bmatrix} \text{identifier-5} \\ \text{index-name-3} \end{Bmatrix} \text{\underline{FROM}} \begin{Bmatrix} \text{identifier-6} \\ \text{index-name-4} \\ \text{literal-3} \end{Bmatrix} \right.$$

$$\text{\underline{BY}} \begin{Bmatrix} \text{identifier-7} \\ \text{literal-4} \end{Bmatrix} \text{\underline{UNTIL} condition-2}$$

$$\left[\text{\underline{AFTER}} \begin{Bmatrix} \text{identifier-8} \\ \text{index-name-5} \end{Bmatrix} \text{\underline{FROM}} \begin{Bmatrix} \text{identifier-9} \\ \text{index-name-6} \\ \text{literal-5} \end{Bmatrix} \right.$$

$$\left. \left. \text{\underline{BY}} \begin{Bmatrix} \text{identifier-10} \\ \text{literal-6} \end{Bmatrix} \text{\underline{UNTIL} condition-3} \right] \right]$$

$$\text{\underline{READ} file-name RECORD} \left[\text{\underline{INTO} identifier} \right] \left[; \text{ AT \underline{END} imperative-statement} \right]$$

$$\text{\underline{READ} file-name} \left[\text{\underline{NEXT}} \right] \text{RECORD} \left[\text{\underline{INTO} identifier} \right]$$

$$\left[; \text{ AT \underline{END} imperative-statement} \right]$$

READ file-name RECORD [INTO identifier] [; INVALID KEY imperative-statement]

READ file-name RECORD [INTO identifier]

  [; KEY IS data-name]

  [; INVALID KEY imperative-statement]

RECEIVE cd-name {MESSAGE / SEGMENT} INTO identifier-1 [; NO DATA imperative-statement]

RELEASE record-name [FROM identifier]

RETURN file-name RECORD [INTO identifier] ; AT END imperative-statement

REWRITE record-name [FROM identifier]

REWRITE record-name [FROM identifier] [; INVALID KEY imperative-statement]

SEARCH identifier-1 [VARYING {identifier-2 / index-name-1}] [; AT END imperative-statement-1]

  ; WHEN condition-1 {imperative-statement-2 / NEXT SENTENCE}

  [; WHEN condition-2 {imperative-statement-3 / NEXT SENTENCE}] ...

SEARCH ALL identifier-1 [; AT END imperative-statement-1]

  ; WHEN {data-name-1 {IS EQUAL TO / IS =} {identifier-3 / literal-1 / arithmetic-expression-1} / condition-name-1}

    [AND {data-name-2 {IS EQUAL TO / IS =} {identifier-4 / literal-2 / arithmetic-expression-2} / condition-name-2}] ...

    {imperative-statement-2 / NEXT SENTENCE}

SEND cd-name FROM identifier-1

SEND cd-name [FROM identifier-1] {WITH identifier-2 / WITH ESI / WITH EMI / WITH EGI}

    [{BEFORE / AFTER} ADVANCING {{{identifier-3 / integer} [LINE / LINES]} / {mnemonic-name / PAGE}}]

$$\underline{SET} \begin{Bmatrix} \text{identifier-1} & [, \text{ identifier-2}] & ... \\ \text{index-name-1} & [, \text{ index-name-2}] & ... \end{Bmatrix} \underline{TO} \begin{Bmatrix} \text{identifier-3} \\ \text{index-name-3} \\ \text{integer-1} \end{Bmatrix}$$

$$\underline{SET} \text{ index-name-4 } [, \text{ index-name-5}] \ ... \begin{Bmatrix} \underline{UP} \ \underline{BY} \\ \underline{DOWN} \ \underline{BY} \end{Bmatrix} \begin{Bmatrix} \text{identifier-4} \\ \text{integer-2} \end{Bmatrix}$$

$$\underline{SORT} \text{ file-name-1 } ON \begin{Bmatrix} \underline{ASCENDING} \\ \underline{DESCENDING} \end{Bmatrix} KEY \text{ data-name-1 } [, \text{ data-name-2}] \ ...$$

$$\left[ON \begin{Bmatrix} \underline{ASCENDING} \\ \underline{DESCENDING} \end{Bmatrix} KEY \text{ data-name-3 } [, \text{ data-name-4}] \ ... \right] \ ...$$

$$\Big[COLLATING \ \underline{SEQUENCE} \ IS \ \text{alphabet-name} \Big]$$

$$\begin{Bmatrix} \underline{INPUT} \ \underline{PROCEDURE} \ IS \ \text{section-name-1} \left[\begin{Bmatrix} \underline{THROUGH} \\ \underline{THRU} \end{Bmatrix} \text{section-name-2} \right] \\ \underline{USING} \ \text{file-name-2} \ [, \text{ file-name-3}] \ ... \end{Bmatrix}$$

$$\begin{Bmatrix} \underline{OUTPUT} \ \underline{PROCEDURE} \ IS \ \text{section-name-3} \left[\begin{Bmatrix} \underline{THROUGH} \\ \underline{THRU} \end{Bmatrix} \text{section-name-4} \right] \\ \underline{GIVING} \ \text{file-name-4} \end{Bmatrix}$$

$$\underline{START} \text{ file-name} \left[\underline{KEY} \begin{Bmatrix} IS \ \underline{EQUAL} \ TO \\ IS \ = \\ IS \ \underline{GREATER} \ THAN \\ IS \ > \\ IS \ \underline{NOT} \ \underline{LESS} \ THAN \\ IS \ \underline{NOT} \ < \end{Bmatrix} \text{data-name} \right]$$

$$\Big[; \ \underline{INVALID} \ KEY \ \text{imperative-statement} \Big]$$

$$\underline{STOP} \begin{Bmatrix} \underline{RUN} \\ \text{literal} \end{Bmatrix}$$

$$\underline{STRING} \begin{Bmatrix} \text{identifier-1} \\ \text{literal-1} \end{Bmatrix} \begin{bmatrix} , \text{ identifier-2} \\ , \text{ literal-2} \end{bmatrix} \ ... \ \underline{DELIMITED} \ BY \begin{Bmatrix} \text{identifier-3} \\ \text{literal-3} \\ \underline{SIZE} \end{Bmatrix}$$

$$\left[, \begin{Bmatrix} \text{identifier-4} \\ \text{literal-4} \end{Bmatrix} \begin{bmatrix} , \text{ identifier-5} \\ , \text{ literal-5} \end{bmatrix} \ ... \ \underline{DELIMITED} \ BY \begin{Bmatrix} \text{identifier-6} \\ \text{literal-6} \\ \underline{SIZE} \end{Bmatrix} \right] \ ...$$

$$\underline{INTO} \text{ identifier-7} \Big[WITH \ \underline{POINTER} \ \text{identifier-8} \Big]$$

$$\Big[; \ ON \ \underline{OVERFLOW} \ \text{imperative-statement} \Big]$$

$$\underline{SUBTRACT} \begin{Bmatrix} \text{identifier-1} \\ \text{literal-1} \end{Bmatrix} \begin{bmatrix} , \text{ identifier-2} \\ , \text{ literal-2} \end{bmatrix} \ ... \ \underline{FROM} \ \text{identifier-m} \Big[\underline{ROUNDED} \Big]$$

$$\Big[, \text{ identifier-n} \Big[\underline{ROUNDED} \Big] \Big] \ ... \ \Big[; \ ON \ \underline{SIZE} \ \underline{ERROR} \ \text{imperative-statement} \Big]$$

SUBTRACT $\left\{ \begin{array}{l} \text{identifier-1} \\ \text{literal-1} \end{array} \right\}$ $\left[\begin{array}{l} \text{, identifier-2} \\ \text{, literal-2} \end{array} \right]$ ... FROM $\left\{ \begin{array}{l} \text{identifier-m} \\ \text{literal-m} \end{array} \right\}$

    GIVING identifier-n [ROUNDED] [, identifier-o [ROUNDED]] ...

   [; ON SIZE ERROR imperative-statement]

SUBTRACT $\left\{ \begin{array}{l} \underline{\text{CORRESPONDING}} \\ \underline{\text{CORR}} \end{array} \right\}$ identifier-1 FROM identifier-2 [ROUNDED]

   [; ON SIZE ERROR imperative-statement]

SUPPRESS PRINTING

TERMINATE report-name-1 [, report-name-2] ...

UNSTRING identifier-1

   $\left[\text{DELIMITED BY [ALL]} \left\{ \begin{array}{l} \text{identifier-2} \\ \text{literal-1} \end{array} \right\} \left[\text{, OR [ALL]} \left\{ \begin{array}{l} \text{identifier-3} \\ \text{literal-2} \end{array} \right\} \right] ... \right]$

    INTO identifier-4 [, DELIMITER IN identifier-5] [, COUNT IN identifier-6]

      [, identifier-7 [, DELIMITER IN identifier-8] [, COUNT IN identifier-9]] ...

   [WITH POINTER identifier-10] [TALLYING IN identifier-11]

   [; ON OVERFLOW imperative-statement]

USE AFTER STANDARD $\left\{ \begin{array}{l} \underline{\text{EXCEPTION}} \\ \underline{\text{ERROR}} \end{array} \right\}$ PROCEDURE ON $\left\{ \begin{array}{l} \text{file-name-1 [, file-name-2] ...} \\ \underline{\text{INPUT}} \\ \underline{\text{OUTPUT}} \\ \underline{\text{I-O}} \\ \underline{\text{EXTEND}} \end{array} \right\}$.

USE AFTER STANDARD $\left\{ \begin{array}{l} \underline{\text{EXCEPTION}} \\ \underline{\text{ERROR}} \end{array} \right\}$ PROCEDURE ON $\left\{ \begin{array}{l} \text{file-name-1 [, file-name-2] ...} \\ \underline{\text{INPUT}} \\ \underline{\text{OUTPUT}} \\ \underline{\text{I-O}} \end{array} \right\}$.

USE BEFORE REPORTING identifier.

USE FOR DEBUGGING ON $\left\{ \begin{array}{l} \text{cd-name-1} \\ \text{[ALL REFERENCES OF] identifier-1} \\ \text{file-name-1} \\ \text{procedure-name-1} \\ \underline{\text{ALL PROCEDURES}} \end{array} \right\}$

   $\left[\text{,} \begin{array}{l} \text{cd-name-2} \\ \text{[ALL REFERENCES OF] identifier-2} \\ \text{file-name-2} \\ \text{procedure-name-2} \\ \underline{\text{ALL PROCEDURES}} \end{array} \right]$ ... .

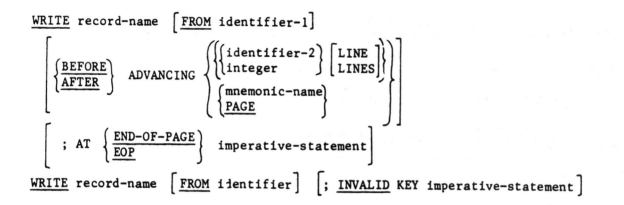

WRITE record-name [FROM identifier] [; INVALID KEY imperative-statement]

GENERAL FORMAT FOR CONDITIONS

RELATION CONDITION:

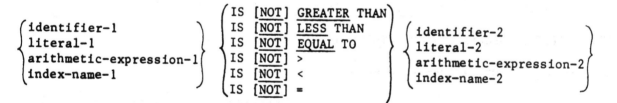

CLASS CONDITION:

$$\text{identifier IS [\underline{NOT}]} \begin{Bmatrix} \underline{\text{NUMERIC}} \\ \underline{\text{ALPHABETIC}} \end{Bmatrix}$$

SIGN CONDITION:

$$\text{arithmetic-expression IS [\underline{NOT}]} \begin{Bmatrix} \underline{\text{POSITIVE}} \\ \underline{\text{NEGATIVE}} \\ \underline{\text{ZERO}} \end{Bmatrix}$$

CONDITION-NAME CONDITION:

condition-name

SWITCH-STATUS CONDITION:

condition-name

NEGATED SIMPLE CONDITION:

<u>NOT</u> simple-condition

COMBINED CONDITION:

$$\text{condition} \left\{ \left\{ \frac{\text{AND}}{\text{OR}} \right\} \text{condition} \right\} \ldots$$

ABBREVIATED COMBINED RELATION CONDITION:

$$\text{relation-condition} \left\{ \left\{ \frac{\text{AND}}{\text{OR}} \right\} [\underline{\text{NOT}}] \; [\text{relational-operator}] \; \text{object} \right\} \ldots$$

MISCELLANEOUS FORMATS

QUALIFICATION:

$$\begin{Bmatrix} \text{data-name-1} \\ \text{condition-name} \end{Bmatrix} \left[\begin{Bmatrix} \text{OF} \\ \text{IN} \end{Bmatrix} \text{data-name-2} \right] \ldots$$

$$\text{paragraph-name} \left[\begin{Bmatrix} \text{OF} \\ \text{IN} \end{Bmatrix} \text{section-name} \right]$$

$$\text{text-name} \left[\begin{Bmatrix} \text{OF} \\ \text{IN} \end{Bmatrix} \text{library-name} \right]$$

SUBSCRIPTING:

$$\begin{Bmatrix} \text{data-name} \\ \text{condition-name} \end{Bmatrix} (\text{subscript-1} \; [, \; \text{subscript-2} \; [, \; \text{subscript-3}]])$$

INDEXING:

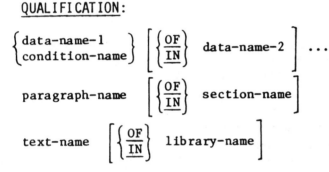

$$\begin{Bmatrix} \text{data-name} \\ \text{condition-name} \end{Bmatrix} (\begin{Bmatrix} \text{index-name-1} \; [\{\pm\} \; \text{literal-2}] \\ \text{literal-1} \end{Bmatrix}$$

$$\left[, \begin{Bmatrix} \text{index-name-2} \; [\{\pm\} \; \text{literal-4}] \\ \text{literal-3} \end{Bmatrix} \left[, \begin{Bmatrix} \text{index-name-3} \; [\{\pm\} \; \text{literal-6}] \\ \text{literal-5} \end{Bmatrix} \right] \right])$$

IDENTIFIER: FORMAT 1

$$\text{data-name-1} \left[\begin{Bmatrix} \text{OF} \\ \text{IN} \end{Bmatrix} \text{data-name-2} \right] \ldots \left[(\text{subscript-1} \; [, \; \text{subscript-2} \; [, \; \text{subscript-3}]]) \right]$$

IBM OS EXECUTION-TIME ERROR MESSAGES D

D.1 INPUT/OUTPUT ERRORS

Errors can occur while a COBOL file is being processed. For example, during data transmission, an input/output error may occur that cannot be corrected. In some situations, this will result in the job being terminated. . . .

Referring to an input area (non-VSAM/QSAM) before both an OPEN and a READ statement are issued can cause unpredictable results, because base locator (BL) cells and registers are not properly initialized.

Another error that can cause termination is an attempt to read a file whose records are of a different size than those described in the source program. . . .

D.2 ERRORS CAUSED BY INVALID DATA

Abnormal termination of a job occurs when a data item with an invalid format is processed in the Procedure Division.

Some of the program errors are:

1) A data item in the Working-Storage Section is not initialized before it is used, causing invalid data to be picked up.
2) An input file or received message contains invalid data or data incorrectly defined by its data description. For example, the contents of the sign position of an internal or external decimal data item in the file may be invalid. The compiler does not generate a test to check the sign position for a valid configuration before the item is used as an operand.
3) If a group item is moved to a group item and the subordinate data descriptions are incompatible, the new data in the receiving field may not match the corresponding data descriptions. (Conversion or editing is not performed in a move involving a group item.)
   Note: A numeric class test, "IF Numeric", for signed data items,

allows C, D, and F as valid signs. For external decimal items this includes X'C1' through X'C9' and X'D1' through X'D9' and X'F1' through X'F9' as valid last bytes. For internal decimal items, this includes X'1C' through X'9C', X'1D' through X'9D', and X'1F' through X'9F' as valid last bytes. Certain invalid numeric data times, such as EBCDIC A through R in the last byte of an external decimal numeric item, and EBCDIC <, *, %, @, (,), —, ', |, □, ?, and "in the last byte of an internal decimal item, are considered valid numeric items for an "IF Numeric" test.

4) The SIZE ERROR option is not specified for the COMPUTE statement and the result of the calculation is larger than the specified resultant COMPUTATIONAL data name. Using the result in a subsequent calculation might cause an error.

5) The SIZE ERROR option is not specified for a DIVIDE statement, and an attempt is made to divide by zero.

6) The USAGE specified for a redefining data item is different from the USAGE specified for the redefined item. An error results when the item is referred to by the wrong name for the current content.

7) A record containing a data item described by an OCCURS clause with the DEPENDING ON *data-name* option, may cause data times in the record to be affected by a change in the value of *data-name* during the course of program execution. This may result in incorrectly described data. . . .

8) The data description in the Linkage Section of a called program does not correctly describe the data defined in the calling program.

9) Blanks read into data fields defined as numeric generate an invalid sign.

10) Some common errors that occur when clearing group items in storage are:
    a. Moving ALL ZEROS to a group level item to clear several counters causes an invalid sign to be generated in all of the elementary fields except the lowest order field.
    b. Moving SPACES to a group level item will put invalid data in any numeric field in that group.
    c. Moving 0 to a group level item moves one zero and pads the rest of the fields with blanks.

11) Failure to initialize counters produces incorrect results. No initial values are generated by the compiler unless specifically instructed to do so with a VALUE clause. If such fields are defined as decimal, internal or external, invalid signs may result in addition to unpredictable initial values. If defined as binary, they will cause unpredictable results and, further, if used in subscripting, may exceed the range of the associated OCCURS clause and cause data to be fetched or stored erroneously. An addressing exception may occur if the uninitialized subscript generates a bad address.

12) Not testing to ensure that a subscript or index does not exceed the range of the associated OCCURS clause may lead to fetching and storing data from and to some incorrect locations.

13) Failure to initialize an index produces incorrect results. No initial values are generated by the compiler unless a SET statement is executed. When indexing is then specified, the range of the

OCCURS clause may be exceeded and cause data to be fetched or stored erroneously. An addressing exception may occur if the initialized index generates an address outside the range of the machine, or a protection exception if data is stored outside the partition of this program.

14) A subscript or index set at zero will address data outside the range of the table.

15) If either HIGH-VALUE or LOW-VALUE is moved to internal or external decimal fields and those fields are used for comparisons, computations, or subscripting, a data exception will occur. HIGH-VALUE and LOW-VALUE are the hexadecimal values X'FF' and X'00', respectively (unless these values have been altered by a user-defined collating sequence).

D.3   OTHER ERRORS

Additional I/O errors may occur that will result in an abnormal termination (these are listed below). For QSAM files, however, the user can employ the FILE STATUS clause to intercept many of these errors; his program can then identify and deal with them, and thus prevent the abend from occurring.

1) No DD statement is included for a file described in the source program and an attempt is made to access the file. When an OPEN statement for the file is executed, the system console message is written. The programmer can elect to direct the operator to continue processing his program, but any READ, WRITE, REWRITE, or START associated with the unlocated file will fail. (A READ for a missing optional file, however, will follow end-of-file processing rules.) A similar situation exists when a file is closed WITH LOCK and an attempt is made to reopen it.

2) A file is not opened and execution of a READ or WRITE statement for the file is attempted, or a MOVE to a record area in the file is attempted.

3) A GO TO statement, with no procedure name following it, is not properly initialized with an ALTER statement before the first execution of the GO TO statement.

4) Reference is made to an item in a file after end of data. This includes the use of the TERMINATE statement of the Report Writer feature, if the CONTROL FOOTING, PAGE FOOTING, or REPORT FOOTING contain items that are in the file (e.g., SOURCE data-name, where data-name refers to an item in the file).

5) Block size for an F-format file is not an integral multiple of the record length.

6) In a blocked and/or multiple-buffered file, information in a record is unavailable after a WRITE.

7) A READ is issued for a data set referenced on a DD DUMMY statement. The AT END condition is sensed immediately and any reference to a record in the data set produces unpredictable results.

8) A STOP RUN statement is executed before all files are closed.

9) A SORT did not execute successfully. The programmer may check SORT-RETURN.

10) An input/output statement is issued for a file after the AT END branch is taken, without closing and reopening the file.

11) A SEND or RECEIVE statement is issued when a message control program is not running.

12) A SEND or RECEIVE statement is issued for a QNAME (i.e., the 'QNAME=' parameter of the DD card) that is unknown to the message control program.

In addition to errors that can result in an abnormal termination, errors in the source program can occur that cause parts of the program to be overlaid and the corresponding object code instructions to become invalid. If an attempt is then made to execute one of these instructions, an abnormal termination may result because the operation code of the instruction is invalid, the instruction results in a branch to an area containing invalid instructions, or the instruction results in a branch to an area outside the program, such as an address protected area.

Some COBOL source program errors that can cause the overlaying are:

1) Using a subscript whose value exceeds the maximum specified in the associated OCCURS clause.

2) Using a data-name as a counter whose value exceeds the maximum value valid for that counter.

D.4   SYSTEM COMPLETION CODES

The following cases represent some of the errors that can occur in a COBOL program and the interrupt or completion code associated with them. These errors do not necessarily cause an abnormal termination at the time they are recognized and do not always hold true. . . .

1) 013-Check register 2 of registers at the entry to ABEND. This address points to the DCB in conflict.

2) 043-Error occurred during the attempted opening of a TCAM application program data set, as described below.

   a. A value of 01 in register 0 indicates the attempted opening of a TCAM application program data set without an active message control program (MCP) in the system.

   b. A value of 02 indicates that the QNAME= parameter of a DD statement associated with an input or output DCB for a COBOL program is not the name of a process entry defined in the terminal table.

   c. A value of 03 indicates that the process entry named by the QNAME= parameter of a DD statement associated with a COBOL program is currently being used by another COBOL program.

   d. A value of 04 indicates that insufficient main storage was available in the MCP to build internal control blocks associated with the COBOL program interface. Specify a larger region or partition size in the JOB statement for the MCP.

   e. A value of 05 indicates that insufficient main storage was available in the COBOL work area to build internal control blocks. Specify a larger region or partition size in the JOB statement for the COBOL program.

3) 046-Error occurred during the termination of the TCAM MCP because the COBOL program data set was still open. Specify the STOP RUN statement when COBOL processing is complete. Ensure that all COBOL programs have terminated processing before deactivating the MCP.

4) OC1-Operation Exception:

   a. When the interrupt is at 000048 or at 004800, look for a missing DD card or an unopened file.

   b. When the interrupt is at 000050, look at register 1 of the registers at entry to ABEND. Add hexadecimal 28 to the address found in register 1. This should point to the DD name of a missing DD statement.

   c. When the interrupt is at 00004A, look for a missing card, i.e.,

   //SYSOUT DD SYSOUT=A

   any missing JCL card, or the wrong name of a JCL card. Add hexadecimal 28 to the address found in register 1 at entry to ABEND. This should point to the DD name of the DD statement in error.

   d. When interrupt is at 00004F, look for inconsistent JCL or check the system-name in the COBOL program.

5) OC4-Protection Exception:

   a. Check for the block size and record size being equal for variable record input or output.

   b. Check for missing SELECT statement.

   c. If interrupt is at 004814, check for an attempt to READ an unopened input file or a missing DD card.

   d. Check for an uninitialized index or subscript.

   e. If a QSAM file with FILE STATUS opened OUTPUT, check for a missing DD card.

6) OC5 and OC6- Addressing and Specification Exception:

   a. Subscript or index value may have exceeded maximum and instruction or table area was overlaid.

   b. check for an improper exit from a procedure being operated on by a PERFORM statement.

   c. Check for duplicate close of an input or output file if DS formatting discontinued.

   d. A sort is being attempted with an incorrect catalog procedure.

   e. Attempting to reference an input/output area before a READ or OPEN statement, respectively.

   f. Check for initialized subscript or index value.

7) OC7-Data Exception:

   a. Data field was not initialized.

   b. Input record numeric field contains blanks.

   c. Subscript or index value exceeded maximum and invalid data was referenced.

   d. Data was moved from the DISPLAY field to the COMPUTATIONAL or COMPUTATIONAL-3 field at group level. Therefore, no conversion was provided.

    e. The figurative constants ZERO or LOW-VALUE moved to a group level numeric field.

    f. Omission of USAGE clause or erroneous USAGE clause.

    g. Incorrect Linkage Section data definition, passing parameters in wrong order, omission or inclusion of a parameter, failure to carry over a USAGE clause when necessary, or defining the length of a parameter incorrectly.

8) 001-I/0 Error:

    a. Register 1 of the SVRB points to the DCB which caused the input/output problem. Look for input record and blocking errors. That is, the input does not agree with the record and blocking descriptions in the DCB, the COBOL file description, or the DD statement LRECL parameter.

    b. Attempted to READ after EOF has been sensed.

    c. Attempted to write to a QSAM file that has previously encountered end of file (taken a B37 exit) and set the file status to X'34' and/or entered the INVALID KEY routine.

9) 002-Register 2 of registers at the entry to ABEND contains the address of the DCB for the file causing the input/output problem. Check the DCB list for the specific file.

10) 013-Error during execution of an OPEN EXTEND statement. Ensure that the system OPEN EXTEND facility is available. OPEN EXTEND requires at least OS/VSI Release 6, or OS/VS2 Release 7 with SU8.

11) 213-Error during execution of OPEN statement for data set on mass storage device, as follows:

    a. DISP parameter of DD statement specified OLD for output data set.

    b. Input/output error cannot be corrected when reading or writing the DSCB. Recreate the data set or resubmit the job.

12) 214-Error during CLOSE for data set on tape; there is an input/output error that cannot be corrected either in tape positioning or value disposition. Resubmit the job and inform the field engineer if error persists.

13) 237-Error at EOV:

    a. Incorrect volume serial number specified in SER subparameter of VOLUME parameter of DD statement.

    b. Incorrect volume mounted.

    c. Incorrect labels.

14) 400-If this completion code is generated during a compile step, the member to be compiled has not been extracted from the source library for compilation.

15) 413-Error during execution of an OPEN statement for a data set on tape:

    a. Volume serial number was not specified for input data set.

    b. Volume could not be mounted on the allocated device.

    c. There is an input/output error in reading the volume label that cannot be corrected.

16) 804-The error occurred during a GETMAIN. If this error occurs when a non-COBOL program (such as IMS or an installation-defined assembler program) links to a COBOL load module many times in a job step, the programmer should determine if

the NOENDJOB option was used; if so, specifying the ENDJOB option may correct the problem.

17) 806-The error occurred during execution of a LINK, XCTL, ATTACH, or LOAD macro instruction. An error was detected by the control program routine for the BLDL macro instruction. The contents of register 15 indicate the nature of the error:

04   The requested program was not found in the indicated private, job, or link library.

08   An uncorrectable input/output error occurred when the control program attempted to search the directory of the library indicated as containing the requested program.

18) 80A-Insufficient contiguous main storage for linkage to some phase of the compiler. The programmer should see if secondary data-set allocation has caused an extra DEB to be built at lower main storage addresses within the region. If so, this problem can be corrected by assigning sufficient primary extends for the data set in question. See "Data Set Requirements" for further information. If this error occurs when a non-COBOL program (such as IMS or an installation-defined assembler program) links to a COBOL load module many times in a job step, the programmer should determine if the NOENDJOB option was used; if so, specifying the ENDJOB option may correct the problem.

19) 813-Error during execution of an OPEN statement in verification of labels:
   a. Volume serial number specified in VOLUME parameter of DD statement is incorrect.
   b. Data set name specified in DSNAME parameter is incorrect.
   c. Wrong volume is mounted.

20) 906-The system use count limit was exceeded during the execution of a LINK, XCTL, LOAD, or ATTACH macro. If this error occurs when an non-COBOL program (such as IMS or an installation-defined assembler program) links to a COBOL load module many times in a job step, the programmer should determine if the NOENDJOB option was used; if so, specifying the ENDJOB option may correct the problem.

PERSONNEL SYSTEM E

E.1 BACKGROUND

The ABC Company uses a computer based system to perform most functions related to payroll and personnel accounting. At the heart of this system is a file called the "Personnel Master File," which contains one record for each current employee. The layout for the records in this file is shown in Figure E.1. The programming exercises in this appendix all relate to this file. Figure E.2 contains a sample data set that you may use to test programs you write. Your instructor will tell you what you must do to make use of this data on your system.

Figure E.1 Record layout for personnel master file

Record Positions	Description	PIC
1-9	Employee social security number	9(9)
10-30	Employee name	
	10-19 Last name	X(10)
	20-29 First name	X(10)
	30 Middle initial	X
31-36	Date hired (*mmddyy*)	9(6)
37-41	Cost center	9(5)
42	Pay type	X
	S Salary	
	H Hourly/full time	
	P Hourly/part time	
43	Marital status	X
	M Married	
	S Single	
44-49	Pay amount	9(4)V99
	Pay type S: Biweekly amount	
	Pay type H/P: Hourly amount	
50-51	Number dependents	99

(*continued on page A-50*)

52-58	Year-to-date gross pay	9(5)V99
59-65	Year-to-date federal income tax	9(5)V99
66-71	Year-to-date social security tax	9(4)V99
72-77	Year-to-date state income tax	9(5)V99
78-80	Unused	XXX

E.2 PROGRAMMING EXERCISES

Note: The chapter reference in parentheses after each exercise indicates the background required to write the program.

1) Write a program to produce a report showing the social security number, name and cost center for each employee. Include appropriate headings as shown on the printer spacing chart illustrated in Figure E.3. (Chapter 2)

2) Write a program to produce a report showing detail of year-to-date pay for all employees including totals for gross pay, federal income tax, social security tax and state income tax as shown in Figure E.4. (Chapter 3).

3) Write a program to produce a detailed listing of the Personnel Master File. Use appropriate labels and editing for each field as shown in Figure E.5. (Chapter 4)

4) Modify the program written for Exercise 2 to compute and print each employee's net income (gross pay minus all withholding amounts). (Chapter 5)

5) Write a program to compute and print the annual bonus amount due each employee based on the following rules:

> Salaried employees receive 5% of their annual income not to exceed $2000.
>
> Full time hourly employees receive one week's pay (40 hours).
>
> Part time hourly employees receive no bonus.

Include totals as shown in the printer layout of Figure E.6. (Chapter 6)

6) Write a program to validate the records contained in the Personnel Master File using the following guidelines:

Numeric Fields

All numeric fields must contain numeric data:
> Employee social security number
> Date hired (the date hired field must contain a valid date: month must be in the range 1 to 12; day must be in the range of 1 to 31)
> Cost center (valid cost centers are shown in Exercise 9 below)
> Pay amount
> Number dependents
> All year-to-date fields

Alphabetic Fields

> Employee name (must contain alphabetic characters, must not contain all spaces)

Pay type (only S, H, and P are valid)

Marital status (only M and S are valid)

Your program should list any record found to contain invalid data with an appropriate error message. Additional sample data that can be used to test this program is shown in Figure E.7. (Chapter 6)

7) Write a program to sort the Personnel Master File into ascending sequence by cost center. Records within each cost center group must be in ascending sequence by employee name. (Chapter 7)

8) Write a program to process the file produced in Exercise 7 to produce a summary of personnel expenditures by cost center. Use the printer spacing chart shown in Figure E.8. (Chapter 8)

9) Modify the program you wrote for Exercise 8 to produce a separate report for each cost center. The heading of each report should contain the cost center identification as in the following table:

Cost Center	Identification
00001	Administration
03000	Manufacturing plant A
03001	Manufacturing plant B
04000	Purchasing
05000	Accounting
06000	Shipping
07000	Advertising

Set up the table shown above as a table of constants in your program. (Chapter 9).

Figure E.2 Sample Data for personnel system programming exercises

Employee Social Security Number	Last Name	First Name	M.I.	Date Hired	Cost Center	Pay Type	M.S.	Pay Amount	Number Dependents	Y.T.D. Gross Pay	Y.T.D. Federal Income Tax	Y.T.D. Social Security Tax	Y.T.D. State Income Tax
100000000	SMITH	LEE	A	031480	04000	S	M	1000 00	02	04000 00	00800 00	0320 00	0053 32
111111111	BARKLEY	WALTER	I	050281	07000	S	M	0875 00	03	03500 00	00700 00	0280 00	0046 66
200000000	CARR	BONNIE	S	120579	05000	H	S	0018 75	01	06000 00	01200 00	0480 00	0079 98
222222222	DREW	VIRGINIA	R	030185	00001	H	M	0015 63	03	05000 00	01000 00	0400 00	0066 65
300000000	BOMAR	CHARLES	B	070783	03000	S	S	1500 00	02	06000 00	01200 00	0480 00	0079 98
333333333	JACKSON	RAMONE	M	100582	03000	P	M	0010 00	02	00900 00	00090 00	0072 00	0000 00
400000000	MOYER	JAMES	E	040185	06000	H	M	0012 50	04	04000 00	00800 00	0320 00	0053 32
400000004	ROWE	ROBERTA	T	050680	03001	S	S	1500 00	01	06000 00	01200 00	0480 00	0079 98
444444444	KAY	RONALD	A	011582	07000	S	S	0012 50	01	04000 00	00800 00	0320 00	0053 32
500000000	MCGEE	CALVIN	S	053085	03000	P	M	0008 00	05	01000 00	00050 00	0080 00	0013 33
500000005	MILLER	DAVID	L	061578	00001	H	M	0015 63	03	05000 00	01000 00	0400 00	0066 65
555555555	PATTERSON	JOHN	J	110182	05000	S	M	1250 00	02	05000 00	01000 00	0400 00	0066 65
566666666	ROBINSON	ANDREW	R	090180	03001	P	S	0007 50	02	00300 00	00030 00	0024 00	0000 00
577777777	GRAY	HELEN	S	071582	00001	P	M	0008 00	02	00500 00	00050 00	0040 00	0000 00
588888888	BEECH	STEVEN	A	080104	06000	S	S	0500 00	01	02000 00	00400 00	0160 00	0026 66
599999999	JORDAN	JOHN	R	030783	05000	S	S	0750 00	01	03000 00	00600 00	0240 00	0039 98
600000000	LEWIS	EUNICE	A	080184	07000	S	M	1000 00	03	04000 00	00800 00	0320 00	0053 32
600000006	MCBRIDE	LEE	S	020185	04000	H	M	0012 50	03	04000 00	00800 00	0320 00	0053 32
611111111	PETERSON	GARRY	J	060183	00001	H	S	0017 19	02	05500 00	01100 00	0440 00	0073 32
622222222	RICH	RICHARD	K	121585	06000	P	S	0008 00	01	00600 00	00060 00	0048 00	0000 00
633333333	TURNER	LAURIE	R	081580	03000	S	M	0750 00	03	03000 00	00600 00	0240 00	0039 99
666666666	WADE	MARY	M	090183	03001	S	M	0875 00	02	06500 00	00700 00	0280 00	0046 66
699999999	WILLIAMS	SONJA	C	051582	07000	H	M	0015 78	02	05050 00	01010 00	0404 00	0067 32
700000000	TODD	DOUGLAS	R	070183	04000	H	M	0019 06	04	06100 00	01300 00	0488 00	0081 31
711111111	ROSE	PETER	M	071582	03000	S	S	1100 00	01	04400 00	00880 00	0352 00	0058 65
722222222	MCGRAW	STEPHEN	T	100184	00001	P	M	0008 00	02	00600 00	00060 00	0048 00	0000 00
733333333	GARCIA	JOSE	A	110183	04000	S	S	1500 00	03	06000 00	01200 00	0480 00	0079 98
744444444	DYE	WILLIAM	J	100183	06000	S	M	1000 00	02	04000 00	00800 00	0320 00	0053 32
755555555	BARNES	ARTHUR	R	010185	03001	H	M	0009 69	03	03100 00	00620 00	0248 00	0041 32
766666666	ALEXANDER	JOSEPH	J	041580	07000	P	S	0008 00	01	01100 00	00220 00	0088 00	0014 66
777777777	BISHOP	RICHARD	R	050682	03000	S	M	0625 00	03	02500 00	00500 00	0200 00	0033 33
788888888	CARROLL	ANNE	B	091580	00001	S	M	0825 00	02	03300 00	00660 00	0264 00	0043 98

Figure E.3 Printer spacing chart for Exercise 1

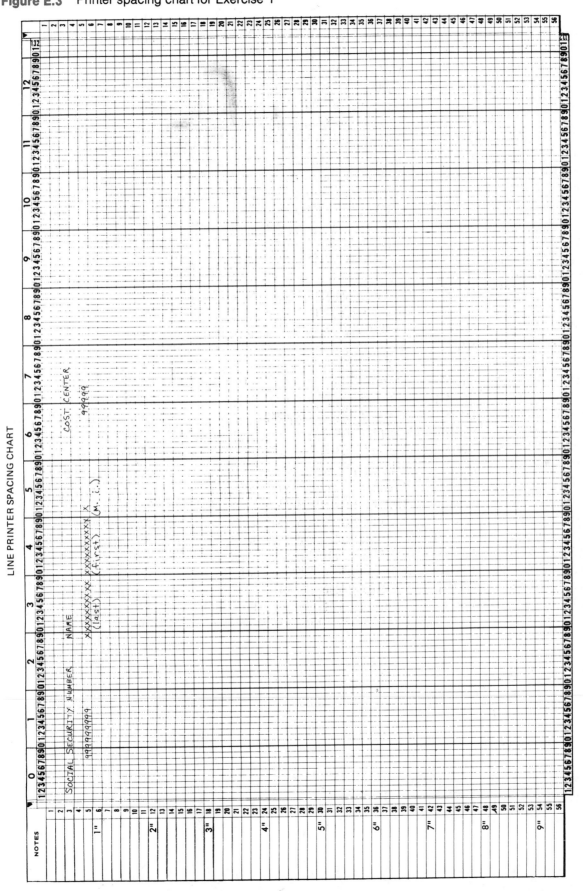

Figure E.4 Printer spacing chart for Exercise 2

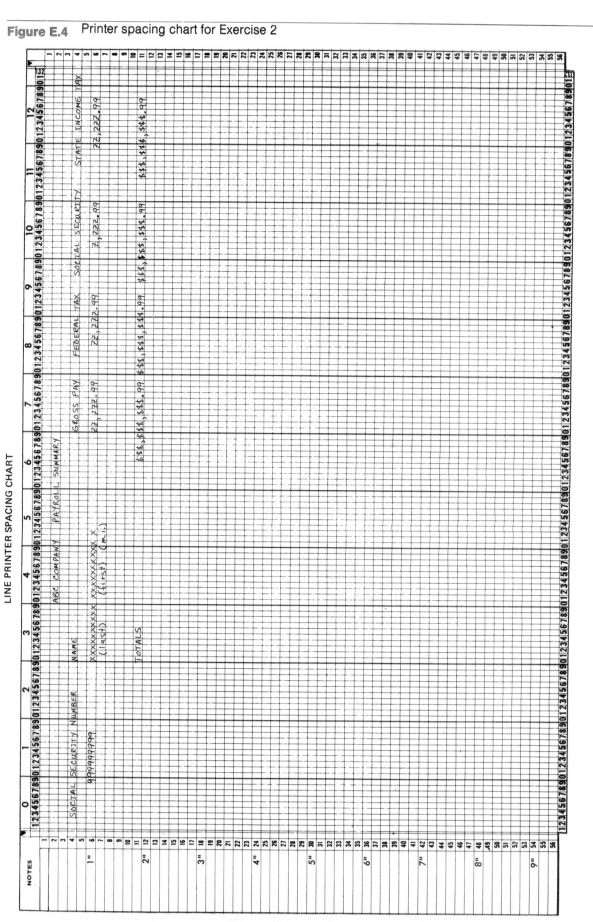

Figure E.5 Printer spacing chart for Exercise 3

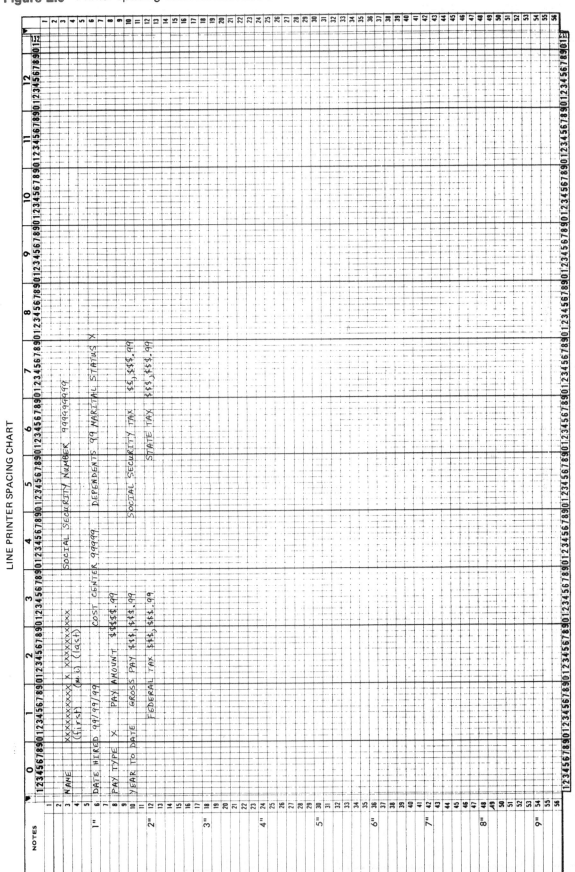

Figure E.6. Printer spacing chart for Exercise 5

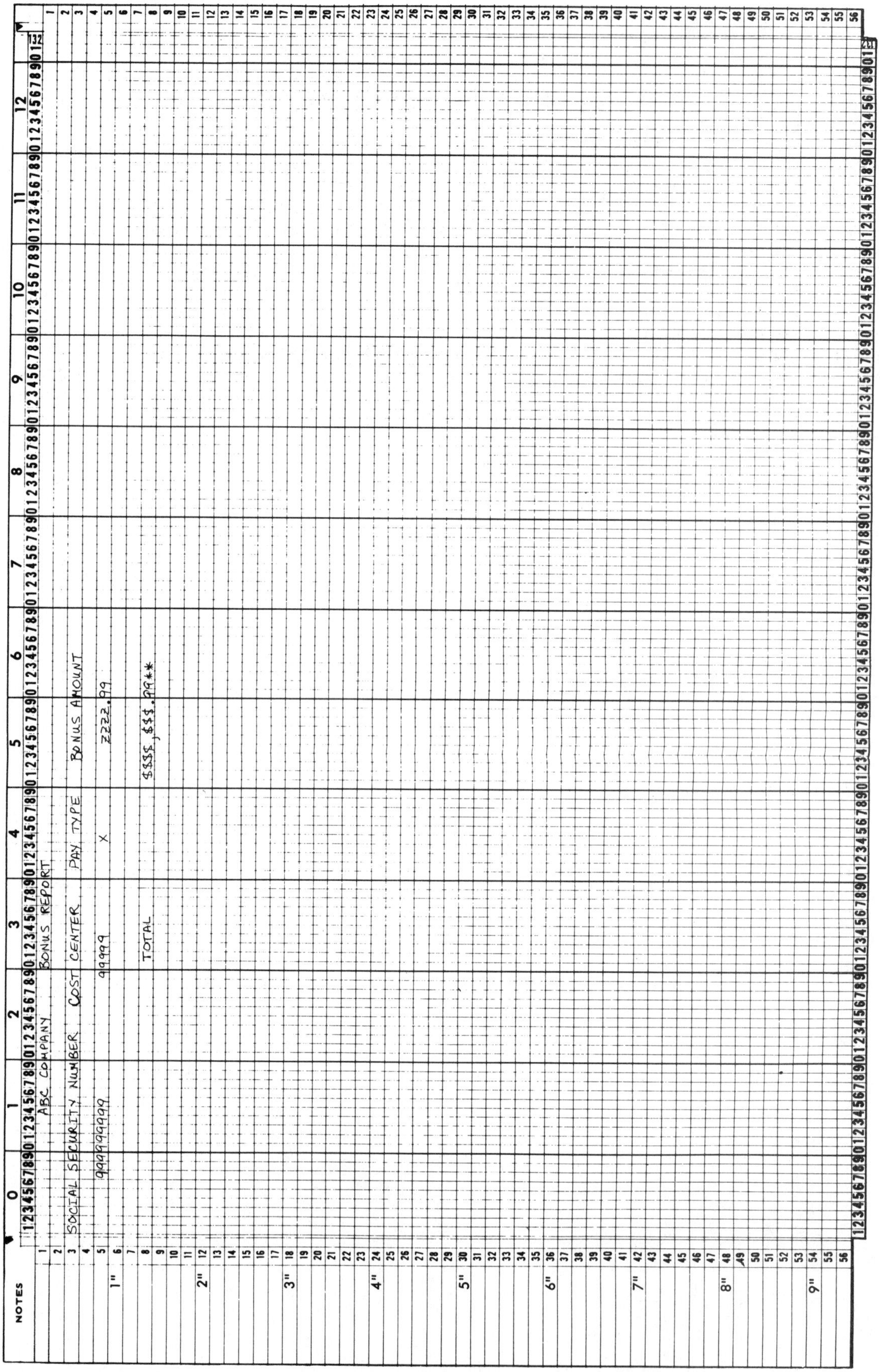

Figure E.7 Additional data to test data validation program

Employee Social Security Number	Last Name	First Name	M.I.	Date Hired	Cost Center	Pay Type	M.S.	Pay Amount	Number Dependents	Y.T.D. Gross Pay	Y.T.D. Federal Income Tax	Y.T.D. Social Security Tax	Y.T.D. State Income Tax	Comment
111111	JONES	JOHN	D	010286	01000	S	M	0900 00	03	00000 00	00000 00	0000 00	0000 00	Non-numeric social security number
200000002	MOORE	MARY	M	010386	02000	M	H	0010 00	01	00000 00	00000 00	0000 00	0000 00	Invalid pay type and marital status
800000000	MORTON	WILLIAM3RD	A	010386	05000	H	M	0008 50	02	00000 00	00000 00	0000 00	0000 00	Non-alphabetic first name
300000033	WARD	MARGRET	S	013386	04000	S	S	1000 00	01	00000 00	00000 00	0000 00	0000 00	Invalid date hired
400000044	KNOTT	DANIEL	W	010486	0C000	P	M	0006 00	03	00000 00	00000 00	0000 00	0000 00	Non-numeric cost center
500000055	HALL	CHARLES	C	010586	04000	S	M	A000 00	02					Non-numeric data in Y.T.D. amounts
600000066	HAND	NANCY	R	000586		S	M		02	00000 00	00000 00	0000 00		Invalid date hired, non-numeric cost center and state income tax
700000077	DALE	CHIP	N	010386	10000	S	M	1200 00	03	00000 00	00000 00	0000 00	0000 00	Invalid cost center
800000088	BOOTH	MARIE	R	010386	00001		S	0010 00	02	00000 00	00000 00	0000 00	0000 00	Invalid pay type
800000888	SPRINGER	DAN	S	010386	00000	S								Invalid cost center, marital status, non-numeric data in pay amount, number dependents, Y.T.D. amounts

Figure E.8 Printer spacing chart for Exercise 8

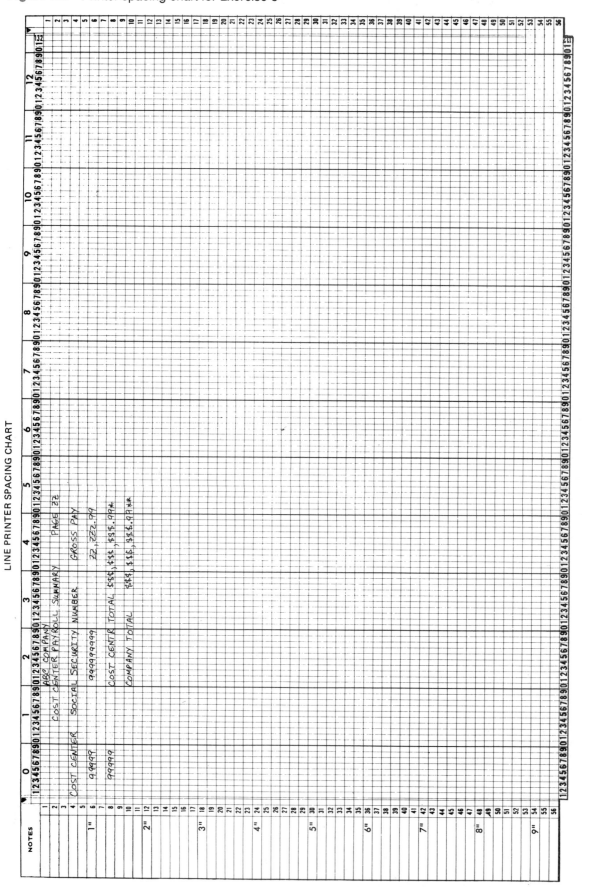

SALES ACCOUNTING SYSTEM F

F.1 BACKGROUND

The ABC Company uses a computer-based system for entering sales information for products which are sold in its stores to both wholesale and retail customers. At the heart of this system is the Sales Detail File which contains one record for each sale. The record layout for this file is shown in Figure F.1. The programming exercises in this appendix all make use of this file. Figure F.2 contains sample data which you may use to test your programs. Your instructor will tell you what you must do to make use of this data on your system.

Figure F.1   Record layout for sales detail file

Positions	Description	PIC
1-9	Item number	9(9)
10-19	Item description	X(10)
20-25	Retail list price (each)	9(4)V99
26-31	Wholesale list price (each)	9(4)V99
32-34	Quantity	999
35	Type of sale	X
	W Wholesale	
	R Retail	
36-38	Sales tax rate	V999
39-43	Salesperson identifier	9(5)
44-45	Store number	99
46-54	Customer account number	9(9)
55-60	Date of sale (*mmddyy*)	9(6)
61	Billing code	X
	C Cash	
	R Credit	

(continued on page A-60)

62	Shipping code	X
	C Customer pick up	
	U UPS	
	P Parcel Post	
63-80	Unused	X(18)

F.2   PROGRAMMING EXERCISES

Note: The chapter reference in parentheses after each exercise indicates the background required to write the program.

1) Write a program to produce a report showing the item number, item description, retail price, wholesale price, type of sale and quantity for each record in the file. Use the printer spacing chart shown in Figure F.3. (Chapter 2)

2) Modify the program written for Exercise 1 to include the total number of items sold. This output should follow the body of the report. (Chapter 3)

3) Write a program to produce a detailed listing of each record in the Sales Detail File. Use appropriate labels and editing for each field as shown in Figure F.4. (Chapter 4)

4) Write a program to produce a report showing the item number, item description, type of sale, price each, quantity, and amount of sale. The price each should be the wholesale list price for a type W sale; for a type R sale the price each should be the retail list price. Include totals as shown in the printer spacing chart illustrated in Figure F.5. (Chapter 5)

5) Write a program to generate an invoice for each record in the Sales Detail File. The amount of sale must be computed as described in Exercise 4 above. Retail sales should have sales tax computed; wholesale sales are not subject to sales tax. Sales which are to be shipped by UPS should have a shipping charge of 1% of the amount of sale for each item; sales which are shipped by parcel post have a shipping charge of 1 ½% of the amount of sale. Use the printer spacing chart shown in Figure F.6. (Chapter 6)

6) Write a program to validate records in the Sales Detail File using the following guidelines:

Numeric fields

All numeric fields must contain numeric data.
> Item number
> Retail list price
> Wholesale list price
> Quantity
> Sales tax rate
> Salesperson identifier
> Store number (only store numbers 01, 02, 04, and 14 are valid)
> Customer account number
> Date of sale (must contain a valid date: month in range of 01 to 12, day in range 01 to 31)

Alphabetic fields

> Type of sale (only W and R are valid)
> Billing code (only C and R are valid)
> Shipping code (only C, U and P are valid)

The item description field may contain alphabetic and/or numeric characters but must not contain all spaces.

Your program must list any record found to contain invalid data with an appropriate error message. Additional sample data that can be used to test this program is shown in Figure F.7. (Chapter 6)

7) Write a program to sort the Sales Detail File into ascending sequence by store number. Records within each store group should be in ascending sequence by salesperson number. (Chapter 7)

8) Write a program to process the file produced in Exercise 7 to produce a summary of sales by store and salesperson. Use the printer spacing chart shown in Figure F.8. (Chapter 8)

9) Modify the program you wrote for Exercise 8 to produce a separate report for each store. The heading of each report should contain the store identifier as shown in the following table:

Store Number	Identifier
01	Main
02	Mall
04	Suburb A
14	Suburb B

Set up the table shown above as a table of constants in your program. (Chapter 9)

Figure F.2 Sample data for sales accounting system programming exercises

Item Number	Item Description	Retail List Price		Wholesale List Price		Quantity	Type	Sales Tax Rate	Salesperson Identifier	Store Number	Customer Account Number	Date of Sale	Billing Code	Shipping Code
111111111	SECR CHAIR	0079	00	0060	00	001	W	050	00002	01	000001000	011386	C	C
222222222	EXEC CHAIR	0129	50	0099	98	003	R	050	00003	01	000009999	011386	R	U
300000000	L DESK	0325	00	0299	00	001	R	050	00011	04	000001000	011386	R	P
300000003	EXEC DESK	0449	00	0421	95	002	W	050	00012	02	000002000	011386	C	C
222222222	EXEC CHAIR	0129	50	0099	98	002	W	050	00002	01	000003000	011386	C	C
300000003	EXEC DESK	0449	00	0421	95	001	R	050	00002	04	000009999	011486	R	U
100000000	DESK LAMP	0035	00	0028	95	004	R	050	00011	14	000008888	011486	R	U
400000000	CREDENZA	0319	00	0291	90	001	R	050	00011	04	000007777	011486	R	P
222222222	EXEC CHAIR	0129	50	0099	98	001	W	050	00003	01	000001000	011486	C	U
300000000	L DESK	0325	00	0299	00	002	W	050	00003	01	000001000	011486	C	U
111111111	SECR CHAIR	0079	00	0060	00	004	R	050	00013	02	000007777	011486	R	P
111111222	SECR CHAIR	0099	00	0070	00	003	W	050	00012	02	000006666	011586	R	P
222222333	EXEC CHAIR	0159	00	0130	90	001	R	050	00002	01	000003000	011586	C	C
300000333	RECPT DESK	0419	00	0389	90	001	W	050	00011	14	000007777	011586	R	U
111111111	SECR CHAIR	0079	00	0060	00	002	R	050	00012	02	000002000	011586	C	C
111111222	SECR CHAIR	0099	00	0070	00	001	R	050	00012	02	000002000	011586	C	C
400000004	CREDENZA	0359	00	0331	95	001	R	050	00013	02	000002000	011586	C	C
500000000	BOOK SHELF	0139	00	0119	90	004	W	050	00011	14	000003000	011586	C	C
500000005	BOOK SHELF	0149	00	0129	95	006	W	050	00002	04	000007777	011586	R	U
300000003	EXEC DESK	0449	00	0421	95	002	W	050	00002	04	000009999	011586	R	U
222222444	EXEC CHAIR	0198	00	0149	90	002	R	050	00003	61	000008888	011586	R	U
111111111	SECR CHAIR	0079	00	0060	00	001	R	055	00011	14	000001000	011686	R	P
500000000	BOOK SHELF	0139	00	0119	90	001	W	055	00012	02	000008888	011686	R	P
222222222	EXEC CHAIR	0129	50	0099	98	002	R	055	00011	04	000009999	011686	C	U
300000333	RECPT DESK	0419	00	0389	90	002	R	055	00011	14	000001000	011686	R	P
300000003	EXEC DESK3	0449	00	0421	95	001	W	055	00012	02	000002000	011686	C	U
222222222	EXEC CHAIR	0129	50	0099	98	001	W	055	00013	02	000002000	011686	C	C
100000000	DESK LAMP	0035	00	0028	95	002	W	055	00011	04	000006000	011686	R	U
300000000	L DESK	0325	00	0299	00	002	R	055	00011	14	000007000	011686	C	C
300000003	EXEC DESK3	0449	00	0421	95	003	W	055	00002	01	000008000	011686	R	P
100000000	DESK LAMP	0035	00	0028	95	001	R	055	00012	02	000002000	011686	C	C

Figure F.3 Printer spacing chart for Exercise 1

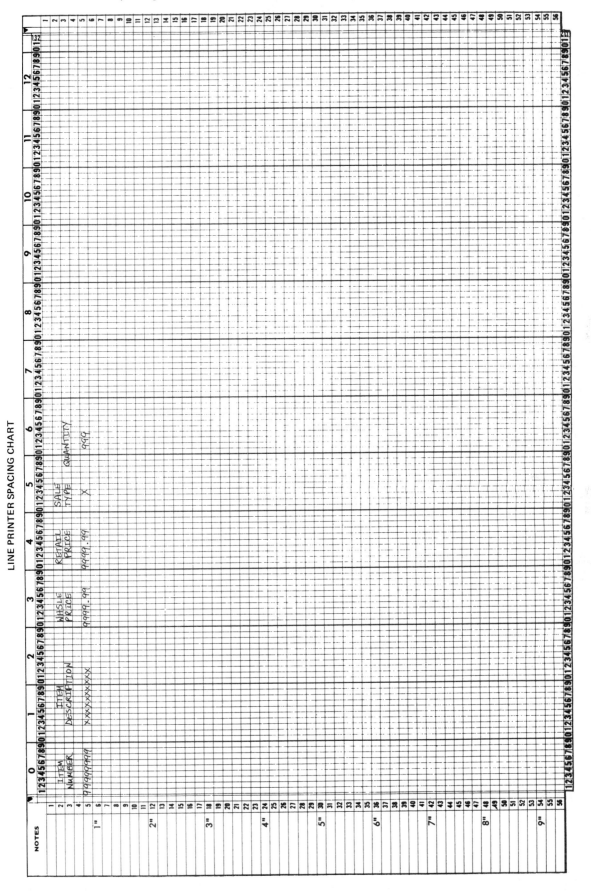

Figure F.4 Printer spacing chart for Exercise 3

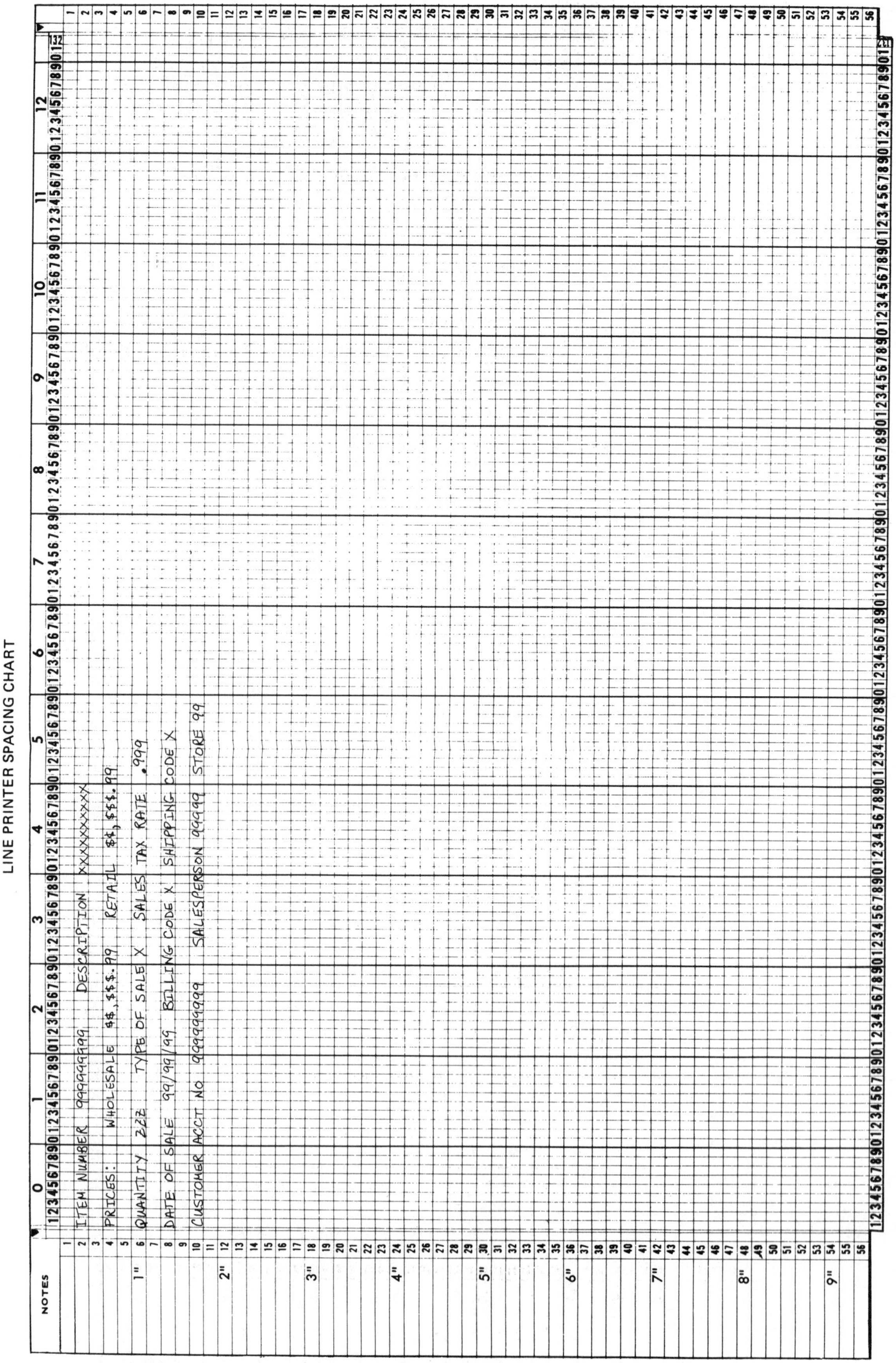

Figure F.5 Printer spacing chart for Exercise 4

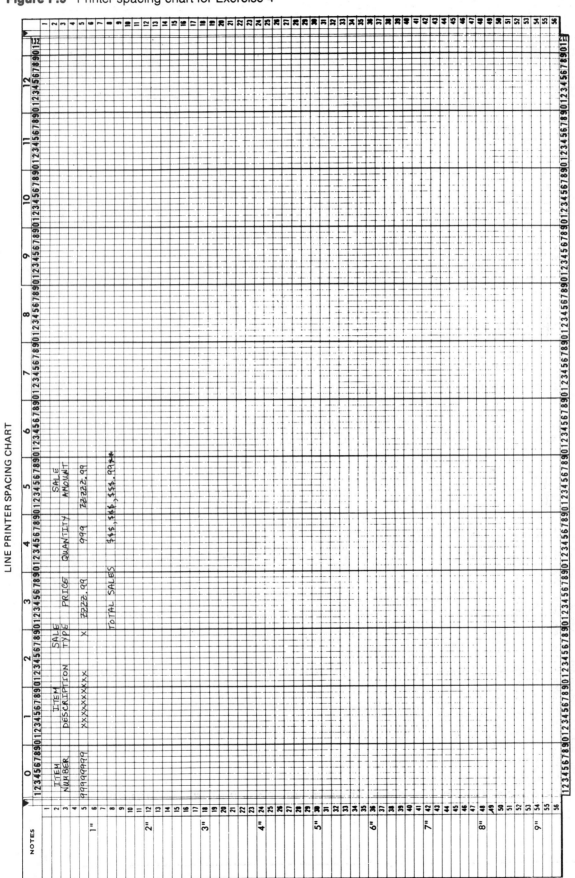

Figure F.6   Printer spacing chart for Exercise 5

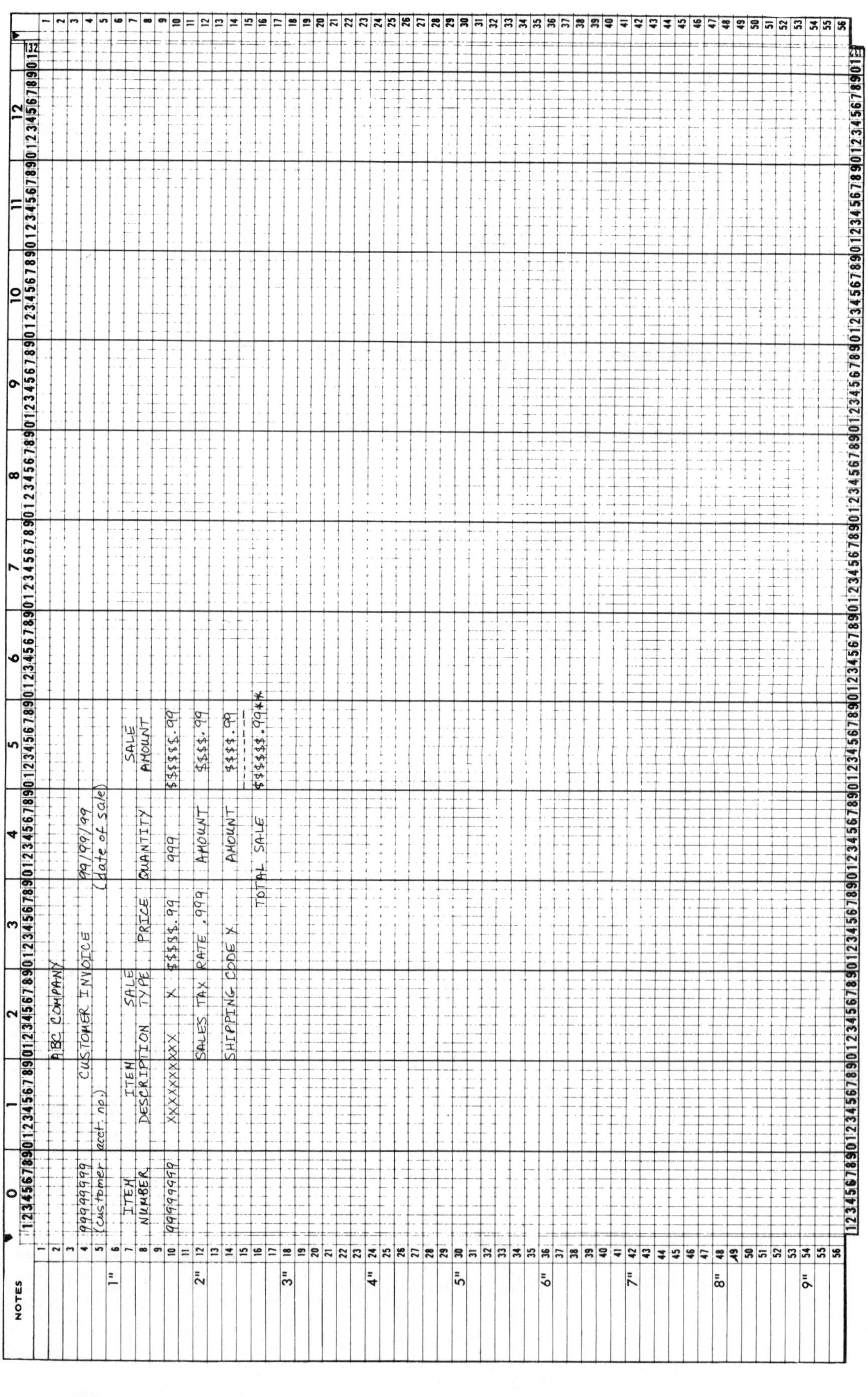

LINE PRINTER SPACING CHART

ABC COMPANY

CUSTOMER INVOICE

9999999
(customer acct. no.)

99/99/99
(date of sale)

ITEM	SALE		SALE
NUMBER	DESCRIPTION	TYPE	PRICE	QUANTITY	AMOUNT
9999999	XXXXXXXXXX	X	$$$$$.99	999	$$$$$$.99

SALES TAX RATE .999   AMOUNT $$$$.99

SHIPPING CODE X   AMOUNT $$$$.99

TOTAL SALE $$$$$$.99**

Figure F.7 Additional data for data validation program

Item Number	Item Description	Retail List Price	Wholesale List Price	Quantity	Type	Sales Tax Rate	Salesperson Identifier	Store Number	Customer Account Number	Date of Sale	Billing Code	Shipping Code	Comment
1111111	SECR CHAIR	0079 00	0060 00	002	W	055	00002	04	000004000	011786	C	P	Non-numeric item number
222222222		129 50	99 98	001	R	055	00011	01	000005000	011786	R	C	Missing item description, non-numeric prices
300000000	L DESK	0325 00	0299 00				00013	02	000005555	011786	C	C	Invalid quantity, type and sales tax rate
300000000	L DESK	0325 00	0299 00	001	R	055				011786	R	C	Invalid salesperson id, store number, cust. acct. no.
300000003	EXEC DESK3	0449 00	0421 95	001	W	055	00002	01	000001111	11786	R	C	Invalid date of sale
222222222	EXEC CHAIR	0129 00	0099 98	001	W	055	00002	01	000001111	011786			Invalid billing and shipping codes
A11111111		0079 00	0060 00	1		055	0000B	15	000001111	011786	C	U	Missing item description, non-numeric quantity, invalid store number

Figure F.8　Printer spacing chart for Exercise 8

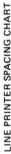

LINE PRINTER SPACING CHART

STORE	SALESPERSON	ITEM NUMBER	ITEM DESCRIPTION	SALE TYPE	PRICE	QUANTITY	AMOUNT	SALES TAX	SHIPPING	TOTAL SALE
							PAGE ZZ			
ABC COMPANY										
SALES REPORT										
99	99999	999999999	XXXXXXXXX	X	ZZZZ.99	999	ZZZZZ.99	ZZZ.99	ZZZ.99	ZZZZZ.99
	SALESPERSON TOTALS						ZZZZZZ.99	ZZZZ.99	ZZZZ.99	ZZZZZZ.99*
99	STORE TOTALS						ZZZZZZ.99	ZZZZ.99	ZZZZZ.99	ZZZZZZ.99**
99	GRAND TOTALS						ZZZZZZ.99	ZZZZ.99	ZZZZ.99	ZZZZZZ.99***

SUBSCRIPTION SYSTEM G

G.1 BACKGROUND

Amalgamated Publishing, Inc., publishes several specialized magazines and distributes them by mail to subscribers. The management wishes to implement a subscription system that would make use of the company's small business computer. The computer is currently used for accounting and payroll; it has both batch and interactive capabilities.

The purpose of the system is to keep track of subscribers–which magazines a subscriber is taking, expiration date for each subscription, amounts paid and owed. The system is also used to determine the number of magazines of each type to print for the production department, and to produce mailing labels for the mailing department. As the company advertises heavily on TV and has a tollfree number for subscribers, the subscription entry portion of the system is to be interactive. Most other portions of the system will be batch-oriented.

The company publishes the following magazines on a monthly basis:

Name	Code
Everyone's Computer	EC
You and Your Garden	YG
Suburban Family Life	SF
Farmer's Guide	FG

From time to time new magazines are added to the list and, rarely, magazines are dropped. The system should be designed to handle a maximum of ten titles. Some subscribers take more than one magazine.

Each subscriber is assigned a 17-character identifier, made up of

Positions	Content
1-5	Zip code
6-11	First 6 characters of street address (with any spaces removed)
12-15	First 4 characters of last name
16-17	Magazine code

Example

John Jones, 123 Maple Street, Anywhere, CA, 00576, who subscribes to *You and Your Garden*, would have as his identifier:

```
 Zip        Last
Code Address Name Magazine
   \    |     |    /
00576123MAPJONEYG
```

The purpose of this identifier is to facilitate retrieval of data as well as production of mailing labels and required reports.

G.2 THE SYSTEM

Two files make up the heart of the system:

Magazine Master File
Subscription Master File

The Magazine Master File is a sequential file containing one record for each magazine published by the company. Each record contains the following fields:

Positions	Content	COBOL Description
1-2	Magazine code	X(2)
3-20	Magazine title	X(18)
21-24	Subscription rate 6 mo.	99V99
25-28	Subscription rate 12 mo.	99V99
29-32	Subscription rate 24 mo.	99V99
33-36	Extra production quantity	9999

The Subscription Master File is an indexed file and contains one record for each subscription. Each record contains the following fields:

Positions	Content	COBOL Description
1-17	Subscription identifier	X(17)
18-30	Subscriber name	X(13)
31-45	Street address	X(15)
46-54	City	X(9)
55-56	State	X(2)
57-60	Subscription date (*mmyy*)	9(4)
61-64	Expiration date (*mmyy*)	9(4)
65-68	Subscription amount	99V99

Positions	Content	COBOL Description
69-69	Billing code	9
70-75	Date of last payment (*mmddyy*)	9(6)
76-79	Total amount paid	99V99
80-80	Payment type	9
	0 No payment received	
	1 Check	
	2 VISA	
	3 Master card	
	4 Returned check	

The system may be divided into five subsystems:

- Magazine Master File Maintenance
- Subscription Master File Maintenance
- Billing and Payment Accounting
- Production and Shipping
- Management Information

Each of the subsystems is described in more detail below.

Magazine Master File Maintenance

A program is needed to perform file maintenance operations–add, change, and delete–on the Magazine Master File. Because the file is sequential and not all of the operations can be made in place, this program will be batch-oriented. The system flowchart for this subsystem is shown in Figure G.1.

Figure G.1   Magazine master file maintenance subsystem

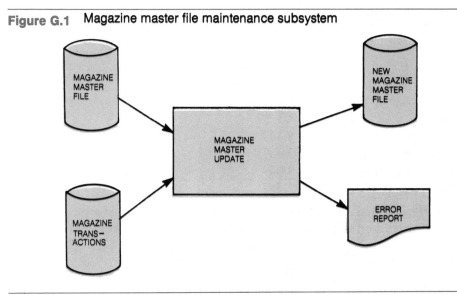

Subscription Master File Maintenance

An interactive program is needed to perform file maintenance operations–add, change, and delete–on the Subscription Master File. This program would be used routinely by personnel who take phoned-in subscriptions and by others who process mailed-in subscriptions and answer inquiries from subscribers. The system flowchart for this portion of the subscription system is shown in Figure G.2.

Billing and Payment Accounting

After a subscription is entered into the system, a bill is sent to the subscriber. This is accomplished in the system by running a program periodically that will generate bills for new subscribers. This program will scan the Subscription Master File for new subscribers, as determined by the Billing Code field; when a bill is produced, the billing code field is updated. This program also produces past-due notices when appropriate.

When payment is received from a subscriber, the appropriate master file record must be updated. Occasionally subscribers' checks are returned; the master file record must be modified accordingly. Payment accounting will be accomplished using an interactive program.

The system flowchart for the billing and payment accounting subsystem is shown in Figure G.3.

Production and Shipping

Amalgamated Publishing contracts with a local printer to print its magazines each month. The printed magazines are returned to Amalgamated's shipping department, which attaches mailing labels.

Because the subscriber base is growing rapidly, the quantities produced must be updated monthly. The subscription system must have a program that determines the number of subscribers for each magazine. The program should add an extra number for wastage, free copies, internal use and promotion.

Mailing labels are a very important product of the subscription system. The labels must be produced for each magazine in zip-code order to comply with post office regulations. In order to do this, the subscription master file must be sorted into the required sequence before mailing labels are printed.

A system flowchart for the Production and Shipping subsystem is shown in Figure G.4.

Management Information

Management of Amalgamated Publishing requires various reports that are used to monitor the ongoing operation of the company. Among the required reports are:

Subscription Activity Report
This report lists new subscribers for each magazine by length of subscription. The report is produced as a batch job and is routinely run once a month to summarize data for that month.

Aged Accounts Receivable Report
This report lists each account with a balance due and summarizes the data according to the time elapsed since receiving a payment of the account. This report is produced as a batch job once a month.

A system flowchart for this subsystem is shown in Figure G.5.

Figure G.2 Subscription master file maintenance subsystem

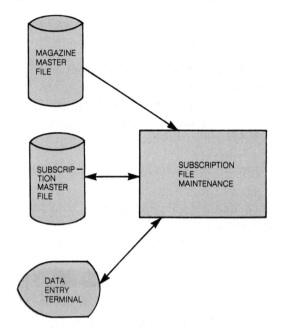

Figure G.3 Billing and payment accounting subsystem

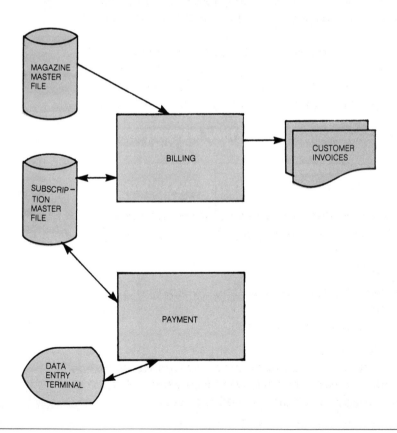

Figure G.4 Production and shipping subsystem

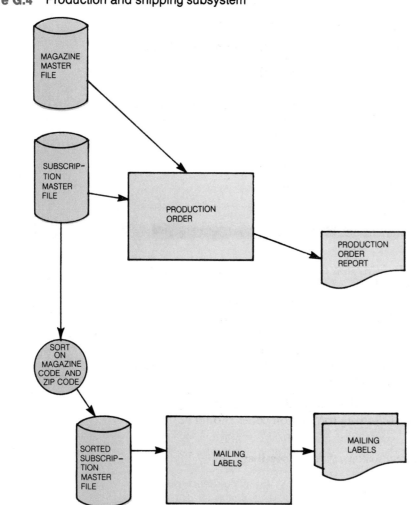

Figure G.5 Management information subsystem

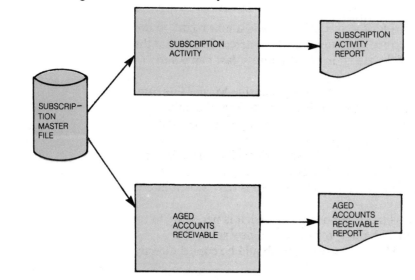

G.3 PROGRAMMING EXERCISES

1. Write a program to perform the Magazine Master Update described in Figure G.1. Record layout for the Magazine Transaction File is as follows:

Positions	Content	COBOL Description
1-2	Magazine code	X(2)
3-20	Magazine title	X(18)
21-24	Subscription rate 6 mo.	99V99
25-28	Subscription rate 12 mo.	99V99
29-32	Subscription rate 24 mo.	99V99
33-36	Extra production	9999
37	Transaction code	X
	A: Add record to file	
	C: Change content of a field	
	D: Delete record from file	

For change transactions, only fields that do not contain spaces should be changed.

Your program should permit multiple transaction types for a given record (i.e., add, change and delete for one magazine in a cycle should be permitted if the transaction records are in this sequence) and multiple change records for one magazine. Be sure to test your program with sufficient invalid transactions and sequences of transactions and to exercise all error messages contained in the program.

2. Write a program to perform the Subscription File Maintenance function described in Figure G.2. The following transaction codes should be implemented:

D   Display content of a record for a given subscriber.
L   List all records in Subscriber Master File.
A   Add a subscription.
K   Delete a subscription.
C   Change address.
E   Extend expiration date for subscription.

Notes

a. In order to access a record for the subscriber or add a new record to the file, all parts of the subscriber identifier must be entered. Recall that the identifier is comprised of the zip code, street address, last name and magazine code.

b. The program should load the content of the Magazine Master File into a table and look up data regarding subscription costs from that table.

c. When a subscription is added to the file, the subscription date should be the current month and year. The expiration date should be computed from the subscription term chosen by the subscriber. The subscription amount should be copied from the table described in Note b above. Positions 69 to 80 should be zeros when the record is first written into the file.

d. When a change of address transaction is processed, it is necessary to delete the old record and add a new record with a new subscriber identifier. Positions 57 to 80 of the new record should be copied directly from the old record.

e. In order to extend the expiration date for a subscription, the term of the subscription should be added to the old expiration date. The subscription amount and other fields should be treated as for a new record. Do not permit a subscription that has a balance due to be extended.

f. The transaction code L should permit a display of records either at the terminal or on the printer.

3. Write a program to perform the billing function described in Figure G.3. Only one invoice should be sent to a given subscriber no matter how many magazines he or she subscribes to. Each entry on the invoice should list the subscription date, expiration date, magazine name (in full), subscription amount, amount paid and balance due. (For an existing subscription, the balance due is the difference between the subscription amount and the total amount paid. For a new subscription, the balance due is the subscription amount.) For an item included in an invoice, add 1 to the billing code in the subscription record. (This field is used to determine how long the account has had an outstanding balance.) Each invoice should contain the customer's name, address, and totals in an appropriate format.

Notes

a. Only new subscriptions and subscriptions for which there is an outstanding balance should be included in an invoice. Paid customers should not receive an invoice.

b. Your program should load the content of the Magazine Master File into a table and look up the full magazine name for an invoice entry as required.

4. Write a program to perform the payment function described in Figure G.3. The program must be interactive and allow the following types of transactions.

D   Display a subscription record.
P   Payment; update a record to reflect payment on account.
R   Returned check; update a record as appropriate.

Notes

a. A payment transaction should cause the amount paid to be added to the total amount paid. The date of the last payment should be changed to the current date, and the payment-type field should be updated as appropriate.

b. A returned check transaction should cause the amount of the check to be deducted from the total amount paid. The payment-type field should be changed to "4".

5. Write a program to perform the production order function described in Figure G.4. The production order report should list the full name of each magazine, the actual number of subscribers, the number of copies to be added and the total production to be ordered.

Note

The content of the Magazine Master File should be loaded into a table and used as a reference to determine the full name of the magazine and added production amount.

6. Write a program to perform the sort on magazine code and zip code function described in Figure G.4. Your program should transform the indexed Subscription Master File into the sequential sorted Subscription Master File, which contains records only for nonexpired subscriptions and which is in sequence by magazine code (primary key) and zip code (secondary key).

7. Write a program to perform the mailing labels function described in Figure G.4. The mailing label should contain the name, full address, subscription identifier and subscription expiration date.

   Note

   If you have access to actual fanfold mailing labels and can construct an appropriate carriage control tape for your printer, this exercise can be made quite realistic.

8. Write a program to perform the subscription activity function described in Figure G.5. The required report should list all new subscriptions entered during the current month and should produce totals for each magazine, as well as grand totals of appropriate fields.

   Note

   Try to put yourself in the manager's position as you design this report. Include as much detail as seems desirable.

9. Write a program to perform the Aged Accounts Receivable function described in Figure G.5. The report should list each account that has a balance due and show whether the account is current (less than 30 days old), 30 to 60 days old, or over 90 days old. Relevant totals should be produced for each magazine and for all magazines. (See Note for Exercise 8.)

10. Modify the organization of the Magazine Master File to a Randomized Relative file. Write Magazine Master Update program that is interactive rather than batch, as in Exercise 1. Revise other programs in the system as required to process the file in its new form, including:

    Subscription File Maintenance
    Billing
    Production Order

GLOSSARY

INTRODUCTION

The terms in this chapter are defined in accordance with their meaning as used in this document describing COBOL and may not have the same meaning for other languages.

These definitions are also intended to be either reference material or introductory material to be reviewed prior to reading the detailed language specifications that follow. For this reason, these definitions are, in most instances, brief and do not include detailed syntactical rules.

DEFINITIONS

Abbreviated Combined Relation Condition.   The combined condition that results from the explicit omission of a common subject or a common subject and common relational operator in a consecutive sequence of relation conditions.

Access Mode.   The manner in which records are to be operated upon within a file.

Actual Decimal Point.   The physical representation, using either of the decimal point characters period (.) or comma (,) of the decimal point position in a data item.

Alphabet-Name.   A user-defined word, in the SPECIAL NAMES paragraph of the Environment Division, that assigns a name to a specific character set and/or collating sequence.

Alphabetic Character.   A character that belongs to the following set of letters: A, B, C, D, E, F, G, H, I, J, K, L, M, N, O, P, Q, R, S, T, U, V, W, X, Y, Z, and the space.

Alphanumeric Character. Any character in the computer's character set.

Alternate Record Key. A key, other than the prime record key, whose contents identify a record within an indexed file.

Arithmetic Expression. An arithmetic expression can be an identifier or a numeric elementary item, a numeric literal, such identifiers and literals separated by arithmetic operators, two arithmetic expressions separated by an arithmetic operator, or an arithmetic expression enclosed in parentheses.

Arithmetic Operator. A single character, or a fixed two-character combination that belongs to the following set:

Character	Meaning
+	addition
−	subtraction
*	multiplication
/	division
**	exponentiation

Ascending Key. A key upon the values of which data is ordered starting with the lowest value of key up to the highest value of key in accordance with the rules for comparing data items.

Assumed Decimal Point. A decimal point position which does not involve the existence of an actual character in a data item. The assumed decimal point has logical meaning but no physical representation.

At End Condition. A condition caused:

1) During the execution of a READ statement for sequentially accessed
   file.
2) During the execution of a RETURN statement, when no next logical record exists for the associated sort or merge file.
3) During the execution of a SEARCH statement, when the search operation terminates without satisfying the condition specified in any of the associated WHEN phrases.

Block. A physical unit of data that is normally composed of one or more logical records. For mass storage files, a block may contain a portion of a logical record. The size of a block has no direct relationship to the size of the file within which contains the block or to the size of the logical record(s) that are either continued within the block or that overlap the block. The term is synonymous with physical record.

Body Group. Generic name for a report group of TYPE DETAIL, CONTROL HEADING or CONTROL FOOTING.

Called Program. A program which is the object of a CALL statement combined at object time with the calling program to produce a run unit.

Calling Program. A program which executes a CALL to another program.

Cd-Name. A user-defined word that names an MCS interface area described in a communication description entry within the Communication Section of the Data Division.

Character. The basic indivisible unit of the language.

Character Position. A character position is the amount of physical storage required to store a single standard data format character described as usage is DISPLAY. Further characteristics of the physical storage are defined by the implementor.

Character-String. A sequence of contiguous characters which form a COBOL word, a literal, a PICTURE character-string, or a comment-entry.

Class Condition. The proposition, for which a truth value can be determined, that the content of an item is wholly alphabetic or is wholly numeric.

Clause. A clause is an ordered set of consecutive COBOL character-strings whose purpose is to specify an attribute of an entry.

COBOL Character Set. The complete COBOL character set consists of the 51 characters listed below:

Character	Meaning
0, 1, ... 9	digit
A, B, ... Z	letter
	space (blank)
+	plus sign
−	minus sign
*	asterisk
/	stroke (virgule, slash)
=	equal sign
$	currency sign
,	comma (decimal point)
;	semicolon
.	period (decimal point)
'	quotation mark
(	left parenthesis
)	right parenthesis
>	greater than symbol
<	less than symbol

COBOL Word. (See Word)

Collating Sequence. The sequence in which the characters that are acceptable in a computer are ordered for purposes of sorting, merging, and comparing.

Column. A character position within a print line. The columns are numbered from 1, by 1, starting at the leftmost character position of the print line and extending to the rightmost position of the print line.

Combined Condition. A condition that is the result of connecting two or more conditions with the AND or the OR logical operator.

Comment-Entry. An entry in the Identification Division that may be any combination of characters from the computer character set.

Comment Line. A source program line represented by an asterisk in the indicator area of the line and any characters from the computer's character set in area A and area B of that line. The comment line serves only for documentation in a program. A special form of comment line represented by a stroke (/) in the indicator area of the line and any characters from the computer's character set in area A and area B of that line causes page ejection prior to printing the comment.

Communication Description Entry. An entry in the Communication Section of the Data Division that is composed of the level indicator CD, followed by a cd-name, and then followed by a set of clauses as required. It describes the interface between the Message Control System (MCS) and the COBOL program.

Communication Device. A mechanism (hardware or hardware/software) capable of sending data to a queue and/or receiving data from a queue. This mechanism may be a computer or a peripheral device. One or more programs containing communication description entries and residing within the same computer define one or more of these mechanisms.

Communication Section. The section of the Data Division that describes the interface areas between the MCS and the program, composed of one or more CD description entries.

Compiling Time. The time at which a COBOL source program is translated, by a COBOL compiler, to a COBOL object program.

Compiler Directing Statement. A statement, beginning with a compiler directing verb, that causes the compiler to take a specific action during compilation.

Complex Condition. A condition in which one or more logical operators act upon one or more conditions. (See Negated Simple Condition, Combined Condition, Negated Combined Condition.)

Computer-Name. A system-name that identifies the computer upon which the program is to be compiled or run.

Condition. A status of a program at execution time for which a truth value can be determined. Where the term "condition" (condition-1, condition-2, . . .) appears in these language specifications in or in reference to "condition" (condition-1, condition-2, . . .) of general format, it is a conditional expression consisting of either a simple condition optionally parenthesized, or a combined condition consisting of the syntactically correct combination of simple conditions, logical operators, and parentheses, for which a truth value can be determined.

Condition-Name. A user-defined word assigned to a specific value, set of values, or range of values, within the complete set of values that a conditional variable may possess; or the user-defined word assigned to a status of an implementor-defined switch or device.

Condition-Name Condition. The proposition, for which a truth value can be determined, that the value of a conditional variable is a member of the set of values attributed to a condition-name associated with the conditional variable.

Conditional Expression. A simple condition or a complex condition specified in an IF, PERFORM, or SEARCH statement. (See Simple Condition and Complex Condition.)

Conditional Statement. A conditional statement specifies that the truth value of a condition is to be determined and that the subsequent action of the object program is dependent on this truth value.

Conditional Variable. A data item one or more values of which has a condition-name assigned to it.

Configuration Section. A section of the Environment Division that describes overall specifications of source and object computers.

Connective. A reserved word that is used to:

1) Associate a data-name, paragraph-name, condition-name, or text-name with its qualifier.
2) Link two or more operands written in a series.
3) Form conditions (logical connectives). (See Logical Operator.)

Contiguous Items. Items that are described by consecutive entries in the Data Division, and that bear a definite hierarchic relationship to each other.

Control Break. A change in the value of a data item that is referenced in the CONTROL clause. More generally, a change in the value of a data item that is used to control the hierarchical structure of a report.

Control Break Level. The relative position within a control hierarchy at which the most major control break occurred.

Control Data Item. A data item, a change in whose contents may produce a control break.

Control Data-Name. A data-name that appears in a CONTROL clause and refers to a control data item.

Control Footing. A report group that is presented at the end of the control group of which it is a member.

Control Group. A set of body groups that is presented for a given value of a control data item or of FINAL. Each control group may begin with a CONTROL HEADING, end with a CONTROL FOOTING, and contain DETAIL report groups.

Control Heading. A report group that is presented at the beginning of the control group of which it is a member.

Control Hierarchy. A designated sequence of report subdivisions defined by the positional order of FINAL and the data-names within a CONTROL clause.

Counter. A data item used for storing numbers or number representations in a manner that permits these numbers to be increased or decreased by the value of another number, or to be changed or reset to zero or to an arbitrary positive or negative value.

Currency Sign. The character "$" of the COBOL character set.

Currency Symbol. The character defined by the CURRENCY SIGN clause in the SPECIAL-NAMES paragraph. If no CURRENCY SIGN is present in a COBOL source program, the currency symbol is identical to the currency sign.

Current Record. The record which is available in the record area associated with the file.

Current Record Pointer. A conceptual entity that is used in the selection of the next record.

Data Clause. A clause that appears in a data description entry in the Data Division and provides information describing a particular attribute of a data item.

Data Description Entry. An entry in the Data Division that is composed of a level-number followed by a data-name if required, and then followed by a set of data clauses as required.

Data Item. A character or a set of contiguous characters (excluding literals) defined as a unit of data by the COBOL program.

Data-Name. A user-defined word that names a data item described in data description entry in the Data Division. When used in the general formats, "data-name" represents a word which can neither be subscripted, indexed, nor qualified unless specifically permitted by the rules for that format.

Debugging Line. A debugging line is any line with "D" in the indicator area of the line.

Debugging Section. A debugging section is a section that contains a USE FOR DEBUGGING statement.

Declaratives. A set of one or more special purpose sections, written at the beginning of the Procedure Division, the first of which is preceded by the key word DECLARATIVES and the last of which is followed by the key words END DECLARATIVES. A declarative is composed of a section header, followed by a USE compiler directing sentence, followed by a set of zero, one or more associated paragraphs.

Declarative-Sentence. A compiler-directing sentence consisting of a single USE statement terminated by the separator period.

Delimiter. A character or a sequence of contiguous characters that identify the end of a string of characters and separates that string of characters from the following string of characters. A delimiter is not part of the string of characters that it delimits.

Descending Key. A key upon the values of which data is ordered starting with the highest value of key down to the lowest value of key, in accordance with the rules for comparing data items.

Destination. The symbolic identification of the receiver of a transmission from a queue.

Digit Position. A digit position is the amount of physical storage required to store a single digit. This amount may vary depending on the usage of the data item describing the digit position. Further characteristics of the physical storage are defined by the implementor.

Division.   A set of zero, one or more sections of paragraphs, called the division body, that are formed and combined in accordance with a specific set of rules. There are four (4) divisions in a COBOL program: Identification, Environment, Data and Procedure.

Division Header.   A combination of words followed by a period and a space that indicates that beginning of a division. The division headers are:

IDENTIFICATION DIVISION.
ENVIRONMENT DIVISION.
DATA DIVISION.
PROCEDURE DIVISION [USING data-name-1 [data-name-2]. . .].

Dynamic Access.   An access mode in which specific logical records can be obtained from or placed into a mass storage file in a non-sequential manner (see Random Access) and obtained from a file in a sequential manner (see Sequential Access), during the scope of the same OPEN statement.

Editing Character.   A single character or a fixed two-character combination belonging to the following set:

Character	Meaning
B	space
0	zero
+	plus
−	minus
CR	credit
DB	debit
Z	zero suppress
*	check protect
$	currency
,	comma (decimal point)
.	period (decimal point)
/	stroke (virgule, slash)

Elementary Item.   A data item that is described as not being further logically subdivided.

End of Procedure Division.   The physical position in a COBOL source program after which no further procedures appear.

Entry.   Any descriptive set of consecutive clauses terminated by a period and written in the Identification Division, Environment Division, or Data Division of a COBOL source program.

Environment Clause.   A clause that appears as part of an Environment Division entry.

Execution Time.   (See Object Time.)

Extend Mode.   The state of a file after execution of an OPEN statement, with the EXTEND phrase specified, for that file and before the execution of a CLOSE statement for that file.

Figurative Constant. A compiler generated value referenced through the use of certain reserved words.

File. A collection of records.

File Clause. A clause that appears as part of any of the following Data Division entries:

File description (FD)
Sort-merge file description (SD)
Communication description (CD)

FILE-CONTROL. The name of an Environment Division paragraph in which the data files for a given source program are declared.

File Description Entry. An entry in the File Section of the Data Division that is composed of the level indicator FD, followed by a file-name, and then followed by a set of file clauses as required.

File-Name. A user-defined word that names a file described in a file description entry or a sort-merge file description entry within the File Section of the Data Division.

File Organization. The permanent logical file structure established at the time that a file is created.

File Section. The section of the Data Division that contains file description entries and sort-merge file description entries together with their associated record descriptions.

Format. A specific arrangement of a set of data.

Group Item. A named contiguous set of elementary or group items.

High Order End. The leftmost character of a string of characters.

I-O CONTROL. The name of an Environment Division paragraph in which object program requirements for specific input-output techniques, rerun points, sharing of same areas by several data files, and multiple file storage on a single input-output device are specified.

I-O Mode. The state of a file after execution of an OPEN statement, with the I-O phrase specified, for that file and before the execution of a CLOSE statement for that file.

Identifier. A data-name, followed as required, by the syntactically correct combination of qualifiers, subscripts, and indices necessary to make unique reference to a data item.

Imperative Statement. A statement that begins with an imperative verb and specifies an unconditional action to be taken. An imperative statement may consist of a sequence of imperative statements.

Implementor-Name. A system-name that refers to a particular feature available on that implementor's computing system.

Index. A computer storage position or register, the contents of which represent the identification of a particular element in a table.

Index Data Item. A data item in which the value associated with an index-name can be stored in a form specified by the implementor.

Index-Name. A user-defined word that names an index associated with a specific table.

Indexed Data-Name. An identifier that is composed of a data-name, followed by one or more index-names enclosed in parentheses.

Indexed File. A file with indexed organization.

Indexed Organization. The permanent logical file structure in which each record is identified by the value of one or more keys within that record.

Input File. A file that is opened in the input mode.

Input Mode. The state of a file after execution of an OPEN statement, with the INPUT phrase specified, for that file and before the execution of a CLOSE statement for that file.

Input-Output File. A file that is opened in the I-O mode.

Input-Output Section. The section of the Environment Division that names the files and the external media required by an object program and which provides information required for transmission and handling of data during execution of the object program.

Input Procedure. A set of statements that is executed each time a record is released to the sort file.

Integer. A numeric literal or a numeric data item that does not include any character positions to the right of the assumed decimal point. Where the term "integer" appears in general formats, integer must not be a numeric data item, and must not be signed, nor zero unless explicitly allowed by the rules of that format.

Invalid Key Condition. A condition, at object time, caused when a specific value of the key associated with an indexed or relative file is determined to be invalid.

Key. A data item which identifies the location of a record, or a set of data items which serve to identify the ordering of data.

Key of Reference. The key, either prime or alternate, currently being used to access records within an indexed file.

Key Word. A reserved word whose presence is required when the format in which the word appears is used in a source program.

Language-Name. A system-name that specifies a particular programming language.

Level Indicator. Two alphabetic characters that identify a specific type of file or a position hierarchy.

Level-Number. A user-defined word which indicates the position of a data item in the hierarchical structure of a logical record or which indicates special properties of a data description entry. A level-number is expressed as a one or two digit number. Level-numbers in the range 1 through 49 indicate the position of a data item in the hierarchical structure of a logical record. Level-numbers in the range 1 through 9 may be written either as a single digit or as a zero followed by a significant digit. Level-numbers 66, 77, and 88 identify special properties of a data description entry.

Library-Name. A user-defined word that names a COBOL library that is to be used by the compiler for a given source program compilation.

Library Text. A sequence of character-strings and/or separators in a COBOL library.

Line. (See Report Line.)

Line Number. An integer that denotes the vertical position of a report line on a page.

Linkage Section. The section in the Data Division of the called program that describes data items available from the calling program. These data items may be referred to by both the calling and called program.

Literal. A character-string whose value is implied by the ordered set of characters comprising the string.

Logical Operator. One of the reserved words AND, OR, or NOT. In the formation of a condition, both or either of AND and OR can be used as logical connectives. NOT can be used for logical negation.

Logical Record. The most inclusive data item. The level-number for a record is 01. (See Report Writer Logical Record.)

Low Order End. The rightmost character of a string of characters.

Mass Storage. A storage medium on which data may be organized and maintained in both a sequential and nonsequential manner.

Mass Storage Control System (MSCS). An input-output control system that directs or controls the processing of mass storage files.

Mass Storage File. A collection of records that is assigned to a mass storage medium.

MCS. (See Message Control System.)

Merge File. A collection of records to be merged by a MERGE statement. The merge file is created and can be used only by the merge function.

Message. Data associated with an end of message indicator or an end of group indicator. (See Message Indicators)

Message Control System (MCS). A communication control system that supports the processing of messages.

Message Count. The count of the number of complete messages that exist in the designated queue of messages.

Message Indicators. EGI (end of group indicator), EMI (end of message indicator), and ESI (end of segment indicator) are conceptual indications that serve to notify the MCS that a specific condition exists (end of group, end of message, end of segment).

Within the hierarchy of EGI, EMI, an ESI, an EGI is conceptually equivalent to an ESI, EMI, and EGI. An EMI is conceptually equivalent to an ESI and EMI. Thus, a segment may be terminated by an ESI, EMI, or EGI. A message may be terminated by an EMI or EGI.

Message Segment. Data that forms a logical subdivision of a message normally associated with an end of segment indicator. (See Message Indicators.)

Mnemonic-Name. A user-defined word that is associated in the Environment Division with a specified implementor-name.

MSCS. (See Mass Storage Control System.)

Native Character Set. The implementor-defined character set associated with the computer specified in the OBJECT-COMPUTER paragraph.

Native Collating Sequence. The implementor-defined collating sequence associated with the computer specified in the OBJECT-COMPUTER paragraph.

Negated Combined Condition. The 'NOT' logical operator immediately followed by a parenthesized combined condition.

Negated Simple Condition. The 'NOT' logical operator immediately followed by a simple condition.

Next Executable Sentence. The next sentence to which control will be transferred after execution of the current statement is complete.

Next Executable Statement. The next statement to which control will be transferred after execution of the current statement is complete.

Next Record. The record which logically follows the current record of a file.

Noncontiguous Items. Elementary data items, in the Working-Storage and Linkage Sections, which bear no hierarchic relationship to other data items.

Nonnumeric Item. A data item whose description permits its contents to be composed of any combination of characters taken from the computer's character set. Certain categories of nonnumeric items may be formed from more restricted character sets.

Nonnumeric Literal. A character-string bounded by quotation marks. The string of characters may include any character in the computer's character set. To represent a single quotation mark character within a nonnumeric literal, two contiguous quotation marks must be used.

Numeric Character. A character that belongs to the following set of digits: 0, 1, 2, 3, 4, 5, 6, 7, 8, 9.

Numeric Item. A data item whose description restricts its contents to a value represented by characters chosen from the digits "0" through "9"; if signed, the item may also contain a "+", "−", or other representation of an operational sign.

Numeric Literal. A literal composed of one or more numeric characters that also may contain either a decimal point, or an algebraic sign, or both. The decimal point must not be the rightmost character. The algebraic sign, if present, must be the leftmost character.

OBJECT-COMPUTER. The name of an Environment Division paragraph in which the computer environment, within which the object program is executed, is described.

Object of Entry. A set of operands and reserved words, within a Data Division entry, that immediately follows the subject of the entry.

Object Program. A set or group of executable machine language instruction and other material designed to interact with data to provide problem solutions. In this context, an object program is generally the machine language result of the operation of a COBOL compiler on a source program. Where there is no danger of ambiguity, the word "program" alone may be used in place of the phrase "object program."

Object Time. The time at which an object program is executed.

Open Mode. The state of a file after execution of an OPEN statement for that file and before the execution of a CLOSE statement for that file. The particular open mode is specified in the OPEN statement as either INPUT, OUTPUT, I-O or EXTEND.

Operand. Whereas the general definition of operand is "that component which is operated upon," for the purposes of this publication, any lowercase word (or words) that appears in a statement or entry format may be considered to be an operand and, as such, is an implied reference to the data indicated by the operand.

Operational Sign. An algebraic sign, associated with a numeric data item or a numeric literal, to indicate whether its value is positive or negative.

Optional Word. A reserved word that is included in a specific format only to improve the readability of the language and whose presence is optional to the user when the format in which the word appears is used in a source program.

Output File. A file that is opened in either the output mode or extend mode.

Output Mode. The state of a file after execution of an OPEN statement, with the OUTPUT or EXTEND phrase specified, for that file and before the execution of a CLOSE statement for that file.

Output Procedure. A set of statements to which control is given during execution of a SORT statement after the sort function is completed, or during execution of a MERGE statement after the merge function has selected the next record in a merged order.

Page. A vertical division of a report representing a physical separation of report data, the separation being based on internal reporting requirements and/or external characteristics of the reporting medium.

Page Body. That part of the logical page in which lines can be written and/or spaced.

Page Footing. A report group that is presented at the end of a report page as determined by the Report Writer Control System.

Page Heading. A report group that is presented at the beginning of a report page and determined by the Report Writer Control System.

Paragraph. In the Procedure Division, a paragraph-named followed by a period and a space and by zero one, or more sentences. In the Identification and Environment Divisions, a paragraph header followed by zero, one, or more entries.

Paragraph Header. A reserved word, followed by a period and a space that indicates the beginning of a paragraph in the Identification and Environment Divisions. The permissible paragraph headers are:

In the Identification Division:
PROGRAM-ID.
AUTHOR.
INSTALLATION.
DATE-WRITTEN.
DATE-COMPILED.
SECURITY.

In the Environment Division:
SOURCE-COMPUTER.
OBJECT-COMPUTER.
SPECIAL-NAMES.
FILE-CONTROL.
I-O-CONTROL.

Paragraph-Name. A user-defined word that identifies and begins a paragraph in the Procedure Division.

Phrase. A phrase is an ordered set of one or more consecutive COBOL character-strings that form a portion of a COBOL procedural statement or of a COBOL clause.

Physical Record. (See Block.)

Prime Record Key. A key whose contents uniquely identify a record within an indexed file.

Printable Group. A report group that contains at least one print line.

Printable Item. A data item, the extent and contents of which are specified by an elementary report entry. This elementary report entry contains a COLUMN NUMBER clause, a PICTURE clause, and a SOURCE, SUM or VALUE clause.

Procedure. A paragraph or group of logically successive paragraphs, or a section or group of logically successive sections, within the Procedure Division.

Procedure-Name. A user-defined word which is used to name a paragraph or section in the Procedure Division. It consists of a paragraph-name (which may be qualified), or a section-name.

Program-Name. A user-defined word that identifies a COBOL source program.

Pseudo-text. A sequence of character-strings and/or separators bounded by, but not including, pseudo-text delimiters.

Pseudo-text Delimiter. Two contiguous equal sign (=) characters used to delimit pseudo-text.

Punctuation Character.   A character that belongs to the following set:

Character	Meaning
,	comma
;	semicolon
.	period
"	quotation mark
(	left parenthesis
)	right parenthesis
	space
=	equal sign

Qualified Data-Name.   An identifier that is composed of a data-name followed by one or more sets of either of the connectives OF and IN followed by a data-name qualifier.

Qualifier

1) A data-name which is used in a reference together with another data-name at a lower level in the same hierarchy.
2) A section-name which is used in a reference together with a paragraph-name specified in that section.
3) A library-name which is used in a reference together with a text-name associated with that library.

Queue.   A logical collection of messages awaiting transmission or processing.

Queue Name.   A symbolic name that indicates to the MCS the logical path by which a message or a portion of a completed message may be accessible in a queue.

Random Access.   An access mode in which the program-specified value of a key data item identifies the logical record that is obtained from, deleted from or placed into a relative or indexed file.

Record.   (See Logical Record.)

Record Area.   A storage area allocated for the purpose of processing the record described in a record description entry in the File Section.

Record Description.   (See Record Description Entry.)

Record Description Entry.   The total set of data description entries associated with a particular record.

Record Key.   A key, either the prime record key or an alternate record key, whose contents identify a record within an indexed file.

Record-Name.   A user-defined word that names a record described in a record description entry in the Data Division.

Reference Format.   A format that provides a standard method for describing COBOL source programs.

Relation.   (See Relational Operator.)

Relation Character. A character that belongs to the following set:

Character	Meaning
>	greater than
<	less than
=	equal to

Relation Condition. The proposition, for which a truth value can be determined, that the value of an arithmetic expression or data item has a specific relationship to the value of another arithmetic expression or data item. (See Relational Operator.)

Relational Operator. A reserved word, a relation character, a group of consecutive reserved words, or a group of consecutive reserved words and relation characters used in the construction of a relation condition. The permissible operators and their meanings are:

Relational Operator	Meaning
IS [NOT] GREATER THAN IS [NOT] >	Greater than or not greater than
IS [NOT] LESS THAN IS [NOT] <	Less than or not less than
IS [NOT] EQUAL TO IS [NOT] =	Equal to or not equal to

Relative File. A file with relative organization.

Relative Key. A key whose contents identify a logical record in a relative file.

Relative Organization. The permanent logical file structure in which each record is uniquely identified by an integer value greater than zero, which specifies the record's logical ordinal position in the file.

Report Clause. A clause, in the Report Section of the Data Division, that appears in a report description entry or a report group description entry.

Report Description Entry. An entry in the Report Section of the Data Division that is composed of the level indicator RD, followed by a report name, followed by a set of report clauses as required.

Report File. An output file whose file description entry contains a REPORT clause. The contents of a report file consist of records that are written under control of the Report Writer Control System.

Report Footing. A report group that is presented only at the end of a report.

Report Group. In the Report Section of the Data Division, an 01 level-number entry and its subordinate entries.

Report Group Description Entry. An entry in the Report Section of the Data Division that is composed of the level-number 01, the option data-name, a TYPE clause, and an optional set of report clauses.

Report Heading. A report group that is presented only at the beginning of a report.

Report Line.   A division of a page representing one row of horizontal character positions. Each character position of a report line is aligned vertically beneath the corresponding character position of the report line above it. Report lines are numbered from 1, by 1, starting at the top of the page.

Report-Name.   A user-defined word that names a report described in a report description entry within the Report Section of the Data Division.

Report Section.   The section of the Data Division that contains one or more report description entries and their associated report group description entries.

Report Writer Control System (RWCS).   An object-time control system, provided by the implementor, that accomplishes the construction of reports.

Report Writer Logical Record.   A record that consists of the Report Writer print line and associated control information necessary for its selection and vertical positioning.

Reserved Word.   A COBOL word specified in the list of words which may be used in COBOL source programs, but which must not appear in the programs as user-defined words or system-names.

Routine-Name.   A user-defined word that identifies a procedure written in a language other than COBOL.

Run Unit.   A set of one or more object programs which function, at object-time, as a unit to provide problem solutions.

RWCS.   (See Report Writer Control System.)

Section.   A set of zero, one, or more paragraphs or entries, called a section body, the first of which is preceded by a section header. Each section consists of the section header and the related section body.

Section Header.   A combination of words followed by a period and a space that indicates the beginning of a section in the Environment, Data and Procedure Divisions.

In the Environment and Data Divisions, a section header is composed of reserved words followed by a period and a space. The permissible section headers are:

In the Environment Division:

CONFIGURATION SECTION.
INPUT-OUTPUT SECTION.

In the Data Division:

FILE SECTION.
WORKING-STORAGE SECTION.
LINKAGE SECTION.
COMMUNICATION SECTION.
REPORT SECTION.

In the Procedure Division, a section header is composed of a section-name, followed by the reserved word SECTION, followed by a segment-number (optional), followed by a period and a space.

Section-Name.   A user-defined word which names a section in the Procedure Division.

Segment-Number.   A user-defined word which classifies sections in the Procedure Division for purposes of segmentation. Segment-numbers may contain only the characters '0', '1', . . . '9'. A segment-number may be expressed either as a one or two digit number.

Sentence.   A sequence of one or more statements, the last of which is terminated by a period followed by a space.

Separator.   A punctuation character used to delimit character-strings.

Sequential Access.   An access mode in which logical records are obtained from or placed into a file in a consecutive predecessor-to-successor logical record sequence determined by the order of records in the file.

Sequential File.   A file with sequential organization.

Sequential Organization.   The permanent logical file structure in which a record is identified by a predecessor-successor relationship established when the record is placed into the file.

Sign Condition.   The proposition, for which a truth value can be determined, that the algebraic value of a data item or an arithmetic expression is either less than, greater than, or equal to zero.

Simple Condition.   Any single condition chosen from the set:

relation condition
class condition
condition-name condition
switch-status condition
sign condition
(simple-condition)

Sort File.   A collection of records to be sorted by a SORT statement. The sort file is created and can be used by the sort function only.

Sort-Merge File Description Entry.   An entry in the File Section of the Data Division that is composed of the level indicator SD, followed by a file-name, and then followed by a set of file clauses as required.

Source.   The symbolic identification of the originator of a transmission to a queue.

SOURCE-COMPUTER.   The name of an Environment Division paragraph in which the computer environment, within which the source program is compiled, is described.

Source Item.   An identifier designated by a SOURCE clause that provides the value of a printable item.

Source Program.   Although it is recognized that a source program may be represented by other forms and symbols, in this document it always refers to a syntactically correct set of COBOL statements beginning with an Identification Division and ending with the end of the Procedure Division. In contexts where there is no danger of ambiguity, the word "program" alone may be used in place of the phrase "source program."

Special Character.   A character that belongs to the following set:

Character	Meaning
+	plus sign
−	minus sign
*	asterisk
/	stroke (virgule, slash)
=	equal sign
$	currency sign
,	comma (decimal point)
;	semicolon
.	period (decimal point)
'	quotation mark
(	left parenthesis
)	right parenthesis
>	greater than symbol
<	less than symbol

Special-Character Word.   A reserved word which is an arithmetic operator or a relation character.

SPECIAL-NAMES.   The name of an Environment Division paragraph in which implementor-names are related to user specified mnemonic-names.

Special Registers.   Compiler generated storage areas whose primary use is to store information produced in conjunction with the use of specific COBOL features.

Standard Data Format.   The concept used in describing the characteristics of data in a COBOL Data Division under which the characteristics or properties of the data are expressed in a form oriented to the appearance of the data on the printed page of infinite length and breadth, rather than a form oriented to the manner in which the data is stored internally in the computer, or on a particular external medium.

Statement.   A syntactically valid combination of words and symbols written in the Procedure Division beginning with a verb.

Sub-Queue.   A logical hierarchical division of a queue.

Subject of Entry.   An operand or reserved word that appears immediately following the level indicator or the level-number in the Data Division entry.

Subprogram.   (See Called Program.)

Subscript.   An integer whose value identifies a particular element in a table.

Subscripted Data-Name.   An identifier that is composed of a data-name followed by one or more subscripts enclosed in parentheses.

Sum Counter.   A signed numeric data item established by a SUM clause in the Report Section of the Data Division. The sum counter is used by the Report Writer Control System to contain the result of designated summing operations that take place during production of a report.

Switch-Status Condition.   The proposition, for which a truth value can be determined, that an implementor-defined switch, capable of being set to an "on" or "off" status, has been set to a specific status.

System-Name.   A COBOL word which is used to communicate with the operating environment.

Table.   A set of logically consecutive items of data that are defined in the Data Division by means of the OCCURS clause.

Table Element.   A data item that belongs to the set of repeated items comprising a table.

Terminal.   The originator of a transmission to a queue, or the receiver of a transmission from a queue.

Text-Name.   A user-defined word which identifies library text.

Text-Word.   Any character-string separator, except space, in a COBOL library or in pseudo-text.

Truth Value.   The representation of the result of the evaluation of a condition in terms of one of two values

true
false

Unary Operator.   A plus (+) or a minus (−) sign, which precedes a variable or a left parenthesis in an arithmetic expression and which has the effect of multiplying the expression of +1 or -1 respectively.

Unit.   A module of mass storage the dimensions of which are determined by each implementor.

User-Defined Word.   A COBOL word that must be supplied by the user to satisfy the format of a clause or statement.

Variable.   A data item whose value may be changed by execution of the object program. A variable used in an arithmetic expression must be a numeric elementary item.

Verb.   A word that expresses an action to be taken by a COBOL compiler or object program.

Word.   A character-string of not more than 30 characters which forms a user-defined word, a system-name, or a reserved word.

Working-Storage Section.   The section of the Data Division that describes working storage data items, composed either of noncontiguous items or of working storage records or of both.

77-Level-Description-Entry.   A data description entry that describes a noncontiguous data item with the level-number 77.

ANSWERS TO SELF-TEST EXERCISES

CHAPTER 1

1. 1. u 2. m 3. s 4. q 5. v 6. f 7. h 8. l 9. n 10. e 11. x 12. p 13. i 14. w 15. t
   16. k 17. g 18. y 19. b 20. o 21. a 22. j 23. c 24. r 25. d 26. z

2. 1. e 2. d 3. f 4. c 5. a 6. b

3.

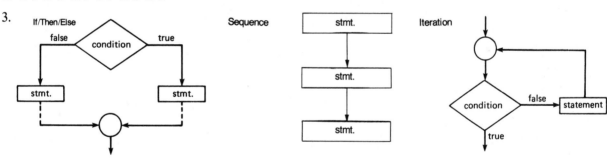

4. See Section 1.6

CHAPTER 2

1. 1. j 2. n 3. e 4. s 5. m 6. r 7. y 8. i 9. f 10. g 11. t 12. a 13. x 14. z 15. d
   16. p 17. h 18. l 19. w 20. b 21. q 22. u 23. o 24. v 25. k 26. c

2.
```
IDENTIFICATION DIVISION.
PROGRAM-ID. SECOND.
AUTHOR. YOUR NAME.
INSTALLATION. YOUR COLLEGE.
DATE-WRITTEN. 1/1/86
DATE-COMPILED.
SECURITY. NONE.
```

3.

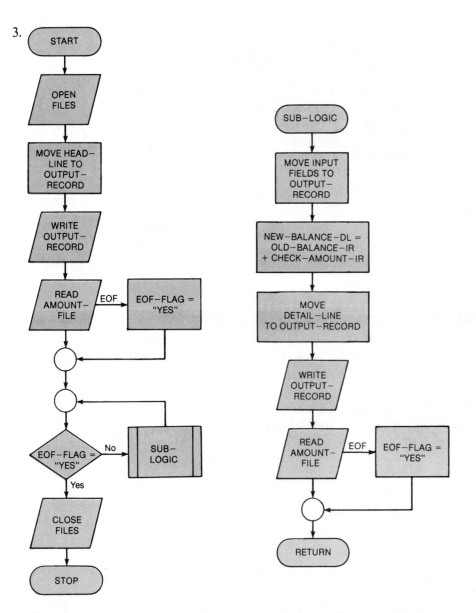

4. Division headers, section headers, paragraph names, FD entries, 01 entries.

5. a. valid b. invalid, no alphabetic character c. invalid, embedded space
   d. invalid, ends with a "−" e. invalid, too long f. invalid, embedded space

6. 1. d 2. a,i 3. i 4. k 5. b,i 6. e 7. c 8. i 9. e 10. f 11. h 12. g,i 13. j 14. j 15. i
   16. i 17. c,i

7.
```
01  NAME-ADDR-REC.
    02  CUSTOMER-NAME-NAR      PIC X(20).
    02  STREET-ADDRESS-NAR     PIC X(15).
    02  CITY-NAR               PIC X(10).
    02  STATE-NAR              PIC XX.
    02  ZIP-NAR                PIC 9(5).
    02  FILLER                 PIC X(28).
```

8.

Where defined in DATA DIVISION

Type of Item	FILE SECTION		WORKING-STORAGE SECTION		
	Used for Input	*Used for Output*	*Used for Input*	*Used for Control*	*Used for Output*
File	AMOUNT-FILE	REPORT-FILE			
Record	INPUT-RECORD	OUTPUT-RECORD			HEAD-LINE DETAIL-LINE
Field	OLD-BALANCE-IR CHECK-AMOUNT-IR			EOF-FLAG FLAGS	OLD-BALANCE-DL CHECK-AMOUNT-DL NEW-BALANCE-DL

CHAPTER 3

1. Numbers in paragraph names are used to help the reader locate paragraphs. They are required by style but not by the syntax of COBOL.

2. A switch is a data item that can contain one of the two values—1 or 0, "yes" or "no," "on" or "off." Switches are used as communication links among paragraphs of a program.

3. An accumulator is a data item which is used to store a running total. Typically, a sequence of values is added to the accumulator one at a time. Accumulators are used to compute totals.

4.
```
PROCEDURE DIVISION.
1000-MAIN-PROCESS.
     PERFORM 2000-INITIAL.
     PERFORM 3000-SUB-LOGIC UNTIL EOF-FLAG = "YES".
     PERFORM 4000-TERMINATE.
     STOP RUN.
2000-INITIAL.
     OPEN INPUT AMOUNT-FILE OUTPUT REPORT-FILE.
     PERFORM 5000-WRITE-HEADINGS.
     PERFORM 6000-READ-AMOUNT-FILE.
3000-SUB-LOGIC.
     PERFORM 7000-COMPUTE-NEW-BALANCE.
     PERFORM 8000-WRITE-DETAIL-LINE.
     PERFORM 6000-READ-AMOUNT-FILE.
4000-TERMINATE.
     CLOSE AMOUNT-FILE REPORT-FILE.
5000-WRITE-HEADINGS.
     MOVE HEAD-LINE TO OUTPUT-RECORD.
     WRITE OUTPUT-RECORD AFTER ADVANCING PAGE.
6000-READ-AMOUNT-FILE.
     READ AMOUNT-FILE AT END MOVE "YES" TO EOF-FLAG.
7000-COMPUTE-NEW-BALANCE.
     ADD OLD-BALANCE-IR CHECK-AMOUNT-IR
         GIVING NEW-BALANCE-DL.
8000-WRITE-DETAIL-LINE.
     MOVE DETAIL-LINE TO OUTPUT-RECORD.
     WRITE OUTPUT-RECORD AFTER ADVANCING 1 LINES.
```

Note to Reader: There are many acceptable solutions to this problem. Use the above code only as an example.

Structure Diagram:

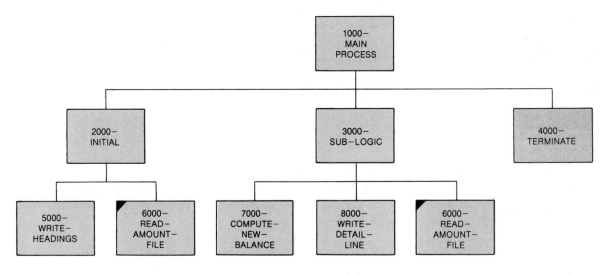

Control Paragraphs:

```
1000-MAIN-PROCESS
2000-INITIAL
3000-SUB-LOGIC
```

Operational Paragraphs:

```
4000-TERMINATE
5000-WRITE-HEADINGS
6000-READ-AMOUNT-FILE
7000-COMPUTE-NEW-BALANCE
8000-WRITE-DETAIL-LINE.
```

5. The program will not enter a loop properly because of the omission of PERFORM/UNTIL at line 4. The program will process only one record because of omission of PERFORM 4000-READ-INPUT-FILE as the last statement of 3000-BUILD-FILE.

1. a. `FD  SALES-RECORD`
   `        LABEL RECORDS ARE STANDARD`
   `        DATA RECORD IS SALESMAN.`

   b. `OPEN INPUT SALES-RECORD.`

   c. `READ SALES-RECORD`
   `        AT END MOVE "YES" TO EOF-FLAG.`

   d. `CLOSE SALES-RECORD.`

2. a. `FD  PAYROLL`
   `        LABEL RECORDS ARE OMITTED`
   `        DATA RECORD IS NET-PAY.`

   b. `OPEN OUTPUT PAYROLL.`

   c. `READ PAYROLL AT END. . . .`

   d. `CLOSE PAYROLL.`

3. a. 0 0 1 2 3

    1 2 3

    0 0 0 0 0 1 2 3

    1 2 3 4 5 0 0

    0 1 2 3 4 5 0

    1

e. 0 0 0 1

    +   1 . 2 3

            1 . 2 3

          1 . 2 3

b.   1 2 3

        $ 1 2 3 . 4 5

      * 1 2 3 . 4

f. $ 3 4 5 6 . 7 8

    1 2 3 4 5 6 . . 7 8 0 0

    2 3 . 4 5 6 . . 7

c. 4 3 2 1

    4 3

          4 3 2 1

    2 1

g. 0 1 2 3 4

    0 1 2 3

    0 1 0 2 3 0 4

    0 1   2 3 4

d.   1 2 . 3 4

            1 2 . 3 4

            1 2 . 3 4 C R

    $ 1 2 . 3 4   D B

h.   3 / 1 1 / 8 2

4.

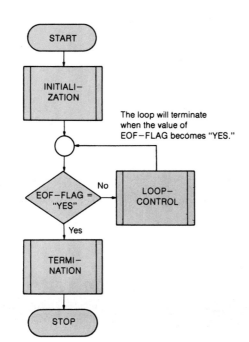

START

INITIALI-
ZATION

The loop will terminate
when the value of
EOF-FLAG becomes "YES."

EOF-FLAG = "YES"

No

LOOP-
CONTROL

Yes

TERMI-
NATION

STOP

5. Major heading
   Column
   Heading
   Detail
   Total

6.

		Receiving field			
		Alphanumeric	*Numeric*	*Numeric edited*	*Alphanumeric edited*
Sending field	*Alphanumeric*	permitted	not permitted	not permitted	permitted
	Numeric	permitted	permitted	permitted	permitted
	Numeric	permitted	not permitted	not permitted	not permitted
	Numeric edited	permitted	not permitted	not permitted	not permitted
	Alphanumeric edited	permitted	not permitted	not permitted	not permitted

CHAPTER 5

1. a. ADD A TO B.
      or
      ADD A B GIVING A.
      or
      COMPUTE A = B + A.
   b. SUBTRACT EXPENSE FROM INCOME GIVING BALANCE.
      or
      COMPUTE BALANCE = INCOME − EXPENSE.
   c. MULTIPLY D BY A.
      or
      MULTIPLY A BY D GIVING A.
      or
      COMPUTE A = A * D.
   d. DIVIDE SALES BY 12 GIVING MONTHLY-AVERAGE.
      or
      DIVIDE 12 INTO SALES GIVING MONTHLY-AVERAGE.
      or
      COMPUTE MONTHLY-AVERAGE = SALES / 12.
   e. COMPUTE VOLUME = 4 / 3 * 3.1459 * R ** 2.
   f. COMPUTE I = P * R * T.
   g. MULTIPLY B BY 0.25 GIVING A
      or
      COMPUTE A = B * 0.25.
   h. COMPUTE A = P * (1 + R) ** N.

2. a. $0\ 7$

      C PIC 99

   b. $1\ 3$

      B PIC 99

   c. $1\ 3\ \bar{4}$

      B PIC S999

   d. $0\ 0\ \bar{1}$ $0\ 0$

      A PIC S99V9   D PIC S99

   e. $0\ 2\ \bar{7}$

      A PIC S999

   f. $0\ 0$

      A PIC V99
      Note: SIZE ERROR because of overflow

g. |0|0|0|
        ∧

A PIC 99V9
Note: SIZE ERROR because of division
by 0.

i. |0|2|0̄|
        ∧

B PIC S99V9

h. |3|3|
       ∧

C PIC 99
Note: loss of sign on result

3.

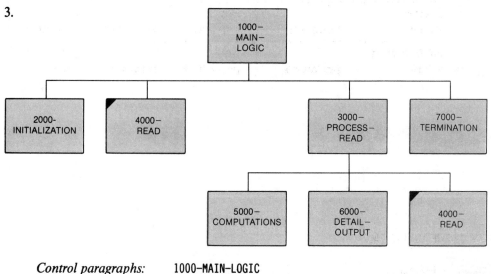

Control paragraphs: 1000–MAIN–LOGIC
                           3000–PROCESS–READ

Operational paragraphs: 2000–INITIALIZATION
                           4000–READ
                           5000–COMPUTATIONS
                           6000–DETAIL–OUTPUT
                           7000–TERMINATION

4. a. The use of group data-items such as 01 COMPUTED-AMOUNTS increases the
      readability of the program.
   b. The use of the VALUE clause for a numeric data item such as WITH-AMT makes
      the program easier to debug and maintain.
   c. The placement of constants such as FICA-FACTOR in WORKING-STORAGE makes
      the program easier to maintain.
   d. The ROUNDED option will ensure that the employee's pay is rounded to the
      nearest penny.

5. COMPUTE JULIAN-DATE = (M − 1) * 30 + D

   Note: This formula is only approximate since not all months have 30 days. In
   some applications the year is also important. The Julian date for the century
   or decade can be computed by

        COMPUTE JULIAN-DATE = Y * 365 + (M − 1) * 30 + D

   where Y represents the year in four-digit or two digit form.

CHAPTER 6

1. a. X < Y OR Y IS NEGATIVE
      True   False
            True

   b. Z IS ALPHABETIC
         True

   c. X IS NUMERIC AND Z IS NOT ALPHABETIC
         True   False
                  False

   d. NOT Y IS POSITIVE
            True
         False

   e. NOT X IS ZERO OR Y IS NOT NEGATIVE
         False   True
            True
                  True

   f. NOT (X > 25 OR Y < 39)
          False   True
               True

   g. X < Y OR X IS ZERO AND Y > 1
      False   False   True
                      False
              False

   h. X < Y AND (Y < 0 OR X > 30)
      True   False   False
                     False
              False

2. a. ITEM-TYPE-1
         False

   b. ITEM-TYPE 1 OR ITEM-TYPE-2
         False   True
              True

   c. XYZ
      True

   d. NOT XYZ
         True
      False

   e. NOT (ITEM-TYPE-1 OR ITEM-TYPE-2)
            False   True
                 True
              False

   f. XYZ AND NOT ITEM-TYPE-1
      True   False
               True
            True

   g. NOT XYZ AND ITEM-TYPE-1 OR NOT ITEM-TYPE-2
         True   False   True
      False   False
                 False
                      False

   h. NOT ITEM-TYPE-OTHER
            False
         True

3. a. A < B AND = C
   b. A < B OR C AND > D
   c. Cannot be abbreviated since subject is not the same. Could be rewritten.

         B > A AND B > C

      and then abbreviated as

         B > A AND C
   d. A > B OR < D
   e. A < B AND C
   f. A NOT > B AND < C AND NOT = C

```
4. IF BALANCE NOT > 20
        MOVE BALANCE TO MINIMUM-PAYMENT
   ELSE
        IF BALANCE NOT > 100
            COMPUTE MINIMUM-PAYMENT =
                20 + (BALANCE - 20) * 0.1
        ELSE
            COMPUTE MINIMUM-PAYMENT =
                36 + (BALANCE - 100) * 0.2.
```

5. a.
```
        IF X > Y
            PERFORM 2000-OUTPUT
            READ FILE-A
                AT END MOVE "YES" TO EOF-A.
```
   b.
```
        IF X > Y
            PERFORM READ-FILE-A
            PERFORM 2000-OUTPUT.
            .
            .
            .
        READ-FILE-A.
            READ FILE-A
                AT END MOVE "YES" TO EOF-A.
```
   c.
```
        IF ERR-CODE = "NO"
            PERFORM COMPUTATIONS.
            .
            .
            .
        COMPUTATIONS.
            ADD A TO B ON SIZE ERROR MOVE 0 TO B.
            ADD C TO D ON SIZE ERROR MOVE 0 TO D.
```

6.
```
   DATA-VALIDATION.
        MOVE "NO" TO VALIDITY-ERROR.
        IF ACCOUNT-NUM-DR NOT NUMERIC
            OR
            ZIP-DR NOT NUMERIC
            OR
            BALANCE-FORWARD-DR NOT NUMERIC
                MOVE "YES" TO VALIDITY-ERROR.
        IF CUSTOMER-NAME-DR = SPACES
            OR
            CUSTOMER-NAME-DR NOT ALPHABETIC
                MOVE "YES" TO VALIDITY-ERROR.
        IF CITY-DR = SPACES
            OR
            CITY-DR NOT ALPHABETIC
                MOVE "YES" TO VALIDITY-ERROR.
        IF STATE-DR = SPACES
            OR
            STATE-DR NOT ALPHABETIC
                MOVE "YES" TO VALIDITY-ERROR.
```

It is not possible to check the field STREET-ADDRESS-DR since it may legitimately contain both alphabetic and numeric characters as well as other characters such as "." "#", and so on.

7. The PERFORM/UNTIL does not have a clause consisting of one or more statements, so it is not a conditional statement.

8. Modify line 3100 as follows:

```
03   BIRTH-DATE-PDR.
     05   FILLER   PIC X(4).
     05   BIRTH-YEAR-PDR   PIC 99.
```

Modify paragraph 3000:

```
3000-DECISION
     IF BIRTH-YEAR-PDR > 20 AND BIRTH-YEAR-PDR < 40
         PERFORM 4000-EMPLOYEE-REPORT.
     READ PERSONNEL-DATA-FILE
         AT END MOVE "YES" TO EOF-FLAG.
```

9. Changes/additions to DATA DIVISION:
   1) change content of HEAD-LINE to reflect new content of report
   2) add counters and accumulators:

```
01   COUNTERS.
     03   NUMBER-MALES    PIC 9999 VALUE 0.
     03   NUMBER-FEMALES  PIC 9999 VALUE 0.
01   ACCUMULATORS.
     03   TOTAL-AGE-MALES    PIC 9(9) VALUE 0.
     03   TOTAL-AGE-FEMALES  PIC 9(9) VALUE 0.
```

   3) add final output record:

```
01   SUMMARY-LINE.
     03   NUMBER-MALES-OUT    PIC Z(5).
     03   NUMBER-FEMALES-OUT  PIC Z(5).
     03   AV-AGE-FEM-OUT      PIC Z(4).
     03   AV-AGE-MALE-OUT     PIC Z(4).
```

   4) Add the following DATA DIVISON item:

```
01   CURRENT-YEAR.
     03   CURR-YR PIC 99 VALUE 86.
PROCEDURE DIVISION.
1000-MAIN-ROUTINE.
     PERFORM 2000-INITIALIZATION.
     PERFORM 3000-DECISION
             UNTIL EOF-FLAG = "YES".
     PERFORM 7000-TERMINATION.
     STOP RUN.
2000-INITIALIZATION.
     no change.
3000-DECISION.
     IF SEX-PDR = "F"
         PERFORM 4000-EMPLOYEE-REPORT
         ADD 1 TO NUMBER-FEMALES
         COMPUTE TOTAL-AGE-FEMALES =
                 TOTAL-AGE-FEMALES + (CURR-YR - BIRTH-YEAR-PDR)
     ELSE
         ADD 1 TO NUMBER-MALES
         COMPUTE TOTAL-AGE-MALES =
                 TOTAL-AGE-MALES + (CURR-YR - BIRTH-YEAR-PDR).
     READ PERSONNEL-DATA-FILE
         AT END MOVE "YES" TO EOF-FLAG.
```

```
4000-EMPLOYEE-REPORT
    no change.
7000-TERMINATION.
    COMPUTE AV-AGE-FEM-OUT = TOTAL-AGE-FEMALES / NUMBER-FEMALES
        ON SIZE ERROR MOVE 0 TO AV-AGE-FEM-OUT.
    COMPUTE AV-AGE-MALE-OUT = TOTAL-AGE-MALES / NUMBER-MALES
        ON SIZE ERROR MOVE 0 TO AV-AGE-MALE-OUT.
    MOVE NUMBER-MALES TO NUMBER-MALES-OUT.
    MOVE NUMBER-FEMALES TO NUMBER-FEMALES-OUT.
    WRITE OUTPUT-RECORD FROM SUMMARY-LINE AFTER 2.
    CLOSE PERSONNEL-DATA-FILE
          EMPLOYEE-REPORT.
```

CHAPTER 7

1. Program 7.4

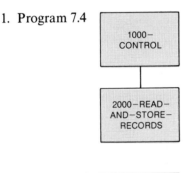

Program 7.5

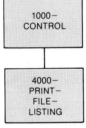

Multiparagraph sections are treated as one program module and represented by one block in a structure diagram.

2. 1. Records from PURCHASE-REQUEST-FILE are copied into SORT-FILE.
   2. Records in SORT-FILE are sorted.
   3. Records from SORT-FILE are copied into PURCHASE-REQUEST-FILE.

3. a. SD entry.
   b. Key field.
   c. The PERFORM contains provision for returning after execution of the paragraph or section; GO TO does not.
   d. Section header which has the form section-name SECTION.
   e. Module.
   f. Branch to the last paragraph in a multiparagraph section.
   g. RETURN
   h. RELEASE
   i. The only statement in a paragraph.
   j. SORT and PERFORM a statement outside the procedure.
   k. Branch to its last paragraph.
   l. Disk

4. a. SORT   SORT-FILE
        ON ASCENDING KEY SS-NUM-SR
        USING DATA-FILE`
        GIVING DATA-FILE.
  b. SORT   SORT-FILE
        ON ASCENDING KEY ZIP-SR NAME-SR
        USING DATA-FILE
        GIVING DATA-FILE

5.   SORT SORT-FILE
        ON ASCENDING KEY STATE-SR
        INPUT PROCEDURE IS 2000-BUILD-FILE
        GIVING DATA-FILE.
        .
        .
        .

```
2000-BUILD-FILE SECTION.
2010-BUILD-FILE-CONTROL.
    MOVE "NO" TO EOF-FLAG.
    OPEN INPUT NEW-DATA-FILE.
    READ NEW-DATA-FILE
        AT END MOVE "YES" TO EOF-FLAG.
    PERFORM 2020-RELEASE-READ
        UNTIL EOF-FLAG = "YES".
    CLOSE NEW-DATA-FILE.
    GO TO 2030-BUILD-FILE-EXIT.
2020-RELEASE-READ.
    MOVE SS-NUM-NDR TO SS-NUM-DR.
    MOVE NAME-NDR TO NAME-SR.
    MOVE ST-ADDR-NDR TO ST-ADDR-SR.
    MOVE CITY-NDR TO CITY-SR.
    MOVE STATE-NDR TO STATE-SR.
    MOVE ZIP-NDR TO ZIP-SR.
    RELEASE SORT-RECORD.
    READ NEW-DATA-FILE
        AT END MOVE "YES" TO EOF-FLAG.
2030-BUILD-FILE-EXIT.
    EXIT.
```

6.   SORT SORT-FILE
        ON DESCENDING KEY ZIP-SR
        INPUT PROCEDURE IS 2000-BUILD-FILE
        GIVING DATA-FILE.
        .
        .
        .

```
2000-BUILD-FILE SECTION.
2010-BUILD-FILE-CONTROL.
    MOVE "NO" TO EOF-FLAG.
    OPEN INPUT DATA-FILE.
    READ DATA-FILE
        AT END MOVE "YES" TO EOF-FLAG.
    PERFORM 2020-COPY-DATA-FILE
        UNTIL
            EOF-FLAG = "YES".
    CLOSE DATA-FILE.
    MOVE "NO" TO EOF-FLAG.
```

```
        OPEN INPUT NEW-DATA-FILE.
        READ NEW-DATA-FILE
            AT END MOVE "YES" TO EOF-FLAG.
        PERFORM 2030-COPY-NEW-DATA-FILE
            UNTIL EOF-FLAG = "YES".
        CLOSE NEW-DATA-FILE.
        GO TO 2040-BUILD-FILE-EXIT.
    2020-COPY-DATA-FILE
        RELEASE SORT-RECORD FROM DATA-RECORD.
        READ DATA-FILE
            AT END MOVE "YES" TO EOF-FLAG.
    2030-COPY-NEW-DATA-FILE.
        MOVE SS-NUM-NDR TO SS-NUM-SR
        MOVE NAME-NDR TO NAME-SR.
        MOVE ST-ADDR-NDR TO ST ADDR-SR.
        MOVE CITY-NDR TO CITY-SR.
        MOVE STATE-NDR TO STATE-SR.
        MOVE ZIP-NDR TO ZIP-SR.
        RELEASE NEW-DATA-FILE
            AT END MOVE "YES" TO EOF-FLAG.
    2040-BUILD-FILE-EXIT.
        EXIT.
```

```
1. FD   DATA-FILE
        LABEL RECORDS ARE STANDARD
        DATA RECORDS ARE DATA-REC-A DATA-REC-B.
   01   DATA-REC-A.
        03 BID-NUMBER-DRA  PIC 9(10).
        03 PROJ-DESC-DRA   PIC X(10).
        03 BID-AMT-DRA     PIC 9(8)V99.
        03 REC-ID          PIC X.
   01 DATA-REC-B.
        03 BID-NUMBER-DRB  PIC 9(10).
        03 BID-AMT-DRB     PIC 9(8)V99.
        03 PROJ-DESC-DRB   PIC X(10).
        03 FILLER          PIC X.
```

```
2.      READ DATA-FILE
            AT END MOVE "YES" TO EOF-CODE.

        .
        .
        .
        IF REC-ID = "A"
            PERFORM PROCESS-REC-TYPE-A
        ELSE
            IF REC-ID = "B"
                PERFORM PROCESS-REC-TYPE-B
            ELSE
                PERFORM ERROR-IN-REC-ID.
```

```
3. SPECIAL-NAMES.
       CURRENCY SIGN IS "Q".
   QQQQ,QQQ.99
```

4. If the last line of the report falls at the last line of a page, page headings will be placed on an otherwise unneeded page. If there were no records in the file, a page containing only page headings and final totals would be produced.

5. If there are no records in the file, a page containing only page headings and final totals would be produced. If the last line of the report falls on the last line of a page, the report would terminate. Because of the potential for producing a superfluous page of output with the method of Program 8.1, and because no special initialization steps to produce page headings on the first page are needed, the method of Program 7.2 is recommended. This method is not compatible with page totals because it would cause a superfluous page total output at the beginning of the program.

6. The number of lines per page should always be defined as a data item in WORKING-STORAGE to facilitate later revision of the program.

7. The value of HOLD-DEPARTMENT should be written. The value of IR-DEPARTMENT is the new department number; the total being produced is for the old department number contained in HOLD-DEPARTMENT.

8.
```
PROCESS-READ.
    IF MAJOR-KEY NOT = MAJOR-KEY-HOLD
        PERFORM MINOR-BREAK
        PERFORM INTERMEDIATE-BREAK
        PERFORM MAJOR-BREAK
    ELSE
        IF INTERMEDIATE-KEY NOT = INTERMEDIATE-KEY-HOLD
            PERFORM MINOR-BREAK
            PERFORM INTERMEDIATE-BREAK
        ELSE
            IF MINOR-KEY NOT = MINOR-KEY-HOLD
                PERFORM MINOR-BREAK.
```

CHAPTER 9

1. a.
```
    PERFORM SEARCH-TABLE
        VARYING INDX FROM 1 BY 1 UNTIL
            PART-NUMBER (INDX) = "9999" OR
            PART-NUMBER (INDX) = KNOWN-PART-NUMBER.
    IF PART-NUMBER (INDX) NOT = "9999"
        MOVE NEW-DESCRIPTION TO PART-DESCRIPTION (INDX).

        .
        .
        .

SEARCH-TABLE.
    EXIT.
```
   b. After a search procedure such as included in part "a" above, include:
```
IF PART-NUMBER (INDX) NOT = "9999"
    MOVE DESCRIPTION (INDX) TO DESCRIPTION-OUT
    MOVE NUMBER-ORDERED TO NUMBER-ORDERED-OUT
    MOVE KNOWN-PART-NUMBER TO PART-NUMBER-OUT
    MULTIPLY NUMBER-SOLD BY PART-PRICE (INDX)
        GIVING INVOICE-AMT-OUT
    WRITE OUT-LINE FROM DETAIL-LINE AFTER 1
ELSE
    PERFORM ERROR-ROUTINE.
```

2. a.

b.

c.

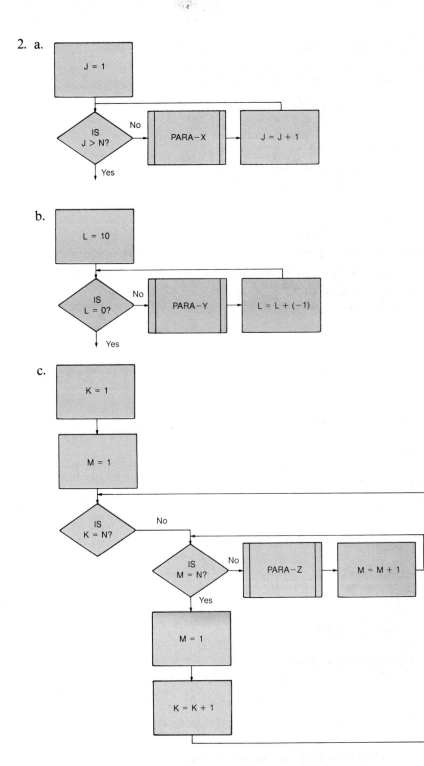

d.

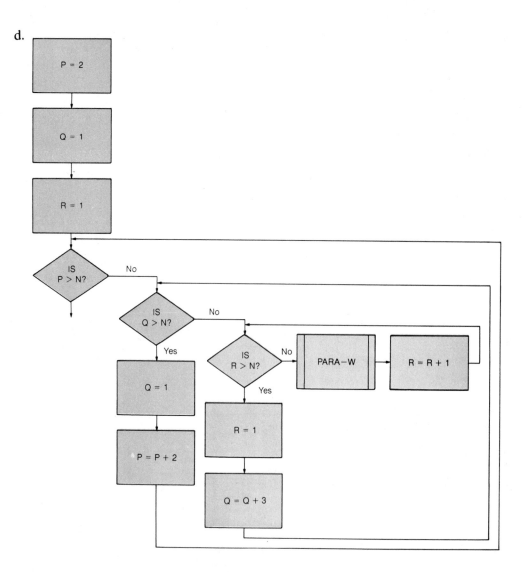

3. a. J | 1 2 3 4 5 6 7   7 times

   b. L | 10 9 8 7 6 5 4 3 2 1   10 times

   c. K 1 1 1 1 1 1 2 2 . . . 2 3 . . . 3 4 . . . 4 5 . . . 5 6 . . . 6   36 times

      M 1 2 3 4 5 6 1 2 . . . 6 1 . . . 6 1 . . . 6 1 . . . 6 1 . . . 6

   d. P 2 2 . . . 2 2 2 . . . 2 2 2 . . . 2 4 . . . 4 4 . . . 4 4 . . . 4 6 . . . 6 6 . . . 6 6 . . . 6   63 times

      Q 1 1 . . . 1 4 4 . . . 4 7 7 . . . 7 1 . . . 1 4 . . . 4 7 . . . 7 1 . . . 1 4 . . . 4 7 . . . 7

      R 1 2 . . . 7 1 2 . . . 7 1 2 . . . 7 1 . . . 7 1 . . . 7 1 . . . 7 1 . . . 7 1 . . . 7 1 . . . 7

4. a. PRODUCTION-OUTPUT.
         MOVE SPACES TO DAILY-OUTPUT.
         PERFORM DETAIL-OUTPUT
             VARYING D FROM 1 BY 1 UNTIL D > NUM-DAYS.
      DETAIL-OUTPUT.
         PERFORM DATA-MOVE
             VARYING L FROM 1 BY 1 UNTIL L > 5.
         MOVE D TO DAY-DO.
         WRITE OUTPUT-LINE FROM DAILY-OUTPUT AFTER 1.
      DATA-MOVE.
         MOVE PRODUCTION (D, L) TO
             DAY-PRODUCTION-DO (L).

b. Assume the table AV-PROD is defined as:

```
01  CONSTANTS.
    02  FILLER PIC X(30) VALUE ALL "0".
01  AV-PROD REDEFINES CONSTANTS.
    02  PRODUCTION-BY-LINE PIC 9(6) OCCURS 5 TIMES.
```

PRODUCTION DIVISION code required:

```
PERFORM SUMMATION
    VARYING INDEX-1 FROM 1 BY 1 UNTIL INDEX-1 > NUM-DAYS
    AFTER INDEX-2 FROM 1 BY 1 UNTIL INDEX-2 > 5.
PERFORM COMPUTE-AVERAGES
    VARYING INDX FROM 1 BY 1 UNTIL INDX > 5.

    .

    .

    .

SUMMATION.
    ADD PRODUCTION (INDEX-1, INDEX-2) TO
        PRODUCTION-BY-LINE (INDEX-2).
COMPUTE-AVERAGES.
    DIVIDE NUM-DAYS INTO PRODUCTION-BY-LINE (INDX).
```

c. Assume the table DAYS-DOWN is defined as:

```
01  CONSTANTS-2.
    02  FILLER PIC X(15) VALUE ALL "0".
01  DAYS-DOWN REDEFINES CONSTANTS-2.
    02  DAYS-DOWN-BY-LINE OCCURS PIC 999 OCCURS 5 TIMES.
```

PROCEDURE DIVISION code required:

```
PERFORM COUNT-ROUTINE
    VARYING INDEX-1 FROM 1 BY 1 UNTIL INDEX-1 > NUM-DAYS
    AFTER INDEX-2 FROM 1 BY 1 UNTIL INDEX-2 > 5.
COUNT-ROUTINE.
    IF PRODUCTION (INDEX-1, INDEX-2) = 0
        ADD 1 TO DAYS-DOWN-BY-LINE (INDEX-2).
```

5.
```
    MOVE 0 TO SUM-OF ELEMENTS.
    PERFORM SUMMATION
        VARYING INDEX-1 FROM 1 BY 1 UNTIL INDEX-1 > 2
        VARYING INDEX-2 FROM 1 BY 1 UNTIL INDEX-2 > 5
        VARYING INDEX-3 FROM 1 BY 1 UNTIL INDEX-3 > 4.

        .

        .

        .

SUMMATION.
    ADD BONUS-AMOUNT (INDEX-1, INDEX-2, INDEX-3) TO
        SUM-OF-ELEMENTS.
```

6. Assume the table AV-BY-TEST-CLASS is defined as

```
01   CONSTANTS-3 PIC X(125) VALUE ALL ZEROS.
01   AV-BY-TEST-CLASS REDEFINES CONSTANTS-3.
     02   CLASS-ENTRY OCCURS 5 TIMES.
          03   TEST-ENTRY OCCURS 5 TIMES.
               04   AVERAGE PIC 9(5).
```

PROCEDURE DIVISION code required would be:

```
PERFORM SUMMATION
     VARYING INDX-1 FROM 1 BY 1 UNTIL INDX-1 > 5
     AFTER INDX-2 FROM 1 BY 1 UNTIL INDX-2 > NUM-STUDENTS (INDX-1)
     AFTER INDX-3 FROM 1 BY 1 UNTIL INDX-3 > 5.
PERFORM COMPUTE-AVERAGES
     VARYING INDEX-1 FROM 1 BY 1 UNTIL INDEX-1 > 5
     AFTER INDEX-2 FROM 1 BY 1 UNTIL INDEX-2 > 5.
     .
     .
     .

SUMMATION.
     ADD GRADE (INDEX-1, INDEX-2, INDEX-3) TO
          AVERGE (INDEX-1, INDEX-3).
COMPUTE-AVERAGES.
     DIVIDE NUM-STUDENTS (INDEX-1) INTO
          AVERAGE (INDEX-1, INDEX-2).
```

7. a. F b. F c. F d. T e. T f. T

8. a. F2 F9 C8
    b. 01 66
    c. 29 8C
    d. 01 66

CHAPTER 10

1. Programmers may be able to contribute to system design because they may be able to forsee problems that others have overlooked. The programmer's work is defined and constrained by the elements of the system design, however.

2. The systems analyst, like the architect, is responsible for the planning and design of the system. The programming manager, like the general contractor, is responsible for implementation of the system. The programmer, like the subcontractor, is responsible for implementation of specific portions of the system.

3. Both the system and the program flowcharts are schematic representations. The major components of the system flowchart are the data files and the processing programs; in a program flowchart the major components are processing steps within a specific program.

4. In a system flowchart, the double-headed arrow is used to signify that a file is used both as an input and an output file by the processing program.

5. The program specification statement is used to communicate the requirements for each program in a system. It usually includes a description of the input and output files, layouts for input and output records, and a description of the processing required of the program.

6. Because the company's computer was capable of handling a limited amount of interactive computing, some portions of the system were interactive, whereas report generation is batch. In general, data acquisition and validation are interactive, whereas report generation is batch.

7. A major advantage to the team approach is that the close coordination among team members helps to ensure that all portions of the system will mesh correctly. A major disadvantage is the time required for the team's meetings and other coordination efforts.

8. The primary purpose of the structured walk-through is to eliminate programming errors before programs are compiled or tested. A major disadvantage is the potential for harming the morale of the programmer whose work is reviewed.

9. "Ego-less" programming refers to the disengagement between the programmer and the program that must take place so that a programmer does not perceive criticism of a program as criticism of the programmer.

10. The data dictionary concept implies that all programs in a system will use the same data names for the same files, records, and fields. The COBOL source statement library can be used to make data descriptions available to each program that must reference the elements.

11. Structured implementation and testing implies that coding and testing are carried out alternately, as opposed to more primitive techniques usually employed by students to completely code a program before beginning to test it.

12. In carrying out structured implementation and testing, strict adherence to a bottom-up approach results in too much work, and strict adherence to a top-down approach may not be useful because of the logic of the program; most programmers use a combination of the two techniques.

13. A "program stub" is a dummy procedure that will later be replaced by the real thing.

14. The COPY statement allows insertion of code from a library into a program. Considerations for use will vary from one installation to another.

15. The classification of cohesion type is not an exact science. A case may be made for a different classification than that offered here:

Paragraph	Cohesive Type
1000-MAIN LOGIC	Sequential
2000-INITIALIZATION	Time
3000-CONTROL	Sequential
4000-READ	Functional
4050-CONTROL-BREAK-CHECK	Control
5000-CHECK-FULL-PAGE	Control
5100-MOVE-FIELDS	Data
5200-ADD-ORDER-COMPONENTS	Functional
5300-WRITE-DETAIL	Sequential
6500-ORDER-NUMBER-BREAK	Sequential

16. In a programming context, the term "black box" implies that each program module should perform its function in a way that does not require other program modules to have knowledge of the inner workings of the module.

17. The paragraph 1000-MAIN-LOGIC takes action based on the setting of EOF-FLAG, which is set by the paragraph 4000-READ.

18. Answers to this exercise will vary greatly.

CHAPTER 11

1. In general, a batch system processes data after it has accumulated over a period of time, whereas an interactive system processes data as it occurs.

2. In designing an interactive program, the programmer must pay close attention to user communications to make sure that users understand what they are expected to do and know how to do it.

3. In a batch system, ACCEPT and DISPLAY are used to handle communication with the system operator. In an interactive system, they are used for the same purpose and may also be used to allow communication with the program user.

4. Instructions may be provided in the form of
   - initial instructions
   - prompts
   - menus

   Another form of user instructions in many systems comes from the help option found on many menus.

5. A submenu gives the user options that relate to the choice made in the main menu.

6. Formatted screens contribute greatly to a program's user friendliness.

7. The answer is system dependent.

8. The answer is system dependent.

9. a. | A B 1 2 * 3 4 A | | | |
      ITM-R

   b. | 1 2 A A B | | |
      ITM-R

   c. | A - 1 2 * A B - 1 2 |
      ITM-R

   d. | A B - C 1 2 * 3 4 |
      ITM-R

10. a.
```
A B C -
```
FLD-A
```
D E * 1 2
```
FLD-B
```
3 - - X Y *
```
FLD-C

b.
```
A B C -
```
FLD-A
```
1 2 3 - -
```
FLD-B
```
Z W
```
FLD-C

c.
```
A B C
```
FLD-A
```
D E * 1 2
```
FLD-B
```
```
FLD-C

d.
```
A B C
```
FLD-A
```
D E * 1 2
```
FLD-B
```
X Y * Z W
```
FLD-C

e.
```
A B C -
```
FLD-A
```
X Y * Z W
```
FLD-B

11.
```
UNSTRING NAME-IN
     DELIMITED BY ALL SPACES
     INTO FIRST-NAME
          MIDDLE-INITIAL
          LAST-NAME.
MOVE SPACES TO NAME-OUT.
STRING LAST-NAME    DELIMITED BY SPACE
          ", "          DELIMITED BY SIZE
          FIRST-NAME  DELIMITED BY SPACE
          " "           DELIMITED BY SIZE
          LAST-NAME    DELIMITED BY SPACE
     INTO NAME-OUT.
```

12. Assume the following DATA DIVISION entries:

```
01   FIRST    PIC 999.
01   SECOND   PIC 99.
01   THIRD    PIC 9999.
UNSTRING SS-NUM
     INTO FIRST SECOND THIRD.
STRING FIRST, "-", SECOND, "-", THIRD
     DELIMITED BY SIZE
     INTO SS-NUM-OUT.
```

or

Assume the following DATA DIVISION entry:

```
03   SS-NUM-OUT    PIC 999B99B9999.
MOVE SS-NUM TO SS-NUM-OUT.
INSPECT SS-NUM-OUT REPLACING
                   ALL " " BY "-".
```

13. a.
```
B B 1 B B B
```

b.
```
B 1 A B A
```

c.
```
A   1 A B A
```

CHAPTER 12

1. COMPUTE-DATE-DIFFERENCE.
        DIVIDE YEAR-1 BY 4 GIVING Q1
                            REMAINDER R1.
        COMPUTE JULIAN-1 =
            365.25 * YEAR-1 +
            DAYS-PREVIOUS-ENTRY (MONTH-1) +
            DAY-1.
        IF R1 = 0 AND MONTH-1 > 2
            ADD 1 TO JULIAN-1.
        DIVIDE YEAR-2 BY 4 GIVING Q2
                            REMAINDER R2.
        COMPUTE JULIAN-2 =
            365.25 * YEAR-2 +
            DAYS-PREVIOUS-ENTRY (MONTH-2) +
            DAY-2.
        IF R2 = 0 AND MONTH-2 > 2
            ADD 1 TO JULIAN-2.
        SUBTRACT JULIAN-1 FROM JULIAN-2.
            GIVING DIFFERENCE.

    Note: The second condition regarding leap years is not incorporated into
    this procedure because only the last two digits of the year are available.

2. Modify the definition of SUPPLIER-TABLE in Program 3.1 as follows:

    01 SUPPLIER-TABLE.
        02 SUPPLIER-ENTRY OCCURS 1 TO 100 TIMES
                    DEPENDING ON NUM-ELEMENTS
            ASCENDING KEY IS SUPPLIER-ID-NUMBER
            INDEXED BY X.

    Omit definition of X at line 4900.

    a. Replace line 12400 by the following:

            SEARCH ALL SUPPLIER-ENTRY
                AT END MOVE "NOT PRESENT" TO SEARCH-FLAG
                WHEN SUPPLIER-ID-NUMBER (X) =
                    SUPPLIER-ID-NUMBER-PRR
                MOVE "FOUND" TO SEARCH-FLAG.

    Note: the table must be in ascending or descending sequence if the SEARCH ALL
    verb is to be used.

    b. Replace line 12400 by the following:

            SET X TO 1.
            SEARCH SUPPLIER-ENTRY
                AT END MOVE "NOT PRESENT" TO SEARCH-FLAG
                WHEN SUPPLIER-ID-NUMBER (X) =
                    SUPPLIER-ID-NUMBER-PRR
                MOVE "FOUND" TO SEARCH-FLAG.

    Note: the table is not required to be in Ascending/Descending sequence in
    order for the SEARCH verb to be used.

3. Low = 0
   High = 20
   Move "CONTINUE" to search flag
   Do while search flag = "CONTINUE"
   　　　Mid = (low + high)/2
   　　　If miles driven < lower limit (mid)
   　　　　　Move mid to high
   　　　Else
   　　　　　If miles driven > upper limit (mid)
   　　　　　　　Move mid to low
   　　　　　Else
   　　　　　　　Move "FOUND" to search flag
   　　　　　End If
   　　　End If
   End Do

4.

	TABLE-ARGUMENT	ACTUAL-ARGUMENT
(1)	4	115
(2)	9	
(3)	17	
(4)	25	
(5)	30	
(6)	45	
(7)	70	
(8)	100	
(9)	105	
(10)	110	

		Values of		
Repetition	LOW	HIGH	MID	Comments
1	0	11	5	115 > TABLE-ARGUMENT (5)
2	5	11	8	115 > TABLE-ARGUMENT (8)
3	8	11	9	115 > TABLE-ARGUMENT (9)
4	9	11	10	115 > TABLE-ARGUMENT (10)
	10	11		HIGH − LOW = 1; therefore element is not in table.

ACTUAL-ARGUMENT

3

		Values of		
Repetition	LOW	HIGH	MID	Comments
1	0	11	5	3 < TABLE-ARGUMENT (5)
2	0	5	2	3 < TABLE-ARGUMENT (2)
3	0	2	1	3 < TABLE-ARGUMENT (1)
	0	1		HIGH−LOW = 1; Therefore element is not in table.

5.

Data	Hash function value
6	7
19	6
23	3
20	7

TABLE

(1)	20
(2)	
(3)	23
(4)	
(5)	
(6)	19
(7)	6

Note: Position 7 is already occupied; therefore position 1 is used.

Data	Hash function value
20	7
6	7
19	6
23	3

TABLE

(1)	6
(2)	
(3)	23
(4)	
(5)	
(6)	19
(7)	20

Note: Positions of items 20 and 6 in the table are interchaned.

6.

Technique	Table Size						
	10	50	100	500	1000	5000	10000
Direct Access	1	1	1	1	1	1	1
Exhaustive Search	10	50	100	500	1000	5000	10000
Sequential Search	5	25	50	250	500	2500	5000
Binary Search	less than 4	less than 6	less than 7	less than 9	less than 10	less than 13	less than 14
Randomized Table	approx. 1	approx. 1	approx. 1	approx. 1	approx. 1	approx. 1	approx. 1

Note: The difference between a sequential search and a binary search become much more pronounced as the table size increases.

7. See Section 12.6.

8. a. An Exhaustive Search in which the most frequently used values are placed at the beginning of the table would be best if space does not permit a randomized table.
   b. A sequenced table with a binary search or if space permits, a randomized table.
   c. A randomized table would provide optimum response time and, since space is not a problem, would be the best solution.

9. The process will enter an infinite loop. The procedure can be modified to terminate if the number of repetitions of the loop equals the table size.

10. a.
```
   LOAD-ROUTINE.
        MOVE "YES" TO MORE-DATA.
        OPEN INPUT TABLE-FILE.
        READ TABLE-FILE
            AT END MOVE "NO" TO MORE-DATA.
        PERFORM MOVE-READ
            UNTIL MORE-DATA = "NO".
        CLOSE TABLE-FILE.
   MOVE-READ.
        ADD 1 TO NUM-ENTRY.
        MOVE TABLE-RECORD TO
            TABLE-ENTRY (NUM-ENTRY).
        READ TABLE-FILE
            AT END MOVE "NO" TO MORE-DATA.
```
   b.
```
   01  TABLE-DATA.
       05  TABLE-ENTRY OCCURS 1 TO 100 TIMES
                       DEPENDING ON NUM-ENTRY
                       ASCENDING KEY IS TABLE-ARGUMENT
                       INDEXED BY INDX.
           10  TABLE-ARGUMENT PIC 9(6).
           10  TABLE-VALUE    PIC X(20).
```
   c.
```
   SEARCH ALL TABLE-ENTRY
       AT END MOVE SPACES TO OUTPUT-VALUE
       WHEN ACTUAL-ARGUMENT = TABLE-ARGUMENT (INDX)
           MOVE TABLE-VALUE (INDX) TO OUTPUT-VALUE.
```

CHAPTER 13

1.

	Mode			
	INPUT	OUTPUT	I/O	EXTEND
Valid Input/Output Statements	READ	WRITE	READ REWRITE	WRITE

2. a. rewind—a tape file is repositioned to its beginning.
   b. key field—a field used as the basis for organizing a file.
   c. audit trail—maintenance of complete records to enable an auditor to retrace and verify actions taken by a data processing system.
   d. file status—a two-character field declared in the SELECT entry and updated automatically after each input/output operation related to a file.
   e. backup—a copy of a file maintained in case of error.
   f. activity—the ratio of transaction records to master file records.
   g. volatility—the ratio of add and delete transaction records to master file records.

3. If a key field can legitimately have a value like 99999 (for example, this value was actually assigned as an account number), the method used in this chapter would have to be modified. It is possible to use other fields, each of which is one digit wider than the key field for the file. Each time a record is read, the key field is moved to its corresponding other field. At end-of-file, the large value is moved to the other field. Only the other fields are

compared when determining action to be taken on a record. In this way, an actual key field value like 99999 will be less than another key field terminal value like 999999, resulting in appropriate processing for the record. For an alphanumeric key field, it will be necessary to use a value like ALL "Z" to signify end-of-file.

4. Open files
   Read FILE-A
   Read FILE-B
   Read FILE-C
   Do until KEY-A = high value and KEY-B = high value and KEY-C = high value
       If KEY-A ≤ KEY-B and KEY-A ≤ KEY-C
           Write new record from FILE-A record
           Read FILE-A
       Else
           If KEY-B ≤ KEY-A and KEY-B ≤ KEY-C
               Write new record from FILE-B record
               Read FILE-B
           Else
               Write new record from FILE-C record
               Read FILE-C
           End If
       End If
   End Do
   Close files
   Stop

5. COBOL provides for sequential and random access to data files. Sequential access is simple, and there is the least possible system overhead when this method is used; however, sequential access makes possible only next record access to the file. Random access provides for access to records on demand; however, there is an added burden of complexity and system overhead.

6. If activity is expected to be high, interactive file updating may place a large burden on a data processing system.

7. If volatility is high, the process of adding and deleting records on demand may place stress on the resources of the computing system.

8. Since add and change records are a subset of all transactions, it is not possible for the volatility ratio to exceed the activity ratio.

9. Change records may be entered in the same format as master file records with unaffected fields left blank, or change records may contain a transaction code specifying the field to be changed. The first method is relatively easy to implement but places a considerable burden on the data entry function, since each field must be placed in exactly the right location. The second method places a somewhat greater burden on the processing program but is simpler to use by data entry personnel.

10. A sequential file is appropriate in batch-oriented file maintenance, when next record access is all that is required, or for backups, logs and other system files, and when tape is to be used as the storage medium for the file. A sequential file would not be appropriate in interactive file maintenance or when records must be accessed on demand.

11. Because backup files are only used to re-create active files, it is usually unnecessary to maintain the indexed or relative file organization. When the active file is re-created, the software can copy the backup into a file with appropriate organization.

12. In a batch update procedure, all transactions are collected in a single file, which is sorted and then used to update the master file. In an interactive update procedure, the master file is updated dynamically as each transaction record is entered.

13. Updating a sequential file in place necessitates the use of a flag in each record to mark deleted records. Records can be added to the end of the file but cannot be merged between existing records. This technique is appropriate when master file records only need to be changed or deleted.

14. In the procedure of Figure 13.6, the item *read flag* is used to determine whether or not a record must be read from the old master file.

15. ERROR 1: ATTEMPT TO ADD RECORD ALREADY PRESENT IN MASTER FILE
    ERROR 2: ATTEMPT TO UPDATE A RECORD NOT PRESENT IN MASTER FILE
    ERROR 3: INVALID TRANSACTION CODE
    ERROR 4: NO ORDER COMPONENT WITH THIS CATALOG NUMBER PRESENT
    ERROR 5: RECORD BLOCK CONTAINS EXCESS DETAIL RECORDS

CHAPTER 14

1.

OPEN MODE

		INPUT	OUTPUT	I/O
FILE ACCESS METHOD	SEQUENTIAL	READ (Format-1) START	WRITE	READ (Format-1) REWRITE START DELETE
	RANDOM	READ (Format-2)	WRITE	READ (Format-1) WRITE REWRITE DELETE
	DYNAMIC	READ (Format-1) READ (Format-2) START	WRITE	READ (Format-1) READ (Format-2) WRITE REWRITE START DELETE

2. a. SEQUENTIAL/OUTPUT
   b. SEQUENTIAL/INPUT
   c. SEQUENTIAL/I-O
   d. RANDOM/I-O
   e. RANDOM/INPUT
   f. RANDOM/OUTPUT
   g. SEQUENTIAL/INPUT
   h. DYNAMIC/I-O

3. The WRITE statement is used to add records to a file; the REWRITE statement is used to change an existing record.

4. Format-1 READ generally includes an AT END clause and is used to read records sequentially. Format-2 READ includes an INVALID KEY clause and is sued to read records randomly.

5. An indexed file can be created only under the sequential access method. Dynamic access can be used to update a file.

6. START I-S-FILE KEY NOT < 200.

7. The statements in the INVALID KEY clause will be executed, since FILE STATUS value "23" indicates that no record was found with the specified key field value.

8.
```
PROCEDURE DIVISION.
1000-MAJOR-LOGIC.
    PERFORM 2000-INITIALIZATION.
    PERFORM 3000-CONTROL UNTIL EOF-FLAG = "YES".
    PERFORM 5000-RE-INITIALIZE.
    PERFORM 6000-LIST-READ UNTIL EOF-FLAG = "YES"
    PERFORM 9000-TERMINATION.
    STOP RUN.
2000-INITIALIZATION.
    OPEN INPUT INPUT-FILE
        OUTPUT INVENTORY-FILE.
    READ INPUT-FILE AT END MOVE "YES" TO EOF-FLAG.
3000-CONTROL.
    MOVE INPUT-RECORD TO INVENTORY-DATA-IRR.
    WRITE INVENTORY-RECORD
        INVALID KEY
            PERFORM 8000-ERROR.
    READ INPUT-FILE AT END MOVE "YES" TO EOF-FLAG.
5000-RE-INITIALIZE.
    CLOSE INPUT-FILE
        INVENTORY-FILE.
    OPEN INPUT INVENTORY-FILE
        OUTPUT PRINT.
    MOVE "NO" TO EOF-FLAG.
    READ INVENTORY-FILE
        AT END
            MOVE "YES" TO EOF-FLAG.
6000-LIST-READ.
    MOVE INVENTORY-DATA-IRR TO PRINT-LINE.
    WRITE PRINT-LINE AFTER 2.
    READ INVENTORY-FILE
        AT END MOVE "YES" TO EOF-FLAG.
8000-ERROR.
    EXIT.
8200-ERROR.
    EXIT.
9000-TERMINATION.
    CLOSE INVENTORY-FILE LOCK
        PRINT.
```

9. PROCEDURE DIVISION.
   1000-MAIN-LOGIC.
      OPEN INPUT INVENTORY-FILE
         OUTPUT PRINT.
      READ INVENTORY-FILE AT END MOVE "YES" TO EOF-FLAG.
      PERFORM 2000-WRITE-READ UNTIL EOF-FLAG = "YES".
      CLOSE INVENTORY-FILE PRINT.
      STOP RUN.
   2000-WRITE-READ.
      WRITE PRINT-LINE FROM INVENTORY-RECORD AFTER 1.
      READ INVENTORY-FILE AT END MOVE "YES" TO EOF-FLAG.

10. PROCEDURE DIVISION.
   1000-MAIN-LOGIC.
      PERFORM 2000-INITIALIZATION.
      PERFORM 3000-UPDATE UNTIL EOF-FLAG = "YES".
      PERFORM 9000-TERMINATION.
      STOP RUN.
   2000-INITIALIZATION.
      OPEN INPUT SALES-FILE
         I-O INVENTORY-FILE
         OUTPUT PRINT.
      READ SALES-FILE AT END MOVE "YES" TO EOF-FLAG.
   3000-UPDATE.
      MOVE INVENTORY-NUMBER-SR TO INVENTORY-NUMBER-IRR.
      READ INVENTORY-FILE
         INVALID KEY
            PERFORM 7000-ERROR.
      SUBTRACT NUMBER-SOLD-SR FROM QUANTITY-ON-HAND-IRR.
      REWRITE INVENTORY-RECORD
         INVALID KEY
            PERFORM 7200-ERROR-RECOVERY.
      READ SALES-FILE AT END MOVE "YES" TO EOF-FLAG.
   7000-ERROR.
      EXIT.
   7200-ERROR-RECOVERY.
      EXIT.
   9000-TERMINATION.
      CLOSE INVENTORY-FILE LOCK
         PRINT
         SALES-FILE.

11.   SELECT INVENTORY-FILE ASSIGN TO DISK
        ACCESS IS DYNAMIC
        ORGANIZATION IS INDEXED
        RECORD KEY IS INVENTORY-NUMBER-IRR.

        .
        .
        .

   PROCEDURE DIVISION.
   1000-MAIN-LOGIC.
      OPEN INPUT INVENTORY-FILE.

```
        MOVE "05000" TO INVENTORY-NUMBER-IRR.
        READ INVENTORY-FILE
            INVALID-KEY PERFORM 3000-ERROR.
        READ INVENTORY-FILE NEXT RECORD
            AT END MOVE "YES" TO EOF-FLAG.
        PERFORM 2000-PROCESS-READ
            UNTIL EOF-FLAG = "YES".
        CLOSE INVENTORY-FILE.
        STOP RUN.
    2000-PROCESS-READ.
        .
        .
        .
        READ INVENTORY-FILE NEXT RECORD
            AT END MOVE "YES" TO EOF-FLAG.
    3000-ERROR.
        EXIT.
12. PROCEDURE DIVISION.
    1000-MAJOR-LOGIC.
        PERFORM 2000-INITIALIZATION.
        PERFORM 3000-UPDATE-READ UNTIL END-OF-TRANSACTIONS.
        PERFORM 4000-TERMINATION.
        STOP RUN.
    2000-INITIALIZATION.
        OPEN INPUT TRANSACTIONS
            I-O INVENTORY-FILE
            OUTPUT PRINT.
        READ TRANSACTIONS
            AT END
                MOVE "YES" TO EOF-FLAG.
    3000-UPDATE-READ.
        IF NOT VALID-TRANSACTION-CODE
            PERFORM 5000-ERROR-IN-TRANS-CODE
        ELSE
            IF ADD-RECORD
                PERFORM 6000-ADD-RECORD-TO-FILE
            ELSE
                IF DELETE-RECORD
                    PERFORM 7000-DELETE-RECORD-FROM-FILE
                ELSE
                    PERFORM 8000-UPDATE-RECORD.
        READ TRANSACTIONS
            AT END
                MOVE "YES" TO EOF-FLAG.
    4000-TERMINATION.
        CLOSE TRANSACTIONS
            INVENTORY-FILE
            PRINT.
    5000-ERROR-IN-TRANS-CODE.
        EXIT.
    6000-ADD-RECORD-TO-FILE.
        MOVE TRANSACTION-RECORD TO INVENTORY-RECORD.
        WRITE INVENTORY-RECORD
            INVALID KEY
                PERFORM 6100-ERROR-IN-ADD.
```

```
    6100-ERROR-IN-ADD.
        EXIT.
    7000-DELETE-RECORD-FROM-FILE.
        MOVE INVENTORY-NUMBER-TR TO INVENTORY-NUMBER-IR.
        DELETE INVENTORY-RECORD
            INVALID KEY
                PERFORM 7100-ERROR-IN-DELETE.
    7100-ERROR-IN-DELETE.
        EXIT.
    8000-UPDATE-RECORD.
        MOVE INVENTORY-NUMBER-ID TO INVENTORY-NUMBER-IR.
        MOVE "YES" TO RECORD-FOUND-FLAG.
        READ INVENTORY-FILE
            INVALID KEY
                MOVE "NO" TO RECORD-FOUND-FLAG.
        IF RECORD-FOUND
            PERFORM 9000-CHANGE-FIELD
        ELSE
            PERFORM 8100-ERROR-IN-UPDATE.
    8100-ERROR-IN-UPDATE.
        EXIT.
    9000-CHANGE-FIELD.
        IF CHANGE-DESCRIPTION
            MOVE DESCRIPTION-TR TO DESCRIPTION-IR.
        IF CHANGE-QUANTITY-ON-HAND
            MOVE QUANTITY-ON-HAND-TR TO QUANTITY-ON-HAND-IR.
        IF CHANGE-REORDER-POINT
            MOVE REORDER-POINT-TR TO REORDER-POINT-IR.
        IF CHANGE-REORDER-AMOUNT
            MOVE REORDER AMOUNT-TR TO REORDER-AMOUNT-IR.
        IF CHANGE-CHANGE-UNIT-SELLING-PRICE
            MOVE UNIT-SELLING-PRICE-TR TO
                UNIT-SELLING-PRICE-IR.
        IF ADD-TO-QTY-ON-HAND
            ADD QUANTITY-ON-HAND-TR TO QUANTITY-ON-HAND-IR.
        IF SUBTRACT-FROM-QTY-ON-HAND
            SUBTRACT QUANTITY-ON-HAND-TR FROM
                QUANTITY-ON-HAND-IR.
        REWRITE INVENTORY-RECORD
            INVALID KEY
                PERFORM 9100-ERROR-IN-PROGRAM.
    9100-ERROR-IN-PROGRAM.
        EXIT.

13. SELECT PERSONNEL-FILE
        ASSIGN TO DISK
        ORGANIZATION IS INDEXED
        ACCESS IS SEQUENTIAL
        RECORD KEY IS SS-NO-IR
        ALTERNATE RECORD KEY IS
            EMPLOYEE-NAME-IR
            WITH DUPLICATES
        ALTERNATE RECORD KEY IS
            DEPARTMENT-NUMBER-IR
            WITH DUPLICATES
        ALTERNATE RECORD KEY IS
            ZIP-CODE-IR
            WITH DUPLICATES.
```

14. SELECT entry is the same as for Exercise 13 above, except ACCESS IS DYNAMIC.

```
PROCEDURE DIVISION.
1000-MAIN.
    OPEN INPUT INVENTORY-FILE.
    MOVE "3" TO DEPARTMENT-NUMBER-IR.
    START INVENTORY-FILE
        KEY IS EQUAL TO DEPARTMENT-NUMBER-IR
        INVALID KEY
            DISPLAY "NO EMPLOYEES IN DEPT. 3"
            CLOSE INVENTORY-FILE
            STOP RUN.
    READ INVENTORY-FILE NEXT RECORD
        AT END MOVE "YES" TO END-OF-DATA.
    PERFORM 2000-LIST-READ
        UNTIL END-OF-DATA = "YES"
        OR DEPARTMENT-NUMBER-IR
            NOT = "3".
    CLOSE INVENTORY-FILE.
    STOP RUN.
2000-LIST-READ.
    DISPLAY INVENTORY-RECORD.
    READ INVENTORY-FILE NEXT RECORD
        AT END MOVE "YES" TO END-OF-DATA.
```

CHAPTER 15

1.

OPEN Mode

Access Type		INPUT	OUTPUT	I-O
	SEQUENTIAL	Sequential READ START	Sequential WRITE	Sequential READ REWRITE START DELETE
	RANDOM	Random READ	Random WRITE	Random READ Random WRITE REWRITE DELETE
	DYNAMIC	Sequential READ Random READ START	Sequential WRITE Random WRITE	Sequential READ Random READ Sequential WRITE Random WRITE REWRITE DELETE START

2. File access: Sequential
   Open Mode: Input
   ```
   Open files
   Read data file
   Do while not end of file
        If deleted record
             Move data file record to output record
             Write output record
        End If
        Read data file
   End Do
   Close files
   Stop
   ```

3. Each time a program is run that accesses the file, the program should compute the ratio of total number of collisions to the number of file accesses required in the execution of the program. This value, along with a time stamp and possibly other information, should be added to a log file. Periodically, the operator or systems programmer would examine the content of the log file. If the ratios are increasing over time, there is an indication that it is possibly time to reorganize the relative file.

4. The DELETE verb cannot be used to remove records from a randomized file without modifying the procedure for adding records to the file because the removed record creates a logical "hole" in the file. If this location were needed for another record, a random READ would result in an INVALID KEY condition, and the REWRITE verb would be invalid if the record did not already exist.

5. New records are added to a randomized file by seeking an unused record and rewriting that record with new information. The random WRITE creates a new record in the file and cannot be used if there is an existing record at that location.

6. *Revision of Figure 15.5*
   ```
   Record address = hash function (key field)
   Move "CONTINUE" to found flag
   Do while found flag = "CONTINUE"
        Read data file
        If active record
             Add 1 to record-address
             If record-address > file size
                  Move 1 to record-address
             End If
        Else
             Move "FINISH" to found flag
        End If
   End Do
   Move actual data to data file record
   Rewrite data file record
   ```

Revision of Figure 15.6

```
Record-address = hash function (transaction key)
Move "CONTINUE" to found flag
Do while found flag = "CONTINUE"
     Read data file
     If record does not contain data
          Move "NOT PRESENT" to found flag
     Else
          If record is active and key field = transaction key
               Move "FOUND" to found flag
          Else
               Add 1 to record-address
               If record-address > file size
                    Move 1 to record-address
               End If
          End If
     End If
End Do
If found flag = "FOUND"
     Move transaction date to appropriate fields in data record
     Rewrite data record
Else
     Take action appropriate for invalid transaction
End If
```

7. An indexed file can be used to store table data by using the table argument as the key field. Look-up can be accomplished using the START verb to locate the record that has the desired relationship with the actual argument.

8. A relative file may be chosen for efficiency of execution time.

9. When relative files are used for randomization, extra unused records must be included. These records occupy space in mass storage.

10.
```
Low = 0
High = table size + 1
Move "CONTINUE" to search flag
Do while search flag = "CONTINUE"
     Record address = (low + high)/2
     If table-argument = actual argument
          Move "FOUND" to search flag
     Else
          If table argument > actual argument
               Move record address to low
          Else
               Move record-address to high
          End If
          If high − low = 1
               Move "NOT PRESENT" to search flag
          End If
     End If
End Do
If search flag = "FOUND"
     Use table-value as appropriate
Else
     Take action appropriate when data is not present in the table
End If
```

11. It would be possible to create a table of error messages and use the value of a flag set at the point an error is detected to pick out the appropriate message from the table. The latter operation would take only one paragraph.

12. If the procedure used to locate a position for a new record were removed from Program 15.2, the program would continue to function, but deleted records could not be reused for new data. This would be a problem if the file were volatile, with numerous additions and deletions.

CHAPTER 16

1. a. A *subprogram* is a program that is executed by another program. A subprogram is sometimes referred to as a "called" program.
   b. A *calling program* is a program that executes another program. A calling program is sometimes referred to as a "main" program.
   c. A *program unit* is a subprogram on a main program.
   d. A *load module* is a set of program units ready for execution.
   e. *Linking* is a process of relocating program units and resolving address references.

2. Program modules may be linked before or during execution.

3. All DIVISIONs must be present in a subprogram.

4. Three features found in subprograms but not in other programs are:
   1) LINKAGE SECTION.
   2) PROCEDURE DIVISION USING . . .
   3) EXIT PROGRAM.

5. The VALUE clause can be used only in conjunction with an 88-level item in the LINKAGE SECTION.

6. Items listed in a PROCEDURE DIVISION USING clause must be defined in the LINKAGE SECTION as 01-level or 77-level items.

7. The name of a subprogram is usually defined in the PROGRAM-ID entry.

8. Subroutines aid program development by enabling many programmers to work on a project simultaneously, by enabling significant portions of a program to be tested independently of other parts, by simplifying the debugging task at each stage of program development, and by saving time if the procedure can be used by another program. Subroutines aid program maintenance by simplifying the propagation of any change in a routine common to several programs in the system.

9. Answers will vary. The student should ascertain the details of crating subprograms and load modules from local documentation.

10. A subprogram can execute another subprogram. A subprogram cannot execute itself or another subprogram that would cause an execution of the calling subprogram.

```
11.  100       IDENTIFICATION DIVISION.
     150

     200       PROGRAM-ID. JULIAN.
     300      *REMARKS.  CONVERT MMDDYY TO JULIAN DATE.
     400      *          ANSWER TO EXERCISE 11 SECTION 8.6.
     450

     500       ENVIRONMENT DIVISION.
     520

     550       CONFIGURATION SECTION.
     570

     600       SOURCE-COMPUTER.
     700       OBJECT-COMPUTER.
     750

     800       DATA DIVISION.
     850

     900       WORKING-STORAGE SECTION.
     950

    1000       01  REFERENCE-CONSTANTS.
    1100           03  FILLER PIC 999 VALUE 0.
    1200           03  FILLER PIC 999 VALUE 31.
    1300           03  FILLER PIC 999 VALUE 59.
    1400           03  FILLER PIC 999 VALUE 90.
    1500           03  FILLER PIC 999 VALUE 120.
    1600           03  FILLER PIC 999 VALUE 151.
    1700           03  FILLER PIC 999 VALUE 181.
    1800           03  FILLER PIC 999 VALUE 212.
    1900           03  FILLER PIC 999 VALUE 243.
    2000           03  FILLER PIC 999 VALUE 273.
    2100           03  FILLER PIC 999 VALUE 304.
    2200           03  FILLER PIC 999 VALUE 334.
    2300       01  REFERENCE-TABLE REDEFINES REFERENCE-CONSTANTS.
    2400           03   DAYS-ELAPSED PIC 999 OCCURS 12 TIMES.
    2500       01  QUOT           PIC 99.
    2600       01  REM            PIC 99.
    2650

    2700       LINKAGE SECTION.
    2750

    2800       01  DATE-IN.
    2900           03  MONTH-IN    PIC 99.
    3000           03  DAY-IN      PIC 99.
    3100           03  YEAR-IN     PIC 99.
    3200       01  JULIAN-DATE     PIC 999.
    3250

    3300       PROCEDURE DIVISION
    3400           USING DATE-IN, JULIAN-DATE.
    3450

    3500       1000-MAIN.
    3550

    3600           COMPUTE JULIAN-DATE = DAYS-ELAPSED (MONTH-IN) + DAY-IN.
    3700           DIVIDE YEAR-IN BY 4 GIVING QUOT REMAINDER REM.
    3800           IF REM = 0 AND MONTH-IN > 2
    3900               ADD 1 TO JULIAN-DATE.
    3950

    4000       2000-EXIT.
    4050

    4100           EXIT PROGRAM.
```

```
12. 100      IDENTIFICATION DIVISION.
    150
    200      PROGRAM-ID. NAMECONV.
    250
    300      *REMARKS. CONVERTS NAME STRING TO SEPARATE FIELDS.
    400      *          ANSWER TO EXERCISE 12 SECTION 8.6.
    450
    500      ENVIRONMENT DIVISION.
    550
    600      CONFIGURATION SECTION.
    650
    700      SOURCE-COMPUTER.
    800      OBJECT-COMPUTER.
    850
    900      DATA DIVISION.
    950
    1000     LINKAGE SECTION.
    1050
    1100     01  FULL-NAME           PIC X(20).
    1200     01  LAST-NAME           PIC X(10).
    1300     01  FIRST-NAME          PIC X(10).
    1400     01  MIDDLE-INITIAL      PIC X.
    1450
    1500     PROCEDURE DIVISION
    1550
    1600          USING FULL-NAME, LAST-NAME, FIRST-NAME, MIDDLE-INITIAL.
    1650
    1700     1000-MAIN.
    1750
    1800       UNSTRING FULL-NAME DELIMITED BY ALL SPACES
    1900          INTO  LAST-NAME, FIRST-NAME, MIDDLE-INITIAL.
    1950
    2000     1100-EXIT.
    2050
    2100       EXIT PROGRAM.
```

CHAPTER 17

1. a. A *data base* is the total of all data collected and stored for a given system.
   b. A *data base management system* is a system designed to aid in the organization and maintenance of a data base.
   c. A *report generator* is a facility designed to simplify the task of writing programs to produce routine reports.
   d. A *Data Base Manager* is that portion of the DBMS that acts as an interface between requests for information and the actual data.
   e. A *Data Definition Language* is a facility provided by the DBMS to allow the description of a data base.
   f. A *schema* is a description of the entire data base.
   g. A *subschema* is a description of a portion of a data base.
   h. A *Data Manipulation Language* is a facility provided by a DBMS to allow programs written in traditional languages to access a data base.
   i. A *query facility* provides on-line responses to ad hoc requests for information from a data base.

2. Some problems with traditional systems that are addressed in DBMS are:
   - complexity of the data base
   - ensuring accuracy and completeness of data
   - redundant storage of data items
   - need to rewrite all programs because of physical changes in data
   - difficulty in retrieving information in a timely fashion
   - ensuring security of the data base

3. A typical request for data is interpreted by the Data Base Manager, which accesses the data base description to determine how to fulfill the request. Once the method of response is determined, appropriate data is retrieved from the data base and returned to the user in an appropriate form.

4. A *Data Base Manager* is software; a *Data Base Administrator* is a person charged with overseeing the DBMS.

5. Utilities are usually provided to (*a*) initialize the data base, (*b*) make an archival copy of all transactions, and (*c*) produce reports on various aspects of the operation of the DBMS.

6. In a hierarchical organization, data is organized into a tree in which data at higher levels is considered to "own" data at lower levels. In a network approach, pointers are used to maintain relations among data items. In a relational approach, data is organized into tables that represent the relations among data items.

7. A file management system has provision for organizing and maintaining data in a single file; a DBMS has a similar capability for many files.

INDEX

Programming books from boyd & fraser

Structuring Programs in Microsoft BASIC
BASIC Fundamentals and Style
Applesoft BASIC Fundamentals and Style
BASIC Programming with Structure and Style
Complete BASIC: For the Short Course
Fundamentals of Structured COBOL
Advanced Structured COBOL: Batch and Interactive
Comprehensive Structured COBOL
Pascal
Pascal Programming: A Spiral Approach
WATFIV-S Fundamentals and Style
VAX Fortran
Fortran 77 Fundamentals and Style
Structured Fortran 77 Programming
Structured Fortran 77 Programming: With Hewlett-Packard Computers
Learning Computer Programming: Structured Logic, Algorithms, and Flowcharting

Also available from boyd & fraser

Data Communications Software Design
Microcomputer Applications: Using Small Systems Software
The Art of Using Computers
Using Microcomputers: A Hands-on Introduction

Shelly and Cashman books from boyd & fraser

Computer Fundamentals with Application Software
Workbook and Study Guide to accompany Computer Fundamentals with
  Application Software
Learning to Use SUPERCALC3, dBASE III, WORDSTAR 3.3: An Introduction
Learning to Use SUPERCALC3: An Introduction
Learning to Use dBASE III: An Introduction
Learning to Use WORDSTAR 3.3: An Introduction
BASIC Programming for the IBM Personal Computer

Structured COBOL — Flowchart Edition
Structured COBOL — Pseudocode Edition
Introduction to Pascal Programming

COBOL CODING FORM

PROGRAM					REQUESTED BY		PAGE	OF
PROGRAMMER					DATE		IDENT.	73 80

GLUE

PLACE CUTOFF EDGE OF TAPE HERE

FRONT

FRONT

NOTES

1"
2"
3"
4"
5"
6"
7"
8"
9"

	0	1	2	3	4

COBOL CODING FORM

COBOL CODING FORM

| PROGRAM | | | | | | REQUESTED BY | | PAGE | OF | |
| PROGRAMMER | | | | | | DATE | | IDENT. | 73 | 80 |

PAGE NO. 1 3

LINE NO. 4

A 7 8

B 11 12

Z 72

01
02
03
04
05
06
07
08
09
10
11
12
13
14
15
16
17
18
19
20

8 12 16 20 24 28 32 36 40 44 48 52 56 60 64 68 72

Boyd & Fraser Publishing Company

COBOL CODING FORM

PROGRAM

PROGRAMMER

PAGE ___ OF ___

REQUESTED BY

DATE

IDENT. 73

80

PAGE NO.	LINE NO.	A	B														

1   3 4   6 7   8   11 12   16   20   24   28   32   36   40   44   48   52   56   60   64   68   72

01
02
03
04
05
06
07
08
09
10
11
12
13
14
15
16
17
18
19
20

4   8   12   16   20   24   28   32   36   40   44   48   52   56   60   64   68   72

Boyd & Fraser Publishing Company